EU...
WON...
LITTLE HOTELS
& INNS,
1998

Great Britain & Ireland

****

Dear Reader

Your reports are vital to the well-being of this guide. Do please
write to us when you have visited a hotel. Even the briefest of
endorsements is useful, but lengthier reports are of greater
value as they enable us to add new life to the entries. You may
use the report forms at the back of the book, but this is not
essential. Each year we award a bottle of champagne to twelve
correspondents, for the literary style, or the generous number –
or both – of their reports.

The Editors

****

EUROPE'S WONDERFUL LITTLE HOTELS & INNS, 1998

Great Britain & Ireland

Editors:

Hilary Rubinstein and Caroline Raphael

Consulting Editor:
Adam Raphael

Editor for Wales and the Channel Islands:
Emily Read

Editor for Scotland:
Caroline David

Editor for Ireland:
John Ardagh

Published in London as part of
THE GOOD HOTEL GUIDE, 1998

St. Martin's Griffin ✵ *New York*

Please send reports on hotels to
The Good Hotel Guide
50 Addison Avenue, London W11 4BR, England
or (posted in UK only)
Freepost PAM 2931, London W11 4BR
Tel/fax: (0171) 602 4182
E-mail: Goodhotel@aol.com

Maps copyright © 1997 David Perrott
Illustrations © 1997 David Brindley

ISBN 0-312-16825-X

Published in Great Britain as *The Good Hotel Guide, 1998* by Ebury Press.

First St. Martin's Griffin Edition: December 1997
10 9 8 7 6 5 4 3 2 1

Contents

A note for new readers

This is an annual guide to hotels, inns, guest houses and B&Bs in the British Isles, Ireland and the offshore Channel Islands that are of unusual character and quality. There's a companion guide to hotels on the Continent. In the UK, it is published under the title *The Good Hotel Guide*.

The *Guide* is completely independent. No cash changes hands at any point; contributors are not rewarded for writing to us; hotels do not pay for their entries; the editors and their staff accept no free hospitality. The entries are based on reports from readers who write to us when they come across an establishment which has given them out-of-the-ordinary satisfaction, and who send us their comments, critical or appreciative, when they visit places already included in the *Guide*. We verify and collate the reports, making inspections where necessary, and select those hotels which we consider make the grade.

We do not attempt to be comprehensive. There are many blank areas on our maps, and a number of major cities and towns lack a single full entry, though many are listed in our Shortlist. We see no point in lowering our standards in order to recommend an indifferent establishment as "the best available". But of course we are particularly glad to receive nominations for hotels in a town or a region that is poorly represented. If you can help to plug our gaps, please do so.

Most of our entries, especially in rural areas, are for small establishments (but never with fewer than three rooms) in the hands of resident owners. We don't have any *prima facie* objection to large hotels or those run by managers, except that, in our experience, they often fail to provide the welcome and care for guests' comfort that can be found in the best of the small individually owned hostelries. And this failure is particularly evident in the case of hotels owned by a chain, which explains why there are few chain hotels in these pages.

The entries in this book cover a wide range. People want different things from a hotel depending on whether they are making a single-night stop or spending a whole vacation in one place, whether they have young children with them, whether they are visiting a city or staying in the remote countryside, and according to their age and means. Many *Guide* establishments are distinctly unhotel-like. Some are very small; many do not have the kind of facilities which are normal in chain hotels. We try to convey the flavour of each place. We make no claims of universal compatibility, but hope that our descriptions will help you to find hotels that suit your tastes, needs and purse. If an entry has misled you, please write to us, or send us a fax or e-mail, so that we can do better next time. We hope also that you will let us know if a hotel has fulfilled your expectations. Both endorsement and criticism are essential if the *Guide* is to achieve its purpose. A hotel is dropped unless we get positive feedback.

We should emphasise that this is a thoroughly personal work. We started the *Guide* 21 years ago because we wanted a book that would tell us honestly what to expect when we make a reservation.

Brochures help, but are often deceptive. Travel agents can be useful if they specialise in particular localities, but they often know at recent first-hand only a fraction of the hotels on their books. Guides full of symbols can only capture a fraction of the character of a place. For many, the most reliable way to choose a hotel is by word-of-mouth recommendation. One way to describe this work is to say that it is the word of mouth in print.

The book's aim is to reflect the discriminating taste of its readers. From the first edition, we have depended on the generosity of those who write to us about the hotels they visit. We could not function without this continuous blood transfusion. We appreciate even the briefest endorsement or comment; but it is of course the stylish, witty, perceptive reports that help to give the *Guide* its special character. We are always grateful, too, for suggestions as to how to make the *Guide* more useful.

Inevitably, the book is full of personal prejudices and preferences, including the editors'. We loathe big anonymous hotels where we might as well be in Los Angeles or Lisbon as in London. We avoid, if we can, boring establishments which lack individuality in their decor and warmth in their welcome. We care about good food, but decry pretentiousness in cooking. We cherish the dedicated hotelier who has a vocation for his work.

Introduction

A coming of age

The *Guide* celebrates its 21st birthday this year, and this coming of age brings a few changes. In the past, readers have often asked us why we did not include any hotels in a number of major cities and towns. Our usual answer was that they did not have hotels of *Guide* standard. This year, we have introduced a Shortlist suggesting hotels in or near such places. Most are not typical *Guide* hotels, but by filling a gap they make the *Guide* more comprehensive. We hope, with your help, to build the list up over the years.

The full entries are slightly longer this year, with more local information than before, and details about public transport in the case of many of the rural hotels. We would like to have more illustrations, but, for reasons of cost and space, we cannot compete with the publishers of glossily illustrated hotel guides, which are often paid for by the hotels. We recommend that, when the description of a hotel in these pages appeals to you, you send for its brochure.

Finally, as we approach the millennium, the *Guide* has acquired an Internet address. Readers may now send us their reports and communicate with us by e-mail at: Goodhotel@aol.com. We also now have a superb on-line site courtesy of one of the biggest Internet service providers, America on Line (AOL). At present this is accessible only to members of AOL. But having tried several other service providers, we have found it easy to use, fast and dependable. If you are on line, please let us know what you think of our site, and how we can improve it in the future.

The changing scene

The hotel scene has changed dramatically over the past 21 years. Smart little town house hotels have sprung up in London; in Edinburgh, elegant New Town houses have been turned into upmarket B&Bs; Jonathan Wix's stylish warehouse conversion, *42 The Calls*, transformed the scene in Leeds; Ken McCullough opened his *Malmaisons* in interesting old buildings in Glasgow and Edinburgh, and others will open this year in Manchester and Newcastle, and within the next four years in Leeds, Birmingham and London. Many hotels nowadays have a good restaurant, which brings in trade at times when rooms are not in high demand. But good budget accommodation in cities remains desperately needed, particularly in London.

The capital has recently had a number of highly publicised openings. In September 1996, Anouska Hempel's hotel, modestly named after herself, opened in West London. It has a minimalist decor ("you can't find the front door," some visitors have complained) and an Italian/Thai restaurant. In January, Singaporean Mrs Ong, owner of the *Halkin* (*qv*), opened the 155-bedroom *Metropolitan*, in Park Lane. "Glamorous and buzzy", it too has a fashionable modern design, and its Nobu Japanese restaurant and Met bar are pulling in crowds. Such is the demand for accommodation in London that many five-star hotels have raised their prices by 20 per cent or more in 1996–97.

London also has some of the dingiest hotels of any western city, with indifferent service, shabby rooms, thin walls and depressing decor. Often, what appears to be a row of small hotels turns out to be a single large one behind different façades. Disgracefully, some of these doss-houses are endorsed by tourist boards and hotel associations which should know better.

No wonder tourists complain about London hotels. We hope that it won't be too long before some entrepreneur steps forward to plug this obvious gap in the market. A budget hotel doesn't have to have a central location, but it should be clean and reasonably quiet, with easy access to public transport.

Ripoffs – added service and VAT

The most frequent complaints from our readers, hardly surprisingly, relate to that most painful part of a hotel visit, the settling of the bill. All too often in the UK, unexpected additions bump up the total. Hotels, particularly in London, often quote tariffs exclusive of VAT. Many nowadays have special credit card slips with a blank space marked "Service", waiting to be filled in. Others, only slightly less blatantly, print "Service not included" at the foot of their bill. Some add a "voluntary" service charge, particularly on meals. Either way, visitors find themselves paying a service percentage on a bill already including VAT.

Friction is generated in other ways, too, by the use of credit cards. When taking a booking, many hotels ask for a credit card number instead of a deposit. As one reader wrote: "Often hotels reserve the right to claim compensation if the reservation is cancelled a week or less before you are due to take up the accommodation (unless it is re-let) or you fail to turn up without notice. This is reasonable enough, and is a matter of contract. Hotels take your card number to place themselves in a position to be able to debit the account with any loss they may incur in these circumstances. However, this also places the hotels in a position to debit your account when it would not be reasonable to do so – for example, when the reservation had been cancelled many weeks ahead."

Some hotels make more startling use of credit card numbers. A *Guide* correspondent recently reserved a room in a hotel in Tenerife, guaranteeing the booking with his credit card number. He was amazed to find that the total cost of his accommodation had been deducted from his card two months in advance of his visit. In the United States some hotel guests have found that amounts in excess of the cost of their room are charged against their credit card to take into account projected spending on room service and in the bar and restaurant.

We believe that it is safer to pay a deposit by cheque, eurocheque or travellers' cheque, in cases where hotels want more than a letter of confirmation. And some hoteliers tell us that they accept credit cards, but fail to warn us that they do so reluctantly, or make a surcharge. This too can lead to embarrassment at the time of reckoning.

Food

This continues to generate much comment. Since the advent of *nouvelle cuisine*, many hotels and restaurants have taken to describing their cooking as "modern British", and experimenting with unlikely combinations of flavours. Many, alas, offer elaborate cooking which they cannot deliver, and prettily displayed concoctions are brought to the table lukewarm due to the time it has taken to achieve such decorative effect. "Pretentious" is a description which features regularly in readers' reports. And this style of cooking can be inflexible. Often menus do not vary over days, if not weeks, and meals become an expensive five- or six-course gastronomic marathon, when guests, particularly those on a long stay, would much prefer something simple, and the option of eating only two or three courses. "Generous" portions are often mentioned, but not always with approval; they are daunting to some. Why do so few hoteliers and restaurateurs oblige when a diner asks for a small helping? Surely they could cater for varieties of appetite, thereby avoiding the depressing return to the kitchen of half-empty plates.

Grading – the row continues

Two years of talks on a common hotel grading system broke up this year because of opposition from the Scottish and Welsh tourist boards. We have considerable sympathy with their view of the grading scheme, because it is too mechanistic and fails to recognise that the quality of a hotel depends more on its ambience and service than on its facilities. Absence of a uniform star grading system has been a source of confusion and complaint since the 1970s. All the more need, therefore, for a reliable guide which tells you, as we try to do, just what you can expect from a hotel. That cannot be done by a series of symbols. No wonder the Scots and the Welsh are up in arms.

A guide to the guides

In January 1997, we were proud to be rated the best of all the hotel guides published in Great Britain, in a survey by *The Sunday Times*. The great strength of the book, they wrote, "lies in its squeaky clean integrity – no free hospitality accepted, no payment solicited from hotels, and no advertisements allowed . . . the *GHG* [*Good Hotel Guide*, our title in the UK] conveys the spirit of a hotel better than any of its competitors. It is easy to tell which will best suit your tastes, needs and purse."

This was gratifying, but we have been surprised to discover how many people, even booksellers, are unaware that many hotel guides on sale in book shops charge hotels for their entries. If readers knew that they were being asked to pay for what amounts to little more than glossy advertising, they might think twice. Regrettably, many buyers of travel books do not know (and deliberately are not told) that large sums of money are the price of an entry in these publications. Guides which fail to disclose the basis on which they are published are, in our view, trading on consumer ignorance.

Promotional publications with full colour pictures look good, but the hotelier who pays the piper invariably calls the tune. "You can more or less write your own entry," a former hotelier wrote about a glossy competing guide, in a recent article in the trade paper, *Caterer and Hotelkeeper*. If you were told, for example, that *Hotel Splendido* had paid £2,500 for a full page colour entry, you would surely want a more impartial source of advice before taking the risk of booking there. But you are not told.

Such selling practices are prohibited by other publications. Advertisements and advertising supplements in newspapers, for example, have to be prominently labelled as such. Why do publishers of "paid-for" hotel guides fail to insist that they carry a similar warning? The reason is obvious. If they admitted on the cover that hotels had to pay for their entries, few copies would be sold. We wrote to the chairmen of a number of leading booksellers to ask whether they felt they had any responsibility for the guide books they sold or was it simply a question of *caveat emptor*. We regret that nearly all of them responded that it was up to the customer to beware.

Please write

Finally, we can never adequately thank all the readers who so generously send us hotel reports. All we can do is ask, like Oliver Twist, for more. The great strength of the *Guide* is the fund of details and impressions you provide, giving a far wider range of information on each hotel than is yielded by an inspector walking around it with a clipboard on a solitary visit. Do please write to us while your visit is fresh in your mind. The report forms at the back of the book are for your convenience; it is not essential that you use them, as you can write to us on anything, or send a fax or e-mail. And we are always happy to supply voluntary inspectors with lists of places on which we need more information, on the understanding that these inspections are anonymous, and that no hospitality is accepted from the hotelier.

HILARY RUBINSTEIN AND CAROLINE RAPHAEL
July 1997

The 1998 César awards

Since 1984, as a way of demonstrating our appreciation for different kinds of excellence among hotels in Britain and Ireland, we have made annual awards called Césars, after the most celebrated of all hoteliers, César Ritz. Hotels of the grandest sort, like the finest restaurants, rarely lack public attention, but there are many more modest establishments that are supremely good in their own way. Their owners are dedicated to their vocation and commonly work from seven in the morning till one the next morning. Their contribution to innkeeping deserves to be recognised and honoured along with that of the professionals at the top of the ladder.

This year, as previously, we have bestowed ten laurel wreaths on a heterogeneous selection of establishments, each of which we consider to be outstanding in its own class, though we have, for the first time, made no awards in the luxury class. Previous César winners, provided the establishments are still in the same hands and as good as ever, are indicated in the text by the symbol of a smaller laurel wreath.

AWARD	WINNER
Quiet rural perfection	Little Barwick House Barwick
	Christopher and Veronica Colley win a long-service award for consistent standards of cooking and hospitality over 17 years, at their Georgian dower house in a quiet corner of Somerset.
Restaurant-with-rooms of the year	Fischer's Baslow Hall Baslow
	Max and Susan Fischer delight gourmets with excellent food both in their restaurant and in their café, amid some of Derbyshire's loveliest scenery, and overnight guests are equally cosseted.

Inn of the year   Hoste Arms
                                         Burnham Market

In addition to the usual comforts, Paul
and Jeanne Whittome's fortunate
guests can enjoy jazz performances and
art exhibitions at this inn, in a lovely
Norfolk village.

Traditional Lakeland   Aynsome Manor
hospitality   Cartmel

Two generations of the Varley family
look after their manor-house guests in a
tranquil Cumbrian setting, in the best of
traditional style.

Best hotel by the sea   Tregildry
                                         Gillan

Lynne and Huw Phillips were previously known for their Lakeland
hospitality. They bring the same professional expertise and care to their new
hotel, in a magnificent setting above
the sea.

Best B&B for   Caterham House
Bard lovers   Stratford-upon-Avon

Dominique and Olive Maury care for
Thespians, critics and theatre-lovers in
exemplary style. And the theatre is only
a short walk distant.

A town house for   Hotel du Vin
wine connoisseurs   Winchester

In one of England's loveliest cathedral
towns, Gerald Basset and Robin Hutson
offer food and accommodation at
reasonable prices, and – a bonus – a
range of wines to delight the most
finicky palate.

Gastronomic wizardry   Carlton House
in the heart of Wales   Llanwrtyd Wells

Alan and Mary Ann Gilchrist's little
restaurant-with-rooms in a mid-Wales
spa town is a budget-priced haven for
lovers of good food and friendly
comfort.

Scottish hotel of the year

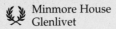 Minmore House
Glenlivet

Belinda Luxmoore may hail from the Antipodes, but here in Scotland, where the air is perfumed by the Glenlivet distillery, she entertains her guests with haggis and Scotch salmon, and the warmest of informal hospitality.

For utterly enjoyable
mild eccentricity

 Castle Leslie
Glaslough

In their impressive 19th-century castle, crammed with mementos of the past, the Leslie family have long entertained distinguished visitors. It is now ebulliently run, in high Victorian style, by Samantha Leslie – plenty of jokes, but plenty of modern comforts too.

Special hotels

City hotels with luxury and/or grandeur

England

Royal Crescent, Bath
42 The Calls, Leeds
Cadogan, London
Capital, London
Connaught, London
Goring, London
22 Jermyn Street, London
Middlethorpe Hall, York

Scotland

One Devonshire Gardens, Glasgow

Town and city hotels of character and/or value

England

Bridge House, Beaminster
Copperfield House, Birmingham
Collin House, Broadway
On the Park, Cheltenham
Evesham, Evesham
Lansdowne, Leamington Spa
D'Isney Place, Lincoln
Basil Street, London
Portobello, London
Angel, Midhurst
Old Parsonage, Oxford
Abbey, Penzance
Mansion House, Poole
Jeake's House, Rye
George, Stamford
Castle, Taunton
Du Vin, Winchester
Wykeham Arms, Winchester
Feathers, Woodstock
Mount Royale, York

Scotland

Malmaison, Edinburgh
Babbity Bowster, Glasgow
Malmaison, Glasgow
Clifton, Nairn
Dungallan House, Oban

Northern Ireland

Ash-Rowan, Belfast

Rural charm and character in the luxury class

England

Hartwell House, Aylesbury
Mallory Court, Bishop's Tachbrook
Lygon Arms, Broadway
Buckland Manor, Buckland
Brockencote Hall, Chaddesley Corbett
Gidleigh Park, Chagford
Bailiffscourt, Climping
Gravetye Manor, East Grinstead
Summer Lodge, Evershot
Stock Hill House, Gillingham
Manoir aux Quat'Saisons, Great Milton
Hambleton Hall, Hambleton
Hintlesham Hall, Hintlesham
Chewton Glen, New Milton
Ston Easton Park, Ston Easton
Cliveden, Taplow
Thornbury Castle, Thornbury
Sharrow Bay, Ullswater

Wales

Bodysgallen, Llandudno
Llangoed Hall, Llyswen

Scotland

Arisaig House, Arisaig
Kinnaird, Dunkeld
Inverlochy Castle, Fort William

Channel Islands

Longueville Manor, St Saviour

Republic of Ireland

Marlfield House, Gorey
Park, Kenmare

Rural charm and character at medium price

England

Rothay Manor, Ambleside

Wateredge, Ambleside
Amerdale House, Arncliffe
Callow Hall, Ashbourne
Little Barwick House, Barwick
Cavendish, Baslow
Netherfield Place, Battle
Lindeth Fell, Bowness
Linthwaite House, Bowness
Woolley Grange, Bradford-on-Avon
Farlam Hall, Brampton
Danescombe Valley, Calstock
Aynsome Manor, Cartmel
Uplands, Cartmel
Castleman, Chettle
Highbullen, Chittlehamholt
Ashwick House, Dulverton
Congham Hall, Grimston
Highfield House, Hawkshead
Heddon's Gate, Heddon's Mouth
Langley House, Langley Marsh
Lastingham Grange, Lastingham
Hope End, Ledbury
Lewtrenchard Manor, Lewdown
Morston Hall, Morston
Beetle and Wedge, Moulsford-on-Thames
Pear Tree, Purton
Stone House, Rushlake Green
Plumber Manor, Sturminster Newton
Calcot Manor, Tetbury
Priory, Wareham
Woodhayes, Whimple

Wales

Gliffaes, Crickhowell
Ynyshir Hall, Eglwysfach
Tyddyn Llan, Llandrillo
Lake, Llangammarch Wells
Portmeirion, Portmeirion
Maes-y-Neuadd, Talsarnau

Scotland

Farleyer House, Aberfeldy
Old Manse, Bridge of Marnoch
Minmore House, Glenlivet
Dunain Park, Inverness
Killiecrankie, Killiecrankie

Channel Islands

Château La Chaire, Rozel Bay

Northern Ireland

Glassdrumman Lodge, Annalong

Republic of Ireland

Temple House, Ballymote
Hilton Park, Clones
Doyle's Townhouse, Dingle
Assolas, Kanturk
Currarevagh House, Oughterard
Coopershill, Riverstown
Ballymaloe House, Shanagarry

Rural charm, simple style

England

Frog Street Farm, Beercrocombe
Bolebroke Watermill, Hartfield
Lydgate House, Postbridge
Parrock Head, Slaidburn
Howtown, Ullswater

Republic of Ireland

Kylenoe, Ballinderry

Hotels by the sea, luxury style

England

Island, Tresco

Channel Islands

Atlantic, St Brelade

Hotels by the sea, medium-priced or simple

England

Burgh Island, Bigbury-on-Sea
Treglos, Constantine Bay
Crantock Bay, Crantock
Boscundle Manor, St Austell
Garrack, St Ives
Tides Reach, Salcombe
Seaview, Seaview
Soar Mill Cove, Soar Mill Cove
Talland Bay, Talland-by-Looe
Trebrea Lodge, Tintagel
Nare, Veryan

Wales

St Tudno, Llandudno

Scotland

Summer Isles, Achiltibuie
Loch Melfort, Arduaine
Balcary Bay, Auchencairn
Crinan, Crinan
Baile-na-Cille, Timsgarry

Republic of Ireland

Zetland House, Cashel Bay
Rosturk Woods, Mulrany

Walking and mountain hotels

England

Grey Friar Lodge, Ambleside
Appletree Holme Farm, Blawith
Seatoller House, Borrowdale
Ivy House, Braithwaite
Mill, Mungrisdale
Swinside Lodge, Newlands
Hazel Bank, Rosthwaite
Howtown, Ullswater
Wasdale Head, Wasdale Head

Wales

Pen-y-Gwryd, Nantgwynant

Scotland

Summer Isles, Achiltibuie

Hotels with a spa/good leisure facilities

England

Hartwell House, Aylesbury
Priory, Bath
Devonshire Arms, Bolton Abbey
Lygon Arms, Broadway
Charingworth Manor, Charingworth
Hintlesham, Hintlesham
Chewton Glen, New Milton
Polurrian, Mullion
Tides Reach, Salcombe
Cliveden, Taplow
Bishopstrow House, Warminster

Wales

Bodysgallen Hall, Llandudno

Scotland

Isle of Eriska, Eriska

Channel Islands

St Brelade's Bay, St Brelade

Ireland

Dunraven Arms, Adare
Aghadoe Heights, Killarney
Rathmullan House, Rathmullan

Fishing hotels

England

Callow Hall, Ashbourne
Holne Chase, Ashburton
Highbullen, Chittlehamholt
Tarr Steps, Hawkridge
Arundell Arms, Lifton
Bishopstrow House, Warminster

Wales

Gliffaes, Crickhowell
Tyddyn Llan, Llandrillo
Lake, Llangammarch Wells
Llangoed Hall, Llyswen

Scotland

Farleyer House, Aberfeldy
Banchory Lodge, Banchory
Kinnaird, Dunkeld
Taychreggan, Kilchrenan
Ballathie House, Kinclaven
Dryburgh Abbey, St Boswells

Republic of Ireland

Mount Falcon Castle, Ballina
Ballylickey Manor, Ballylickey
Caragh Lodge, Caragh Lake
Enniscoe House, Crossmolina
Sheen Falls Lodge, Kenmare
Delphi Lodge, Leenane
Longueville House, Mallow
Newport House, Newport
Currarevagh House, Oughterard
Ballynahinch Castle, Recess

Hotels for golfers

England

Budock Vean, Budock Vean
Highbullen, Chittlehamholt
Hintlesham Hall, Hintlesham
South Lodge, Lower Beeding
Chewton Glen, New Milton

Scotland

Banchory Lodge, Banchory
Balbirnie House, Markinch

Ireland

Ballycormac House, Aglish

Channel Islands

Atlantic, St Brelade

Hotels with tennis

England

Little Hemingfold, Battle
Netherfield Place, Battle
Lindeth Fell, Bowness
Woolley Grange, Bradford-on-Avon
Frogg Manor, Broxton
Charingworth Manor, Charingworth
Highbullen, Chittlehamholt
Bailiffscourt, Climping
Corse Lawn House, Corse Lawn
Summer Lodge, Evershot
Stock Hill House, Gillingham
Manoir aux Quat'Saisons, Great Milton
Congham Hall, Grimston
Hambleton Hall, Hambleton
Homewood Park, Hinton Charterhouse
Huntsham Court, Huntsham
Upper Court, Kemerton
South Lodge, Lower Beeding
Alexandra, Lyme Regis
Old Bell, Malmesbury
Polurrian, Mullion
Romney Bay House, New Romney
Old Wharf, Newbridge
Ravenwood Hall, Rougham
Stone House, Rushlake Green
Greenway, Shurdington
Gabriel Court, Stoke Gabriel
Ston Easton Park, Ston Easton
Calcot Manor, Tetbury
Island, Tresco
Wallett's Court, West Cliffe

Wales

Porth Tocyn, Abersoch
Gliffaes, Crickhowell
Bodysgallen Hall, Llandudno
Lake, Llangammarch Wells
Llangoed Hall, Llyswen
Egerton Grey, Porthkerry

Scotland

Inverlochy Castle, Fort William
Torbeag House, Banavie
Minmore House, Glenlivet
Ballathie House, Kinclaven
Skirling House, Skirling
Baile-na-Cille, Timsgarry

Channel Islands

Atlantic, St Brelade
Longueville Manor, St Saviour

Ireland

Caragh Lodge, Caragh Lake
Cashel House, Cashel Bay
Zetland House, Cashel Bay
Grangebeg House, Dunlavin
Marlfield House, Gorey
Assolas Country House, Kanturk
Sheen Falls Lodge, Kenmare
Rathmullan House, Rathmullan
Tinakilly House, Rathnew
Ballynahinch Castle, Recess
Ballymaloe House, Shanagarry

Hotels with a swimming pool

(see also hotels with a spa)

England

Frog Street Farm, Beercrocombe
Little Hodgeham, Bethersden
Mallory Court, Bishop's Tachbrook
Blakeney, Blakeney
Winterbourne, Bonchurch
Woolley Grange, Bradford-on-Avon
Collin House, Broadway
Aynsome Manor, Cartmel
Corse Lawn House, Corse Lawn
Summer Lodge, Evershot
Manoir aux Quat'Saisons, Great Milton
Congham Hall, Grimston
Hambleton Hall, Hambleton
Cockle Warren Cottage, Hayling Island
Headlam Hall, Headlam
Homewood Park, Hinton Charterhouse
Upper Court, Kemerton
Polurrian, Mullion
Cornish Cottage, New Polzeath
Ravenwood Hall, Rougham
Boscundle Manor, St Austell
Greenway, Shurdington
Gabriel Court, Stoke Gabriel
Talland Bay, Talland-by-Looe
Calcot Manor, Tetbury
Island, Tresco
Curdon Mill, Vellow

Hollington House, Woolton Hill
Mount Royale, York

Wales

Porth Tocyn, Abersoch
Portmeirion, Portmeirion

Scotland

Minmore House, Glenlivet
Dunain Park, Inverness
Dryburgh Abbey, St Boswells

Channel Islands

Atlantic, St Brelade
Longueville Manor, St Saviour
Petit Champ, Sark
Stocks Island, Sark

Ireland

Ballymaloe House, Shanagarry

Friendly informality/run like a private house

England

Little Hemingfold, Battle
Frog Street Farm, Beercrocombe
Little Hodgeham, Bethersden
Appletree Holme Farm, Blawith
Bourne Eau House, Bourne
Burghope Manor, Bradford-on-Avon
Chilvester Hill House, Calne
Hancocks Farmhouse, Cranbrook
Old Cloth Hall, Cranbrook
Coach House, Crookham
Upper Court, Kemerton
Bowerfield House, Otley
Stone House, Rushlake Green
Stratton House, Swaffham
Thomas Luny House, Teignmouth

Wales

Old Rectory, Llansanffraid Glan Conwy

Scotland

Campsie Hill, Guildtown
Viewfield House, Portree
Baile-na-Cille, Timsgarry

Republic of Ireland

Temple House, Ballymote
Tullanisk, Birr
Hilton Park, Clones

Castle Leslie, Glaslough
Cullintra House, Inistioge
Delphi Lodge, Leenane
Roundwood House, Mountrath
Coopershill, Riverstown

Hotels that welcome children

England

Elms, Abberley
Rothay Manor, Ambleside
Cavendish, Baslow
Eagle House, Bathford
Blakeney, Blakeney
Woolley Grange, Bradford-on-Avon
Lygon Arms, Broadway
Gidleigh Park, Chagford
Charingworth Manor, Charingworth
Tudor Farmhouse, Clearwell
Corse Lawn, Corse Lawn
Crantock Bay, Crantock
Evesham, Evesham
Manoir aux Quat'Saisons, Great Milton
Highfield House, Hawkshead
Combe House, Holford
Lastingham Grange, Lastingham
Great House, Lavenham
Arundell Arms, Lifton
Basil Street, London
Connaught, London
22 Jermyn Street, London
Old Bell, Malmesbury
Beetle and Wedge, Moulsford-on-Thames
Mill, Mungrisdale
Ennys, St Hilary
Seaview, Seaview
Soar Mill Cove, Soar Mill Cove
Cliveden, Taplow
Island, Tresco
Nare, Veryan
Wallett's Court, West Cliffe
Inn at Whitewell, Whitewell

Wales

Porth Tocyn, Abersoch
St Tudno, Llandudno

Scotland

Loch Melfort, Arduaine

Isle of Colonsay, Colonsay
Enmore, Dunoon
Creebridge House, Newton
  Stewart
Cringletie House, Peebles
Dryburgh Abbey, St Boswells
Baile-na-Cille, Timsgarry
Burrastow House, Walls

Channel Islands

St Brelade's Bay Hotel, St Brelade's
Bella Luce, St Martin

Republic of Ireland

Roundwood House, Mountrath
Coopershill, Riverstown
Ballymaloe House, Shanagarry
Inch House, Thurles

No-smoking hotels

England

Abbey House, Abbotsbury
Haydon House, Bath
Holly Lodge, Bath
Somerset House, Bath
Frog Street Farm, Beercrocombe
Appletree Holme Farm, Blawith
Bradford Old Windmill, Bradford-
  on-Avon
Cokerhurst Farm, Bridgwater
Twelve Angel Hill, Bury St
  Edmunds
Pickett Howe, Buttermere
Cross Keys, Cautley
Cleeve Hill Hotel, Cleeve Hill
Manor Farm, Crackington Haven
Hancocks Farmhouse, Cranbrook
Stone Close, Dent
Little Parmoor, Frieth
Old Rectory, Fulletby
Ashfield House, Grassington
Bolebroke Watermill, Hartfield
Farthings, Hatch Beauchamp
Northleigh House, Hatton
Windrush House, Hazleton
Old Rectory, Hopesay
Holmfield, Keswick
Molesworth Manor, Little
  Petherick
New House Farm, Lorton
Old Rectory, Lynton
Swinside Lodge, Newlands
Newstead Grange, Norton-on-
  Derwent

Bowerfield House, Otley
Cotswold House, Oxford
Roseland House, Portscatho
Hazel Bank, Rosthwaite
Nanscawen House, St Blazey
Ennys, St Hilary
Slough Court, Stoke St Gregory
Upper Green Farm, Towersey
Old Millfloor, Trebarwith Strand
Shieldhall, Wallington
Old Parsonage, West Dean
Bales Mead, West Porlock
Archway, Windermere
4 South Parade, York

Wales

Dol-llyn-wydd, Builth Wells
Tan-y-Foel, Capel Garmon
Gilfach Goch Farmhouse,
  Fishguard

Scotland

Torbeag House, Banavie
Arran Lodge, Callander
Brook Linn, Callander
Priory, Callander
Chirnside Hall, Chirnside
Todhall House, Dairsie
Drummond House, Edinburgh
17 Abercromby Place, Edinburgh
Crolinnhe, Fort William
Grange, Fort William
Skirling House, Skirling
Altnaharrie, Ullapool
Grange House, Whiting Bay

Hotels that welcome dogs

England

Holne Chase, Ashburton
Bracken House, Bratton Fleming
Lygon Arms, Broadway
Crantock Bay, Crantock
Glewstone Court, Glewstone
Worsley Arms, Hovingham
Morston Hall, Morston
Hall, Newton-le-Willows
Rose-da-Mar, St Just-in-Roseland
Swan, Southwold
Mortal Man, Troutbeck
Prince Hall, Two Bridges
Inn at Whitewell, Whitewell

Wales

Lake, Llangammarch Wells

Scotland

Baile-na-Cille, Timsgarry

Hotels for gourmets

England

Fischer's Baslow Hall, Baslow
Mallory Court, Bishop's
  Tachbrook
Waterside Inn, Bray
Buckland Manor, Buckland
Gidleigh Park, Chagford
White Moss House, Grasmere
Manoir aux Quat'Saisons, Great
  Milton
Hambleton Hall, Hambleton
Hintlesham Hall, Hintlesham
Gordleton Mill, Hordle
Northcote Manor, Langho
Langley House, Langley Marsh
Capital, London
Connaught, London
Halkin, London
Lovells at Windrush Farm, Minster
  Lovell
Morston Hall, Morston
Beetle and Wedge, Moulsford-on-
  Thames
Chewton Glen, New Milton
Seafood Restaurant, Padstow
Sandgate, Sandgate
McCoy's, Staddlebridge
Castle, Taunton
Howard's House, Teffont Evias
Sharrow Bay, Ullswater
Old Beams, Waterhouses
Miller Howe, Windermere
Winteringham Fields,
  Winteringham

Wales

Old Rectory, Llansanffraid Glan
  Conwy
Carlton House Llanwrtyd Wells
Plas Bodegroes, Pwllheli

Scotland

Summer Isles, Achiltibuie
Crinan, Crinan
Harlosh House, Dunvegan
Cross, Kingussie
Airds, Port Appin
Knockinaam Lodge, Portpatrick
Altnaharrie, Ullapool

Channel Islands

Longueville Manor, St Saviour

Republic of Ireland

Doyle's Townhouse, Dingle
Marlfield House, Gorey
Park, Kenmare
Rathmullan House, Rathmullan
Ballymaloe House, Shanagarry
Aherne's, Youghal

Hotels with facilities for ♿

England

Rothay Manor, Ambleside
Callow Hall, Ashbourne
Hartwell House, Aylesbury
Priory, Bath
Park House, Bepton
Devonshire Arms, Bolton Abbey
Millstream, Bosham
Bracken House, Bratton Fleming
Brockencote Hall, Chaddesley
  Corbett
Coach House at Crookham,
  Crookham
Old Manor, Cropredy
Casterbridge, Dorchester
Duxford Lodge, Duxford
Borrowdale Gates, Grange-in-
  Borrowdale
Northill House, Horton
Northcote Manor, Langho
Knightsbridge Green, London
New House Farm, Lorton
South Lodge, Lower Beeding
Angel, Midhurst
Beeches, Norwich
Ravenwood Hall, Rougham
Garrack, St Ives
Albright Hussey, Shrewsbury
Stonor Arms, Stonor
Gilpin Lodge, Windermere
Old Vicarage, Worfield
Grange, York

Wales

Porth Tocyn, Abersoch
Penbontbren Farm, Glynarthen

Scotland

Farleyer House, Aberfeldy
Loch Melfort, Arduaine
Roman Camp, Callander

Forss House, Forss
Kilmichael, Glen Cloy
Obinan Croft, Laide
Dryburgh Abbey, St Boswells
Isle of Barra, Tangusdale
Burrastow House, Walls

Republic of Ireland

Mustard Seed at Echo Lodge,
   Ballingarry
Milltown House, Dingle
Hibernian, Dublin
Park Hotel Kenmare, Kenmare
Glenview House, Midleton
Rosturk Woods, Mulrany
Tinakilly House, Rathnew
Aherne's, Youghal

Hotels licensed for civil weddings

England

Burgh Island, Bigbury-on-Sea
Millstream, Bosham
Linthwaite House, Bowness
Waterside Inn, Bray
Budock Vean, Budock Vean
Haley's, Leeds
Lewtrenchard Manor, Lewdown
Mains Hall, Little Singleton
Mackworth, Mackworth
Pear Tree, Purton
Thornbury Castle, Thornbury
Curdon Mill, Vellow

Wales

Egerton Grey, Porthkerry
Lake, Llangammarch Wells

Hotels that offer a Christmas package

England

Rothay Manor, Ambleside
Rowanfield, Ambleside
Holne Chase, Ashburton
Somerset House, Bath
Little Hemingfold, Battle
Linthwaite House, Bowness
Bridge House, Beaminster
Burgh Island, Bigbury-on-Sea
Biggin Hall, Biggin by Hartington
Ivy House, Braithwaite

Lygon Arms, Broadway
Buckland Manor, Buckland
Danescombe Valley, Calstock
Aynsome Manor, Cartmel
Ashwick House, Dulverton
Summer Lodge, Evershot
Hambleton Hall, Hambleton
Hintlesham Hall, Hintlesham
Lewtrenchard Manor, Lewdown
Old Bell, Malmesbury
Cottage in the Wood, Malvern
   Wells
Lea Hill, Membury
Burgoyne, Reeth
Garrack, St Ives
Parrock Head, Slaidburn
Soar Mill Cove, Soar Mill Cove
Swan, Southwold
George, Stamford
Cliveden, Taplow
Castle, Taunton
Howard's House, Teffont Evias
Steppes, Ullingswick
Nare, Veryan
Wasdale Head, Wasdale Head
Gilpin Lodge, Windermere
Hollington House, Woolton Hill
Middlethorpe Hall, York

Wales

Ynyshir Hall, Eglwysfach
Milebrook, Knighton
Tyddyn Llan, Llandrillo
Lake, Llangammarch Wells
Egerton Grey, Porthkerry
Portmeirion, Portmeirion

Scotland

Loch Melfort, Arduaine
Auchendean Lodge, Dulnain
   Bridge
Woodwick House, Evie
Taychreggan, Kilchrenan
Kildrummy Castle, Kildrummy
Dryburgh Abbey, St Boswells

Channel Islands

Bella Luce, St Martin

Republic of Ireland

Park Hotel Kenmare, Kenmare
Aghadoe Heights, Killarney
Tinakilly House, Rathnew

How we choose our hotels

We are often asked about our principles of selection and rejection. This is a fair question, since the hotels included in the *Guide* cater for a wide spectrum of ages, income, tastes and prejudices, and have been nominated by a miscellaneous collection of individuals, whose own predilections and standards of judgment cannot be known to us. How then can there be any coherent standard behind our choices?

There clearly is no single standard. Our own tastes are eclectic, and the only thing which all these hotels have in common is that the editors would be happy to stay in them. Nevertheless the process of selection is by no means arbitrary. Among the factors which assist us are the following:

• The consensus of recent reports on a hotel that already has an entry in the *Guide*, and the tone of the nominating letter in the case of a candidate for first-time selection. If someone whose judgment we know and trust tells us of an exciting new find or that a particular hotel does not deserve its entry, he or she obviously carries more weight than a nominator or complainant out of the blue.
• The hotel's brochure. Its pitch will usually reveal the kind of custom it is hoping to attract, and its photographs or drawings, while no doubt always aiming to beguile, may indicate instantly that this one is not for us.
• Menus. Very instructive in subtle as well as in obvious ways.
• Hoteliers' responses to our questionnaire. We invite them to expand on their answers by telling us what sort of custom they hope to attract; relatively few take the trouble; the replies of those who do are of great help to us.
• Whether and how a hotel features in other guides.
• Inspections. In cases of doubt (due to unconvincing or ambivalent reports), we carry out an anonymous inspection. We have a limited inspection budget, but a number of readers have generously volunteered to do unreimbursed inspections for us.

Of course, such a pragmatic system is open to error, but the fact that we get far more endorsements than blackballs encourages us to think that we are on the right lines.

Hotels are dropped when it is clear that there has been a fall in standards or – a tricky question this – when we feel that they are no longer offering value for money. We also omit a hotel after a change of ownership or management, if we do not have enough evidence that the new regime is maintaining previous standards. And hotels are dropped – often unfairly – when we have had inadequate feedback. We are used to getting a spate of letters asking: "Why on earth have you left out — ?" If the case is well made, we reinstate the place in the next edition. As we have said *ad nauseam*, we wish that readers who find the *Guide* useful would make a habit of sending reports after staying in a *Guide* hotel.

A common practice is for hotels to give departing guests a report form and invite them to send us an "unsolicited" recommendation. Sometimes we receive a rash of fulsome reports on a particular establishment, all from people who have never written to us before. Some hotels photocopy our report forms, and, having prevailed on their guests to fill them in, post them to us in a batch. One hotel designed a special postcard for the purpose. The owners of a French hotel once asked their English customers to fill in a special questionnaire which they then posted to us. They did not take the trouble to read these first, or else their English was not up to the job; many of the so-called reports contained more insults than compliments. We wish that hoteliers would desist from these collusive and counter-effective practices.

How to read the entries

The long and the short of it Entries vary in length. A long entry need not necessarily imply an especially good hotel, nor a short one a marginal case. Sometimes it takes a lot of words to convey a hotel's special flavour, and sometimes we can't resist quoting at length from an amusing report, since we aim to be entertaining as well as informative. In general, city hotels get less space than country ones because the ambience of a hotel matters less in towns, and also because it is often helpful, when a hotel is in a relatively remote or little-known area, for the entry to comment on the location.

Names The italicised names and initials in brackets at the end of an entry are those of people who have nominated that hotel or endorsed the entry that appeared in a previous edition. We don't give the names of writers of adverse reports – though their contributions are every bit as important as the laudatory ones.

Maps and index You will find these at the end of the book. We list hotels not by county or district, but country by country under the name of the town or village. If you remember the hotel's name but not its precise location you should consult the alphabetical list of hotels.

Nuts and bolts The factual material varies in length. Some hotels have lots of facilities, others few. We don't give detailed information about bedroom facilities. Most hotel bedrooms nowadays have telephone, TV and *en suite* bathroom; many have tea-making facilities. If any of these is vital to your comfort you should discuss it with the hotel at the time of booking. A "double room" may be double- or twin-bedded; you should mention which you prefer when booking. We try to give accurate information about facilities for the disabled, but again these must be discussed with the hotel. We also aim to provide accurate information about opening times, but hotels, particularly small ones, do sometimes close on the spur of the moment. Finally, hotels don't always give us reliable information about whether they take credit cards or which ones; please check with the hotel if this is vital to you.

Italic entries These describe hotels which are worth considering but which we feel, for various reasons – inadequate information, lack of feedback, ambivalent reports – do not at the moment deserve a full entry. Reports on these hotels are particularly welcome.

Symbols This is an unashamedly wordy guide. We are against providing a lot of information in complicated, hard-todecipher hieroglyphic form. Days and months are abbreviated; "B&B" means bed and breakfast, "D,B&B" means dinner, bed and breakfast, and "alc" is *à la carte*. The "full alc" price is the hotel's estimate per person for a three-course meal and a half bottle of modest wine, including service and taxes; "alc" indicates the price excluding the wine. We say: "Unsuitable for ♿" when hotels tell us that, but it is vital that you check details with the hotel. We have a "New" label for hotels making their debut in the *Guide* or being readmitted after an absence, and a "Budget" label for hotels which offer dinner, bed and breakfast at around $80 per person (or its Irish punt equivalent) or B&B for about $48 and dinner for around $32. *V* indicates hotels in the UK and Ireland which have agreed to take part in our Voucher scheme.

Vouchers Once again we offer our readers an opportunity to obtain discounts at many British and Irish *Guide* hotels. At the end of the book you will find six vouchers which may be used at any hotel in the UK and Ireland with *V* at the end of its entry. A voucher will entitle you to a discount of 25 per cent from the normal price for bed and breakfast (or the price of a room in the case of hotels that charge for breakfast separately). It won't apply if you are already on a bargain break or special deal, and you will be expected to pay the full price for all other services. The discount will apply whether you use the voucher for one night or for a longer visit, and is for one room. You must produce two vouchers if you are booking two rooms. The vouchers remain valid till the publication of the 1999 edition in the UK in early September 1998. *Important*: It is essential that you request a voucher booking at the time of reservation, and participating hotels may refuse a voucher reservation or accept the voucher for one night only if they expect to be fully booked at the full room price at that time.

Tariffs Terms are regrettably complicated. Some hotels have a standard rate for all rooms regardless of season and length of stay, but many operate a complex system which varies from low season to high (some have a medium-high season as well), and according to length of stay, whether there is a bathroom *en suite* and whether the room is in single or double occupancy. To complicate matters further, most hotels offer breaks of one kind or another, but rarely of the same kind. When figures are given without mention of single or double rooms they indicate the range of tariffs per person; otherwise we give a room rate. Lowest rates are what you pay for the simplest room, sharing a double, or out of season, or both; highest rates are for the "best" rooms – and for the high season if the hotel has one. Meal prices are per person.

One crucial point must be emphasised with regard to the tariffs: their relative unreliability. We ask hotels when they complete our questionnaire in the spring of one year to make an informed guess at their tariffs for the following year. This is a difficult exercise. Many prefer to quote their current rates.

Please *don't* rely on the figures printed. You should *always* check at the time of booking and not blame the hotel or the *Guide* if prices are different from those printed.

Special offers If you wish to spend two days or more at a hotel in the British Isles, it is worth asking about special offers. The bargain terms can be amazing value, and may apply throughout the year. And the voucher scheme should help you to find accommodation at cheaper rates.

We end with our customary exhortation, imploring readers to tell us of any errors of omission or commission in both the descriptive and informative parts of the entries. Our entries are written in good faith, but we can't guarantee that, after we have gone to press, a hotel won't close or change its owners. We make constant efforts to improve our information under Location, especially with out-of-the-way places, and would like to hear from readers who have found our directions inadequate. We recognise what an imposition it is to ask readers to write us letters or fill in report forms, but it is essential that people let us know their views if the *Guide* is to continue to meet consumer needs as well as it can.

England

Fischer's Baslow Hall, Baslow

Almost all the establishments in the *Guide* are independently owned and run. There are a few exceptions: some large hotels, and some in cities, are in the hands of managers, and we include a small number of hoteliers who own more than one hotel.

Many *Guide* hotels, however, belong to a consortium for the purposes of marketing and promotion, and it may be useful to identify the more important of these groupings. The most famous, also the most expensive, is Relais & Châteaux, French-owned but world-wide. All Relais establishments, be they grand castles, lush country houses or gourmet restaurants, are privately owned. But so strong is the Relais brand image that they are sometimes mistaken for a chain. Some well-heeled folk, who like to be assured of the acme of luxury when they travel abroad, use the Relais booklet extensively or exclusively. Others steer clear, not caring for the swank – and sometimes the snootiness – which they detect in these posh places, and feel they are being asked to pay too high a price for the grand trappings. The present Relais contingent in the UK are in general an impressive lot, more dependable in our view than their associates across the Channel. Because the style is so distinctive, we always mention a hotel's membership in its *Guide* entry.

Pride of Britain, a similar consortium, is exclusively British. It was formed by a breakaway group from Relais who resented the French domination of the latter, and the high prices they were being asked to pay for the privilege of membership. Not all Pride of Britain establishments are independent entities – they include a Hebridean Cruise company and the Royal Scotsman. About two-thirds of their members have an entry in the *Guide*.

The Virgin consortium is gradually expanding, and we include five of its members in the UK; though luxurious, they are not, on the whole, prohibitively expensive. The consortium's overseas members include the smart *Residencia*, in Mallorca, which has an entry in our European volume. Mr Branson is also half owner of the *Manoir aux Quat'Saisons* in Great Milton (*qv*).

The Best Western group, world-wide but strongest in the US, insists on independence for its members, but they are less homogeneous than those of the groups mentioned above. In the US, Best Western hotels are often motels; in the UK they are mostly what in the old AA parlance would be called two- or three-star establishments. There are not many Best Westerns in the *Guide*; most of them cater for a market very different from ours.

The self-explanatory Relais du Silence, long established on the Continent, is now expanding in the UK; a few of our British hotels are members. Consortiums of cheaper hotels include Logis of Great Britain, with 378 members in the UK and 61 in Ireland, and Minotel, with 250 members in the UK.

In recent years more of our readers have chosen to stay in sophisticated B&Bs operated in private homes, the number of which has been increasing all the time. Some function alone, others belong to various groups. A leading one is Wolsey Lodges, a non-profit-making consortium, which was launched in 1981. It is named for Henry VIII's cardinal, who toured the country expecting to be entertained in style. Its members are defined as "an Englishman's home where you are welcome to stay as a guest for a night or more". Today it has more than 200 members scattered throughout the UK, as well as half a dozen on the Continent – though none in Ireland. They are private guest houses catering for travellers who like to socialise with their hosts and enjoy the lottery of eating, dinner party style, with fellow guests. Some have only two bedrooms and are therefore too small to qualify for a *Guide* entry. There are some splendid examples of the species scattered through these pages.

Other groups include Bed and Breakfast for Garden Lovers, which lists 82 properties that have a particularly attractive garden, and Definitely Different. This small group was founded by Peter and Priscilla Roberts, of *Bradford Old Windmill* at Bradford-on-Avon (see page 38). Its members offer accommodation in old mills, a lighthouse, an old railway carriage and a number of former industrial buildings. The National Trust has 70 tenants, mostly on working farms, who offer B&B at low prices. Some of the B&B groups which operate in London are listed on page 403.

As usual, if a hotel or a restaurant-with-rooms has a *Michelin* star, or a red "Meals" for a good meal at a moderate price, we mention this in the text. When we list an inn that also has an entry in our sibling publication, *The Good Pub Guide*, we mention that fact.

Our experience is that chain hotels do not normally provide the personal style that our readers seek, so they do not qualify for these pages. One shining exception was *Leeming House*, on Ullswater, owned by Forte, where an exceptional manager, Christopher Curry, headed a superb staff. Sadly, the Granada take-over of Forte's hotels has led to a restructuring in which all general managers have been abolished, to be replaced by area managers, each in charge of a group of hotels. Mr Curry has been made redundant, and we can only fear for the future of *Leeming House*.

ABBERLEY Worcestershire

Map 3

The Elms NEW
Abberley WR6 6AT

Tel (01299) 896666
Fax (01299) 896804

This harmonious Queen Anne mansion, with lawns in front and formal gardens behind, was built in 1710 by Gilbert White, a pupil of Sir Christopher Wren. Two modern wings were added when it became a hotel in 1946. For years, it was the first hotel in the *Guide*, but it then went through several changes of ownership and was omitted. Now it is in the hands of Corinna and Marcel Frichot from the Seychelles, formerly the César-winning owners of *Knockinaam Lodge*, Portpatrick, Scotland (*qv*). They have extensively renovated. The ornate plasterwork in the public rooms has been restored; there are some interesting time-pieces in the foyer; the bedrooms have antique furniture, while the bathrooms are smart and modern. "No honeymooning couple could have found a more relaxing retreat after a hectic wedding," write its nominators. "We crunched our way up the drive to a warm welcome. Room 3, which looks out on to the Teme valley and towards Wales, is so large we felt dwarfed. The service was friendly but not overly informal. The lunch and dinner menus were original and well executed; there is a good wine cellar and the staff enjoy advising guests about their wines." Other guests have admired the surrounding countryside. Witley Court, "one of the most spectacular country house ruins in England", and its attached baroque church of Great Witley are a short drive away. *The Elms* won an AA "Courtesy and Care" award in 1997. Children are welcomed. (*AM, and others*)

Open All year.
Rooms 14 double, 2 single.
Facilities Lounge/hall, drawing room, bar, restaurant (occasional musician Sun). 10-acre grounds: tennis, croquet. "Every effort made to help disabled guests."
Location 10 miles NW of Worcester on A443 to Tenbury Wells. Local bus.
Restrictions No smoking in restaurant. No dogs in public rooms.
Credit cards All major cards accepted.
Terms [1997] B&B: single £75–£90, double £110–£135. Set lunch: weekdays £10, Sun £15.95, dinner £25–£32. Special breaks.

Important reminder: terms printed in the *Guide* are only a rough indication of the size of the bill to be expected at the end of your stay. It is vital that you check the tariffs when booking.

ABBOTSBURY Dorset   **Map 1**

Abbey House   **BUDGET**   Tel (01305) 871330
Church Street   Fax (01305) 871088
Abbotsbury DT3 4JJ

In a previous existence, Jonathan and Maureen Cooke charged £12 a
night for B&B at their transport café, *The Greasy Spoon*, on an industrial
estate on the outskirts of Bristol. Now they preside over this picturesque guest house, 15th-century in origin, with 17th- and 18th-
century additions, in what was once the infirmary of a Benedictine
abbey. Its garden goes down in terraces to the largest tithe barn and the
only surviving Benedictine water mill in England. Not all the bathrooms are *en suite*, and one visitor found the attic bedroom uncomfort-
able, but other guests have been enthusiastic: "The views are delicious
– the sea distantly visible – and the Cookes are perfect dears, and most
obliging." "Our bedroom had a cushioned window-seat, pretty
colours, soft carpets, and an unpretentious bathroom. We had delicious
lunches, with fresh-caught fish, simply grilled, on the lawn." The
Cookes go in for house parties and themed weekends, and serve cream
teas in a large tearoom or, in summer, in the garden. For an evening
meal, the *Ilchester Arms*, a big coaching inn in the village, is recommended. Abbotsbury is a pretty stone and thatch village, with sub-
tropical gardens and a swannery with 800 mute swans (it formerly
supplied the abbey's kitchen). Nearby are unspoiled countryside and
excellent coastal walks (Chesil Bank is 15 minutes on foot), and a
monument to Admiral Hardy, Nelson's flag captain at the battle of
Trafalgar. (*Margot and David Holbrook, and others*)

Open All year. Restaurant closed Oct–Apr.
Rooms 1 family suite, 4 double.
Facilities Reception (taped music), lounge, TV/breakfast room. 1½-acre
grounds: stage for classical concerts and plays. Unsuitable for ♿.
Location Abbotsbury is on B3157 half-way between Weymouth and Bridport.
Turn left at sign to swannery; after 100 yds left through abbey arch; *Abbey House*
on right. Train: Dorchester/Weymouth; then taxi.
Restrictions No smoking. No dogs.
Credit cards None accepted.
Terms [1997] B&B £27–£30. Set lunch £7–£15. Themed weekends ("Murder in the
abbey", etc). 1-night bookings sometimes refused in high season. Children
under 13 half-price in parents' room.

ALDEBURGH Suffolk *See SHORTLIST*   **Map 2**

ALSTON Cumbria   **Map 4**

Lovelady Shield   Tel (01434) 381203
Nenthead Road   Fax (01434) 381515
nr Alston CA9 3LF

"A charming hotel. Attentive but not bothersome hosts. Excellent
dinner, charmingly served, supported by a sound wine list. Above-
average breakfast." "For such a remote place, so lacking in pretension,
the sophistication of the food came as a surprise. The dawn chorus
of birds was unforgettable." "Warm and sheltered in the bleak

midwinter. Log fires inside, frozen river and blizzards on the moors." "Relaxed atmosphere. No piped music, no organised entertainment; a place to 'get away from it all'." Praise this year and last for Kenneth and Margaret Lyons' handsome white 19th-century house in a remote setting in the High Pennines, at the foot of majestic fells. It is reached up a long tree-lined drive; the river Nent borders its grounds. It makes a good base for visiting Hadrian's Wall and touring the border country. The bedrooms have a home-like feel, and are well equipped (two are quite small). Chef Barrie Garton's cooking on a daily-changing menu is mainly English in style and served in generous portions; there's always a hot dessert. Plenty of half bottles of wine. Breakfast includes freshly squeezed orange juice, home-made marmalade, kedgeree and mixed grills. (*JDH Mackenzie, Ruth West, Mr and Mrs WA Pedder*)

Open 4 Feb–3 Jan.
Rooms 10 double, 2 single.
Facilities Drawing room, library, bar, restaurant. 2½-acre grounds: tennis, croquet. Golf, fishing, riding nearby. Unsuitable for &.
Location 2½ miles E of Alston. Take A689 to Nenthead. Hotel 2 miles on left, at junction with B6294.
Restrictions No smoking: drawing room, restaurant. No dogs in public rooms.
Credit cards All major cards accepted.
Terms B&B £55–£60; D,B&B £78.50–£88.50. Set dinner £26.95. Christmas, New Year, winter, spring breaks. *V*

AMBERLEY West Sussex   Map 2

Amberley Castle   Tel (01798) 831992
Amberley, nr Arundel BN18 9ND   Fax (01798) 831998

12th-century castle, in prime condition, owned by Joy and Martin Cummings. In pretty village 4 miles N of Arundel, amid lovely countryside on a bend of the river Arun. 12-acre grounds; serene garden behind portcullis. Glorious views from battlements. 15 luxurious bedrooms, in manor house, tower and castle wall; all with jacuzzi. 5 suites planned. Cosy reception rooms. "Unexceptional" country house cooking served in magnificent barrel-vaulted, lancet-windowed restaurant (no smoking). Visitors in late 1996 experienced delays at reception and in restaurant "and lack of visible management", but recent reports more favourable; we'd like more, please. Unsuitable for &. No children under 12. No dogs. All major credit cards accepted. B&B double £130–£300. Set lunch £18.10, dinner £27.50; full alc £45 [1997].

AMBLESIDE Cumbria   Map 4

Grey Friar Lodge   BUDGET   Tel/Fax (01539 4) 33158
Clappersgate   E-mail gflodge@aol.com
Ambleside LA22 9NE

Ambleside is a market town and tourist centre at the head of Lake Windermere. It gets crowded in season, but this former vicarage, built in traditional Lakeland stone, is set well back from a fairly busy road, in sloping gardens on the wooded flanks of Loughrigg Fell, with lovely views over the Brathay River Valley. It is "well run, and pleasantly home-like, with antiques and interesting pictures and curios". Bedrooms, some with four-poster, have pine furniture, flowery fabrics,

---

lots of storage space, and good views. The gregarious hosts, Tony and Sheila Sutton, run the place informally; first names tend to be used. "Our tenth visit revealed no change in the high standard of accommodation," write one couple. "Same warm welcome, and easy relaxed atmosphere. The Suttons work their socks off to ensure that all guests enjoy their stay." Others have admired the immaculate housekeeping, and the "excellent but healthy dinners, a blend of traditional English and mildly exotic, frequently capped by a brilliant old-fashioned hot pudding". There is no choice, "but they will provide alternative dishes". The dining room is small, with tables quite close together, which leads to socialising. "Marvellous value for money." (*Marc and Margaret Wall, and others*)

Open Easter–end Oct; weekends Feb, Mar. Dining room closed midday and to non-residents.
Rooms 8 double. No telephone.
Facilities 2 lounges, dining room (piped "easy listening" music). 1-acre garden: patio, sun terrace. River, fishing 500 yds; Lake Windermere 1 mile. Golf, pony trekking, cycling nearby. Unsuitable for &.
Location 1½ miles SW of Ambleside on A593. Train: Windermere; then taxi or bus.
Restrictions No smoking, except 1 lounge. No children under 10. No dogs.
Credit cards None accepted.
Terms B&B £22–£33; D,B&B £39–£50. Set dinner £17. Special breaks; winter weekend tariffs. 1-night bookings refused if too far in advance.

Rothay Manor Tel (01539 4) 33605
Rothay Bridge Fax (01539 4) 33607
Ambleside LA22 0EH
♦ *César award in 1992*

A Georgian house, "full of English atmosphere", with many original architectural features. It stands in immaculate gardens half a mile from Lake Windermere, in a valley surrounded by fine mountain scenery. It is run by the Nixon brothers, Nigel and Stephen; Colette Nixon and Jane Binn are in charge of the restaurant. This "thoroughly deserves its high reputation", according to a recent visitor, who also admired the friendly reception, and the relaxing lounges with deep carpets, flowers, and plenty of books and magazines. Most bedrooms are spacious; best ones lead off an imposing first-floor verandah with cast iron railings; they have soft pastel colours and are well supplied with fruit, bottled water, and so on. At dinner, served by candlelight on polished wooden tables, with heavy glass and tableware, you can choose from two to five courses; cooking is a mixture of English and French, served in generous portions. There's an interesting vegetarian menu. The wine list is excellent, "but you cannot beat the bottles, some very cheap, recommended on the menu". Breakfast is "copious and excellent". Weekday lunch is a generous buffet or a selection of cooked dishes. Children are welcomed: there are family rooms, free cots, baby-listening, and a decent children's tea. A grandmother was impressed: "When Katy Bear, battered but much loved, was accidentally left behind, she was returned by special delivery, in a beautiful box which was personally addressed to my small grandson." There's a busy one-way traffic system close by, but rooms have double-glazing. (*John Rowlands, and others*)

Open All year, except 3 Jan–6 Feb.
Rooms 3 suites (in annexe, 20 yds: 1 honeymoon; 2 family, 1 with &. access), 13 double, 2 single.
Facilities Ramps. 2 lounges, bar lounge, 2 dining rooms. 1-acre garden: croquet. Free use of nearby leisure centre. Near river Rothay and Lake Windermere: sailing, water-skiing, fishing, riding, golf.
Location On A593 to Coniston, ¼ mile SW of Ambleside. Garden-facing rooms quietest. Train: Windermere; then taxi or bus.
Restrictions No smoking: dining rooms, 1 lounge. No very young children in restaurant at night. No dogs.
Credit cards All major cards accepted.
Terms B&B: single £76–£79, double £118–£122, suite £166–£173; D,B&B: single £100–£106, double £155–£177, suite £220–£226. Set lunch £13, dinner (2–5 courses) £25–£31. Reductions for children. Winter rates. Off-season breaks: music, antiques and fine arts, painting, walking, etc. Christmas, New Year programmes. 1-night bookings sometimes refused.

Rowanfield   NEW/BUDGET   *Tel* (01539 4) 33686
Kirkstone Road   *Fax* (01539 4) 31569
Ambleside LA22 9ET

"The find of our holiday week," runs an enthusiastic nomination for this unassuming Lakeland period house. "Worthy of a *Guide* entry not just for location, but also for food, child-tolerance (to over-fives) and price. It is in a gorgeous hillside setting on the northern edge of Ambleside, on the steep road to the start of Kirkstone Pass (a stiff walk up from the town centre). Our comfortable double room had a Laura Ashley-type decor, and a view of distant lake and woodlands. The owners are very friendly." "Real food", cooked by Philip Butcher, is served at 7 pm by his wife, Jane, in a dining room with the original flagstone floor and an old pine dresser. There is a choice of meat, fish or a vegetarian dish, and two alternative starters and desserts (you make your choice at 5 pm). Breakfasts are lavish. Unlicensed: bring your own drinks. (*Kate Kelly*)

Open Mid-Mar–mid-Nov, Christmas/New Year.
Rooms 8 double. No telephone.
Facilities Lounge, dining room (taped classical music). ¾-acre garden. Lake Windermere 1 mile.
Location NE of Ambleside. Turn off A591 towards Kirkstone almost opposite Bridge House; *Rowanfield* ¾ mile on right. Train: Windermere; then taxi.
Restrictions No smoking. No children under 5. No dogs in house.
Credit cards Access, Visa.
Terms B&B £30; D,B&B £47. Single supplement £20. 1-night booking sometimes refused. Half-board breaks all year.

Wateredge Hotel   *Tel* (01539 4) 32332
Borrans Road   *Fax* (01539 4) 31878
Waterhead, Ambleside LA22 0EP

"A super family-run hotel. The proprietors and staff are friendliness itself, and this seems to rub off on the guests." Praise from a returning visitor to this traditional hotel, run by Mr and Mrs Cowap, their two sons, and their daughter and daughter-in-law. It is a rambling building, which has undergone numerous conversions down the centuries, "resulting in some interesting nooks and crannies". The bedrooms in the old part are sometimes an odd shape; those in the newer part are larger and more conventional; most have a view of the lake. There are two small lounges, a large one with picture windows overlooking the lake, and a tiny cocktail bar – "a delight". "Everywhere is well furnished. Bathroom towels are changed frequently; beds are made during breakfast. The food, served in the smallish dining room, is interesting and beautifully presented. Five courses for dinner, followed, if you can manage it, by cheese. Portions not excessive. Croissants, good brown bread, memorable muesli and whisky porridge for breakfast." Only reservation: "Surely they could rise to fresh orange juice." The hotel recently acquired an adjacent plot of land thereby increasing its lake frontage. (*David Jervois, Shirley Tennent; also O Lynes, and others*)

Open Mid-Jan–mid-Dec.
Rooms 5 suites (across small courtyard), 14 double, 3 single. Some on ground floor.
Facilities Ramp. 3 lounges, TV room, bar, restaurant (taped music in evening); patio. ½-acre grounds: lake frontage, private jetty, rowing boat, fishing, bathing. Fishing permits for local rivers; complimentary use of nearby leisure club with swimming pool, sauna etc. Unsuitable for &.
Location ½ mile S of town; off A591 Kendal–Keswick at Waterhead (roadside rooms can be noisy).
Restrictions No smoking: restaurant, 2 lounges. No children under 7. Dogs by arrangement; not in suites, public rooms.
Credit cards Access, Amex, Visa.
Terms B&B £35–£74; D,B&B £55–£94. Set dinner £26.90. Winter breaks. 1-night bookings sometimes refused Sat.

ARNCLIFFE North Yorkshire   Map 4

Amerdale House   *Tel/Fax* (01756) 770250
Arncliffe, Littondale
Skipton BD23 5QE

❧ *César award in 1995*

"A quiet centre of excellence." "Good value for money. Friendly without being intrusive; very pleasant staff, mostly Australians over for the summer." "No false attempt at bonhomie or house party atmosphere." "Wonderful breakfast: fresh orange juice, good brown toast, nice croissants, excellent grill." Praise this year and last for Nigel and Paula Crapper's Victorian manor – they have been here ten years. It is in a tiny unspoilt hamlet amid the spectacularly beautiful countryside of one of the quietest dales, "with the sound of curlews, lambs grazing in green fields with huge trees, parkland to gaze upon while dining, tranquil fields and hills to calm and restore as one walks". There is wonderful birdwatching. Nigel Crapper's cooking (he has a *Good Food Guide* entry) continues to draw plaudits: "Wonderful and artistic." "Imaginative to a degree; classy ingredients." Meat is local, some of fish is from the Yorkshire coast, herbs, vegetables and fruit are home-grown. The wine list is wide-ranging and fairly priced. The bedrooms are comfortable if not luxurious; some are on the small side. Two were refurbished recently. Fountains Abbey, Harewood House and Skipton Castle are nearby; the start of the Settle–Carlisle railroad is 14 miles away – a spectacular drive. (*John Campbell, Helen Brandes, Beverly Brittan, and others*)

Open Mid-Mar–mid-Nov. Dining room closed for lunch.
Rooms 11 double. 1 on ground floor in converted stables.
Facilities Lounge, library, bar, restaurant. 2-acre grounds. Unsuitable for &.
Location 17 miles N of Skipton; fork left off B6160 to Arncliffe.
Restrictions No smoking: restaurant, library. No dogs in house.
Credit cards Access, Visa.
Terms [1997] D,B&B £59.50–£62.50. Set dinner £27. Special breaks: 4 nights for the price of 3. 1-night bookings refused bank holidays, high-season weekends.

ASHBOURNE Derbyshire   Map 3

Callow Hall   *Tel* (01335) 343403
Mappleton Road   *Fax* (01335) 343624
Ashbourne DE6 2AA

This large Victorian house stands up a tree-lined drive in large grounds just outside Ashbourne, a pretty market town at the southern edge of the Peak District National Park. It has views of rolling fells and dales, and of the valley of the river Dove and its tributary, the Bentley Brook, on which it has fishing rights. The interior is impressive: fine fireplaces, moulded ceilings, antique and period furniture, flowered fabrics, potted plants and flowers. The bedrooms are reached up an imposing staircase. One couple this year, who booked late, were given a room called Violet, which was small and not particularly well furnished. But another room, Anthony, is praised: "Typically Victorian, with high ceilings, moulded cornices, striped wall paper, massive furniture, including a large carved bed with apricot and white swags hung from a coronet, and a large, well-equipped bathroom. The window overlooked woodland gardens carpeted with fat white snowdrops, where a colourful pheasant pursued his drab mate with noisy determination." Breakfast, served in "a charming room, decorated in springtime colours", has a generous buffet and plenty of cooked items. The family owners, David, Dorothy and son Anthony Spencer, are praised: "They could not have been more welcoming and helpful." "Despite the house's grandeur, they are unpretentious hosts and, with their long-serving staff, create a caring atmosphere." Children are welcomed. The dining room has a strikingly red and pink decor, setting off white table cloths. The cooking, by the father and son, is based on high-quality materials: home-produced meat, home-grown garden produce, local fish; bread is home-baked. "Some of the best food we have had," wrote one couple. Stately homes nearby include Chatsworth, Kedleston, Hardwick and Haddon Halls, and Calke Abbey. (*Patricia Flynn, Kate and Brendan McCann; also Meriel Packman, and others*)

Open All year, except Christmas, 1 week Feb. Restaurant closed midday Mon–Sat, evening Sun to non-residents.
Rooms 1 suite, 15 double. 1 on ground floor, equipped for &.
Facilities Lounge, bar, restaurant; function/conference facilities. 42-acre grounds: garden, woodland, farm, stables; fishing (tuition available).
Location ¾ mile from Ashbourne: A515 to Buxton; sharp left at top of 1st hill by *Bowling Green* pub, 1st right to Mappleton; cross bridge; drive is on right. Train: Derby; then taxi.
Restrictions No smoking in restaurant. Dogs by arrangement, not in public rooms.
Credit cards All major cards accepted.
Terms B&B: single £73–£97.50, double £110–£136.50, suite £168; D,B&B: single

£108–£132.50, double £180–£206.50, suite £238. Set Sun lunch £17, dinner £35; full alc £37. Weekend, midweek breaks. *V*

ASHBURTON Devon   Map 1

Holne Chase   NEW   *Tel* (01364) 631471
Ashburton   *Fax* (01364) 631453
Newton Abbot TQ13 7NS   *E-mail* info@holne-chase.co.uk

The former hunting lodge of nearby Buckfast Abbey has a peaceful set-ting in large grounds in the Dartmoor National Park. It was dropped from the *Guide* last year when it changed hands, but a correspondent who lives in Madeira has spent four happy visits here since Sebastian and Philippa Hughes took over, and warmly recommends its rein-statement. "The superb food is complemented by the magnificent situ-ation on the river Dart, with acres of beautiful private woodland to wander through. The hosts are a delightful, hard-working couple, who keep us laughing with their zany sense of humour, even on the gloomi-est of Devon days. Their small son Henry and Batty the basset hound are just as genuinely welcoming." Another visitor waxed lyrical about the view: "Every conceivable shade of green in springtime; every kind of wild flower." Front bedrooms look across wide croquet lawns and through tall trees to distant blue hills. The public rooms are warmed by log fires; there's a well-stocked library. Breakfast is continental or English; light or full lunches and lavish teas are served. The cooking of Wayne Pearson is traditional British with modern touches, using local meat and fish and home-grown vegetables. The place remains dedi-cated to sporting activities: it has a mile of fishing on the river Dart; rid-ing and shooting on Dartmoor can be arranged, and the stable suites are particularly suitable for visitors with sporting gear or dogs. (*Thoma and Michael Smallthwaite*)

Open All year.
Rooms 6 suites (4 in stables), 11 double, 1 single. 1 on ground floor.
Facilities Ramp. Drawing room, library, bar, restaurant; private dining room. 70-acre grounds: croquet, putting, river, fishing.
Location From N and E: M5 to Exeter, A38, 2nd Ashburton turn-off; pass Pear Tree garage on left; after 2 miles cross Holne bridge; hotel ¼ mile on right. From Plymouth: leave A38 at 1st Ashburton turn-off. Train: Newton Abbot; then taxi or hotel may meet.
Restrictions No smoking in restaurant. No children under 10 in restaurant at night. Dogs in public rooms "by consent".
Credit cards All major cards accepted.
Terms B&B £57.50–£80; D,B&B (2 nights min.) £65.50–£110. Set lunch £20, dinner £25; full alc £39.50. Child in parents' room: B&B £15.50. Cookery, painting, fly-fishing courses; shooting packages; garden tours. *V*

ASKRIGG North Yorkshire   Map 4

The King's Arms   NEW   *Tel* (01969) 650258
Market Place   *Fax* (01969) 650635
Askrigg DL8 3HQ   *E-mail* rayliz@kahaskrigg.prestel.co.uk

In a tiny Wensleydale village, this old building was once the stables of an 18th-century racehorse owner, John Pratt (who was painted by Stubbs). In 1810, it became a coaching inn on the Richmond to

Lancaster turnpike. It retains a strong period feel and, writes a recent visitor, "specialises in tranquil pleasures – the log fire in the low-beamed front bar, the softly chiming grandfather clock on the main staircase, the creaking of uneven wooden floors". The bedrooms are scattered around the building; those on the higher floors look over slate rooftops. They have antique furniture, a brass half-tester or four-poster bed, a bath or shower, telephone and TV. They vary in size; two are on the road, but there is little traffic; most are "blessedly quiet". John Barber's cooking has won many awards, and there are plenty of options for eating: a generous three-course meal in the panelled restaurant, a casual dinner in the front bar, or a butty in the atmospheric basement pub. "Breakfasts are enormous and excellent. If you want to know what hard work means, have a look at Ray and Liz Hopwood, now in their 15th year here; they attend to every detail." One of the three bars, the back parlour, which has an inglenook fireplace and oak settles, played the part of the *Drovers' Arms* in "Darrowby" (nearby Thirsk in real life) of the TV series *All Creatures Great and Small*. Outside is a small courtyard on two levels, with tables and chairs. There is beautiful scenery all around, which Turner painted in the early 19th century, and much to visit, including Middleham, Bolton and Skipton castles and the abbeys at Fountains and Jervaulx. (*Kathryn Jourdan, David and Anna Berkeley; also Good Pub Guide*)

Open All year.
Rooms 1 suite, 10 double.
Facilities Lounge, 3 bars (live jazz/pop monthly), restaurant; function facilities. Courtyard. Fishing, shooting nearby. Unsuitable for &.
Location 1 mile N of A684 Leyburn–Sedbergh. Train: Carlisle, Settle; hotel will meet.
Restrictions No smoking in restaurant. No dogs in restaurant.
Credit cards Access, Amex, Visa.
Terms [1997] B&B £39.50–£70; D,B&B £64.50–£95. 2-night weekend breaks. Set lunch £12.50, dinner £25. Bar meals *c.* £17.50. *V*

AYLESBURY Buckinghamshire   Map 2

Hartwell House   *Tel* (01296) 747444
Oxford Road   *Fax* (01296) 747450
Aylesbury HP17 8NL

This serene country mansion (where King Louis XVIII of France held court in exile between 1809 and 1814) was restored to its original splendour by Historic House Hotels Ltd (see also *The Cadogan*, London, *Middlethorpe Hall*, York, and *Bodysgallen Hall*, Llandudno, Wales). It stands in huge landscaped grounds, with a trout lake, a ruined church, lots of statuary, and an orangery-style spa with a buttery for light lunches. Behind its impressive Jacobean and Georgian façades, there is a splendid interior, with fine paintings and plasterwork, a Jacobean central staircase, a spectacular 18th-century great hall, a fine library, and a maze of corridors, corners and different levels. Bedrooms are spacious, some huge. Some have magnificent panelling and a four-poster; newer ones on the Hartwell wing are less well designed. Despite the grandeur, the friendliness of the manager, Jonathan Thompson, and his mainly young staff creates an unintimidating atmosphere. "A very nice hotel," one visitor wrote; another detected "an endearing touch of the fawlties".

Modern English cooking is served in the formal restaurant. It is admired by some, but others have thought it pretentious and over-elaborate. A couple spending a few days would have liked some light alternatives to the elaborately sauced dishes; while the breakfast is thought "not up to that served in many less expensive establishments". And corporate bookings can detract from the country-house feel. But the champagne breaks are considered good value. Nearby Aylesbury has suffered at the hands of developers, though some attractive old houses round a church survive, and the award-winning Buckinghamshire County Museum is worth a visit – it has a charming art gallery and a Roald Dahl Children's Gallery (he lived at Great Missenden, nine miles away). (*Sir Timothy Harford, and others*)

Open All year.
Rooms 13 suites, 32 double, 1 single. Some in stable block. Some on ground floor. 1 equipped for &.
Facilities Lift, ramp. Hall (pianist Fri/Sat evening), great hall, morning room, drawing room, library, bar, buttery, restaurant; conference facilities; spa: indoor swimming pool, whirlpool, sauna, beauty salon, bar/buttery. 90-acre grounds: tennis, croquet, lake (fishing), woodlands.
Location 2 miles S of Aylesbury on A418 towards Oxford; hotel on right. Train: Aylesbury; then taxi.
Restrictions No smoking: dining rooms, morning room, some bedrooms. No children under 8. No dogs in public rooms.
Credit cards Access, Amex, Visa.
Terms Rooms: single £110–£140, double £180–£300, suite £300–£500. Breakfast: continental £10.50, English £14. Set lunch (2–4 courses) £19.75–£26.50, dinner £42; full alc £49. Winter champagne breaks (D,B&B from £123 per person per night); summer breaks; spa breaks; Christmas, New Year house parties.

BARNSTAPLE Devon   Map 1

Lynwood House   NEW   *Tel* (01271) 43695
Bishop's Tawton Road   *Fax* (01271) 79340
Barnstaple EX32 9EF

Restaurant-with-rooms in yellow-brick Victorian hotel (outwardly no beauty) on outskirts of town. Run for 27 years by Roberts family, John and Ruth, Matthew and Lisa; admired for cooking (Good Food Guide entry), especially fish, in tastefully furnished dining room. Light lunches in well-appointed bar. "Lived-in and unpretentious; warm and personal welcome, but no time wasted on ceremony." 5 bedrooms with shower, modestly furnished, but with cafetière, fresh milk, biscuits, fruit, etc. Large carpark. Closed 1–3 Jan; Sun supper for residents only. Unsuitable for &. No dogs in public rooms. All major credit cards accepted. B&B: single £47.50, double £67.50; full alc £30. More reports, please. ***V***

BARWICK Somerset   Map 2

 Little Barwick House   *Tel* (01935) 423902
Barwick, nr Yeovil BA22 9TD   *Fax* (01935) 420908

César award: quiet rural perfection

Barwick is a tiny village near Yeovil, noted chiefly for the 18th-century follies – pillars, towers and arches – on the edge of its park. This

Georgian dower house is in a secluded corner, set in a peaceful garden. A perennial *Guide* favourite, it represents "quiet perfection" to regular visitors: "You don't get that without a lot of care and attention, which is exactly what Christopher and Veronica Colley have been giving us for the last ten years. I cannot imagine anywhere else as special. The rooms aren't grand but they are comfy. The food is delicious – nothing flashy, just first-class ingredients, lovingly and simply cooked. The wine list has a wide, but not excessive, choice. Marvellous value for money." "Our visits are the highlight of the year, and we are never disappointed." Others have written gratefully of the first class service and the pleasant, relaxed atmosphere. "There's nothing phony or pretentious; the dining room is not a temple. Meals are balanced, steamed vegetables crunchy, puddings indulgent." "Christopher Colley is an ideal front-of-house, always friendly, never overbearing. Veronica's food is superb." Mrs Colley cooks mainly British dishes using local ingredients. There are choices at each stage of the four-course set menu; you can opt for two and pay less. The lounge is small, so are some bedrooms, but they are quiet and well equipped, with comfortable chairs and good lights. Breakfasts include good toast, ample coffee, nothing packaged. Afternoon tea with crumpets is free. Winter breaks are excellent value. There are plenty of houses and gardens to visit nearby, and the Colleys offer folly-hunting breaks. (*Sebastian Chamberlain, Stephen Potts, Celia and Andrew Payne, PE Carter, and others*)

Open All year, except Christmas, New Year. Restaurant closed midday, to non-residents Sun.
Rooms 6 double.
Facilities Lounge, bar, restaurant. 3½-acre garden. Unsuitable for &.
Location Left off A37 Yeovil–Dorchester at *Red House* pub. Hotel ¼ mile on left.
Restrictions No smoking: dining room, bedrooms. No dogs in public rooms.
Credit cards Access, Amex, Visa.
Terms [1997] B&B from £42; D,B&B from £62. Set dinner (2–4-course): £19.90–£27.90. Reductions for 2 nights or more. Winter breaks Oct–Apr. 1-night bookings sometimes refused Sun off-season. Children accommodated free in parents' room. ***V***

BASLOW Derbyshire   Map 3

The Cavendish   *Tel* (01246) 582311
Baslow DE45 1SP   *Fax* (01246) 582312

This hotel, which has been run since 1975 by Eric Marsh, is on the edge of a village on the northern edge of the Chatsworth estate, the family seat of the Duke and Duchess of Devonshire. It backs on to a busy road, but all the bedrooms overlook the park. The best ones, in the newer Mitford wing, are named for members of the duchess's famous family. Their decor, wrote recent visitors, is "modern, but not OTT". The public rooms have log fires, impressive flower arrangements, antiques (many from Chatsworth) and an interesting collection of paintings. Some recent reports: "The hotel and the courtesy of its staff are like a time bubble of England as it used to be." "A very friendly place; most unusually they did not ask for a deposit. Our bedroom was comfortable and quiet." "Two genuinely comfortable chairs in the bedroom (most unusual); we applaud their practice of serving breakfast all morning." But there are also comments about amateurish service, and "a feeling of complacency", and some of the older bedrooms are thought to be in need of redecoration. In the main restaurant, Nick Buckingham's cooking ranges from traditional to sophisticated. One couple said it was "probably best on robust, rather than delicate, flavours", but others have thought it over-ambitious. The wine list is "intelligently arranged, with a fair mark-up". Meals are priced according to the number of courses taken. For £39.95 a head you can eat in the kitchen, watching the chef at work. Simpler food, from late breakfast and *plats du jour* to soups and sandwiches, is served in the Garden Room between 11 am and 11 pm. In winter, if you book for Friday and Saturday nights you can stay for Sunday night at no extra charge, paying only for meals. Children are welcomed. Mr Marsh recently bought and refurbished *The George*, in the nearby village of Hathersage. (*Jonathan Palfrey, Ian and Francine Walsh, Carolyn Mathiasen, and others*)

Open All year.
Rooms 1 suite, 23 double.
Facilities Lounge with bar, 2 restaurants; private dining room, conference room. 2-acre grounds: putting green. Fishing nearby. Unsuitable for ♿.
Location On A619 in Chatsworth grounds. M1 exit 29. Train: Chesterfield; then bus or taxi.
Restrictions No smoking in restaurant. No dogs.
Credit cards All major cards accepted.
Terms [1997] Rooms: single £84–£99, double £104–£124, suite £139. Breakfast: continental £4.95; English £9.20. Light meals in Garden Room. Restaurant: set lunch/dinner £32.25; kitchen table £39.95; full alc £45. Winter bonus weekends.

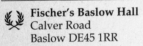

Fischer's Baslow Hall	*Tel* (01246) 583259
Calver Road	*Fax* (01246) 583818
Baslow DE45 1RR	

César award: restaurant-with-rooms of the year

In their Edwardian manor, up a tree-lined drive in a village on the edge of the Chatsworth estate, Max and Susan Fischer run a *Michelin*-starred restaurant-with-rooms alongside a less formal café (with *Michelin*'s red "Meals"). The house is furnished in personal style, with Victorian and country pine furniture, bold colours, good fabrics; ornaments, fresh flowers, plants and bowls of pot-pourri abound, and there is much evidence of the Fischers' passion for antiques. The lounge can get crowded, as it serves non-resident diners as well as residents. "A charming manageress takes the dinner orders," explains a regular visitor. "In the restaurant, which has a fine plaster ceiling, Max Fischer's cooking is modern and eclectic; many dishes are rich and complicated; fish is a speciality; portions are generous. Service is by helpful young waiters. The atmosphere is cheerful, with much chatting among the guests; no church-like feel here." Others have written: "Food was first class, ending with a cheese board, properly served. The wine list is extensive and fairly priced. Without our asking, a newspaper was pushed under our door. The breakfast scrambled egg, served in a dome shape with smoked salmon, was the finest I have ever tasted." Delicious oven-fresh brioches and croissants too. The bedrooms, up a carved oak staircase, are as crammed with ornaments as the rest. One couple's was "lovely and small"; another's was "spacious and extremely comfortable, and its Edwardian bath and shower/body spray both beautiful and effective". Warm tributes are paid to Mrs

Fischer: "A natural hostess. She remembers everyone's name. There's never a sign of stress, however busy they are. Though we arrived in the middle of a wedding party, she came to greet us, offered us coffee, and found someone to help with our luggage. When we left, she came out to bid us goodbye." Haddon Hall is four miles away; Hardwick Hall and Kedleston are a comfortable drive. (*PF, Jeffrey Reed; also Stephen and Ellise Holman*)

Open All year, except 25/26 Dec. Restaurant closed to non-residents Sun evening. Café closed Sat evening/Sun.
Rooms 1 suite, 5 double.
Facilities Lounge/bar, breakfast room, restaurant, café (taped light music). 5-acre grounds. Fishing 3 miles. Unsuitable for &.
Location Take A623 Baslow–Stockport. Last entrance on right within village boundary. Train: Chesterfield, 12 miles; then taxi.
Restrictions No smoking in restaurant. No children under 12 in restaurant after 7 pm. Guide dogs only.
Credit cards All major cards accepted.
Terms B&B: single £75–£90, double £100–£130, suite £130. Restaurant: set lunch (2/3-course) £18–£22, dinner £42; café: full alc £25. 2-night packages; weekend breaks. 1-night bookings refused New Year.

BATH Somerset   Map 2

Dukes' Hotel   BUDGET   *Tel* (01225) 463512
Great Pulteney Street   *Fax* (01225) 483733
Bath BA2 4DN

Grade I listed Georgian house in one of the town's premier streets, just across river from Abbey (quietest rooms at rear). Many original features, including fine staircase (no lift). Exceptionally kind American owners, Tim and Rosalind Forester. Unpretentious regional English cooking, well prepared and served, in no-smoking basement restaurant (piped classical music). "Cheerfully served hearty breakfasts." Garage, unrestricted street parking. Closed 24–26 Dec; restaurant closed Sun evening. 23 rooms (5 family). Unsuitable for &. No dogs in public rooms. All major credit cards accepted. B&B: single £55–£75, double £70–£95; D,B&B single £65–£85, double £90–£115. Set dinner (2/3-course) £14.50/£18.50. Recently endorsed, but we'd like more reports, please. *V*

Haydon House   BUDGET   *Tel/Fax* (01225) 427351 and 444919
9 Bloomfield Park
Bath BA2 2BY

"We arrived at 10 pm after a hideous journey and were warmly greeted, ushered in and given a welcome tray of tea," writes a grateful visitor to Gordon and Magdalene Ashman-Marr's B&B, a semi-detached Edwardian house (dovecote outside) in a quiet residential area above the city. It has a chintzy lounge, crammed with family photos, china ornaments and dried flowers. At the back is a colourful garden with statues, lit up at night; in summer, drinks may be taken on the terrace. The immaculate bedrooms, also well endowed with ornaments, have home-made shortbread, a decanter of sherry and a hot-water bottle. One has a four-poster; a large one at the top is suitable for a family. Bathrooms have a good-sized tub and/or a power shower.

Breakfast is served at flexible times. "I rather dreaded the communal eating," one guest said, "but the group of guests was delightful, and the conversation wide-ranging, with Gordon (who likes to crack a joke) adding his comments while serving." The menu includes whisky or rum porridge, scrambled eggs with smoked salmon, eggs Benedict, and home-made mango and orange marmalade, all served with good china, silver and crystal. A continental breakfast may be taken in the bedrooms. Help is offered with dinner reservations. No parking problems; an agreeable walk down to the centre; a stiffish one back. In low season, guests who book for two nights may stay free for a third, except Friday. (*Jill McLaren, and others*)

Open All year.
Rooms 5 double.
Facilities Sitting room, study, breakfast room; sun terrace. ½-acre garden. Sports/leisure centre nearby. Not really suitable for &.
Location From centre take A367 (to Exeter) *c.* ½ mile up Wells Rd. Right into shopping area (*Bear* pub on right). At end of short dual carriageway fork right into Bloomfield Rd; Bloomfield Pk 2nd right. Street parking. Bus 14 from centre.
Restrictions No smoking. Children by arrangement. No dogs.
Credit cards Access, Amex, Visa.
Terms B&B: single £45–£55, double £60–£80. 3 nights for price of 2 (except Fri/Sat) Nov–Mar. 1-night bookings occasionally refused weekends. ***V***

Holly Lodge   *Tel* (01225) 424042
8 Upper Oldfield Park   *Fax* (01225) 481138
Bath BA2 3JZ

This no-smoking B&B is a large Victorian house, high above the city in a tree-lined road containing a number of B&Bs. It has a "charming owner", George Hall, and is "beautifully quiet", according to a recent visitor. "Our bedroom was sumptuously decorated; it had views of the city and the terraced garden. The bathroom was large and well appointed." Some rooms have a four-poster. Generous breakfasts are served in a conservatory. There is a pretty sitting room, with a chandelier, antique furniture and newspapers and glossy magazines. It takes about ten minutes to walk to the centre; there are local buses for the uphill return journey. More reports, please.

Open All year.
Rooms 6 double, 1 single. 1 on ground floor.
Facilities Lounge, breakfast room. ½-acre garden: gazebo.
Location ½ mile SW of centre. 1st right off Wells Rd (A367). Private parking. Bus 200 yds.
Restrictions No smoking. No dogs.
Credit cards All major cards accepted.
Terms B&B: single £46–£48, double £75–£85. 2-night breaks Nov–Feb: £70 per person. 1-night bookings sometimes refused bank holidays.

The Priory   *Tel* (01225) 331922
Weston Road   *Fax* (01225) 448276
Bath BA1 2XT

Grade II listed 19th-century Gothic-style house, in 3-acre grounds 1 mile W of centre, off A4 to Bristol. Centre reached by bus, or easy walk through Victoria Park. Country house decor, "atmosphere of quiet good taste": antiques, splendid flower arrangements, log fires. Courteous, welcoming service. Excellent

French/English classical cooking in formal restaurant by long-serving chef, Mike Collom; brasserie-style meals in Garden Room/orangery. Leisure centre: swimming pool, gym, sauna; 2-acre grounds: swimming pool, croquet. No smoking in restaurants. No dogs. All major credit cards accepted. 29 rooms, 1 adapted for &. B&B: single £120, double £140–£195, suite £230; D,B&B: single £150, double £200–£250, suite £285. Set lunch £17, dinner £30. Weekend breaks; Christmas programme. New manager, Tim Pettifer, arrived in early 1997. More reports, please. *V*

The Queensberry　　　　　　　　　　　　*Tel* (01225) 447928
Russel Street　　　　　　　　　　　　　　*Fax* (01225) 446065
Bath BA1 2QF

Stephen and Penny Ross's upmarket small hotel, bedecked in summer with myriad flower baskets, is in a residential street not far from the Assembly Rooms. The finely proportioned house was designed by John Wood for the Marquis of Queensberry in 1772, and its decor complements the 18th-century stucco ceilings, cornices and panelling. "A cool, calm courtyard stretches along the rear, making an oasis for some ground-floor bedrooms and the small, clubby bar." Teas are served in the cream-coloured drawing room. Bedrooms on the first floor are large. "Ours felt spacious even when two child's beds were added," one couple wrote. Another visitor admired his, with the bathroom down a flight of steps, "which gave an airy feeling". Rooms at the top are smaller, and priced accordingly. In the basement restaurant, *The Olive Tree*, Mathew Prowse's modern British/Mediterranean cooking is "a treat, with friendly, caring service". The wine list is "interesting and affordable". (*Sue Cooper, Prof. RS Cormack and Dr WM Beard, Robin Houston*)

Open All year, except 1 week Christmas.
Rooms 22 double. Some on ground floor.
Facilities Drawing room, bar, restaurant (occasional taped jazz); meeting room. Courtyard garden.
Location Central. Take Bennett St left off Lansdown Rd, then 1st right. Street parking.
Restrictions No smoking in restaurant. Guide dogs only.
Credit cards Access, Visa.
Terms B&B: single £89–£110, double £90–£175. English breakfast £7.50. Set lunch (2/3-course) £11.50/£13.50, dinner £19; full alc £32. 2-night winter breaks. 1-night booking sometimes refused.

Royal Crescent Hotel　　　　　　　　　*Tel* (01225) 739955
The Royal Crescent　　　　　　　　　　　*Fax* (01225) 339401
Bath BA1 2LS

This luxurious hotel sits in the middle of Bath's most glorious crescent, its entrance discreetly marked by bay trees. It was skilfully created from two adjoining Georgian houses; many period features have been retained. There are antiques and fine paintings in the grand public rooms. The suites are grand, too, and lavishly equipped, and most doubles are large. The main restaurant, the bar, and further bedrooms are in the Dower House, Pavilion and Garden Villa, across the peaceful garden. The hotel was recently taken over by Cliveden plc, and an extensive refurbishment is underway. By the end of 1997 a second, less formal restaurant, and a holistic spa, the Bath House, will have been added. "Everything perfect," wrote a 1997 visitor. "The staff are friendly and helpful. But we thought that at these prices breakfast should have been included in the room rate." We'd like reports on the meals cooked by chef Steven Blake, please. "They will be classical and creative," promises Ross Stevenson, the general manager. (*Prof. Wolfgang Stoeke*)

Open All year.
Rooms 16 suites, 26 double. In 5 separate buildings. Some on ground floor.
Facilities Lift. 3 drawing rooms, bar, 2 restaurants; function facilities. 1-acre garden: plunge pool, croquet. River launch. hot air balloon trips, theatre tickets arranged. Holistic spa planned for 1998.
Location ½ mile from centre. Valet parking.
Restriction No smoking: restaurants, 2 drawing rooms, 8 bedrooms.
Credit cards All major cards accepted.
Terms [1997] Rooms: double £160–£260, suite £330–£675. Breakfast: continental £11, English £13.50. Set lunch £19.50, dinner £39.

Somerset House **BUDGET**   *Tel* (01225) 466451
35 Bathwick Hill   *Fax* (01225) 317188
Bath BA2 6LD

This handsome listed Regency house is a short drive or a stiffish walk uphill from the centre. It has been run for many years by Jean and Malcolm Seymour, with son Jonathan (the chef), and a parrot, which greets arriving guests at the door. There is a flowery garden with a large Judas tree. The bedrooms, named for George III's children, retain their original dimensions, and one double and the single are small; each has a bathroom or shower (there can be problems with water pressure in rooms at the top). The restaurant is open to the public. Dinner, served at 7 pm (7.30 on Saturday), with two or three choices for each course, is traditional English family cooking, with occasional ethnic or themed menus. One couple this year complained of a cool welcome and of being rushed at mealtimes, but otherwise reports are positive. "The Seymours strike a nice balance between friendliness and professionalism. We enjoyed pre-dinner drinks in the drawing room, sharing the fireside with the family pets. There was a good vegetarian dish on the menu, and a fruity bread-and-butter pudding. Good house wines too (an eccentric pamphlet in the bedroom describes how the wines are chosen)." "Excellent and varied food; in two weeks not a single dish was repeated on the menu." "We particularly enjoyed the meals themed to suit the composer of the opera weekends." "Breakfast is an experience: sideboard laden with cereals, home-made muesli, bread, jams, marmalades; every cooked dish one could expect." "Informality the trademark. Younger members of the family continue to appear." "The friendly gathering of guests before dinner is a great start to the evening." (*Sarah Chrisp, and many others*)

Open All year. Restaurant closed Sun evening.
Rooms 9 double, 1 single. 2 on ground floor. 3 with TV.
Facilities 2 lounges, restaurant, conservatory. 1-acre garden: miniature railway. Kennet and Avon Canal, fishing, boat trips nearby.
Location ¾ mile from centre. Junction of Bathwick Hill (leading to university) and Cleveland Walk. Carpark. Mini-bus no.18/418 from centre.
Restrictions No smoking. No dogs in public rooms.
Credit cards Access, Amex, Visa.

Terms B&B: single £20.50–£32, double £41–£64; D,B&B: single £43.50–£51, double £82–£102. Set lunch £11, dinner £19. Midweek bargain breaks. Opera, Brunel, canal weekends in low season. Christmas, New Year house party. *V*

BATHFORD Somerset   Map 2

Eagle House   BUDGET   *Tel/Fax* (01225) 859946
Church Street
Bathford BA1 7RS

Bathford, a pretty conservation village spread up a steep hill, three miles east of Bath, makes a pleasant alternative to staying in the city; you can avoid parking problems there by taking a bus. Informally run by John and Rosamund Napier, this B&B is a beautiful listed Georgian building by John Wood the Elder, quietly set in a large garden (complete with treehouse, sandpit, swing and grass tennis court). It has a handsome drawing room with a fine marble fireplace and moulded ceiling, and "old family furniture – good, but not too smart"; a beautiful curving staircase leads to the bedrooms upstairs. "I have rarely stayed in a hotel with such a nice atmosphere," one guest wrote. "We were in a large party, with five children. The welcome could not have been friendlier. Our rooms were large and pretty, with beautiful views. Everything had been thought of, down to fresh milk in a thermos for tea-making.

The bathrooms were great. Breakfast was plentiful, with a ridiculously small extra charge for cooked dishes. The children loved the garden. We enjoyed every minute." Two bedrooms are in a cottage with its own walled garden and kitchen. Breakfast is until 10 am on weekdays, 10.30 on Sunday. (*CT and others*)

Open All year, except 20–31 Dec.
Rooms 1 family, 6 double, 1 single. 2 double in cottage with sitting room, kitchen, walled garden.
Facilities Drawing room, breakfast room. 2½-acre garden: tennis, croquet, sandpit, treehouse, swings. Unsuitable for &.
Location First right off Bathford Hill; 200 yds on right behind high stone wall and wrought iron gates (conservation area; no sign permitted). Ample parking. 3 buses an hour from Bath.
Restrictions No smoking in 1 bedroom. Generally no dogs in public rooms.
Credit cards Access, Visa.
Terms B&B: single £35–£47, double £46–£72, suite £75–£98. Cooked breakfast £2.80 added. Winter breaks mid-Nov–mid-Mar. 1-night bookings sometimes refused Sat, bank holidays. Children accommodated free in parents' room. *V*

The Lodge   *Tel* (01225) 858467 and 858575
Bathford Hill   *Fax* (01225) 858172
Bathford BA1 7SL

"We could not have been more impressed. Our bedroom was pretty, elegant and comfortable, its bathroom spotless. Even in October the garden was lovely. No matter how hard we looked for a flaw we could not find one." "On a return visit, we were treated like old friends. We noticed new touches: a bowl of butterscotch, a jug of fresh milk on the tea tray every day, more toiletries. The buffet-style breakfast is superb, from exotic fresh fruits, cereals and yogurt, to a huge and varied cooked plateful." "A fabulous place, with a personal atmosphere." Recent praise from both sides of the Atlantic for Keith and Mary Johnson's B&B on the village's steep hill. In the lounge, visitors may browse through the papers over tea or a complimentary sherry. In the award-winning landscaped garden (with sheltered swimming pool) they may socialise with the owners' dogs and cats. The Johnsons own a narrow boat, which guests may hire, on the Kennet and Avon canal. They specialise in house parties. The *Crown* pub, just down the road, is recommended for an evening meal. (*Mark and Marissa Martin, Jean and John Hinton, Karen M Harvey*)

Open All year, except Christmas, New Year.
Rooms 1 suite, 6 double. 1 on ground floor.
Facilities Lounge, breakfast room. 3-acre garden: swimming pool (heated May–Oct).
Location Up Bathford Hill, on right, 100 yds after *Crown* inn. Bus or taxi from Bath.
Restriction No dogs in public rooms.
Credit cards Access, Visa.
Terms B&B: single £50–£90, double £65–£110. Weekend breaks "negotiable". Children under 5 accommodated free in parents' room. 1-night bookings some-times refused weekends in high season. *V*

BATTLE East Sussex   Map 2

Little Hemingfold   *Tel* (01424) 774338
Telham, Battle TN33 0TT   *Fax* (01424) 775351

Paul and Allison Slater's informal hideaway is a higgledy-piggledy, not very *soigné* mixture of old buildings up a bumpy track, in a bucolic posi-tion by a lake. It is not equipped for very small children, but for older ones there is plenty to do. There's a grass tennis court, good walking, "with two labradors for those needing an incentive", and "ravishing countryside" all around. Bedrooms, some with a small wood-burning stove, are spacious; though plainly furnished, they have a telephone, TV, and an electric blanket. Dinner, "no-frills cooking, with some choice, using fresh produce from the garden, and served by charming students", is at 7.30 pm; vegetarians are catered for. Communal eating is the norm, but you can ask for a separate table. Most 1996/97 visitors have been well pleased: "Charming owners. Rooms and bathrooms a bit rough in places, but beds comfortable and hot water plentiful. Beautiful walks through bluebell woods. Rowing on pretty lake good fun. Lovely light lounges with interesting books for browsing. Well-cooked food, with skilful sauces. Excellent English breakfasts." "Delightful sur-roundings; congenial atmosphere." Battle, close by, is a charming town which grew up round the abbey (now ruined) which was founded by Duke William of Normandy to celebrate his victory over King Harold at the battle of Hastings, fought here in 1066. The Newhaven ferry is 40 minutes' drive away. (*NM Mackintosh, Bruce Douglas-Mann*)

Open All year, except 5 Jan–12 Feb. Lunch not served, except for previously booked parties.

Rooms 13 double. 10 with *en suite* facilities. 9 in adjoining coach house.
Facilities 2 lounges, bar, dining room (piped classical music at night). 40-acre grounds: tennis, croquet, woods, lake (swimming, fishing, boating). Golf nearby. Unsuitable for &.
Location 1½ miles S of Battle off A2100; blue hotel sign on left by road sign indicating sharp bend. Train: Battle; then bus/coach, and ½-mile walk up bumpy drive.
Restrictions No smoking: dining room, 1 lounge. No dogs in public rooms.
Credit cards All major cards accepted.
Terms B&B: single £36–£61, double £72–£78; D,B&B: single £56–£80, double £112–£116. Set dinner £21.50. Children under 4 accommodated free in parents' room. Special breaks; house parties; Christmas, New Year packages. 1-night bookings generally refused Sat night, bank holidays in season.

Netherfield Place   *Tel* (01424) 774455
Battle TN33 9PP   *Fax* (01424) 774024

Michael and Helen Collier's Georgian-style 1920s country house is set up a long drive in extensive, well-kept grounds with formal gardens and plenty to do (see below). It has attractive public rooms and a traditional decor. Bedrooms, with light colours and chintzy fabrics, vary in size and are well supplied with flowers, fresh fruit, chocolates etc; their old-fashioned carpeted bathrooms have capacious towels and bathrobes, and good toiletries. The panelled restaurant, popular locally, serves modern English cooking, "not *haute cuisine*, but freshly prepared", using ingredients from the large kitchen garden. Recent visitors enjoyed their stay: "Our room was bright and attractively decorated, though we had to do a bit of repair work on the stand for the TV; we will pack glue next time. The staff were friendly but respectful. Room service very good. Breakfast and afternoon tea terrific, everything home-made and tasty – bread and cakes are a speciality. Dinner was also good, particularly the duck and the venison; and the puds more than compensated for a little over-adventurousness with flavours. The setting is beautiful; at Easter there were newborn lambs, and seas of daffodils and cowslips." (*Ruth and John Pearson*)

Open All year, except Christmas–early Jan.
Rooms 10 double, 4 single.
Facilities Lounge, bar, restaurant (piped light classical/modern music); conference facilities. 30-acre grounds: gardens, tennis, putting, croquet, clay pigeon-shooting, woodland walks. Golf, fishing, riding nearby. Sea 8 miles. Unsuitable for &.
Location 2 miles NW of Battle. Turn left towards Netherfield off A2100. Hotel is 1½ miles on. Train: Battle; then taxi.
Restriction Dogs by arrangement, in bedrooms only.
Credit cards All major cards accepted.
Terms B&B: single £70, double £105–£160; D,B&B: single £100, double £160–£190. Set lunch £15, dinner £27; full alc £38–£40. 2-night breaks. 1-night bookings refused Sat Apr–Nov. *V*

Powder Mills   *Tel* (01424) 775511
Powdermill Lane   *Fax* (01424) 774540
Battle TN33 0SP

Lovely listed 18th-century house with Mediterranean feel – Doric columns, Greek statues – in 150-acre park and woodlands, 1 mile up lane opposite Battle railway station. 4 lakes (coarse fishing), unheated swimming pool. Antiques,

*log fires, books in public rooms. Informal style; country atmosphere. Light
lunches, snacks in library. Good modern cooking in Orangery restaurant
(closed Sun evening Jan/Feb); dinner-dance on Fri in winter/spring; venue for
weddings, conferences, etc. 35 rooms: best in main house, 12 in mill, 5 on
ground floor (1 with facilities for &). No smoking in some bedrooms. All major
credit cards accepted. B&B: single £60–£65, double £85–£115. D,B&B: single
£75–£80, double £120–£150 [1997]. Maintenance of bedrooms and grounds
criticised this year, "but it would take little to make it excellent". More reports,
please.* *V*

BEAMINSTER Dorset   **Map 1**

Bridge House   *Tel* (01308) 862200
3 Prout Bridge   *Fax* (01308) 863700
Beaminster DT8 3AY

"Consistently good food, accommodation and service; fair prices."
"Atmosphere that of a visit to attentive friends; proprietor and staff
there when needed. Tea by a fire on a winter afternoon. Dinner menu
just what we like: not too ambitious, nor too long to be believably fresh,
and using largely local produce. Excellent wine list. Enormous, enjoyable breakfast, with a good selection of uncooked and cooked items
and home-made preserves." "Large, well-lit bedroom with beautiful
decor, upmarket tea bags and fresh milk." Recent praise for this small
hotel in a 13th-century building, once a priest's house, in an old country town in the west Dorset hills. It has mullioned windows, old beams
and inglenook fireplaces, and a pretty walled garden. Its popular
restaurant, which has a pink decor, serves traditional mainly English
cooking by proprietor/chef Peter Pinkster and Jacky Rae. Light
lunches are served in a conservatory extension. Bedrooms are in the
main house, converted stables and a new wing. Beaminster, pronounced Bemminster, is in the heart of Hardy country (it is Emminster
in *Tess of the D'Urbervilles*). Its stone manor, Parnham House, now the
John Makepeace Furniture Workshops, stands in formal gardens three-
quarters of a mile to the south; many stately homes and gardens are
close by; and the coast is ten miles away. (*John Campbell, EB, and others*)

Open All year, except 28/29 Dec.
Rooms 13 double, 1 single. 5 in coach house. 4 on ground floor.
Facilities Sitting room, lounge/bar, sun room, restaurant, conservatory; patio.
⅓-acre walled garden.
Location 2 mins' walk from centre. Windows on road double-glazed. Private
carpark. Train: Crewkerne, 8 miles; then taxi.
Restrictions No smoking in restaurant. No dogs in public rooms, unattended in
bedrooms.
Credit cards All major cards accepted.
Terms B&B: single £56–£76, double £65–£107; D,B&B (min. 2 days): single
£75–£92, double £101–£140. Snack lunches available. Set lunch (2/3-course)
£13/£15, dinner £20.50. Winter breaks; Christmas, New Year packages. 1-night
bookings sometimes refused weekends. *V*

Deadlines: nominations for the 1999 volume should reach us
not later than 25 May 1998. Latest date for comments on existing entries: 1 June 1998.

BECKINGTON Somerset   **Map 2**

The Woolpack Inn   *Tel* (01373) 831244
Beckington, nr Bath BA3 6SP   *Fax* (01373) 831223

This 16th-century coaching inn is in the centre of an agreeable,
Domesday-old stone village near Bath (now quiet, thanks to a bypass).
Legend has it that condemned villains were allowed a final drink here
as they were wheeled to the gibbet; more recently Tina Turner and
Annie Lennox stayed while using a nearby recording studio. There are
new owners this year, and a new manager, Andrew Morgan, so we sent
an inspector. "Reception was adequately friendly," she wrote, "but I
was not offered help with bags up to my room in the eaves – not the
easiest of manoeuvres. The room had low beams, good lighting and a
small shower, and it was quiet at night. In the cosy, candlelit dining
room the atmosphere was cheerful and service prompt; there's a reasonably priced, eclectic wine list. I felt quite comfortable dining alone
on a Saturday night." Modern English/French cooking with oriental
influences, on a short menu, is served by Mark Nacchia, who was
trained by his predecessor, the much-admired David Woolfall. There is
an attractive no-smoking lounge, with antique furnishings and pictures, and a lively flagstoned public bar with stripped pine tables
and a log fire. Breakfast includes undyed kippers, real toast and non-
packaged butter. Summer meals are served on two small rear patios.
All manner of attractions are nearby, including Salisbury and Wells,
Longleat and Stourhead, the Cheddar Gorge and Wookey Hole caves,
and racing at Wincanton. (*Good Pub Guide, and others*)

Open All year.
Rooms 12 double.
Facilities Lounge, bar, garden room, 2 dining rooms; patio. Unsuitable for &.
Location In village off A36, 10 miles SE of Bath. Carpark. Train: Frome, 3
miles/Bath, 10 miles; then bus.
Restrictions No smoking: lounge, 1 dining room. No children under 5. No dogs.
Credit cards Access, Amex, Visa.
Terms [1997] B&B: single £54.50–£64.50, double £64.50–£84.50; D,B&B: single
£75, double £90–£110. Full alc £25–£30.

BEERCROCOMBE Somerset   **Map 1**

Frog Street Farm   **BUDGET**   *Tel/Fax* (01823) 480430
Beercrocombe, Taunton TA3 6AF

❦ *César award in 1988*

"A perfect couple of days." "Such peace combined with such generosity! Superb breakfasts." "One of the best small-scale establishments we
have come across. What made it special was Veronica Cole's jolly personality, and the excellence of her cooking – straightforward English at
its best. Ingredients, almost all locally produced, were as fresh as is possible, with vegetables more flavoursome and meat more tender than
one generally gets nowadays. Our bedroom was spacious and pleasantly decorated. Downstairs there are three delightful lounges. Henry
Cole is a racehorse trainer of some note; his horses add interest to the
fields around." Praise this year and last for a long-time *Guide* favourite,
an unpretentious listed 15th-century farmhouse (the name comes from

a Saxon word for a meeting place). It is on a large working farm, deep in rural Somerset, with fields and woods on one side, orchards on the other, and a heated pool under cherry trees. It has beams, panelling, inglenook fireplaces, "and furnishings and fittings appropriate to its style". There are never more than six guests. Dinners, by arrangement, are generally served at separate tables, but guests may eat together if they prefer. The menus include traditional roasts, wild salmon and pheasant, and "wicked" desserts. No licence: bring your own wine. Plenty of National Trust properties in the area: Barrington Court, Montacute, Brampton D'Evercy and Tintinhull House; the busy market town of Ilminster is nearby; the north and south coasts are about 21 miles away. (*Carole J Levensohon, James H Small, and others*)

Open Apr–Oct.
Rooms 3 double. No telephone/radio/TV.
Facilities 2 lounges, dining room. Garden: swimming pool. On 130-acre working farm with trout stream. Unsuitable for &.
Location 7 miles SE of Taunton. M5 exit 25, A358 to Ilminster. In Hatch Beauchamp, at *Hatch Inn*, take Station Rd; left down no through road. Signposted.
Restrictions No smoking. No children under 11. No dogs.
Credit cards None accepted.
Terms [1997] B&B £27. Set dinner £16 (unlicensed: bring your own wine). Reductions for 4 or more nights. Weekly rates. 1-night bookings sometimes refused weekends.

BEPTON West Sussex   Map 2

Park House NEW   *Tel* (01730) 812880
Bepton, nr Midhurst GU29 0JB   *Fax* (01730) 815643

In attractive South Downs village, 3 miles SW of Midhurst, handy for Cowdray Park polo, Goodwood racecourse and Chichester, rambling, red-roofed hotel, run by O'Brien family for over 50 years. "Beautifully kept, reassuringly traditional in classic country house style." Relaxing feel; welcoming service. Immaculate 9-acre grounds: tennis, croquet, swimming pool, 9-hole par 3 pitch-and-putt golf course; small barn for conferences/functions; golf courses nearby. 14 bedrooms, most spacious, with pretty decor; 1 on ground floor with facilities for &. Bar with sporting and theatrical photographs; mellow, elegantly furnished drawing room. Tomato-coloured dining room with splendid sideboard and "resolutely English" cooking, on spoken menu, which inspectors thought unremarkable. Alfresco meals on wisteria-covered terrace in summer. Access, Amex, Visa accepted. B&B £45–£70; D,B&B £62.50–£90. More reports, please. *V*

BETHERSDEN Kent   Map 2

Little Hodgeham BUDGET   *Tel* (01233) 850323
Smarden Road
Bethersden TN26 3HE

Ω *César award in 1994*

"Erica Wallace's faultless hospitality and meticulous attention to detail are unique. She seems to have followed William Morris's dictum: 'Have nothing in your house which is neither useful nor beautiful.'" So write returning visitors to Miss Wallace's half-timbered

Tudor cottage, set in a flower-filled garden with a swimming pool, a pond stocked with carp and tench, and a water garden, in this pretty conservation village. Inside are more ancient beams, fresh flowers, and log fires in cold weather. Both house and garden are lovingly tended. The public rooms are spotless, with shining antique furniture. Bedrooms are "charming and original; the four-poster one is like something out of *The Princess and the Pea*". Breakfasts are generous "and can be English, French or Australian (ie, a mixed grill)," says Miss Wallace. Guests admire the personal touch and the attention to detail: "A tea basket when you go touring, and the loan of wellies when it rains." "Excellent value for money." Full hotel amenities are not on offer, and an evening meal is no longer served, though 1997 visitors were given a supper "in every way as good as the gourmet dinners of yore"; guests are advised on local eating places. There are more than 80 stately homes, castles and gardens to visit in the area; Canterbury is 40 minutes' drive, and the Eurostar station at Ashford is 15 minutes away. (*John and Isabel Turner*)

Open Mid-Mar–1 Sept.
Rooms 3 double. No telephone/TV.
Facilities Drawing room, library/TV room, breakfast room, conservatory. ½-acre garden: swimming pool, pond, water garden. Tennis, fishing, golf nearby. Unsuitable for &.
Location 10 miles W of Ashford. From Bethersden, at *Bull* pub, take Smarden road for 2 miles.
Restrictions No smoking in dining room. Dogs in barn and garden only.
Credit cards None accepted.
Terms B&B £35–£40 (£32.50 for 4 nights or more).

BIGBURY-ON-SEA Devon   Map 1

Burgh Island Hotel   *Tel* (01548) 810514
Bigbury-on-Sea TQ7 4BG   *Fax* (01548) 810243

♨ *César award in 1993*

Standing offshore from the wide beaches of Bigbury Bay, this 22-acre property, with its rocky cliffs, is truly an island only at high tide, when visitors are carried out by a giant sea tractor – "a magical experience". At low tide you walk across the sand. On it is Tony and Beatrice Porter's lovingly restored Art Deco extravaganza, "a fantasy world of the 1920s". It has had many famous visitors, including Edward, Prince of Wales and Wallis Simpson, and Agatha Christie, two of whose books are based on the island. The hotel's splendours include a palm court with peacock dome, a 1920s bar serving exotic cocktails, and a glass sun lounge where residents take tea. Accommodation is in suites with one or two bedrooms and a sitting room; most have a balcony and sea view; there is also a two-bedroom beach house. Dinner is served in a 1920s ballroom – in deference to its splendour guests are asked to dress formally. Recent praise: "The personal touch of the amiable, caring host made our stay memorable. The staff's enthusiasm adds to the fun." "A very special hotel. Our suite, with authentic Art Deco decor, was simple, almost stark, with breathtaking views. On Saturday night a crooner entertained us with twenties and thirties songs. Cliff walks also breathtaking, particularly in a high wind." "Faded elegance rather than plush modern furniture; superb breakfast – both the continental and the fry-up." A new chef took over in January 1997, so we'd like reports on the food, a mixture of traditional and modern.

Open All year, except Feb.
Rooms 18 suites. 1-bedroom beach house 100 yds.
Facilities Lift. Sun lounges, palm court bar, breakfast room, restaurant/ball-room (taped 20s/30s music; dinner-dance Sat), games room, billiards; sauna. On 22-acre island: pub, tennis, tidal swimming pool; beach: safe bathing, water sports, cliff walks, bird sanctuary. Unsuitable for &.
Location Leave A38 at Modbury exit. Through Modbury to Bigbury-on-Sea (telephone for collection). Free parking on mainland. Train: Plymouth; then bus to Bigbury.
Restrictions No smoking in breakfast room. No dogs.
Credit cards All major cards accepted.
Terms [1997] D,B&B double £198–£248. Set lunch £22.50, dinner £35. Reductions for longer stays. Christmas, New Year, Easter packages. 1-night bookings some-times refused weekends.

BIGGIN BY HARTINGTON Derbyshire   Map 2

Biggin Hall `BUDGET`   *Tel* (01298) 84451
Biggin by Hartington   *Fax* (01298) 84681
Buxton SK17 0DH   *E-mail* 100610.1573@compuserve.com

This 17th-century house, with stone walls, mullioned windows, old beams and antique furniture, has a peaceful setting in the Peak District National Park. It is a family-run affair with a cheerful atmosphere. "Those looking for a posh hotel would be happier elsewhere," says the owner, James Moffett, who nevertheless notes one change this year: the dining room has been extended, "so breakfast is now more organised". He is a "courteous and gregarious man", say *Guide* correspondents. They enjoyed the unstuffy atmosphere – "at mealtimes guests chat freely between tables" – and the "simple and well cooked" traditional food. Dinner is served at 7 pm, in an attractive room with a fireplace and a picture window. The emphasis is on free-range wholefood and natural flavours; no choice of main course; seconds are sometimes offered. Slabs of butter are left on the table and you help yourself from a cheese board. The continental breakfast has a huge selection of cereals, and home-made hot croissants, jams and marmalade; guests not on a special break pay a small supplement for the cooked one. Cream teas and packed lunches are available. Most bedrooms are spa-cious, with old beams and chintz, TV and a well-appointed bathroom. Some are in converted outbuildings. There are two sitting rooms, one with TV and books, the other with a large open fireplace. The winter "Icebreaker Special", with hot porridge for breakfast and Glühwein round a log fire at night, is considered "amazing value". A good base for visiting the market towns of Ashbourne, Buxton and Bakewell, and stately homes such as Chatsworth and Haddon Hall; Alton Towers is 16 miles away. (*Diana and Michael Smith*)

Open All year.
Rooms 15 double, 2 single. 9 (including 5 apartments) in outbuildings. 3 on ground floor. No telephone.
Facilities Sitting room, TV room, dining room; meeting room. 7-acre grounds. River Dove 1½ miles. Not really suitable for &.
Location 8 miles N of Ashbourne, ½ mile W of A515.
Restrictions No smoking: dining room, sitting room. No children under 12.

Dogs in apartments only, not in public rooms.
Credit cards Access, Visa.
Terms B&B £22.50–£49.50; D,B&B £32.50–£59.50. English breakfast £3.50. Set dinner £14.50. Christmas, New Year, winter breaks. 1-night bookings sometimes refused. ***V***

BINBROOK Lincolnshire   Map 4

Hoe Hill   BUDGET   *Tel* (01472) 398206
Swinhope, Binbrook LN8 6HX

This unassuming guest house, 18th-century in origin, was once the home of the local warren bailiff (ie, rabbit catcher). The best bedroom, overlooking the garden, has an *en suite* bathroom with a spa bath and a power shower. Breakfast includes home-made muesli, local sausages and eggs, and home-made bread and marmalade. A sherry or a glass of wine is included in the price of the "plentiful" dinner (by arrangement; no choice of main course); a light supper is also available. "I have seldom been made to feel more welcome," wrote a visitor last year. "My bedroom was simple but adequate. The hosts, Erica and Ian Curd, are charming. I shared an excellent dinner (main course roast poussin) with my fellow guests, a music examiner and a circuit judge. We drank the wine I had brought (*Hoe Hill* is unlicensed), and afterwards had some good conversation over coffee. Such experiences make me wonder why anyone would want to stay in a Post House. Stunning value." Breakfast includes kippers, fruit compote and home-made marmalade. Binbrook, which has an old market place and an impressive Victorian church, is set amid the unspoilt Lincolnshire Wolds; there's excellent walking, including the Viking Way. (*CK*)

Open Feb–Dec (B&B only Christmas/New Year). Closed during owners' holiday. Lunch/dinner by arrangement only.
Rooms 3 double, 1 with *en suite* bathroom. No telephone/TV.
Facilities Lounge, dining room. 1-acre garden. Unsuitable for &.
Location On B1203 1 mile NE of Binbrook, towards Grimsby; quiet at night.
Restrictions No smoking: dining room, bedrooms. No children under 5. No dogs.
Credit cards None accepted.
Terms [1997] B&B £18–£25. 4-course dinner £14; light supper £5. Reductions for 3 or more nights. Children charged £1 for each year of their age.

BIRCH VALE Derbyshire   Map 3

The Waltzing Weasel   BUDGET   *Tel* (01663) 743402
New Mills Road
Birch Vale SK12 5BT

This stone built inn, sympathetically extended, is in some of Derbyshire's most beautiful countryside, yet only 40 minutes' drive from Manchester. The owner, Michael Atkinson, is a former philosophy lecturer; Linda, his wife, is an artist. "They generate a relaxed and civilised atmosphere," wrote an inspector, "and successfully combine a popular local pub and a small, more sophisticated restaurant. They have excellent taste and they love antiques, which are plentifully scattered in all the rooms. The well-equipped bedrooms are named after local hills and dales; ours was generous in size with a large bathroom, soft colours,

Victorian furniture, and a welcoming feel." Good simple food is served in hearty portions in a pretty (and machine-free) bar with an open fire, and in the mullion-windowed dining room, which overlooks the garden and has superb views across to Kinder Scout, one of the highest peaks in the county. It has lady and unicorn tapestries, and burgundy-red walls, "which create an intimate feel at night, but are a bit oppressive in the morning", one visitor thought. The wine list is reasonably priced. Service is "friendly if a bit speedy". Plenty of choice on the menu for breakfast, which can be served on a patio in fine weather. Local stately homes include Chatsworth and Haddon Hall. Some passing traffic, but the road is not a busy one. (*ANR, Good Pub Guide*)

Open All year.
Rooms 7 double, 1 single. Some on ground floor.
Facilities Reception (piped classical music midday/evening), bar, restaurant. Small garden. Shooting, golf, fishing nearby.
Location On A6015, ½ mile west of Hayfield. Local buses.
Restrictions Smoking discouraged in restaurant. No children under 7.
Credit cards Access, Amex, Visa.
Terms [1997] B&B: single £45–£75, double £65–£95. Bar meals. Set lunch £10, dinner (2/3-course) £19.50/£22; full alc £29. 30% reduction for 2 or more nights.

BIRMINGHAM West Midlands   Map 3

Copperfield House   NEW/BUDGET   *Tel* (0121) 472 8344
60 Upland Road   *Fax* (0121) 415 8655
Selly Park B29 7JS

"A cheerful no-nonsense ambience; value for money; a yes for the *Guide*." An inspector's verdict on John and Jenny Bodycote's red brick, mid-Victorian house in a residential suburb. "It has been restored lovingly and tastefully, with new furniture, new carpeting, smart wallpaper and curtains; everything done with great attention to detail. The bedrooms are all different, and all attractive. Some are in the attic, a steepish climb. Ours, on the ground floor, was light and airy, and looked over a very attractive back garden with trees and shrubs, squirrels cavorting on the grass, chairs and parasols. Breakfast was extremely satisfactory: juice and cereals on a dresser, a good selection of fresh fruit and a cooked breakfast (perfect eggs) kept warm in a trolley. Mr Bodycote exudes warmth, and runs things in debonair style." The owners' daughter, Louise, who trained with Prue Leith, cooks traditional English/French dishes on a menu ending on a rich note with such delights as sticky gingerbread pudding with a ginger wine and brandy sauce. Nearby are the BBC's Pebble Mill studios, Birmingham University, the Barber Institute of Fine Arts, and Cadbury World (the hotel offers Chocolate Weekend rates).

Open All year, except Christmas, New Year. Restaurant closed Sun.
Rooms 12 double, 5 single. 2 on ground floor.
Facilities Ramp. Lounge/bar, restaurant (piped jazz/classical music). ½-acre garden.
Location 2 miles SW of centre. Take A38; through 2 sets of lights; left into Pebble Mill, right on to A441; Upland Rd 2nd on right. Carpark.
Restrictions No smoking in restaurant. Guide dogs only.
Credit cards Access, Amex, Visa.
Terms B&B: single £55, double £67.50; D,B&B: single £70, double £97.50. Set dinner £15–£18. Weekend rates. *V*

BISHOP'S TACHBROOK Warwickshire   Map 3

Mallory Court   *Tel* (01926) 330214
Harbury Lane   *Fax* (01926) 451714
Bishop's Tachbrook   *E-mail* mallorycourt@dial.pipex.com
nr Leamington Spa CV33 9QB

"A happy house, built in the exuberant jazz age. No 'faded charm' here, but elegance in all its clean-lined, mirrored glory. We felt like extras in a *Poirot* film. The owners were not much in evidence, but the mainly French young staff were friendly and attentive, and the food was delicious. Only gripe: no non-smoking lounges; but we enjoyed every moment." "Must be one of the best country house hotels in the UK. Sarah Fletcher, the manager, is a great asset." Reports in 1997 on this luxurious 1920s mansion (Relais & Châteaux), which has been owned and run by Jeremy Mort and Allan Holland for 20 years, and has had a *Guide* entry since 1980. It has an impressive decor: large entrance hall with soft sofas, chesterfields and glossy magazines; cosy lounge looking through leaded panes on to a formal garden with statuary, ponds, croquet lawns, box-hedged herb garden, and unheated swimming pool. The dining room has oak panelling and sliding doors to make it large or intimate, depending on numbers. Here, Allan Holland serves traditional English/French food, "with a Mediterranean influence and some interesting modern twists, particularly on the lighter lunch dishes". Bedrooms are "skilfully designed and extremely comfortable", though some are on the small side, and one above the kitchen is noisy. The luxurious Blenheim Suite has a painted ceiling and two tubs in its bathroom. There is a generous continental breakfast, and in the afternoon lavish teas are served, on a terrace in fine weather. Despite its rural setting, *Mallory Court* is close to Birmingham and Stratford-upon-Avon; it arranges trips to the Royal Shakespeare Theatre. (*Christina Sausman, Pat and Jeremy Temple, and others*)

Open All year, except 1–9 Jan.
Rooms 1 suite, 9 double.
Facilities Lounge, drawing room, conservatory, restaurant; conference facilities in stable block. 10-acre gardens: swimming pool (unheated), tennis, squash, croquet. Balloon trips, riding, golf nearby. Unsuitable for &.
Location 2 miles S of Leamington Spa. M40 exit 13 (from S), 14 (from N). Hotel on unmarked road to Harbury off B4087. Train: Leamington Spa; then taxi.
Restrictions No smoking in restaurant. No children under 9. No dogs (kennels nearby).
Credit cards All major cards accepted.
Terms B&B: single £120–£140, double £180–£235, suite £395. Set lunch £26, dinner £30; full alc £60. 2/3-day winter breaks. ***V***

BLAKENEY Norfolk   Map 2

The Blakeney Hotel   *Tel* (01263) 740797
Blakeney, nr Holt NR25 7NE   *Fax* (01263) 740795

Until its harbour filled with silt, this village, with cobbled streets and picturesque cottages, was a port. Nowadays it is a popular yachting centre, and offers excellent birdwatching at the Blakeney Point nature reserve, owned by the National Trust. This "good, solid traditional hotel" has a wonderful position on the quay, with fine views across the estuary and salt marshes, "and perfect blessed silence at night". Its decor is simple. Bedrooms vary greatly in style and are priced accordingly. Estuary views are at a premium. There are spacious ones in a modern annexe, some with a private patio. The hotel welcomes families ("we expect parents to ensure that their children do not spoil the enjoyment of others"), providing cots, high chairs and early meals. It has a safe garden, an indoor pool and a games room; at low tide the estuary is excellent for children, and there are magnificent beaches close by. The elderly and the disabled are welcomed too. The staff is friendly and vigilant. "Food good though not sophisticated," wrote a regular visitor. "Breakfasts decent also. Good cream teas." (*Barbara Blake*; also A and CR.)

Open All year.
Rooms 51 double, 9 single. 10 in annexe across drive. 1, on ground floor, with access for &.
Facilities Lift, ramps. Lounge, sun lounge, cocktail bar, games room, restaurant; function facilities; indoor swimming pool, spa bath, sauna. ¼-acre garden: table-tennis, swings.
Location On quay. Off A149 coast road between Cromer and Wells-next-the-Sea.
Restrictions No smoking in sun lounge. No dogs in public rooms.
Credit cards All major cards accepted.
Terms D,B&B £57–£94. Light lunches Mon–Sat. Set lunch (Sun) £12, dinner £17; full alc £25. 1-night bookings sometimes refused weekends/public holidays. 2/3 and 4/7-day breaks. Midweek breaks for senior citizens. Christmas, New Year house parties.

BLAWITH Cumbria   Map 4

Appletree Holme Farm   *Tel* (01229) 885618
Blawith, nr Ulverston LA12 8EL

"We spend eight days here every spring and autumn. Our enthusiasm for the welcome and kindness of the hosts, and the excellence of the cooking remains undimmed." So writes a regular visitor to Roy and Shirley Carlsen's old stone farmhouse (motto: "A fine example of living life the way it was meant to be lived") in a remote corner of the south-western part of the Lake District. It has an idyllic fellside setting, amid carefully tended gardens and orchard; the immediate surroundings are a designated site of special interest, where flora and fauna are protected. All the bedrooms have a fell view and private facilities (one bathroom is across a corridor). The suite, on two floors, has a large bed/sitting room upstairs, a bathroom with a "sybaritic" double bath downstairs, and a private patio and separate entrance. There's a "home-like" lounge, with log fire, brasses, silver and paintings, and a well-stocked library. The Carlsens do not offer hotel-style facilities – there is no reception, and visitors are asked not to arrive between 2 and 5 pm without prior arrangement – but this is one of the attractions in the eyes of devotees. The food is traditional British, with Mediterranean influences; no choice on the five-course menu, preferences discussed in advance. Breakfast includes a good selection of cooked dishes, and home-made marmalade. "The Carlsens are charming and highly professional," wrote a recent visitor. "They strike just the right balance between formality and informality. The facilities are excellent, the food is varied and delicious, the wine list splendid and reasonably priced." Coniston Water is three miles away; many other

sporting activities are available (see below); and there are stately
homes, art galleries and market towns to visit. (*JL Prichard*)

Open All year. Dining room closed for lunch (picnics/light lunches available).
Rooms 1 suite (adjacent to main building), 3 double.
Facilities Sitting room, library, dining room. 5-acre grounds: gardens, orchards.
Lake, tarn, swimming, fishing, boating, golf, pony-trekking, shooting nearby.
Unsuitable for &.
Location M6 exit 36; A590 to Greenodd; A5084 to Blawith church; up lane
opposite church; right after farm; left 1 mile, at sign. Train/bus: Ulverston; hotel
will meet.
Restrictions No smoking. Small children by arrangement. No dogs in house.
Credit cards Access, Visa.
Terms D,B&B £61.50–£70.50. £3 reduction for 2 or more nights (except bank
holidays).

BLORE Staffordshire   Map 3

The Old Rectory   NEW   *Tel/Fax* (01335) 350287
Blore, nr Ashbourne DE6 2BS

*Attractive stone house, a Wolsey Lodge, in 2-acre grounds in hamlet on
Staffordshire border, 4 miles NW of Ashbourne. Lovely views of Dovedale and
Manifold valley. Run in old-fashioned style by genial hosts, Stuart and
Geraldine Worthington ("a talented cook"), with her mother, a shy spaniel and
a pushy cat. Formal dress required for pre-dinner drinks (generously poured)
and communal dinner, shared with hosts – good home cooking, elegantly
served; ladies retire when port circulates. Home-like atmosphere: family
photos, Malaysian mementos, unsmart bedroom decor. Good walking, many
historic buildings nearby. Closed Christmas; dinner not served Sun.
Unsuitable for &. No smoking: dining room, bedrooms. No children under 15.
Dogs in cars only. B&B £38–£50.50. Set dinner £21.50.*

BOLTON ABBEY North Yorkshire   Map 4

The Devonshire Arms   *Tel* (01756) 710441
Bolton Abbey, nr Skipton BD23 6AJ   *Fax* (01756) 710564

The Augustinian priory that once stood in this Wharfedale village fell
into ruin after the dissolution of the monasteries, when the huge estate
passed to the Cavendish family. This smart hotel, built as a coaching
inn in the 17th century, is now owned by their descendants, the Duke
and Duchess of Devonshire, and managed by Jeremy Rata, who was
admired by *Guide* readers during his time at *Rookery Hall*, Nantwich. It
is set back from the road on the edge of the estate (wonderful walking;
plenty of wildlife). Many antiques and pictures come from Chatsworth,
the family seat. "A jewel in a gorgeous setting – the grounds, and the
nearby moors and ruins are so spectacular it could have been constructed by a Hollywood set designer," wrote American visitors last
year. "It has a real country home feel. Public rooms are cosy, and bedrooms well provisioned." A 1997 visitor concurs: "A satisfying, relaxing visit. The staff were without exception helpful and friendly. The
porter willingly drove us several miles up the valley, so that we could
walk back. We enjoyed watching a match on the adjacent cricket field."
Best bedrooms, overlooking the garden, are in the main house; those in

the newer wing have less character and are nearer the road. One couple this year were critical of room maintenance, and thought some rooms over-priced. The *Burlington Restaurant*, named for another member of the family, the 18th-century patron of the arts whose architectural drawings hang on the walls, overlooks the Yorkshire Dales National Park. It serves traditional and modern English dishes, including game in season, which are generally enjoyed, though the menu does not have daily variations. Informal meals are available in the bar, lounges or bedrooms. Guests have free membership of the health club, and free use of wellington boots for riverside walks. At times, the hotel is busy with conferences and functions. (*Dr and Mrs Viola, Alan Greenwood, and others*)

Open All year.
Rooms 3 suites, 38 double. 2 suitable for &, 2 for lady executives.
Facilities 3 lounges, bar, pub, restaurant; function/conference facilities; health club: swimming pool, sauna, gym, beauty treatments, tennis court. 12-acre grounds in 10,000-acre estate: walking, croquet, helipad. River fishing 200 yds; golf nearby.
Location On B6160 5 miles E of Skipton; 250 yds N of junction with A59. Train: Skipton; then taxi.
Restrictions No smoking: restaurant, 13 bedrooms. No children under 12 in restaurant.
Credit cards All major cards accepted.
Terms [1997] B&B: single £105–£130, double £150–£190, suite £230–£250. Set lunch £20, dinner £39. Special breaks: active, romantic, etc.

BONCHURCH Isle of Wight   Map 2

Winterbourne   BUDGET   *Tel* (01983) 852535
Bonchurch, nr Ventnor PO38 1RQ   *Fax* (01983) 853056

The Isle of Wight was a favourite holiday resort of many Victorians; the Queen had a house here, as did Lord Tennyson. And Charles Dickens worked on *David Copperfield* at this creepered house, now owned by Mr and Mrs O'Connor. "The prettiest place I ever saw in my life, at home or abroad," Dickens wrote. It has a quiet setting near a tiny church, on the south side of the island. Its terraced gardens, with stream, pools, waterfalls, sheltered swimming pool and sea views, slope down a hillside. A gate at the bottom leads to the path to the shore. "The setting is delightful," writes a recent guest. "The hotel was a haven, comfortable, though not luxurious. The welcome was warm and genuine. We were well looked after, and with time I even found the piped music enjoyable. A pity about the wines, though; we thought them overpriced, particularly in view of the otherwise reasonable rates. Benefits not mentioned in the brochure: the sighting of two badgers on the lawns, and a sleek fox visiting late one evening." Other visitors have thought the staff "pleasant, though not what one might describe as professional, probably the right approach for this place", and have praised the "atmosphere of happiness, elegance and charm" and the Victorian decor of the public rooms. However, one couple in 1997 were critical of the dinners. Bedrooms, most with a sea view, vary greatly in style; the singles are quite basic; the garden suites are good for families. Dogs are welcomed. Ventnor's botanic garden, nearby, is worth a visit. The National Trust owns 4,000 acres of the island, and there are many marked footpaths. (*Fr Gordon Murray, and others*)

Open Mar–beginning Nov.
Rooms 2 family (in annexe), 9 double, 3 single.
Facilities Lounge, bar, restaurant (piped music); patio. 4-acre grounds: gardens, swimming pool (heated Apr–Oct), stream. Shingle/sand beach, riding, fishing, golf, tennis, bowls nearby. Unsuitable for &.
Location 1 mile NE of Ventnor. Right off A3055 into Bonchurch Shute; sharp left at bottom of road. Bus from Ventnor.
Restrictions No smoking in restaurant. No children under 5 in the restaurant at night (high tea 6.30 pm). No dogs in restaurant.
Credit cards All major cards accepted.
Terms [1997] D,B&B: single £46–£55, double £92–£111, suite £112–£130. Light lunch available. *V*

BORROWDALE Cumbria   **Map 4**

Seatoller House　**BUDGET**   *Tel/Fax* (01768 7) 77218
Borrowdale, Keswick CA12 5XN

Ԓ *César award in 1984*

This unpretentious establishment has a glorious setting at the head of the Borrowdale valley (much of which is owned by the National Trust). Many spectacular fell walks start nearby. Over 300 years old, it has been a guest house for more than a century. Its many regular visitors love the "warmth of welcome, the mixture of 'low-key-ness' and style", and the home-like atmosphere; it offers "tremendous value for money". A returning visitor this year thought the food, cooked by the "exceptionally pleasant and efficient" manager, Ann Pepper, better than ever, "with particularly delicious soups and puddings, and an excellent cheeseboard". Because visitors eat together, "the place buzzes with friendliness". Meals are served at two long oak tables, breakfast at 8.30 am and dinner (no choice) at 7 pm. There's a well-chosen wine list. No TV; socialising and board games are the order of the evening. Bedrooms, some quite large, are simple, but spotless, and sympathetically decorated; all have a private bathroom, though not always *en suite*. No special concessions (high tea, games room, etc) are made to children, "but they fit in very well and respond to the civilised atmosphere". (*TR Mann*)

Open Mar–Nov. Dining room closed midday, Tues all day.
Rooms 9 double. 1 in garden annexe, 2 on ground floor. No telephone/tea-making facilities.
Facilities Lounge, library, dining room, tea room; drying room. 2-acre grounds: pond. Unsuitable for severely &.
Location 8 miles S of Keswick on B5289. Regular bus service.
Restrictions Smoking in 1 lounge only. No children under 5. No dogs in public rooms.
Credit cards None accepted.
Terms [1997] D,B&B £36.50–£38.50. Packed lunches available. Weekly rates. Children under 12 half-price in parents' room. 1-night bookings sometimes refused.

****

    Traveller's tale Cambridgeshire: The owner looked down his nose at all the guests as though they were parasites. We wondered what he was doing in the hotel business.

****

BOSHAM West Sussex **Map 2**

The Millstream
Bosham Lane
Bosham, nr Chichester PO18 8HL

Tel (01243) 573234
Fax (01243) 573459

"The charming setting added an extra dimension to the outing." "Service throughout professional and friendly. Excellent cooked dishes complemented the limited breakfast buffet." Recent reports on this hotel in an old fishing and sailing village at the head of Chichester Harbour. It is composed of a small manor and an 18th-century malt house cottage, set in tranquil gardens, on a stream complete with ducks. The sea is just 500 yards away. The public rooms and bedrooms have a pretty, unfussy decor, with pale colours, antique and period furniture, potted plants and unexceptional pictures. Non-residents come for bar lunches and teas (served outdoors in summer), and for dinners in the restaurant overlooking the garden, where good traditional English/French dishes are served. "The assistant manageress was very competent, and the two young Italian waiters gave quick and deft service with great charm," wrote one recent visitor. But she found the bedroom reading lighting inadequate. The hotel is licensed for weddings; it is handy for Chichester (theatre-goers may order a late supper) and Goodwood. Bosham, pronounced Bozzum, is full of history: its church, which is still standing, was visited by King Harold before he set off to visit Duke William of Normandy in 1064 (this is depicted in the Bayeux Tapestry), and the incident of King Canute and the tide is said to have occurred here. (*Ian Marshall, and others*)

Open All year.
Rooms 1 suite, 27 double, 5 single. 7 on ground floor, 2 with ♿ access.
Facilities Lounge (pianist Fri, Sat night), bar, restaurant (taped classical music); conference room. ½-acre garden.
Location In village 3½ miles W of Chichester. Follow signs for Bosham Quay. Carpark. Station/bus-stop in village.
Restrictions No smoking: dining room, 16 bedrooms. No dogs in public rooms.
Credit cards All major cards accepted.
Terms B&B: single £69–£72, double £109–£112, suite £139–£145; D,B&B (min. 2 nights): single £55–£75, double £110–£150, suite £140–£180. Set lunch £13.50, dinner £19.50. 3-day breaks. Falconry, murder/mystery packages, Christmas, New Year breaks. 1-night bookings refused Sat. ***V***

BOUGHTON MONCHELSEA Kent **Map 2**

Tanyard
Wierton Hill, Boughton Monchelsea
Maidstone ME17 4JT

Tel (01622) 744705
Fax (01622) 741998

"From the moment you arrive, you feel like a much valued guest at a private house party. All our requests were cheerfully met. High standards of care and professionalism throughout." "Charming building and setting; a good overnight stop before the Channel crossing." Regular visitors' praise for this beautiful medieval yeoman's house, peacefully set on a sheltered hillside, amid orchards in the Weald of Kent. It has landscaped grounds with a pond and stream, and pleasing views. Inside, the feel is intimate, with ancient beams, open-hearth fireplaces, antiques, designer pastels and chintzes. There is a "cosy small bar, almost dwarfed by its fireplace". A narrow staircase, "best negoti-ated with a clear head", leads to the bedrooms; some are small, and sound insulation is not always perfect. The suite, with far-reaching views and a bathroom with a spa bath, occupies the entire top floor. The restaurant is in the beamed former kitchen. Here, owner/chef Jan Davies serves modern English cooking on a menu with four choices for each course. The main courses are sometimes thought "bland", but puddings are good, "and there is an excellent cheese board". Breakfast (served until 9.30) includes "delicious 'Kentish Korker' sausages". There is good walking all around. Boughton Monchelsea Place, a battlemented 16th-century manor house set in a landscaped deer park, is open to the public; Leeds Castle and Sissinghurst are nearby. (*Mr and Mrs AJ Gatham, David and Patricia Hawkins; also Dr R Feltham*)

Open All year, except 2 weeks in winter. Restaurant open for lunch Wed, Thurs, Fri, Sun only, for pre-booked groups of 6 or more.
Rooms 1 suite, 4 double, 1 single.
Facilities Reception/hall, lounge, bar, restaurant (taped classical music "when few people are in"). 10-acre grounds: garden, pond, stream. Unsuitable for &.
Location From B2163 at E edge of Boughton Monchelsea, turn opposite *Cock* pub into Park La; first right towards Wierton, bear right down Wierton Hill. *Tanyard* on left at bottom.
Restrictions No smoking in restaurant. No children under 6. No dogs.
Credit cards All major cards accepted (Amex, Diners *with surcharge*).
Terms [1997] B&B: single £65–£85, double £100–£110, suite £140. Set lunch £20.50; dinner £27.50. 1-night bookings generally refused Sat.

BOURNE Lincolnshire   Map 2

Bourne Eau House   `BUDGET`   *Tel* (01778) 423621
30 South Street
Bourne PE10 9LY

Bourne is small Fenland market town, near the source of a winding stream, the Bourne Eau, for which this Wolsey Lodge is named. It is a listed Elizabethan/Georgian house, set in a beautiful garden in a con-servation area. It looks across the stream, complete with swans and ducks, to a Norman abbey and the ruins of a castle said to be the birth-place of the Saxon leader, Hereward the Wake. "Dr and Mrs Bishop make you feel wanted and cared for," writes a recent guest. "We were welcomed with tea and home-made cakes, elegantly served. We had a lovely Jacobean bedroom, with a carved oak bed, flowers, fruit, books, etc, and an enormous bathroom." The public rooms are light and pretty, with period furniture. There is a music room with a concert piano. Dinner ("well cooked if not gourmet, and excellent value"), is served at 7.30 pm at a long refectory table "with candles, and silver and cut glass glinting in the light of a huge log fire". Couples are split up, to encourage conversation. Breakfast includes fresh grapefruit, cereals, "and very good cooked items if required". Only snag: traffic noise from the busy A15 road nearby. (*Mrs J Keeble, Diane Sumner; also RMJ Kenber*)

Open All year, except Christmas, New Year, Easter. Lunch not served.
Rooms 3 double. 2 with bathroom *en suite*.
Facilities Drawing room, music room, breakfast room, dining room. 1-acre gar-den. Unsuitable for &.
Location 200 yds from traffic lights in centre; concealed entrance opposite ceno-taph in park. Courtyard parking. Train: Peterborough; then bus.

Restrictions No smoking in dining room. No dogs.
Credit cards None accepted.
Terms B&B £35. Set dinner £22.50 (including wine).

BOWNESS-ON-WINDERMERE Cumbria   Map 4

Lindeth Fell   *Tel* (01539 4) 43286
Lyth Valley Road   *Fax* (01539 4) 47455
Bowness-on-Windermere LA23 3JP

Bowness is a busy tourist centre on Lake Windermere – many lake cruis-
ers set off from here – but this turn-of-the-century house is tranquilly set
above the bustle. "It must be one of the best situated hotels in
Lakeland," one couple has written, "and it has a cheerful atmosphere."
It is reached by a tree-lined drive, and the large grounds have rhododendrons and azaleas, lawns for tennis, putting and croquet, and a
small tarn with trout. The place is owned and run by Pat Kennedy (ex-
RAF) and his wife Diana. "They are relaxed hosts, who treat you like
members of the family," wrote regular visitors. "Food is excellent and
the cellar broad-ranging." Family photographs, bric-à-brac, books and
log fires add to the home-like feel in the lounges. One has a fine plaster
ceiling and large windows looking over the treetops towards distant
Windermere. In the picture-windowed restaurant, modern English
cooking is served on a five-course dinner menu; the kitchens are under
the supervision of Mrs Kennedy, and there's a new chef, Thomas Rowe,
this year. "Breakfasts are copious and delicious," writes a 1997 visitor
but vegetables and desserts at dinner a bit bland. However, every effort
is made to give what one wants, without having to ask. Bedrooms vary
in size and are priced accordingly. Best ones enjoy the lake view; top
ones are quite small, with a sloping ceiling; one couple this year thought
that some were in need of attention. (*Tony Cockroft, Dame Jennifer Jenkins*)

Open All year.
Rooms 1 suite, 12 double, 2 single. 1 on ground floor, with access for &.
Facilities 2 lounges, dispense bar, 2 dining rooms. 7-acre grounds: gardens, ten-
nis, croquet, putting, tarn with fishing. Lake Windermere 1 mile.
Location 1 mile S of Bowness on A5074.
Restrictions No smoking: dining rooms, 1 lounge. No children under 7. Dogs in
grounds only.
Credit cards Access, Visa.
Terms B&B: single £50–£65, double £100–£140; D,B&B: single £60–£75, double
£120–£160. Light lunch available. Set dinner £21. Christmas, New Year packages.
1-night bookings sometimes refused bank holidays. *V* (in winter)

Linthwaite House   *Tel* (01539 4) 88600
Crook Road   *Fax* (01539 4) 88601
Bowness-on-Windermere LA23 3JA   *E-mail* admin@
                                              linhotel.u.net.com

"A wonderful place to escape the rat-race of the nearby tourist areas.
Owner, Mike Bevans, involved and enthusiastic. Staff very helpful. The
whole place oozes good humour. We had a divine dinner and enjoyed
reading the wine list. Breakfast was huge, with fish, porridge, the full
fry-up. Drinks outside on a summer's evening a very pleasurable experience." So writes a recent visitor to this timbered stone and white

Edwardian house, in an exceptionally tranquil position overlooking Lake Windermere. The extensive grounds include well-tended gardens, woods, and a trout-stocked tarn where guests may fish. Indoors, the public rooms have an Edwardian flavour, with potted palms, cabin trunks, wicker furniture, and interesting antiques and memorabilia. Plenty of choice on Ian Bravey's menus (modern British cooking), served in the candlelit, mahogany-tabled restaurant; always an unusual vegetarian dish and a hot traditional pudding; rolls are home-baked. The bedrooms are impressively equipped, but vary in size; the best ones have a king-size bed and a lake view, but some look on to the carpark, and some bathrooms are tiny; towel rails can be scaldingly hot. The hotel boasts an impressive list of recent awards, including the AA's for care and courtesy. It is licensed for weddings. Local attractions include Wordsworth's Dove Cottage, Beatrix Potter's Hill Top, and Levens Hall topiary gardens. (*LM, and others*)

Open All year.
Rooms 1 suite, 16 double, 1 single. 5 on ground floor.
Facilities Lounge, bar, restaurant (piped music), conservatory; function facilities. 14-acre grounds: garden, croquet, putting green, woods, tarn (fishing); guests have access to nearby leisure spa.
Location ¾ mile S of Bowness, off B5284, on left past Windermere Golf Club. Train: Windermere; then taxi.
Restrictions No smoking: restaurant, some bedrooms. No children under 7 in restaurant (early meal provided). Dogs in grounds only.
Credit cards Access, Amex, Visa.
Terms B&B: single £90–£100, double £130–£190, suite £200–£220; D,B&B: single £99–£125, double £138–£240, suite £254–£280. Set dinner £32. Weekend, mid-week, romantic, Christmas, New Year, Easter breaks. 10% reduction on 7-night stay. 1-night bookings often refused weekends. ***V***

BRADFIELD COMBUST Suffolk   Map 2

Bradfield House   *Tel* (01284) 386301
Bradfield Combust   *Fax* (01284) 386177
Bury St Edmunds IP30 0LR

This village's curious name is said to date from the burning down of its hall in riots in the 14th century. Nowadays it makes a peaceful base for touring Suffolk. Douglas Green's restaurant-with-rooms is a pale pink, half-timbered 17th-century house, which stands in a well-tended garden, with yew hedges, listed trees and a summer house. Its interior is decorated in a mixture of styles, "with a home-like feeling": strong colours, eclectic furniture, mostly Edwardian and Victorian, old French wood-burning stoves, and lots of pictures. Best bedrooms overlook the garden; roadside ones are double-glazed. Dinners are "innovative and delicious", making good use of home-grown herbs; there's a well-chosen, reasonably priced wine list. Light lunches are served in the bar. Very good croissants for breakfast, and the full cooked works if wanted. "Very friendly service." (*JJ Edwards; also Richard Stuart-Prince*)

Open All year. Restaurant closed Sun evening/Mon.
Rooms 3 double, 1 single.
Facilities Lounge, bar, 2 dining rooms (piped jazz, classical music). 1½-acre garden. Golf, shooting, riding nearby. Unsuitable for &.
Location 5 miles S of Bury St Edmunds on A134 to Sudbury (front windows double glazed). Train: Bury St Edmunds; regular buses.

Restrictions No smoking: restaurant, bedrooms.
Credit cards Access, Visa.
Terms B&B: single £55, double £65–£80. Set lunch £8.50, £17.50, £21.50, dinner £16.95, £21.50; full alc £30. 2-day breaks.

BRADFORD-ON-AVON Wiltshire   Map 2

Bradford Old Windmill   *Tel* (01225) 866842
4 Masons Lane   *Fax* (01225) 866648
Bradford-on-Avon BA15 1QN

Bradford is a small Cotswold town on the river Avon. Seventeenth-and 18th-century stone houses and cottages line its steep streets; it has three old churches (one Saxon), and a bridge with a chapel in the middle. Overlooking all this, Peter and Priscilla Roberts's converted windmill stands in a small hillside garden. Full of atmosphere, and run in relaxed style, it is filled with old pine furniture, and an eclectic collection of *objets trouvés* acquired during travels around the world. Only three bedrooms, with patchwork quilts and books. They vary in shape and size: one has a round bed, another a water bed. The suite is suitable for families; children are accommodated in a minstrels' gallery up a ladder. Priscilla Roberts sometimes cooks vegetarian/ethnic dinners by arrangement, and a bread and soup tray is available for £6. Breakfast, communally served (outdoors in fine weather), offers alternatives "to suit carnivores, vegetarians, vegans, healthy and unhealthy eaters". No smoking. Unlicensed: bring your own wine. We'd like more reports, please.

Open All year. Evening meal by arrangement, generally available Mon, Thurs, Sat.
Rooms 1 suite, 2 double. No telephone.
Facilities Lounge, dining room. Small garden. 5 mins' walk to river Avon. Unsuitable for &.
Location Entering town on A363 from N find *Castle* pub; go down hill towards centre. Left after 100 yds into private drive immediately before first roadside house (no sign or number).
Restrictions No smoking. No children under 6. No dogs.
Credit cards (*With commission charge*) Access, Amex, Visa.
Terms (*Not VAT-rated*) B&B: single £65–£79, double £75–£85, suite £89; D,B&B: single £83–£97, double £111–£121, suite £125. Set dinner £18. Child in family room £15. Honeymoon package. 1-night bookings sometimes refused Sat, bank holidays. ***V***

Burghope Manor   *Tel* (01225) 723557
Winsley   *Fax* (01225) 723113
nr Bradford-on-Avon BA15 2LA

"The nicest of all the B&Bs on our trip," writes an American visitor. "John Denning is a great host; his humour and repartee keep you smiling. His two friendly dogs make you feel at home right away." This beautiful house, part Tudor, gabled and creepered, is set back from the road in a large garden, in a village overlooking the river Avon. It is John Denning's ancestral home, complete with family portraits and antiques, and a huge Elizabethan fireplace. He runs it with his wife, Elizabeth, on house party lines. The large, light bedrooms have a sofa, easy chairs, plenty of storage space and a bathroom *en suite*. The

English breakfast is served at flexible times. An evening meal, served dinner party-style, is available by arrangement, for groups only. Many eating places are nearby, including a local pub, the *Hop Pole*. A good base for visiting Bath, five miles away, and there are plenty of castles, stately homes and gardens to visit in the area. (*James and Andrea Bleecker*)

Open All year, except Christmas/New Year.
Rooms 2 suites, 6 double. No telephone.
Facilities Drawing room, breakfast room. 2½-acre garden. Unsuitable for &.
Location Village 1½ miles W of Bradford-on-Avon. From B3108, pass through new part of village. In old part, pass war memorial, *Seven Stars* pub, and Winsley House. Turn right into small lane marked: "Except for access." Follow high wall on left to gates. From Bath, turn left into lane immediately after 30 mph signs.
Restrictions No smoking: dining room, bedrooms. No children under 10. No dogs.
Credit cards Access, Amex, Visa.
Terms B&B: single £55–£60, double £65–£75.

Woolley Grange
Woolley Green
Bradford-on-Avon BA15 1TX

Tel (01225) 864705
Fax (01225) 864059
E-mail woolley@cityscape.co.uk

♀ *César award in 1992*

"We greatly enjoyed our stay at this charming country house sanatorium for Yuppies with Young Children," wrote 1997 visitors to Nigel and Heather Chapman's famously child-friendly hotel. Others have enjoyed "the wonderful gardens and grounds", which have "just the right degree of informality, a children's vegetable and flower garden, a beautifully situated swimming pool, and all manner of bicycles for adult and child use". Indoors, informal antiques and amusing primitive paintings adorn the public areas. There is a "cosy panelled hall with every imaginable newspaper and magazine". Bedrooms, with beams and windows in odd places, have been fitted into the mainly Jacobean structure; some are spacious, others "small, but cleverly designed"; some have a gas log fire. Parents pay by the room, squeezing in as many children as they can tolerate. The place is geared to giving children a good time while providing sophisticated comforts for their parents. From 10 am to 6 pm, there is a nanny in the Woolley Bears' Den, where children's meals ("good basic fare") are provided, and reliable baby-sitting is available in the evening. This year, a huge Victorian hen house has been equipped as a refuge for older children, with table tennis, pool, music and videos. The hotel's relaxed atmosphere and its friendly young staff are praised, but this year there are some complaints of poor organisation, and room maintenance has been criticised. Eating arrangements are flexible. Light meals are served in the terrace restaurant, more formal ones in the main restaurant. These are generally enjoyed, though the hotel can be overrun by business visitors at lunchtime. For couples without children there are honeymoon packages and local activity holidays. The Chapmans' other hotel, *The Old Bell* at Malmesbury (*qv*), is run on similar lines. (*Mr and Mrs R Osborne, Bruce Douglas-Mann, and others*)

Open All year.
Rooms 3 suites, 18 double, 1 single. 8 in outbuildings round courtyard. Some on ground floor.

40 ENGLAND

Facilities 4 lounges, restaurant with conservatory; children's playroom/nursery, games rooms. 14-acre grounds: gardens, swimming pool, tennis, badminton, croquet, children's play area. Cycling, riding, golf, fishing, hot-air ballooning nearby.
Location 1 mile NE of Bradford-on-Avon on B3105. Train: Bath/Bradford-on-Avon.
Restrictions No smoking in restaurant. No dogs in restaurant.
Credit cards Access, Visa.
Terms B&B: single £90, double from £100, suite from £160. Light meals available; set lunch £15, dinner £29. Off-season reductions; Christmas, New Year packages. 1-night bookings refused weekends. Children accommodated free in parents' room.

BRAITHWAITE Cumbria   Map 4

Ivy House   BUDGET   *Tel* (01768 7) 78338
Braithwaite, Keswick CA12 5SY   *Fax* (01768 7) 78113
♦ *César award in 1997*

This small 17th-century hotel (green walled, not creeper-covered) is in a picturesque Lakeland village with streams and stone bridges and surrounded by high fells. "In spring," writes a regular *Guide* correspondent, "there are enough daffodils around to keep Wordsworth happy." Nick and Wendy Shill have presided for a decade, and again this year have earned much praise: "Lived up to every expectation, inexpensive and charming. Wonderful food. We were impressed that the staff did not repeatedly come round asking if everything was satisfactory. There was no need. They remembered returning visitors (there were many) from years back." "The exceptionally nice owners have an effortless way of including guests in the general chatter." The kindness to children and dogs is also admired. The double lounge is predominantly red, with a beamed ceiling, and log fires at each end. In the dark green galleried restaurant, dinner is served by candlelight on fine linen with silver, crystal and good china. The cooking, on a fixed-price four-course menu which changes daily, attracts an enthusiastic local clientele and, thinks one regular, "has become more adventurous." There's a comprehensive wine list. The bedrooms vary in size, and have a less dramatic decor; one is "very pink, with roses everywhere and a four-poster the size of a caravan". The garden is small, but there is spectacular walking from the door. Guests may use the leisure facilities at a nearby club. Bassenthwaite Lake and Derwent Water are nearby. (*Padi and John Howard, DH Evans; also M Firth*)

Open All year, except Jan. Lunch not served.
Rooms 10 double, 2 single.
Facilities Lounge, bar, dining room. Access to nearby leisure club. Unsuitable for &.
Location 2½ miles W of Keswick. Take B5292 off A66; turn left down narrow road by *Royal Oak* inn; hotel straight ahead. Private carpark. Train: Penrith, 18 miles; coach: Keswick, 2 miles.
Restrictions No smoking in dining room. No children under 6 at dinner. Dogs by arrangement.
Credit cards All major cards accepted.
Terms [1997] B&B: single £30–£35, double £60–£78. Set dinner £19.95. 3-night midweek breaks Feb–Apr; Christmas package. 1-night bookings sometimes refused Fri/Sat.

BRAMPTON Cumbria   Map 4

Farlam Hall   *Tel* (01697 7) 46234
Brampton CA8 2NG   *Fax* (01697 7) 46683

"A magical place." "Goes from strength to strength." "All six Quinions provide the warmest welcome imaginable." "Unpretentious outside; family atmosphere within – informal without being matey." Recent encomiums for this cosseting country hotel (Relais & Châteaux) not far from Hadrian's Wall. It is a mellow building surrounded by a landscaped Victorian garden with huge trees, a stream and a lake. A true family affair (a rarity in Britain), it is run by Alan and Joan Quinion, their son Barry (the chef) and his wife Lynne, and their daughter Helen and her husband, Alastair Stevenson. The public rooms are Victorian and ornate, with dark wallpaper, heavy furniture, and lots of trimmings and ornaments. Bedrooms, which vary considerably in size and shape and are priced accordingly (best ones have a whirlpool bath), "manage to be both Victorian and whimsical"; and "everything has been thought of, from high-quality linen, good lighting, dishes of sweeties, bowls of fresh fruit, books and new magazines, to unobtrusive staff who tidy up quietly while you are out". Drinks are served in the lounge (no bar). Dinner is formal, starting punctually at 8 pm. The four-course menu, country house cooking based on local produce, changes daily. "The food gets better all the time. It is imaginative and substantial, never prissy or over-decorated. Sauces complement, but never overwhelm. Platters of fresh vegetables are left on the table for guests to help themselves." "Excellent breakfast." Bedrooms on the road hear traffic, but there's effective double-glazing. Brampton village was founded by Augustinian monks in 1166; it has an old church (mostly 13th-century), and an ancient border fortress, Naworth Castle. Hadrian's Wall is four miles away. (*Michael and Maureen Heath, Stephen and Ellise Holman, Eve and Ron Jones*)

Open All year, except: hotel 24–30 Dec, restaurant 26–30 Dec. Restaurant closed midday (light meal for residents by arrangement).
Rooms 12 double. 1 in converted stable block. 2 on ground floor.
Facilities 2 lounges, restaurant. 12-acre grounds: croquet. Golf nearby. Unsuitable for &.
Location On A689, 2½ miles SE of Brampton (*not* in Farlam village). Rooms double-glazed.
Restriction No children under 5.
Credit cards Access, Amex, Visa.
Terms [Until May 1998] D,B&B £100–£125. Light and packed lunches by arrangement. Set dinner £31. Winter, spring breaks; New Year package.

BRATTON FLEMING Devon   Map 1

Bracken House   **NEW/BUDGET**   *Tel* (01598) 710320
Bratton Fleming
nr Barnstaple EX31 4TG

This former rectory has a glorious setting, high up on the western edge of Exmoor amid rolling country, with views across to distant Taw Estuary and Hartland Point. The owners, Prue and Lawrie Scott, "aim to provide good value at a modest tariff, with relative informality, in a simple decor". The Victorian house is set in large grounds, with wood-land and paddocks, a small lake, animals and birds, and hens on the lawn for fresh eggs. "A find!" wrote the enthusiastic nominator. "Friendly, personal welcome with tea and fruit cake. Lots of taxidermy in the house, which is spotless. Large selection of local guides, etc, in the lounge. Bedrooms vary greatly in size. Ours was large and well dec-orated: melamine matching furniture, but of good quality, and TV; bathroom with power shower. Attractive dining room; starched nap-kins placed in ladies' laps by Lawrie Scott. Delicious dinner, cooked by Prue Scott, is ordered after breakfast, and served at 7 pm: real English-style menu, with wonderful Aga-cooked vegetables – no *al dente* here; different potatoes every night. Three choices of dessert, including plum crumble and apricot tart, all with custard, cream or ice cream. Super breakfast with plenty of choice, and hot toast. The Scotts formerly ran a far larger hotel on the coast; their experience shows. The efficient booking form even asked the type of bedding required." "Well-behaved dogs" are welcomed. Nearby is much natural beauty, as well as fine beaches, the Rosemoor and Marwood Hill gardens, and two National Trust properties, Arlington Court and Knightshayes Court. (*Janice Carrera*)

Open Late Mar–early Nov.
Rooms 8 double. No telephone. 2 on ground floor; 1 suitable for &. 1 self-cater-ing cottage.
Facilities Ramps. Drawing room/bar, library, dining room (piped music, mainly classical, during dinner). 8½-acre grounds: aviary. Riding, boating nearby.
Location On edge of village 6 miles NE of Barnstaple. Bus from Barnstaple.
Restrictions No smoking: dining room, library. No children under 8.
Credit cards Access, Visa.
Terms B&B £29–£36 per person; D,B&B £44–£51 per person. Supplement for single person in room £0–£15, depending on circumstances.

BRAY Berkshire   Map 2

Monkey Island Hotel   `NEW`   *Tel* (01628) 23400
Old Mill Lane,   *Fax* (01628) 784732
Bray, nr Maidenhead SL6 2EE

This hotel full of character and history has a lovely setting on a small island in the Thames. It is accessible only by a narrow suspension bridge; you leave your luggage in your car on the mainland and it is car-ried over. Built by the third Duke of Marlborough in the 18th century, it started life as a "fishing lodge" and a "fishing temple" (now called the Pavilion and the Temple, and Grade I listed). By 1840 it had become a popular inn. King Edward VII and Queen Alexandra enjoyed tea on the lawn; HG Wells and Rebecca West visited. Nowadays it goes in for weekday conferences and Saturday weddings, and offers good-value packages at the weekend, when generous breakfasts are served until 11 am. The two stately white buildings are set in well-maintained gar-dens, with peacocks strutting. The Pavilion houses the lounge, where an 18th-century painted ceiling represents monkeys, dressed in the fashion of the day, in sporting scenes, and the Regency-style restaurant. Function rooms and bedrooms, some in sympathetic 20th-century extensions, are in the Temple. "We were delighted with the hotel and its setting," write regular *Guide* contributors. "The public rooms are interesting, the bedrooms tastefully decorated, and dinner overlooking the pleasure traffic on the river, under a canopy of laden walnut trees, could not be faulted. There is a wide-ranging *table d'hôte* as well as a *carte*, and an excellent wine list ranging from reasonably priced to 'over the top'. Service was attentive and friendly. The hotel is not under a Heathrow flight-path, so is less prone to aircraft noise than nearby Windsor." Eton, Henley, Ascot and Cliveden are within easy reach. (*PJ and BA D'Arcy*)

Open All year, except 26–31 Dec. Restaurant closed Sat midday.
Rooms 2 suites, 20 double. Some on ground floor.
Facilities Lounge, bar, restaurant (piped music); function facilities; gym. 4½-acre grounds: fishing, boating, launch for hire. Unsuitable for &.
Location From M4 exit 8/9, A308 to Windsor, left on B3058 to Bray. Right down Old Mill Lane. Park and take footbridge to island. Train: Maidenhead; then taxi.
Restriction No dogs.
Credit cards All major cards accepted.
Terms Rooms: single £70–£95, double £95–£165, suite £145–£165. Breakfast: continental £7.50, English £11. Bar lunches. Set lunch £20, dinner £28. Weekend breaks (2 days min.): D,B&B £75–£140 per person per night. Sunday night discounts.

The Waterside Inn	*Tel* (01628) 20691
Ferry Road	*Fax* (01628) 784710
Bray SL6 2AT	*E-mail* 100552.1641@compuserve.com

This old Thames-side village was immortalised in the song about the adaptable 16th-century vicar of its large old church. Nowadays it is equally renowned for Michel Roux's *restaurant-avec-chambres*, a Relais & Châteaux member with three *Michelin* stars and four crossed spoon-and-forks. "The setting, on the banks of the river, with a willow tree hanging over the water, is charming," one visitor wrote, "and the ducks must be the best fed in the country." The restaurant has green walls, and formal service by French waiters. A honeymoon couple praised the food: "It was at the incredible end of excellence; all courses perfectly displayed." But some have thought it very rich. Drinks and coffee may be served in a summer house on the water, or on an electric launch. Accommodation is in smallish bedrooms, and in one suite on the river bank. The best rooms, La Tamise and La Terrace, share a river-side terrace where breakfast may be served. Le Nid Jaune, the cheapest, is "very small", according to an inspector, who reported last year: "It is dominated by an iron-framed bed, with a bathroom designed for the slim, only one chair, and no table, so the tray with a rather indifferent continental breakfast had to be perched on the bed. Very noisy plumbing." "This hasn't changed," says a 1997 correspondent. There are kitchen facilities on each landing where drinks may be made. The hotel is licensed for weddings. Heathrow airport is 45 minutes' drive away. (*RM O'Brien, and others*)

Open All year, except 26 Dec–31 Jan. Restaurant closed bank holidays, Mon; also Sun evening, Tues midday mid-Oct–mid-Apr.
Rooms 1 suite (in cottage, 30 yds), 8 double.
Facilities Restaurant; private dining room in cottage; launch for drinks/coffee. Unsuitable for &.
Location On Thames, just SE of Maidenhead. M4 exit 8/9 towards Maidenhead Central. At 2nd roundabout follow sign to Windsor/Bray. Left after ½ mile on to B3028. In Bray 2nd right into Ferry Rd; hotel on left. Train: Maidenhead; then taxi.
Restrictions No children under 12. No dogs.

Credit cards All major cards accepted.
Terms [1997] B&B: single/double £135–£165, suite £215. Set lunch £30.50 week-days, £45.50 weekend, dinner £69.50; full alc £80.

BRIDGWATER Somerset   Map 1

Cokerhurst Farm   BUDGET   *Tel/Fax* (01278) 422330
87 Wembdon Hill
Bridgwater TA6 7QA

This unpretentious small B&B, a 16th-century farmhouse overlooking a lake, is set on a large farm on the fringe of the Quantocks. "The owners, Derrick and Diana Chappell, are very friendly," wrote the nominator. "The bedrooms are well up to *Guide* standard." This is endorsed: "We were impressed by little touches, such as the tray of sweets replenished each day. The breakfasts would put many grander hotels to shame." Others have admired the sheltered walled garden and the interesting collection of "bygones", including a polyphon, a barrel organ, and a pennyfarthing bicycle. No dinners, but good pub meals nearby. Pick your own strawberries and raspberries in season. All the bedrooms now have *en suite* facilities. The old town of Bridgwater, nearby, is an inland port at the head of the Parrett estuary, with a large market place, a medieval church, and some attractive Georgian houses. It stages an annual carnival in November. Exmoor, Wells, Glastonbury and Taunton are all within easy reach. (*Michael Crick, David Cornish; also Georgina Brooks*)

Open All year, except Christmas.
Rooms 3 double.
Facilities Lounge. ⅓-acre garden on 100-acre farm. Riding, fishing, 3 leisure centres nearby.
Location 1½ miles W of Bridgwater.
Restrictions No smoking. Dogs in cars only.
Credit cards None accepted.
Terms [1997] B&B £22.50. 10% discount on 7 nights' accommodation.

BRIGHTON East Sussex   Map 2

Topps   *Tel* (01273) 729334
17 Regency Square   *Fax* (01273) 203679
Brighton BN1 2FG

"I had not been for three years, and I'd forgotten how good it is. Why stay in a big hotel when here you can get almost everything you need for half the price? You have in your bedroom and bathroom all creature comforts: a *good large* TV, flowers, chocolates, trouser press, bathrobe, excellent shower, etc. Delicious breakfast. Charming service. Splendid location. *Topps* is still just that." High praise from a returning visitor to Paul and Pauline Collins's conversion of two Regency terrace houses a block away from the sea, opposite a small green square. It is eclectically furnished, and decorated in soft colours. The only public room acts as reception, library and meeting place. Bedrooms are warm (11 have a gas fire) and well lit. The best one is spacious and high-ceilinged, with a four-poster, a huge bay window and a small balcony on which to breakfast. Bathrooms have large towels and generous toiletries. The restaurant has now closed, but snacks may be served in the bedroom from 10 am to 10 pm. (*Braham Murray*)

Open All year.
Rooms 14 double, 1 single. Some on ground floor.
Facilities Lift. Reception/lounge, breakfast room. Near sea: safe bathing. Unsuitable for &.
Location 200 yds from centre, opposite West Pier, but quiet. NCP carpark nearby. 5 mins by taxi from station.
Restriction No dogs.
Credit cards All major cards accepted.
Terms B&B: single £45, double £49–£109. Reductions for 2 nights or more; weekly rates. Children accommodated free in parents' room. 1-night bookings sometimes refused Sat.

See also SHORTLIST

BRISTOL *See SHORTLIST*   Map 1

BROADWAY Worcestershire   Map 3

Collin House   *Tel* (01386) 858354
Collin Lane
Broadway WR12 7PB

This unpretentious Cotswold stone house, not far from *the* showplace Cotswold village, was built by a prosperous wool merchant in the 15th century. "Neither too posh nor too casual", it is run by John Mills and a helpful staff. It has a picturesque setting, amid trees, lawn and gardens, and an equally beguiling interior, "more private house than hotel": mullioned windows, flagstones, beams, fine fireplaces, antique furniture and china, and interesting prints and pictures. The bedrooms, with flowery fabrics and wallpaper, vary in size and style. A recent visitor praised hers as "large yet cosy, with every comfort". Some, particularly the single, are small. Lunches are served in a lounge bar with beams and armchairs round an inglenook fire, or in the garden. Evening meals are taken in the oak-beamed candlelit dining room; there is a *carte* with plenty of choice, priced according to the main course, and a simpler supper menu (not available on Saturday). Cooking is dependable traditional English, served in generous portions, with old-style puddings; local produce is used, and fresh fish is delivered daily. Breakfasts, too, are generous. *Collin House* does not have extensive facilities for small children. "But," says Mr Mills, "they are very welcome provided parents control them and accept certain modest limitations." A good base for visiting the villages of the north Cotswolds, Warwick and Sudeley castles, Blenheim Palace, and many other houses and gardens. (*Patricia Mack*)

Open All year, except 24–28 Dec.
Rooms 6 double, 1 single. No telephone; TV on request.
Facilities Lounge, lounge bar, restaurant. 3-acre grounds: swimming pool (unheated). Riding, golf nearby. Unsuitable for &.
Location 1 mile NW of Broadway on A44. Turn right down Collin La. Train: (from south) Moreton-in-Marsh, 9 miles; (from north) Evesham, 6 miles, Cheltenham, 15 miles; then taxi.

Restrictions No smoking in restaurant. Children under 7 by arrangement. No dogs.
Credit cards Access, Visa.
Terms [1997] B&B: single £46, double £88–£98. Bar lunches. Set lunch £16, dinner £16–£24. 2-night breaks all year except bank holiday weekends and New Year. 1-night bookings sometimes refused Sat. Child sharing parents' room: B&B £20. *V*

The Lygon Arms	*Tel* (01386) 852255
High Street	*Fax* (01386) 858611
Broadway WR12 7DU	*E-mail* info@the-lygon-arms.co.uk

This handsome building is in the centre of this sometimes touristy village. Its guest register includes Cromwell and Charles I, but it is named for General Sir William Lygon, who bought it after the battle of Waterloo. Nowadays, it is owned by the Savoy Group; Kirk Ritchie is managing director. It has beamed ceilings, panelled public rooms, fine fireplaces, polished stone floors and antique furniture. "Lots of little lounges, most with a fire; you can happily sit in your own nook." The bedrooms vary greatly. Traditional ones, some with a four-poster, are in the main building; modern ones are in rear extensions; some overlook the carpark; and one visitor this year complained of noise from a kitchen extractor fan. Formal meals are served in the Great Hall, which has a barrel ceiling, a minstrels' gallery, stags' heads and a heraldic frieze. You should specify that you wish to dine there, not in the less attractive adjacent room. The food is "good, particularly if you are not in search of the latest fashion – puddings, for example, sherry trifle and spotted dick, hark back more than a few years". Light meals may be taken in the wine bar. The hotel has a pretty walled garden, and good leisure facilities (see below), though these can become crowded with outside visitors. Children and dogs are welcomed. Some *Guide* correspondents have found the place wholly congenial: "Such history." "Staff universally nice." "Stunning restaurant." But one winter visitor concluded: "Higher levels of supervision are required; for our next visit we shall double-check in advance any aspects that are important to us, and then settle back and accept philosophically whatever happens." Many packages are available, including a visit to the Royal Shakespeare Theatre in Stratford-upon-Avon, half-an-hour's drive away.

Open All year.
Rooms 5 suites, 57 double, 3 single. Some on ground floor.
Facilities 5 lounges, cocktail bar, wine bar, restaurant; function facilities. 3½-acre grounds: tennis (lessons available), croquet, archery; Country Club: swimming pool, spa bath, sauna, solarium, fitness room, beauty salon, light meals. Fishing, golf, riding, hunting etc, nearby.
Location Central (front rooms double-glazed; quietest ones at rear; Broadway bypass under construction). Garage, large carpark. Train: see above.
Restrictions Smoking discouraged in restaurant. No dogs in bar, restaurant.
Credit cards All major cards accepted.
Terms [1997] (*Excluding VAT*) B&B: single £98–£128, double £155–£225, suite £245–£330; half board £36 per person added. Cooked breakfast £9.20. Set lunch £25.50, dinner £40; full alc £50. Weekend, midweek breaks; Shakespeare, Christmas package.

If you find details of a hotel's location inadequate, let us know.

BROXTON Cheshire   Map 3

Frogg Manor   *Tel* (01829) 782629
Fullers Moor, Nantwich Road   *Fax* (01829) 782238
Broxton, Chester CH3 9JH

❡ *César award in 1997*

In his white Georgian manor in a deeply prosperous rural area near
Chester, John Sykes styles himself "chief frog". He offers an unlikely
combination of eclectic furnishings, old-time music and over 100 frogs
(ceramic, straw, brass, etc), scattered around among a plethora of *objets*.
He likes to greet his guests wearing a frock coat, and adds a tall top hat
to deliver a champagne breakfast to the honeymoon suite (entered
through the bookcase in the sitting room, and endowed with an "amazing" bathroom). His César was for utterly acceptable mild eccentricity,
and the quirky charm of it all, as well as the thoughtfulness (emergency
supplies in the bedrooms include hangover remedies, gripe water and
spare stockings) continue to impress. "Mr Sykes is a wonder to behold.
He deals with everything in a highly personal way, ranging from his
bugle call to dinner to his stimulating conversation." "What really
stands out is his obvious pleasure in having guests. Bedrooms are lavish. There is a charming dining room, and the sitting room has wall-to-
wall frogs of every shape and form. The garden is romantically floodlit
at night." Cooking is "unfussy, but modern"; dinner is served between
7 and 10 pm, but a light supper may be arranged for late arrivals.
Breakfast *à la carte* is served round the clock Monday to Saturday, and
9 to 10.30 am on Sunday. (*Mrs Jo Murray, CR Smith, and others*)

Open All year. Restaurant closed to non-residents 1 Jan.
Rooms 1 suite, 5 double.
Facilities Lounge, restaurant (piped 1930/40s music). 10-acre grounds: tennis.
Unsuitable for &.
Location 15 miles SE of Chester. From A41, take A534 to Nantwich. Hotel on
right.
Restriction Dogs by arrangement; not in public rooms.
Credit cards All major cards accepted.
Terms Rooms: single £50–£92, double £66–£90, suite £120. Breakfast alc from
c £3.50. Set lunch £16, dinner £26. Discounts for 2 or more nights (except
Christmas, New Year). ***V*** (room only)

BUCKLAND Worcestershire   Map 3

Buckland Manor   *Tel* (01386) 852626
Buckland, nr Broadway WR12 7LY   *Fax* (01386) 853557

"Our dream place; cosseting, tranquil, beautiful and welcoming. We
had a glorious time. Tea in front of the fire in our room, drinks with
canapés in front of another fire. Dinner one of the best we have ever
enjoyed; the vegetables were a picturesque delight." A rave review in
1997 for this beautiful 13th-century manor (Relais & Châteaux) in a harmonious Cotswold village. Much gabled, it stands in large grounds,
with formal flower gardens, a stream and a swimming pool. Other visitors have admired the public rooms "with a clutter of antique furniture, fabulous flower displays, and light falling through mullioned
windows". Bedrooms vary in size from spacious to quite small. "The

Oak Room has lots of panelling and chintz, and a gorgeous view of the
landscaped and water-cascaded terraced garden. No key, which gave
us a curious sense of security." Two couples encountered coolness
when paying their bill, and one guest wrote: "We felt after dinner that
we were expected to retire, as the lights were switched off around us."
But most have found the staff friendly. "And dining was a delightful
experience. Martyn Pearn's cooking well deserves its *Michelin* star.
Much pleasure, too, could be derived from the wine list." Dinner is *à la
carte*, each course served on a plate with a different design. The "charm-
ing" manager, Nigel Power, will take guests on a tour of the cellars.
Only church bells at 9 am on Sunday interrupt the peace. An early sup-
per may be served for visitors to the Royal Shakespeare Theatre at
Stratford-upon-Avon, 16 miles away. Sudeley and Warwick castles and
Hidcote Manor are nearby. *Buckland Manor*'s owners, Roy and Daphne
Vaughan, recently bought two other Cotswold hotels, *Lower Slaughter
Manor*, and *Washbourne Court*, both in Lower Slaughter. (*Ruth and Derek
Tilsley, and others*)

Open All year.
Rooms 13 double. Some on ground floor.
Facilities Ramp. Lounge, morning room, restaurant. 10-acre grounds: gardens,
stream, waterfall, tennis, putting, swimming pool, croquet. Golf, riding nearby.
Location Centre of quiet village off B4632, 2 miles SW of Broadway. Train:
Moreton-in-Marsh, 11 miles; then taxi.
Restrictions No smoking in restaurant. No children under 12. No dogs.
Credit cards All major cards accepted.
Terms B&B: single £168–£315, double £178–£325. Set lunch £27.50; full alc from
£50. Winter breaks; Christmas package. 1-night bookings refused Sat.

BUDOCK VEAN Cornwall   Map 1

Budock Vean Hotel   *Tel* (01326) 250230
Mawnan Smith, Falmouth TR11 5LG   *Fax* (01326) 250892

*Traditional hotel, owned by Barlows of Treglos, Constantine Bay (qv); man-
aged by Alan Tookey. 5 miles S of Falmouth, in designated area of outstanding natural beauty. 65-acre grounds: private waterfront on Helford Passage,
fishing, water sports; large swimming pool, enclosed in winter, open in summer; "challenging" 9-hole golf course; tennis, croquet, archery. Good amenities for children; special arrangements for families during school holidays, half
term. Licensed for weddings. Traditional food in generous portions on varied
five-course dinner menu; seafood, local lobsters, oysters often available; pianist
in dining room at night; Country Club restaurant for less formal meals.
"Helpful staff, good atmosphere" most visitors say, but decor has been criticised. Open 9 Feb–2 Jan. 58 rooms, 3 self-catering cottages. Unsuitable for ⟨&⟩.
No children under 7 in dining room for dinner. No dogs in public rooms.
Access, Visa accepted. B&B £50–£70; D,B&B £60–£80. Set dinner £19.50;
full alc £39.*

"Set meals" indicates fixed-price meals, with ample, limited or
no choice on the menu. "Full alc" is the hotel's estimated price
per person of a 3-course *à la carte* meal, with a half-bottle of
house wine. "Alc" is the price of a *carte* meal excluding the cost
of wine.

BURNHAM MARKET Norfolk   Map 2

 The Hoste Arms   *Tel* (01328) 738777
The Green   *Fax* (01328) 730103
Burnham Market PE31 8HD   *E-mail* 106504.2472@compuserve.com

César award: inn of the year

Lord Nelson used to collect his dispatches from this pub (now named for a *protégé* of his) on the green of the lovely Georgian village where he was born. In 1989, it was bought and extensively restored by Paul Whittome, formerly a potato merchant. Nowadays it buzzes, even in low season. Live jazz and picture exhibitions reflect the owner's interests. The first floor houses an impressive shell collection. There's a nautical flavour to the bar decor. Bedrooms are stylish, with old features preserved, and period furniture. The restaurant is full of character, with red walls, wooden floors and panels. It serves modern cooking with oriental influences; there's a comprehensive, well-presented wine list. "We could not praise the place highly enough," wrote recent visitors. "We had a spacious bedroom, with a bed as comfortable as the one we left at home, and a splendid bathroom. The attention to detail is impressive. We loved the relaxed environment, and enjoyed being able to choose where to eat, either in the lovely dining room or in the less formal conservatory." "Delightful. The bright young staff, from Australia, South Africa, etc, were without exception obliging." "Charming decor. Excellent breakfast. Free help-yourself coffee all day for residents. Good food." "A friendly atmosphere and a generous spirit." Mr Whittome writes in the brochure: "Please speak up! I am very deaf, and this is sometimes mistaken for rudeness." Not a complaint we have ever heard. The surrounding area is one of designated natural beauty, with nature reserves, historic buildings, golf courses, etc. Mr Whittome recently bought and restored the Burnham Market station house, to make a bedroom annexe with cheaper accommodation. (*Carol Clark, David and Anna Berkeley, Oliver and Delia Millar, and others; also Good Pub Guide*)

Open All year.
Rooms 17 double, 3 single. Some on ground floor, 1 with access for ♿.
Facilities 2 lounges, bar, 4 dining rooms, conservatory, art gallery; conference facilities. Walled garden. Sea, golf, bird sanctuaries nearby.
Location Central. Large carpark. Train: Norwich/Kings Lynn; then hotel car (small charge).
Restrictions No smoking: conservatory, 1 dining room. No dogs in restaurant.
Credit cards Access, Visa.
Terms [1997] B&B: single £60, double £86–£98. Bar meals; full alc from £17. Child 2–14 sharing parents' room £15. Short breaks all year.

BURPHAM West Sussex   Map 2

The Burpham Country Hotel   **NEW**   *Tel* (01903) 882160
Burpham, nr Arundel BN18 9RJ   *Fax* (01903) 884627

This handsome 18th-century house is set in a small garden, in an unspoilt South Downs hamlet (pronounced Ber'-fum). It is said once to have been a shooting lodge of the dukes of Norfolk, the owners of nearby Arundel Castle. Later, it was a vicarage. George and Marianne

Walker, who previously ran the *George and Dragon* pub down the road (recommended for lunch), bought it in 1995 and have extensively renovated. "They are charming hosts, who greet you personally on arrival," writes the nominator. "The decor throughout is in soft colours, with well-chosen fabrics and fresh flowers. The lounge is small, which makes for a friendly atmosphere; it includes the bar, where George Walker amiably presides. The bedrooms are large, and decorated in the style one might expect in the spare room in a friend's house. Many have lovely country views." The food, served in two small dining rooms, is "imaginative and sophisticated"; the menus include dishes from Mrs Walker's native Switzerland. The wine list is "eclectic and well chosen". The staff "exude the same charm and friendliness as the owners". There is excellent walking all around; the Arundel Wild Fowl Trust is close by; Chichester and Goodwood are within easy reach. (*Brian and Li Jobson, Lianne Jarrett, and others*)

Open All year, except early Jan. Restaurant closed midday, Mon.
Rooms 9 double, 1 single. 1 on ground floor.
Facilities Hall (piped classical music at night), lounge, bar, restaurant; function room; patio. ¾-acre garden: croquet. Coast 6 miles: sand/shingle beaches, safe bathing.
Location NE of Arundel, down country lane. Left off A27 Arundel–Worthing towards Warningcamp and Burpham just after railway bridge. Hotel on right after 2½ miles.
Restrictions No smoking: restaurant, bedrooms. No children under 10. No dogs.
Credit cards Access, Amex, Visa.
Terms B&B: £37–£41.50, D,B&B £57–£61.50. Set dinner £20. 2-night breaks. Christmas package. *V*

BURY ST EDMUNDS Suffolk   **Map 2**

Ounce House   *Tel* (01284) 761779
Northgate Street   *Fax* (01284) 768315
Bury St Edmunds IP33 1HP   *E-mail* pott@globalnet.co.uk

Named for King Edmund the Martyr, who was murdered by Danes in the 9th century, this bustling town was once an important pilgrimage site; the impressive ruins of its 14th-century abbey stand in large gardens in the centre. Among its many handsome buildings is Simon and Jenny Pott's Victorian house, which has been found "highly civilised, yet utterly unpretentious, with charming hosts" by *Guide* reporters: "Our bedroom overlooking the garden was beautifully quiet at night. Breakfasts were perfectly cooked and presented." Others have admired the "welcoming family atmosphere, the first-rate fabrics, antiques, pictures and prints and the inviting colour schemes". Traditional English dinners (by arrangement) are served communally round a large table. The off-street parking is a huge attraction. Light sleepers might be disturbed by traffic noise in the front rooms. More reports, please.

Open All year.
Rooms 3 double, 1 single.
Facilities Drawing room, snug, bar/library, dining room. ⅔-acre walled garden. Unsuitable for &.
Location Central. Leave A14 (formerly A45) at 2nd Bury exit. Left at 1st roundabout into Northgate St; house at top of hill. Private parking.
Restrictions Smoking in bar/library only. No dogs.

Credit cards Access, Visa.
Terms B&B: single £40–£45, double £64–£80. Set dinner (by arrangement) £18–£22. Reductions for weekends/3 or more nights.

Twelve Angel Hill   *Tel* (01284) 704088
12 Angel Hill   *Fax* (01284) 725549
Bury St Edmunds IP33 1UZ

This no-smoking B&B, a Georgian house with Tudor origins, stands on the north side of Bury's busy main square, near the abbey ruins and the cathedral. Its bedrooms are named after wines – Claret, Chablis, etc – and have colour schemes to match, with bold floral prints, odd knick-knacks, and a bath or shower *en suite*. One has a large four-poster. The owners, Bernadette and John Clarke, take a keen interest in their guests, and first names tend to be used. "They make you feel wonderfully pampered, and the place has a real family feel," writes a regular visitor. The Clarkes have an inexhaustible knowledge of local eating places, many of which offer discounts to their guests. Breakfast includes freshly squeezed fruit juice, fruit salad, cereals, an enticing variety of hot dishes cooked to order, and home-made marmalade. (*Mrs RJ East, IC, and others*)

Open All year, except Jan.
Rooms 1 suite, 4 double, 1 single.
Facilities Lounge, bar, breakfast room; meeting room. Small walled garden. Unsuitable for &.
Location Central, on main square (front rooms double-glazed). Parking for 3 cars at rear. Free collection from station.
Restrictions No smoking. No children under 16. No dogs.
Credit cards All major cards accepted.
Terms [1997] B&B: single £45, double £70–£80. Weekend breaks.

BUTTERMERE Cumbria   **Map 4**

Bridge Hotel   **NEW**   *Tel/Fax* (01768 7) 70252
Buttermere CA13 9UZ

250-year-old hostelry, by ancient pack horse bridge, which numbers Thomas Carlyle and Alfred Wainwright among past guests. Recently extensively upgraded by resident owners, Mr and Mrs McGuire. Traditional beamed bars serving walkers, residents and locals. Comfortable lounge. English/French traditional cooking in restaurant; vegetarians catered for. Children welcomed. Lake Buttermere and Crummock Water 3 mins' walk. Smoking in bars only. Unsuitable for &. No dogs in public rooms. Access, Visa accepted. 22 bedrooms. B&B £36–£42; D,B&B £52–£62. Bar meals. Set dinner £20. More reports, please.

Pickett Howe   *Tel* (01900) 85444
Buttermere CA13 9UY   *Fax* (01900) 85209

There is excellent walking right from the door of this farmhouse hotel on a hillside in a beautiful, untouristy setting, near a small village between Lake Buttermere and Crummock Water. You approach down a rough track through trees. In 1977 the owners, David and Dani Edwards (she is chef), won the Booker Prize for Excellence in

Independent Catering. It is "small and cosy, personal and romantic", with slate floors, mullioned windows, antique furniture, and all manner of comforts. The bedrooms have low beams, tiny windows, sprigged wallpaper, fine china teapot and cups, home-made biscuits and fresh fruit. The immaculate bathrooms have a jacuzzi bath or a power shower. Dinners, by candlelight, with good crystal and silver on oak tables, are semi-communal (two tables for four; safest, perhaps, to come with friends). The eclectic menu, "a treat for both eyes and palate, with unobtrusive service", draws on English, French and Mediterranean styles, and features local cheeses and Cumbrian puddings. "Very more-ish" truffles with coffee in the lounge or garden afterwards. There's a huge choice at breakfast, including a plentiful Cumbrian cooked affair and home-made preserves. "The only sounds were gentle classical music in the background, and the hoot of an owl at night." "Helpful hosts, full of suggestions about what to do. No smoking – hurrah! Excellent value." More reports, please.

Open Mar–Nov.
Rooms 4 double.
Facilities Lounge, study, dining room (piped classical music at night). 15-acre grounds: garden; direct access to hills. Boat for hire on Crummock Water. Unsuitable for &.
Location From Lorton, follow signs to Buttermere, going south on B5289. Track on right about ⅓ mile after turning to Buttermere.
Restrictions No smoking. No children under 10. Dogs in cars or barn.
Credit cards Access, Visa.
Terms B&B £37. Picnic lunches available. Set dinner £22. 1-night bookings sometimes refused.

CALNE Wiltshire   Map 2

Chilvester Hill House   `BUDGET`   *Tel* (01249) 813981 and 815785
Calne SN11 0LP   *Fax* (01249) 814217

♦ *César award in 1992*

This spacious Victorian house, filled with antiques and mementos of a lifetime, is the family home of John and Gill Dilley. Set in a large garden amid fields, it overlooks the vast grounds of the Bowood estate, landscaped by Capability Brown. No brochure; enquirers get a friendly letter describing the facilities, and discussing dietary requirements. The Dilleys join their guests for pre-dinner drinks or coffee, and occasionally for the four-course no-choice dinner ("honest English fare", with home-grown vegetables), which is served round one splendidly set table and couples may be invited to split up to keep the conversation going. Light meals can sometimes be arranged. There's no obligation to dine in; the Dilleys will help with reservations at local eating places. The guest bedrooms are large, with a lovely view, and generously kitted out. The *en suite* bathrooms have a hand-held shower, and a large shower room is available (bathrobes provided). The Dilleys have many fans. One visitor called them "a lovely couple". Another wrote: "I know them so well that we eat together in the kitchen if I am the only guest." "The most relaxing stay I can remember," said a third. "Combines the best elements of a B&B and a fine small hotel." Cooked-to-order breakfasts – what you want, when you want – are "as generous as the rest". Dr Dilley has an encyclopaedic knowledge of local sights, which include the Neolithic stone circle at Avebury, and Lacock, the National Trust village loved by makers of Jane Austen films. (*AC, Chris Kay, WK Moulding, and others*)

Open All year, except 1 week off-season (autumn or spring).
Rooms 3 double. No telephone.
Facilities Drawing room, sitting room with TV, dining room. 2½-acre grounds (also 5 acres used for cattle). Golf, riding locally. Unsuitable for &.
Location From Calne, A4 towards Chippenham. Right after ½ mile to Bremhill; drive immediately on right (gateposts with stone lions).
Restrictions No smoking in dining room. Generally no children under 12, except babes in arms. Guide dogs only.
Credit cards All major cards accepted.
Terms B&B: single £45–£55, double £70–£85, triple £90–£105. Packed or snack lunches. Set dinner £18–£25. 10% discount for B&B 1 week or longer.

CALSTOCK Cornwall   Map 1

Danescombe Valley Hotel   *Tel* (01822) 832414
Lower Kelly, Calstock PL18 9RY   *Fax* (01822) 832446
                    E-mail Danescombe@compuserve.com

Martin and Anna Smith's Victorian villa is set on a steep wooded hill-side on a meander of the river Tamar, in a designated area of outstanding natural beauty. Its grounds adjoin the Cotehele estate, which is owned by the National Trust. There are lovely views up and down the river from the veranda and most bedrooms. The house is filled with *objets d'art*, books and paintings. The airy bedrooms have antique and traditional furniture, and an *en suite* or adjacent private bathroom. The charms of the tranquil setting are enhanced by the absence of TV, the "warm and personal welcome" (first names tend to be used), and the good food, modern British with Californian and Italian overtones, which draws heavily on local produce. Anna Smith has now retired from the kitchen, and three chefs, Christine Dew, Melissa Haywood and Jill Urwin, are cooking in rotation. Dinner (no choice) is at 7.30 for 8 pm, and ends with a huge choice of British cheeses. The informative wine list offers excellent, mainly Italian wines with a modest mark-up. The simple breakfast – juice, muesli, yogurt, etc – is a leisurely affair. Rates include morning coffee, afternoon tea, mineral water, etc. Alternative health treatments – aromatherapy, massage, reflexology, etc – are available; "Calstock is a forerunner into the Aquarian age," writes Mr Smith. Dartmoor, Bodmin Moor, and many National Trust properties are nearby. (*JK Lunn*).

Open All year.
Rooms 5 double. No telephone/TV. 1 self-catering cottage down lane.
Facilities Lounge, bar, dining room. 4 acres steep woodland; steps to river Tamar: moorings, fishing, walking. Golf, riding nearby. Unsuitable for &.
Location ½ mile W of Calstock village. Go under viaduct, past Methodist church, sharp right; follow road parallel to river for ½ mile. Train: Plymouth, then Tamar Valley line to Calstock.
Restrictions No smoking in dining room. No children under 12. No dogs.
Credit cards All major cards accepted (*with surcharge*).
Terms B&B: single by arrangement, double £125. Set dinner £35. 1-night bookings sometimes refused weekends. 4-night Christmas break.

Give the *Guide* positive support. Don't leave feedback to others.

CAMBRIDGE, Cambridgeshire *See SHORTLIST*　　　　　　Map 2

CAMPSEA ASHE Suffolk　　　　　　　　　　　　　　　Map 2

The Old Rectory ▓BUDGET▓ 　　　　　*Tel/Fax* (01728) 746524
Campsea Ashe
nr Woodbridge IP13 0PU

♥ *César award in 1992*

In a village near Woodbridge, this restaurant-with-rooms, a Wolsey Lodge member, is a spacious Georgian rectory in a large garden with statuary. It has high ceilings, grandiose antiques set off by rich terra-cotta walls, "and a benign ambience". The proprietor/chef Stewart Bassett – of whom one guest wrote: "He is like a favourite uncle" – runs it in house party style. Bedrooms range "from the wonderful four-poster room overlooking the garden to the 'au pair's room', which is used *in extremis*"; the one above the kitchen can be noisy. There is an honesty bar in the large drawing room. Dinner (no choice), at 7.30 pm, is accompanied by outstanding wines on an impressive, reasonably priced list. "The food is delicious and innovative," wrote a recent visitor. "Mr Bassett knows what he is about. But fresh fruit might be a welcome alternative to the creamy puds, and you have to be prepared to linger. After dinner, wearing a different pinny each night, Mr Bassett appeared to meet the guests; he is an expert Scrabble player. The domestic side of things is taken care of by Tina Morford, the talented wife of the church warden; she is also the church organist and a writer." Breakfast ("sometimes a bit haphazard") includes an extensive buffet and "delicious dark marmalade". The place is too casual for some, but others find it "enjoyably idiosyncratic", "a haven of peace", and excellent value. Children are welcomed; high tea must be booked in advance. Guests should not arrive between 2 and 4 pm. Snape and Aldeburgh are 15 minutes' drive away; the RSPB reserve at Minsmere is nearby. (*Lady Levinge, Miss ER Bowmer; also Joan A Powell*)

Open All year, except Christmas. Restaurant closed midday, Sun; bedrooms closed Sun in winter.
Rooms 8 double, 1 single. No telephone, radio, TV (payphone in hall).
Facilities Lounge/TV room, bar, restaurant; function facilities. 2-acre garden: croquet. Riding, golf nearby. Unsuitable for &.
Location In village 1½ miles E of A12 on B1078. Next to church. Train: Wickham Market, via Ipswich.
Restrictions No smoking: restaurant, bedrooms. No dogs in public rooms.
Credit cards All major cards accepted.
Terms [1997] B&B: single £35, double £55–£65; D,B&B: single £51, double £87–£97. Set dinner £16 (£18.70 to non-residents). Half board obligatory on Sat. Winter mid-week breaks; house parties.

CARLISLE Cumbria　　　　　　　　　　　　　　　　Map 4

Avondale ▓BUDGET▓ 　　　　　　　　　　*Tel* (01228) 523012
3 St Aidan's Road
Carlisle CA1 1LT

"Equivalent in quality to many highly rated hotels, but at a much more sensible tariff." "Maintains its high standards. Food is all 'real', and freshly cooked." Recent endorsements for Michael and Angela Hayes' civilised guest house. It is a large Edwardian building in a quiet road in a residential area, ten minutes' walk from the centre of this interesting border city. It has many original features – fireplaces, stained glass, elaborate ceilings, even door handles – and an unostentatious decor. Only three bedrooms; the largest, overlooking the garden, has a private bathroom. There's a good choice for breakfast. A simple evening meal is available by arrangement – traditional dishes, served in generous portions. The hotel's unlicensed: bring your own wine. (*Michael Blanchard, Kate Kelly*)

Open All year, except Christmas.
Rooms 3. 1 with bathroom *en suite*. No telephone.
Facilities Lounge, dining room. Small garden. Unsuitable for &.
Location From M6 exit 43 go into Carlisle. Turn right just past church after 4th traffic lights. Parking. Train/bus stations nearby.
Restrictions Smoking discouraged in bedrooms. Not really suitable for small children. No dogs.
Credit cards None accepted.
Terms (*Not VAT-rated*) B&B £20–£25; evening meal £8.

CARTMEL Cumbria   Map 4

 Aynsome Manor   `BUDGET`   *Tel* (01539 5) 36653
Cartmel   *Fax* (01539 5) 36016
nr Grange-over-Sands LA11 6HH

César award: for traditional Lakeland hospitality

"I cannot improve on the *Guide* entry except to emphasise the perfect silence of the surrounding countryside, particularly at night. The misty, chilly days of our stay gave a good opportunity to assess the hosts' attitude toward heating and open fires. Their generosity could not be faulted." "Soothing views. Rooms well equipped. House-keeping impeccable." "Comfortable, relaxing, good value for a longer stay. Consistently high standards." "Personal service. Excellent in every way." Recent praise for this handsome 16th-century house in a cobbled courtyard, run by two generations of the Varley family, Tony, Margaret, Chris and Andrea. It has a pastoral setting in a picturesque village on the edge of the Lake District, well away from the busy holiday resorts but near enough for a visit. From the small garden there is a view across meadows with livestock towards the ruined 12th-century priory. The decor is cheerful and traditional. There are two spacious, well-lit lounges; the one upstairs has a fine old marble fireplace. The oak-panelled restaurant, with large bay windows, moulded plaster ceiling and distinctive oil paintings, serves four- or five-course dinners with choice, generally at 7 pm. The unpretentious English country house-style cooking is "not brilliant, but far better than acceptable". On Sunday there is a traditional lunch and a generous supper (soup, cold buffet, etc). The long wine list "should suit most pockets". The bedrooms vary in size; some are suitable for a family; on the top floor, there is a heavily beamed one with sloping ceilings; two are in a cottage with a sitting room, across the courtyard. Local attractions include Holker Hall, Levens Hall and Sizergh Castle. (*Ann and Norman Leece, Dr John Rowlands, and others*)

Open All year, except 2–30 Jan. Lunch served Sun only.
Rooms 12 double. 2 in cottage across courtyard.
Facilities 2 lounges, bar, dining room. ¾-acre garden. Lake Windermere 4 miles: watersports; outdoor/indoor swimming pools, golf nearby. Unsuitable for &.
Location 12 miles from M6 exit 36. Leave A590 at Cartmel sign. Hotel on right, ½ mile before village. Train: Grange-over-Sands; then taxi.
Restrictions No smoking in restaurant. No children under 5 in restaurant at night. No dogs in public rooms, unsupervised in bedrooms.
Credit cards Access, Amex, Visa.
Terms D,B&B £46–£62. Set Sun lunch £11.95, dinner from £16. Weekend, mid-week, Christmas breaks; bonus breaks for returning guests. 1-night bookings occasionally refused. *V*

Uplands   *Tel* (01539 5) 36248
Haggs Lane   *Fax* (01539 5) 36848
Cartmel
nr Grange-over-Sands LA11 6HD

"A serene base in the Lake District, with pastel-colour furnishings and a sunny outlook to a well-trimmed garden. The house is small, but Tom and Di Peter provide a warm welcome and a pair of gorgeous mar-malade cats on which to stroke away the tension of a long journey. Tom is an outstanding and generous chef and produces an almost over-whelming selection of garnishes and fresh vegetables to accompany delicious main courses. Di is cheerfully front-of-house." So write hotel experts of this mustard-coloured pebbledash house perched on a hill-side with fine views over Morecambe Bay. The Peters co-own it with John Tovey of *Miller Howe*, Windermere (*qv*). It is run "in the *Miller Howe* manner", but is less grand, less theatrical and less expensive. Mealtimes are more flexible than at the parent hotel. The walls of the pink and grey dining room are crammed with Impressionist prints from the Metropolitan Museum of Art, New York. There is limited choice on the four-course fixed-price dinner menu (modern English cooking "of the good dinner party variety", served in generous por-tions). Bedrooms are simply furnished, and comfortable if not spa-cious; three have a small shower room, the others a bathroom; two enjoy the view. Other visitors have written of the "wonderful breakfast, with toaster at table and superb home-made bread", and praised the young staff, "who seem genuinely to enjoy their work", and the gar-dens, "a delight, reinforcing the feel of care and attention to detail". (*Ron and Eve Jones, P Flynn, and others*)

Open Mar–end Dec. Restaurant closed Mon, midday Tues, midday Wed.
Rooms 5 double.
Facilities Lounge, dining room. 2-acre garden. Golf nearby. Unsuitable for &.
Location In Cartmel, opposite *Pig & Whistle*, take road to Grange-over-Sands for 1 mile; hotel on left. Private parking. Train: Grange-over-Sands; then taxi.
Restrictions No smoking in dining room. No children under 8. No dogs in pub-lic rooms.
Credit cards Access, Amex, Visa.
Terms D,B&B £60–£80. Set lunch £15, dinner £27. Reductions (£10–£20) for 2 or more nights Nov–Apr. Christmas package. 1-night bookings occasionally refused Sat. *V*

Report forms (Freepost in UK) are at the end of the *Guide*.

CASTLE CARY Somerset   Map 1

Bond's BUDGET   *Tel/Fax* (01963) 350464
Ansford Hill
Castle Cary BA7 7JP

"Worthy of unstinted praise, particularly in terms of value. Just the sort
of place one hopes to find in the *Guide*." "These folks take cooking seriously. Dinner was creative and very tasty." Recent enthusiasm for this
listed, creeper-covered Georgian former coaching inn, in an agreeable
mid-Somerset town whose name refers to its Norman castle, now in
ruins, and its river, the Cary. It has kindly hosts, Kevin and Yvonne
Bond, and a period feel, with William Morris wallpaper in the dining
room, an open fire in the bar, antique furniture, and knick-knacks dotted around. Mrs Bond cooks imaginative English dishes on the reasonably priced, constantly changing menu. Cheese is a special feature.
Vegetarians are happily accommodated, but it is wise to give advance
warning. The short wine list includes some excellent bottles at moderate prices. Breakfast is generous and varied: continental, traditional,
healthy etc. . . . Bedrooms are small, but generally considered "delightful". Room 3 has come in for some criticism this year, although "its
bathroom is superb". "Mr Bond is a punctilious, informative host; he
will gladly show you his immaculate classic cars and charming garden.
High standard of service from quiet, friendly local staff." Some traffic
noise in front rooms. (*Irene Zelle and Kathleen Akin, and others*)

Open All year, except 1 week Christmas.
Rooms 7 double.
Facilities Lounge/bar, restaurant. Small garden. Unsuitable for &.
Location ½ mile N of Castle Cary, on A371. Large carpark. Train: Castle Cary;
then footpath 300 yds.
Restrictions No smoking in restaurant. No children under 8, except babes in
arms. No dogs.
Credit cards Access, Visa
Terms [1997] B&B £30–£38; D,B&B £50.50–£59. Lunch from £3.90, set dinner
from £13.50; full alc £26.50. 2-day breaks. *V*

CHADDESLEY CORBETT Worcestershire   Map 3

Brockencote Hall   *Tel* (01562) 777876
Chaddesley Corbett   *Fax* (01562) 777872
nr Kidderminster DY10 4PY

Chaddesley Corbett's village street is a harmonious blend of houses
dating from the 16th to the 19th century, and its interesting old church
is part Norman. On the edge of the village, this serene turn-of-the-
century mansion is set by a lake in large grounds. It is an engaging
Anglo-French set-up, with owners Alison and Joseph Petitjean ("they
could give a course on hotel management") and chef Didier Philipot.
Half the staff are French. The interior is airy, with well-proportioned
rooms, honey-coloured panelling, open fires, potted plants and a
restrained country house decor. "We enjoyed our stay in every way,"
write recent guests. "Meals were consistently delicious. Excellent continental breakfast." This endorses last year's praise: "A flawless visit.
Our bedroom was full of grace and light, with fresh flowers and fruit,

excellent sherry, up-to-date magazines, immaculate bathroom. A spirit of generosity pervades: delicious bites accompanied our drinks; coffee and petits fours are included in the dinner price. You can mix and match between the menus. Breakfast, served at hours reflecting the accommodating spirit of the staff, was perfect, too, with home-made marmalade and jam, flavourful Cumberland sausages, perfectly cooked eggs." "I have never eaten a meal here that I do not remember with pleasure. The food suited all our party, from children wanting simple dishes, to those for whom nothing is too rich or strange. The Petitjeans were much in evidence, and the staff helpful and kind – never in the way, never out of the way. Very good for a family; excellent value." Birmingham airport is only 40 minutes' drive away. (*Joy and Raymond Goldman, and others*)

Open All year.
Rooms 17 double. Some, on ground floor, adapted for &.
Facilities Lift, ramps. Lounges, restaurant, conservatory. 70-acre grounds: gardens, lake, croquet. Golf nearby.
Location On A448 between Kidderminster and Bromsgrove. M42 exit 1; M5 exit 4. Train: Kidderminster; then taxi.
Restrictions No smoking in restaurant. No dogs.
Credit cards All major cards accepted.
Terms [1997] B&B: single £85–£99, double £120–£145. Set lunch £19.50, dinner £24.50. Weekend breaks; aromatherapy, shooting, golfing breaks. Christmas, Easter, Whitsun packages. Children under 12 accommodated free in parents' room. ***V***

CHAGFORD Devon   **Map 1**

Easton Court   BUDGET   *Tel* (01647) 433469
Easton Cross, Chagford TQ13 8JL   *Fax* (01647) 433654
                                             E-mail stay@easton.co.uk

Grade II listed Tudor house, thatched and creeper-covered, on A382 Whiddon Down–Moretonhampstead; 1½ miles E of old market town on E edge of Dartmoor. Granite walls, oak beams, inglenook, large library. Small green garden. Literary connections: Evelyn and Alec Waugh and Patrick Leigh Fermor stayed and worked here. Enthusiastic owners, Gordon and Judy Parker, supply "solid comfort and excellent hospitality". Good dinners; breakfast "well up to standard". Fishing, riding, golf nearby. Open Feb–Dec. 8 bedrooms (rear ones quietest), 2 on ground floor. No smoking: dining room, library, bedrooms. No children under 12. No dogs in public rooms. Access, Amex, Visa accepted. B&B £40–£52; D,B&B £50–£70 [1997]. Recently endorsed, but we'd like more reports, please. ***V***

Gidleigh Park   *Tel* (01647) 432367 and 432225
Chagford TQ13 8HH   *Fax* (01647) 432574
                                    E-mail gidleighpark@gidleigh.co.uk

《♥ *César award in 1989*

"We could probably buy a luxury yacht with the money we have spent here over the last 17 years, but we treasure our visits to *Gidleigh* more than we would a yacht." So write regular visitors to Paul and Kay Henderson's luxurious mock-Tudor hotel (Relais & Châteaux), which caters for an affluent international clientele in a remote setting on the edge of Dartmoor, near the little market town of Chagford. The Teign river runs through its grounds, which have carefully laid out woodland walks, a water garden, a tennis court, four croquet lawns and a "golf garden". Others have written of public rooms "with rich fabrics in vibrant colours, good antiques, and exquisite watercolours, mainly of Dartmoor". The "sumptuously comfortable" bedrooms are priced by size and view; courtyard-facing ones are cheapest. But some rooms are small, and there are reports of problems with water pressure. In the *Michelin*-starred restaurant, Michael Caines cooks "with *élan* and enthusiasm, underpinned by classical technique". Desserts are outstanding; the marvellously interesting wine list is sensibly priced. Breakfasts, which have been criticised in the past, are liked too: "A charming young French waiter looked after us. We had delicious thin slices of exotic fruits and yogurt; for cooked breakfast enthusiasts the 'Full Monty' is excellent." Some visitors have found the atmosphere impersonal, but others praise the staff, led by manageress Catherine Endacott: "They are friendly and attentive, but not overly so, and kind to babies, children and dogs." Another plus point: "The terms were inclusive; we felt under no obligation to tip." (*Padi and John Howard, A Wright, and others*)

Open All year.
Rooms 2 suites, 12 double. Also 3-roomed cottage.
Facilities Hall, lounge, bar, 2 dining rooms. 45-acre grounds: gardens, croquet, tennis, bowls, putting green, walks. Fishing, riding nearby. Unsuitable for &.
Location Approach from Chagford, *not* Gidleigh. From main square, facing Webbers with Lloyds Bank on right, turn right into Mill St. After 150 yds fork right; downhill to Factory Crossroad; straight across into Holy St; follow lane 1½ miles to end. Train: Exeter, 20 miles; then taxi.
Restrictions No smoking in restaurant. No dogs in public rooms.
Credit cards All major cards accepted.
Terms [1997] D,B&B: single £200–£360, double £300–£410, suite £325–£410. Set lunch £30, dinner £57.50. Winter discounts. Walking holidays, shooting weekends. 1-night bookings sometimes refused.

CHARINGWORTH Gloucestershire   Map 3

Charingworth Manor   *Tel* (01386) 593555
Charingworth   *Fax* (01386) 593353
nr Chipping Campden GL55 6NS

A beautiful house, early 14th-century with Jacobean additions, mullioned windows, oak beams and open fireplaces. It is set on a ridge with far-reaching views, in beautiful gardens amid a huge Cotswold estate. The best bedrooms, and some less good attic ones, are in the main building; their insulation is not always perfect. Cheaper, modern rooms, well appointed and spacious but with less character and no view, are in converted stables. Recent praise: "Lovely bedroom, well equipped with sherry, fruit, home-made biscuits, and a stunning view. We liked the laid-back approach, country style, of the staff. Breakfast was brought smartly to the bedroom at 10 am. Very good snack lunches and teas, too. The swimming pool, in a tasteful extension, is excellent in every respect." "A perfect retreat from stress. Small enough to avoid a corporate atmosphere, and with no bar to attract noisy groups." "Warm and comfortable sitting rooms – nice for dozing in front of a fire on a rainy day." "They could not have been kinder to our baby." One couple thought the dining room cold in winter, and another was critical of the wines, but they agreed: "The food and service at dinner were excellent." The chef, Matthew Laughton, offers an unusually varied choice of veg-etarian dishes. Hidcote Manor with beautiful gardens (National Trust), and Chipping Campden, a lovely old town made prosperous in the Middle Ages by wool, are nearby. (*EY, and others*)

Open All year.
Rooms 3 suites, 23 double.
Facilities 3 lounges, billiard room, restaurant; function facilities; leisure spa (indoor pool, sauna, etc). 50-acre grounds: tennis. Unsuitable for &.
Location 2½ miles E of Chipping Campden, on B4035. Train: Moreton-in-Marsh/Evesham; then taxi.
Restrictions No smoking in restaurant. No children under 10 in restaurant after 6.30 pm. No dogs.
Credit cards All major cards accepted.
Terms [1997] B&B: single from £95, double from £132, suite from £239. Set lunch from £17.50, dinner £35. Weekend and midweek breaks. 1-night bookings some-times refused.

CHELTENHAM Gloucestershire   Map 3

Hotel on the Park   *Tel* (01242) 518898
38 Evesham Road   *Fax* (01242) 511526
Cheltenham GL52 2AH

Once a fashionable spa, Cheltenham claims to be "the most complete Regency town in Britain". It has tree-lined avenues and many handsome houses including this one, painted white, opposite Pittville Park, a short walk from the centre. The decor is sumptuous, with swagged and draped chintz, strong colours, and many antiques. The coral-and-cream drawing room and the dignified library have French windows over-looking the secluded garden. Bedrooms and bathrooms are large, and as chic as the rest. "Wonderful," is one recent visitor's verdict. There was one report of a cool reception, but another guest praised the welcome she received from the owner, Darryl Gregory, and the staff's kind treatment of her young daughter. The hearty English breakfast is also liked. The high-ceilinged restaurant, pale green, with striped fabrics, is run as a

concession by Graham Mairs. The meals (English with Mediterranean influences) are "beautifully presented, and the ingredients fresh and interest-ing". Cheltenham is home to Europe's largest boarding school for girls, a famous race course, and an annual literary festival. (*John Hall, Vicky Maltby, and others*)

Open All year.
Rooms 2 suites, 10 double.
Facilities Lounge with bar, library, restaurant (piped classical music). Tiny gar-den. Unsuitable for &.
Location 5 mins' walk from centre. On A435 towards Evesham (front rooms double-glazed). Carpark.
Restrictions No smoking in restaurant. No children under 8. No dogs in public rooms.

Credit cards All major cards accepted.
Terms [1997] Rooms: single from £74.50, double from £89.50, suite from £119.50.
Breakfast: continental £6, English £8.25. Set lunch £15.95, dinner £22.50; full alc
£38. Weekend rates.

CHESTER Cheshire *See SHORTLIST*   **Map 3**

CHETTLE Dorset   **Map 2**

Castleman   NEW/BUDGET   *Tel* (01258) 830096
Chettle   *Fax* (01258) 830051
nr Blandford Forum DT11 8DB

Chettle, on the edge of Cranborne Chase, a designated area of outstanding natural beauty, is one of the few remaining feudal villages in
England. Owned by the Bourke family for over 150 years, it has a fine
Queen Anne manor house (open to the public), set in five-acre grounds
amid farmland. The former dower house is now this unpretentious
little hotel. It was much remodelled in Victorian days, and has been
carefully converted to preserve its galleried hall, plasterwork ceilings
and Jacobean fireplace. "It is not super-smart," writes the nominator,
himself an experienced hotelier. "It shows the simple good taste that I
thought had been eradicated for ever from the English country house
hotel scene, and a laid-back atmosphere. The large restaurant serves
carefully chosen, unfussy dishes, all well cooked. Very good value."
The owners Edward Bourke and Barbara Garnsworthy, who previously ran a restaurant, the *Moonacre* in Alderholt, write: "Our intention
is to offer high quality, comfortable accommodation with good food at
reasonable prices. We do not offer frills, expensive fabrics, swimming
pool, 24-hour room service, etc." There are lovely country walks from
the door. Salisbury Cathedral and many historic houses, including
Wilton, Kingston Lacy, Stourhead and Longleat, are within easy reach,
as well as plenty of action for the sportingly inclined (see below).
(*Stephen Ross; endorsed by A and CR*)

Open All year, except Feb.
Rooms 8 double.
Facilities 2 drawing rooms, bar, restaurant. 1-acre grounds. Golf, riding, fishing,
shooting, cycling nearby. Only restaurant suitable for &.
Location Chettle is 1 mile off A345 Salisbury–Blandford. Hotel signposted in vil-
lage. Train: Salisbury; then bus (stop 1 mile from hotel).
Restrictions No smoking: restaurant, 1 lounge. No dogs.
Credit cards Access, Visa.
Terms [1997] B&B: single £35, double £55–£65. Full alc £22. 5% discount for 3 or
more nights; 10% for 7 or more.

CHICHESTER West Sussex   **Map 2**

Suffolk House   NEW   *Tel* (01243) 778899
3 East Row   *Fax* (01243) 787282
Chichester PO19 1PD

Unpretentious hotel in Georgian house in centre of old town; two theatres 5
mins' walk away. Friendly owners, Michael and Rosemary Page; children

welcomed. Small garden. Some bedrooms large and bright; top ones are small; some overlook garden or nearby Priory Park; some get early morning noise from factory opposite. Decor not to everyone's taste, "but innocuous". Acceptable traditional cooking. 11 rooms, 4 on ground floor. 24-hour carpark nearby. No smoking: lounge, restaurant, 3 bedrooms. No dogs. All major credit cards accepted. B&B: single £52–£77, double £79–£114; set dinner £14.75. Theatre package available.

CHIPPING CAMPDEN Gloucestershire   Map 3

Cotswold House   *Tel* (01386) 840330
The Square   *Fax* (01386) 840310
Chipping Campden GL55 6AN

This lovely town grew rich on the wool trade in medieval times. Among its many fine houses is Christopher and Louise Forbes's Relais du Silence, which overlooks a little square. Inside there is a beautiful central staircase, an airy dining room with a plaster ceiling and tall French windows leading to the walled garden, and a bright (some say garish) decor. Chef Raymond Boreham's modern English cooking is mostly enjoyed, though one couple observed: "We would have preferred more emphasis on serving food hot than on the current fashion for display." The house dinner menu, included in the half-board rate, has two choices for each course; there is also a longer, more expensive *table d'hôte* menu. Simpler meals are served in a brasserie. In summer, guests take drinks and meals in a willow-shaded courtyard. Some visitors have remarked that the owners are not much in evidence, and functions can overwhelm the place at times, but there is praise too: "Good welcome, staff efficient and unobtrusively helpful throughout our stay. Our rooms were simple, in a flowery style, and practically equipped. Breakfast included almost anything we wanted. The management take care to entertain their guests: one night a pianist played during dinner, and on our last evening there was a French wine-tasting with staff in national costume and a special menu." The area is rich in gardens, historic buildings, and interesting towns and villages. (*Margaret and Charles Baker*)

Open All year, except 3 days over Christmas
Rooms 12 double, 3 single.
Facilities Hall/lounge, sitting room, restaurant (occasional pianist), brasserie; private dining/conference room; courtyard. 1¾-acre grounds: croquet. Golf, riding, fishing, shooting, cycling, hot air ballooning nearby. Unsuitable for &.
Location Central (front rooms sound-proofed). Private parking. Train: Moreton-in-Marsh, 6 miles.
Restrictions Smoking banned in restaurants, discouraged in bedrooms. No children under 7. No dogs.
Credit cards All major cards accepted.
Terms [1997] B&B £55–£72; D,B&B (min. 2 nights) £60–£85. Restaurant: set Sun lunch £16, dinner £19, £28; brasserie: set dinner £17. Weekend, midweek, off-season breaks. 1-night bookings sometimes refused weekends Apr–Oct.

There are many expensive hotels in the *Guide*. We are keen to increase our coverage at the other end of the scale. If you know of a simple place giving simple satisfaction, please write and tell us.

CHITTLEHAMHOLT Devon   Map 1

Highbullen Hotel   *Tel* (01769) 540561
Chittlehamholt   *Fax* (01769) 540492
Umberleigh EX37 9HD

♥ *César award in 1991*

Hugh and Pam Neil's Victorian Gothic mansion is set high up between
the Mole and Taw valleys (glorious views). An 18-hole golf course undu-
lates through the immaculate grounds, and the public rooms are sometimes busy with golfing groups. There are two small outdoor swimming
pools and a tiny indoor one. Fishing on the two rivers can be arranged,
and the many amenities in the huge grounds, sporting and other (see
below), make *Highbullen* ideal for a family holiday. The loyal clientele,
some of whom have been coming for 25 years, admire the tranquillity,
the "mixture of relaxed informality and good service when it is needed",
and the many small generosities. One couple wrote: "It is a splendid
place to unwind; you are left to your own devices. The comfortable decor
makes you feel at home." Others have praised the "experienced, kindly
and friendly" staff and the bar snacks, and called a stay here "marvellous
value". Bedrooms in the main house are traditional, many are large, with
glorious views; those in the converted farm buildings are modern (insulation is not always perfect); a four-bedroom house with a kitchen has
an idyllic riverside setting. The Neils' daughter, Colette Potter, is chef,
and the food, on an eclectic menu, is said to be "good home-entertaining
cooking of the ambitious kind". Breakfast, mainly self-service, is a
generous buffet; cooked dishes cost extra. Rosemoor garden, Dartington
Hall, and three National Trust properties are within half-an-hour's drive.
(*Brian and Eve Webb; also A and CR, Simon Jones, and many others*)

Open All year.
Rooms 36 double, 1 single. 24 in converted farm buildings and cottages. Some
on ground floor.
Facilities 2 sitting rooms (1 in annexe), library, bar (piped music in evening),
billiard room, breakfast room, restaurant; indoor swimming pool, steam room,
sunbed, exercise room, table-tennis, squash. 200-acre grounds: 85-acre woodland, garden, croquet, putting, swimming pool, 18-hole golf course, tennis
(golf/tennis tuition), 10 miles river fishing (ghillie available).
Location M5 exit 27. A361 to South Molton. B3226 for 5 miles, up hill to
Chittlehamholt; through village, ½ mile to hotel. Train: Tiverton Parkway, then
taxi; Exeter St David's to connect with North Devon branch line to King's
Nympton; hotel will meet, "but remember to ask the guard to stop the train."
Restrictions No smoking: restaurant, breakfast room. No children under 8.
No dogs.
Credit cards Access, Visa.
Terms [1997] D,B&B: single £60–£85, double £100–£170. Cooked breakfast: £2.50–
£4. Snack lunches £5. Set dinner £18.50. Off-season breaks. Midweek reductions.

CHOBHAM Surrey   Map 2

Knap Hill Manor   NEW   *Tel* (01276) 857962
Carthouse Lane, Chobham   *Fax* (01276) 855503
nr Woking GU21 4XT

"A perfect retreat," writes the American nominator of this large 18th-
century house. "It is an ideal place to recover from jetlag – Kevin and

64 ENGLAND

Teresa Leeper understand their guests' need for a quiet space on arrival. This is truly a family home, welcoming and beautifully decorated, which over the years has accrued a patina of traditional English country house comfort and charm. The gardens are special; acres of them, some formal, some rustic, all with a magical, peaceful quality. I was welcomed in the delightful large sitting room with a glass of sherry. The spacious bedrooms of varying shapes are well appointed and overlook the garden, as does the panelled room where wonderful breakfasts are served, with fruit compotes, cereals, and all manner of traditional fare, accompanied by home-made marmalade and preserves. Kevin Leeper is a charming host, full of local knowledge." B&B only; there are pubs and restaurants in Chobham, a delightful old village, Saxon in origin, with a small village green and a large common. Heathrow Airport is 30 minutes' drive away, Gatwick is 40 minutes, and London is 25 minutes away by train from nearby Woking. (*Lynn S Hay*)

Open All year, except Christmas, Easter.
Rooms 3 double.
Facilities Lounge, breakfast room. 6-acre garden: tennis, croquet. Golf nearby.
Location 1 mile from Chobham, which is 3 miles NW of Woking. With Chobham church on left, go S along Castle Grove Rd towards Knaphill. Left after 1 mile, and sharp bend, into Carthouse La. Hotel 150 yds on right at top of driveway.
Restrictions No smoking: breakfast room, bedrooms. No children under 8. No dogs.
Credit cards Access, Visa.
Terms [1997] B&B £32.50–£42.50.

CLEARWELL Gloucestershire   Map 3

Tudor Farmhouse   **NEW/BUDGET**   *Tel* (01594) 833046
Clearwell, nr Coleford GL16 8JS   *Fax* (01594) 837093

Deborah and Richard Fletcher's 13th-century house, with oak beams, original panelling, stone walls, open fire; cottage garden, 14-acre fields at rear. In village with neo-Gothic castle and iron-mining museum, in Forest of Dean. Close to rivers Severn and Wye, and Welsh border. Fishing, golf, canoeing, cycling nearby. 13 bedrooms, warm and comfortable; some (no-smoking, up spiral staircase) in main house; some in garden cottages, 3 on ground floor. Jolly atmosphere. Children welcomed. Good and varied home-cooked dinners in pretty, candlelit restaurant (closed Sun evening, except bank holidays); breakfast less good (packaged jams etc). Lunch not served, but picnics provided. Closed 24–30 Dec. No smoking: restaurant, main house bedrooms. B&B: single £47.50, double £57–£67; D,B&B: single £60, double £82.50–£92.50 [1997]. More reports, please.

CLEEVE HILL Gloucestershire   Map 3

Cleeve Hill Hotel   *Tel* (01242) 672052
Cleeve Hill
nr Cheltenham GL52 3PR

John and Marian Enstone's informal, no-smoking B&B is set high up in an area of outstanding natural beauty. It has glorious views across a valley to the Malvern hills and over Cleeve Common. Behind are fields with sheep and horses. There is direct access to the Cotswold Way (excellent walking). It is admired for the bedrooms, "large, comfortable, clean, with heavy curtains, beautiful fabrics, and all that one could require"; the lounge, "decorated in excellent taste", with a licensed bar; and the kindness and thoughtfulness of the proprietors. "Superb breakfasts, after which you can't eat all day", are served in a conservatory-style room, overlooking the pretty garden. *Wesley House (qv)*, in nearby Winchcombe, is recommended for meals. Cleeve Common Golf Club, with a spectacular course, is close by; Cheltenham is ten minutes' drive, and its famous National Hunt racecourse is 1½ miles away. (*S Gates, and others*)

Open All year.
Rooms 2 suites, 6 double, 1 single.
Facilities Lounge with bar (piped light classical music "when appropriate"), breakfast room; patio. ¼-acre garden. Golf, riding nearby. Unsuitable for &.
Location 4 miles NE of Cheltenham on B4632. Bus or taxi.
Restrictions No smoking. No children under 8. No dogs.
Credit cards Access, Amex, Visa.
Terms [1997] B&B: single £45, double £60–£65, suite £75. 10% discount off season for 2 or more nights. 1-night bookings sometimes refused.

CLIMPING West Sussex   **Map 2**

Bailiffscourt   *Tel* (01903) 723511
Climping BN17 5RW   *Fax* (01903) 723107

This "medieval" house was built in the 1920s by Lord and Lady Moyne, of the Guinness brewing family, who, with the architect Amyas Phillips, erected it on the site of a 13th-century house and chapel – the name refers to the monk who was sent as bailiff to protect the interests of the Norman abbey that owned them. It was recently expensively refurbished by the current owners, Sandy and Anne Goodman, who call it "the genuine fake". The large grounds (with a good-sized swimming pool) stretch down to a pebble beach. "A haven of peace," wrote recent visitors. "Romantic and stylish, with an intimate maze of rooms, corridors, and courtyards, and peacocks adding a touch of class." "A comfortable country house ambience, without the country house pretensions that too often are a barrier to true relaxation." The interconnecting lounges have warm colours, tapestries, and log fires. The bedrooms (each with a medieval name) are spacious; many have a fireplace, some a four-poster – several of these are narrow, and the one in Monksfoyle is said to be due for retirement. Bar lunches are served, except on Sunday. The elegant restaurant is now in the hands of Richard Vowell, formerly of the *Michelin*-starred *36 on the Quay* at Emsworth in Hampshire. "He is a serious, sophisticated chef," wrote 1997 inspectors. "But the restaurant service was haphazard and the canapés and petits fours were unsuccessful. Housekeeping, too, was a bit casual at times. We did not see the manager, but the staff were keen, if not very experienced, and the clientele was an engaging mix, including young couples with children and dogs. It lacks the hard gloss often encountered in expensive establishments. An enjoyable visit." The Goodmans own two other Sussex hotels: *Ockenden Manor*, at Cuckfield (*qv*) and the *Spread Eagle* at Midhurst, on which we'd like reports, please. (*Jane Bailey, Gary Crossley, and others*)

Open All year.
Rooms 1 suite, 25 double, 1 single. 17 in buildings in grounds; 2 with ♿ access.
Facilities 3 lounges, bar, restaurant (piped classical music at night). 22-acre grounds: tennis, croquet, golf practice, unheated swimming pool, beach 200 yds.
Location 3 miles S of Arundel. Train: Littlehampton.
Restrictions No smoking in restaurant. No dogs in public rooms.
Credit cards All major cards accepted.
Terms B&B: single £120–£125, double £125–£199, suite £285–£300; D,B&B £87–£170 per person. Bar lunches. Set lunch £19.50, dinner £35; full alc £50. Child in parents' room £25.

COLN ST ALDWYNS Gloucestershire   Map 3

The New Inn   *Tel* (01285) 750651
Coln St Aldwyns   *Fax* (01285) 750657
nr Cirencester GL7 5AN

A creeper-clad, flower-bedecked inn (a Relais du Silence) in an unspoilt Cotswold village. "It was old when Wren built St Paul's cathedral," write the owners, Brian and Sandra-Anne Evans. "Queen Elizabeth I decreed that there should be a coaching inn within a day's travel of every major centre of population. Through 20 changes of monarch, neither the purpose nor the fabric of the building has changed." Inside are a small lounge, a long bar with an inglenook fireplace, where light meals are served, and a restaurant on two levels, with open fires, low beams and oriental rugs. The chef, Stephen Morey, has worked at *Gravetye Manor*, East Grinstead (*qv*); his cooking is admired, though some guests have bemoaned the lack of change on the quite short dinner menu, and others have described the mealtime service as "adequate; sometimes indifferent". Each chintzy bedroom (some are small) is named after a local village, river or estate. "They are beautifully furnished, and a pleasure to relax and sleep in," wrote regular visitors." Our favourite has a beamed pointed ceiling and a downstairs bathroom *en suite*." The "genuinely old-fashioned atmosphere and the caring, concerned owners" are admired. So are the breakfasts, and the two labradors who will accompany guests on walks. (*Good Pub Guide, and others*)

Open All year.
Rooms 1 suite, 12 double, 1 single. 6 in dovecote.
Facilities Lounge, bar, breakfast room, restaurant; function facilities; terrace. River 100 yds; golf nearby. Unsuitable for ♿.
Location In village 8 miles E of Cirencester, between Bibury and Fairford.
Restrictions No smoking in restaurant. No children under 8 in restaurant. Dogs in bar only.
Credit cards Access, Amex, Visa.
Terms [1997] B&B: single £59, double £87, suite £104; D,B&B £60–£80 per person. Bar meals. Set Sun lunch £15.50, dinner £22.50. Midweek winter breaks.

****

Traveller's tale Wales: At breakfast in this bummer of an expensive hotel, the toast was burnt. When I pointed this out to the waitress, she offered to return it to the kitchen to be scraped. She was surprised when I suggested that a new batch might be more appropriate.

****

CONSTANTINE BAY Cornwall   Map 1

Treglos Hotel   *Tel* (01841) 520727
Constantine Bay   *Fax* (01841) 521163
Padstow PL28 8JH
Ɋ *César award in 1994*

"My twenty-first annual visit. *Treglos* goes marching on in high style."
One of many tributes to this well-run traditional seaside hotel ("by no
means luxurious, but consistent, with good old-fashioned service"),
which has been owned and run by the Barlow family for 32 years. It has
a choice position, near a wide sandy beach and the coastal footpath.
The peaceful atmosphere (no canned music, no entertainment), the
long-serving staff and the old-fashioned courtesies – carrying luggage,
tidying rooms during dinner, cleaning shoes – are all admired. In low
season it is a favourite of retired people; the disabled and children are
welcome. The decor – brick fireplaces, log fires, chintzy furniture, patterned carpets – is conventional. Bedrooms, many with a sea view,
some with a balcony, have light colour-schemes and built-in white furniture. The west-facing terrace, surrounded by flowers, "is a perfect
place for tea with the chef's delicious home-made scones". There is a
sheltered sunken garden and a warm indoor pool. The six-course dinner is generally liked: "The starters and desserts have style"; "for true
traditionalists, there is even a savoury to finish." The menu is adaptable, and special diets are catered for. "Very good breakfasts. And they
remember not only your likes and dislikes, but also birthdays and
anniversaries." The hotel has concessions at a number of local golf
courses. Many National Trust properties are nearby. (*IC Dewey, Kay
Thomson, and others*)

Open 12 Mar–early Nov.
Rooms 4 suites, 32 double, 8 single. 1 on ground floor. 4 self-catering flats in
grounds.
Facilities Lift, ramps. Lounges, bridge/TV room, restaurant; children's den,
snooker room; indoor swimming pool, whirlpool. 3-acre grounds: croquet.
Sandy beach, golf, tennis, riding, watersports nearby.
Location 4 miles W of Padstow. Avoid Bodmin, Wadebridge. From crossroads
at St Merryn take B3276. Train: Bodmin; then bus or taxi.
Restrictions No smoking: dining room, 1 lounge, 10 bedrooms. No children
under 7 in dining room after 7.30 pm. No dogs in public rooms.
Credit cards Access, Visa.
Terms D,B&B: single £53–£77, double £106–£154, suite £146–£196. Bar lunches.
Set lunch £12.50, dinner £23; full alc £31. Weekly rates; weekend, midweek
breaks, bridge, golf packages. Children accommodated free in parents' room
during school holidays, half term. ***V***

CORSE LAWN Gloucestershire   Map 3

Corse Lawn House   *Tel* (01452) 780771
Corse Lawn GL19 4LZ   *Fax* (01452) 780840

"Twenty-eight members of my family stayed three nights over
Christmas; we enjoyed our stay enormously. Nice, comfortable bedrooms; pleasant sitting rooms and bar; good breakfasts – four-minute
boiled eggs were spot on; attentive staff. All in all, an excellent choice,
and good value for money." A recent tribute to this elegant Grade II

listed Queen Anne coaching inn, set back from the green of an unspoiled hamlet in lovely countryside, with a large pond (once the coach wash) and assorted wildfowl in front. Though much extended, it retains its country house atmosphere, and has an agreeably under-stated decor to match. The owners are Baba ("her warm, outgoing per-sonality infects her staff") and Denis Hine, he ("an imperious character") of the cognac family; son Giles is front-of-house. Bedrooms, some named for brandies, are large and airy, with high ceiling, king-sized bed, good storage, shortbread biscuits, real tea and coffee, and a smart bathroom. The restaurant, run by Baba Hine with Tim Earley, is popular for its modern French/English cooking, served on set menus, including an attractive vegetarian one, or from a *carte*. The wine list "could make one weep at some of the names and their prices, but there are some first-class choices at a reasonable cost". Snacks and light meals are served in the brightly upholstered, informal bistro where no dish costs more than £10. Breakfast can be served in the bedroom from 7 am until 11. Plenty to see nearby, including Tewkesbury's beautiful abbey and interesting old buildings, the Westonbirt Arboretum, and the Wildfowl Trust and Wetlands centre. (*RMJ Kenber, and others*)

Open All year.
Rooms 2 suites, 17 double. 5 on ground floor.
Facilities 2 lounges, bar, bistro, restaurant; small conference facilities. 12-acre grounds: croquet, tennis, badminton, swimming pool. Golf, fishing, riding nearby.
Location 5 miles SW of Tewkesbury on B4211.
Restrictions No smoking in restaurant. No dogs in réstaurant.
Credit cards All major cards accepted.
Terms B&B: single £70, double £100, suite £135; D,B&B: single £85, double £130, suite £165. Set meals: lunch (2/3 courses) £14.95/£16.95, dinner £24.50; full alc £35–£45. 2-day breaks. *V*

COVENTRY West Midlands *See SHORTLIST*   **Map 2**

COWAN BRIDGE Lancashire   **Map 4**

Hipping Hall   *Tel* (01524 2) 71187
Cowan Bridge   *Fax* (01524 2) 72452
Kirkby Lonsdale LA6 2JJ

This fine old house on the Cumbrian border is named for the "hipping" or stepping stones used by drovers to ford the stream that now runs, complete with ducks, through its well-maintained grounds. "Elegantly restored and bursting with charm", it is run in house party style by Ian and Jocelyn Bryant (she is chef). Guests are introduced at drinks in a pretty conservatory (with parakeets). The communal dinner (no choice) is informally served ("wear anything", says the brochure) at 8 pm at a refectory table in the beamed Great Hall. This magnificent room, with a minstrels' gallery and an enormous fireplace, serves as restaurant and lounge. The host waits at table, pouring wines selected by himself – "he never fails to provide something a little different" – to match the five-course meal, which is "well balanced, with a host of flavours, and beautifully presented". A traditional breakfast is served at separate tables in another attractive room. The spacious bedrooms have flowery wallpaper, antique furniture, a sofa, fresh flowers, TV, plenty of storage space, excellent lighting, and a large, well-lit bath-room. Two cottages can be rented on a self-catering basis. There is excellent walking from the door. Charlotte Brontë's unhappy days at the School for Clergymen's Daughters in Cowan Bridge are vividly evoked in *Jane Eyre*. (*Judith Brannen and Larry Machum, Dr and Mrs JH Jones, and others*)

Open Mar–Nov, and for private parties in winter (not Christmas).
Rooms 5 double. 2 cottage suites (with sitting room, kitchen) across courtyard.
Facilities Lounge, Great Hall (piped classical music/jazz at night, often chosen by guests), breakfast room, conservatory; small function facilities; terrace. 3-acre grounds: croquet. Unsuitable for &.
Location On A65, 2 miles E of Kirkby Lonsdale. 8 miles from M6 exit 36.
Restrictions No smoking in breakfast room, dining area. No children under 12. No dogs in public rooms.
Credit cards Access, Amex, Visa.
Terms [1997] B&B: single £69, double £84, suite £94; D,B&B: £65–£92 per person. 5-course dinner (Tues–Sat) £23, 3-course supper (Sun, Mon) £16. Half-board rates all year for stays of more than 1 night. 1-night bookings sometimes refused. *V*

CRANBROOK Kent   **Map 2**

Hancocks Farmhouse   **BUDGET**   *Tel* (01580) 714645
Tilsden Lane
Cranbrook TN17 3PH

❧ *César award in 1997*

This 16th-century Grade II listed timber-framed house is set amid farm-land with oast houses and pear orchards. Inside there are old beams, low doorways, antiques, fine fabrics and an inglenook fireplace; fresh flowers everywhere, even in the bathrooms. "We try to look after our guests as if they were staying with friends in the country," write the proprietors, Bridget and Robin Oaten. "We respond to their likes and dislikes; eg, we ask in advance whether they prefer a duvet or blankets and sheets." They have been warmly praised again this year: "They are terribly nice. If you have an award for 'not fussing', they should win it." "The best breakfasts we have had anywhere. Copious fresh orange juice, decent tea, toast served when you want it, home-made preserves; we never have room for cooked dishes." "They understand the true meaning of hospitality." No charge is made for early morning tea trays, pots of tea and coffee at any time, and sherry before dinner. The bed-rooms have TV, fruit, a decanter of Madeira or sherry, and a private bathroom (two are *en suite*) with expensive toiletries. Dinner (by arrangement) is traditional English with a French influence, with limited choice; it could include "a chocolate mousse to die for – *and* they will share the recipe". Guests usually dine communally; breakfast is at separate tables. Hole Park, an early 20th-century garden at Rolvenden nearby, is worth visiting; and the gardens at Sissinghurst and Great Dixter, and Bodiam, Hever, Leeds and Scotney castles are within easy reach. (*Robin McKinlay, PE Carter, David F McEwen; also Karin and Jörg Wohrwag, G and M Bailey, and others*).

Open All year, except Christmas, occasional unfixed times.
Rooms 2 suites, 1 double. 1 on ground floor. No telephone.

Facilities Drawing room/dining room. ½-acre garden.
Location From Cranbrook take Tenterden road; fork right towards Benenden (Tilsden La). *Hancocks* up first track on left. Train: Staplehurst, *c.* 6 miles; then taxi.
Restrictions No smoking. Generally no children under 9 ("but we remain flexible"). Dogs in ground-floor bedroom only, not in public rooms.
Credit cards None accepted.
Terms B&B: single £35–£40; double £50–£65, suite £56–£70; D,B&B: single £50–£65, double £90–£110, suite £96–£120. Set dinner £20–£25. 1-night bookings sometimes refused weekends.

Kennel Holt NEW
Goudhurst Road
Cranbrook TN17 2PT

Tel (01580) 712032
Fax (01580) 715495

This part Tudor, part Edwardian house in the Weald of Kent has "a very beautiful location," wrote one nominator. Another rhapsodised: "Atmosphere so embracing, ambience so intoxicating, setting so idyllic, we found it difficult to leave." The owner, Nigel Chalmers, whose wife, Sally, is front-of-house, and whose giant schnauzer, Clovis, "extends a friendly welcome", writes: "We are not boring or homogenised; we do not have fitness suites and the like. We concentrate on old-fashioned service." Though just off a busy road, the house is quiet. It has well-maintained gardens, with a pond and topiaried yew hedges, a beamed lounge, a panelled library "with a superb selection of pre-war books of the *Boys' Own* variety – very nostalgic" – and a large collection of vinyl discs which guests may play. The host's eclectic cooking is admired: "It included the best bread-and-butter pudding I have ever tasted – always a dish to sort the real chef from the phoney." The bedrooms (some are large) have good antique furniture; some have exposed timbers; two have a four-poster. Twenty-eight houses and 37 gardens open to the public, notably Sissinghurst, are within easy reach; the sea at Hastings is a half-hour drive. (*Richard Creed, Alastair Clement*)

Open All year, except 5–29 Jan; restaurant closed Mon.
Rooms 8 double, 2 single. 1 on ground floor.
Facilities Sitting room, drawing room/library, dining room (music, "largely on old-fashioned vinyl", selected by guests), 5-acre grounds. Golf, fishing, walking, cycling nearby.
Location 1 mile NE of Cranbrook, off A262. Train: Staplehurst.
Restrictions Smoking banned in restaurant, discouraged in bedrooms. No children under 7 in restaurant at night. No dogs.
Credit cards Access, Amex, Visa.
Terms [1997] B&B: single £85, double £125–£150. Set 2/3-course lunch/dinner (*excluding "optional" 10% service charge*) £22.50–£27.50. 3-night breaks in low season.

The Old Cloth Hall
Cranbrook TN17 3NR

Tel/Fax (01580) 712220

"Perfect for relaxing in peaceful surroundings. Katherine Morgan went out of her way to make us welcome. We felt we'd known her for years. We enjoyed tea with delicious home-made cakes in front of a roaring log fire." A recent tribute to this Elizabethan house with later extensions (a Wolsey Lodge), deep in the country. Its large grounds have gardens noted for roses, rhododendrons and azaleas, an unheated swimming pool and a tennis court. Inside are low-ceilinged, panelled public rooms with highly polished floors. Books, magazines and flower arrangements abound, with "a miscellany of relics from a lifetime of journeys, sitting next to mellow antiques, family portraits and personal whimsy objects, all reflecting the originality and strong artistic sense of the owner". The three guest bedrooms are scattered among those of the hostess and her absent family; the best has a four-poster. Guests dine with Mrs Morgan by candlelight. Many are regulars who enjoy both the cooking – "simple dinner party stuff; desserts are the strongest point; second helpings are offered" – and the "absence of the anonymity of an ordinary hotel". Unlicensed: bring your own wine. Plenty of castles, stately homes and gardens are nearby. (*Endorsed this year by Patricia Albo*)

Open All year, except Christmas.
Rooms 3 double. No telephone (portable one available).
Facilities Drawing room, dining room. 13-acre grounds: swimming pool (unheated), tennis, croquet. Sea 25 mins. Unsuitable for &.
Location 1 mile SE of Cranbrook on Golford Rd to Tenterden. Private road on right, immediately before cemetery. Train: Staplehurst.
Restrictions Smoking discouraged. Children by arrangement. No dogs.
Credit cards None accepted.
Terms B&B: single £45–£55, double £65–£95. Set dinner £22. 1-night bookings sometimes refused Sat, bank holidays.

CRANTOCK Cornwall   Map 1

Crantock Bay Hotel   BUDGET   *Tel* (01637) 830229
Crantock, Newquay TR8 5SE   *Fax* (01637) 831111

This unpretentious seaside hotel has a stunning setting on West Pentire headland, facing the Atlantic and a huge sandy beach. The North Cornwall Coastal Path runs through the garden. A large extension houses a warm swimming pool, spa bath, toddlers' pool, sauna and exercise room. Bedrooms are comfortable with adequate facilities; most have a sea view (partly obscured, on the first floor, by a large flat roof). Many guests are faithful regulars; the long-serving owners, Brenda and David Eyles ("a delightful host"), welcome all generations, and dogs too. They are admired for their "adaptability combined with total professionalism", and for their "unsurpassed" attention to detail. The food, served by friendly waitresses, is traditional, and there is general agreement that meals have improved greatly in recent years. Lunch is a self-service buffet; freshly baked scones and home-made biscuits are served with afternoon tea. Entertainments are organised in season. Special breaks of all kinds are offered. Crantock, a mile away, is a pretty old village with an ancient church and thatched cottages. There are six golf courses nearby. (*Frank and Joyce Davies, and others*)

Open Mar–early Nov, winter weekends, New Year.
Rooms 25 double, 9 single. 1 on ground floor. 1 self-catering cottage.
Facilities 2 lounges, bar lounge (piped classical/light music at night), bar, restaurant; games room, indoor swimming pool, exercise room; dances, competitions, children's parties in season. 4½-acre grounds: tennis, croquet, adventure playground. Sea, sandy beach, safe bathing 200 yds. Riding, golf nearby.
Location 5 miles SW of Newquay, 1 mile beyond Crantock. Train: Truro; hotel will meet.
Restrictions No smoking: dining room, 1 lounge. No dogs in public rooms.
Credit cards All major cards accepted.

Terms [1997] D,B&B £51.50–£64. Set Sun lunch from £8.50; weekday buffet from £3. Set dinner £16.95. Discounts for returning visitors; winter weekend breaks; spring garden breaks. Children under 2 accommodated free in parents' room. *V*

CROOKHAM Northumberland   Map 4

The Coach House at Crookham   **BUDGET**   Tel (01890) 820293
Crookham   Fax (01890) 820284
Cornhill-on-Tweed TD12 4TD
🐾 César award in 1997

In an area with magnificent scenery near the Scottish border, this sympathetic guest house is a complex of venerable farm buildings set back from the road around a courtyard. "We don't claim to offer hotel-type service or atmosphere," writes the owner, Lynne Anderson. "This is our home, and we shall do our best to ensure that you are content here." And *Guide* visitors regularly praise "the charming hostess, revered by her staff". "It's like staying with an aunt – tapestry cushions, Lloyd Loom tub chairs, etc. Super free tea with home-made cakes on arrival." Guests meet for pre-dinner drinks in the drawing room. Dinner at 7.30 pm is in two attractive rooms, with antique tables, good paintings and large fireplaces. No regular choice of main course, but individual needs are catered for. Soups, ice-creams, preserves, etc, are home-made; masses of vegetables; free-range, quality ingredients. "Some dishes rather quirky, all distinctive. Breakfast delicious with lots of choice." "Our small daughter and our dogs were made welcome. Our bedroom was large, with a large bathroom, and plainly but pleasantly furnished, and it had a fridge in a cupboard, with real milk in a jug." Very good facilities for the disabled. Service includes dog-sitting for those wishing to spend a day in Edinburgh, an hour's drive away. A good base for exploring Northumberland's National Trust coastline and the Tweed valley; many of the county's 189 castles and stately homes are nearby. (*AJW and HM Harvey, and others*)

Open Easter–end Oct.
Rooms 7 double, 2 single. 7 with bath/shower. No telephone.
Facilities Lounge with honesty bar, TV lounge, 2 dining rooms; large terrace. 3-acre grounds. Golf, fishing, riding, gliding, birdwatching nearby.
Location On A697, 3½ miles N of Milfield.
Restrictions No smoking in dining rooms. No dogs in public rooms.
Credit cards Access, Visa.
Terms B&B: single £20–£36, double £46–£72; D,B&B: single £36.50–£39.50, double £79–£103.

CROPREDY Oxfordshire   Map 2

The Old Manor   **BUDGET**   Tel (01295) 750235
Cropredy, nr Banbury OX17 1PS   Fax (01295) 758479
                              E-mail old manor@cropredy.force9.net

Liz and John Atkins' mellow manor is in a pretty farming village in the Cherwell valley, the site, because of its bridge, of a battle between Royalists and Roundheads in 1644. Its fields, which border the Oxford canal, are stocked with Gloucester Old Spot pigs and thoroughbred

horses; ducks and geese patrol the moat. It has a private motor museum
with vintage and classic cars and "automobilia" (Silverstone is nearby).
"A lovely spot," wrote the nominator. "I never tire of looking round the
beautiful old rooms. There are books everywhere. The bedrooms have
antiques, magazines, sherry, etc. The Atkinses share the honours with
two Airedale dogs and three cats." A full English breakfast is served in
the 15th-century dining room, which has antique furniture and a collection of clocks. The guests' sitting room (with TV) is stocked with games
and local information. A barn, which can sleep up to five people, has
been converted to accommodate disabled visitors, and has a fully
equipped kitchen. Two pubs in the village serve meals. (*Linda Brook*)

Open All year, except Christmas/New Year.
Rooms 3 double (2 with private facilities). Barn with kitchen (sleeps 4/5; suitable
for &).
Facilities Lounge, breakfast room. 3-acre grounds: moat and canal (coarse fish-
ing), motor museum.
Location 4 miles N of Banbury. M40 exit 11, A361 to Daventry; left, after
2½ miles, to Cropredy. Follow lane to T-junction; B&B sign 25 yds on left.
Restrictions No smoking. No dogs in public rooms.
Credit cards Access, Visa.
Terms B&B: single £25–£28, double £42–£50; barn suite £30 per person. Very
small children accommodated free. 1-night bookings refused during British
Grand Prix. *V*

CROSBY-ON-EDEN Cumbria   Map 4

Crosby Lodge   *Tel* (01228) 573618
High Crosby, Crosby-on-Eden   *Fax* (01228) 573428
nr Carlisle CA6 4QZ

"It is lovely," writes a fellow *Guide* hotelier of this castellated 18th-
century country house near the Scottish border and the M6 motorway.
"Comfortable, welcoming and dependable; a good overnight stop on
the way to Scotland," say regular visitors. It is a family affair – Michael
and Patricia Sedgwick have run it since 1970; their son James is co-chef
with his father; daughter Pippa is in charge of the wide-ranging wine
list (plenty of half bottles). Most bedrooms are in the main house and
are reached by a carved staircase; two are in converted stables, overlooking the walled garden. The wooded grounds overlook the river
Eden. Guests have found the atmosphere personal, but never intrusive,
and enjoyed the decor: "Our spacious bedroom had a dazzling combination of wallpapers and wonderful drapes. Real fires in the lounge;
antiques, fine fabrics, bowls of fruit everywhere. Lots of help when we
wanted to plan an outing. There was plenty of choice, and coffee *ad lib*,
for breakfast." The restaurant serves traditional British and continental
cooking in generous portions, on set menus and a *carte*; seafood, local
game and desserts are a speciality; much is home-made, including the
bread. There is a wide range of bar snacks. Good walking nearby. (*Jane
Pullee, John and Helen Wright*)

Open All year, except 24 Dec–24 Jan. Restaurant closed midday Sun.
Rooms 10 double, 1 single. 2 in courtyard.
Facilities 2 lounges, bar, restaurant. 4-acre grounds: woodland, walled garden.
River Eden ½ mile. Unsuitable for &.
Location 4½ miles NE of Carlisle, just off A689, on right (pass hotel; take right
turn just before left bend).

Restrictions No smoking in restaurant. Dogs by arrangement; not in main house.
Credit cards Access, Amex, Visa. None accepted for weekend breaks.
Terms [1997] B&B: single £75, double £95–£120; D,B&B £75.50–£103. Set lunch £16, dinner £28; full alc £38–£40. Midweek, winter weekend breaks.

CUCKFIELD West Sussex   **Map 2**

Ockenden Manor   NEW   *Tel* (01444) 416111
Ockenden Lane   *Fax* (01444) 415549
Cuckfield
nr Haywards Heath RH17 5LD

Sixteenth-century manor house, with later additions, in 9-acre informal gardens with views of downs, on edge of charming town. Exceptionally helpful manager, Kerry Turner; kind, efficient staff. Elegant sitting room: antiques, flowers, fire. Modern English cooking in no-smoking panelled restaurant with moulded ceiling, stained glass; meals willingly adapted for special diets. 22 chintzy bedrooms, 3 with 4-poster; well-equipped bathrooms. Unsuitable for &. No dogs. All major credit cards accepted. B&B (continental breakfast): single £85, double £160, suite £225; D,B&B (2-day break, English breakfast) £95–£130. Set lunch £18.50, dinner £29.50: full alc £40. Brighton, Gatwick within easy reach. More reports, please.

DALTON Lancashire   **Map 4**

Prescott's   NEW   *Tel* (01257) 464137
Lees Lane
Dalton, nr Wigan WN8 7RB

Farm restaurant with friendly owners, Cesare and Angela Marchesan, in locality 2 miles NE of Skelmersdale, 8 miles W of Wigan (hotel will provide directions). Creepered old house in pretty 2-acre grounds: garden, orchard, stream. 5 bedrooms, quite plain, but warm and clean; 3 on ground floor in 16th-century granary with separate entrance off cobbled path. Careful French/Italian cooking in black-and-white beamed restaurant. Closed 2 weeks summer, 1 week winter. No dogs. Access, Amex accepted. B&B: single £45, double £65–£70. Full alc £30.

DEDHAM Essex   **Map 2**

Maison Talbooth   *Tel* (01206) 322367
Stratford Road   *Fax* (01206) 322752
Dedham, Colchester CO7 6HN

In the heart of Constable country, Gerald Milsom presides over two luxurious establishments which combine to offer dinner and accommodation. *Le Talbooth* is the restaurant, a half-timbered building in a lovely setting by a bridge across the river Stour, with a flowery terrace and swans gliding by. It serves traditional English cooking by Terry Barber, on set-price menus and a *carte*. Those who can spend the night stay in *Maison Talbooth* ten minutes' walk away (there's also a courtesy car). This is a Victorian country house on a bluff looking over Dedham Vale. Accommodation is in suites, "principal and standard", named for poets. They range from Shakespeare, which is enormous, with a large sunken bath in its opulent bathroom and a terrace leading into the garden, to the much smaller Brooke and Kipling. All have lavish fabrics and wallpaper, sherry, mineral water, fruit, and plenty of reading matter. "The staff were unfailingly cheerful and helpful both here and at the restaurant," say recent visitors. "We had three enjoyable dinners. Breakfast, served in the bedroom, included light croissants, very good cooked dishes and excellent coffee." Snacks and drinks are available during the day. There is a beautifully proportioned sitting room with squashy chairs and settees, and a large garden, mainly lawns, with loungers. The two-night break offers an option of dining at another Milsom restaurant, *The Pier at Harwich* (*qv*), 20 minutes' drive away. (*Joy and Raymond Goldman*)

Open All year. Restaurant closed Sun evening Oct–end May.
Rooms 10 suites. Some on ground floor.
Facilities Drawing room; function facilities. 3-acre grounds: giant chess, croquet. Restaurant, garden on banks of Stour, 10 mins' walk (courtesy car provided).
Location 6 miles NE of Colchester, just E of A12 exit Stratford St Mary. Train: Colchester; then taxi.
Restriction No dogs.
Credit cards All major cards accepted.
Terms B&B: single £90–£130, double £110 –£170. Cooked breakfast £7. Set lunch £14.50, dinner £23.50; full alc £34.50. 2-night breaks. 1-night bookings refused Sat.

DENT Cumbria   Map 4

Stone Close   NEW/BUDGET   *Tel* (01539 6) 25231
Main Street
Dent, nr Sedbergh LA10 5QL

In picturesque village (narrow cobbled streets) in remote setting in Yorkshire Dales National Park. Kay and Peter Rushton's "cottagey and cosy" tea shop in 17th-century listed building: flagstone floors, cast-iron ranges, pine tables. Delicious home-baking. Well-presented wholefood breakfast with vegetarian option; teas, lunches. Small selection of wines. No evening meal, but cooked high tea £10. 2 CAMRA pubs nearby. 5 guests max, in 3 small, simple bedrooms, which share a bathroom ("you can see down a lovely valley while showering"). Amazing value – book early. Carpark adjacent. Closed mid-week Nov–Feb. Unsuitable for &. No smoking. No dogs in public rooms. Access, Visa accepted. B&B £16.25–£18.50 [1997]. More reports, please.

DIDDLEBURY Shropshire   Map 3

Delbury Hall   BUDGET   *Tel* (01584) 841267
Diddlebury, Craven Arms SY7 9DH   *Fax* (01584) 841441
                              E-mail wrigley@delbury.demon.co.uk

This handsome 18th-century red brick house stands by an ornamental pond, complete with ducks, in a large park amid lovely countryside. It has two trout-stocked lakes, gardens, a tennis court, and a small farm and a vegetable garden which supply the kitchen. The interior is impressive, with fine plasterwork and a striking hall with an open-string staircase leading to a spectacular gallery. It is the family home of

Lucinda and Patrick Wrigley. He is a former amateur jockey who learned to cook at Leith's cookery school in London. Dinners "of restaurant standard, imaginative, and immaculately presented", are served in house party style – there is no menu, but choices are discussed in advance. "Breakfasts are exemplary, and our bedroom was comfortable," says a 1997 visitor. Others have enjoyed the warm welcome and the generous log fire in the guests' sitting room. Close by are Offa's dyke, Much Wenlock, Stokesay Castle, and all the charms of Ludlow. (*NJ Thomas, Robin and Olivia Collet, and others*)

Open All year, except Christmas. Lunch not served.
Rooms 3 double, all with *en suite* or private bathroom.
Facilities Drawing room, sitting room, dining room. 12-acre grounds in 80-acre parkland: tennis, dovecote, lake. Unsuitable for &.
Location In village 5 miles NE of Craven Arms. Train: Ludlow, 8 miles.
Restrictions No smoking: dining room, bedrooms. No dogs in house (kennels available).
Credit cards Access, Visa.
Terms B&B £42.50–£55. Set dinner £28.

DORCHESTER Dorset   Map 1

Casterbridge Hotel   BUDGET   *Tel* (01305) 264043
49 High East Street   *Fax* (01305) 260884
Dorchester DT1 1HU

This B&B, in the centre of the pleasant town on which Thomas Hardy modelled Casterbridge, has been owned by the Turner family for 80 years. It is a Georgian house, with period furnishings and original paintings. Some bedrooms (quite small, with a low doorway) are in the main house; the four front ones are double-glazed. The quietest are in a modern annexe across a small courtyard. There is good family accommodation; children are welcome. "Exemplary" breakfasts, served in a pretty conservatory with a fountain, include freshly squeezed orange juice, cereals, muffins, and a good choice of cooked items, including kedgeree. No restaurant, but tea and coffee are served all day, guests may picnic in the conservatory, and there are plenty of eating places nearby. The kindly owners, Stuart and Rita Turner, are admired: "They drove me around to see the local sights," wrote an American, travelling on her own without a car. Others have praised the friendly staff, and the "relaxed, essentially English ambience". The Turner family also owns *The Priory*, Wareham (*qv*). (*Barbara Messenger; also David and Anna Berkeley, and others*)

Open All year, except 25/26 Dec.
Rooms 10 double, 5 single. 6 in annexe across courtyard; 3 on ground floor.
Facilities Ramps. Lounge, bar/library, breakfast room, conservatory; small courtyard.
Location Main street, just below town clock (front rooms double-glazed). 2 garages; free overnight parking in public carpark in adjacent street. Station 1 mile.
Restrictions Smoking discouraged in breakfast room, banned in 11 bedrooms. No dogs.
Credit cards All major cards accepted.
Terms [1997] B&B: single £36–£45, double £56–£75. Discounts for extended stays; off-season breaks. *V*

Yalbury Cottage   *Tel* (01305) 262382
Lower Bockhampton   *Fax* (01305) 266412
nr Dorchester DT2 8PZ

Lower Bockhampton is a tiny village near Dorchester, with 20 or so
houses and a pretty bridge over the river Frome; no pub, no church, no
shop. "If you have been seriously ill," a recent visitor writes, "this
would be a marvellous place to recuperate. It is incredibly rustic, on the
road to nowhere." This "excellent small hotel, long, low, thatched and
pretty", is a clever conversion of two old cottages, with a flower-filled
garden. Inside are inglenook fireplaces and low, beamed ceilings.
Bedrooms are in a discreet modern wing. They are spacious and airy,
with pretty bedclothes and much use of pine furniture, adding warmth
and naturalness – "almost Quakerish in feel". "Everything runs like
clockwork," says a returning devotee. "Heather and Derek Furminger,
attentive, caring, and full of know-how, don't 'try to please', they do it
in the most natural way. Nick Larby's cooking uses fresh local ingredients, and is successfully designed to highlight their quality rather than
show off the chef's cleverness. Lovely walks through Hardy country,
and a sense of rural tranquillity made this a memorable stay." Cream
teas are served, in the garden in fine weather. The village is "Mellstock"
in Thomas Hardy's *Under the Greenwood Tree* (his birthplace, now
owned by the National Trust, is close by). (*Margot and David Holbrook,
Katie Plowden; also Peter Cass, Thérèse Descloux*)

Open 23 Jan–27 Dec. Restaurant closed for lunch.
Rooms 8 double.
Facilities Lounge, restaurant. ½-acre garden. River Frome 200 yds (no fishing
rights). Unsuitable for ♿.
Location In hamlet 2 miles E of Dorchester. Turn S off A35 Bournemouth–
Dorchester. Train: Dorchester; then taxi.
Restrictions No smoking: restaurant, 6 bedrooms. No dogs in public rooms.
Credit cards Access, Visa.
Terms B&B £35–£46; D,B&B (min. 2 nights) £53–£63. Set dinner £19. Discounts
for 3 or more nights. Christmas package. 1-night bookings occasionally
refused. ***V*** (Nov–May inclusive)

DORRINGTON Shropshire   **Map 3**

Country Friends   **BUDGET**   *Tel* (01743) 718707
Dorrington, nr Shrewsbury SY5 7JD

*Half-timbered restaurant-with-rooms, with owner/chefs Charles and Pauline
Whittaker (has had a* Good Food Guide *entry for many years). In ¼-acre
grounds in hamlet 6 miles S of Shrewsbury, on A49; good walking in
Shropshire hills close by. Modern cooking, with emphasis on local produce.
Half board rate includes breakfast with Bucks Fizz, smoked salmon and scrambled eggs. 3 simple rooms over converted coach house; 1 with private shower,
shared bathroom for the others; 1 double-glazed. Praised in the past – "warm
welcome, attentive service, lovely food" – but we lack recent reports. Closed
Sun/Mon, 2 weeks early July. Only restaurant open Christmas, New Year.
Unsuitable for ♿. No smoking in restaurant. No dogs. Access, Amex, Visa
accepted. D,B&B: single £65, double £102. Set lunch/dinner (3/4-course)
£23/£26 [1997].*

DOVER Kent *See SHORTLIST*   **Map 2**

DREWSTEIGNTON Devon   **Map 1**

Hunts Tor House   `BUDGET`   *Tel/Fax* (01647) 281228
Drewsteignton EX6 6QW

Castle Drogo, the impressive 19th-century edifice built by Lutyens for
Julius Drewe, now run by the National Trust, looms on a granite out-
crop above this picturesque, tiny village. This restaurant-with-rooms in
the main square is an architectural oddity, a large 18th-century house
enclosing a smaller 17th-century one. The decor is a blend of Victorian
and Edwardian furniture, Art Deco and Art Nouveau ornaments and
Habitat ("great fun"). There is a comfortable lounge with an interesting
selection of books, a low-ceilinged, heavily beamed dining room, and a
smaller bar/dining room, with a huge old fireplace, beams and a large
kitchen-type table. *Hunts Tor* is run almost single-handedly by Chris
Harrison and his wife, Sue, a "marvellous, subtle and imaginative
cook". No brochure, and hotel-style facilities are not available, but the
Harrisons offer a high level of personal service. "And all so reasonable,"
exclaims one returning guest. *Michelin* awards a red "Meals" for the
modern cooking "with a tendency to the healthy". Dinner (no choice, 24
hours' notice required) is at 7.30 pm; the short wine list is well chosen
("but no half bottles"). Separate tables, but the smallness of the place
encourages socialising. Breakfast at 9 am includes freshly squeezed
orange juice, home-made croissants and preserves, and a good choice of
cooked dishes. On the first floor are three suites, with TV, plenty of storage space, good lights and a "warm, spotless and well-lit" bathroom.
There's good walking from the front door. (*Sarah Curtis, Nadia Young*)

Open Probably Mar–end Oct (please check). Dining room closed for lunch; 24
hrs notice needed for dinner.
Rooms 3 suites. No telephone.
Facilities Lounge, bar/dining room, dining room (piped classical music/jazz,
when required). River Teign nearby: fishing. Unsuitable for &.
Location On square in village 3 miles N of Moretonhampstead.
Restrictions No smoking in restaurant. No children under 10. No dogs in public
rooms.
Credit cards None accepted.
Terms [1997] B&B: single £40–£45, double £60–£70. Set dinner (3/4-course)
£20/£23. 1-night bookings sometimes refused bank holidays.

DULVERTON Somerset   **Map 1**

Ashwick House   *Tel/Fax* (01398) 323868
Dulverton TA22 9QD

✵ *César award in 1994*

This lovingly cared-for small Edwardian house has a magnificent position high up in the Exmoor National Park, overlooking the Barle valley.
It has large grounds with mature trees, water gardens and lily ponds,
an old-fashioned, colourful decor, and a caring, quietly spoken host,
Richard Sherwood, who has been warmly praised again this year: "He
greets you as you enter the galleried hall, which is richly decorated

with original William Morris wallpaper. He also mows the sweeping
lawns, prepares imaginative dinners, and is always available to rustle
up a tray of afternoon tea. As you sit on the delightful south-facing terrace (where breakfasts and dinners are served in fine weather) the
peace is almost tangible; deep silence punctuated only by the bleating
of sheep and the occasional whinny of a pony. Sleep comes easily in the
bedrooms, furnished in Edwardian style; bed warmed by a teddy bear
hot-water bottle." "Words cannot describe the unique atmosphere. The
weather forecast on the breakfast menu is thoughtful. The handwritten
personalised menus at dinner are a delight. The waitress at dinner was
warm, friendly, informative. The list of items stolen by previous guests
is alarming." Guests are expected to dine in. An "affordable wine list,
with some nice bottles" accompanies the four-course, limited choice
dinner. "Food not always hot enough," wrote one visitor this year.
Generous breakfasts include freshly made apple juice and good brown
toast. Bedrooms are stocked with "everything you could possibly
want", including binoculars, a portable electric heater, Scrabble, and
speak-your-weight scales in the bathroom. (*Philippa Roberts, DG; also
Maxine Taylor, and others*)

Open All year.
Rooms 6 double.
Facilities 2 lounges, library, dining room. 6-acre grounds: water garden, croquet,
woodland. Unsuitable for &.
Location 2½ miles NW of Dulverton. Take B3223 towards Lynton; up steep hill,
over 2 cattle grids; signpost on left. Train: Tiverton; then bus.
Restrictions No smoking: library, dining room. No children under 8. No dogs.
Credit cards None accepted.
Terms B&B £48–£60; D,B&B £55–£75. Set lunch £14, dinner £22.75. 2/5-day
breaks. Christmas, New Year house parties. 1-night bookings sometimes refused
bank holidays. ***V***

DUXFORD Cambridgeshire   Map 2

Duxford Lodge   *Tel* (01223) 836444
Ickleton Road   *Fax* (01223) 832271
Duxford CB2 4RU

Suzanne and Ron Craddock's unpretentious hotel is in a village about
20 minutes' drive from both Cambridge and Newmarket. The M11 runs
nearby, but not within earshot of this square red brick house, set back
in its garden. Downstairs walls are hung with pictures of fighter aircraft
(the Imperial War Museum's magnificent aircraft collection is close by).
Bedrooms, recently redecorated, are neat and well lit, with flowery fabrics and efficient bathroom; four have a four-poster; some are across the
garden. The restaurant *Le Paradis*, which is popular with outside diners
and business lunchers, serves modern (but not exaggeratedly so) cooking by Kevin Bingham. There's a fixed-price menu with plenty of
choice, as well as a *carte*, and dishes may be simply served on request.
The wine list is keenly priced. The welcome is friendly, "but don't
expect luggage carrying or evening bedroom tidying". Audley End, the
largest Jacobean mansion in England, is nearby. (*NW, and others*)

Open 2 Jan–24 Dec.
Rooms 13 double, 2 single. 4, on ground floor, across garden. 4 with access for &.
Facilities Lounge with TV, bar, restaurant (piped music during restaurant
hours); conference facilities. 1-acre garden.

Location From M11 exit 10, go E on A505; take 1st right to junction, then right fork. Entrance 700 yds on left. Train: Whittlesford, 2 miles; then taxi. Bus from Cambridge.
Restriction Dogs in garden rooms only, not in public rooms.
Credit cards All major cards accepted.
Terms [1997] B&B: single £40–£75; double £75–£90; D,B&B: single £58.50, double £112. Set lunch/dinner £18.50; full alc £29. Weekend discounts.

EAST BUCKLAND Devon   **Map 1**

Lower Pitt Restaurant   BUDGET   *Tel/Fax* (01598) 760243
East Buckland
Barnstaple EX32 0TD

"Perfect hosts." "They are welcoming, yet discreet, with that instinct of all good hoteliers of knowing when a chat would be welcome and when to let people be." "Food was memorably good." "We enjoyed everything: the room was so comfortable and clean; the arrangements for early morning tea, including fresh milk in a vacuum flask, were just right; the evening meals were super, and the breakfasts wonderful." "Jerome and Suzanne Lyons sensibly have not introduced the frills and furbelows so beloved of interior decorators and so wholly inappropriate to a country setting." Praise this year and last for this restaurant-with-rooms in a peaceful hamlet set in the fold of a hillside, surrounded by the walled fields of south Exmoor. It is a 16th-century white-washed stone farmhouse, Grade II listed, with low doorways, an open fire and an old bread-oven in the small sitting room, and books in the cosy bar lounge. The small bedrooms are simple, with pine furniture, duvet, electric blanket and radio. In the two dining rooms, one a conservatory, all green and white, residents have the run of the *carte*. Mrs Lyons' cooking is original but not gimmicky, using local produce and home-grown herbs. The good wine list has plenty of half bottles. The Tarka Trail, a 180-mile route around Devon, passes the door. Arlington Court, a popular National Trust property set in a large park, is eight miles away. (*Brian Singleton, CJ Alpe, Carol Gourlay, and others*)

Open All year, except Christmas. Restaurant closed to non-residents Sun/Mon. Lunch by arrangement.
Rooms 3 double. 1 with bath, 2 with shower. No telephone; portable available.
Facilities Lounge, lounge bar, dining room, conservatory dining room; terrace. 2-acre grounds. Unsuitable for &.
Location 45 minutes' drive from M5 exit 27. 3 miles NW of South Molton off A361.
Restrictions No smoking: dining rooms, bedrooms. No children under 12. No dogs.
Credit cards Access, Amex, Visa.
Terms D,B&B £50–£62.50. Full alc £30. Residents are expected to dine in. *V*

EAST GRINSTEAD West Sussex   **Map 2**

Gravetye Manor   *Tel* (01342) 810567
East Grinstead RH19 4LJ   *Fax* (01342) 810080
  ❧ *César award in 1991*

"Everything we would like our home to be, complete with perfect peace." "Peter and Sue Herbert provide the ultimate hotel experience;

you feel like an invited guest in their extraordinary home. The elegant interior with comfortable antiques, combined with the aroma of polished oak, the huge wood-burning fireplace and the beautiful flowers, enhances the feeling of enchantment. The bedrooms are soothing havens of comfort. The dining room, with its fine panelling and beautiful table settings, provides another treat for the senses. Topping off all this is the marvellous staff; an exceptionally well-trained, mainly young group." "Every meal superb; breakfast in the garden not to be missed." Apart from one caveat about the food ("best stick to the simpler dishes") and one about the wine list ("impressive, but mark-up ridiculous"), there is much praise this year for this renowned Elizabethan manor house hotel, over which Peter Herbert has presided for 40 years. It is set in magnificent grounds, designed by William Robinson, pioneer of the English natural garden. Bedrooms, some in a new wing imperceptibly melded on to the old house, are all decorated in the same style. The chef, Mark Raffan, is generally thought to be "on top form"; many ingredients for his eclectic modern cooking are home-grown. "We liked being able to choose just one or two items from the *carte*, rather than eat a heavy meal day after day." A good place to see in the millennium – the meridian line passes close by. The lovely gardens of Wakehurst Place (National Trust) are four miles away. (*Walter Avery, Emily and Bob Hanna, Ngaere Mackay, and many others*)

Open All year. Restaurant closed to non-residents Christmas evening.
Rooms 16 double, 2 single.
Facilities 3 sitting rooms, bar, restaurant; private dining room. 35-acre grounds: gardens, croquet, lake: trout-fishing. Unsuitable for &.
Location 5 miles SW of East Grinstead, off B2110 to West Hoathly. From M23 exit 10 take A264 to East Grinstead. At roundabout after 2 miles, take 3rd exit to Turners Hill; after village fork left, then turn 1st left. Train: East Grinstead, 5 miles, Gatwick Airport, 12 miles; then taxi
Restrictions No smoking in restaurant. No children under 7, except babies. No dogs in house (kennels in grounds).
Credit cards Access, Visa.
Terms [1997] (*Excluding VAT*) Rooms: single from £105, double £140–£215. Breakfast: continental £10; English *c.* £15. Set lunch £24, dinner £30; full alc £58. Off-season rates. 1-night bookings sometimes refused weekends May–Sept.

EAST STOKE Dorset   **Map 2**

Kemps   NEW   *Tel* (01929) 462563
East Stoke, nr Wareham BH20 6AL   *Fax* (01929) 405287

Victorian rectory in village on A352, 6 miles W of Wareham. Not smart or luxurious, and close to road and railway, but admired by inspector for warm, friendly feel; charming hands-on proprietors Paul and Jill Warren; and excellent food, both dinner and breakfast, served in pretty restaurant with conservatory. 14 bedrooms: most characterful ones in main house; 4 in coach house (furthest from road); 6 in new extension (some with jacuzzi); 2 have access for &. No smoking in dining room. Dogs by arrangement. All major credit cards accepted. B&B: £37–£76. Set lunch £9.95, dinner £19.95 [1997]. Child under 7 accommodated free in parents' room. *V*

We are particularly keen to have reports on italicised entries.

ERPINGHAM Norfolk   Map 2

The Ark   `BUDGET`   *Tel* (01263) 761535
The Street
Erpingham NR11 7QB

This welcoming restaurant-with-rooms is a typical brick-and-flint
Norfolk house, in the middle of a quiet village. It has a pretty garden
where many ingredients are organically grown for its much-admired
restaurant. Here Sheila Kidd and her daughter Becky cook "imaginative and flavourful dishes, using the freshest of ingredients", in the
style of Elizabeth David. Sheila's husband, Mike, waits at table, and
they are supported by a friendly staff. There is an extensive wine list,
ranging from reasonably priced house wines up to the £80 mark. Only
three bedrooms. One (suitable for dog-owners) has large windows
leading on to the garden; the Attic Room, furnished in cottage style,
"with an excellent bathroom under the eaves", is good for a family; the
smaller Tulip Room has a shared bathroom. "Breakfast-time is flexible," say the Kidds. "There is no menu. Ask and it shall be yours" –
which includes fresh croissants and home-baked bread, and excellent
home-made marmalade. The grounds of two estates owned by Lord
Walpole – Wolterton Park just outside Erpingham and Mannington
Hall two miles to the north-west – are worth visiting. Two fine National
Trust houses, Blickling Hall and Fellbrigg Hall, and some wonderful
beaches are nearby. (*JR*)

Open All year, except perhaps Christmas. Oct–Mar: restaurant closed Mon,
rooms closed Mon/Tues (unless guests are on an extended stay).
Rooms 3 double. 2 with *en suite* facilities; 1 with shared bathroom. 1 on ground
floor. No telephone.
Facilities Reception/bar, lounge, restaurant, private dining/breakfast room. 1-
acre garden: croquet. Sea 8 miles.
Location 4 miles N of Aylsham. Left off A140, just before Alby Centre.
Restrictions No smoking: restaurant, bedrooms. No very young children in
restaurant at night. Dogs in garden bedroom only, not in public rooms.
Credit cards None accepted.
Terms [1997] D,B&B: single £65–£75, double £100–£125. Full alc £32.00. Off-
season breaks.

EVERSHOT Dorset   Map 1

Summer Lodge   *Tel* (01935) 83424
Evershot DT2 0JR   *Fax* (01935) 83005
                          E-mail summerlodge@sumlodge.demon.co.uk

🅠 *César award in 1985*

Nigel and Margaret Corbett, now in their 19th year at this ever-popular
dower house, have had a *Guide* entry since 1981. They started on quite a
simple scale; now they are Relais & Châteaux members, with lavish bedrooms full of luxurious extras and gardens much improved by Penelope
Hobhouse, and prices are high. But regular visitors report: "The personal
touch has not been lost: they continue to wave goodbye to guests until
the car is out of sight. Shoes can still be left out for cleaning at night. The
splendid afternoon tea (included in the half board rate) is still laid out in
the lovely drawing room." "The Corbetts have a real gift for hospitality.

We are better looked after here than in any other hotel we know." "Delightful young staff, supervised by charming manager, Alison Burden." There is general admiration for the cooking of Tim Ford, who has spent some time at *Sharrow Bay*, Ullswater (*qv*): "The best chef *Summer Lodge* has had"; "his cooking cannot be faulted." But several visitors complained: "The *table d'hôte* included in the half-board rates has limited choice; if you prefer the mouth-watering dishes on the *carte* there's an extra charge"; and there are occasional reports of slow meal service. But the introduction of light options to the set lunch is welcomed, the generous breakfasts are admired (apart from the coffee), the off-season rates are thought good value, and there is a rave review of an "utterly spoiling" five-day Christmas break – "we left with a feeling of real gratitude for this little oasis of charm." Evershot starred as Highbury in the film version of *Emma*. "Many locals were used – few needed to get into costume," writes Mr Corbett. Local attractions include gardens from cottages to Stourhead, Parnham House and Hardy's cottage. (*Edwin Prince, Elizabeth Biggs, JH Bell, Dr and Mrs B Webb; also Pat and Jeremy Temple, Heather Sharland, AS-M, and many others*)

Open All year.
Rooms 1 junior suite, 13 double, 3 single. 6 in coach house 20 yds (3 on ground floor, 2 with private terrace).
Facilities Ramps. 2 lounges, bar, dining room. 5-acre garden: swimming pool, croquet, tennis. Golf, fishing nearby; sea, shingle beach 12 miles.
Location 10 miles N of Dorchester. On entering village turn left into Summer La, then right into drive. Train: Yeovil/Dorchester; then taxi, or hotel will meet.
Restrictions No smoking in dining room. No dogs in public rooms.
Credit cards All major cards accepted.
Terms B&B: single £115, double £155–£215; suite £245; D,B&B: normal rate: single £150, double £225–£285, suite £315; winter break: single £88.30, double £145, suite £315. Set lunch £12.50, dinner £32.50; full alc £45. Christmas, New Year packages. 1-night bookings occasionally refused Sat.

EVESHAM Worcestershire — Map 3

The Evesham Hotel
Cooper's Lane, off Waterside
Evesham WR11 6DA

Tel (01386) 765566
Fax (01386) 765443
Freephone (0800) 716969 (reservations only)

César award in 1990

This friendly hotel has a secluded setting a short walk from the centre of the main market town, Saxon in origin, of a fruit-growing area (attractive old houses, walks along the river Avon). Run for the past 22 years by the Jenkinson family and a long-serving staff, it is genuinely welcoming to children. Under-twelves are charged £2 in winter and £3 in summer for each year of their age; items on the children's menu are costed according to size of portion and age of child. The convivial sitting room is well supplied with board games. The jokey style (the hotel's César was for "utterly acceptable mild eccentricity") includes a wise-cracking brochure and menu, countless teddy bears, toy ducks and boats in the baths, and a huge wine list devoid of French and German vintages. Behind this is genuine professionalism and will to please. The popular restaurant, overlooking a large garden with a huge old cedar of Lebanon, offers exotic dishes from around the world (with some startling combinations), as well as plain grills; at lunchtime there is also a 50-dish buffet – "wonderful value". Recent praise: "A life-enhancing place. We loved it. John Jenkinson is very much in evidence, joking and jollying all parties, while keeping a vigilant eye on the show." "We have visited regularly since 1981. Service is excellent. Bedrooms of a high standard: comfortable beds, good lighting, coffee, bubble bath, etc, in large jars (no horrid sachets). Consistently good food." "Very good vegetarian meals." There are plenty of local attractions – historic towns including Stratford-upon-Avon (13 miles); old villages; houses and gardens, etc. (*HR, and others*)

Open All year, except 25/26 Dec.
Rooms 1 family, 33 double, 6 single. 10 on ground floor. Some no-smoking.
Facilities Bar, 2 lounges, restaurant; small indoor swimming pool. 2½-acre grounds: croquet, putting, children's play area. "Though not officially suitable for &, we manage to cope."
Location Off Riverside Rd. 5 mins' walk from town centre, across river. Parking.
Restrictions No smoking: restaurant, 3 bedrooms, pool area. No dogs in public rooms.
Credit cards All major cards accepted.
Terms B&B: single £58–£66, double £76–£90, suite £120–£130; D,B&B £49–£63 per person. Buffet lunch £6.85; full alc £25. Off-season breaks. 1-night bookings sometimes refused. Children under 12 charged £2–£3 for each year of their age.

EXETER Devon   **Map 1**

St Olaves Court   NEW/BUDGET   *Tel* (01392) 217736
Mary Arches Street   *Fax* (01392) 413054
Exeter EX4 3AZ

Raymond and Ute Wyatt's 19th-century Georgian town house near cathedral, with quiet walled garden with fountain. Omitted last year following criticisms of upkeep and food, but recently refurbished, and cooking by new chef John Winston is liked. "Friendly welcome; delightful bedroom"; breakfast "generous and adequate". 15 rooms; 1 on ground floor. No smoking in restaurant. No dogs in public rooms. All major credit cards accepted. B&B: single £55–£80, double £65–£95. Cooked breakfast £6 extra. Set lunch/dinner (2/3-course) £11.50/£15; full alc £30 [1997]. *V*

EYTON Herefordshire   **Map 3**

The Marsh   *Tel* (01568) 613952
Eyton, Leominster HR6 0AG

"Pack your first edition of AE Housman and head for this delightful hotel. It's a quintessential medieval manor house in a tranquil location, with elegant bedrooms and a most cordial host, Martin Gilleland. We arrived on an evening of 'gardening entertainment', with a special dinner, which was charming. We spent much time in the ravishing garden: leisurely reading of papers after breakfast, a cake/scone/jam/cream extravaganza on our return from a lovely walk to ancient hilltop forts, champagne and crudités before dinner. Special praise for my wife's vegetarian dinner: home-grown vegetables in series of individual tartlets, pasta with wild mushrooms, and local cheeses." "Our fifth visit. Delicious food; how gratifying to see the vegetables, freshly dug, being brought in from the garden." Praise this year for this 14th-century black and white house, sensitively restored by the owners Jacqueline and Martin Gilleland. It stands in a peaceful garden with a stream and a lily pond. The stone-flagged, two-storey medieval hall is now used as the lounge. There is a well-stocked library. Comfortable bedrooms, named after birds, have fresh flowers, and fresh fruit, replenished daily. Residents on half board have a choice of starters and desserts and a fixed main course. The wine list is extensive, with reasonable mark-up. Good breakfast, with a wide choice. There are fine walks locally: Offa's Dyke, Wenlock Edge, Long Mynd; and further afield on the Welsh borders and the Malvern Hills. Leominster, nearby, is a well-known antiques centre. *Jon Hughes, AE Crossley; also Michael Forrest*)

Open All year, except last 3 weeks Jan.
Rooms 4 double.
Facilities Lounge, bar, dining room. 1½-acre garden: croquet. Unsuitable for &.
Location 2 miles NW of Leominster. From A49 by-pass, take B4361 to Richards Castle; left after ¾ mile towards Eyton/Lucton. Continue along lane to common; hotel on right. Train: Leominster; then taxi.
Restrictions No smoking: dining room, bedrooms. No children under 12. No dogs.
Credit cards All major cards accepted.
Terms B&B: single £85, double £120–£130. Set Sun lunch £19.95, dinner £24.75. Off-season breaks.

FOWEY Cornwall   **Map 1**

Carnethic House   BUDGET   *Tel/Fax* (01726) 833336
Lambs Barn, Fowey PL23 1HQ

David and Tricia Hogg's unassuming guest house is close to the sea and the Cornish Coastal Path. It has peaceful, award-winning gardens, a heated swimming pool, ample parking for cars and boats, an unexceptional decor and a loyal following. "It is a wonderful home from home," say a couple on their fifth annual visit. "The Hoggs go out of their way to ensure that everyone is happy. All ages are made welcome." The extrovert David Hogg welcomes guests, makes introductions, takes them to and collects them from walks, and organises games and quizzes in the evening. "He breaks down the British reserve in newcomers, persuading even snooty Londoners to join in," said one devotee. Another wrote: "Good decor and furnishing. Food of high quality; the varied menu always includes local fish. The wine list offers value for money." "No white-tied waiters or deferential doormen here; we aim to provide a carefree holiday at a reasonable cost," say the Hoggs. Agatha Christie spent much of her adult life in Fowey (pronounced Foy), and her fans come here on pilgrimage. It has narrow streets, old houses, a pretty estuary and lots of boats; there are many National Trust properties nearby. (*Mrs G Cham, and others*)

Open 1 Feb–30 Nov.
Rooms 7 double, 1 single. 1 on ground floor. No telephone.
Facilities Lounge/bar, dining room (occasional piped classical/"easy listening" music). 2-acre grounds: swimming pool, tennis, putting, croquet, badminton. Sandy beach 1 mile, river 1 mile; boating, sailing, bathing, fishing; golf nearby.
Location ½ mile from centre. Off A3082 St Blazey–Fowey, opposite "Welcome to Fowey" sign.
Restrictions No smoking: dining room, 2 bedrooms. Dogs by arrangement.
Credit cards All major cards accepted.

Terms B&B £25–£40; D,B&B £40–£55. Set dinner £15. 2–5-day breaks. Winter weekend house parties. ***V***

FRANT Kent   **Map 2**

The Old Parsonage   BUDGET   *Tel/Fax* (01892) 750773
Church Lane
Frant, nr Tunbridge Wells TN3 9DX

In 1820, Lord Abergavenny built a spacious parsonage for his son, parish priest of this quiet hilltop village. The house remained in the hands of clerics until 1989, when Mary and Tony Dakin set about sensitively restoring it. Guests now find it both impressive and welcoming. "Arriving in the dark we found an imposing Georgian house with both drive and house floodlit. The entrance was through two sets of oak double doors. The entrance hall and staircase are best described as grand." Inside, it is "beautifully furnished with antiques, and tastefully decorated". A balustraded terrace leads to the well-kept garden. The bedrooms, two with a four-poster, have TV and a luxuriously

equipped bathroom. There's a large lounge and a sunny Victorian conservatory. Breakfast is continental, with ham, cheese and croissants, or English, with a choice of eggs, bacon, etc, or kedgeree. Evening meals are available by arrangement; good restaurants and pubs are nearby. (*HC Medcalf*)

Open All year. Dining room open for dinner by arrangement (groups only).
Rooms 3 double. No telephone.
Facilities Drawing room (piped classical music in evening), conservatory, dining room. 3-acre grounds: terrace, lawns, croquet. Lake, trout fishing 3 miles; reservoir, leisure facilities 5 miles. Unsuitable for &.
Location By church in village 300 yds off A267, 2 miles S of Tunbridge Wells. Train: Tunbridge Wells; then taxi.
Restrictions No smoking, except conservatory. No dogs in public rooms.
Credit cards Access, Visa.
Terms B&B: single £39–£49, double £59–£69. Set dinner (by arrangement) £17. 1-night bookings sometimes refused weekends in season.

FRIETH Oxfordshire   **Map 2**

Little Parmoor   NEW/BUDGET   *Tel* (01494) 881447
Frieth   *Fax* (01494) 883012
nr Henley-on-Thames RG9 6NL

This tall red brick Georgian house is in the middle of open farmland on the edge of the Chiltern Hills, in a designated area of outstanding natural beauty. Its lovingly tended gardens contain a profusion of herbaceous plants, mature trees and old roses, and a small walled garden, bounded by brick walls and yew hedges. "We cannot recommend this place too highly," write experienced hotel-goers. "It makes a stylish base for visiting the Thames valley, and is a treasure trove of beautiful antique furniture. Our room had a magnificent painted folding screen, an antique chest of drawers, and pretty cream-and-white painted panelled walls. The guests' sitting room has a splendid fireplace, and pale green panelling. Interesting portraits and water colours are everywhere, and there's a catholic collection of books. The owners, Wynyard and Julia Wallace, are a hospitable couple who allow their guests space and privacy. They produced tea on arrival, took us on a tour of the garden, of which they are justly proud, and gave us a key to the house." Mrs Wallace serves a substantial breakfast, which in summer may be taken on a vine-shaded patio. One double room has a bath, the other a shower. "We cannot offer hotel-style facilities," writes Mrs Wallace, "This is our family home. Five guests is our maximum." A simple evening meal is available by arrangement, and some gastro-pilgrims have used the house as a base for dining at the *Michelin* two-starred *Ortolan* near Reading. Though very quiet (it is on a small road with almost no traffic) *Little Parmoor* is convenient for the M4, the M40, Heathrow airport and Windsor. (*David and Kate Wooff*)

Open All year.
Rooms 2 double, 1 single. No telephone/TV.
Facilities Drawing room, dining room. 1-acre garden. Unsuitable for &.
Location 1 mile SW of village, which is NE of Henley. Follow road through village and left at sign for Hambleden/Henley; house ¾ mile on right.
Restrictions No smoking. No children under 5. Dogs by arrangement.
Credit cards None accepted.
Terms B&B £25; D,B&B £38.

FULLETBY Lincolnshire   Map 4

The Old Rectory   NEW/BUDGET   *Tel/Fax* (01507) 533533
Fulletby, nr Horncastle LN9 6JX

In lovely setting in unspoilt Lincolnshire Wolds (a designated area of outstanding natural beauty), 1 mile from Fulletby, which is 4 miles NE of Horncastle. Beautiful 16th-century house with 19th-century additions in 5-acre grounds on hillside (lovely views). Welcoming (but not overwhelming) hosts, Michael and Jill Swan. 4 attractive bedrooms (Tennyson, Marwood, Maud and Somersby), some spacious. Generous breakfasts; evening meal by arrangement (£15). Good walking, cycling, fishing, etc, nearby; also churches, medieval villages, gardens, etc. Closed Christmas/New Year. Unsuitable for &. No smoking. No children. Dog house in stables. Credit cards not accepted. B&B £26 [1997]. More reports, please.

GATESHEAD Tyne and Wear   Map 4

Eslington Villa   BUDGET   *Tel* (0191) 4876017 and 4200666
8 Station Road   *Fax* (0191) 48200667
Low Fell, Gateshead NE9 6DR

On south bank of Tyne opposite Newcastle, in not particularly prepossessing setting, Mr and Mrs Tulip's Edwardian country house is "an oasis". Friendly atmosphere; caring, dedicated owners and staff. Good public rooms, with some original features. Agreeably furnished bedrooms, well-planned bathrooms. English/French traditional food in smart, popular restaurant; variable breakfasts. Piped "easy listening" music in public rooms not always liked. Mainly business visitors on weekdays; weekend reductions. 12 bedrooms, some on ground floor. 1½-acre grounds. Closed bank holidays. No smoking in restaurant. No dogs in public rooms. Access, Amex, Visa accepted. B&B: single £40–£54.50 double £50–£64.50. Set lunch from £9.95, dinner £20.95 [1997]. *V*

GILLAN Cornwall **Map 1**

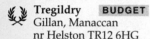 **Tregildry** BUDGET
Gillan, Manaccan
nr Helston TR12 6HG

Tel (01326) 231378
Fax (01326) 231561

César award: best hotel by the sea

This small hotel has a glorious setting on a peninsula in a designated area of outstanding natural beauty, with magnificent views over Gillan Bay. A private path leads down to a small stony cove; the coastal path is nearby. It was taken over in mid-1995 by Lynne and Huw Phillips, who previously ran another popular *Guide* hotel, *Quarry Garth* in Windermere. They have refurbished from top to bottom, and recent visitors have approved: "A beautifully appointed hotel, with an ambience of the Mediterranean." "The lounge and dining room are irregular in shape and spacious, with panoramic views in all directions. The lounge has a beautiful, unusual colour scheme. The dining room has exceptional amounts of space between tables; its airy tranquillity is enhanced by wide archways; the comfort of its upholstered Indonesian chairs reconciled me to their dramatic, un-Cornish shape." "The menu includes original starters and imaginative main dishes, as well as perfectly cooked steak and chips. Hot puddings are a speciality. The low fat option at breakfast is imaginative, too." The bedrooms, some of which are small, now have rattan furniture, bright fabrics and good lighting. "The great plus is the amiability of the management: no reproach when we unavoidably arrived late for dinner; no notices telling us what we couldn't do." "They are most welcoming, and thoroughly professional, but never intrusive; the emphasis is on peace and quiet. Not a place for those requiring 'entertaining'." (*Heather Sharland, Ann Lawson Lucas, JA Fisher, Anne Laurence, Shirley Tennent*)

Open 1 Mar–31 Oct.
Rooms 10 double.
Facilities 2 lounges, bar, restaurant (piped light classical music at night). 4-acre grounds. Private path to coastal path and cove: bathing, sailing, fishing, windsurfing. Golf nearby. Unsuitable for &.
Location 12 miles E of Helston. Take A3083 towards the Lizard. 1st left for St Keverne; follow signs for Manaccan/Gillan.
Restrictions No smoking: restaurant, 1 lounge, bedrooms. No children under 8 in restaurant at night. No dogs in public rooms.
Credit cards Access, Visa.
Terms [1997] D,B&B £55–£60. Set dinner £19.50. 1-night bookings sometimes refused bank holidays. Special breaks. *V*

Most hotels have reduced rates out of season and offer "minibreak" rates throughout the year. It is always worth asking about special terms.

GILLINGHAM Dorset   Map 2

Stock Hill House   *Tel* (01747) 823626
Stock Hill   *Fax* (01747) 825628
Gillingham SP8 5NR   *E-mail* reception@stockhill.net
♥ *César award in 1991*

"From the moment we were greeted to the time we waved goodbye, the service could not be faulted. It was like being family guests in a manor house. No one could call it run of the mill. The food was superb, on a varied menu, and the surrounding countryside is charming. The hosts work hard to achieve high standards." "Lovely hotel with excellent restaurant. We visit whenever we need a few days to recharge." Two recent tributes to Peter and Nita Hauser, whose *César* was for "dedicated hotelmanship" – still well deserved in the view of *Guide* readers. They are exuberant and gregarious hosts. Their Victorian manor (Relais & Châteaux) is quietly situated in parkland and gardens, with a stream, a fountain, old and rare trees and lots of wildlife. It is "shining clean and sumptuously if somewhat eccentrically decorated", with heavy drapes, elaborate chandeliers, and *objets d'art* (eg, Indian horses, immense Siamese cats, buddhas). Bedrooms, in similar style, vary in size. Dinner is an occasion, for which guests are expected to dress, and leisurely. Using locally produced ingredients and home-grown herbs and vegetables, Peter Hauser cooks a mixture of English and Austrian dishes, served in generous portions; Viennese-style desserts are particularly admired. There is plenty of choice; wines are reasonably priced. "It is the house for perfectionists," one guest wrote. "I was even offered help with unpacking and packing. Every meal tray brought to the room had a miniature vase of fresh flowers." Others have praised the "charming staff". Breakfasts are "excellent, if rather protracted, with eggs from the Hausers' ultra-free-range hens". When he has the time, Mr Hauser will play the zither for his guests. This Gillingham is pronounced with a hard G, unlike Gillingham in Kent. (*John Gardner, RM Scott; also Hanna Dobias*)

Open All year. Restaurant closed Mon midday.
Rooms 8 double, 1 single. 3 in coach house.
Facilities Foyer, lounge, breakfast room, restaurant. 11-acre grounds: croquet, tennis, putting, stream, lake (fishing), wildlife; chauffeur service. Unsuitable for &.
Location On B3081 1½ miles W of Gillingham, 3 miles S of A303.
Restrictions No smoking: restaurant, breakfast room, bedrooms. No children under 6. No dogs (kennels nearby).
Credit cards All major cards accepted.
Terms D,B&B: single £105–£145, double £200–£280. Set lunch £19.50–£22, dinner £30–£32.50. Winter breaks; wine and food weekends. 1-night bookings sometimes refused.

GLEWSTONE Herefordshire   Map 3

Glewstone Court   *Tel* (01989) 770367
Glewstone, nr Ross-on-Wye HR9 6AW   *Fax* (01989) 770282

Bill and Christine Reeve-Tucker's part Victorian listed house in 4-acre gardens with orchard near Welsh border, 3 miles SW of Ross-on-Wye. Home-like decor: photos, old pictures and family clutter. Log fires in lounge, taped music in public areas. 7 large well-furnished bedrooms. Leisurely breakfasts served until 10 am (excellent granary toast). Bar meals; dinner in Georgian restaurant; variable cooking (adequate choice) on unchanging menu. Children and dogs welcomed. River Wye ½ mile. Good walking, plenty of outdoor activities locally. Breezy style, too informal for some (first names used, etc). Closed 25–27 Dec. Access, Amex, Visa accepted. B&B: single £40, double £85–£98. Set dinner £25.

GLOSSOP Derbyshire   Map 3

The Wind in the Willows   NEW   *Tel* (01457) 868001
Derbyshire Level   *Fax* (01457) 853354
off Sheffield Road
Glossop SK13 9PT

This Victorian house, willow tree in front, is set amid fields in the Pennine foothills. It is run by a mother-and-son team, Anne and Peter Marsh. He earlier worked at his brother Eric's hotel, the *Cavendish*, Baslow (*qv*), long a *Guide* favourite. "He is a charming and ebullient host, who had already gained brownie points by not charging us when bad weather obliged us to cancel a visit earlier in the year," writes an inspector. "Tall, slim and smartly dressed, he bounded out of the office to meet us. The decor is a bit hectic, perhaps, but colourful and welcoming, with much evidence of a love for Thailand. Our bedroom and bathroom were large and thoughtfully equipped. Before dinner (served at 7 pm) we sat and chatted with Peter Marsh in a lounge which had the feel of a family room – flowers, books, newspapers and a huge drink-stocked oak dresser. A most acceptable dinner, no choice, prepared by Hilary Barton, a sweet-natured local lady, was served in the pretty blue and beige dining room. Breakfast was cooked to perfection by our host – if all else failed he could run an excellent café. Toast came in hot relays. The place is run with old-fashioned courtesy and excellent housekeeping. We thoroughly enjoyed our stay." The hotel won an AA Courtesy and Care award in 1996 and again in 1997. "We specialise in peace, quiet and relaxation, with no background music," the Marshes write. Old Glossop is mainly 17th-century, with narrow streets and pretty houses; the current town centre, and the cotton mills which brought prosperity, were built in the early 19th century. There is beautiful mountain and moorland scenery all around, with excellent walking. Chatsworth and Haddon Hall are 40 minutes' drive away.

Open All year, except Christmas.
Rooms 12 double.
Facilities Drawing room with dispense bar, study, dining room, conference room. 1-acre garden, 4 acres fields. Golf course adjacent; pot-holing, horse riding, gliding, boating nearby. Unsuitable for &.
Location 1 mile E of Glossop. Turn left off A57 opposite *Royal Oak* pub. Hotel 400 yds on right. Train: Glossop.
Restrictions No smoking: restaurant, study. No children under 10. No dogs in public rooms.
Credit cards All major cards accepted.
Terms B&B: single £65–£85, double £80–£105. Set dinner £20.

All our inspections are carried out anonymously.

GOLANT Cornwall   **Map 1**

The Cormorant   NEW   *Tel/Fax* (01726) 833426
Golant, nr Fowey PL23 1LL

*Small pink hotel, owned by George and Estelle Elworthy, perched above sail-
ing village 3 miles N of Fowey (steep driveway). Picture windows with stunning views over tidal estuary. 11 simple bedrooms: pine furniture, small
bathroom. Swimming pool with sliding glass doors and motorised roof, open
all year (residents only). 4-course dinners with emphasis on local fish; light
lunches, picnics available. "Charming, friendly family service; excellent
value." Good fishing for bass, salmon, sea trout nearby; also sailing.
Unsuitable for &. No dogs in public rooms. Close to railway – goods trains
only, quiet at night. Access, Amex, Visa accepted. B&B: single £42–£57,
double £70–£84. Set dinner £18 [1997]. More reports, please.*

GRANGE-IN-BORROWDALE Cumbria   **Map 4**

The Borrowdale Gates   *Tel* (01768 7) 77204
Grange-in-Borrowdale   *Fax* (01768 7) 77254
Keswick CA12 5UQ

*Terry and Christine Parkinson's rambling Victorian house on the edge of
ancient hamlet in Borrowdale valley, at head of Derwent Water. In 2-acre
wooded grounds amid magnificent scenery; craggy peaks close by; good walking and climbing. Attractive lounges: antique and period furniture, flowers,
fires in winter. Dining room, with picture windows, serves modern
English/French cooking on menu with plenty of choice; wide-ranging wine
list. Some bedrooms in main building; larger, if less characterful, ones in modern wing. 1996 visitors praised "efficient, friendly" style, and food – "better
than ever". But 1997 brought reports of lack of welcome, and a regimented feel.
Open 1 Feb–2 Jan. 37 rooms, 10 on ground floor; 1 adapted for &. No smoking in restaurant. No dogs. Access, Amex, Visa accepted. B&B: single
£42.50–£64, double £75–£130; D,B&B: single £57.50–£79, double
£105–£160. Set Sun lunch £14.50, dinner £26; full alc £40.*

GRASMERE Cumbria   **Map 4**

Michael's Nook   *Tel* (01539 4) 35496
Grasmere LA22 9RP   *Fax* (01539 4) 35645

"Upon a forest side at Grasmere Vale/There dwelt a shepherd, Michael
was his name." Wordsworth's poem (he lived at nearby Dove Cottage)
was the inspiration for the name of this hotel, perched on a hill well
back from the A591, in large landscaped gardens. The owner since
1969, Reg Gifford, who runs it with a friendly staff, is a former antiques
dealer. There's plenty of evidence in the decor of his collector's eye for
furniture, rugs, prints and porcelain. A grand piano in the lounge, a
spinet in the hall, impressive flower displays, potted plants, great
danes (one a Cruft's medal-winner) and exotic cats add to the slightly
eccentric atmosphere. A fine mahogany staircase leads up to bedrooms
of varying sizes furnished in elegant country house style: antiques,
chintzes, flowers and plants, and a smart bathroom. One suite opens on

to a terrace with lovely views; the other has a private patio. The dining room, where white cornices contrast with the deep red walls, has a collection of antique tables and a log fire. This is the only hotel in the north of England to have the AA's four-rosette accolade. The cooking of the young chef, Mark Treasure, is "modern, with a European influence", with plenty of choice on the five-course set-price menu. The wide-ranging wine list includes many half bottles. Guests may use the health facilities and swimming at the *Wordsworth Hotel* nearby, under the same ownership. More reports, please.

Open All year.
Rooms 2 suites, 12 double.
Facilities Lounge/hall, lounge, bar, 2 dining rooms; conference room. 3-acre garden adjoining 10-acre woodland: croquet. Access to leisure facilities at *The Wordsworth* nearby. Free river/lake fishing nearby. Unsuitable for &.
Location Turn up between *Swan* hotel and its carpark on A591 just N of village. Hotel 400 yds on right. Train/bus: Windermere; then bus/taxi.
Restrictions No smoking in restaurant. No dogs.
Credit cards All major cards accepted.
Terms D,B&B: single £130–£140, double £160–£280, suite £310–£390. Set lunch £31.50, dinner £41.50 and £48.50. Midweek, weekend breaks off-season. Christmas, New Year house parties. 1-night bookings sometimes refused Sat, bank holidays in high-season. ***V*** (not on discounted winter rates)

White Moss House
Rydal Water, Grasmere LA22 9SE

Tel (01539 4) 35295
Fax (01539 4) 35516

Peter and Susan Dixon's grey stone, creepered Lakeland house, in a little garden, looks across the A591 to Rydal Water. William Wordsworth bought it for his son, and used to compose poetry on the porch. Nowadays it is renowned as a restaurant-with-rooms – it has had a *Good Food Guide* entry for 24 years. Peter Dixon and co-chef Colin Percival serve a fixed-price five-course dinner, with no choice until dessert. The cooking is light, modern English in style, "extraordinary in quality and consistency" according to a recent guest: "You can stay a week without feeling bloated. The meal is well paced, with a welcome pause after the main course." The extraordinary wine list has 200 bins, fairly priced, and many wines are offered by the glass. Dinner is at 7.30 for 8 pm, and afterwards guests take coffee together in the small lounge. Breakfasts include the full cooked works (kippers, Cumberland sausage, etc). The bedrooms are well appointed, but mainly small, with tiny bathrooms. This year two larger ones, which share a lounge and terrace, have been added. Two bedrooms (let as a unit) are in a late 18th-century cottage up the hill, with spectacular fell views. There is walking "of all levels" from the door. The gardens of nearby Rydal Hall are worth visiting. More reports, please.

Open Mar–Dec. Restaurant closed midday, Sun.
Rooms 7 double, 2-room cottage on hillside (10 mins' drive or direct footpath).
Facilities 2 lounges, dining room; terrace. 1-acre garden. Near Rydal Water, river Rothay: swimming, fishing, boating. Free use of nearby leisure club: swimming pool, sauna, gym, etc. Unsuitable for &.
Location 1 mile S of Grasmere on A591 (heavy lorries banned; double-glazing); cottage rooms quietest. Train: Windermere, 8 miles; then bus to door.
Restrictions No smoking in dining room. No toddlers at dinner. No dogs.
Credit cards Access, Visa.
Terms D,B&B double £110–£180. Set dinner £27.50. Longer stay rates and special breaks Nov, Mar, Apr. 1-night bookings refused bank holiday weekends, occasional Sat.

GRASSINGTON North Yorkshire   Map 4

Ashfield House ⬛ BUDGET ⬛   *Tel/Fax* (01756) 752584
Grassington, nr Skipton BD23 5AE

This "friendly little guest house, cottagey, cosy and relaxed", is a
creeper-covered 17th-century stone building, tucked away from the
centre of the principal village in Upper Wharfedale, which can be
tourist-ridden in summer. It is informally run by Linda and Keith
Harrison, and so popular that you need to book well in advance. The
decor is simple: old oak and pine furniture, modern fabrics, log fires.
Seasonal produce, and vegetables from the garden are used in the traditional English dishes on the four-course menu, which has limited
choice and is served punctually at 7 pm. Bedrooms are compact. There
is a pretty garden. Praise this year from returning visitors: "The
Harrisons are dedicated hosts who create an atmosphere that is intimate without being claustrophobic. Fellow guests are introduced, but
there is no forced jollity. Dinners (not communal) are simple but tasty,
and carefully presented. Second helpings are offered. The short wine
list is reasonably priced, and wines by the glass are, for once, a bargain." "Comfortable upstairs and down. Two cats, Rupert and Rosie, as
friendly as their owners. Good value." "Generous breakfast." No
smoking. (*Trevor Lockwood, RAL Ogston, Kate Kelly*)

Open Feb–Dec, New Year.
Rooms 7 double. No telephone (payphone for guests).
Facilities 2 lounges (1 with small bar), dining room; drying room. ⅓-acre garden.
Free midweek membership of local leisure centre. River, fishing ¼ mile.
Unsuitable for &.
Location Village centre: turn left into Summers Fold when coming *up* main
street. Private parking. Train/bus: Skipton, via Leeds; then bus.
Restrictions No smoking. No children under 5. No dogs.
Credit cards Access, Visa.
Terms B&B £26.50; D,B&B £40–£56. Set dinner £16.50. Spring breaks; Dickensian
festivities in Dec. 1-night bookings refused bank holidays, some Sats.

GREAT DUNMOW Essex   Map 2

The Starr   *Tel* (01371) 874321
Market Place   *Fax* (01371) 876337
Great Dunmow CM6 1AX

An old inn, black-and-white and beamed, now a smart restaurant-
with-rooms with a caring owner, Brian Jones, and an enthusiastic staff.
It stands in the village's old market place, where two roads converge.
Bedrooms, with names such as Rose, Poppy, Pine and Blue, and decor
to match, are in converted stables in a rear courtyard; four are above
bays where guests may park their car. They are well supplied with local
information, books, magazines, mineral water, etc. Some have antique
or period furniture; one has a freestanding, curtainless bath in the
middle ("you can relax in it and watch TV") as well as a conventional
shower room. Beds include four-posters and ones with brass or
wooden heads. The cooking is mostly liked: the daily-changing menu
is "traditional English with a Mediterranean feel". Fish is a speciality.
Good breakfasts. Not for those in search of peace and quiet; there is

noise from passing traffic, and insulation between bedrooms is imperfect. Easton Lodge, with beautiful gardens, recently restored, is close by. In Little Dunmow, two-and-a-half miles away, are the remains of Dunmow Priory, where an old custom allowed a couple who had survived a year of marriage unscathed to claim a flitch of bacon. Stansted airport is 15 minutes' drive away.

Open All year, except 2–9 Jan.
Rooms 8 double, all in rear courtyard. 2 on ground floor.
Facilities Reception/bar, restaurant (piped classical music/jazz/blues); function/conference facilities.
Location Central (some traffic noise). Courtyard parking. Train: Bishops' Stortford, 8 miles; then taxi.
Restrictions No smoking: restaurant, bedrooms. "Well-behaved dogs only, by arrangement."
Credit cards All major cards accepted.
Terms [1997] B&B: single £60, double £90–£105. Set lunch £21.80, dinner £21.50 and £32.50; full alc £34.50. Weekend rate for diners. *V*

GREAT MILTON Oxfordshire   Map 2

Le Manoir aux Quat'Saisons   *Tel* (01844) 278881
Great Milton OX44 7PD   *Fax* (01844) 278847

Q *César award in 1985*

This celebrated manor (Relais & Châteaux), with an international clientele and two *Michelin* stars for Raymond Blanc's inimitable cooking, stands by the church in a peaceful village near Oxford. Its immaculate gardens have statue-dotted lawns, a Japanese water garden and large vegetable and herb gardens. Inside, fine fabrics and antique furniture abound. The bedrooms "contain every luxury". Some, in the main house, face the front and the carpark; those in the extension have a private terrace; there's a romantic round one in a converted dovecote. Children are welcomed and have their own menu; vegetarians are well catered for too. Such is the *Manoir*'s fame, that it can be difficult to book a room at short notice, but those who succeed continue the eulogies, apart from muttering about the cost of extras: "A palace of excellence. M. Blanc makes sure his guests get their money's worth. Food is a sublimation of the erotic. Everything – table settings, lighting, sculptures, paintings, drapery, beds, carpets – blends together to form a total menu for mind, body and soul." "It could be pretentious and stuffy, but the staff are relaxed and friendly. The cooking is outstanding: fresh, vivid flavours, lightness, creativity." "A paradigm of the English country house hotel for the nineties, more innovative and less stuffy than some of the older generation." Richard Branson is a partner in *Le Manoir*, but Raymond Blanc is in control. This year there is a new head chef, Jonathan Wright. M. Blanc hopes for planning permission to build a new cookery school and to create more lounge space. Thirteen new bedrooms are planned for 1998. (*Louise Chase, David and Kate Wooff, HR, and others*)

Open All year.
Rooms 3 suites, 16 double. 9 in garden extension. Some on ground floor.
Facilities 2 lounges, restaurant, conservatory restaurant; function room. 27-acre grounds: gardens, swimming pool, croquet, tennis, lake, fishing.
Location 7 miles SE of Oxford. From London: M40 exit 7, 1 mile, 2nd right. From Oxford: A40, A329 at Milton Common towards Wallingford, 2nd right. Coach service from *Lanesborough Hotel*, Hyde Park Corner, London, 11 am/6 pm (£35

return). Train: Oxford; then taxi.
Restrictions No smoking: 1 dining room, 1 lounge. Only guide dogs in house (free kennels).
Credit cards All major cards accepted.
Terms [1997] No single rates. Double room £195–£360, suite £425. Breakfast: continental £9.50, cooked £14.50. Midweek breaks. Set lunch (3 courses) Mon–Sat £32; *menu gourmand* (lunch and dinner) £69; full alc £88–£116. Child's menu £12. Cooking courses.

GREAT SNORING Norfolk   Map 2

The Old Rectory   *Tel* (01328) 820597
Barsham Road   *Fax* (01328) 820048
Great Snoring, Fakenham NR21 0HP

This old manor, peacefully set beside the church in an unspoilt Norfolk village, is owned by Mrs Tooke and her daughter and son-in-law, Mr and Mrs Scoles. Elizabethan in origin, it has a hexagonal tower, a terracotta frieze and Victorian additions. It is surrounded by a large walled garden with old trees; a magnificent beech is floodlit at night. Inside are polished floor tiles, lots of dark wood furniture, and flowers. The dining room has mullioned windows, heavy beams and oak tables set with good silver, plate and glass. Inevitably in such a venerable house the bedrooms vary in size: some are quite small; others are spacious. One couple in 1997 was critical of the decor but others admired their bedrooms; they are comfortable rather than luxurious, but all have bath, telephone and TV. "It was prettily furnished, and had two armchairs, a comfortable bed, and lots of local information. Lighting not what it should be, but is it ever? Early morning tea was brought punctually to the room. The food (no choice of main course) was good dinner party style, always with Melba toast on the table and a selection of three cheeses to finish. We were looked after by the charming Mrs Scoles, who made us feel really at home." "Don't go if you are in a hurry. A place for a quiet, take-your-time stay." Five serviced cottages nearby are under the same ownership. A good base for the Heritage Coast, Sandringham and Holkham Hall. (*Moira Jarrett, BJ Elliott*)

Open All year, except 24–27 Dec. Dining room closed for lunch.
Rooms 6 double.
Facilities Sitting room, dining room. 1½-acre walled garden. Unsuitable for ♿.
Location Behind church on road to Barsham, in village off A148, 3 miles NE of Fakenham. Train: King's Lynn, 23 miles.
Restrictions No smoking in dining room. Children by arrangement. No dogs.
Credit cards Access, Amex, Diners.
Terms B&B: single £69.50, double £89.50–£91. Set dinner £22. Special breaks negotiable.

GRIMSTON Norfolk   Map 2

Congham Hall   *Tel* (01485) 600250
Lynn Road   *Fax* (01485) 601191
Grimston, King's Lynn PE32 1AH

🎖 *César award in 1994*

Trevor and Christine Forecast's handsome Georgian manor has large, manicured grounds with a colourful country garden, an impressive

herb garden (open to the public), a cricket pitch, a swimming pool and
a tennis court. "It has a pleasant country house feel," writes a 1997 visitor. "Wellies by the front door, glossy magazines, lovely arrangements
of home-grown flowers, plants in big china *jardinières*, deep green carpets with brilliant white-painted winding staircase and bannisters."
"Hospitable owners. Staff could not have been more attentive and careful," adds another. On the food side, all appetites are catered for. There
are bar snacks, light room-service meals (£2 charge), and a flexible *carte*
for lunch, which may be taken alfresco in fine weather. In the formal
orangery-style dining room, modern British cooking is served by chef
Stephanie Moon on two- and three-course fixed-price dinner menus
with choice. Opinions on the food vary: one guest thought it undistinguished, but another, though expressing surprise that the menu did not
change over four days, was enthusiastic: "Everything very *nouvelle* and
artistic; dessert like a David Hockney painting." The bedrooms vary in
size; some are small; impressive suites have luxurious bathrooms.
Nearby attractions include Sandringham, Houghton Hall ("newly
refurbished, a must") and the RSPB reserve at Titchwell. King's Lynn,
close by, was called Bishop's Lynn until Henry VIII renamed it during
the dissolution of the monasteries in the 16th century. The town has an
attractive waterfront and many fine old buildings. (*Minda Alexander,
and others*).

Open All year.
Rooms 2 suites, 11 double, 1 single.
Facilities Hall/lounge, lounge, bar, restaurant; meeting room. 40-acre grounds:
swimming pool, jacuzzi, tennis, cricket, parklands, orchards, stables. Coast,
sandy beaches 10 miles; nature reserves, fishing, golf, riding nearby. Unsuitable
for &.
Location 6 miles NE of King's Lynn. Right towards Grimston off A148; hotel
2½ miles on left. Do not go to Congham. Train: King's Lynn; then taxi.
Restrictions No smoking in restaurant. No children under 12. Dogs in kennels
only.
Credit cards All major cards accepted.
Terms [1997] B&B: single £74–£95, double £115–£145, suite £180–£198. Light
lunch from *c.* £6; set lunch (2/3-course) £9.50/£15, dinner £27.50/£35. Weekend
breaks all year; racing, shooting, Christmas packages.

GRITTLETON Wiltshire   **Map 3**

Church House   NEW/BUDGET   *Tel* (01249) 782562
Grittleton   *Fax* (01249) 782546
nr Chippenham SN14 6AP

A spacious, Grade II listed Georgian rectory, reputedly the largest in
Wessex, "rather grand for the average vicar". It is quietly set in large
gardens and pasture, in a delightful village on the edge of the
Cotswolds. Here Anna and Michael Moore offer country house accommodation with a house party atmosphere. It was dropped from the
Guide for lack of reports, but 1997 inspectors were enthusiastic: "Dr and
Mrs Moore treat their guests with exactly the right degree of friendliness and interest. We stepped from a night of wind and lashing rain
into a blast of warmth. The public rooms are filled with beautiful
things, particularly pictures; the drawing room's huge bay window
overlooks a gently lit terrace. Our bedroom, with an attractive, if not
luxurious, chintzy decor, was up a beautiful spiral staircase with a roof

light (not for the infirm). The *en suite* facilities were screened off only by
wooden louvred screens, so ablutions had to be discreet – the view
from the loo, aided by mirrors, was extraordinary. In the dining room,
which has raspberry-coloured walls, we dined at a long William IV
table – a memorably good Aga-cooked meal, accompanied by a crisp
Chardonnay, included in the price. Good breakfast too, with eggs provided by the hens on the lawn." Others, too, have enjoyed the "elegant
but unpretentious meals", for which much use is made of organically
home-grown vegetables; no choice – requirements are discussed in
advance. There is a heated indoor swimming pool. Only gripe: "UHT
milk and ordinary teabags in the bedroom." Good walking and riding
locally, and plenty of interesting sightseeing: Avebury, Stonehenge,
etc; Badminton is four miles away, Bath 12 miles.

Open All year.
Rooms 4 double.
Facilities Drawing room, dining room, conference/music room (occasional clas-
sical radio music); indoor swimming pool. 11-acre grounds: garden, croquet,
helipad. Unsuitable for ♿.
Location North of M4, 3½ m W of exit 17. Train: Chippenham; then taxi.
Restrictions No children under 12, except babies under 1. No dogs.
Credit cards None accepted.
Terms B&B: single £32.50, double £54.50. Packed lunch £8, set dinner (including
wine) £16.50. Low-season midweek breaks. 3-day Christmas package. 1-night
bookings sometimes refused Sat, bank holidays.

GULWORTHY Devon   **Map 1**

The Horn of Plenty   *Tel/Fax* (01822) 832528
Gulworthy, Tavistock PL19 8JD

This beautifully proportioned, mellow stone Georgian house, creeper-
covered, and with long windows, is approached up a sweeping drive,
through gardens filled with camellias, azaleas and rhododendrons. The
views across the surrounding fields to the Tamar valley are glorious. It
is a popular restaurant-with-rooms, which our inspectors thought altogether delightful. "The owners, Ian and Elaine Gatehouse, are very
friendly; she is a natural host, smart and sophisticated, with a wry
humour; he is responsible for the excellent wine list." The main building houses two pretty drawing rooms and the restaurant, which has a
pink and green colour scheme as "fresh and pretty" by day as it is at
night. "Chef Peter Gorton is an enthusiastic traveller, who cheerfully
plunders the styles of many countries. His cooking is decorative without being contrived; fish dishes are especially good, with vibrant
flavours and textures. You can order a plateful of minuscule portions
of the delicious puddings; the lemon tart was the best I have ever eaten.
Service is by local ladies, who care for the guests with efficient enthusiasm." The bedrooms are in converted stables, a few yards away. Each
is spacious and well furnished, with arched, beamed ceiling, muted
colour scheme, a well-stocked mini-bar, a balcony overlooking the
view (where breakfast can be served in fine weather) and a small but
adequate bathroom. Other visitors, too, have written of the "exquisite
food", and admired the "impeccable attention to detail", and the breakfasts. On Monday there's a cheaper three-course "pot luck" menu. Sir
Francis Drake was christened in the parish church of nearby Tavistock,
a market town on the edge of Dartmoor.

Open All year, except 25/26 Dec. Restaurant closed Mon midday.
Rooms 7. 6 in coach house. Some on ground floor with ♿ access.
Facilities Ramps. Drawing room, bar area, restaurant; function room. 4-acre grounds: garden, orchards. Golf, riding, fishing, walking, sailing nearby.
Location 3 miles W of Tavistock. Right at Gulworthy Cross; 1st left.
Restrictions No smoking: restaurant, bedrooms. No children under 13 (except Sun lunch). No dogs in public rooms.
Credit cards Access, Amex, Visa.
Terms [1997] B&B: single £63–£83, double £88–£98. English breakfast £7.50. Set lunch £18.50, dinner £31 (Mon £21). 2-day breaks.

HAMBLETON Rutland   Map 2

Hambleton Hall   *Tel* (01572) 756991
Hambleton, Oakham LE15 8TH   *Fax* (01572) 724721

☯ *César award in 1985*

"We could not fault this hotel: the staff, particularly reception, were outstanding. Our perfect bedroom overlooked Rutland Water; even the loo had a view. Super atmosphere – peace combined with coddling. Lovely grounds." "Everything was marvellous; much to admire, both inside and out. Expensive, but worth every penny." Recent visitors pay tribute to this grand Victorian mansion (Relais & Châteaux), which Tim and Stefa Hart have owned and run for nearly 20 years. It has a magnificent setting in manicured gardens with mature trees, on a peninsula in Rutland Water (the largest man-made lake in northern Europe, with fishing, sailing and water sports). The decor is sophisticated: fine fabrics, good antiques and paintings, flowers everywhere. Customers' likes and dislikes are recorded on a database. *Michelin* awards a star for the modern British cuisine of chef Aaron Patterson, which our readers find "very accomplished, with first-class ingredients, served by knowledgeable and charming waiters, many French". "There is a long *à la carte* menu, but we found we got the most balanced meal by sticking to the set menu." "Breakfast is impeccable, though the continental one, included in the room rate, is fairly basic." In fine weather it is served on a terrace overlooking Rutland Water, "everything superbly laid out". The hotel is licensed for weddings. The attractive little town of Oakham, nearby, is a famous fox-hunting centre. Some of Britain's greatest treasure houses, Burghley, Belton, Boughton and Belvoir, are nearby. (*Kenneth Smith, Meriel Packman; also Sir William Goodhart, Michael Schofield*)

Open All year.
Rooms 15 double.
Facilities Lift, ramp. Hall, drawing room, bar, restaurant; small conference facilities, 2 private dining rooms. 17-acre grounds: swimming pool, tennis, cycling, lake with trout-fishing, windsurfing, sailing. Riding, shooting by arrangement.
Location 2 miles E of Oakham. Follow the Hambleton sign off A606 to Stamford. Train: Peterborough/Kettering/Oakham (branch line); then taxi.
Restriction Dogs by arrangement; not in public rooms, alone in bedrooms.
Credit cards All major cards accepted.
Terms B&B: single £115–£140, double £165–£285. English breakfast £12. Set lunch (2-course) £14.50, dinner (3-course) £35; full alc £55. 2-day break any time. Winter rates; Christmas package. 1-night bookings sometimes refused Sat.

We need detailed fresh reports to keep our entries up to date.

HAROME North Yorkshire   Map 4

The Pheasant   NEW   *Tel* (01439) 771241
Harome, Helmsley YO6 5JG   *Fax* (01439) 771744

Once a blacksmith's premises, this old inn stands by the church in a village near the attractive old market town of Helmsley, at the beginning
of Ryedale and the North Yorkshire moors. It looks over a millstream
and a village pond complete with ducks and ducklings. "The bedrooms
are spacious and well equipped – they even have wing armchairs,"
write the nominators "The Binks family owners are practical and
unpretentious. The service was a delight, at both dinner and breakfast,
and the food exceeded our expectations – in four dinners there was
nothing we could fault, whether smoked seafood, pheasant, wild
mushroom paté or sorbets. All had a touch of originality. Good toast
and coffee at breakfast, too. And to cap all this, there is an indoor swimming pool." Rievaulx and Byland abbeys and the North York Moors
National Park are nearby. More reports, please.

Open Mid-Mar–mid-Nov.
Rooms 3 suites (across courtyard), 10 double, 2 single. 1 on ground floor.
Facilities Lounge, bar, dining room; indoor swimming pool. ½-acre garden.
Golf, riding, fishing nearby.
Location Centre of village 3 miles SE of Helmsley. Carpark.
Restrictions No smoking in dining room. No children under 5. Dogs by arrange-
ment, not in public rooms.
Credit cards Access, Amex, Visa.
Terms [1997] D,B&B £57–£65. Bar lunches. Set dinner £20.

HARROGATE North Yorkshire   Map 4

The White House   NEW/BUDGET   *Tel* (01423) 501388
10 Park Parade   *Fax* (01423) 527973
Harrogate HG1 5AH

Mrs Jennie Forster's handsome 19th-century Venetian-style villa was
the home of a mayor of this old spa town (now a popular conference
venue). It has a prime position, near the 200-acre park, The Stray, and is
five minutes' walk from the centre. "It is quirky, original and beautifully decorated," writes the nominator, "and not over-formal. It has the
feel of a family home: lots of photographs and a collection of antique
and modern board games in the sitting room, and frogs, made from
every sort of material, dotted all around. In the hall, there is a cage with
two beautiful chinchillas. Mrs Forster is charming, and informative
about the town. Although we hadn't booked it, she upgraded us to her
bridal suite, a large and splendid room with a huge, luxurious bathroom. She is a skilful cook. Dinner, served at well-spaced tables, was
simple but exciting, with four choices for each course. Only let-down
was the breakfast, with slow service, weak coffee, and packaged orange
juice." Fellow hoteliers add: "Scrumptious bedrooms, first-class food
and a welcome that is warm and friendly." (*Eileen Engelmann, Patricia
and Geoffrey Noble*)

Open All year. Restaurant closed Sun evening.
Rooms 1 suite, 7 double, 2 single.
Facilities Lounge/bar, lounge, restaurant (piped music all day). Garden.
Unsuitable for &.

Location Central. Park Parade is reached from Skipton Rd (A59), or York Pl, which runs along The Stray.
Restrictions No smoking: restaurant, bedrooms. No dogs.
Credit cards All major cards accepted.
Terms B&B: single £68.50–£88.50, double/suite £90–£135; D,B&B (min. 2 nights) from £47.50. Set lunch £14.95; full alc £25. 1-night bookings refused during major conferences. *V* .

HARTFIELD East Sussex   Map 2

Bolebroke Watermill   NEW/BUDGET   *Tel/Fax* (01892) 770425
Edenbridge Road
Hartfield TN7 4JP

"You need sharp eyes to spot the B&B sign which leads you down an unmade track to this peaceful place," writes an inspector. "It stands on a tree-lined stream flowing through pastureland towards a section of Ashdown Forest much trampled by devotees of AA Milne in search of the Five Hundred Acre Wood and the Pooh Sticks bridge. But you don't have to be a fan of the winsome bear to enjoy this delightful 17th-century watermill, which David and Christine Cooper have skilfully converted into a most appealing and distinctive guest house. Two bedrooms are up steep loft ladders in the main building of tile-hung brick and white weather boarding; three are in the detached Elizabethan barn. All are different, but similarly furnished with cottagey charm, bristling with dried flower arrangements and rustic beams. Each building has its own spacious sitting room, with comfortable sofas and bookshelves amid a startling array of agricultural implements, assorted hunting trophies, African carvings and ancient weaponry, suggesting an ex-service life. The bedrooms are thoughtfully equipped with mod cons and many extras, including a coolbox with fresh milk for morning tea. Bedlinen veers toward the frilly, and the hygienically synthetic but unforgiving pillows could be improved. Breakfasts are served communally in the main house, and offer imaginative creations, such as huge stuffed mushrooms as an alternative to routine fry-ups; jams are home-made. The old mill machinery has been carefully restored and incorporated in the surroundings. With steep stairs and many changes of level, *Bolebroke* is suitable only for the nimbler sort of guest, but its romantic four-posters and secluded setting make it a memorable hideaway." No smoking.

Note The hordes of visitors to the bridge have led to defoliation of the nearby trees. Bring your own twigs if you wish to play Pooh Sticks.

Open Feb–mid-Dec.
Rooms 5 double.
Facilities 2 lounges, 2 breakfast rooms. 6½-acre grounds: garden, millpond, woodland walks. Unsuitable for &.
Location A264 E Grinstead–Tunbridge Wells for 6 miles. Turn right at crossroads on to B2026 towards Hartfield. After 1 mile, left into unmade lane, just past Perryhill Nursery. Follow signs.
Restrictions No smoking. No children under 7. No dogs.
Credit cards Access, Visa *(2½% surcharge)*, Amex *(5% surcharge)*.
Terms B&B: single £52–£59, double £57–£74.

For details of the Voucher scheme see page xxviii.

HARVINGTON Worcestershire   Map 3

The Mill at Harvington   *Tel/Fax* (01386) 870688
Anchor Lane
Harvington, nr Evesham WR11 5NR

"A delightful hotel in a marvellous situation, quietly elegant but
simple, with a most friendly staff. The food, on imaginative menus,
was beautifully cooked and well presented, and dishes are willingly
adapted for those who prefer something simpler." So writes an octogenarian visitor to this hotel, which is composed of a Georgian house and
a red brick mill with original features, such as cast iron bakery doors
and wooden beams. It has a peaceful setting outside an agreeable village near Evesham. Its large garden, with hard tennis court, croquet
lawn, and heated swimming pool, runs down to the river Avon, where
guests may fish for chub, roach, dace and barbel, and moor their boats.
The hotel is owned and enthusiastically run by Simon and Jane
Greenhalgh, with partners Richard and Sue Yeomans. All the bedrooms enjoy the view of the river. There are six new ones this year
across the garden, and the older ones have been refurbished (insulation, previously a gripe in these pages, has been attended to). The
restaurant and the lounge, which has log fires in winter, overlook the
garden. Cooking is a mixture of English and French, modern and traditional, and makes use of local suppliers. The wine list is helpfully
annotated, and each day two high-quality wines are offered for sam-
pling by the glass. Breakfast
is a generous affair, with
excellent wholemeal toast.
Third Night Special Offers
are considered "fabulous
value". Local attractions include Stratford-upon-Avon,
only ten miles away, the
medieval castles of Warwick,
Kenilworth, and Sudeley,
and the Cotswolds. (*Mrs MG
Munro Glass and others*)

Open All year, except 24–27 Dec.
Rooms 21 double. 6 in garden annexe. 3 on ground floor.
Facilities Ramp. Lounge, restaurant; private dining room. 8-acre grounds:
swimming pool, tennis, 200 yds river frontage, fishing.
Location Turn S off B439 down Anchor La (from Stratford do not go into
Harvington). Train: Evesham; then taxi.
Restrictions No smoking in restaurant. No children under 10. No dogs.
Credit cards All major cards accepted.
Terms [1997] B&B: single £58, double £92–£115; D,B&B (min. 2 nights): single
£75, double £108. Set lunch £13.95, dinner £22.50. 3-night breaks. 1-night book-
ings sometimes refused. *V*

The second volume of the *Guide*, containing 1,000 continental
hotels, will be published early in 1998. Deadline for reports on
continental hotels: 6 November 1997; for new nominations:
18 October 1997.

HARWICH Essex   Map 2

The Pier at Harwich   *Tel* (01255) 241212
The Quay   *Fax* (01255) 551922
Harwich CO12 3HH

Handsome Victorian building (built for passengers on packet boats to Holland),
overlooking busy harbour. Now owned by Richard Wheeler, with Gerald
Milsom of Maison Talbooth, Dedham (qv), it houses renowned fish restau-
rant and 6 neat bedrooms. Nautical decor, fine collection of railway posters,
assorted piped music in bar and restaurant. "Charming, helpful management
and staff; food exceptional by any standard." Parking. Closed 24–26 Dec
(restaurant open 24 Dec). Unsuitable for &. No dogs. All major credit cards
accepted. B&B: single £50–£65, double £70–£80. English breakfast £4. Set
lunch £14, dinner £18 (plus 10% service) [1997]. More reports, please.

HATCH BEAUCHAMP Somerset   Map 1

Farthings   `BUDGET`   *Tel* (01823) 480664
Hatch Beauchamp   *Fax* (01823) 481118
nr Taunton TA3 6SG

This elegant white-painted Georgian house with a wrought-iron
veranda is set in a pretty walled garden in a quiet old village. It has new
owners this year, Mr and Mrs Sparkes, with daughter and son-in-law,
Mr and Mrs Tindall, but many of the staff have remained from the old
regime, and visitors in early 1997 were pleased: "Genuinely friendly
owners. Splendid building; bedroom one of the best I have had, with
sitting area and excellent bathroom. Good traditional food too, cooked
by chef Jason Harmer." Light meals may be served in the bedrooms.
The whole place is now smoke-free. Close by are the village cricket
pitch and Hatch Court, a Palladian Bath stone mansion set in award-
winning gardens in a large deerpark. Bath, Wells, Exeter, many
National Trust properties, and the Somerset and Devon coasts are
within easy reach. The M5 is three miles away. (*RAL Ogston*)

Open All year.
Rooms 2 suites, 6 double.
Facilities Lounge, bar (piped music at night), restaurant. 3-acre grounds: cro-
quet. Golf, cricket, fishing, riding nearby. Unsuitable for &.
Location Centre of village 4 miles SE of Taunton, signposted from A358
Taunton–Ilminster. Train: Taunton; then bus or taxi.
Restrictions No smoking. No dogs in public rooms.
Credit cards None accepted.
Terms [1997] B&B: single £50–£55, double £70–£80, suite £80–£90. Set dinner
£18.50. Short breaks; Christmas, New Year packages.

HATTON Warwickshire   Map 3

Northleigh House   `BUDGET`   *Tel* (01926) 484203
Five Ways Road   *Fax* (01926) 484006
Hatton, Warwick CV35 7HZ

"A charming house in a lovely Cotswold setting, decorated in exquisite taste, with a gracious and accommodating hostess," say Anglophile

American visitors to this no-smoking B&B. "Superb value," other guests have written. In a rural setting near Warwick, but only 30 minutes' drive from Birmingham, it was the family home of the owner, Sylvia Fenwick. She is an enthusiastic decorator, and each bedroom has a different theme. The Blue Room (the priciest) has a bed in a blue-curtained alcove, blue couches, pine furniture, a bamboo coffee table, and a huge *en suite* bathroom "with masses of hot water, big soft towels, etc". Others include the Chinese Room, the Gold Room, Victoria, Poppy and (new this year) the Italian Room, which has a Mediterranean feel. All bedrooms have a fridge; the Blue Room has a kitchenette. A hearty English breakfast (with a toaster at each table) is served in the pretty dining room overlooking the garden. The panelled lounge has a wood-burning stove, books and original paintings. A home-cooked evening meal or a supper tray can be arranged; plenty of pubs and restaurants nearby. Stratford-upon-Avon is only 12 miles away. (*Caroljo and David Henderson*)

Open Feb–mid-Dec. Evening meals by arrangement.
Rooms 6 double, 1 single. 1 with kitchenette. 2 on ground floor. Payphone for guests.
Facilities Sitting room, dining room. Small garden; access to fields. Unsuitable for &.
Location 5 miles NW of Warwick off A4177. At Five Ways roundabout take Shrewley road for ½ mile.
Restrictions No smoking. No dogs in public rooms.
Credit card Access, Visa.
Terms [1997] B&B: single £33–£40, double £46–£58. Supper tray from £6.50; evening meal £15.

HAWKRIDGE Somerset   Map 1

Tarr Steps Hotel   *Tel* (01643) 851293
Hawkridge, Dulverton TA22 9PY   *Fax* (01643) 851218

This Georgian ex-rectory is named for the rough stone Cyclopean bridge, owned by the National Trust, that crosses the river Barle nearby. Approached by switchback country roads, it is peacefully set above the river valley, has magnificent views and is a sporting hotel *par excellence*, with six miles of salmon- and trout-fishing (and tuition for beginners), stabling for guests' horses, rough and formal shooting, and hunting. It was taken over in October 1995 by Sue and Shaun Blackmore, local people, who are "friendly, practical hosts". They have carried out extensive repairs and redecoration. Some find the dining room's new decor "a bit startling", but new windows have made it lighter. There is a new flower-covered pergola, and the walled Victorian garden has been cleared to make a vegetable garden and an orchard. Recent visitors have found it "still comfortable and pleasant, with good, conventional, carefully prepared food". "In the drawing room, with open fire, games, local history books, you can be private or convivial. No sound at night except river and owls." The bedrooms now have a telephone, but remain "blissfully free of radio and TV". Children and dogs are welcomed. Bar lunches are available. Tea is included in the half-board rate. More reports, please.

Open All year.
Rooms 9 double, 2 single. 1 on ground floor. Self-catering 3-bedroom cottage.
Facilities Lounge, bar, 2 dining rooms. 11-acre grounds: garden, stables/

paddocks for guests' horses, kennels. 6 miles river fishing, 500 acres rough shooting. Hunting, tennis, squash, golf nearby.
Location 7 miles NW of Dulverton. Go to Hawkridge, then follow signs to Tarr Steps. Do *not* follow earlier signs to Tarr Steps; they lead to wrong side of river. Train: Dulverton; then taxi.
Restrictions No smoking in dining room. No dogs in lounge, dining room.
Credit cards Access, Visa.
Terms [1997] B&B: single £35–£45, double £80–£90; D,B&B: single £50–£59, double £110–£118. Snack lunch from £2; set lunch from £13.50, dinner from £22.75. Special offers all year. *V*

HAWKSHEAD Cumbria   Map 4

Highfield House   *Tel* (01539 4) 36344
Hawkshead Hill   *Fax* (01539 4) 36793
Hawkshead LA22 0PN

Pauline and Jim Bennett's unpretentious Lakeland stone house stands on high ground in large gardens with fine trees and shrubs and a glorious view over the fells. It has a simple decor (one couple thought it rather basic), a small bar, and a lounge well supplied with books and local information. The many regular visitors praise the "cheerful hospitality and well-thought-out bedrooms", the "commitment of the owners, and the superb setting", the peace and quiet, and the "supreme cleanliness". Breakfast is called "copious and very enjoyable". The restaurant, open to the public for dinner, serves English cooking with choices for each course and a vegetarian option. It is generally admired. "Varied and imaginative, with high quality ingredients and generous portions. We like the tradition of offering second helpings of dessert, though we can rarely contemplate the pleasure." But one couple wrote of "some bizarre combinations of flavours" and unattractive lighting in the dining room, while another regretted the introduction of piped background music. Children of all ages are welcomed: cots, baby seats, high teas are provided. Washing and drying facilities are available. William Wordsworth went to school in Hawkshead, and the National Trust runs the Beatrix Potter Gallery here (she lived at Near Sawrey, close by). (*Derek Wilson, David Askew, and others*)

Open 31 Jan–20 Dec, 26 Dec–3 Jan. Restaurant closed midday (snack/packed lunches available).
Rooms 9 double, 2 single.
Facilities Lounge, bar, restaurant (piped music during dinner); laundry facilities, drying room. 2½-acre garden. Fishing nearby. Unsuitable for &.
Location ¾ mile W of Hawkshead on B5285 to Coniston. Infrequent bus service, taxi.
Restrictions No smoking in restaurant. No dogs in public rooms.
Credit cards Access, Visa.
Terms [1997] B&B £35–£43.50; D,B&B £51–£60. Set dinner £17.50. Winter breaks. 3-night New Year package. Children under 2 free; 2–12 sharing with parents: B&B £12.50.

Rough Close   BUDGET   *Tel* (01539 4) 36370
Hawkshead LA22 0QF

This unassuming guest house, just outside Hawkshead, overlooks Esthwaite Water (excellent birdwatching; no powered craft allowed).

There is good walking from the grounds. The *Guide* correspondent who first told us about it many years ago writes this year to say that everything is just as good as ever: "I never cease to wonder at the high standards maintained by Tony and Marylin Gibson. We have stayed twice already and have just booked again for October." Other visitors, too, praise the "excellent hosts, always smiling and obliging", and the "consistently varied and enticing food, English at its best, in generous servings, with a wide choice of vegetables and mouthwatering home-made puddings". Dinner is at 7 pm, five courses; no choice except alternative desserts. The Gibsons share the cooking, and Mr Gibson serves and acts as wine waiter (each menu suggests a wine to match the food). Coffee is taken round the fire in the sitting room; later guests may adjourn to the small bar. Substantial breakfasts, between 8.45 and 9.15 am, "set you up for the day". All the bedrooms have private facilities, but one bathroom is not *en suite*; they were all given a television set this year. Beatrix Potter's home, Hill Top, is one mile away. "Peter Rabbit is very popular with Japanese visitors," write the Gibsons. (*Elizabeth Sandham, WE Lees, Gillian Crossland*)

Open Late Mar–early Nov, New Year. Lunch not served.
Rooms 5 double. No telephone.
Facilities Lounge, bar with TV, dining room. 1-acre garden: *boules*. Lake, boating, fishing nearby. Unsuitable for ♿.
Location 1¼ miles S of Hawkshead on Newby Bridge road. Infrequent bus service.
Restrictions No smoking: dining room, bedrooms. No children under 12. No dogs.
Credit cards Access, Visa.
Terms B&B: single £36–£39.50, double £52–£59; D,B&B: single £48–£51.50, double £76–£83. Set dinner £12 (£14 to non-residents). Reductions for long stays.

HAWORTH West Yorkshire   Map 4

Weaver's **BUDGET**   *Tel* (01535) 643822
15 West Lane   *Fax* (01535) 644832
Haworth BD22 8DU

The Brontë sisters grew up in the parsonage (now a museum) of this old town on the edge of the Pennine Moors. Its tea rooms and souvenir shops cater to some 250,000 of their fans each year. The steep cobbled main street is lined with old stone weavers' cottages, three of which compose this cheerful restaurant-with-rooms. "It goes from strength to strength," writes a regular visitor, and other guests concur: "We felt welcomed and comfortable from the moment we arrived." The decor is "a delight": old photographs, modern paintings, antiques, bric-à-brac, and mementos of the Yorkshire spinners' craft. The "stylish and idiosyncratic" bedrooms, up a narrow staircase, are supplied with fresh milk, tea and a cafetière with ground coffee, and satellite TV. "The bar and lounge can be crowded in a friendly sort of way. The young staff are without exception willing and pleasant. Colin Rushworth is an archetypal bluff Yorkshireman, who fulfils the front-of-house role perfectly, but has little tolerance of pretension. Jane Rushworth is a talented chef. The food, northern cooking with a light touch, is difficult to fault, particularly at these prices. The unobtrusive background music is an interesting blend of jazz, blues and opera." Everything from bread to ice-cream is made on the premises. There are always vegetarian options. The wine list is wide-ranging, with some unusual vintages, a good selection of half bottles, and a low mark-up. There's a reduced-price menu on weekdays if you order by 7.15 pm. English breakfast is served at flexible times. Calderdale, the Yorkshire Dales, Bradford, Leeds and York are nearby. (*Chris Kay, Mrs T Biggs, and others*)

Open All year, Tues–Sat from 6.45 pm, except 24 Dec–2 Jan, 1 week June. Restaurant open for Sun lunch in winter.
Rooms 2 double, 2 single.
Facilities Lounge, bar, restaurant (piped music at night). Unsuitable for &.
Location By Brontë Parsonage Museum: use its pay-and-display carpark. Ignore sign for Brontë village/Tourist Information. Train: Keighley; then bus or taxi.
Restrictions No smoking in restaurant. No dogs.
Credit cards All major cards accepted.
Terms B&B: single £49.50, double £69.50. Set menu (6.45–7.15 pm, Sun lunch) £12.50; full alc £25. ***V***

HAYLING ISLAND Hampshire   Map 2

Cockle Warren Cottage   *Tel* (01705) 464961
36 Seafront   *Fax* (01705) 464838
Hayling Island PO11 9HL

This two-by-four-mile island, reached by a bridge from the mainland, is in Chichester and Langstone harbours on the Hampshire/Sussex border. It became a resort in the 19th century, and is known for its warm climate. Its five-mile beach has a Blue Flag award for clean and safe bathing, and it is said to be the birthplace of windsurfing. David and Diane Skelton's pretty tile-hung cottage hotel, bedecked in summer with geraniums, is on the seafront. In winter a log fire burns in the large lounge, which has antique furniture, magazines and games. The conservatory dining room overlooks the heated swimming pool (lit at night). Mrs Skelton's English/continental dinner menus use local fish and vegetables; portions are generous. No choice until you reach the luscious desserts, but prior discussion is encouraged. Breads and brioches are home-made. Wines are reasonably priced. Bell pushes at table summon the next course. Bedrooms are decorated in country style; each has a trouser press, an iron, playing cards, chocolates, and a carafe of Madeira; two bedrooms have a sea view and a four-poster. More reports, please.

Open All year.
Rooms 1 suite, 4 double. 2 in barn annexe. Some on ground floor.
Facilities Lounge, conservatory restaurant. ⅓-acre garden: swimming pool. Sea, sandy beach 70 yds: bathing, fishing, sailing; golf nearby.
Location Over bridge, S to seafront, turn left; *c.* 1 mile on left. Carpark.
Restrictions No smoking: restaurant, bedrooms. No children under 12, except babies. No dogs in public rooms.
Credit cards Access, Amex, Visa.
Terms B&B: single £55–£75, double £68–£98; D,B&B: single £65–£95, double £123–£153. Cooked breakfast £3.50–£9.50. Set dinner £26.50. 1-night bookings sometimes refused. ***V***

If the *Guide* is unavailable, or poorly displayed, in your local bookshop, please complain to the manager and/or let us know.

HAZLETON Gloucestershire   Map 3

Windrush House   `BUDGET`   *Tel* (01451) 860364
Hazleton, nr Cheltenham GL54 4EB

"An excellent establishment," writes a recent visitor to Mrs Sydney Harrison's modern stone-built guest house, which others have called "cosy and appealing". Set on the edge of a village high up in the heart of the north Cotswolds, it offers peace and quiet, wonderful views, and "food which puts many plusher establishments to shame: soft dark home-made bread, tender young vegetables, flavoursome meat and delicious sweets". "Delicious breakfasts too – whisky in the porridge if you wish." The small bedrooms are modestly but attractively furnished; some have a sloping ceiling. The house is licensed, but guests may bring their own wine; no corkage charge. Northleach, close by, has a beautiful church and many stone and timber-framed buildings. (*EA Thwaite, Mrs S Baker, and others*)

Open Mid-Jan–mid-Dec approx.
Rooms 4 double. 2 with *en suite* facilities. 2 on ground floor.
Facilities 2 lounges, dining room. ¾-acre garden. Unsuitable for &.
Location On edge of village 3 miles NW of Northleach. Turn off A40 on minor road marked Hazleton. 1st left; then 1st right. House is 4th on left.
Restrictions No smoking. No children. No dogs.
Credit cards None accepted.
Terms [1997] B&B £22–£25, D,B&B £41–£45. Light supper from £10, set dinner £20–£22. 4% reduction in Feb. Riding weekends in winter.

HEADLAM Co. Durham   Map 4

Headlam Hall   *Tel* (01325) 730238
Headlam, Gainford   *Fax* (01325) 730790
Darlington DL2 3HA

On the edge of a charming rural village in lower Teesdale, in a maze of minor roads, stands this creeper-covered manor house, part Jacobean, part Georgian – "a perfect example of its kind," said Pevsner. Privately owned until the Robinson family turned it into a hotel in 1979, it is peacefully set in mature gardens within its own large farm. It is admired for its fine setting, its excellent facilities (see below), and its "courteous, considerate staff". The public rooms have huge log fires in cold weather. In the pretty dining room, popular with locals, the tables are immaculately set. The cooking, mainly English with plenty of choice and accompanied by a well-chosen, reasonably priced wine list, is described as "enjoyable, if not *haute cuisine*", by a correspondent on his tenth visit, who adds: "And the atmosphere of friendliness created by John Robinson and his daughter, Mrs Metcalf, brings us back again and again." The best bedrooms are well furnished, with thick fitted carpets (but one room has been called "small and stuffy"). Good breakfasts. The hotel's conference and banqueting trade is kept well away from residents. (*Simon Jones; also Sir Alan Cook, Sydney Downs*) Only drawback: "very audible plumbing."

Open All year, except Christmas.
Rooms 2 suites, 26 double. 3 on ground floor. 9 in coach house 20 yds.

Facilities Ramps. Lounge, 2 bars, restaurant (occasional piped music), conservatory; ballroom, conference facilities; snooker room; indoor swimming pool. 100-acre farm: 4-acre garden, croquet, tennis, trout lake, fishing.
Location 7 miles W of Darlington. 1 mile N of Gainford off A67 to Barnard Castle. Train: Darlington; then taxi.
Restriction Dogs in coach house bedrooms only; not in public rooms.
Credit cards All major cards accepted.
Terms [1997] B&B: single £55–£68, double £70–£83, suite £83–£98. Set lunch £12.50, dinner £22.50; full alc £27. 2-night breaks: D,B&B £49–£54 per person per night.

HEDDON'S MOUTH Devon   Map 1

Heddon's Gate Hotel   *Tel* (01598) 763313
Heddon's Mouth, Parracombe   *Fax* (01598) 763363
Barnstaple EX31 4PZ

César award in 1990

"A wonderful hotel. It has lost none of its quality over the years. It has real character, without affectation, and a marvellously quiet atmosphere. The cosseting happens without contrivance. Bedrooms are serviced with great attention to detail: beds made during breakfast, fresh fruit daily. I can only echo the praise that has been heaped on it in successive editions of the *Guide*." "Delightful situation in the middle of nowhere. Lovely (if slightly neglected) gardens. Marvellous food, thoughtfully prepared. Beautiful bedroom. Large, inviting bathroom, a pleasant contrast to the utilitarian cubby-holes often encountered. Fine lounges. Warm hospitality." Apart from a few demurs about the food, the eulogies continue for this Swiss/Victorian lodge in large grounds with steeply terraced gardens, on the edge of Exmoor. It has been run for 29 years by proprietor/chef Robert Deville, who in 1997 married Heather Hurrell, front-of-house manager since 1991; the staff are long-serving. Bedrooms, named for their original use, Grandmama's Room, Nursemaid's Room, etc, vary greatly, and are priced accordingly. There is a Victorian-style sitting room with large French tapestries, a well-stocked library, and a large dining room where dinner with limited choice is served promptly at 8 pm. No midday meal, but packed lunches are available. A generous afternoon tea is included in the half-board rates. The cottages in the garden are good for dog-owners. Some of Exmoor's most spectacular coastal scenery is close by. (*JA Fisher, Brian and Li Jobson; also PE Carter, JP Berryman, and others*)

Open 4 Apr–2 Nov. Dining room closed for lunch.
Rooms 4 suites (3 in cottages with access for &), 9 double, 1 single.
Facilities Lounge, library, piano/card room, bar, dining room; table-tennis room. 20-acre grounds. River, fishing, riding, pony-trekking nearby. Sea 1 mile.
Location 6 miles W of Lynton. From A39, after 3 miles, take road to Martinhoe/Woody Bay; follow signs for Hunter's Inn; hotel drive on right. Train: Barnstaple, 16 miles; then taxi.
Restrictions No smoking in dining room. Children "must be old enough to dine at 8 pm". No dogs in dining room.
Credit cards Access, Amex, Visa.
Terms D,B&B £51–£75.50. Set dinner £26.50. 3-day breaks. 1-night bookings occasionally refused. Children accommodated in parents' room: 50% reduction.

Make sure the hotel has included VAT in the prices it quotes.

HINTLESHAM Suffolk   Map 2

Hintlesham Hall   *Tel* (01473) 652268
Hintlesham, Ipswich IP8 3NS   *Fax* (01473) 652463

A stunning country house in a village near Ipswich. Grade I listed,
Tudor in origin with a Georgian façade, it is "both classy and welcoming". Its interior is sumptuous and impeccably maintained, with panelling and mouldings, fine fabrics and antiques. The bedrooms vary in
size and style; some are huge and opulent; some have a gas log fire,
some the real thing. Guests' accommodation is upgraded at no extra
cost when possible. In the vast grounds there is a leisure club, and an
18-hole championship golf course, well hidden by trees (its clubhouse
is an agreeable place for a light lunch, though one visitor this year took
exception to its dress code. Many other outdoor pursuits are available
(see below). "Close to perfection for a relaxing country weekend," say
regular visitors. "It is extremely well managed by Tim Sunderland.
Many of the staff have been there for years; relaxed service of a remarkably high level. Breakfasts are impeccable." Chef Alan Ford cooks
meals "in elegant country house style", with first-class raw materials,
"which live up to the surroundings". The wine list is "superb – the
house recommendations are always worth trying". The breaks are
thought good value. (*Kate and David Wooff, Pat and Jeremy Temple*)

Open All year.
Rooms 4 suites, 29 double. 11 in courtyard wing 20 yds. 8 on ground floor.
Facilities 4 lounges, 3 dining rooms; conference/function facilities; snooker
room. 175-acre grounds: leisure club, swimming pool, tennis, croquet, 18-hole
golf course with club house, trout lake, fishing, riding, shooting. Unsuitable
for &.
Location 5 miles W of Ipswich on A1071 to Sudbury.
Restrictions No smoking in dining rooms. "Good children and good dogs welcomed", but no under-10s at dinner, no dogs in house.
Credit cards All major cards accepted.
Terms [1997] B&B: single from £89, double from £115, suite from £225. English
breakfast £7.50. Set lunch £19.50, dinner £25; full alc £38. 2-day breaks; golf
breaks; Christmas package. 1-night bookings refused bank holidays. Child
accommodated in parents' room £10.

HINTON CHARTERHOUSE Somerset   Map 2

Homewood Park   *Tel* (01225) 723731
Hinton Charterhouse   *Fax* (01225) 723820
nr Bath BA3 6BB

This mainly 18th-century house, with skilful later additions, is set in
immaculate grounds in a village on the edge of the Limpley Stoke valley, a designated area of outstanding natural beauty near Bath. It is
owned by the Fentum family and run by their daughter Sara, with her
husband, Frank Gueuning. The country house decor includes fine fabrics, antiques and oriental rugs, and there are works by local artists on
display; log fires warm the lounge and bar in winter. Bedrooms are
priced according to style and outlook; most are spacious and overlook
the garden. One of the two suites has been sponsored by Marks and
Spencer. Chef Gary Jones, who has worked at *Le Manoir aux
Quat'Saisons*, Great Milton (*qv*), and *The Waterside Inn*, Bray (*qv*), cooks

modern English dishes which are admired. "Total excellence and professionalism, yet relaxed and friendly, a rare mix," wrote a recent visitor. "The owners were in evidence, but not pushy. The bedrooms were the best of our trip." Others have thought it "pricey, but worth every penny". The Fentums recently bought *Hunstrete House*, a Georgian mansion in magnificent 100-acre grounds with woodlands and a deer-park, at Hunstrete nearby. Hayden Fentum will be manager, and the chef will be Clive Dixon, formerly of the *Michelin*-starred *Lords of the Manor*, Upper Slaughter. We'd like reports on this venture, please. (*TR, and others*)

Open All year.
Rooms 2 suites, 17 double. 2 on ground floor.
Facilities Drawing room, study, bar, restaurant; private dining room, conference room. 10-acre grounds: tennis, swimming pool, croquet, parkland.
Location 6 miles SW of Bath opposite Hinton Priory. Left off A36 at Freshford. Some traffic noise; rooms double-glazed. Train: Bath; then taxi.
Restrictions No smoking in restaurant. No dogs.
Credit cards All major cards accepted.
Terms [1997] B&B: single £95–£105, double £105–£115, suite £235–£255. Set lunch £22; full alc £45. Seasonal breaks.

HOCKLEY HEATH Warwickshire   Map 3

Nuthurst Grange   *Tel* (01564) 783972
Nuthurst Grange Lane   *Fax* (01564) 783919
Hockley Heath B94 5NL   *E-mail* 106220.1743@compuserve.com

In a large village on the Stratford-on-Avon Canal, handy for Birmingham, this Edwardian house is approached by an immaculate drive through well-maintained, spacious grounds. "It is low and pleasant," writes an inspector, "with a terrace, creeper-clad walls, bay windows with leaded panes, and dormer windows in the roof. The front looks down from its elevation across the M40 [half a mile away; some traffic noise] to open country. The overall impression of the common rooms is of warmth, comfort and pinkness, with lavish use of fabrics, and stylish flower arrangements. Two light sitting rooms overlook the garden. The restaurant is set out in a string of rooms, with well-spaced tables. We had been impressed by the hotel's informative professionalism when we booked; our reception was friendly, and all the staff were pleasant. Our large bedroom, with a sitting area, continued the feel of affluent, traditional suburbia. It was well decorated, with reproduction furniture and useful extras. We chose fairly simple dishes from the wide-ranging *à la carte* menu. They were well handled, but we thought the meal was expensive. Breakfast is good; you order what you want, and it appears. They prefer you to take it in the bedroom, but will serve it in the dining room if asked." Cooking by owner/proprietor David Randolph is modern British; there is an impressive wine list. "Suitable for children who are well behaved," says the brochure. Three impressive castles, Warwick, Broughton and Berkeley, are nearby.

Open All year. Restaurant closed midday Sat.
Rooms 2 suites, 13 double.
Facilities Ramp. 2 lounges, restaurant; 2 private dining rooms, function room. 7½-acre grounds: croquet, helipad. Riding, hunting, tennis, golf, clay pigeon-shooting, canal boating nearby.
Location Off A3400 ½ mile S of Hockley Heath. Turn right at hotel sign.

Restrictions No smoking: restaurant, 1 lounge. No dogs.
Credit cards Access, Amex, Diners.
Terms [1997] B&B: single £99, double £125–£140, suite £150. English breakfast £9.90. Set dinner £26.90; full alc c £32. Weekend breaks. *V*

HOLFORD Somerset   Map 1

Combe House NEW/BUDGET   Tel (01278) 741382
Holford
nr Bridgwater TA5 1RZ

*Unpretentious, convivial hotel (converted 17th-century tannery, with water-wheel), in wooded valley in the Quantocks. "Amusingly sharp" owner Richard Bjergfelt; long-serving staff. Public rooms with beams, open fires; not large or chic, sometimes crowded. Straightforward cooking in huge portions on menu with choices. Variable bedrooms upstairs, some large, most with facilities en suite. Indoor swimming pool (closed in middle of day), sauna. 3-acre grounds: tennis, croquet; golf, riding, excellent walking nearby. Children welcomed. Loved by some: "A secluded haven." "Lovely garden." "No fuss." Too casual for others. Open mid-Mar–end Oct. 19 rooms (3 in cottage). No smoking: lounge, restaurant. No dogs in public rooms, except bar. Access, Amex, Visa accepted. B&B £29–£35. Bar lunches from £2.50. Set dinner £18.25 [1997]. *V*

HOPESAY Shropshire   Map 3

The Old Rectory BUDGET   Tel (01588) 660245
Hopesay, Craven Arms SY7 8HD   Fax (01588) 660502

This 17th-century ex-rectory stands in landscaped gardens by a 12th-century church in a hamlet above the Clun valley – the heart of Housman country. The lounge, recently refurbished, has an Adam fireplace, Georgian sash windows opening on to a terrace, and antique and period furniture. The spacious bedrooms, all with *en suite* bathroom, have TV, armchairs, and electric blankets; two have an emperor-size bed. It is a Wolsey Lodge member, and recent visitors admired the "lovely house, beautifully decorated and equipped" and wrote warmly of the "charming and courteous" owners: "We felt like family friends after only two days. Roma Villar is an excellent cook and Michael Villar is justly proud of his breakfasts." The Aga-cooked dinners (no choice until dessert) are served at 8 pm at an oak refectory table. "I try to use food in season and adjust menus to suit individual tastes and also weather conditions," writes Mrs Villar. Breakfast includes home-made yogurt and preserves, fruit salad, home-baked bread, and traditional cooked items. A complimentary afternoon tea, with home-made biscuits and cakes, is included in the rates. The church clock strikes regularly "but unobtrusively", write the Villars. There is good walking close by on National Trust land; good birdwatching too, both in the garden and from local RSPB bird hides. Powis and Stokesay castles, Offa's Dyke and Long Mynd are near. (*RH; also Mrs M Kershaw, and others*)

Open All year, except Christmas.
Rooms 1 suite, 2 double. No telephone.
Facilities Drawing room, dining room. 2-acre grounds. Unsuitable for &.

Location 3 miles W of Craven Arms. B4368 to Clun. At Aston-on-Clun turn right over humpback bridge to Hopesay. Hotel 1½ miles, by church.
Restrictions No smoking. No children. No dogs.
Credit cards None accepted.
Terms [1997] B&B £32; D,B&B £50.

HORDLE Hampshire   Map 2

Gordleton Mill   NEW   *Tel* (01590) 682219
Silver Street   *Fax* (01590) 683073
Hordle, nr Lymington SO41 6DJ

William Stone's converted 17th-century water mill is set on the banks of the river Avon, with sluice gates, ponds, water lilies, rustic bridges and formal gardens. The old mill, its machinery still apparent, houses two lounges. The upstairs one, for smokers, has heavy ancient beams, nautical maps, and plenty of character. The downstairs one is smarter, with mirrors and plants. A veranda-corridor leads to the purpose-built newer part, which houses the restaurant. This gained a *Michelin* star in 1997 for the modern French cooking of manager/chef Toby Hill, who trained with Raymond Blanc. "A first class establishment in a heart-breakingly lovely Monet-style setting," wrote an inspector in early 1997. "It has been done up with great flair, and is smart without being pretentious. The restaurant is one of the most attractive we have ever eaten in. The bedrooms, above, are not large, but impeccable, with tra-ditional style yew furniture, well-chosen fabrics and pictures, fresh flowers, fruit, bottled water, etc. Each has a well-appointed bathroom with stacks of towels, generous quality toiletries and even toothpaste-impregnated toothbrushes. Free tea and coffee are available on demand. The food is imaginative and delicious. Puddings are all vari-ations on chocolate; there is an excellent cheese board. Breakfast, in a pretty pale-panelled room, had exceptional orange juice, the lightest croissants imaginable, and artistically sliced fruit, as well as the full cooked works. Service, however, was very slow at both meals, and a bit detached, and the 24-hour piped muzak was a bit much: Elgar's *Pomp and Circumstance* for breakfast, the *Dam Busters* with pre-dinner drinks, and piano *ad nauseam* for dinner." Lymington, nearby, is a popular yachting base; a lively Saturday market takes place in its handsome, mostly Georgian high street.

Open All year, except Mon; restaurant also closed Sun evening.
Rooms 1 suite, 6 double.
Facilities 2 lounges, breakfast room, restaurant (constant piped music); function facilities; terrace. 5½-acre grounds on river. Unsuitable for ♿.
Location 3½ miles NW of Lymington. Take Sway road off A337 by *Toll House* inn. Regular buses from Lymington.
Restrictions No smoking: 1 lounge, restaurant, 4 bedrooms. Lapdogs only; ken-nels on premises.
Credit cards All major cards accepted.
Terms [1997] B&B: single £97, double £116–£123; suite £129–£136. Set lunch £19.50, dinner £45; full alc £55. Low season midweek break (2 nights min.): D,B&B £130–£140.

Before making a long detour to a small hotel, do check that it is open. Some are known to close on impulse.

HORLEY Surrey   Map 2

Langshott Manor   *Tel* (01293) 786680
Langshott, Horley RH6 9LN   *Fax* (01293) 783905

An airport hotel with a difference, close to Gatwick, but not on a flight path. It is a Grade II listed Elizabethan manor in a traditional English garden with roses, herbaceous borders and a lake. The New Zealand-born owners, Geoffrey, Rish and Christopher Noble, cosset travellers. They offer airport collection/delivery service in the house Jaguar, and guests may leave their car at the hotel for up to two weeks. Early morning tea comes with newspapers and shortbread. Breakfasts include fresh fruit, a variety of compotes, excellent cooked dishes, "and properly brewed tea". "Dinners continue to delight," says a regular visitor from America. "There is a short, seasonally changing menu of traditional English/French dishes, and lighter alternatives, such as an omelet and a salad, are always available. The Nobles have a natural talent for hospitality. Staying here is the only way we can consider beginning or ending a holiday." *Langshott* has spacious reception rooms with log fires, and large bedrooms with books, magazines, sewing basket, bath salts in large jar, plants and flowers. One is the old nursery at the top: "Comforting and homelike as a nursery should be; its bathroom has a freestanding, claw-footed bath, a Victorian-style loo, and lots of humorous touches." The rooms in the converted mews may lack the character of those in the main house, but they have "a soothing decor, and pretty views over gardens or fields and treetops". (Mrs *Romney Bathurst*)

Open All year, except 25–30 Dec.
Rooms 9 double. 2 in mews 50 yds. 1, on ground floor, with ♿ access.
Facilities Sitting room, morning room/bar, 2 dining rooms; conference/private dining room. 3-acre garden: croquet. 2 weeks' free parking; courtesy car to Gatwick (2½ miles).
Location From A23 in Horley take Ladbroke Rd (*Chequers* hotel roundabout) to Langshott. Hotel ¾ mile on right.
Restrictions No smoking: restaurant, bedrooms. No children under 7, except babes in arms. No dogs.
Credit cards All major cards accepted.
Terms B&B: single £98.50, double £125. Set lunch £17.50, dinner £32.50; D,B&B: single £131, double £190–£200. 2-day breaks Oct–end Mar.

HOVINGHAM North Yorkshire   Map 4

The Worsley Arms   *Tel* (01653) 628234
Hovingham YO6 4LA   *Fax* (01653) 628130

Old coaching inn overlooking green of unspoilt village surrounded by forest, 17 miles N of York. Traditional decor: chintz, antiques, hunting and cricketing prints. Comfortable bedrooms with champagne, mineral water, bathroom goodies. Modern British cooking in pleasant restaurant; less formal meals in bistro bar. Adequate breakfasts. ½-acre garden. Local sightseeing includes Hovingham Hall, Castle Howard, moors and dales. No smoking: restaurant, bedrooms. No dogs in public rooms. 18 bedrooms, some in cottages. All major cards accepted. B&B: single £55–£65, double £75–£80; D,B&B: single £80–£85, double £125–£135. Set lunch £16, dinner £25. ***V***

HUDDERSFIELD West Yorkshire *See SHORTLIST* **Map 4**

HUNTINGDON Cambridgeshire **Map 2**

The Old Bridge NEW
1 High Street
Huntingdon PE18 6TQ

Tel (01480) 452681
Fax (01480) 411017

John Hoskins' handsome 18th-century building, once a bank, now an inn, on bank of river Ouse in centre of Cromwell's birthplace. Modern international cooking in formal no-smoking panelled restaurant and terrace room (with mural); award-winning wine list; well-trained young staff. Lounge/bar popular with locals. Small garden: jetty on river; private mooring. "Better for an overnight stop than an extended stay." Extensive business trade. Traffic noise from bridge, but windows double-glazed. 25 well-appointed bedrooms with attractive decor (2 on ground floor); some are large. No smoking in restaurant. All major cards accepted. B&B: single £79.50–£99.50, double £89.50–£120. Full alc £24. Weekend break: D,B&B £69.50. More reports, please. *V*

HUNTSHAM Devon **Map 1**

Huntsham Court
Huntsham Valley
nr Tiverton EX16 7NA

Tel (01398) 361365
Fax (01398) 361456

César award in 1988

This unique establishment, in a secluded Devon setting, received its César for "utterly acceptable mild eccentricity". It is run in laid-back style by Mogens Bolwig, who is Danish, and his Greek wife, Andrea, with a friendly Australian staff. The house is a choice example of high-Victorian architecture, with huge rooms, massive fireplaces, impressive panelling and marble pillars. It is eclectically furnished, and dedicated to music. There are pianos everywhere – a grand in the hall, uprights in the drawing room and bar and a pianola in the dining room, and there is a vast collection of records and cassettes. The bedrooms (no locks on doors, no telephone or TV) are named after composers, and each has a pre-war radio. Beethoven has a log fire, a seven-foot-wide bed, a baby grand piano, and two free-standing old bathtubs, with silver claws, side by side in its bathroom (most bathrooms are huge). The five-course dinner (good home-cooking) is communal, served by candlelight at a long Victorian table; there's no menu and no wine list. Bottles are chosen from the amazing wine cellar (convivial wine-tastings are often held). Breakfast is served until noon; free tea and coffee are available all day in the butler's pantry. *Huntsham*'s motto is *Dulce nihil facere* (how sweet it is to do nothing). It is too casual for some; others find it addictive. The whole place is often taken over for house parties or conferences. More reports, please.

Open All year.
Rooms 3 suites, 11 double. 2 in converted barn. No telephone/TV, etc.
Facilities Drawing room, music room, bar, great hall/dining room (piped classical music), library/snooker room; mini-gym, sauna. 8-acre grounds: tennis, croquet, lake, bicycles. Golf, shooting, riding, fishing nearby.
Location From M5 exit 27, A373 to Tiverton, 500 yds turn left to Sampford

Peverell. Sharp right on bridge at *Globe Inn*. 2 miles to Uplowman, then 4 miles
to Huntsham.
Restriction No dogs.
Credit cards Access, Amex, Visa.
Terms [1997] B&B: single £75, double/suite £125–£150. Set dinner £30. House
parties, wine weekends; midweek breaks. *V*

IPSWICH Suffolk   Map 2

The Marlborough   *Tel* (01473) 257677
73 Henley Road   *Fax* (01473) 226927
Ipswich IP1 3SP

The birthplace of the butcher's son who became Cardinal Wolsey is a
busy inland port on the river Orwell and an agricultural centre. Despite
modernisation, it retains some fine old buildings, and it makes a good
base for touring Suffolk. The *Marlborough*, a Victorian building in a residential area opposite Christchurch Park, is owned by Mrs Mary
Gough, who also owns the *Angel*, Bury St Edmunds, and has been run
for four years by her son and daughter-in-law, Robert and Karen. Its
decor is traditional, with pastel colours and antique or period furniture. The restaurant, with well-spaced tables, and impeccable napery
and flowers, overlooks a pretty garden (floodlit at night). Regular visitors in 1997 had a happy break: "The Goughs are very welcoming, and
the charming head receptionist, Leena Goshal, is most efficient. Some
bedrooms have been refurbished; the new bathrooms are impeccable.
Room service is good. The bedroom television sets have a low maximum volume, so neighbours do not disturb each other. Excellent reading lights. The food is now good, with some unusual dishes, and the
restaurant service is deft and speedy. Breakfast includes tender kidneys, and especially good marmalade." (*Moira Jarrett*)

Open All year.
Rooms 1 suite, 17 double, 4 single. Some on ground floor.
Facilities Ramps. Lounge, bar (piped music), restaurant; private dining/confer-
ence room. ⅓-acre garden.
Location N of Christchurch Pk; turn S off A1214. Private parking.
Restrictions No smoking in restaurant. No dogs in public rooms.
Credit cards All major cards accepted.
Terms [1997] Room (single/double) £68–£78, suite £85–£95. Breakfast
£6.65–£8.95. D,B&B £56.50–£76.50 per person. Set lunch £15.50, dinner £19.50;
full alc £32. Christmas, New Year, Easter package.

KEMERTON Gloucestershire   Map 3

Upper Court   *Tel* (01386) 725351
Kemerton, nr Tewkesbury GL20 7HY   *Fax* (01386) 725472

This beautiful Georgian manor, an informally run Wolsey Lodge, is by
the church in a lovely village on Bredon Hill. It stands in showpiece
gardens with a sheltered swimming pool and tennis court, and a lake
with two islands, rainbow trout and water fowl. The owners, Bill and
Diana Herford, have an antiques and interior decorating business;
something is always for sale, and they can offer advice about other
dealers in the area. Their house is filled with antiques, oriental rugs,
porcelain, and accumulated clutter; the chintzy guest bedrooms in the

main house, twin-bedded or with a four-poster, are in similar style. Others, in cottages and stables, are generally self-catering. "There is a smart sitting room for guests," writes an inspector. "The bedrooms are delightful. Dinner, by arrangement and served communally at 8 pm (no choice; guests' requirements are discussed in advance), was good home fare, in copious portions, ending with cheese and port. Breakfast was standard English, entirely satisfactory, with lovely preserves. The Herfords are a very pleasant couple, interested in their guests and helpful about local attractions, but things can be a little disorganised at times." *Upper Court* is often taken over by house parties and small

 conferences. John Moore, whose writing vividly evoked this part of the world, lived in Kemerton. There are many historic buildings nearby, including Tewkesbury Abbey, Sudeley and Warwick castles; handy for the races at Cheltenham, and its literary festival.

Open All year, except Christmas. Lunch not served; dinner by arrangement.
Rooms 3 suites. 9 more in cottages/converted stables (can be self-catering). 1 on ground floor. No telephone.
Facilities 2 drawing rooms, dining room, conservatory. 15-acre grounds: walled garden, swimming pool (heated May–Sept), tennis, croquet, archery, lake: fishing, boating. Riding, clay pigeon-shooting, good walking nearby.
Location From Cheltenham N on A46; right to Kemerton 1 mile past junction with A438. Turn off main road at war memorial; house behind church. Bus from Cheltenham.
Restrictions No smoking in bedrooms. Dogs in cottages only.
Credit cards Access, Visa.
Terms [1997] B&B: single £50–£65, double £75–£95, suite £115. Set dinner £25. 1-night bookings sometimes refused summer weekends.

KENDAL Cumbria   **Map 4**

Holmfield   NEW/BUDGET   *Tel/Fax* (01539) 720790
41 Kendal Green, Kendal LA9 5PP

Unassuming B&B in large Edwardian house, 20 minutes' uphill walk from centre of old market town (said to be birthplace of Catherine Parr). "Home-like atmosphere; interesting artefacts; exuberant proprietor, Eileen Kettle. Excellent value. Good for a short stay." Residents' lounge with TV. Communal breakfasts ("but not too forced"). 1-acre garden: views of Kendal Castle and Lake District hills, heated swimming pool, croquet; carpark. Closed Christmas, sometimes New Year, occasionally at other times. Unsuitable for ♿. No smoking. No children under 12. No dogs. Credit cards not accepted. 3 bedrooms, 2 with private bathroom, all with TV. B&B £21–£30. More reports, please.

By sending us reports you automatically qualify for the Report of the Year competition; each one of 12 winners is awarded a bottle of champagne.

KINTBURY Berkshire   **Map 2**

The Dundas Arms   NEW   *Tel* (01488) 658263
53 Station Road   *Fax* (01488) 658568
Kintbury RG17 9UT

Restaurant-and-pub-with-rooms in charming position at junction of river
Kennet with Kennet and Avon canal. 5 good-sized "appealingly unsmart"
bedrooms in converted stables, with sliding doors that open on to riverside
terrace – "lovely, peaceful setting; delightful walking". Well-balanced, eclectic
menu, extensive, reasonably priced wine list, in rustic-style dining room.
Lighter meals in small bar ("with friendly feel"). Breakfast well cooked, but
sometimes haphazardly served. Owner/chef David Dalzell-Piper, not someone
to cross swords with, has presided for over 30 years. Closed Christmas, New
Year; restaurant closed Sun/evening Mon. Unsuitable for &. Smoking dis-
couraged in restaurant. Dogs by arrangement, but not in public rooms.
Access, Amex, Visa accepted. B&B double £65–£75; full alc £30–£35. More
reports, please.

KIRKBYMOORSIDE North Yorkshire   **Map 4**

The George and Dragon   BUDGET   *Tel/Fax* (01751) 433334
Market Place
Kirkbymoorside YO6 6AA

This civilised old coaching inn is on the main street of a market town in
the Vale of Pickering. It is handy for the moors, and a good staging
point on the journey to Scotland. The owners, Stephen and Frances
Colling, have spent some time in France, and the bedroom decor and
wine list benefit from this connection. The lively pub, with gleaming
woodwork, log fires, newspapers and the owners' collection of sporting memorabilia, has a bistro blackboard menu. Traditional meals,
with the emphasis on simple flavours and fresh local ingredients, are
served in large portions in the restaurant (formerly the brewhouse).
"Delicious stews, pies, fishcakes, intensely flavoured sauces, vegetables cooked to perfection", were enjoyed by a regular *Guide* correspondent. "The wine list is adventurous and inexpensive. A dozen or so (not
just the cheaper ones) are available by the glass." Substantial Yorkshire
breakfasts include home-made bread. Views of the accommodation are
mixed. The bedrooms are in a converted corn mill and old vicarage
across a courtyard, well away from the pub. One couple's was "the size
of a flat, with a vast, unusually comfortable three-piece suite (I got used
to the pink damask); everything scrupulously clean, plain and attractive." But some ground-floor rooms lack sound-proofing, and plumbing can be noisy and bedside lighting inadequate. Muddles over
bookings have also occurred, but much is forgiven because of the
"delightful, never overbearing" staff and the "first-rate" food. (*Claire*
Wrathall, John and Joan Wyatt; also Good Pub Guide)

Open All year.
Rooms 18 double, 1 single. In 2 separate buildings, at rear. 5 on ground floor.
Facilities Ramp. Residents' lounge, bar/bistro (piped classical music/jazz),
restaurant. ¼-acre walled garden. Golf nearby.
Location Town centre. Carpark.
Restrictions No smoking in restaurant. No dogs in public rooms.

Credit cards Access, Visa.
Terms B&B: single £45–£49, double £78–£88. Bar meals. Full alc £20. 2/4-day breaks. Activity breaks: microlight, gliding, golfing, riding, etc. Children accommodated free in parents' room. *V*

KNUTSFORD Cheshire   **Map 3**

La Belle Epoque   NEW/BUDGET   *Tel* (01565) 633060
60 King Street   *Fax* (01565) 654150
Knutsford WA16 6DT

Knutsford (where King Canute is said to have forded the river Lily in 1016) is a small market town on a road to Manchester, 18 miles away. Birthplace of the Victorian writer Mrs Gaskell, who used it as the model for *Cranford*, it retains its cobbled alleys and courtyards, and its narrow streets are rich in antique shops, pubs and interior designers, This building, with a quirky tower, was designed by Richard Watts, an architect active locally at the turn of the century, and is now a stylish restaurant-with-rooms. Much of its Art Nouveau character has been maintained. The decor is dramatic – walls are painted in deep greens and purples, fabrics are lavish and dark. Tables are set with heavy cloths, good cutlery and glassware, and flowers in tall glass vases, and have comfortable wicker chairs. "A quintessential *Guide* candidate," say inspectors. "The proprietors, Keith and Nerys Mooney, greet customers, eat in the dining room, and supervise everything. Their son David is chef, and his straightforward brasserie-style cooking, using high-quality ingredients, is justly popular. Service from the young team is friendly and mostly efficient. There is an attractive garden behind the building, used for alfresco meals in fine weather. Our bedroom upstairs, though simple, shared the restaurant's emphasis on dark and dramatic decor (some are plainer). It was idiosyncratic, stylish and comfortable, but drawer space was non-existent and the lighting was poor. Breakfast was fair, with packaged juice and tea-bag tea, but good brown toast and well-prepared cooked dishes. When paying the bill, we were surprised to notice that we had been charged for our coffee top-ups at dinner." Residents are expected to dine in. Knutsford has two Palladian mansions (both National Trust): Tatton Park, set in a large park with magnificent gardens by Humphry Repton and a working farm, and Tabley House.

Open All year, Mon–Sat, except Christmas, New Year, bank holidays.
Rooms 6 double, 1 single.
Facilities Restaurant (piped music); function rooms. Small garden. Unsuitable for &.
Location Town centre. Street parking. Regular trains from Manchester.
Restrictions No children under 14. No dogs.
Credit cards All major cards accepted.
Terms [1997] B&B: single £40, double £50. Set lunch £9.50; full alc £25.

Longview Hotel   NEW/BUDGET   *Tel* (01565) 632119
51 and 55 Manchester Road   *Fax* (01565) 652402
Knutsford WA16 0LX

Pauline and Stephen West's small hotel (a Logis of Great Britain), composed of 2 Victorian houses separated by a private house. Looks across busy road to

*common where Martin Bell was famously confronted by Neil and Christine
Hamilton during 1997 election campaign. Welcoming feel: open fire in reception, cosy cellar bar. 23 pretty bedrooms, thoughtfully equipped (rear ones quietest). Careful cooking served in restaurant with dressers, clock with resonant
chime, piped classical music. Breakfast adequate, but marred by banging
kitchen doors. Light room-service meals available. Closed Christmas/New
Year; restaurant closed midday, Sun dinner. Unsuitable for &. No dogs in
public rooms. Access, Amex, Visa. B&B £30–£57. Full alc £20 [1997].*

LAMORNA Cornwall   **Map 1**

Lamorna Cove Hotel   NEW/BUDGET   *Tel* (01736) 731411
Lamorna, nr Penzance TR19 6XH

*Malcolm and Lisa Gray's 19th-century country house near Land's End, idyl-
lically set above wooded valley and sea in 5½-acre grounds with terraced gardens, swimming pool, path to cove; beautiful views. Attractive lounges (1 a
former chapel) with antiques, paintings by Newlyn artists, family photos.
Traditional cooking, with emphasis on local produce, especially fish, in dining
room with picture windows; attentive service, good wine list. Open late
Feb–end Oct, 4 days New Year. 12 bedrooms, some with balcony or patio. No
smoking. Unsuitable for children, &. No dogs, except in garden bedroom.
Access, Amex accepted. B&B £29.50–£34.50; D,B&B £44.50–£49.50 [1997].*

LANGAR Nottinghamshire   **Map 2**

Langar Hall   *Tel* (01949) 860559
Langar NG13 9HG   *Fax* (01949) 861045

*Charming Regency house by venerable church of village in Vale of Belvoir,
12 miles SE of Nottingham. 30-acre grounds: gardens, ponds, parkland.
Classical/modern cooking on seasonally structured menu; after-dinner entertainment (last Fri of month) by local professional singers and actors. Bedrooms
vary in size; best ones in the main house, newer ones off courtyard. Weddings,
parties, catered for. Utterly beguiling to some – "delightful hostess, Imogen
Skirving; tranquil, gently eccentric feel" – but altogether too casual for others.
Possibly closed Christmas. No smoking: sitting room, function room, bedrooms. All major credit cards accepted. B&B: single £75–£85, double
£85–£150. Set lunch £10–£20, dinner £15–£25; full alc £35.* *V*

LANGHO Lancashire   **Map 4**

Northcote Manor   *Tel* (01254) 240555
Northcote Road   *Fax* (01254) 246568
Langho, nr Blackburn BB6 8BE

"Some of the best food we have ever had, with wonderful home-grown
herbs" was eaten by a *Guide* correspondent at this *Michelin*-starred
restaurant-with-rooms owned by Craig Bancroft and Nigel Haworth.
The British cooking of the latter, who is also the chef, makes the most
of local ingredients, and has robust regional overtones – black pudding
and apple crumble feature on the menu alongside more modern items.
There is an extensive wine list. The turn-of-the-century red brick manor

is set in two-acre wooded grounds with views across to Pendle Hill, above the county town of Clitheroe, but it is close to the busy A59 road – windows are double-glazed. The interior is Victorian in feel, with beams, oak panelling, a handsome staircase, and deep leather arm-chairs and open fires in the public rooms. The bedrooms, mostly spacious, are well furnished, with good-quality fabrics, antique and period furniture, knick-knacks and games; some are in a 1993 exten-sion. Breakfasts are "exceptional and generous". The place is infor-mally run by a helpful staff. Children are welcomed. Serious foodies might like to take advantage of Langho's "Back to Back" offer of a two-night stay, with dinner one night at Paul Heathcote's two-starred restaurant at Longridge, 12 miles away (transport is included). Close by is the beautiful Ribble Valley, with wonderful walking, ruined abbeys, interesting museums and historic villages, many associated with witches. (*Eric Lee*)

Open All year, except 25 Dec, 2 Jan.
Rooms 1 suite, 13 double. 4 on ground floor, 1 adapted for &.
Facilities Lounge, drawing room, bar, restaurant; private dining/meeting room. 2-acre grounds. Shooting, hunting, fishing, golf nearby.
Location From M6 exit 31 take A59 to Clitheroe for 9½ miles; turn left immedi-ately before large roundabout at Langho. Train: Preston; good bus service.
Restrictions Smoking discouraged in dining room. No dogs.
Credit cards All major cards accepted.
Terms [1997] (*Excluding 10% optional service charge*) B&B: single £80, double £100, suite £120. Set lunch £15; dinner £37; full alc £45–£50. 1/2-night gourmet breaks.

LANGLEY MARSH Somerset   **Map 1**

Langley House   *Tel* (01984) 623318
Langley Marsh   *Fax* (01984) 624573
Wiveliscombe TA4 2UF

Peter and Anne Wilson's Grade II listed house stands at the edge of a small town amid the Brendon Hills, on the eastern side of Exmoor, in "some of the most magnificent countryside in the south-west". A hand-some gold grasshopper sign marks the entrance to the gravel drive. "Its gardens are a delight," wrote one visitor, "with a pond, tiny stream, and walled vegetable and herb garden, all surrounded by soft hills dot-ted with sheep. The decor, with emphasis on comfort as well as ele-gance, has been done with flair, using vibrant colours, antique furniture and rich fabrics; dainty ornaments and fresh and dried flow-ers abound. Bedrooms, up a curved staircase, are of medium size, with floral fabrics, flowers, books, magazines and excellent bedside lighting. We heard owls in the garden at night and awoke to the sound of sheep, lambs and birdsong." "Absolute perfection," says another. "One feels like the most pampered guest in a private home with a model hostess. Delicious food. Fantastic breakfast obviated the need for lunch." Dinner, at 8.30 pm, in the small beamed pink and green dining room, consists of three or four courses on weekdays, and five at weekends; no choice until dessert or cheese. One visitor thought the wine list unimag-inative, but Peter Wilson's "beautifully presented" modern English cooking has earned a *Michelin* red "Meals". Extra charges, for after-din-ner coffee and chocolates, morning tea and newspapers, etc, can bump up the bill. (*Hillary de Ste Croix, and others*)

Open All year.
Rooms 1 suite, 6 double, 1 single.
Facilities 2 drawing rooms, bar, restaurant, conservatory. 4½-acre garden: cro-
quet. Unsuitable for ♿.
Location ½ mile N of Wiveliscombe. Turn left at town centre. Train: Taunton;
then bus to Langley Cross.
Restrictions No smoking: restaurant, 2 bedrooms. No dogs in public rooms.
Credit cards Access, Amex, Visa.
Terms B&B: single £72.50–£75, double £90–£125, suite £145–£165. Set dinner: 3-
course £25.50, 4-course £30.65. Discount all year for 2 or more nights. 1-night
bookings sometimes refused weekends.

LASTINGHAM North Yorkshire   Map 4

Lastingham Grange   *Tel* (01751) 417345 and 417402
Lastingham YO6 6TH   *Fax* (01751) 417358

"What a place! Such individuality and charm, and a great position.
Efficient and friendly service; everything clean and well looked after."
A recent tribute to this unpretentious hotel, whose hosts, Dennis and
Jane Wood, pride themselves on "preserving traditional values of
country hospitality". Their old creeper-covered house, surrounded by
well-kept gardens, fine old trees and fields, stands in an old village,
where St Cedd built an abbey in the 7th century. This is the heart of the
North York Moors National Park, and there is wonderful walking from
the door. First opened in 1946 by Mr Wood's father, it has had a *Guide*
entry since the first edition. Inside, the decor is thoroughly traditional,
and well maintained, but again this year there are reports of beds that
are "on the lumpy side". The food has been described in the past as
"wholesome and generous"; but both dinner (not cheap) and breakfast
have been criticised this year. The wine list is straightforward and
reasonably priced. Newspapers, morning coffee, afternoon tea and
shoe-cleaning are included in the rates. Children are welcomed – they
have their own playground and ponies. "Teens," one guest wrote, "are
treated with respect that elicits adult behaviour"; there is baby-
listening at night. (*WL, and others*)

Open Beginning Mar–end Nov.
Rooms 10 double, 2 single.
Facilities Hall, lounge, dining room; laundry facilities. 10-acre grounds: garden,
adventure playground. In National Park, near moors and dales; riding, golf,
swimming nearby. Unsuitable for ♿.
Location Off A170, 5 miles NE of Kirkbymoorside. Turn N towards Appleton-le-
Moors 2 miles E of Kirkbymoorside.
Restrictions No smoking in dining room. No dogs in public rooms.
Credit cards None accepted.
Terms [1997] B&B: single £70.50–£76, double £131.25–£143; D,B&B: single
£85.25–£98, double £158.75–£181. Set lunch £15.50, dinner £27.75. Light, picnic
lunches available. Reductions for long stays; winter breaks. Children accommo-
dated free in parents' room. *V*

Letter to *The Times* Recently, in a lift in a Sydney hotel, I spotted
a button marked "Cancel Muzak". Can we hope that this brilliant idea will catch on in the UK?

LAVENHAM Suffolk   Map 2

The Great House   BUDGET   *Tel* (01787) 247431
Market Place   *Fax* (01787) 248007
Lavenham CO10 9QZ

Lavenham is an unspoiled medieval wool town, with a splendid
church and many lovely old houses, including this 15th-century building with a Georgian façade. Once the home of Stephen Spender, it is
now a French restaurant ("you could be in Normandy," one reader has
written) and a Logis of Great Britain. Other correspondents have
praised the kind proprietors, Régis and Martine Crépy, the courteous
all-French staff, and the welcome accorded to children. M. Crépy
serves traditional French dishes in the oak-beamed, candlelit dining
room, which still has its original inglenook fireplace. The *carte* can be
pricey, but the *prix fixe* offers plenty of choice "and is very good value".
The mainly French wine list includes plenty of reasonably priced bottles. Once a month there is an international week, with a guest chef. In
addition to a little sitting room/bar, there's a leafy rear garden with a
patio, where tea can be served. Up a creaky oak staircase are four
suites, each with a lounge or sitting area, individually controlled heating, and a "homey" decor – floral fabrics, antiques, old beams.
Windows may be on the small side and hard to shut tight, and sloping
floors are another period feature, but this year the bathrooms have
been given a face-lift. And the restaurant and bar have acquired a new
colour scheme, and been hung with new paintings, bought from local
art galleries. We'd like reports on these developments, please. One
visitor this year was surprised to be given shop-sliced bread and no
croissants at breakfast.

Open Feb–Dec. Closed Sun night/Mon, except bank holidays.
Rooms 4 suites.
Facilities Lounge/bar, restaurant (piped music all day); patio. ½-acre garden:
swings. Unsuitable for &.
Location Behind Market Cross, near Guildhall. Carpark.
Restrictions Smoking discouraged in restaurant. No dogs in public rooms.
Credit cards Access, Amex, Visa.
Terms [1997] B&B: single £45–£55, double £66–£88; D,B&B £49.95–£71.95. Set
lunch £12.95, dinner £16.95; full alc £32.75. Midweek breaks; off-season rates.
Children under 4 accommodated free in parents' room; 5–12 £15.

LEAMINGTON SPA Warwickshire   Map 3

The Lansdowne   BUDGET   *Tel* (01926) 450505
87 Clarendon Street   *Fax* (01926) 421313
Leamington Spa CV32 4PF

♀ *César award in 1989*

The medicinal powers of its water made this delightful town on the
river Leam a fashionable resort in the 18th and 19th centuries. Many
Regency town houses still survive, including David and Gillian Allen's
small hotel, which stands, fronted by a monkey-puzzle tree, at a busy
crossroads near the centre. Some rooms are very small, and not all have
en suite facilities, but it continues to be popular with our readers. "I was
impressed by the genuine welcome," runs one of this year's warm

endorsements. "The owner was efficient, pleasant and genuine, not at all fawning. I arrived too late for dinner, so I was given sandwiches and an agreeable half bottle of wine in my room. Breakfast included really good toast, jams in proper pots, and a simple cooked affair – no choice, but it was fine. I felt I had done very well for under £30." Others have written: "The atmosphere was excellent and the simple evening meal beautifully cooked – there was an entertaining cross-section of fellow diners, including locals – always a good sign. The wines were well chosen, with plenty of half bottles, and good value too." Public rooms are not large, but "delightfully done, with period pieces". Bedrooms, some very small, have pine furniture, spriggy fabrics and "every facility: alarm clock, fresh milk offered, etc"; but storage space can be limited. They are well insulated against traffic noise. There is a pretty, small garden. Convenient for Warwick Castle, the National Exhibition Centre (25 minutes by car) and the National Agricultural Centre (10 minutes). (*Andrew Davis, WS Rogers, and others*)

Open All year, except 24/25 Dec.
Rooms 10 double, 5 single. 2 on ground floor.
Facilities Lounge, bar (piped music at night), restaurant. Small garden. Discounts for local attractions. Not really suitable for &.
Location Central, on A425 (rear rooms quietest). Small private carpark.
Restrictions No smoking in restaurant. Preferably no children under 5. No dogs.
Credit cards Access, Visa.
Terms B&B: single £29.95–£49.95, double £39.90–£64.90; D,B&B £37.90–£67.90 per person. Lunch by arrangement. Set dinner from £17.95. 2/5-day breaks.

LECK Lancashire   **Map 4**

Cobwebs   *Tel/Fax* (01524 2) 72141
Leck, Cowan Bridge
nr Kirkby Lonsdale LA6 2HZ

"*Cobwebs* cheers, warms and comforts," write enthusiastic inspectors of this small restaurant-with-rooms. "It is a stone-built house, domestic in scale, much extended, in peaceful open countryside, amid fields with sheep. It is warm, clean, and professionally run in a personal style. Paul Kelly, pleasant, chatty and informal, greets guests and carries bags. The sitting rooms are closely packed with couches, armchairs and tables. The bedrooms are quite small with a Victorian/Edwardian feel. Ours had busy wallpaper, floral fabrics of various kinds, and framed coloured prints (sentimental Victorian-style portraits and views). It looked over a bucolic landscape. The bathroom had marble-ised plastic cladding that was not to our taste, but it was well equipped, with good lighting, loads of towels, unlimited hot water and adequate shelf space. The restaurant seats only 16, so its atmosphere is intimate. Yvonne Thompson's cooking is modern and highly competent, with excellent presentation. The selection of wines (Paul Kelly's passion) is exceptional, with a good-value Antipodean section, as well as some very expensive bottles. Breakfast was excellent, with a huge choice. Prices are modest." Other visitors have praised the "stunning home-made breads" and the "kindly hostess", and found the decor "hectic, with much pink, but not a cobweb". Some bathrooms are tiny. An eight-mile walk along Leck Beck starts close by. The market town of Kirkby Lonsdale, two miles away, has a 12th-century bridge across the river Lune, and a Norman church. Two national parks, the Lake District, and Ingleton, with caves and waterfalls, are nearby.

Open Mid-Mar–end Dec.
Rooms 5 double.
Facilities 2 lounges, conservatory restaurant (piped classical music). 4-acre grounds. Golf, riding, fishing nearby. Unsuitable for &.
Location 2 miles SE of Kirkby Lonsdale. A65 to Cowan Bridge. Left at General Store, signposted Leck. Go under railway bridge; *Cobwebs* on left.
Restrictions No smoking in restaurant. No children under 12. No dogs.
Credit cards Access, Visa.
Terms [1997] B&B: single £45, double £60. Set dinner £28. Gourmet wine weekends.

LEDBURY Herefordshire   Map 3

Hope End   *Tel* (01531) 633613
Ledbury HR8 1JQ   *Fax* (01531) 636366
♢ *César award in 1992*

John and Patricia Hegarty's idiosyncratic hotel (Relais du Silence) was the childhood home of Elizabeth Barrett Browning. It is set amid romantic, wild gardens with rambling roses, courtyards, gothic temples and a grotto, in a hidden valley near the harmonious old market town. A vast walled organic vegetable and fruit garden supplies the kitchen. The internal decor is of upmarket simplicity: wood-burning stoves, polished floors, modern pine, woven fabrics, autumn colours, books everywhere. There is a romantic suite in a minaret – all that remains of an earlier Moorish fantasy. "This must be the most peaceful hotel in England" is one recent compliment. "No TV, no radio. Absolute bliss." But some bedrooms have "paper-thin" walls, and though one couple felt safe – "our fellow guests did not look as though they had come for a weekend of unbridled lust" – others were less fortunate. The cooking "in modern British style", on a three-course dinner menu with choice at each stage, is admired: "Classy and original, with imaginative use of herbs. Breakfast one of the best anywhere: fresh juice, local yogurt, a perfect grill." *Hope End* does not suit those in search of conventional hotel facilities and a gushing welcome. "It operates to suit its own convenience," some say. "If you accept that, all will be well." But the "lack of false effusiveness" is one of the charms for the many regular visitors: "A lovely place; not cheap, but worth the money." "I enthusiastically endorse all the praise in the *Guide*. We felt quite at home – if only home were like that." The Hegartys operate a standby rate for last-minute bookings. (*AB, DW Tate. Mary Milne-Day, Bruce Douglas-Mann, and others*)

Open Feb–mid-Dec. Lunch not served.
Rooms 8 double. 1 in cottage 200 yds, 1 in minaret.
Facilities 3 lounges, dining room. 40-acre grounds: garden, walled garden, parkland. Unsuitable for &.
Location 2 miles N of Ledbury, just beyond Wellington Heath; signposted after railway station.
Restrictions No smoking in dining room. No children under 12. Dogs in car only.
Credit cards Access, Visa.
Terms [1997] B&B: single £87–£110, double £123–£144. Set dinner £30. Reductions for 2 or more nights; off-season breaks. 1-night bookings sometimes refused Sat.

LEEDS West Yorkshire   Map 4

42 The Calls   *Tel* (0113) 244 0099
42 The Calls   *Fax* (0113) 234 4100
Leeds LS2 7EW

Ϙ *César award in 1995*

"Can a more perfect hotel exist? Everything is exquisite, down to the
tiniest detail (hi-fi speakers in the bathroom, needles in the sewing kit
– a lacquered box – already threaded, books of short stories, current
magazines). Our spacious room at the back overlooked the river Aire.
Superb room service breakfast. I hope to spend all future holidays in
Leeds." "All the rooms are different; the more expensive ones are
exceptional. Extremely friendly staff." Two recent accolades for
Jonathan Wix's luxurious warehouse conversion in the lively waterfront area of central Leeds. It has a stunning ultra-modern decor. Each
bedroom has original pictures, a desk, a CD player, satellite TV, *three*
telephones, a lavish bathroom, and jokey touches (frog soaps, smarties
on pillows). Continental breakfast is delivered via a hatch; downstairs
there's an impressive buffet and a good selection of cooked items. The
adjacent restaurant, *Pool Court at 42*, serving *"haute cuisine* with an
Italian influence", has a *Michelin* star. In summer, meals can be taken on
its distinctive waterfront balcony. The popular *Brasserie 44* (swings for
bar seats, tables close together, loud jazz) serves modern, ungimmicky
food with a Mediterranean influence. "Exemplary cooking, chaotic but
delightful service," one visitor wrote of it this year. The hotel is busi-
ness-orientated during the week, and offers generous weekend reductions to pilgrims to this now trendy city, visited for its nightlife, its
opera and theatre, its Victorian architecture and new Harvey Nichols,
and its proximity to the Yorkshire Dales. (*Claire Wrathall, Mrs M Dwan*)

Open All year, except 3 days Christmas. Restaurants closed Sat midday/Sun,
bank holidays (24-hour room service).
Rooms 3 suites, 32 double, 6 single. 1 suitable for ⅏.
Facilities Lift. Lounge, bar, breakfast room, 2 restaurants; conference facilities.
Location Central, near Corn Exchange (rooms double/triple-glazed; quiet
ones overlook river). Hard to find; hotel will send directions. Private and street
parking.
Restrictions Smoking discouraged in restaurants; banned in 6 bedrooms.
"Friendly dogs only"; not in public rooms (except guide dogs).
Credit cards All major cards accepted.
Terms [1997] Rooms: single £95 (£65 weekend), double £140 (£70 weekend), suite
£220 (£130 weekend). Breakfast: continental £6.95, English £11. Cot for child £5.
Restaurant: set lunch £12.50–£17.50, dinner £24.50–£39.50; brasserie: set lunch
£7.95–£11.95, dinner (7.15–8.15 pm) £8.75–£11.95; full alc £26.50. ***V***

Haley's   *Tel* (0113) 278 4446
Shire Oak Road   *Fax* (0113) 275 3342
Headingley, Leeds LS6 2DE

"Quiet surroundings. Warm welcome. Tempting, if relatively small
dinner menu. Well-trained young staff." "No sycophancy; real friendliness." Recent praise for John Appleyard's turreted Victorian mansion,
named after a master stonemason prominent in Leeds at the turn of the
century. It is in a quiet road in the leafy suburb near the university.

Though "country house" in style, it is only two miles from the city centre and eight miles from the airport. Carefully restored to its original Victorian splendour, it has a large hall, a bay-windowed drawing room, a fine staircase, open fires, period furniture, lavish drapes, and pictures everywhere, many with a cricketing theme in tribute to the famous cricket ground nearby. The hotel caters to a business clientele during the week, and each bedroom has two telephones, one on a desk; extras range from a trouser press to Harrogate toffee. The best rooms are in the turrets, with large curving windows; some are small. The restaurant, which has a striking brown-and-cream decor, appears in the *Good Food Guide*. Chef Jon Vennell serves "light modern cooking with a classical base" on a monthly-changing menu. Breakfast (Yorkshire or continental) is "a generous repast". *Haley's* is licensed for civil weddings. This year an annexe, with seven new bedrooms and a meeting room, was due for completion, so we'd like more reports, please.

Open All year, except 26–30 Dec. Restaurant closed midday Mon–Sat, to non-residents evening Sun.
Rooms 2 2-room suites, 10 double, 8 single. 7 more in annexe planned for late 1997.
Facilities Lounge, lounge/bar, restaurant (piped classical music/jazz); function room. Small front lawn. Unsuitable for &.
Location 2 miles N of centre. Turn off A660 Leeds–Otley between Yorkshire and Midland banks in Headingley. Private parking.
Restrictions No smoking: restaurant, library, some bedrooms. No dogs.
Credit cards All major cards accepted.
Terms [1997] B&B: single £110 (£63 weekend), double £125 (£89 weekend), suite £170 (£220 weekend). Set Sun lunch £14.50; full alc £29. Weekend break (2 nights min.): D,B&B from £145 per person. Child in cot in parents' room £10. ***V***

LEONARD STANLEY Gloucestershire   Map 3

The Grey Cottage   **BUDGET**   *Tel/Fax* (01453) 822515
Bath Road
Leonard Stanley
Stonehouse GL10 3LU

"Enclosed by a nine-foot-high yew edge, a beautiful garden surrounds this 1807 cottage, probably once owned by a weaver, and now lorded over by a hundred-foot sequoia, planted in 1864 to commemorate Wellington's victory at Waterloo. The hosts, Andrew and Rosemary Reeves, charming, capable and dedicated but never intrusive, have restored the beauty of the old building and furnished it with interesting and appropriate pieces. The balloon dining chairs are 140 years old, and a writing bureau was used by a general in the Crimean War. Flowers, mostly from the garden, fill the public rooms. The food is of premium quality, abundant and imaginatively prepared. There is a huge choice at breakfast. We were offered tea and scones in the afternoon." "Never have we been so cosseted, in such a sensitive manner." That enthusiasm is endorsed by praise from New York: "Everything is of high quality, down to china, silver and crystal, and bed-linen and towels which are changed daily. The bedrooms have a large selection of hot drinks, biscuits, chocolates, fruit, fresh flowers, magazines, local information, dressing gowns, even ear plugs in case of early-morning tractors in summer." Meals are taken at a polished dining table in front of a log fire, or in a sunny conservatory. Dinner – "good and varied home-cooking" – is by prior arrangement. No licence; guests may bring

their drinks, and there is an honesty bar. Advance booking essential. A
fine Norman church is all that remains of the medieval priory which
once stood in the village. Wildfowl Trust at Slimbridge, Berkeley
Castle, and the Westonbirt Arboretum are nearby. (*Bob H Marshall, Mrs
SV Smith, Robin Oaten, and others*)

Open All year, except Christmas and occasionally at other times.
Rooms 2 double, 1 single. No telephone.
Facilities Sitting room with conservatory, honesty bar, dining room. ¼-acre gar-
den. Unsuitable for &.
Location 3 miles W of Stroud. 1 mile S of A419, between King's Stanley and
Leonard Stanley. Train: Stonehouse, 1½ miles; then local bus.
Restrictions No smoking: dining room, bedrooms. No dogs.
Credit cards Credit cards not accepted.
Terms B&B: single £29–£32, double £46–£54; D,B&B: single £45–£50, double
£78–£90. Reductions for 2/3 nights.

LEWDOWN Devon   Map 1

Lewtrenchard Manor   Tel (01566) 783256
Lewdown, nr Okehampton EX20 4PN   Fax (01566) 783332

"A beautiful house in lovely, slightly neglected gardens that add to its
Secret Garden-ish charms. It is furnished with taste and slight eccentricity. Chef Jason Buck's modern English/French cooking is above
average; service in the restaurant is charming, and the breakfasts are
particularly good. The hotel has its own spring, and the water is delicious. In May the bluebells and primroses in the garden are a beautiful
sight. The proprietors seem to be around all the time, caring for their
guests." That report by a regular *Guide* correspondent on Sue and
James Murray's grey stone manor is endorsed by most visitors this
year, though one complained: "The menu did not change during our
stay," and another thought the food pretentious. The place is run on
house party lines. Elizabethan in origin, with mullioned windows and
a dovecote, it stands near a church in a peaceful Devon valley. It was
once the home of the Revd Sabine Baring-Gould, author of the hymn
"Onward Christian Soldiers". His renovations have given it a predominantly Victorian interior: ornate plaster ceilings, dark oak panelling,
large fireplaces with log fires; there are portraits everywhere, knick-
knacks, gleaming brass door-handles and locks, and cats and dogs.
Bedrooms are on the first floor off a long gallery, reached by an impressive staircase. It is worth paying extra for a garden-facing one. No key,
but you can bolt yourself in. (*RCJ Gordon, and others*)

Open All year.
Rooms 1 suite, 8 double.
Facilities Stair lift. 2 lounges, bar lounge, 2 dining rooms (classical music); ball-
room. 11-acre grounds: garden, croquet, fishing lake, clay pigeon-shooting.
River fishing nearby; sea 4 miles.
Location Off A30 between Okehampton and Launceton. Follow signs for
Lewtrenchard.
Restrictions No smoking in dining rooms. Children by arrangement. No dogs in
public rooms.
Credit cards All major cards accepted.
Terms [1997] B&B: single £80–£95, double £105–£140, suite £145. Set lunch £16,
dinner £28. Off-season discounts, Christmas house party. 1-night bookings
refused bank holidays.

LEWES East Sussex   Map 2

Berkeley House   `BUDGET`   *Tel/Fax* (01273) 476057
2 Albion Street
Lewes BN7 2ND

This small B&B is a Grade II listed house, part of a Georgian terrace in
a small street near the centre of the county town of East Sussex. It
makes a good base for visiting Glyndebourne, close by. "The owner,
Roy Patten, an opera enthusiast, is accommodating and unassuming,"
write returning visitors. "There are many touches over and above what
is normally expected." Breakfast is a generous affair, "with *hot* toast,
but weak coffee". One couple had a "minuscule" room in the eaves,
which they thought overpriced, but others have written: "The epitome
of a *GHG* hotel, with that 'home from home' feeling. Roy Patten does
all he can to make your stay memorable." (*B Nicol, Mrs JC Smye, Roger
Diamond, and others*)

Open All year, except Christmas.
Rooms 1 suite, 4 double. All with shower. No telephone.
Facilities Lounge, breakfast room; roof terrace. Unsuitable for &.
Location Near centre. Carpark opposite.
Restrictions No smoking: breakfast room, 1 bedroom. No dogs.
Credit cards Access, Amex, Visa.
Terms B&B: single £40–£47.50, double £47.50–£55, suite £70. Special breaks: 25%
discount. More reports, please. *V*

LIFTON Devon   Map 1

The Arundell Arms   *Tel* (01566) 784666
Lifton PL16 0AA   *Fax* (01566) 784494

This traditional creeper-covered coaching inn stands on a road in a
small Devon town, with a pretty terraced garden behind, complete
with one of the few remaining cockpits in England. It is well known
for its fishing – Ann Voss-Bark, the owner for over 35 years, and her
husband Conrad, a former BBC political correspondent, are expert fly-
fishers, and both have written books on the subject. The hotel has
20 miles of trout-, sea trout- and salmon-fishing on the river Tamar
and four of its tributaries, and a three-acre stocked lake. There are full-
time fishing instructors, and courses of all kinds are offered (you need
to book early); fisherfolk set off for the day with a packed lunch in a
wicker basket. There is good shooting, too, and the hotel also welcomes families, and non-sporting guests, one of whom, a regular
visitor, writes: "We love staying here. It is not really luxurious, but it
has many good points which we consider more important. The staff,
almost all local, are delightful. The food, both in the dining room and
in the bar, is excellent, and the wines are reasonably priced. Service is
genuinely friendly. An excellent stop on the way to Cornwall." Others,
too, have admired the "modern English cooking, with a traditional
French influence", of chef Philip Burgess, who has presided over the
kitchens for 15 years. A refurbishment of the bedrooms was recently
completed. They vary greatly in size and style; quietest ones are at the
back. There's a variety of off-season packages; functions and conferences are catered for. Two contrasting National Trust properties,

Lutyens's Castle Drogo and 15th-century Cotehele, are close by. (*LF Leech, A and CR, and others*)

Open All year, except 2 days over Christmas.
Rooms 20 double, 8 single. 5 in annexe opposite.
Facilities Ramp. Lounge, cocktail bar, public bar, 2 dining rooms; conference/meeting rooms; games room, skittle alley. ½-acre terraced garden. 20 miles fishing rights on river Tamar and tributaries, 3-acre stocked lake, fishing school for beginners. Only restaurant suitable for &.
Location ½ mile off A30, 3 miles E of Launceston, Road-facing rooms double-glazed. Train: Exeter, 40 miles; then taxi.
Restrictions No smoking in restaurant. No dogs in restaurant.
Credit cards All major cards accepted.
Terms B&B: £42–£68; D,B&B (min. 2 nights) £66–£85. Bar meals. Set meals (2/3 courses): lunch £15.50/£19, dinner £27.50–£35. 2–6-night breaks all year; off-season breaks: sporting, gourmet, etc. Children under 16 accommodated free in parents' room.

LINCOLN Lincolnshire   Map 4

D'Isney Place Hotel   *Tel* (01522) 538881
Eastgate   *Fax* (01522) 511321
Lincoln LN2 4AA

David and Judy Payne's Georgian B&B, with Victorian extensions, is in the heart of the city; the wall of the cathedral close forms the southern boundary of its garden. It has no public rooms, but a good breakfast (English or continental) is served in the bedrooms. These vary greatly in size and style: some are quite basic, others "charming, with a spacious bathroom"; one has a four-poster, and three have a jacuzzi. Some get traffic noise, others are praised for their quietness. Reports to the *Guide* therefore tend to be mixed, but those who are fortunate with their accommodation write with enthusiasm: "Quite excellent." "Beautifully warm on a freezing day." "Unpretentious, pretty and comfortable. Fresh flowers and pretty china on breakfast tray. Service unobtrusive but solicitous. Weekend bargain break excellent value." The *Wig and Mitre*, a pub/café/restaurant, and *The Jew's House* (in one of the oldest inhabited houses in Britain) are recommended for meals. (*C Beadle, and others*)

Open All year.
Rooms 16 double, 1 single. 2 in cottage annexe with sitting room, kitchen, dining room. Some on ground floor.
Facilities Ramps. 1-acre garden adjoining cathedral.
Location By cathedral. Front rooms double-glazed; back ones quietest. Limited private parking; street parking after 6 pm. Bus, taxi from station.
Restriction No smoking in 10 bedrooms.
Credit cards All major cards accepted.
Terms B&B: single £57, double £72–£92. Weekend breaks. ***V***

LITTLE MALVERN Worcestershire   Map 3

Holdfast Cottage   *Tel* (01684) 310288
Marlbank Road   *Fax* (01684) 311117
Little Malvern WR13 6NA

"A charming place, with welcoming hosts, and excellent home-cooked meals. Our bedroom was small and rather busily furnished, but well equipped." This report on Stephen and Jane Knowles' 17th-century cottage, pretty, long and low, with Victorian extensions, endorses earlier praise: "They combine professional expertise with a caring manner. Food is original without being pretentious. Sweets are particularly delicious. Breakfast is in the best English tradition; no plastic containers. Service is exemplary." "Odd little staircases abound, leading to small, pretty bedrooms; teddy bear on chair, duck and small boat in well-equipped bathroom. Warm throughout." There is a small beamed hall, and a diminutive bar opening on to a wisteria-covered terrace with lovely views of the Malvern Hills. In the dining room, which has prints on the walls and candles, flowers and knick-knacks on tables, Mrs Knowles offers three choices for each course. Rolls are home-baked, ice-creams home-made, herbs home-grown. Children are welcomed. The setting is agreeably rural, amid trees and farmland. Sir Edward Elgar is buried in the Roman Catholic cemetery in the village. Gloucester, Worcester, Hereford and Tewkesbury are all within easy reach. (*Jan Wansell, and others*)

Open All year, except Christmas, 3 weeks Jan.
Rooms 7 double, 1 single.
Facilities Lounge, conservatory, bar, restaurant. 2-acre grounds: small wood, croquet. Unsuitable for &.
Location On A4104 midway between Welland and Little Malvern. Train: Great Malvern.
Restrictions No smoking: dining room, bedrooms. No dogs in public rooms, except conservatory.
Credit cards Access, Visa.
Terms B&B: single £42–£44, double £76–£85; D,B&B £52–£73 per person. Set dinner £19. Short breaks all year; 10% reduction for weekly stays. New Year package. *V*

LITTLE PETHERICK Cornwall   Map 1

Molesworth Manor   NEW/BUDGET   *Tel* (01841) 540292
Little Petherick
nr Padstow PL27 7QT

"A wonderful hideaway", in a village at the head of the Camel estuary. It is a Grade II* listed 17th-century rectory, converted into a manor house in the 19th century by Sir Hugh Molesworth; his coat of arms features in the tall windows on the main staircase. It has a period feel and an interesting decor. "We visit often and are never disappointed by the warmth of welcome from Peter Pearce and Heather Clarke, and the high standards," writes the nominator. "The house is tastefully furnished throughout. Accommodation varies from grand to simple, as evidenced by the bedroom names: Her Ladyship's, His Lordship's, Butler's, Maid's, etc. We've yet to discover one without space and ambience. There are separate lounges for reading, TV and music, which makes for a peaceful atmosphere. The breakfast spread obviates the need for lunch; and afternoon tea on the terrace is a real treat." No dinners, but the dining room table is willingly laid for guests who choose to bring their own food, and the owners are licensed to sell wine. There is a two-room family suite, but not much in the way of entertainment for children. Many pubs, bistros, and restaurants nearby, including the famous *Seafood Restaurant* (*qv*) in Padstow, which can be reached on foot by a coastal path. The Heritage Coastline and

Lanhydrock House (National Trust) are nearby; good bird-watching.
(*R Hoseason*)

Open Jan–Oct.
Rooms 2 suites (1 family), 7 double, 2 single. No telephone/TV.
Facilities Library/drawing room, morning room, TV room, music room, study,
conservatory, breakfast room, dining room. 1-acre garden; gym. Close to sea:
fishing, boating, sailing, etc. Unsuitable for &.
Location 2 miles SE of Padstow. From A39 Wadebridge–Truro, take A389 to
Padstow; through St Issey into Little Petherick; over hump-back bridge; hotel
300 yds on right. Train: Bodmin, 14 miles.
Restrictions No smoking. No dogs.
Credit cards None accepted.
Terms [Until 30 Apr 1998] B&B £20–£28.

LITTLE SINGLETON Lancashire   Map 4

Mains Hall   *Tel* (01253) 885130
86 Mains Lane   *Fax* (01253) 894132
Little Singleton   *E-mail* mains.hall@Blackpool.net
nr Blackpool FY6 7LE

Handy for those who cannot stand the rigours of staying in nearby
Blackpool, this white-walled Grade II listed house on the river Wyre
was built by monks in the 16th century. In the 18th century, it was the
home of Maria Fitzherbert, who was courted and married here by
Prince George, later George IV. Today, couples marry in the marquee-
style conservatory (also used for conferences and other functions) and
are photographed in sheltered gardens, which feature orchards, walnut trees and a fountain. The decor of *Mains Hall* is in keeping with the
date of the house. Some of the bedrooms have a four-poster or half-
tester bed, and all are stocked with mineral water and fresh fruit. In the
attic are three simple rooms, "suitable for teenagers". The nominator,
who describes the owner, Roger Yeomans, as "a lovely chap who will
look after your every need", adds: "Helpful staff, convivial atmosphere, a little like a weekend country house party. The restaurant is
beautiful, and the wine list is extensive, with tastes and prices to suit all
pockets." This year there is a new chef, Gary Marsland, who has introduced a simpler, brasserie-style menu. We'd be grateful for reports on
this development.

Open All year.
Rooms 11 double.
Facilities Garden room, library, bar, 2 dining rooms (piped "easy listening"
music); conservatory (for functions). 5-acre garden: river frontage.
Location 6 miles NE of Blackpool. From M55 exit 3, follow signs for Fleetwood
(A585) for 5 miles. Hotel is ½ mile on right, past 2nd set of traffic lights. Train:
Blackpool; then taxi.
Restrictions No smoking in some bedrooms. No dogs in public rooms.
Credit cards All major cards accepted.
Terms [1997] B&B: single £40–£70, double £50–£100. Full alc £20. ***V***

Don't trust out-of-date editions of the *Guide*. Hotels change
hands, deteriorate or go out of business. Many hotels are
dropped and new ones added every year.

LITTLEBURY GREEN Essex   Map 2

Elmdon Lee   `BUDGET`   *Tel/Fax* (01763) 838237
Littlebury Green
nr Saffron Walden CB11 4XB

Diana Duke's large 18th-century farmhouse is a Wolsey Lodge on the
outskirts of village near Saffron Walden, 16 miles from Cambridge. The
M11 is close by, but the house has a quiet setting in a 900-acre working
farm, managed by Mrs Duke's son Robert. "It is attractive, welcoming
and unpretentious," writes a returning visitor, "and very good value.
We enjoyed sitting by an open fire in the large drawing room. A good
home-cooked dinner, by arrangement, was served *en famille* at 7.30 pm.
The wine mark-up is remarkably low. Our bedroom was large, with
views of trees. Breakfast is of the high cholesterol variety." "A kind and
thoughtful hostess," add 1997 visitors. "We thoroughly enjoyed our
stay." Audley End, the impressive house built by Thomas Howard,
Earl of Suffolk, in a landscaped park, is nearby. (*Andrew Palmer, Dawn
and Geoffrey Loyd*)

Open All year, except Christmas Day.
Rooms 3 double, 1 single. No telephone.
Facilities Sitting room, TV room, dining room; craft shop. 1-acre garden.
Unsuitable for &.
Location Outskirts of Littlebury Green, between villages of Littlebury on B1383,
and Elmdon, just off B1039. Travelling from north, M11 exit 10, from south,
exit 8.
Restrictions No children. No dogs.
Credit cards Access, Diners, Visa.
Terms B&B: single £30–£35, double £60–£65. Set dinner £16.50.

LIVERPOOL Merseyside *See SHORTLIST*   Map 4

LODDISWELL Devon   Map 1

Hazelwood House   `BUDGET`   *Tel* (01548) 821232
Loddiswell   London office: (0171) 538 5633
nr Kingsbridge TQ7 4EB   *Fax* (01548) 821318

This early Victorian house is set up a long drive in huge, rambling
grounds, above a valley sweeping down to the river Avon. The trio of
owners, Jane Bowman, Gillian Kean and Anabel Watson, are involved
in the Dandelion Trust which organises conservation and cultural projects in the UK, and "Through Heart to Peace" projects in Ethiopia,
Bosnia and Armenia. At *Hazelwood* they run a busy programme of
courses and lectures, and there are regular musical weekends involv-
ing groups such as the Medici String Quartet. Some visitors have found
the "Mystic Path atmosphere" and the emphasis on organic food too
much. But one seasoned traveller dubbed it "a delightful spot".
Another said: "It won't suit everyone, but it worked for me. The setting
is magnificent. The welcome, including that by the 'outside concierge',
a soft labrador, could not be faulted. The sense of peace and friendliness has to be experienced to be appreciated fully." A third praised
"the staff's tolerance, and marvellous sense of fun". The decor is

"delightful mix" of simple furniture and antiques and paintings. The small bedrooms "are clean and fresh". Simple meals, with little choice, are prepared in the enormous Victorian kitchen and served communally, accompanied by the house's own spring water, and organic wines, one red, one white. Sandy beaches, fishing and moorland walks are nearby. (*Michael Crick, Chris Kay, Maryly La Follette*)

Open All year.
Rooms 1 suite, 11 double, 4 single. 1 with bath, 1 with shower. 1 on ground floor. No telephone/TV. 4 self-catering cottages.
Facilities Lounge, reading room (with payphone), TV room, dining room. 67-acre grounds, river.
Location 4 miles E of Loddiswell. From California Cross on B3207 Dartmouth–Modbury take road to Kingsbridge/Loddiswell. Left after *c.* ¾ mile to Hazelwood. Gate with stone pillars on right. Train: Totnes, 14 miles; then taxi.
Restrictions No smoking: bedrooms, public rooms sometimes. Dogs by arrangement.
Credit cards None accepted.
Terms B&B £23.50–£32.90, full board from £42. Set lunch £7.50, dinner £14; full alc £28. Children 4–12 half price. Cultural events and courses. Negotiable rates for parties, groups, etc. *V*

LONDON   Map 2

The Abbey Court   NEW   *Tel* (0171) 221 7518
20 Pembridge Gardens, W2 4DU   *Fax* (0171) 792 0858

This smart little town house B&B is in a relatively quiet street near Notting Hill Gate and Portobello Road, convenient for transport to the West End and the City. Outside are window-boxes, bay trees and carriage lamps, inside antique and period furniture and imposing flower arrangements. Bedrooms are mostly medium-sized, though one single is extremely small. They vary from grand to cottagey in style; some have a four-poster, others a brass bed; some also have armchairs and a desk. All have a marble bathroom with a whirlpool bath. Breakfast, light meals and tea are brought to the room (£7 surcharge) or served in a conservatory, which, say recent visitors, "is charming, but crowded at times". Not for the infirm – five storeys, no lift, and stairs up to the entrance and down to the basement. (*John and Susan Colby, and others*)

Open All year.
Rooms 3 suites, 13 double, 6 single.
Facilities Lounge, conservatory/bar/breakfast room ("mellow" piped music). Small patio garden. Access to nearby private health club. Unsuitable for &.
Location Central. Meter parking. (Underground: Notting Hill Gate.)
Restrictions No smoking: conservatory during meals, 11 bedrooms. Guide dogs only.
Credit cards All major cards accepted.
Terms [1997] B&B: single £88–£118, double £120–£145, suite £157–£175. Light alc meals and teas available. Room service £7 surcharge. *V*

Basil Street Hotel   *Tel* (0171) 581 3311
8 Basil Street, SW3 1AH   *Fax* (0171) 581 3693
 Ω *César award in 1993*

This Edwardian hotel in Knightsbridge is beloved by its many regulars for its "delightful Englishness" and its country house feel. Privately owned by one family for 85 years, it has old-fashioned public rooms with antiques, oriental rugs, mirrors and paintings. The dining room is traditional, with formally dressed waiters and immaculate linen. Female guests have their own domain, the Parrot Club. Under the regime of the new manager, David Brockett, there have been changes, such as the introduction of double-glazing and air-conditioning, which not everyone welcomes. And an American guest who first visited 20 years ago thought the place rather expensive now for what it offers, but others consider it "good value for a taste of gracious old-world standards, especially if you opt for a bedroom that does not have an *en suite* bathroom". The ever-efficient room service and shoe-cleaning, and the much improved food and service in the dining room are praised, and so are staff: "pleasant as always". "The welcome may not be personal, but it is charming and efficient," wrote long-standing *Guide* hoteliers. Other visitors enjoyed the breakfast – "no buffet, nothing packaged; you are waited on." Bedrooms are not lavishly endowed with extras, and they vary greatly. Some are spacious, with a large bathroom; some have noise from traffic, a nearby fire station or neighbouring bedrooms (earplugs can be provided). Some, overlooking a courtyard, are "exceptionally quiet, if small". Children are warmly welcomed. (*Jenny Parks, Richard Creed, Nigel and Margaret Corbett, and others*)

Open All year.
Rooms 4 family, 42 double, 41 single. 76 with facilities *en suite*.
Facilities Lift. Lounge bar, ladies' club, dining room (pianist at night); function facilities. Unsuitable for &.
Location Central; public carpark nearby. (Underground: Knightsbridge.)
Restrictions No smoking in 2 bedrooms. No dogs in public rooms.
Credit cards All major cards accepted.
Terms [1997] (*Excluding VAT on accommodation*) Rooms: single £115, double £170. Extra bed £15. Breakfast: continental £9.50, English £13.50. Set lunch (2-course) *c.* £10 approx, set dinner (2/3-course) *c.* £17–£21; full alc £27.50. Concessions to regular visitors; special rates Aug, winter, bank holidays; long-stay rates.

Bloom's   NEW   *Tel* (0171) 323 1717
7 Montague Street, WC1B 5BP   *Fax* (0171) 636 6498
                              E-mail blooms@mermaid.co.uk

18th-century town house in heart of Bloomsbury, at side of British Museum (Underground: Russell Square). Cosy small lounge with library-like air and bagatelle board; varied breakfast (but poor coffee) in smallish no-smoking room leading to patio garden; helpful staff. 24-hour piped classical music in public rooms. Light meals available in lounge or bedroom. 27 bedrooms, recently refurbished, some large; most are bright and well appointed and overlook patio. Unsuitable for &. No dogs. All major cards accepted. B&B: single £110, double £165–£175. Full alc £22 [1997]. More reports, please.

The Cadogan   *Tel* (0171) 235 7141
75 Sloane Street, SW1X 9SG   *Fax* (0171) 245 0994

In a prime position, handy for smart shops, restaurants, museums and Hyde Park, this has been a distinguished hotel for over 100 years. Lily Langtry (mistress of King Edward VII) was a visitor; Oscar Wilde was arrested while staying here, an event immortalised in a poem by John Betjeman: "...The door of the bedroom swung open / And TWO

PLAIN-CLOTHES POLICEMEN came in: / 'Mr Woilde, we 'ave come
for tew take yew / Where felons and criminals dwell: / We must ask
yew tew leave with us quoietly / For this is the *Cadogan Hotel.*'" In 1990
the hotel was taken over by Historic House Hotels Ltd, which exists to
conserve buildings of historical and architectural interest (see also
Hartwell House, Aylesbury, *Middlethorpe Hall,* York, and *Bodysgallen
Hall,* Llandudno). It is managed by Malcolm Broadbent. An extensive
restoration will be completed by 1998. The nominator, who liked the
"nice clubby atmosphere and pleasant staff", added: "The lounge is
agreeable for reading newspapers and taking coffee or tea. Bedrooms
are well designed and comfortable, without being OTT." And there is
a warm endorsement this year: "Two women with rucksacks in hand
are probably a nightmare for most Knightsbridge hotels. But here we
were made welcome. We admired the antique elevator, and enjoyed
the view of the garden square opposite, to which guests have access."
The Edwardian-style restaurant serves traditional British cooking
by Graham Thompson. Well placed for Sloane Square, Knightsbridge
and Hyde Park. In August a Buckingham Palace weekend (including a
visit to the palace's state apartments) is offered. (*Paul Henderson,
Kathryn Jourdan*)

Open All year. Restaurant closed Sat midday.
Rooms 5 suites, 56 double, 4 single. Some air-conditioned.
Facilities Drawing room, bar, restaurant; function facilities. Access to Cadogan
Square gardens opposite: tennis. Unsuitable for &.
Location Central (rear rooms quietest). Meter parking; NCP carpark opposite.
(Underground: Sloane Square, Knightsbridge.)
Restrictions No smoking in 20 bedrooms. No dogs.
Credit cards Access, Amex, Visa.
Terms [1997] Rooms: single £140–£190, double £185–£215, suite £290. Breakfast:
continental £10.50, English £14.50. Set lunch £17.90, dinner £25.50; full alc £40.
Weekend rates. Theatre packages, Buckingham Palace weekends.

The Capital   *Tel* (0171) 589 5171
22–24 Basil Street, SW3 1AT   *Fax* (0171) 225 0011

David and Margaret Levin's "grand hotel in miniature" (their description) is in a narrow but busy side street near Harrods. It has lavishly
decorated bedrooms with heavy fabrics, original oil paintings, flowers,
double-glazing, air-conditioning (which can be noisy), smart marble
bathroom and 24-hour room service. Some are quite dark. The public
rooms are lighter in style. There's a small lounge (where tea may be
served) and a pale-panelled bar. The restaurant has chandeliers, mirrors, honey-coloured walls and tapestry chairs, and a *Michelin* star for
Philip Britten's inventive cooking, which is served on four different
menus. Best value is the lunchtime *table d'hôte.* In the evening there are
two "tasting" menus ("Temptation" with seven courses, "Seduction"
with nine), and a long *carte* on which main dishes cost about £25. The
hotel's residents may also eat in the *Metro* wine bar in the basement of
its much cheaper sister, *L'Hotel (qv),* almost next door. A reporter this
year wrote of a visit when a number of things went wrong, but others
would never stay anywhere else in the city. One said: "Service probably the best in London, with old-fashioned courtesy. The restaurant is
lovely; food very good, if exorbitantly expensive." We'd like more
reports, please.

Open All year.
Rooms 8 suites, 28 double, 12 single.
Facilities Lift. Lounge, bar, restaurant; 2 private dining rooms, business facilities.
Location Central (rooms double-glazed; rear ones quietest). Garage for 12 cars (£20 per night). (Underground: Knightsbridge.)
Restriction Dogs at management's discretion, not in public rooms.
Credit cards All major cards accepted.
Terms [1997] (*Excluding VAT on accommodation*) Rooms: single £167, double £207–£260, suite £310. Breakfast: continental £12.50, English £16.50. Set lunch £25, dinner £55 and £75; full alc £60. Weekend rates.

The Connaught   *Tel* (0171) 499 7070
Carlos Place, W1Y 6AL   *Fax* (0171) 495 3262

This grand old London institution in Mayfair celebrated its centenary in style in 1997, when the Queen came to dinner (it is named for her great-great uncle, Prince Arthur, Duke of Connaught, the third son of Queen Victoria). One of London's most exclusive hotels, it is owned by the Savoy Group. For 24 years it was managed by Paolo Zago; he will be succeeded in October 1997 by Duncan Palmer. With its uniformed staff, the hotel offers what readers have called "a standard of discreet service almost unknown these days, without a hint of pretension". Guests' privacy is jealously guarded, bedrooms are often booked months in advance. Public rooms are panelled and staid, with formal, fragrant flower arrangements, and a splendid mahogany staircase. "We have been visiting the *Connaught* for over 16 years, and consider it the best hotel in the world," say veteran hoteliers. "The restaurant manager, M. Chevallier, is the most courteous, considerate and efficient we have ever encountered." The *Michelin*-starred kitchen serves both the restaurant, grandly elegant with gleaming panels, arched windows and glittering chandeliers, and the more intimate green-walled Grill Room. Formal dress is *de rigueur*. Michel Bourdin's cooking has been described as "maintaining links with the classic traditions that have been all but obliterated by the quick tricks of 'modern British' cuisine". On the wide-ranging *carte*, classic French dishes rub shoulders with traditional English fare. There is also a small daily-changing *table d'hôte* menu for lunch and dinner in both restaurants. Recent praise: "The restaurant service is impeccable. As many waiters as diners, all busy – carving the joint on the trolley, flambéeing dishes at the table, pouring wine; no rush, no delays." "One of the most *home-like* hotels we have stayed in. The staff were friendly and warm. We had a magnificent suite – high-ceilinged, with good lighting, and immaculate marble bathroom." "Top-class breakfast." Children of all ages are warmly welcomed. (*Francis Coulson and Brian Sack, CR, and others*)

Open All year.
Rooms 24 suites, 36 double, 30 single.
Facilities Lift. 2 lounges, cocktail bar, Grill Room, restaurant; private dining room.
Location Central. Limited private parking. (Underground: Bond St.)
Restrictions Guests asked to refrain from smoking in restaurants. No dogs.
Credit cards All major cards accepted.
Terms [1997] (*Excluding VAT on accommodation*): Rooms: single £215, double £285–£310, suite £570. Breakfast: continental £16.50 (*plus 15% service charge*); English alc. Set lunch £25 (Sun £30), dinner: Grill Room: £35, restaurant £55; full alc from £50.

The Covent Garden Hotel `NEW`   *Tel* (0171) 806 1000
10 Monmouth St, WC2H 9HB   *Fax* (0171) 816 1100
                                E-mail firmdale@dircon.co.uk

Former French hospital in Seven Dials (where seven streets converge), close to Covent Garden, theatres, interesting shops (Underground: Leicester Sq, Covent Gdn). Cleverly converted into luxurious hotel with stylish decor. Smiling reception. Classy foyer; wrought-iron staircase leads to large, colourful lounge. 50 spacious bedrooms (some on two levels), with cellular phone, fax, CD player, TV/video, luxurious bathroom, double-glazing. Light meals and continental breakfast served in lounge or bedroom; cooked breakfast, lunch and dinner in small ground-floor brasserie (intrusive piped music; service sometimes over-stretched). Lift; gym. Public carpark nearby. No dogs. Access, Amex, Visa accepted. Rooms: single £165, double £190–£245, suite £280–£495 (excluding VAT). Breakfast: continental £12, English alc. More reports, please.

Dukes `NEW`   *Tel* (0171) 491 4840
35 St James's Place SW1A 1NY   *Fax* (0171) 493 1264
                              E-mail: dukeshotel@compuserve.com

On tiny courtyard off quiet street in St James's, near palaces, parks, National Gallery, smart shops, theatres. Luxurious hotel owned by David Naylor-Leyland, also owner of Egerton House (qv). Recent extensive refurbishment. High-quality traditional decor: antiques, oil paintings, porcelain, marble bathrooms; also air-conditioning. High standard of management and service. Bar claims to serve best martinis in London. Adequate meals in dining room (residents only); restaurants of all kinds close by. All major credit cards accepted. Unsuitable for ♿. No smoking at breakfast. No dogs. 64 rooms: single from £165, double £175–£215, suites £225–£450. Breakfast: continental £9.50, English £14 [1997] (excluding VAT). More reports, please.

Durrants   *Tel* (0171) 935 8131
George Street, W1H 6BJ   *Fax* (0171) 487 3510

"Quintessentially English and old-fashioned in style." "Delightful and well maintained." Recent comments on one of London's oldest privately owned hotels, which has been run by the Miller family since 1921. Composed of a row of terraced houses, it has a quaint and rambling interior: small panelled lounges with leather settees and chairs lead off a corridor. It is decorated with original paintings, prints and engravings of London, and antique furniture. Bedrooms are well maintained, but vary greatly (some are extremely small): the largest ones, at the front, get some traffic noise; and insulation between rooms is not always perfect. But *Durrants* is liked for its convenient location, its generally helpful staff, and the traditional meals with good service in the panelled restaurant. Good breakfasts too. Women visitors on their own have spoken warmly of their kindly reception. Oxford, Harley and Baker streets and the Wallace Collection (one of the world's finest art collections) are close by. The Miller family also own the *Red Lion* at Henley-on-Thames. (*IM, CW, and others*)

Open All year.
Rooms 4 suites, 69 double, 16 single. Some on ground floor. Some air-conditioned.

Facilities 3 lounges, bar, restaurant; function facilities. Sports centre nearby.
Location Central (rear rooms quietest). Public carpark 5 mins' walk. (Underground: Bond St.)
Restriction No dogs.
Credit cards Access, Amex, Visa.
Terms [1997] Rooms: single £87.50–£92.50, double £115–£125, suite £235. Breakfast: continental £7.75, English £10.75. Set lunch/dinner (2/3-course) £17/£21; full alc £40 (*plus 12½% "optional" service charge*).

Egerton House   *Tel* (0171) 589 2412
Egerton Terrace, SW3 2BX   *Fax* (0171) 584 6540

"Represents some kind of perfection in the town house category." "Smiling faces everywhere. Nothing is too much trouble. Scores eleven out of ten." Recent praise from Manchester and Vancouver for this smart little Knightsbridge hotel, "whose international clientele know a good thing when they find it". A red brick Victorian house on four floors, on a residential side-street – remarkably quiet for London – it is filled with good antiques, pictures and fabrics. Bedrooms (with impressive marble-clad bathroom) vary in size; most overlook private gardens to which guests have access. "Impeccable" breakfasts are taken in the bedrooms or in a pretty basement room. Afternoon tea is served in the drawing room; there is an honesty bar ("pricey"), and an extensive room-service menu, ranging from snacks to full meals. Shoe-cleaning and a newspaper are included in the rates. Accommodation is upgraded when possible. The *Egerton*'s owner, David Naylor-Leyland, also owns the *Franklin*, nearby, and *Dukes Hotel*, St James's, which makes its *Guide* debut this year. (*David and Kate Wooff, David Lodge*)

Open All year.
Rooms 21 double, 9 single. All air-conditioned.
Facilities Lifts. Drawing room, bar, breakfast room. 24-hour room service. Access to private gardens. Unsuitable for &.
Location Central. Valet parking. (Underground: South Kensington, Knightsbridge.)
Restrictions No smoking in breakfast room. No children under 8. No dogs.
Credit cards All major cards accepted.
Terms [1997] (*Excluding VAT*) Rooms: single £130, double £170–£210. Breakfast: continental £9, English £14. Light meals; full alc £20–£25.

The Goring   *Tel* (0171) 396 9000
Beeston Place   *Fax* (0171) 834 4393
Grosvenor Gardens, SW1W 0JW

❧ *César award in 1994*

"A terrific hotel; service is sensational." "Friendly, able staff. Bedrooms – even the singles – attractive: pretty mouldings, striped wallpaper, handsome chintz curtains, writing desk and easy chairs. Smashing bathrooms, with pink marble and dark wood." Recent praise from American visitors to this discreet, traditional hotel in a small quiet street near Victoria, handy for Buckingham Palace and Westminster. Unique among London hotels, it has been a family fief for 87 years. It was built in 1910 by the grandfather of the present Mr Goring, George the Third, who was born in Room 114. The staff are long-serving – William Cowpe has been general manager for 27 years. Many bedrooms face the pretty private garden (not accessible to guests); some have a balcony. Guests tend to be upgraded when rooms better than those they booked are available. Meals in the restaurant, accompanied at night by a pianist, are traditional English, "good and well served"; there's an extensive, fairly priced wine list. Generous bar lunches and teas are served in the "plush" lounge. (*Alfred Knopf Jr, and others*) We'd like more reports, please, particularly on the breakfast.

Open All year.
Rooms 64 suites, 47 double, 23 single. Most with air-conditioning.
Facilities Lifts, ramps. Lounge with bar, restaurant (pianist at night); function facilities. Free use of nearby health club.
Location Central, by Buckingham Palace (front rooms double-glazed). Garage and mews parking. (Underground: Victoria.)
Restriction No dogs.
Credit cards All major cards accepted.
Terms [1997] Rooms: single £135–£155, double £160–£180, suite £250–£275. Breakfast: continental from £10.50, English from £14.50. Bar meals. Set lunch £24, dinner £35. Christmas, Easter, weekend breaks.

Halkin Hotel   *Tel* (0171) 333 1000
Halkin Street, SW1X 7DJ   *Fax* (0171) 333 1100
                                           E-mail sales@halkin.co.uk

"Must be the best hotel in London. Marvellous staff. Altogether wonderful, though the unbridled technology takes some getting used to. The best breakfast bread basket that I have encountered." "Exquisite cooking; *Michelin* star well deserved." Praise this year for an expensive small hotel in a residential street in Belgravia, near Hyde Park Corner. It has an ultra-modern Italian decor and a showbiz/business clientele. A Reuters area supplies up-to-date financial news. Bedrooms have a sitting area, fax, video, two telephone lines, and 24-hour room service. In the restaurant, which overlooks a private garden, serious, black-clad waiters serve the outstanding modern Italian cooking of chef Stefano Cavallini. The staff are dressed by Armani – the *Halkin*'s owner, Singaporean Christina Ong, runs a fashion empire which includes all the Armani shops in Britain. In 1997 she opened a second London hotel, the 155-bedroom *Metropolitan* in Park Lane, which has a similarly modern decor and quickly acquired a fashionable, moneyed clientele. (*Jonathan Wix, CR*)

Open All year. Restaurant closed Christmas, Easter, bank holidays (24-hour room service).
Rooms 11 suites, 30 double.
Facilities Lobby (live harp/guitar at night), bar, restaurant. Only restaurant suitable for &.
Location Central (double-glazing). (Underground: Hyde Park Corner.)
Restriction No dogs.
Credit cards All major cards accepted.
Terms [1997] (*Excluding VAT on accommodation*) Rooms: single £240–£270, double £270–£300, suite £350–£450. Breakfast: continental £10.25–£10.75, cooked £14.25–£15. Set lunch £18.50; full alc £50–£60. Weekend rates.

L'Hotel   NEW   *Tel* (0171) 589 6286
28 Basil Street, SW3 1AS   *Fax* (0171) 823 7826

This upmarket B&B, now extensively refurbished, is owned by David and Margaret Levin of *The Capital* (*qv*), next door but one. It was dropped from the *Guide* some years ago for lack of reports, but recent guests were impressed. "We loved the decor – magnificent curtains and shutters – and the subdued atmosphere." It is relatively inexpensive for this part of London, having dispensed with porterage, room service, bathroom extras, etc. Reception during the day is friendly; at night it is shared with the *Capital*, "which can be a bit of a puzzle". There is no residents' lounge. The busy basement wine bar, the *Metro*, "Conran-ish in style", serves good-value meals to all comers, and breakfast ("very French, apart from limp, dull toast") to *L'Hotel*'s residents. Its menus are supervised by the *Capital*'s *Michelin*-starred chef, Philip Britten. The bedrooms have a country-style decor, and each has a kettle, crockery and a fridge; best ones have a gas fire. Rooms above the *Metro* can be noisy until late. The suite at the top ("with a sumptuous large sofa") is the quietest. (*R Hoseason, NM Mackintosh*)

Open All year. *Metro* closed Sun, bank holidays, except for residents' breakfast.
Rooms 1 suite, 11 double. 1 on ground floor.
Facilities Lift. Wine bar ("intermittent relaxed instrumental background music").
Location From Underground (Knightsbridge, Harrods' exit) turn left into Hans Cres, then 1st left. Rear rooms quietest. NCP opposite.
Restriction No dogs.
Credit cards All major cards accepted.
Terms (*Excluding VAT on accommodation*) Rooms £140, suite £160. English breakfast £6.50. Set lunch £14.95; full alc £22.50.

Knightsbridge Green Hotel   *Tel* (0171) 584 6274
159 Knightsbridge, SW1X 7PD   *Fax* (0171) 225 1635
                              E-mail theKGHotel@aol.com

This unassuming hotel on Knightsbridge, handy for Hyde Park, has been owned by the Marler family for over 30 years; a new manager, Paul Fizia, arrived in September 1996. The best accommodation is in large suites with a double bedroom, sitting room and bathroom. The quietest rooms are at the back, overlooking a courtyard. Breakfast, delivered to the room, is "express" at 7 am, with croissants, and continental or cooked from 7.30 on weekdays, 8 on Sunday, until 10. The only public room, on the first floor, provides free tea and coffee during the day. Recent improvements include air-conditioning and double-glazing, and an arrangement for guests to use a nearby health club. The place has many devotees, who consider it "better than ever since the improvements", and admire the "clean and comfortable rooms, simply but attractively furnished", the "unique sense of privacy" and the "excellent" hot breakfast. But the praise is not unanimous; whereas some visitors have described the staff as "friendly, quick and efficient", others have reported a cool reception, and one visitor complained of a lingering smell of cigarette smoke on the bedclothes. But there is no questioning the value for money. (*Martin and Karen Oldridge, Desmond Balmer*)

Open All year, except 24–27 Dec.
Rooms 12 suites, 8 double, 7 single. All air-conditioned. 1 with ♿ access.
Facilities Lift. Club Room with complimentary refreshments 9 am–8 pm. Access to nearby health club.
Location Central (rooms double-glazed; quietest ones at rear). NCP carpark nearby. (Underground: Knightsbridge.)
Restriction No dogs.
Credit cards All major cards accepted.

Terms Rooms: single £90–£100, double £130, suite £150. Breakfast: express £3.50, continental £6, English £9.50. *V*

Langorf Hotel   *Tel* (0171) 794 4483
20 Frognal   *Fax* (0171) 435 9055
Hampstead, NW3 6AG

An Edwardian house with a sloping rear garden in a residential area of north London, five minutes' walk from Hampstead village, and a quick tube journey to the centre. It has good-sized bedrooms, some suitable for a family. "A good alternative to swisher places," writes a recent visitor. "Staff friendly, informal and mostly female. My room, at the back, was quiet, with a pleasant decor, but it was hard to adjust the shower in the small bathroom to the 'just right' between burn and freeze. The buffet breakfast with packet juice, etc, was OK apart from poor coffee." Light evening meals are available; there is 24-hour room service. *Mamma Rosa*, an Italian restaurant nearby, is warmly recommended. Street parking only, said to be expensive. (*Dr AT Winterbourne; also ME Goldby*)

Open All year.
Rooms 30 double, 1 single. Some on ground floor. Also 5 serviced apartments.
Facilities Lift. Lounge area, bar, restaurant (piped popular/classical music at night); walled garden. Unsuitable for &.
Location Between Finchley Road and Fitzjohn's Avenue. Street parking. (Underground: Finchley Road.)
Restrictions No smoking in restaurant. No dogs.
Credit cards All major cards accepted.
Terms B&B: single £68–£78, double £85–£95. 50% reduction for children under 8 sharing parents' room.

The Leonard   *Tel* (0171) 935 2010
15 Seymour Street, W1H 5AA   *Fax* (0171) 935 6700
                             E-mail rbc45@dial.pipex.com

This smart town house hotel, "neither so small as to be claustrophobic, nor so large that it lacks a personal feel", has a central position, just off Portman Square, near Hyde Park and Oxford Street. The accommodation is mostly in suites, some very large, "with all the comfort and luxury one could want". Antiques, fine fabrics, paintings, plants and flowers, combine with the latest technology: video, hi-fi and (in the suites) a dedicated line for fax or modem. "The rooms are beautiful," says an American visitor. "And though a famous rock group and journalists from a reputable American magazine were staying, we were treated as if we were the most important guests. We were pleasantly surprised by the reasonable prices of the room service food, and relieved to be able to do our laundry in the utility room, at a fraction of the price of the hotel's laundry service." Others, too, have admired the decor – "it is like staying in a rich Victorian aunt's home" – and have praised the "attentive staff, who do everything they can to please the guests". The café/bar serves light meals and drinks all day, and there is a 24-hour room service menu. (*Sisi Sabeti, Ruth Schaefer, Amir Vahabzadeh, and others*)

Open All year.
Rooms 20 suites, 6 double, 2 single.
Facilities Lift, ramp. Lobby, café/bar; function facilities; exercise room.

Location Central, near Marble Arch (rooms double-glazed). NCP 2 mins' walk. (Underground: Marble Arch.)
Restrictions No smoking in some bedrooms. No dogs.
Credit cards All major cards accepted.
Terms (*Excluding VAT*) Rooms: single £117, double £170, suite (1/2 bedrooms) £225. Breakfast: continental £10, English £14. Light meal £10. Weekend rates.

Number Sixteen   *Tel* (0171) 589 5232
16 Sumner Place, SW7 3EG   From US: 1-800 592 5387
                                                               Fax (0171) 584 8615

Conversion of four late-Victorian town houses in residential street near South Kensington station. Willing staff. Traditional decor. Lift, lounges, conservatory (tea and breakfast service), flowery garden with fountain and fishpond. 36 bedrooms (quietest overlook garden), some on ground floor. Access to nearby health and fitness club. Paid parking 5 mins' walk. No children under 8. No dogs. All major credit cards accepted. B&B: single £80–£115, double £150–£180, suite £190 [until Feb 1998]. English breakfast £8. Recently endorsed: "Like staying in someone's home, creaky floors and all." But we'd like more reports, please.

Park Consul   NEW   *Tel* (0171) 225 7500
Ixworth Place, SW3 3QX   *Fax* (0171) 225 7555

Former police hostel, opened as hotel in June 1996. On quiet residential street in Chelsea, 5 mins' walk from South Kensington Underground station; handy for Knightsbridge and Sloane Square. Polite, if not personal, reception. Bright decor, with Thai influence, in interestingly shaped bedrooms. Conservatory-style restaurant for breakfast, lunch, tea; drinks, light meals served in drawing room or bedrooms. Classical/"moody jazz" in public rooms "when appropriate". Function/conference facilities. All major credit cards accepted. 46 rooms (20 no-smoking): single £115–£125, double £135–£145, suite £165 (excluding VAT). Breakfast: continental £8.75 English £12.75. Full alc meals £35–£40 [1997]. Children under 12 accommodated free in parents' room.

Pembridge Court   *Tel* (0171) 229 9977
34 Pembridge Gardens, W2 4DX   *Fax* (0171) 727 4982

Civilised town house, recently redecorated, in tree-lined setting near Notting Hill Gate, handy for travel to centre. "Neither dauntingly luxurious nor vastly expensive." 20 stylish bedrooms, ranging from large to poky, some on ground floor. Pretty lounge. Resident ginger cats, Spencer and Churchill. Excellent service by pleasant staff, led by long-serving manager, Valerie Gilliat. Basement restaurant serves light meals (residents only). Special rates at nearby health club. Unsuitable for ⅙. No dogs in public rooms. All major credit cards accepted. B&B: single £110–£140, double £130–£170. Full alc £30. More reports, please. ***V*** *(1 night only)*

The Portobello   NEW   *Tel* (0171) 727 2777
22 Stanley Gardens, W11 2NG   *Fax* (0171) 792 9641

Tim Herring's hotel "of wayward charm" is in two six-floor Victorian terrace houses on a quiet residential street, a short stroll from the

Portobello Road market. It numbers many famous rock stars among its trendy clientèle. The design, by Julie Hodgess, is an eclectic mix of styles, Victorian to Gothic, with gilt mirrors, marble fireplaces, four-posters, palms, Edwardiana, cane and wicker furniture. There is a Victorian-style seashell grotto outside the restaurant. Some of the rooms, called cabins, are tiny, with "an interesting decor of mahogany and brass to resemble a pre-war ship's cabin", but they squeeze in colour TV, a minute fridge and a micro-bathroom. Lower down are normal-sized rooms and ritzy suites – the Bath Room has mirrors above the bed and painted clouds on the ceiling, the Round Room has a round bed and free-standing Edwardian bathing machine. Porterage and room service operate only between 8 am and 4 pm, but reception is open day and night. Breakfast, with a reasonable choice, is served in the basement bar/restaurant. Other meals, too, are available round the clock, from a short menu. "The unconventional style of the place and the staff may come as a shock to the average traveller," one regular visitor has written, "but I am not alone in enjoying its uniquely relaxed style." The Herrings also own *Julie's* restaurant in nearby Clarendon Cross (known for its arty little shops). More reports, please.

Open 2 Jan–24 Dec.
Rooms 9 suites, 9 double, 4 single.
Facilities Lift. Lounge, bar, restaurant (open 24 hours to residents).
Location Central. Meter parking. (Underground: Notting Hill Gate.)
Restriction No dogs in public rooms.
Credit cards All major cards accepted.
Terms [1997] Rooms: cabin single £100, double £150, suite £200. English breakfast *c.* £8. Full alc £20.

Sandringham Hotel   *Tel* (0171) 435 1569
3 Holford Road, NW3 1AD   *Fax* (0171) 431 5932

Four-storey Victorian town house B&B in quiet residential street, handy for Hampstead Heath and tube station (20 mins to central London). Smart country house-style public rooms (piped classical music all day). Pretty bedrooms vary in size. One tiny single has open-plan bathroom. Some overlook pretty garden, with pond, flower borders, view of nearby church steeple. Good breakfast. Private parking. 17 rooms, 2 on ground floor. No smoking: dining room, bedrooms. No dogs. All major cards accepted. B&B: single £70–£85, double £115–£140, suite £145–£155. Cooked breakfast £3.50 added. New owners, since mid-1996, Mr and Mrs Long; entry recently endorsed with some reservations; we'd like more reports, please.

Swiss Cottage Hotel   *Tel* (0171) 722 2281
4 Adamson Road, NW3 3HP   *Fax* (0171) 483 4588

Idiosyncratic establishment in residential area of north London, convenient for transport to the centre (2 mins' walk from Swiss Cottage Underground, Eton Ave exit; regular buses). Victorian decor: public rooms have antiques, oriental rugs, original 19th-century paintings, piped classical music. 63 bedrooms, greatly varied: some doubles with sitting room overlooking small walled garden; some cheap singles with shared shower; some on ground floor. Cheerful, helpful staff; but breakfast room and room maintenance sometimes criticised. Small carpark. 24-hour snack service. No smoking in breakfast room. No dogs. All major credit cards accepted. B&B: single £75–£130, double £85–£140

[1997]. Children under 10 accommodated free in parents' room. No recent reports; we'd like some, please. ***V***

Tophams Ebury Court   *Tel* (0171) 730 8147
28 Ebury Street, SW1W 0LU   *Fax* (0171) 823 5966
                           E-mail 106010.1706@compuserve.com

Family-owned for over 56 years, this hotel rambles through five adjoining houses on a busy road near Victoria Station (rooms at the back are quietest). The bedrooms are mostly small; not all have facilities *en suite*, but bathrobes are provided for the trip down the corridor. The public rooms are small, too. There's a pleasant basement bar, open to all, and a restaurant serving traditional English dishes, with an emphasis on fish. The hotel is run by Marianne Topham, of the third generation of Tophams, with her husband, Nicholas Kingsford, "both much in evidence". Many of the staff are long-serving. "Though they have modernised to some necessary degree," writes a regular visitor, "it retains much of its old-fashioned style." An American, who stayed for ten days, thought it "a gem, impeccably clean, with a calm country house atmosphere, and a competent staff", and a visitor from the Netherlands called it his favourite hotel in London. (*RAL Ogston, Nancy T Elmer, Prof. Wolfgang Stroebe, and others*)

Open All year, except Christmas, New Year. Restaurant closed 2 weeks Aug.
Rooms 2 suites, 26 double, 11 single. Most with facilities *en suite*. Some on ground floor.
Facilities Sitting room, bar, restaurant (piped light music); private dining/function room.
Location Central (front rooms double-glazed). Meter parking. (Underground: Victoria.)
Restriction No dogs.
Credit cards All major cards accepted.
Terms [1997] B&B: single £85–£110, double £115–£135, suite £150–£230. Set lunch £15, dinner £20; full alc £18–£25.

---

22 Jermyn Street   *Tel* (0171) 734 2353
22 Jermyn Street, SW1Y 6HL   *Fax* (0171) 734 0750
                                E-mail office@22jermyn.com

♙ *César award in 1996*

"I cannot recommend this wonderful hotel too highly. We have visited regularly for seven years, and only wish that everywhere we go had a hotel half as good. The attention to detail is phenomenal; comfort and service are the watchword. Every single member of staff is helpful. Their sheer unadulterated niceness will keep me faithful to 22." "A gem of a place. Understated elegance. Unobtrusive staff. Never a hint of seeking gratuities." More endorsements this year for this small hotel in a prime position in St James's ("acceptably quiet for such a central location"). Owned by the same family since 1915, it is run by Henry Togna with manager Laurie Smith (new this year). No public rooms; accommodation is in spacious suites and studios; the decor is an appealing blend of contemporary furniture and fabrics with antiques, potted plants and flowers. The bathrooms are "marvellously luxurious". West End theatres and shops, and many good restaurants, are nearby. An impressive folder gives plenty of information about what is on. Mr Togna's art-historian niece, Louise Hayward, will take guests on tours of the galleries and museums. He is a fitness fanatic: guests may use the sporting facilities at a luxurious club nearby, or borrow a mountain or a racing bike. For the technology buff there is an Internet/CD-ROM room, with help for those who need research done. Light meals are served in the rooms. Children are welcomed: there are games, videos and teddy-bear dressing gowns, and a list of local child-friendly restaurants. (*Lesley Evans, AA van Straubenzee; also John T McCann*)

Open All year.
Rooms 13 suites, 5 double. 24-hour room service.
Facilities Lift. Small conference facilities. Access to pool, gym, squash courts at nearby club.
Location Central. Valet parking. (Underground: Piccadilly Circus.)
Credit cards All major cards accepted.
Terms (*Excluding VAT*) Room £199, suite £260–£290. Extra bed £30. Continental breakfast £12.

The Wilbraham   *Tel* (0171) 730 8296
1 Wilbraham Place   *Fax* (0171) 730 6815
Sloane Street, SW1X 9AE

This long-established privately owned hotel, which *Guide* readers have called "useful but not luxurious", is remarkably reasonable in price for its prime position near Sloane Square. "The epitome of an old London house," one guest wrote. "Generally quiet and warm, with agreeable public rooms, nice pictures, pretty wallpaper. Several staircases; you have to remember which is yours. Good breakfast, with brown bread and scones, brought to the room." Some bedrooms are "large and handsome", others are small. Many have been refurbished this year; all now have facilities *en suite*. Some visitors have reported abrasive telephone conversations when booking, but on arrival they have received a genuine welcome – "no charm school here" – and "old-fashioned service", with a porter available to carry bags. The "lovely cotton sheets and luscious towels" and the 24-hour room service have also been appreciated. The hotel has a regular clientele, so booking well in advance is advised. But we need more reports, please.

Open All year, except Christmas, bank holidays. Bar/buttery closed Sun.
Rooms 6 triple, 37 double, 2 single. 5 on ground floor.
Facilities 2 lifts. Residents' lounge, bar/buttery. 24-hour room service. Unsuitable for &.
Location Central, near Sloane Square. Public garage nearby. (Underground: Sloane Square.)
Restriction No dogs.
Credit cards None accepted.
Terms [1997] (*Excluding VAT*) Rooms: single £60, double £75–£88. Breakfast: continental £4, English £5.95. Set lunch £9, dinner £12; Full alc £15. *V*

See also SHORTLIST

LORTON Cumbria   Map 4

New House Farm   **BUDGET**   *Tel/Fax* (01900) 85404
Lorton, Cockermouth CA13 9UU

Neither new nor a farm, Hazel and John Hatch's unassuming guest
house is 17th-century and Grade II listed, with oak beams and rafters,
flagged floors and stone open fireplaces. It is on the edge of a traditional village, in large grounds with a garden, fields, woodland and a
stream. All around is some of the Lake District's most spectacular and
unspoilt scenery. There is easy access to Loweswater, Crummock
Water and Buttermere. Inside are two lounges, one with an open fire,
and good-sized bedrooms with flowery fabrics and sporting prints. A
returning visitor was "delighted to report a consistent picture of high
standards, and "the most cheerful and personal" service: "Bedside
lights are turned on during dinner; there are hot-water bottles and a
torch in each bedroom, *and* extra heating. Drinks are available in the
sitting room before dinner, which can be an occasion for conversation
between guests. So far this has not been problematic, I suspect
because those who stay here have mutual interests in this unspoilt
corner of the Lake District." The traditional dinners (no choice of main
course) might include local pheasant shot by Mr Hatch or locally
caught fish, and end with ginger pudding with butterscotch sauce, or
spotted dick. There is a "short, intelligent" wine list. "Above-average"
lunches and teas are served in a lovely old barn next door. This year
there is a new bedroom, suitable for wheelchair-users. (*Dr CH
Maycock; also Mrs JEG Wood, Brenda McDowell, and others*)

Open All year.
Rooms 3 double, 1 single. 1, suitable for ♿, in annexe. No TV.
Facilities Lounge, dining room. 15-acre grounds.
Location Off B5289 S of Lorton.
Restrictions No smoking. No children under 12. No dogs in public rooms.
Credit cards None accepted.
Terms [1997] B&B £30–£45, D,B&B £45–£65.

LOWER BEEDING West Sussex   Map 2

South Lodge   *Tel* (01403) 891711
Brighton Road   *Fax* (01403) 891766
Lower Beeding   *E-mail* inquiries@
nr Horsham RH13 6PS   southlodgehotel.dial.gl.co.uk

An impressive wisteria-clad mansion in the Sussex Downs, peaceful,
but handy for Gatwick airport. It was originally the home of Frederick
Ducane Godman, a Victorian explorer and botanist who planted rare
trees and shrubs, including some magnificent rhododendrons, in the
vast grounds. It is now owned and run by a father-and-son team, the
Pecorellis. The interior is elegant, with wooden floors, panelling,
moulded ceilings, chandeliers and antiques. The bedrooms are large
(except for one called Ronnie Corbett), and some have views of the
downs; bathrooms are lavishly marbled. Our correspondents have
found the place welcoming and good value. Some recent reports:
"We'd booked the least expensive rooms. They were quiet and huge,
with all the goodies one expects of a luxury hotel, but packaged in a

homely way, eg, cotton buds in pretty Thai pottery. Excellent lighting. Lavish marble bathrooms. Cooking by chef Timothy Neal was a sort of revisited English cuisine, extremely good, served in a room with lovely views. Breakfast also good, with nice bread." "The staff were genuinely concerned that we should have exactly what we wanted, particularly during meals." "Afternoon tea one of the finest ever." Small conferences are sometimes held, but they are organised so as not to impinge on the private guest. There are lots of outdoor pursuits (see below), and guests have members' rights at Mannings Heath Golf Club nearby, under the same management. Two lovely gardens, Leonardslee, and Nymans, are close by; Brighton, Arundel and Petworth are not far. More reports, please.

Open All year.
Rooms 4 suites, 34 double, 1 single. 1 on ground floor, suitable for &.
Facilities Ramp. Lounge (pianist Fri/Sat evening, Sun lunch), bar, restaurant; conference/function facilities. 93-acre park: gardens, tennis, croquet, *pétanque*, clay pigeon-shooting. Golf, coarse fishing, riding nearby.
Location On A281, 6 miles S of Horsham. Train: Horsham, 12 miles, Gatwick, 14 miles; then taxi.
Restrictions No smoking in restaurant. No children under 9 in restaurant at night. No dogs.
Credit cards All major cards accepted.
Terms [1997] Rooms: single £120–£145, double £165–£185, suite £265–£295. Breakfast: continental £8.50, English £10.95. Set lunch from £17, dinner from £27.50; full alc £45.

LUDLOW Shropshire   Map 3

Dinham Hall   *Tel* (01584) 876464
Dinham, Ludlow SY8 1EJ   *Fax* (01584) 876019

Ludlow is one of the most beautiful towns in England, crammed with historic buildings. It is known for its horse races, and it makes an excellent base for touring Shropshire's many attractions. In a quiet street near the Norman castle (where plays by Shakespeare are produced during Ludlow's annual festival) this handsome 18th-century house is owned by the Mifsuds of *The Lake*, Llangammarch Wells, Wales (*qv*). It is run by James Warlow with a young staff. "I was most impressed by their charm and helpfulness," says a recent visitor. Others have concurred: "They are nicely attentive, but unobtrusive, just as we like. The location is delightful, with peace and quiet, and views over the surrounding countryside." One guest thought there was a slightly functional air about the upstairs areas, but another admired her bedroom: "sunny, spacious, bright and clean, with good views." There is an agreeable garden. In the restaurant, which has pastel colours and gas lighting, Gareth Williams' modern English/French cooking is thought "highly satisfactory, we particularly enjoyed a flavourful and tender lamb cassoulet". Good breakfast, too "with butter and marmalade in pots, and very good coffee". (*Dr CH Maycock, and others*)

Open All year.
Rooms 10 double, 2 single.
Facilities 2 lounges, dining room; 2 private dining rooms; gym, sauna. ½-acre garden. Fishing, riding, golf nearby. Only public rooms suitable for &.
Location By castle. Private parking.

Restrictions No smoking in dining room. No children under 12 in dining room at night. No dogs in public rooms.
Credit cards All major cards accepted.
Terms B&B: single £62–£72, double £90–£125; D,B&B £68–£85 per person. Set lunch £14.50, dinner £25.50. Winter, Christmas breaks. *V*

Number Twenty Eight   NEW/BUDGET   *Tel/Fax* (01584) 876996
28 Lower Broad Street
Ludlow SY8 1PQ

Patricia and Philip Ross's B&B consists of three houses in the same street, in a quiet part of town close to the river Teme. Broadgate Mews is two Tudor cottages; Number Twenty Eight (where breakfast is served) is early Georgian; West View is part of a small Victorian terrace (said to have had the first internal water closets in Ludlow). Each house has a garden, a sitting room with an open fire, books, maps, etc, and two bedrooms. Our inspectors admired theirs, in the Mews: generously proportioned with a fresh decor, good lighting, a fridge and a toaster, more books, and bathroom extras ranging from razors to pain-killers. Breakfast, in a pretty room with dusky pink walls, a pale blue frieze and family photographs, included a generous buffet, "the best bacon we'd eaten for years", and local honey. "With their natural warmth the Rosses create a genuinely friendly atmosphere. He is charming, with a keen sense of humour; she is delightful, slender and well-groomed, and cannot do enough for her guests. Their labrador, Daisy, is friendly too." Eating places of all kinds are close by, including Shaun Hill's *Michelin*-starred *Merchant House*.

Open All year.
Rooms 6 double, in 3 different houses.
Facilities 3 lounges, breakfast room (piped classical music). 3 gardens. Unsuitable for &.
Location 200 yds from centre; close to Ludford Bridge.
Restrictions No smoking. No dogs in public rooms.
Credit cards Access, Amex.
Terms [1997] B&B double £50–£65. 1-night booking sometimes refused weekends.

LYME REGIS Dorset   **Map 1**

Hotel Alexandra   BUDGET   *Tel* (01297) 442010
Pound Street   *Fax* (01297) 443229
Lyme Regis DT7 3HZ

Lyme Regis is the attractive seaside town made famous in literature by the Cobb, the 18th-century artificial harbour where the French Lieutenant's Woman waited, and from which Louisa Musgrove took her fateful jump in *Persuasion*. In a superb position overlooking the Cobb, is this large white "rather old-fashioned" hotel, set in a well-kept garden where cream teas and snacks are served in fine weather. It is a Georgian dower house, with later additions (it became a hotel in 1901), and has many flights of stairs, and long corridors ("you should note carefully the route to your room"). Bedrooms vary greatly in size and quality. No.12 is said to be "a stunner, very large with a marvellous bay window looking over the garden to the sea". Others have been described as "small, but charmingly decorated". Some, on the other hand, "show signs of shabbiness", and some have thin walls. The restaurant serves good traditional English cooking, with a wide choice, and vegetarians are well catered for; there is a comprehensive, fairly priced wine list. Breakfast has "an extensive buffet, including particularly good fish". There is a lounge, with games and current magazines, and a sunny conservatory. While there are those who feel that the owners, Mr and Mrs Haskins, keep too low a profile, thus creating an impersonal atmosphere, not all share this view. "The service was exceptionally good," say 1997 visitors. "The staff went out of their way to be helpful on many occasions." Children are welcomed. Excellent walks start just down the road from the hotel. Parking in the forecourt can be "a squeeze". (*JA Fisher, DGA and ME Thomas, Helen Anthony, and others*)

Open End Jan–Christmas.
Rooms 25 double, 2 single. 3 on ground floor. 1 on garden, with private patio.
Facilities Lounge, conservatory, bar, restaurant. 1-acre garden. Beach 300 yds; fishing, tennis, golf, riding nearby.
Location 200 yds from centre. Courtyard parking. Train: Axminster, 6 miles; then bus/taxi.
Restrictions Smoking discouraged in restaurant, banned in some bedrooms. No very young children at dinner. No dogs in public rooms, unattended in bedrooms.
Credit cards All major cards accepted.
Terms [1997] B&B: single £35–£48, double £70–£112; D,B&B: single £50–£63, double £85–£142. Bar lunches. Set lunch £12.50 (Sun £10.50), dinner £22.50; full alc £25. 7 nights for price of 6. Off-season breaks.

LYNMOUTH Devon   Map 1

The Rising Sun   *Tel* (01598) 753223
Lynmouth EX35 6EQ   *Fax* (01598) 753480
                    E-mail risingsunlynmouth@easynet.co.uk

Hugo Jeune's picturesque hostelry is on the harbour of a tiny fishing village at the foot of dramatic wooded cliffs – "a position second to none". It consists of a 14th-century inn and a row of thatched cottages. The poet Shelley, it is claimed, stayed with his bride, Harriet Westbrook, in one of the latter, now a suite. A terraced garden has been cut into the hill at the back. "The place's charm is that it is wholly unsuited to the modern concept of providing comfortable accommodation," writes a 1996 visitor. "Narrow passages, low ceilings, uneven creaky floors, steep stairs. We have never stayed in a smaller hotel bedroom. But it has an idiosyncratic charm. The Antipodean staff were cheery and efficient, and the atmosphere was uplifting." Others have described the bedrooms and bathrooms as "pretty", and enjoyed lying in bed looking at the sea. The oak-panelled, beamed restaurant is small, with tables close together; guests on half-board terms get an allowance of £27 towards the *à la carte* menu. The food is praised by some – "it lifts the place from 'nice' to 'worth a trip'" – but others have thought it over-elaborate, and complained: "No daily variation on the menu." The lounge is said to be unwelcoming, and parking can be awkward. Lynmouth is paired with Lynton, 500 feet above (see next entry). (*AR Wiltshire, Mrs CA Peters; also Good Pub Guide*)

Open All year.
Rooms 1 suite (in cottage), 13 double, 2 single. 4 in annexes.
Facilities Lounge, bar, restaurant (piped classical/"easy listening" music). Small terraced garden. Rock beach; sea fishing. Salmon-fishing ¼ mile. Unsuitable for &.
Location On harbourside. Public carpark nearby. Train: Barnstaple, 20 miles; then bus.
Restrictions No smoking: dining room, 6 bedrooms. No dogs.
Credit cards All major cards accepted.
Terms B&B £41.50–£65; D,B&B £63.50–£87. Bar lunches. Full alc £29. Off-season breaks. Christmas, New Year packages. 1-night bookings sometimes refused. *V*

LYNTON Devon   **Map 1**

Old Rectory   *Tel* (01598) 763368
Martinhoe, nr Lynton EX31 4QT   *Fax* (01598) 763567
                     E-mail john@johnbrad.demon.co.uk

John and Suzanne Bradbury's unpretentious small hotel (no smoking) is set in tranquil gardens in a Domesday-old hamlet just outside Lynton, on the edge of the Exmoor National Park. The surrounding land is owned by the National Trust, and the North Devon Coastal Footpath is close by, giving access to some of the most beautiful scenery in the county. Much praise this year: "We have stayed twice in the last two years, and have found it quite exceptional in the unobtrusive friendliness of its atmosphere and the imaginative excellence of its food. The feeling is that of a small country house, rather than of a hotel. This is enhanced by the fact that it is family run, and its friendliness matched by efficiency and helpful knowledge of the surrounding countryside." "Good bedrooms, comfortable lounges, delightful conservatory/vinery, charming owners." "When we left after four days it was like parting from relatives." The menu, with limited choice, is accompanied by a short, carefully selected wine list with a modest mark-up. No charge for morning coffee and afternoon tea with home-made cake. All details are carefully attended to: elegant table settings, fresh flowers and fruit in bedrooms, beds turned down at night. Two bays with good swimming are within walking/driving distance. Much of the furniture is made by the Bradburys' talented cabinet-maker son, Daniel, who also waits at table. (*Sir Geoffrey Chandler, Sir John Herbecq, Peter Briault, and others*)

Open Easter–end Oct. Lunch not served.
Rooms 1 suite, 7 double. 2 on ground floor. No telephone.
Facilities 2 lounges, dining room, vinery. 3½-acre garden. Sea 1½ miles. Sea and game fishing, riding, golf nearby.
Location From M5 exit 27 take A361; bypass South Molton, right on to A399 for Blackmore Gate; right on to A39 for Parracombe/Lynton, bypass Parracombe; at Martinhoe cross, 3rd unclassified road on left for Woody Bay/Martinhoe.
Restrictions No smoking. No children under 14. No dogs.
Credit cards None accepted.
Terms [1997] B&B £45; D,B&B £56.50–£67.50. Set dinner £25.

> Always let a hotel know if you have to cancel a booking, whether you have paid a deposit or not. Hotels sustain huge losses due to "no-shows".

MACKWORTH Derbyshire   Map 3

The Mackworth   **NEW/BUDGET**   *Tel* (01332) 824324
Ashbourne Road   *Fax* (01332) 824692
Mackworth DE22 4LY

On edge of old village 3 miles NW of Derby, on A52 to Ashbourne, red brick
building much extended. Unexciting exterior, some bedrooms basic, but excel-
lent manager, Pascal Arnoux; genuinely welcoming staff; immaculate house-
keeping. "Efficient and enthusiastic" Scots chef, Tom Robertson, serves
substantial traditional food in no-smoking restaurant with rustic decor: local
game and meat, fresh fish, on large menu; sauces a strong point. Bar lunches
available, except Sun. Generous breakfast, including porridge. Piped instru-
mental music in public rooms all day. Large rear garden with striped marquee
for conferences, functions (hotel has wedding licence). 10 miles from East
Midlands airport; handy for Peak District, Alton Towers, American
Adventure Theme Park. Closed in evening Christmas Day/New Year's Day.
14 bedrooms, 1 on ground floor. No dogs in public rooms. Access, Amex, Visa
accepted. B&B £31–£46 (£25–£29 weekends). Set lunch £5.95, dinner from
£6.95; full alc £24.

MALMESBURY Wiltshire   Map 3

The Old Bell   *Tel* (01666) 822344
Abbey Row   *Fax* (01666) 825145
Malmesbury SN16 0AG

This beautiful old town, perched above the river Avon, grew up
around an abbey founded in the 9th century; its 12th-century church
incorporates a magnificent Norman nave. Its inn, one of the oldest in
Britain, was built in the 12th century for visitors to the abbey's library.
Extensions over the years have given it a rambling character, but some
original features have survived. Owned now by Nicholas Dickinson, it
is run on the same lines as its sister hotel, *Woolley Grange* at Bradford-
on-Avon (*qv*). providing civilised comforts for adults while happily
accommodating their children. "A winning formula," wrote 1997 visitors. "The place was alive with contented parents, affluent enough to
afford the wonderful welcome to children. The staff coped admirably
with all their demands." Others have written of the good atmosphere
and the attractive decor: antiques, interesting pictures and artefacts,
plants and flowers. "A perfect balance between modern comfort
(power showers) and being lived in (resident cat, a few threadbare
patches on the carpet); helpful if unsophisticated staff." The oldest part,
the "Great Hall" (now a collection of small rooms), serves light lunches,
teas and evening snacks. A twisting corridor leads to two lounges with
comfortable chairs and sofas, books, magazines, newspapers and
games. Bedrooms vary in size and style; those in the modern annexe
have a Japanese-style decor, and were reported this year to have noisy
plumbing. Some get traffic noise by day, but it is quiet at night. At no
extra charge, children may be left all day under trained supervision in
the Den, with games and a huge TV screen with Nintendo; and they
have their own supper. Later, the sophisticated listening system takes
over, and parents dine in a large, high-ceilinged Edwardian restaurant,
with huge mirrors and old oil paintings. Cooking by chef David

Richards (new in 1997) is modern British, "and excellent, if a little on the *nouvelle* side". Behind the house there is a patio with tables and chairs, and a small garden with a separate children's play area. (*Elizabeth Biggs, Leslie Farhangi, and others*)

Open All year.
Rooms 3 suites, 25 double, 3 single. 15 in coach house. 6 on ground floor.
Facilities 2 lounges, Great Hall, bar (piped music), children's playroom (supervised 10 am–6 pm), restaurant; patio. Small garden. Riding, tennis, golf, gliding, dry skiing, water-sports, cycling nearby.
Location Central, by abbey. Carpark.
Restrictions No smoking in restaurant. No dogs in public rooms.
Credit cards All major cards accepted.
Terms [1997] B&B: single £60–£70, double £85–£135, suite £145–£160. Set lunch £15, dinner £18.50–£26. Special interest, off-season breaks. Christmas, New Year packages. 1-night bookings refused Sat. Children accommodated free in parents' room.

MALVERN WELLS Worcestershire   **Map 3**

The Cottage in the Wood   *Tel* (01684) 575859
Holywell Road   *Fax* (01684) 560662
Malvern Wells WR14 4LG

This Georgian dower house stands amid woods and shrubbery, high on the slopes of the Malvern Hills, where Edward Elgar loved to walk. It has stunning views over the Severn valley to the distant Cotswolds and Wales, and is in a designated area of outstanding natural beauty. From its grounds you can follow a sign, "To the Hills", and walk straight out to a nine-mile range of the Malverns and more than a hundred miles of tracks. The hotel is a family concern, run by the resident owners, John and Sue Pattin ("genial hosts"), with daughter Maria as manager; son Dominic is *sous chef*, and his wife Romy is housekeeper. It was awarded the AA's Courtesy and Care award both in 1996 and in 1997. Public rooms have fine antique furniture. Bedrooms in the main house (some are small) are decorated in traditional style, "with extras you really need, including binoculars, plenty of local information and delicious home-made shortbread". Others, modern, smallish but with huge picture-windows and terrace or balcony, are in a converted coach house, and there are four cottagey ones in Beech Cottage. The pretty restaurant, hung with Indian paintings, serves modern English cooking on the large menu. The half-board rates include a £23 allowance for dinner, which some visitors have thought "slightly stingy". "Some dishes very good, others less successful," is a recent verdict on the food. "Breakfast excellent, with lovely fruit and a large range of cooked dishes." Light lunches are available on weekdays; on Sunday there is a traditional three-course menu. (*Philippa and Edward Howells, and others*)

Open All year.
Rooms 20 double. 4 in Beech Cottage 70 yds, 8 in Coach House 100 yds.
Facilities Lounge, lounge bar, restaurant; function facilities. 7-acre grounds leading to Malvern Hills. Golf, squash nearby. Unsuitable for &.
Location Off A449 to Ledbury, 3 miles S of Malvern; turn right opposite Gulf/Rover petrol station. Do not approach from S end of Holywell Rd.
Restrictions No smoking in restaurant. No dogs in main house.
Credit cards Access, Amex, Visa.
Terms B&B: single £70–£76, double £89–£140; D,B&B (min. 2 nights) £52–£82 per

person. Set lunch: £13 Mon–Sat, £15 Sun; full alc £33. Bargain breaks all year. Christmas, New Year packages. 1-night bookings sometimes refused Fri/Sat. *V*

MANCHESTER *See SHORTLIST*   **Map 4**

MARKINGTON North Yorkshire   **Map 4**

Hob Green   NEW   *Tel* (01423) 770031
Markington, nr Harrogate HG3 3PJ   *Fax* (01423) 771589

Eighteenth-century country house, peacefully set in prize-winning gardens amid 870-acre farm and woodland (lovely views), outside village 9 miles NW of Harrogate. Agreeable ambience, elegant public areas, pleasant staff. 12 thoughtfully planned bedrooms. Delicious breakfasts; traditional English/French cooking in formal dining room. Unsuitable for &. No dogs in public rooms. All major credit cards accepted. B&B: single £80, double £90–£99. Full alc £30 [until Apr 1998]. More reports, please.

MATLOCK BATH Derbyshire   **Map 3**

Hodgkinson's Hotel   BUDGET   *Tel* (01629) 582170
150 South Parade   *Fax* (01629) 584891
Matlock Bath DE4 3NR

♀ *César award in 1994*

Once a spa town, Matlock Bath is now a tourist centre for the Derby dales, with amusement arcades and fish-and-chip shops. This, its first hotel, stands on the main Matlock to Derby road which most bedrooms overlook. The original oval hotel sign still hangs outside, and much of the ground floor has not changed greatly since the hotel was built in 1698. It has been lovingly restored by Nigel Shelley, an interior designer, and Malcolm Archer, who has a hairdressing salon on the first floor. A collector's treasure trove, unashamedly dedicated to Victoriana, it won its *César* for the enjoyably eccentric atmosphere and decor behind its plain façade. William Morris wallpaper, Victorian prints, and Staffordshire china adorn the public rooms. Fox furs, hats, gloves, shoes, Dinky toys, Minton china, figurines, Art Nouveau relics, dress-maker's dummy, birdcages, old shoes and exotic paintings enliven the climb up the stairs – four floors, no lift. The bedrooms, each with a small *en suite* shower room, are similar in style, and priced according to size; some are spacious, there are some magnificent beds. The owners share the cooking, which our readers consider to be "as eclectic and imaginative as the rest, with impeccable vegetables, succulent desserts and willing service". More reports, please.

Open All year. Restaurant closed midday, to non-residents Sun.
Rooms 7 double.
Facilities 2 lounges, bar, restaurant. ¼-acre garden. Opposite river Derwent: fishing. Unsuitable for &.
Location Central (2 quiet rooms at rear). Private carpark.
Restrictions No smoking in restaurant. No dogs in public rooms.
Credit cards Access, Amex, Visa.
Terms [1997] B&B: single £30–£35, double £50–£90. Set dinner £19.50–£24.50.

2-day break; 4-day midweek break. 1-night bookings sometimes refused weekends.

MAWNAN SMITH Cornwall   Map 1

Meudon NEW   *Tel* (01326) 250541
Mawnan Smith   *Fax* (01326) 250543
nr Falmouth TR11 5HT

This conventional hotel is a mellow stone mansion with massive granite pillars, mullioned windows and an unattractive modern wing. Its chief glories are a garden with rare sub-tropical flowering shrubs and plants, which was laid out in the 18th century by Capability Brown, and its location in 200 acres of protected Cornish coastline between the Fal and Helford rivers, at the head of a lovely valley leading down to a private beach. Run by Harry Pilgrim, who founded it over 30 years ago, and his son Mark, it offers old-fashioned service: cases carried, beds turned down at night, shoes cleaned, early morning tea brought to the room (tea-making facilities are also available). The five-course dinner menu is traditional. "Everything was well executed," wrote our inspector, "and the real star was the usual Cinderella, the vegetables. There is a dessert trolley full of lush dishes, an excellent cheeseboard, and a good range of reasonably priced wines. But the dinner service was very swift. We got through three courses between 8.30 and 9, and were made to feel the staff were wanting to clear away. The bedrooms are good-sized and well equipped, but not luxurious. Breakfast was exemplary Cornish; black pudding with the huge mixed grill; toast and coffee kept coming." Extras bump up the bill: £8 added to the £25 dinner menu for steak or lobster; £2 for fresh orange juice at breakfast. Another lovely garden, Trebah, is close by.

Open Mar–Nov.
Rooms 3 suites, 26 double. Some on ground floor.
Facilities Lift, ramp. 3 lounges, bar, sun loggia, restaurant; 8-acre grounds: gardens, private beach, fishing. Golf nearby.
Location 4 m S of Falmouth. From Truro: A39 towards Falmouth for about 9 miles. Right at Hillhead roundabout; follow signs for Meanporth (*ignore* signs for Mawnan Smith). Follow narrow, winding road (marked "Unsuitable for long vehicles"). Hotel on left ½ mile after Meanporth beach, 1 mile before Mawnan Smith. Carpark; 2 lock-up garages £5. Train: Truro; then taxi/hire car.
Restriction No dogs in public rooms.
Credit cards All major cards accepted
Terms [1997] B&B £65–£95; D,B&B £90–£120. Set lunch £12.50, dinner £25. 3-day breaks. Reductions for children in adjoining rooms July/Aug.

MEMBURY Devon   Map 1

Lea Hill Hotel   *Tel* (01404) 881881 and 881388
Membury, nr Axminster EX13 7AQ

"A super place. Nice room. Good food. Very pleasant hosts." A recent endorsement for this 14th-century thatched longhouse, with ancient beams, flagstone floors, inglenook fireplaces and a pretty decor. It is set high up, with stunning views, in large grounds in a designated area of outstanding natural beauty, and reached by narrow lanes. The owners, Hilary and Jim Reaney, "are easy and welcoming," said the nominators. "Most bedrooms are in smartly converted barns; most have a private garden or patio. Ours had quality fabrics, nice prints, good china for tea, excellent lighting, and a modern bathroom with lots of goodies. Public rooms have old furniture, copper, brass, flowers, etc. There's a pub-like bar, with leather furniture. The dining room has a cottagey feel; Mrs Reaney cooks good dinner party food; there is a set menu with no choice of main course, or they make an allowance towards dishes from the *carte*. Small, inexpensive wine list. Good breakfasts, with fruit, wide choice of cooked items, bowls of marmalade and jam. Duvets on beds, but you can ask for blankets." Children are welcomed; two suites are suitable for a family. Membury, a pretty village on the borders of Devon, Somerset and Dorset, was a Quaker centre in the 17th and 18th centuries. The coast and an abundance of National Trust properties are close by. (*Jonathan Palfrey, Heather Sharland*)

Open Feb–Dec.
Rooms 2 suites, 9 double. 9 in converted barns. Most with private patio or garden. 3 on ground floor.
Facilities Lounge, bar, study, restaurant (piped music "depending on guests and mood"). 8-acre grounds: croquet. Riding, hunting, fishing nearby; sea, safe beaches 10 miles.
Location 2½ miles NW of Axminster. A35 towards Honiton; turn right opposite *Old Inn*, Kilmington, to Stockland; following signs to Membury, cross Yarty River, turn left at T-junction. Driveway on left, after ½ mile. If you reach Membury you have gone too far. From Membury: ¾ mile S; ¼ mile after trout farm.
Restrictions No smoking, except in bar. Dogs by arrangement, in bar, 2 bedrooms only.
Credit cards Access, Amex, Visa.
Terms B&B £43–£58; D,B&B £61–£74. Set lunch £15, dinner £22; full alc £30. 3-night breaks; walking, painting, wine and food weekends; Christmas, New Year packages. 1-night bookings refused weekends in season.

MIDDLECOMBE Somerset   Map 1

Periton Park   *Tel/Fax* (01643) 706885
Middlecombe
nr Minehead TA24 8SW

Richard and Angela Hunt's Victorian house in peaceful setting in 4-acre grounds 1½ miles from Minehead (off A39 to Porlock), on edge of Exmoor National Park. Large, attractive lounge. Good country house cooking in panelled no-smoking dining room, sunny at breakfast, candlelit at night. Riding, shooting, fishing, golf available. Open Feb–Dec. 8 smart bedrooms, 3 no-smoking, 1 on ground floor with access for &. No children under 12. No dogs in public rooms. Access, Amex, Visa accepted. B&B: single £52–£58, double £84–£96; D,B&B: single £69–£76, double £118–£132 [1997]. More reports, please.

MIDDLEHAM North Yorkshire   Map 4

The Millers House   *Tel* (01969) 622630
Middleham DL8 4NR   *Fax* (01969) 623570
                              E-mail millers house.demon.co.uk

Just off the cobbled market square of this quiet Dales village, overlooking an impressive ruined Norman castle, stands Judith and Crossley

Sunderland's pretty grey stone house. "It is decorated in homage to Victoriana," writes a recent visitor. "Our bedroom was done with meticulous attention to detail, everything elaborately swagged and coordinated. It had a four-poster bed, a free-standing Victorian roll-top bath in the room (with screens for the bashful), and a magnificent cornice painted a multitude of colours." Other rooms are smaller and less elaborate; bathrooms vary in size. Another guest praised "the charming hosts, who cannot do enough to help", and added: "We still love it, though they've dropped their apostrophe." The food, which came in for some criticism last year, is now mostly considered excellent. "Unusual and delicious starters; very good main courses; varied and excellent puddings." Fresh local produce and home-grown vegetables, herbs and fruit are used, and vegetarians are catered for. But more than one guest has been irritated by the piped music that accompanies dinner: "It switched abruptly from opera, rather pretentious for the cottagey atmosphere, to overloud thirties jazz, quite inappropriate for a relaxing meal." Middleham has been an important racehorse training centre ever since the monks of nearby Jervaulx Abbey trained their horses on the moors centuries ago; it has three Grand National winners to its credit. The Sutherlands offer a racing weekend as one of their special breaks. Castles, stately homes, ruined abbeys, and many Herriott-associated places are nearby. (*CW, Moira Jarrett, and others*)

Open All year, except Jan. Lunch not served (picnic hamper available).
Rooms 6 double, 1 single.
Facilities Lounge with bar, restaurant (piped music), conservatory. Small garden. Fishing nearby. Unsuitable for &.
Location Centre of small village. Private parking.
Restrictions No smoking: dining room, conservatory. No children under 10. No dogs.
Credit cards Access, Visa.
Terms [1997] B&B £37–£45; D,B&B £55–£62. Set dinner £19.50. Special breaks: wine-tasting, racing, romantic, autumn, spring, Christmas, New Year. *V*

Waterford House   *Tel* (01969) 622090
19 Kirkgate   *Fax* (01969) 624020
Middleham DL8 4PG

Restaurant-with-rooms in Grade II listed house crammed with antiques and knick-knacks, in village centre. "Warmly welcoming" hosts, Brian and Everyl Madell (she is chef). Colourful flowers in pots in front. Cosy lounge, with grand piano, log fire, huge pine dresser, 3-legged cat, Tripod. Attractive restaurant, with large bay windows. Good food, with a Spanish touch; generous portions; amazing wine list. Ample breakfast, wide choice of cooked dishes, quality preserves. 5 bedrooms, quite spacious, eclectically decorated, with fruit, sherry, chocolates. Walled garden. Unsuitable for &. No smoking: restaurant, 1 lounge. No dogs in public rooms. Access, Visa accepted. B&B: single £50–£55, double £65–£85. Set lunch £17.50, dinner £19.50; full alc £29.50. No recent reports; we'd like some, please.

Many hotels put up their prices in the spring. Tariffs quoted in the text may therefore be more accurate before April/May 1998 than after.

MIDHURST West Sussex   Map 2

The Angel   *Tel* (01730) 812421
North Street   *Fax* (01730) 815928
Midhurst GU29 9DN
♥ *César award in 1995*

"A splendid hotel, comfortable and welcoming. The bedrooms are exemplary, and the young staff charming, if occasionally a bit rattled by the pressure of success. Early morning tea is served with a dish of delicious fresh fruit salad, a gracious perk we have not encountered before. The clever contrast of decor in restaurant and brasserie, and the intimacy of the claret walls in the residents' lounge, create an air of relaxed and understated elegance." A recent accolade for an old coaching inn (said to have been visited by the Pilgrim Fathers), which has sprawled in all directions behind its Georgian front. The owners, Peter Crawford-Rolt and Nicholas Davies, have retained the original atmosphere while adding "sophistication without gimmicks". Situated in the main street of a historic West Sussex market town, with the ruins of Cowdray House and the famous polo lawns behind, it caters for all tastes and pockets. Locals call in for a drink, or tea or coffee; it is popular with "the polo crowd". The brasserie (*Michelin* red "Meals") has simple wooden tables and chairs, a daily changing menu, with a good choice of char-grilled meat and fish, and a casual feel. The spacious, handsome *Cowdray Room* serves modern British-based, French-influenced cooking. The bedrooms are in harmony with the house's age; some are large, with good lighting, quality fabrics and pictures, and antiques. There's a quiet rear garden. The operation is overseen by manager, Jonathan Ritchie; Darren Tidd, who took over the kitchens in January 1997, has an impressive CV, including time at two other *Guide* hotels, *Chewton Glen* and *Cliveden*. Some fine National Trust properties, including Uppark and Petworth, are nearby; there is good walking on the South Downs. (*Godfrey and Mary Smith*)

Open All year.
Rooms 2 suites, 19 double, 3 single. 4 across courtyard (2 on ground floor). Some suitable for &.
Facilities Ramps. 2 residents' lounges, bar (piped music midday, evening), brasserie, restaurant (pianist Sat night); 2 function rooms. 2-acre walled garden.
Location Town centre (Union Jack flying). Front rooms double-glazed. Carpark. Train: Haslemere/Petersfield.
Restriction No dogs (kennels nearby).
Credit cards All major cards accepted.
Terms B&B: single £75–£85, double £105–£145. Set lunch £16.25, dinner £18.25; full alc £35. 2-night breaks; 3-day Christmas packages. 1-night bookings refused during "Glorious Goodwood" (29 July–2 Aug).

MINCHINHAMPTON Gloucestershire   Map 3

Burleigh Court   **NEW**   *Tel* (01453) 883804
Burleigh, Minchinhampton   *Fax* (01453) 886870
nr Stroud GL5 2PF

Eighteenth-century Cotswold stone manor in landscaped gardens above Frome valley (extensive views). 2 miles SE of Stroud, approached by tiny country lane. Recently renovated by new owners, Ian and Fiona Hall. Dignified public rooms. 17 bedrooms, most spacious; some, in converted coach house, with access for &. Traditional English cooking, "with a continental twist", served in no-smoking dining room. "Top class breakfasts; excellent service." 3½-acre grounds: Victorian plunge pool. No dogs in public rooms. All major cards accepted. B&B: single £57.50–£67.50, double £80–£90; D,B&B: single £75–£85, double £105–£115. Set lunch £15.95, dinner £21.50 [1997]. More reports, please. ***V***

MINSTER LOVELL Oxfordshire   **Map 2**

Lovells at Windrush Farm   NEW   *Tel* (01993) 779802
Old Minster Lovell   *Fax* (01993) 776212
nr Witney OX8 5RN

One of Britain's prettiest rivers, the Windrush, runs through this lovely village with old cottages, a fine church with medieval stained glass, a 15th-century bridge, and the romantic ruins of a medieval fortified manor, Minster Lovell Hall. On the opposite bank, set amid park and woodland, is Norma Cooper and Mark Maguire's informally run idyll, a 16th-century gentleman farmer's house with a *Michelin*-starred restaurant and just three guest bedrooms. It is probably worth going for one of the two larger ones (the best has a large bathroom with a jacuzzi, the other a shower); the cheapest is considerably smaller. The price includes afternoon tea, dinner, B&B and a newspaper. "Our room was lovely," wrote our beguiled inspector, "with superior linen, fruit, home-made biscuits, and big windows overlooking a well-tended garden. The lounges have teak floorboards and open fires, and there is a full-size antique snooker table. Dinner is at 8.30 pm. The dining room is both pretty and elegant, with everything *comme il faut*, but not stuffily so. Only 16 covers; you must book weeks ahead for Saturday night. The young chef, Marcus Ashenford, serves seven sophisticated courses (no choice). This might be daunting for some, but all were well judged in portion, balanced in composition and well timed in serving. There is a splendid wine list with a reasonable mark-up. Breakfast, just as good, included freshly squeezed orange juice, a beautifully presented plate of fresh fruit, home-made conserves, home-baked rolls. The whole experience was made highly agreeable by the enthusiasm and smileyness of the two owners; we considered it excellent value." Lunch is simpler than dinner. Guests may walk by the river, and fish and picnic there; horse trials are sometimes held in the park.

Open All year, except Jan, Sun night/Mon.
Rooms 3 double.
Facilities Lounge, restaurant. 60-acre grounds. Unsuitable for &.
Location From Minster Lovell, with *White Hart* on right, take 2nd left. *Lovells* is 250 yds on right. Train: Oxford, 16 miles; then taxi.
Restriction No smoking in restaurant.
Credit cards All major cards accepted.
Terms [1997] D,B&B: single £95, double £175. Set lunch £21, dinner £35.

We need feedback on all hotels: big and small, far and near, famous and first-timers.

MORSTON Norfolk   Map 2

Morston Hall   *Tel* (01263) 741041
Morston, Holt NR25 7AA   *Fax* (01263) 740419

This small flint-walled house is in a hamlet on the Norfolk coast near
Blakeney, in gardens with a lily pond and fountain, roses, a croquet
lawn, and a sunny terrace. Its two lounges are small; one has a lovely
old fireplace. The bedrooms, recently refurbished, are spacious and
quiet, each with a large bathroom. The centre of the operation is the
restaurant, which runs the width of the house, with garden views, well-
spaced tables, and a *Michelin* red "Meals" for good food at a reasonable
cost. The owners, Galton Blackiston (the chef), his wife Tracy, and
Justin Fraser, all trained at *Miller Howe*, Windermere (*qv*). *Morston Hall*
is less grand and expensive than the Tovey operation, but it shares the
same approach to dinner: no choice until dessert, and one sitting at
8 pm. This has led to some complaints about "regimentation", to which
the owners reply: "The timing ensures that the food is at its best; the
bread rolls, for example, are timed to come out of the oven just before
8." That criticism apart, our readers have nothing but praise for the
cooking: "I have rarely encountered such high standards." "Extraordinary flavours, textures and presentation." "Friendly, warm and
efficient." "The owners were genuinely interested in the clientele,
unlike many gushingly insincere hoteliers nowadays. The atmosphere
of trust creates a relaxing feel." Breakfast, ordered the previous
evening, can include porridge, kippers and black pudding. Dogs are
welcomed; a small charge is made for those accommodated in the
house, but kennels are free. Morston is in a designated area of outstanding natural beauty; local sights include the seal sanctuary at
Blakeney Point, Sandringham, the Queen's country retreat, and some
fine National Trust properties, including Felbrigg Hall and Blickling
Hall. (*Niki Dixon, WEJ Uttridge, and others; also Barbara Jones*)

Open All year, except Jan. Restaurant closed for lunch, except Sun.
Rooms 6 double.
Facilities 2 lounges, restaurant, conservatory. 3-acre garden: large pond, cro-
quet. Sea, beaches, sailing, birdwatching nearby. Only restaurant suitable for &.
Location On A149 coast road, 2 miles W of Blakeney. Private parking. Train:
Sheringham, via Norwich; then taxi.
Restrictions No smoking in restaurant. No dogs in public rooms.
Credit cards Access, Amex, Visa.
Terms [1997] D,B&B £70–£110. Set Sun lunch £16, dinner £27.50. 3-night bargain
breaks. Christmas package. Cookery courses. Children accommodated free in
parents' room. 1-night bookings sometimes refused Sat.

MOULSFORD-ON-THAMES Oxfordshire   Map 2

The Beetle and Wedge   *Tel* (01491) 651381
Ferry Lane   *Fax* (01491) 651376
Moulsford-on-Thames OX10 9JF

♥ *César award in 1993*

Kate and Dick Smith's much refurbished old ferry inn is on the lovely
stretch of the Thames immortalised in *The Wind in the Willows*. And
Jerome K Jerome lived here when he wrote *Three Men in a Boat*. Most

bedrooms overlook the river. So does the pretty conservatory-style dining room, with sparkling blue glass and flowers on tables, which serves sophisticated classical cooking accompanied by an excellent selection of French wines. No half bottles, but a "dipstick" principle applies: you can order a full bottle and pay for what is consumed plus a surcharge of £1.25. The informal restaurant, the beamed *Boathouse* (which has a different chef and kitchen), is open seven days a week, serving grills from an open charcoal fire, salads, casseroles, traditional puddings, etc, in large portions. There is a water garden for summer meals. Such is the *Beetle*'s popularity that the *Boathouse* is often crowded; long waits can occur at mealtimes, and reception is sometimes disorganised. But most reports are strongly positive. Visitors from Canada write: "It is our favourite bolt-hole in the UK. Lovely bedroom a stone's throw from the river; bathroom nearly as big as the bedroom, with a wonderful free-standing bath. Superlative breakfast, served on exquisite porcelain, with fresh orange juice, fruit, and a good choice of cooked dishes." The dinner, "beautifully cooked and presented but not pretentious", is admired; so are the "self-assured, friendly and attentive staff".

Other guests liked the trusting feel: "They did not ask for a deposit, they upgraded our accommodation, and when we asked about hiring a boat they lent us theirs." Children are welcomed. A good base for Henley and Ascot. (*David Lodge, Marion Fanthorpe; also Eric Dodson, Mrs JC Smye, and others*)

Open All year, except 25 Dec, Restaurant closed Sun evening/Mon.
Rooms 1 suite, 9 double. 4 in adjacent cottage. Some on ground floor.
Facilities Lounge, bars, dining room, *Boathouse* restaurant; function facilities. ½-acre grounds on river: water garden, boating, fishing, mooring.
Location From M4 junction 12 take A4 S; at 2nd roundabout take A340 Pangbourne/Streatley/Moulsford. In village turn to river on Ferry La. Parking. Train: Reading/Goring; then taxi.
Restrictions No smoking: dining room, bedrooms. No dogs.
Credit cards All major cards accepted.
Terms [1997] B&B: single £90, double £110–£135. Bar meals. Set lunch £25 (£27.50 Sun), dinner £35 (dining room); full alc (*Boathouse*) from £25. Champagne weekends; cooking tutorials, etc. *V*

MULLION Cornwall　　　　　　　　　　　　　　　　**Map 1**

Polurrian Hotel　**NEW**　　　　　　　　　　Tel (01326) 240421
Mullion, nr Helston TR12 7EN　　　　　　　　Fax (01326) 240083

In magnificent clifftop position on Lizard peninsula, amid glorious National Trust scenery, large white Edwardian building with excellent facilities for children of all ages and adults too: nanny, crèche, teenagers' room, leisure club, snooker, spa, sauna; indoor and outdoor swimming pools, tennis, squash, etc; 12-acre grounds; small private beach. Golf, riding, windsurfing nearby. "Exceptionally friendly, willing, happy staff." Well-equipped bedrooms (some poorly insulated). Excellent breakfasts; adequate dinners. 39 bedrooms; best ones with sea view; others cheaper. Closed 6 Jan–1 Feb. No smoking: restaurant, reading room. No dogs in public rooms. All major credit cards accepted. B&B £35–£138; D,B&B £45–£145 [1997]. Bar snacks. Set dinner £20. Children under 5 sharing parents' room free if adults are on half board; 6–14s charged for meals only. More reports, please.

MUNGRISDALE Cumbria   Map 4

The Mill Hotel `BUDGET`   *Tel* (01768 7) 79659
Mungrisdale, Penrith CA11 0XR   *Fax* (01768 7) 79155
ꙭ *César award in 1993*

Richard and Eleanor Quinlan's former mill cottage, with a millrace, waterfall and trout stream, is in a hamlet at the foot of the Skiddaw range of mountains – "a delightfully peaceful setting". There is excellent walking from the door. Public rooms are small, and crowded at busy times. Bedrooms are immaculate; some are small. Two, with a shared sitting room, are in the old mill itself; they are bright and airy, with a sloping ceiling and a skylight – "you can lie in bed looking at the stars while listening to the stream." Traditional dinners in generous quantities, with some choice, are cooked by Mrs Quinlan, and served at 7 pm by her husband. Bread is home-baked. Apart from one unhappy letter about a booking not honoured, there is nothing but praise again this year for "the consistency of the hospitality" that the Quinlans provide. "Their sheer professionalism is matched by their warmth and their concern that guests really enjoy their stay. The dinners satisfy and delight. The approach and the setting, in sweeping north lakes countryside, are appropriate preparation for the relaxed comfort that greets you. Richard Quinlan caters for his guests with quiet charm and a delightful sense of humour. We recall each visit with a warm glow." "First-class breakfasts." Children are welcomed. The Penrith exit of the M6 is only 12 miles away. (*Margaret and Alan Clarke, and others*)
    Note: Not to be mistaken for the *Mill Inn*, with which it confusingly shares an entrance.

Open Feb–Oct. Dining room closed for lunch.
Rooms 9 double. Some on ground floor. No telephone.
Facilities 3 lounges, dining room (piped classical music at night); drying room. 2-acre grounds: millrace, waterfall, trout stream. Ullswater 5 miles, fishing, sailing. Unsuitable for &.
Location 2 miles N of A66 Penrith–Keswick. M6 exit 40.
Restrictions No smoking in dining room. Dogs at proprietors' discretion, not in public rooms.
Credit cards None accepted.
Terms B&B: single £30–£35, double £55–£70; D,B&B £50–£65 per person. Set dinner £25. Reductions for 5 or more nights. `*V*`

NEAR SAWREY, Cumbria   Map 4

Ees Wyke   *Tel/Fax* (01539 4) 36393
Near Sawrey
nr Ambleside LA22 0JZ

Near Sawrey and Far Sawrey are tiny villages close to Lake Windermere. Beatrix Potter's small farmhouse, Hill Top (managed today by the National Trust), is in the former, where she is also known to have holidayed in this Georgian house. With its colonnaded doorway, white walls and black window frames, it is now a cheerful guest house, with hardworking hosts John and Margaret Williams. It has a tranquil setting above Esthwaite Water, with views of mountains, forests, fells and sheep, and spectacular sunsets. "It is run with good humour and lightness of touch," wrote a recent visitor. "Guests assemble for drinks at 7 pm, on a terrace in warm weather; dinner is at 7.30. John's cooking (which rates an entry in the *Good Food Guide*) is straightforward and competent, if a little robust for those who haven't climbed Great Gable or Helvellyn earlier in the day. But we learned to ask for small portions, so as to enjoy the perfect vegetables. There is a modest, reasonably priced wine list." Breakfasts are "amazing", with five or six cereals and a wonderful choice of fruit; "and having produced eggs and bacon, Margaret appears with a large platter with mushrooms, tomato, three sorts of sausage, fried bread, black pudding, etc". Bedrooms, all but one with a lake view, are good-sized and "nicely decorated". Each has a compact but charming bathroom and is named for its colour scheme. More reports, please.

Open Mar–Dec.
Rooms 8 double. 1 on ground floor. No telephone.
Facilities 2 lounges, dining room. 2-acre garden. Access to lake; fishing.
Location SE of Hawkshead on road to Windermere ferry; on edge of village. Local bus, "the Coniston Rambler", in summer.
Restrictions No smoking in dining room. No children under 8. No dogs in public rooms.
Credit card Amex.
Terms B&B £44–£54; D,B&B £56–£66. Set dinner £12 (£21 to non-residents). 3-day breaks Mar, Nov; 4-day Christmas house party.

NEW MILTON Hampshire   Map 2

Chewton Glen   *Tel* (01425) 275341
Christchurch Road   *Fax* (01425) 272310
New Milton BH25 6QS   *E-mail* 100547.3423@compuserve.com

An 18th-century red brick mansion (Relais & Châteaux), large and luxurious, "but not intimidating", in huge grounds, with parkland, woodland, lawns and gardens, on the southern fringe of the New Forest. The sea is a short walk away, along a footpath. *Chewton Glen* has been owned for over 30 years by Martin and Brigitte Skan, who run it with a courteous staff. Lounges are large and light, with antiques and fine fabrics. Suites and bedrooms, some vast, are equally lavish, and have fruit, sherry, biscuits, plentiful toiletries, huge towels, bathrobes, etc. Some have a balcony or terrace; the two-storeyed suites in the coach house have a private garden. Almost all of the outstanding health and sporting facilities (see below) are free to residents. The restaurant, named for Captain Marryat, who wrote *The Children of the New Forest* here, has a pretty conservatory extension, and a *Michelin* star for Pierre Chevillard's modern cooking. Recent admirers have found it "difficult to fault": "The food is exquisite, the waiters are great fun and professional. The young *sommelier*, Mark Walter, does an excellent job with the wines, which are memorable." Breakfasts offer a wide choice. But one regular visitor this year complained: "Service is no longer included in the prices, which represents a significant increase of the already high prices." (*JS Rutter, and others*)

Open All year.
Rooms 16 suites (2 in grounds), 37 double. Some on ground floor.
Facilities Ramps. 3 lounges (pianist in 1 on weekdays), bar, 4 dining rooms; function rooms; snooker room; health club: indoor tennis, swimming pool, gymnasium, beauty salon. 70-acre grounds: lake, tennis, croquet, 9-hole golf course, jogging course, swimming pool, helipad; bicycle hire. Beach, fishing, sailing, shooting, riding nearby. Chauffeur service.
Location From A35 *don't* follow New Milton signs; turn off to Walkford and Highcliffe. As you leave Walkford, the road dips; turn into Chewton Farm road (immediately before roundabout sign). Entrance on right. Station 5 mins' drive.
Restrictions No smoking in restaurant. No children under 7. No dogs (kennels nearby).
Credit cards All major cards accepted.
Terms [Until end Mar 1998] B&B: single £224.50, double £323–£368, suite £398–£563. Set lunch £23.50, dinner £42. 5-night breaks; healthy breaks; golfing, Christmas, Easter packages. 2-night bookings preferred weekends.

NEW POLZEATH Cornwall   Map 1

The Cornish Cottage   NEW   *Tel* (01208) 862213
New Polzeath, nr Rock PL27 6UF   *Fax* (01208) 862259

Set amid National Trust land in group of houses above holiday village, Clive and Christine Mason's hotel with restaurant serving sophisticated, beautifully presented cooking (including good vegetarian dishes) by Tim Rogers. Spacious conservatory lounge; 12 cottagey bedrooms. Decor may not be to everyone's taste (plastic as well as fresh flowers, holiday souvenirs). 1½-acre grounds with swimming pool (heated June–Sept). Near coastal path and clean sandy beaches. 5 golf courses within 15 miles. Unsuitable for &. No children under 12. No dogs. All major credit cards accepted. B&B £48; D,B&B £68. Set lunch £17.50, dinner £28.50; full alc Sun lunch £34.50. More reports, please. *V*

NEW ROMNEY Kent   Map 2

Romney Bay House   *Tel* (01797) 364747
Coast Road   *Fax* (01797) 367156
Littlestone, New Romney TN28 8QY

♥ *César award in 1997*

Romney Marsh is a strange, flat area, full of history. When Caesar landed in 55 BC it was a sea bay; the Romans started its reclamation, and it is now protected by sea walls and dykes. Helmut and Jennifer Gorlich's white-walled, red-roofed house stands alone a few feet from the beach, with a golf course behind – a spectacular setting. It was built in the 1920s by Sir Clough Williams-Ellis for the American actress and journalist Hedda Hopper. The Gorlichs have "lavished love on it in every nook and cranny". "The view of the English Channel is glorious," runs one of this year's many encomiums. "It can be enjoyed from the 'look out', a lounge at the front of the hotel complete with telescope, and even from the four-poster bed in Room 1. The Gorlichs make you feel instantly at home. Dinner (four courses, no choice) is excellent:

delightful starter, exquisite main course, fine selection of English cheeses, sumptuous dessert. A full English breakfast is available, and the continental version includes cold meats, cheese, fruits and two kinds of croissants. The house is a treasure trove of antiques, pictures and knick-knacks. At night, white candles burning in the public rooms and a log fire crackling in the lounge create a romantic atmosphere." "An oasis of tranquillity", "excellent value", others have written. Bedrooms have "everything you need": flowers, hot-water bottle, bathrobe, etc. Cream teas are served, on the terrace in fine weather. Two boxer dogs, Lewis and Harriet, will take guests for walks. The Channel Tunnel is 20 minutes' drive away. (*Riccard Parsonson, Jill Johnson, David Langrish, and many others*)

Open All year, except 24–30 Dec. Restaurant closed 2 weeks mid-June, some mid-winter evenings.
Rooms 8 double, 2 single.
Facilities 2 sitting rooms, bar, 2 dining rooms; small function facilities. 1½-acre garden: tennis, croquet, *boules*. Next to sea (safe bathing), golf course. Unsuitable for &.
Location From New Romney, follow signs to Littlestone; at sea, turn left. Continue as far as possible. Hotel alone, opposite sea, on left.
Restrictions No smoking except main lounge, bar. No children. No dogs.
Credit cards Access, Diners, Visa.
Terms [1997] B&B: single from £45, double £70–£105. Snack lunch from £6.50; set dinner £28. Off-season, midweek breaks. 1-night bookings sometimes refused weekends.

NEWBRIDGE West Sussex   **Map 2**

The Old Wharf   NEW/BUDGET   *Tel/Fax* (01403) 784096
Newbridge
nr Billingshurst RH14 0JG

An inspector writes: "Halfway between Billingshurst and Wisborough Green, a track hairpins off the busy A272 through quiet, low-lying farmland. *The Old Wharf* is a pleasant squarish building, wider than it is high, at the edge of a sleepy watercourse. Once a canal warehouse at the terminus of the Arun Navigation Company, it now earns its living as a working farm and an exceptionally agreeable B&B. The bedrooms are light and freshly painted in pastel colours, with simple country furniture and knick-knacks. Bedlinen consists of well-filled duvets and crackling pillows. Each room has its own bathroom, with ample towels on heated rails. Peaceful views extend over water-meadows or gardens. The best room, the Primrose Suite, has a separate sitting room. A large restored hoist wheel from cargo-hauling days makes an eye-catching feature above the open stairway. Guests may use a spacious downstairs sitting room with board games, a piano and an open fireplace. Breakfast is served in a sprig-stencilled, quarry-tiled room overlooking an attractive walled garden. David and Moira Mitchell make you welcome, conveying an infectious enthusiasm for their interesting home and its surroundings. They are keen on conservation and wildlife. The breakfast eggs will be free-range, the muesli home-made, and you are asked not to smoke." Nearby attractions include the Sussex Downs and coast, historic houses such as Petworth and Parham, Arundel Castle, some famous gardens, including Wisley, Nymans and Leonardslee, racing at Goodwood and polo at Cowdray Park.

Open All year, except 2 weeks Christmas/New Year.
Rooms 1 suite, 3 double.
Facilities Drawing room with TV. 15-acre grounds: tennis, river, fishing; swimming pool planned. Unsuitable for &.
Location A272 W from Billingshurst for 2 miles; over narrow bridge; hotel 75 yds on left. Train: Billingshurst; then taxi.
Restrictions No smoking. No children under 12. No dogs.
Credit cards Access, Amex, Visa.
Terms [1997] B&B: single £40, double £55, suite £70. Weekly rates on application.

NEWCASTLE UPON TYNE Tyne and Wear   Map 4

Horton Grange   *Tel* (01661) 860686
Seaton Burn   *Fax* (01661) 860308
Newcastle upon Tyne   *E-mail* andrew@horton.onyxnet.co.uk
NE13 6BU

Though only six miles from the centre of the commercial and cultural hub of north-east England, Sue and Andrew Shilton's hotel stands in open, if flat, farmland, and is "blissfully quiet at night". "We wouldn't stay anywhere else in Newcastle," say regular visitors. "The Shiltons are assiduous hosts, hard-working, professional, and responsive. For a modest price, they provide everything we value in a hotel. Rooms (which are serviced in the evening) are not luxurious, but are pleasantly furnished with antiques; beds are comfortable, with crisp cotton bedding. There is always a small vase of flowers from the garden. Bathrooms are reasonably supplied with toiletries; water is reliably hot. The sitting room is a beauty, with two fires, comfortable sofas and chairs arranged to provide privacy, attractive lighting from table lamps, and arrangements of flowers and foliage. Breakfasts, especially the cooked ones, are excellent." "The Shiltons have mastered that difficult task of supplying perfect hospitality without being intrusive. We were served delicious tea with freshly baked biscuits in front of the fire, specially lit for us on a miserable day." The single suites in a garden annexe have a desk, and the airport is nearby. The place always had a good reputation for its food. This year, the Shiltons have made a new dining room overlooking the garden, and are restructuring their menus to provide less formal meals, with bistro-type cooking. We'd like reports, please (*David and Kate Wooff, and others*)

Open All year, except 25/26 Dec.
Rooms 4 suites (on ground floor in garden annexe, with & access), 7 double, 2 single.
Facilities Ramps. Lounge, restaurant (piped music at night). 3-acre grounds. Lake, fishing 10 mins' walk.
Location 6 miles N of centre. From A1 western by-pass take A19 Ashington/Tyne Tunnel exit. At roundabout take 1st exit; left after 1 mile to Dinnington/Ponteland/Airport. Hotel 2 miles on right. Large carpark. Taxi: from airport 4 miles; from station 6 miles.
Restrictions No smoking in restaurant. No dogs.
Credit cards Access, Amex, Visa.
Terms B&B: single £59, double £90; D,B&B £70 per person. Set dinner from £25.

Hotels are dropped if we lack positive feedback. If you can endorse an entry, we urge you to do so.

NEWLANDS Cumbria   Map 4

Swinside Lodge   *Tel/Fax* (01768 7) 72948
Grange Road
Newlands, nr Keswick CA12 5UE
♀ *César award in 1996*

Graham Taylor's Victorian Lakeland house, at the foot of Catbells, continues to inspire enthusiasm. "My fifth visit in five years. Only one word to describe it, 'perfection'." "We enjoyed every minute. Such sensitive attention to detail." "Books, magazines, interesting company, all helped to make an excellent break." "Blissfully peaceful setting, surrounded by fells and fields. Comfortable bedroom with chocolates, mineral water and a Teasmade. After dinner one could in theory take a five-minute stroll to the shores of Derwent Water, but in practice we only made it to one of the comfortable armchairs." "The food was remarkable. First courses, desserts and soups were particularly unusual. We liked being able to bring our own wine (*Swinside* is unlicensed)." *Michelin* awards a red "Meals" for Chris Astley's cooking, on a five-course no-choice-until-dessert menu, which ends with "not-to-be-missed" cheeses. Complimentary sherry is served before dinner at 7.30 pm. Graham Taylor is an "amenable host", helping new arrivals with their cases and offering them tea with home-made biscuits. "Interesting" packed lunches are available for walkers. Breakfast is a hearty Cumbrian affair, with fresh orange juice. "No hidden extras: very good value." Keswick, the largest town in the Lake District, is close by. (*AT Tulloch, Dr and Mrs RR Evans, Marc and Margaret Wall, Alice Sennett, and others*)

Open Feb–Nov, Christmas. Dining room closed midday.
Rooms 7 double. No telephone.
Facilities 2 sitting rooms, dining room. ¾-acre garden. Derwent Water 5 mins' walk: shingle beach, safe bathing. Unsuitable for ♿.
Location 3 miles SW of Keswick. A66 for Cockermouth; left at Portinscale; follow road to Grange and Lingholm Gardens (do *not* turn off at Swinside sign). Train: Penrith, 18 miles; then taxi.
Restrictions No smoking. No children under 10. No dogs.
Credit cards None accepted.
Terms D,B&B: single £72–£85, double £128–£160. Packed lunches. Set dinner £25. Off-season and longer stay rates. 4-day Christmas package. 1-night bookings sometimes refused.

NEWTON-LE-WILLOWS North Yorkshire   Map 4

The Hall   NEW   *Tel* (01677) 450210
Newton-le-Willows   *Fax* (01677) 450014
nr Bedale DL8 1SW

In quiet village 3 miles W of Bedale (not to be confused with Merseyside town of same name), lovely Georgian house, with caring, informal hostess, Oriella Featherstone. Elegant decor: antiques, tapestries, oriental rugs, objets d'art; house party atmosphere. 3 spacious, well-furnished bedrooms. Traditional home-cooked evening meal (no choice, but prior consultation) communally served. Breakfast a wholesome feast, served at flexible times and sometimes including goose eggs. 2-acre gardens, 12 acres fields (good for dog-walking), stables for visiting horses. Family car with driver available (will collect from Teesside airport, Darlington station). Dales, moors, castles, ruined abbeys, gardens, golf, fishing, riding close by. Unsuitable for &. Smoking discouraged in restaurant, banned in bedrooms. No children under 13. No dogs. B&B £40–£45; D,B&B £60–£65.

NORTH BOVEY Devon   **Map 1**

Blackaller Hotel   BUDGET   *Tel/Fax* (01647) 440322
North Bovey
nr Moretonhampstead TQ13 8QY

This converted woollen mill, long, low and white, stands at the end of a long lane. It is "a special, peaceful place, with a gentle, genial host", Peter Hunt, who also keeps bees, spins wool from his own Jacob sheep, and plays the sitar, and a "jolly hostess", Hazel Phillips, who is "a wonderful cook". Its well-kept garden has a smooth lawn running down to the river, and garden furniture dotted about. Here cream teas are served in fine weather. The public rooms are unpretentious, with antiques, china, flowers and family photos – "more like a home than a hotel". Bedrooms, some up a steep staircase, have a simple decor, with oak beams and quality fabrics, and a clean, bright bathroom. In the pretty candlelit dining room, dinners are well balanced, with excellent sauces and vegetables, and accompanied by reasonably priced wines on a predominantly New World list. Recent praise: "Charming hosts; first-class food." "One of the most enjoyable meals I have eaten recently. Breakfast with toast to die for (a real test)." "Despite its simple appearance, this is a sophisticated operation." North Bovey is a delightful village in the Dartmoor National Park, with granite and thatch houses and a large green with oak trees. Castle Drogo (National Trust) is close by; glorious walking all around. (*Mr and Mrs DG Elliott, and others*)

Open Mar–Jan. Restaurant closed Mon.
Rooms 4 double, 1 single. Family annexe. No telephone.
Facilities Lounge, bar (piped classical music at night), restaurant. 3-acre garden on river: coarse fishing. Trout-fishing, golf nearby. Unsuitable for &.
Location From Moretonhampstead follow sign to North Bovey. Hotel sign on wall at edge of village. Train: Exeter St David's, 14 miles; hotel will meet.
Restrictions Smoking in bar only. No children under 12. No dogs in public rooms.
Credit cards None accepted.
Terms [1997] B&B £29–£36; D,B&B £50–£57. Autumn, spring, Christmas, New Year breaks. *V*

NORTH HUISH Devon   **Map 1**

Brookdale House   *Tel* (01548) 821661
North Huish, South Brent TQ10 9NR   *Fax* (01548) 821606

Listed Tudor-style Victorian rectory with fine moulded ceilings, marble fireplaces, traditional decor: antiques, country house furnishings, light colours. Piped music in public rooms. 4½-acre wooded grounds, with brook, waterfall, in remote Devon valley 7 miles SW of Totnes. Dartmoor 10 mins' drive, beaches 15 mins; fishing, sailing, golf nearby. Hospitable managers, Mike and

Gill Mikkelsen (he is chef). Traditional dishes (with Scandinavian touch): organic vegetables and meat, freshly caught fish; generous portions; extensive wine list. Small conference/function facilities. 8 bedrooms, 3 no-smoking, 2 in cottage 25 yds. Unsuitable for &. Children not encouraged, but over 12 accepted. Dogs in cottages only. Access, Amex, Visa accepted. B&B £50–£65; D,B&B £65. Set Sun lunch £10.50; full alc £25. Recently endorsed, but we'd like more reports, please.

NORTON-ON-DERWENT North Yorkshire   Map 4

Newstead Grange   BUDGET   *Tel* (01653) 692502
Beverley Road   *Fax* (01653) 696951
Norton-on-Derwent
nr Malton YO17 9PJ

Pat and Paul Williams' old stone Georgian house, with Victorian extensions and many original features retained, is set in a large, mature garden. It has a period decor, with antiques, comfortable chairs, settees and chandeliers; watercolours painted by Mrs Williams are hung throughout. Bedrooms, named for previous owners of the house, are decorated in similar style and have "beautifully appointed bathrooms". There are open fires in the sitting rooms, and one has a grand piano. The dining room is spacious, with lace table-cloths and Victorian chairs. This is a friendly place, where guests tend to socialise in the evening; many are on a return visit. Dinners (no choice) at 7.30 pm, cooked by Mrs Williams, are praised: "well balanced and wholesome, with delicious soups and beautifully presented puddings". Some of the fruit and vegetables are organically home-grown. "Excellent, old-fashioned breakfasts, too." Malton is an ancient market town in the heart of race-horse training country. There is beautiful countryside all around: dramatic moors to the north, the softer Wolds to the south; also ancient abbeys and stately homes, including Castle Howard. More reports, please.

Open Mid-Feb–early Nov.
Rooms 8 double. No telephone/TV.
Facilities 2 lounges, dining room (piped music). 2½-acre garden. Unsuitable for &.
Location 1½ miles SE of Malton. Follow signs to Beverley. Hotel on B1248 ½ mile beyond last houses, at junction with road to Settrington. Train: Malton; then taxi.
Restrictions No smoking. Children under 10 by arrangement. No dogs in house.
Credit card Access.
Terms B&B £32.50–£44. Set dinner £16.50. 2-night breaks. 1-night bookings sometimes refused. ***V*** (Feb–Apr, Oct, Nov)

NORWICH Norfolk   Map 2

The Beeches   BUDGET   *Tel* (01603) 621167
4–6 Earlham Road   *Fax* (01603) 620151
Norwich NR2 3DB   *E-mail* beeches.hotel@paston.co.uk

Just ten minutes' stroll west of the historic city centre is a lovely wooded italianate Victorian garden set in a deep hollow, with a gothic fountain, terraces and a massive rockery with cascades. Once sadly neglected, it has been brought back to life by the Plantation Garden

Preservation Trust. Plantation House, the more imposing of the two listed Victorian mansions which comprise this hotel, is set in the heart of the garden, "which makes for a peaceful stay". The other, with a modern extension, is near a busy road. The hotel is run by Keith and Lis Hill with their daughter, Kate, who is the manager. The bedrooms, all no-smoking, are simple but clean, with all mod cons; some are spacious. "This hotel doesn't try to be something it isn't, and it succeeds within its own lights," wrote one visitor. Another was critical of the breakfast, but said: "The atmosphere is agreeable, and the staff are extremely helpful." The informal restaurant serves contemporary bistro-style dinners, to classical/jazz background music. For those with gastronomic aspirations, the *Michelin*-starred *Adlard's* is five minutes' walk away. The garden is open to the public on Sunday, but visitors to the hotel may wander there at any time. (*RB, Helen Brandes, and others*)

Open Closed 23–30 Dec. Restaurant closed for lunch.
Rooms 3 suites, 14 double, 8 single. In 2 buildings. 10 on ground floor, 1 designed for &.
Facilities Lounge/bar, restaurant (piped classical music/jazz). 3-acre grounds (open to public on Sun).
Location On B1108, 10 minutes' walk from centre (roadside rooms double-glazed). Ample parking.
Restrictions Smoking in bar only. No dogs.
Credit cards All major cards accepted.
Terms B&B: single £46–£55, double £59–£65, suite £69–£75. Set dinner £12; full alc £20.

NOTTINGHAM Nottinghamshire   Map 2

Hotel des Clos   NEW   *Tel* (0115) 986 6566
Old Lenton Lane   *Fax* (0115) 986 0343
Nottingham NG7 2SA

Conversion of old farm buildings on banks of river Trent, 10–15 mins' taxi ride from centre. Setting less than bucolic – between two electricity pylons; opposite A52 flyover. But quiet interior (apart from background classical music); pleasant decor. 10 comfortable bedrooms, most facing carefully planted courtyard. Friendly, humorous owner/chef, John Abbey; friendly dog, Sammy. Modern French cooking (a bit rich for some) in popular restaurant; amazing wine list, heavy on Chablis. Good breakfast. Difficult to find; ask for directions. Rooms: single £75, double £75–£90, suite £110–£125. Breakfast £4.95–£8.50. Set lunch £16.95; full alc £27.50. Weekend break: D,B&B £54 [1997]. *V*

Walton's   NEW   *Tel* (0115) 947 5215
2 North Road   *Fax* (0115) 947 5053
The Park, Nottingham NG7 1A6

"How pleasant to find a hotel in Nottingham that is an antidote to modern hotel life," writes an inspector. "It is a pleasing early 19th-century lodge, turned into a thriving hotel and restaurant, full of character. It has been decorated with flair throughout, and antiques of all kinds have been effectively used in the public rooms as well as in the comfortable bedrooms. Our meal was mixed: one main course good, the other over-ambitious. But service was cheerful and discreet. Breakfast, in a sunny morning room, was adequate. There is a busy road in front, but my room at the back was quiet. A delightful stay." "The bar is a pleasant place for lunch," adds another visitor. "Good and plentiful food and a fire in winter." *Walton's* is named for its architect owner, Keith Walton who, with his partner, Gwen Flanders, was responsible for its restoration and decoration. The hotel is on the edge of The Park, once a royal hunting park, now an exclusive residential area with large Victorian villas. Many of the city's attractions are within easy walking distance.

Open All year. Restaurant closed Sat midday.
Rooms 2 suites, 13 double, 4 single. 2 on ground floor. 3 in annexe across road.
Facilities 2 lounges, bar, restaurant (piped music all day; live pianist Fri/Sat night); terrace; conference/function room.
Location On edge of The Park, on A52 (rear rooms quietest). Carpark.
Restrictions No smoking in 6 bedrooms. No dogs where food is served.
Credit cards All major cards accepted.
Terms [1997] B&B: single £65, double £75, suite £90; full alc £23. Children under 6 accommodated free in parents' room; under 12 half price. Reduced rates for week or more.

OAKAMOOR Staffordshire   Map 3

Bank House   BUDGET   *Tel/Fax* (01538) 702810
Farley Lane, Oakamoor   *E-mail* john.orme@dial.pipex.com
nr Stoke-on-Trent ST10 3BD

Enticing guest house, "grandly decorated, yet exuding warmth and comfort". 1 mile from Alton Towers, in lovely Churnet valley, within Staffordshire moorlands, on edge of Peak National Park. Excellent walks from door. Run on house party lines by welcoming hosts, Muriel and John Egerton-Orme, with 2 friendly dogs. 1-acre garden in 4 acres woodland. Pastoral views. Tranquil atmosphere. Elegant home-cooked dinners (menu agreed in advance with guests). 4 bedrooms with telephone, TV and many extras. Good family accommodation. Closed Christmas. Unsuitable for ♿. No smoking: library, bedrooms. Dogs by arrangement. Access, Visa accepted. B&B £26–£36. Set dinner £20 [1997]. More reports, please.

OTLEY Suffolk   Map 2

Bowerfield House   BUDGET   *Tel* (01473) 890742
Helmingham Road   *Fax* (01473) 890059
Otley, nr Ipswich IP6 9NR

Lise and Michael Hilton's listed 17th-century barn and stable conversion is set well back from the road, overlooking fields, in a village in the heart of rural Suffolk. The long drive passes through a mature garden with a pond with koi carp and golden orf. The hotel is run on Wolsey Lodge lines. The decor is home-like: antiques and a wood fire in the sitting room, where guests may play the grand piano; spacious bedrooms, with antiques, fresh flowers, TV, and bathrooms well endowed with toiletries and medicaments. There's a billiard room with a fine table. Michael Hilton will give guests a game of snooker, or play croquet with them on the manicured lawn. Dinner ("excellent home cooking, impeccably served," say our readers) is available on weekdays by arrangement; dishes from Mrs Hilton's native Denmark often appear on the menu. It is communally served at an elegantly appointed table in the beamed dining room; the Hiltons sometimes eat with their guests. No licence: guests bring their own wine. Breakfasts are also admired: "Delicious, thick Danish bacon, proper brown bread, home-made marmalade and strong coffee. Meals and accommodation of a style that 'great' hotels might emulate. Altogether marvellous value." Otley Hall, in the village, a stunning 15th-century moated building in formal gardens (occasionally open to the public), was the home of Bartholomew Gosnold, who discovered Cape Cod, named Martha's Vineyard after his wife, and then went on to found Jamestown, Virginia. Aldeburgh, Snape, and the Minsmere bird reserve are nearby. More reports, please.

Open Mid-Mar–Oct. Dining room closed evening Sat/Sun, midday.
Rooms 3 double. 2 in carriage house across courtyard. 2 on ground floor.
Facilities Drawing room, billiard room, dining room. 2-acre grounds: pond, cro-quet. Golf, fishing, riding nearby. Unsuitable for &.
Location On B1079, in village 6 miles NW of Woodbridge. Hotel 6th house on right after post office. Bus (infrequent) from Ipswich.
Restrictions No smoking. No children under 12. Dogs in cars only.
Credit cards None accepted.
Terms [1997] B&B: single £34–£36, double £42–£46. Set dinner £18. 1-night book-ings sometimes refused weekends.

OXFORD Oxfordshire   Map 2

Bath Place Hotel & Restaurant   `NEW`   *Tel* (01865) 79182
4/5 Bath Place, Holywell Street   *Fax* (01865) 791834
Oxford OX1 3SU

Kathleen and Yolanda Fawsitt's restaurant-with-rooms, composed of three 17th-century cottages, pink and blue, grouped round tiny flagstone courtyard (Elizabeth Siddal, of Pre-Raphaelite fame, was born in one). Down alley between New and Hertford colleges; limited parking, booked in advance. 12 small bedrooms, impeccably decorated, many with exposed timbers. French-inspired modern cooking by Jeremy Blake O'Connor. Restaurant closed Sun evening/Mon/midday Tues. No smoking: restaurant, bedrooms. No dogs in public rooms. Access, Amex, Visa accepted. B&B: single £75–£95, double £90–£125. Cooked breakfast from £6. Set lunch £17.50, dinner £29.50; full alc £40 [1997].

Cotswold House   `BUDGET`   *Tel/Fax* (01865) 310558
363 Banbury Road
Oxford OX2 7PL

"A blessing in overpriced, never-discounted Oxford hotel land." "Jim and Anne O'Kane's constant but unobtrusive attention to detail is without equal. Substantial, delectable breakfast, traditional or vegetar-ian." "An excellent base, and a haven of peace and quiet at the end of the day. We were given maps and detailed instructions about how to get the most out of Oxford." Regular visitors' praise for this modest, welcoming B&B, a double-fronted Cotswold stone house, with flower baskets hung all around. It is in the leafy environs of North Oxford, an easy two-mile bus ride from the city centre. Bedrooms are modern, clean and comfortable, with pastel linens and flounces, pink dolls, pot-pourri, TV, a fridge, fruit, "and the odd pious tome by the bed". Duvet or blankets at your choice. One single room is very small. Bathrooms are well provided with towels; masses of piping hot water. Guests have access to the well-kept garden at the rear of the house. *La Dolce Vita* and the *Greek Taverna* in Summertown, close by, are recommended for an evening meal. (*Braham Murray, Daniel and Susan Davidson, Doreen Attwood, and others*)

Open All year, except 10 days over Christmas/New Year.
Rooms 5 double, 2 single, all with shower. 1 on ground floor. No telephone.
Facilities Lounge, breakfast room. Small rear garden. Unsuitable for &.
Location 2 miles N of centre, just inside ring road (A40), on A423. Carpark. Frequent bus services to centre.
Restrictions No smoking. No children under 5. No dogs.
Credit cards None accepted.
Terms [1997] B&B: single £39–£41, double £57–£61.

Old Parsonage　　　　　　　　　　　*Tel* (01865) 310210
1 Banbury Road　　　　　　　　　　　*Fax* (01865) 311262
Oxford OX2 6NN　　*E-mail* oldparsonage@dial.pipex.com

"A sense of calm greets the weary traveller who enters the foyer of this hotel, a stone's throw from the centre of the historic city. Jeremy Mogford, who also owns the unmissable bistro-style *Brown's* restaurant across the road, and the conservatory-style *Gee's* nearby, has retained all that one loves in charming old manor houses – the character, the comfort, the warmth. He has removed the draughts and the bats in the attic, and has added an impressive bar, an adequate and well-cooked menu and an exemplary staff. The cheapest rooms are smaller than one would expect for the price, but otherwise faultless. A little more detail in the mechanics, rather than the appearance, of the plumbing would make bathing less hazardous. Take your plunger, and don't leave without trying the pear tarte tatin." A recent report on this venerable creeper-clad 17th-century parsonage. Other visitors have praised the "beautifully finished modern bedrooms" and the breakfasts. The large bar, its walls densely hung with pictures, serves snacks and informal meals all day from a short menu, and does a busy local trade; there's a fairly priced wine list. In fine weather, residents may sit

 in the roof garden; alfresco meals, including breakfast, are served on the terrace. The hotel has its own punt and provides picnics. A few snags: some bedrooms face the carpark; the road can be busy; one winter visitor thought the place was overheated "and beds were on the small side". (*Philippa Morgan, Brian Cornwell, and others*)

Open All year, except 25/26 Dec.
Rooms 4 suites, 25 double, 1 single. 10 on ground floor.
Facilities Small lounge, bar/restaurant (piped "easy listening" music); terrace, roof garden. Walled garden. Unsuitable for &.

Location NE end of St Giles (some traffic noise). Parking for 16 cars.
Restriction No dogs.
Credit cards All major cards accepted.
Terms B&B: single £120, double £145–£160, suite £185–£200. Full alc £32. 2-night breaks.

PADSTOW Cornwall   Map 1

The Seafood Restaurant   *Tel* (01841) 532700
  and St Petroc's House   **BUDGET**   *Fax* (01841) 533344
Riverside, Padstow PL28 8BY

Rick Stein's seafood restaurant has a ringside view over the harbour of this attractive fishing village on the Camel estuary. The decor is cheerful: white walls, lots of plants, modern pictures, cane chairs; tables close together. Pre-dinner drinks are taken in a delightful conservatory. Above the restaurant are pleasant bedrooms, priced according to size and view, with a modern decor; two have a balcony. Cheaper rooms and a bistro are in *St Petroc's House*, one of the oldest buildings in Padstow, just up the hill. There are three inexpensive bedrooms, let on a B&B basis, above the Steins' coffee shop, the *Middle Street Café*. They also run a delicatessen, stocked with Stein's Jams, Stein's Pickled Products, Stein-embroidered aprons, etc; his recipe books and cassettes of his TV programmes are for sale everywhere. Mr Stein's fame is such that Padstow is nowadays sometimes called Padstein. You have to book weeks in advance for the restaurant, and there are two sittings for dinner, at 7.30 and 9.30 pm. Inevitably, perhaps, the success has led to reports of disorganised, sometimes unfriendly, service, with diners being given preference over residents, and of complaints unsympathetically dealt with. But the enthusiasm continues too: "One of the best meals I have ever eaten. The restaurant has a real buzz. Breakfast really good too. Our room overlooking the harbour was small but stylish and well planned, with a brilliant bathroom." "Sublime food; fresh, natural tastes are allowed to shine through; the atmosphere is informal. The hotel side was well run; our tastefully furnished room made a comfortable base. This is an unpretentious place, but the personal fingerprints everywhere give it character." The genial Mr Stein, who confessed in one of his television programmes to being disorganised, has advertised for an "extremely hands-on" general manager, so we'd like more reports, please. (*Rosemary Wright, John Rowlands*)

Open Feb–mid-Dec. Restaurant closed Sun.
Rooms 25 double, 1 single. 13 in *St Petroc's*, 3 above coffee shop.
Facilities *Seafood*: conservatory bar, restaurant. *St Petroc's*: lounge, reading room, bar, bistro. Sandy beaches ¼ mile. Unsuitable for &.
Location Central. *Seafood* on harbour; *St Petroc's* in New St (150 yds). Garage, parking. Train: Bodmin Parkway, 15 miles; then bus (infrequent) or taxi.
Restrictions No smoking in restaurant. No children under 5 in restaurant.
Credit cards Access, Visa.
Terms B&B: single £28–£35, double £90–£100. Set meals: bistro £18.95; restaurant: lunch £24.50, dinner £33; full alc £50. 2-day breaks in low season. Children under 6 accommodated free in parents' room.

If you think we have over-praised a hotel or done it an injustice, please let us know.

PAULERSPURY Northamptonshire   Map 2

The Vine House   *Tel* (01327) 811267
100 High Street   *Fax* (01327) 811309
Paulerspury
nr Towcester NN12 7NA

A restaurant-with-rooms in a 300-year-old limestone house and adjoining cottage, with a large garden. Many original features of the interior have been preserved. There is a tiny bar with an open fire, and a peaceful residents' lounge where afternoon tea is served. The spacious restaurant has a light decor, and a *Michelin* red "Meals" for chef/proprietor Marcus Springett's modern English cooking. Much of the food, from bread to petits fours, is home-made; ginger beer is home-brewed. "Julie Springett, front-of-house, is efficient and very friendly," wrote a regular visitor. "Cooking and presentation are of a high standard." Others have said: "One of the best meals we had in two weeks' travelling. Amazing value." "Vegetables some of the best I have eaten; food and wine reasonably priced." The small bedrooms are named after varieties of grape; they have antique beds, a frilly decor, and a tiny shower room. Some overlook the "rather nondescript main street", but traffic noise has not bothered our reporters. Paulerspury, known for its Rolls-Royce enthusiasts' club, is handy for the horse-racing at Towcester, the Grand Prix motor racing at Silverstone, and also for Milton Keynes, Stowe, Althrop and Castle Ashby. (*Chris Kay; also Bill and April Hancock, and others*)

Open All year, except 24 Dec–6 Jan. Lunch served Thurs/Fri (Mon–Fri in Dec); dinner Mon–Sat.
Rooms 5 double, 1 single.
Facilities Lounge, bar, 2 dining rooms. ¾-acre garden. Golf, riding, fishing, shooting nearby. Unsuitable for &.
Location In village 3½ miles SE of Towcester, just off A5. Rear carpark. Train: Milton Keynes; then taxi.
Restrictions No smoking in restaurant. No dogs.
Credit cards Access, Visa.
Terms [1997] B&B: single £39, double £66. Set lunch £16, dinner £23.50.

PENZANCE Cornwall   Map 1

The Abbey Hotel   *Tel* (01736) 366906
Abbey Street   *Fax* (01736) 351163
Penzance TR18 4AR

♦ *César award in 1985*

Jean and Michael Cox's 17th-century house, painted turquoise, and with Gothic windows, stands in one of the narrow streets that run down to the sea from the centre of this resort/fishing port, the most westerly town in Britain. It is crammed with curios, oriental rugs, paintings and photographs, magazines, books and flowers. The drawing room is inviting, with flowered sofas, a fire, and a window looking on to a lovely garden. Some bedrooms also overlook the garden, while others face the harbour (some get street noise); one or two are small, with a small shower room. Room 1 is huge, with antiques and a working fireplace, and a wood-surrounded bath in its large bathroom. There's a light, airy suite. In the pretty white-panelled dining room, the menu has three choices at each stage; there is always a vegetarian main course. The hotel is run in laid-back style. The Coxes are often away, and visitors are generally ably looked after by manager/chef/factotum Glyn Green, but the welcome can be "non-existent" when he too is away. *Guide* readers' reactions over the years have ranged from ecstatic to thumbs-down. "The friendliest of welcomes," write supporters this year. "The staff could not have been more helpful – to three octogenarians." "A comic place. Very good breakfast." "Worth visiting for the sheer eccentricity." Some have thought the dinner excellent; others have found it expensive and unimaginative, and have been critical of the housekeeping. Some bedrooms and bathrooms are "a bit small for comfort". (*Barbara Blake, DK Bewley*)

Open All year, except 1 week at Christmas. Dining room closed midday.
Rooms 1 2-bedroom suite (in adjoining building), 4 double, 2 single. No telephone.
Facilities Drawing room, dining room (piped classical music). Small walled garden. Sandy beach ¼ mile. Unsuitable for &.
Location Take road marked Sea Front; pass carpark on left; right after 300 yds, just before bridge, then left, up slipway, to hotel. Courtyard parking for 7 cars.
Restrictions No smoking in 1 bedroom. No children under 3. No dogs in public rooms.
Credit cards Access, Amex, Visa.
Terms B&B: single £65–£130, double £85–£140. Set dinner £24. Weekend breaks; winter rates. New Year package. 1-night bookings sometimes refused bank holidays. *V*

Tarbert Hotel   NEW/BUDGET   *Tel* (01736) 363758
11–12 Clarence Street   *Fax* (01736) 331336
Penzance TR18 2NU   *E-mail* Tarbert Hotel@compuserve.com

Former sea captain's residence, now a good-value simple hotel (Logis of Great Britain), personally run, with small staff, by Julian and Patti Evans. Good food, particularly fish, served to easy-listening tapes in no-smoking restaurant. Bar snack lunches. Small patio; small carpark. Near centre, but no view. Closed 23 Dec–4 Jan. Unsuitable for &. No children under 7. No dogs. Access, Amex, Visa accepted. 12 bedrooms. B&B £24–£32; D,B&B £38–£46.

PICKHILL North Yorkshire   **Map 4**

The Nags Head   BUDGET   *Tel* (01845) 567391
Pickhill, nr Thirsk YO7 4JG   *Fax* (01845) 567212

Welcoming village inn in heart of Herriot country, run for 25 years by Boynton brothers, Raymond and Edward. 9 miles NW of Thirsk, 1 mile E of A1; a useful stop on way to or from Scotland. 15 bedrooms, 7 in annexe, 3 on ground floor, all with simple decor and en suite facilities. Excellent English/European meals (generous portions) in traditional bar (with necktie collection) and smart restaurant – food award in Good Pub Guide. Small lounge. Beer garden. Handy for Jervaulx, Rievaulx and Fountains abbeys. Golf, shooting, hunting, fishing, hang-gliding, gliding, swimming nearby. Closed 25 Dec. No smoking: restaurant, some bedrooms. No dogs in public rooms, or alone in bedrooms. Access accepted. B&B: single £36, double £50. Set lunch £11, dinner £17 [1997]. Weekend breaks: 3 nights for price of 2. Recently endorsed, but we'd like more reports, please.

PLYMOUTH Devon *See SHORTLIST*   **Map 1**

POOLE Dorset   **Map 2**

The Mansion House   *Tel* (01202) 685666
Thames Street   *Fax* (01202) 665709
Poole BH15 1JN

This handsome Georgian town house is in a quiet cul-de-sac near the
town's old parish church and bustling quay. It has a welcoming air,
and a grand sweeping staircase leading up from the entrance hall to a
stylish residents' lounge. Reports this year are strongly positive: "The
discreet luxury and the dedication of the young staff – no fawning, no
spurious first-name business – remain the dominant impression." "The
remarkable manageress, Jackie Godden, runs the place in the most efficient way. Her husband Gerry, the chef, produces outstanding food."
The panelled restaurant is a fashionable dining club, of which residents
are temporary members; they may also eat in the bar/bistro; the menu
in both is extensive and reasonably priced. Cooking is traditional and
modern English. Vegetarian dinners are "unusually good"; on
Saturday evening and at Sunday lunch there is an impressive hors
d'oeuvre table. Following criticism in last year's entry, the decision has
been taken not to let the restaurant for private functions. Most bedrooms are good-sized and luxurious, with fresh fruit, thermos with ice,
and a telephone in the bathroom, but singles can be small. No charge is
made for room service. Poole's magnificent natural harbour makes it a
popular boating centre, and its beach has been graded one of the clean-
est in Britain. There is good sightseeing nearby, including Brownsea
Island, Kingston Lacey, Athelhampton House, Edmonsham House,
Corfe Castle and Sherborne Castle. (*Canon Michael Bourdeaux; also Dr T
McGhie, and others*)

Open All year.
Rooms 1 suite, 19 double, 9 single. 2 on ground floor.
Facilities Lounge, bar/bistro, restaurant (piped music); private dining room.
Poole Quay 100 yds: fishing, boating, sailing. Unsuitable for &.
Location Follow signs to channel ferry. Left at Poole Bridge, then 1st left, sign-
posted to parish church. 2 private carparks. Train/bus ½ mile.
Restrictions No children under 5 in restaurant. Dogs by arrangement; not in
public rooms.
Credit cards All major cards accepted.
Terms [1997] B&B: single £52–£78, double £85–£115, suite £130–£150. Set lunch
£11.85, dinner £21.50. Weekend rates. Children under 12 accommodated free in
parents' room. *V*

PORLOCK Somerset   **Map 1**

The Oaks   NEW   *Tel/Fax* (01643) 862265
Porlock TA24 8ES

This gabled Edwardian pebbledash house is set amid lawns and, of
course, oak trees, above the village, overlooking Porlock Bay, with
views towards Porlock Weir to the south and the steep hills of Exmoor
above. The owners, Tim and Anne Riley, have been here 12 years; she
cooks, he is front-of-house. "It is wonderful," wrote the nominator.

"The hosts so friendly, the rooms so comfortable." In the dining room, which has picture windows overlooking the view, "good, uncomplicated, well-thought-out" meals on a four-course menu (with choice) feature local fish, meat and game, "and scrumptious puddings, always including a hot one, with clotted cream". "The sort of food you could happily eat for several days without feeling bloated or bored," one reporter wrote. There is a good selection of half bottles of wine on a varied wine list. The public rooms are liked too: "Welcoming log fire in hall, tiny bar, light lounge with fire, magazines, books; interesting oil paintings and prints everywhere." The bedrooms, each with an efficient bathroom, are charmingly furnished, with pretty fabrics, patterned wallpaper, old pine furniture, sherry, fruit and magazines. "Log fires in the public rooms add to the unhurried atmosphere," add inspectors. "Not for those in search of bright lights. The atmosphere is sedate and quite old-fashioned." Porlock has a narrow main street with a variety of old buildings. One of the smallest churches in England is at Culbone, three miles away. (*Christian Millward, Mrs MA Humphries, and others*)

Open Mar–Nov.
Rooms 9 double.
Facilities 2 lounges, bar, restaurant (piped classical music during dinner). 1-acre garden. Sea 1 mile. Unsuitable for &.
Location ¼ mile from village 6 miles W of Minehead.
Restrictions No smoking: restaurant, 1 lounge, bedrooms. No children under 8. No dogs in public rooms.
Credit cards Access, Amex, Visa.
Terms B&B: single £52.50, double £85; D,B&B (2 days min.): single £72.50, double £125. Set dinner £26.

PORTSCATHO Cornwall   **Map 1**

Roseland House   BUDGET   *Tel* (01872) 580644
Rosevine, Portscatho TR2 5EW   *Fax* (01872) 580801

"Amazing value. Pleasing, restful atmosphere. Friendly staff. Food good to excellent with brilliant sweets; some great bargains on the rather vague wine list. Our good-size bedroom had a stunning sea view, a cafetière with a sachet of real coffee and – most unusual – lights bright enough to read by." A recent endorsement for Mr and Mrs Hindley's period house with modern extensions. It is quietly set above Gerrans Bay in the lovely Roseland peninsula, near the little fishing village of Portscatho. A path leads through its sloping grounds to a private beach. The nominator, on a return visit, found it as good as ever: "The decor is simple but attractive. The lounge, bar and dining room are informal and comfortable. The proprietors are experienced and innovative chefs. It is a real pleasure to stay here." The five-course dinner, traditional English/French cooking, is served between 7.30 and 8 pm. Picnic lunches and cream teas are available. Miles of National Trust-protected cliff walks are nearby, as are unspoilt beaches, the Fal estuary, with sailing and boating, several National Trust properties, and the recently restored Heligan gardens. (*Stephen and Judy Parrish, JF Thompson*)

Open All year, except about 1 week early Nov.
Rooms 2 family, 8 double. 1 on ground floor. Also 2 self-catering chalets.

178   ENGLAND

Facilities 2 lounges, bar, restaurant (piped classical music at night), conservatory. 6½-acre grounds: private beach, safe bathing. Sailing, golf, nearby. Not
really suitable for &.
Location N side of Portscatho. On A3078 to St Mawes, look for hotel sign on
right, two miles after Ruan High Lanes. Train: Truro/St Austell, both 15 miles;
then taxi, or hotel will meet.
Restrictions No smoking. No dogs.
Credit cards Access, Amex, Visa.
Terms [1997] D,B&B: single £40–£78, double £80–£120. Short breaks. Children 12
and under half price in parents' room.

PORTSMOUTH Hampshire *See SHORTLIST*   **Map 2**

POSTBRIDGE Devon   **Map 1**

Lydgate House   `BUDGET`   *Tel* (01822) 880209
Postbridge, Yelverton PL20 6TJ   *Fax* (01822) 880202

"One of the nicest hotels in the south-west, full of warm character and
idiosyncratic charm. The secret moorland position is quite unrivalled.
The two young people who run it, Hilary Townsend and Judy Gordon
Jones, provide an unfailingly warm welcome; visitors sit in the log-fire-
warmed lounge, wearing expressions of relaxation and contentment."
So writes a veteran of many visits to this "magical place". It is set in its
own wild Dartmoor valley, rough and boulder-strewn, with superb
walking all around. The river Dart (with bathing and fishing) runs
through the grounds, as does a bridle path. You can walk straight on to
the moor, with the owners' collie if you want company; Postbridge,
with its famous clapper bridge, is accessible by foot along the river. The
sitting room, which has a log-burning stove, magazines, books, and
games, is warm and airy; pots of tea or coffee are available at any time
for no charge. The short dinner menu, served at 7.30 pm, has two
choices for each course, with a vegetarian alternative to the main dish.
One visitor found the dining room lacking in atmosphere, "but the
good, wholesome food (second helpings offered), made up for this, and
the wine list was very acceptable". Bedrooms are "comfortable and
unfussy, not luxurious, but none the worse for that". Some are small,
but all have a private bath or shower (most *en suite*). (*June and Peter
Glover, Alison and Keith Tiley; also Michael Crick, Dr and Mrs McGhie,
Jennifer Harte, and others*)

Open All year, except Feb.
Rooms 7 double, 1 single. 1 on ground floor.
Facilities Sitting room with bar (piped classical music before dinner), dining
room/conservatory. 37-acre grounds: river, trout/salmon-fishing, bathing.
Pony-trekking nearby.
Location Small turning off B3212 in village, between humpback bridge and *East
Dart* pub. Train: Exeter/Newton Abbot; then taxi.
Restrictions Smoking banned in dining room, discouraged elsewhere. No dogs
in dining room (or sitting room if other guests object).
Credit card Access, Visa.
Terms B&B: single £31.00, double £56–£62. Packed lunches £4.50. Set dinner
£16.00. Weekly rates; Christmas, New Year packages.

If you find details of a hotel's location inadequate, let us know.

PRESTBURY Cheshire   **Map 3**

The White House   *Tel* (01625) 829376
  Manor and Restaurant   *Fax* (01625) 828627
The Village, Prestbury SK10 4HP

"Lives up to the *Guide*'s description in every way. Gorgeous food, interesting menu and wine list, friendly staff. It is close to Manchester (17 miles away) and to the ring of motorways reaching into Lancashire and across the Pennines, hence swiftly accessible from quite a distance." This year's endorsement for Ryland and Judith Wakeham's restaurant-with-rooms-just-down-the-road, "a highly enjoyable place to stay", in one of Cheshire's prettiest villages, set on the river Bollin. The restaurant, now in its 14th year, is in a listed white building. It has a high reputation locally for its contemporary British cooking, "with a dash of Asian, Italian and Californian", served amid silk, lace and greenery. Bedrooms, in a redbrick manor a short walk away, are themed: Trafalgar is military in style, Glyndebourne has a sophisticated music centre, Earl Grey has a blue and yellow decor and a vast range of teas and tisanes, Minerva, with an accent on sport and health, has a Turkish steam room and a collection of antique sporting equipment, The Studio is arty. This may sound twee, but the consensus is that it works: "The rooms are quiet and stylish, with quality linen and good antiques." Two have a four-poster. Some of the bathrooms have a power shower with body jets. Breakfast – continental with fresh orange juice, muffins, croissants, etc, "full Cheshire" or "Healthy" – is served "properly laid out" in the bedrooms, or in the manor's new lounge. (*Fr Gordon Murray, and others*)

Open All year, except Christmas.
Rooms 6 double, 3 single.
Facilities Lounge/conservatory/bar, breakfast lounge, restaurant (piped music, mainly jazz); function rooms. ½-acre garden. Unsuitable for &.
Location Edge of village, 2 miles N of Macclesfield.
Restriction No dogs in public rooms.
Credit cards All major cards accepted.
Terms Rooms: single £40–£95, double £65–£120. Breakfast: continental £5, English £8.50. Set lunch £12.95, dinner £16.95; full alc £30.

PURTON Wiltshire   **Map 3**

The Pear Tree at Purton   *Tel* (01793) 772100
Church End   *Fax* (01793) 772369
Purton, nr Swindon SN5 9ED   *E-mail* peartreepurton@msn.com

Francis and Anne Young's old stone house was once the rectory of the unusual twin-towered parish church nearby. It is in a peaceful village, amid rolling Wiltshire farmland, but only four miles from the M4. The large grounds contain a traditional Victorian garden, where herbs are grown for the modern British cookery of chef Catherine Berry. There's an *à la carte* lunch menu, which always includes a traditional pudding, and a fixed-price dinner menu with plenty of choice. One couple this year, visiting on a weekday, when the trade is generally business-oriented, thought the food bland, and they were unhappy with their bedroom, which was in an extension and faced a steep bank and a fire escape.

Another wrote: "Food not always hot enough." But weekend visitors have enthused: "Combines the efficiency and polish of a top notch hotel with the charm and friendliness of a family business. We were made to feel most welcome: bags carried, tea offered. Throughout our stay every consideration was shown. Lovely leisurely breakfast in plant-filled conservatory restaurant: Purton honey on table, Purton church bells peeling, sun streaming through windows overlooking gardens with catmint walks, sunken water garden and herbacious beds. Purton means a pear enclosure, and the pear theme is tastefully developed throughout the hotel." "Calm, fresh, young atmosphere. Lots of pink, flowers everywhere. Enticing green view from bedroom with well-appointed bathroom and a big bowl of fresh fruit. Delicious dinner; smiley service." "Mrs Young and the receptionists are very friendly; the interested Francis Young is around to offer tea and answer local questions." A good base for visiting Avebury, Barnsley House (Rosemary Verey's gardens), and the Cotswolds. (*Sarah Barrington, Minda Alexander, and others*)

Open All year, except 25–30 Dec. Restaurant closed midday Sat.
Rooms 2 suites, 15 double, 1 single. Some on ground floor.
Facilities Ramps. Lounge bar, library, conservatory restaurant; function facilities. 7½-acre grounds: croquet.
Location 5 miles NW of Swindon. From M4 exit 16 follow signs to Purton; through village, right at Spar grocer. Train: Swindon; then taxi.
Restriction No dogs in public rooms, unattended in bedrooms.
Credit cards All major cards accepted.
Terms B&B: single £85, double £85–£105, suite £105. Children in parents' room £10. Alc lunch *c.* £15 (excluding wine); set dinner £27.50. Weekend breaks. ***V***

REETH North Yorkshire
Map 4

Arkleside NEW/BUDGET
Reeth, nr Richmond DL11 6SG

Tel/Fax (01748) 884200

Reeth is a picturesque village in the middle of Swaledale, mostly peaceful though it can be crowded in summer. There is beautiful scenery and wonderful walking all around. This unpretentious hotel, once a row of miners' cottages, is just off the green. Its owners, Dorothy Kendall and Richard Beal, offer walking weekends, led by a Yorkshire Dales specialist, Richard Musgrave, which start with a convivial dinner party on the Friday night. "It is a delightful place, with a home-like decor, a friendly atmosphere, and a well-trained staff," writes the nominator. "The food is traditional English; the dinner menu is not extensive, but it is changed every evening and the quality and presentation of the dishes is excellent and imaginative." Other visitors wrote: "Charming proprietor, with great warmth of manner. Everything looked pretty and comfortable. The reception rooms have a beautiful view over the hills, as do some bedrooms." A good base for visiting Barnard Castle, Teesdale and Wensleydale. (*Maureen and Eric Race, MJ*)

Open All year, except 1 Jan–10 Feb, Christmas. Restaurant closed midday.
Rooms 1 suite in mews, 8 double.
Facilities Lounge, conservatory bar, restaurant (piped "easy listening" music). Small grounds. Trout-fishing rights on river Swale. Unsuitable for &.
Location 10 miles W of Richmond. Top right corner of village green. Parking. Bus: limited service from Richmond.
Restrictions Smoking in bar only. No children under 10. Dogs in public rooms only with consent of other guests.

Credit cards Access, Visa.
Terms [1997] B&B: single £39–£47.50, double £59–£75; D,B&B (3 nights min.): £46.50–£56.50. Set dinner £16.50. Painting breaks, grouse shooting parties, Christmas package. 1-night bookings refused New Year, Easter.

The Burgoyne   *Tel/Fax* (01748) 884292
On the Green
Reeth, nr Richmond DL11 6SN

"A highly civilised establishment, in which one may indulge oneself gloriously and receive excellent value for money." "A memorable three days' hospitality. The joint proprietors, Peter Carwardine and Derek Hickson, welcomed us, offered us tea by a log fire, and showed us to our beautifully appointed bedroom. The food is a gastronomic delight. Each meal was presented with love and dedication. It takes real commitment to reach such standards." Apart from two visitors who found the meals too rigid –"everyone goes in at 8, and plates are not cleared till everyone has finished" – enthusiasm continues for this Grade II listed Regency house set on Reeth's large green. The lounges have a pleasing blend of antique and modern decor. The bedrooms are named after local hamlets; most are large, with a superb view of the village green and hills beyond; three have their bathroom across a corridor (bathrobes and slippers are provided). In the candlelit dining room, green with pink touches, Peter Carwardine's cooking is traditional English, served in generous portions; there is plenty of choice on the menu. The wine list has plenty of half bottles, or you can order a full bottle of the house wine and pay only for what is consumed. Breakfast "is a minor miracle of perfection". (*Trevor Lockwood, JW and M Airey; also JH Astle-Fletcher, Simon Jones, Richard and Sheila Owen, and others.*)

Open 13 Feb–2 Jan. Restaurant closed midday.
Rooms 9 double. 1 on ground floor, suitable for partially &.
Facilities 2 lounges, restaurant (piped classical music at night). ⅓-acre grounds. Trout-fishing rights on river Swale.
Location Centre of village, 10 miles W of Richmond. Parking.
Restrictions No smoking: 1 lounge, dining room, bedrooms. No children under 10. No dogs in dining room, unattended in bedrooms.
Credit card Access.
Terms [1997] B&B: single £57.50–£80, double £67.50–£90; D,B&B: single £80–£102.50, double £112.50–£135. Set dinner £22.50. Reduced rates for child in parents' room. Off-season breaks, grouse shooting parties, Christmas package. 1-night bookings refused New Year, Easter.

REIGATE Surrey *See SHORTLIST*   **Map 2**

ROADWATER Somerset   **Map 1**

Wood Advent Farm   NEW/BUDGET   *Tel/Fax* (01984) 640920
Roadwater, Watchett TA23 0RR

Guest house on 340-acre working farm in Exmoor National Park, at foot of Brendon hills. Swimming pool, tennis, footpaths, riding, fishing. Sea 3 miles. Kindly hosts, John and Diana Brewer: smiling service. Chintzy lounge with games and TV; drawing room with books. Traditional country cooking (with choices): seasonal home-produced ingredients, generous portions, served in dining room with inglenook fire. 4 large bedrooms with simple decor, facilities en suite. Unsuitable for &. No smoking: dining room, 1 lounge, bedrooms. No children under 10. No dogs in house (kennels provided). Access, Visa accepted. B&B £20–£25. Set Sun lunch £12, dinner £13. More reports, please.

ROMALDKIRK Co. Durham   **Map 4**

The Rose and Crown   *Tel* (01833) 650213
Romaldkirk   *Fax* (01833) 650828
nr Barnard Castle DL12 9EB

A civilised old coaching inn on the oak-shaded green (complete with stocks and water pump) of a quiet Dales village whose ancient church is dedicated to St Rumwald. Inside are log fires, panelling, brass and copper, old farming implements, prints, maps and etchings, and fresh flowers; the small lounge is equipped with magazines, books and games. The beamed, traditional bar, with old-fashioned seats facing a log fire, is popular with locals. The oak-panelled restaurant – "a lovely room" says one guest – has earned a *Good Food Guide* entry for proprietor/chef Christopher Davy's cooking (English, with modern and regional influences) on a menu with limited choice. Our readers have thought the food "beautifully cooked and presented, in generous but not excessive portions; puddings are delicious and never pretentious". Alison Davy expertly oversees a local staff. "The welcome is always friendly, and a room upgrade is standard when they are not busy," say recent guests. "The bedrooms are planned for maximum comfort." Those with most character are in the main house. The purpose-built ones in the courtyard open directly on to the carpark and are handy for walkers, dog-owners and business people. Christopher Davy is knowledgeable about local attractions. Good birdwatching, historic buildings, and some of Britain's finest grouse moors are nearby. (*Mr and Mrs DE Powell, Carolyn Mathiasen; also Good Pub Guide*)

Open All year, except Christmas. Restaurant closed Sun evening to non-residents.
Rooms 2 suites, 10 double. 5 in courtyard annexe. Some on ground floor.
Facilities Lounge, lounge bar, Crown Room (bar meals), restaurant. Fishing, grouse-shooting, birdwatching nearby.
Location Centre of village, 6 miles NW of Barnard Castle on B6277. Ample parking. Hourly bus from Barnard Castle.
Restrictions No smoking in restaurant. No dogs in main lounge, restaurant.
Credit cards Access, Visa. (Not accepted for special breaks.)
Terms [1997] B&B: single £58, double £80, suite £88. Set lunch £12.95, dinner £23. Special breaks all year. *V*

ROMSEY Hampshire   **Map 2**

Spursholt House   NEW/BUDGET   *Tel* (01794) 512229
Salisbury Road   *Fax* (01794) 523142
Romsey SO51 6DJ

This beautiful old house was built for one of Cromwell's generals; later additions turned it into a mellow country home set in lovely gardens with paved terraces, lawns, topiary, geranium-filled urns, and a view of Romsey Abbey beyond. It has an impressive sitting room, with stained-glass windows which came from the Palace of Westminster, and a Victorian-style dining room. There are just three bedrooms (one is panelled), with antique furniture, sofa, large bed and garden views. "Mine was palatial, with every creature comfort and a sumptuous bathroom," wrote an inspector. "Anthea Hughes is a delightful hostess who makes you feel welcome from the initial telephone enquiry through to your departure." Home-cooked meals are available by arrangement, and *Old Manor House* restaurant, in the village, the proprietor of which, Mauro Bregoli, is a wild mushroom expert, is warmly recommended for dinner. One of England's great fishing rivers, the Test, flows through the village past Broadlands, the home of Lord Palmerston and later of Lord Mountbatten.

Open All year, except 23 Dec–2 Jan.
Rooms 1 suite, 2 double. No telephone/TV.
Facilities Drawing room, dining room. 7-acre grounds: 2½-acre garden. River 1 mile (fishing).
Location 1 mile NW of Romsey, off A27 to Salisbury. Bus; or hotel will meet at station.
Restrictions No smoking. No dogs in public rooms.
Credit cards None accepted.
Terms [1997] B&B: single £25, double £44, suite £48. Evening meal (by arrangement) £14.50. 5% discount for stays over 4 nights. 1-night bookings refused weekends.

ROSTHWAITE Cumbria   Map 4

Hazel Bank BUDGET   *Tel* (01768 7) 77248
Rosthwaite, nr Keswick CA12 5XB   *Fax* (01768 7) 77373

Gwen and John Nuttall have been 18 years at their no-smoking Victorian guest house. It is quietly set in large landscaped grounds above a pretty village (much of which is owned by the National Trust) in the Borrowdale valley. It has fine views of surrounding mountains and fells, and is popular with walkers and ramblers, to whom it offers efficient drying facilities, abundant hot water, "and meals to suit those who spend their days exploring the Lakeland mountains". Regular visitors continue to enthuse: "A gem. The Nuttalls are thoroughly professional and most friendly; they treat their guests as individuals." "Our spacious bedroom was a delight; simple and immaculate, with an excellent bathroom and a lovely view. You help yourself to drinks in the lounge before the home-cooked dinner, which is served at 7 pm. At least five vegetables accompany the main course, there are delicious old-fashioned puddings. The house wine is reasonably priced. Coffee afterwards in the lounge, where a house party atmosphere prevails. Breakfast (8.30 to 9 am) is equally delicious, with a self-service buffet followed by cooked items." (*Dr and Mrs Naylor, and others*)

Open 10 Apr–end Oct.
Rooms 5 double, 1 single. 1 self-catering cottage. No telephone.
Facilities Lounge, honour bar, dining room; drying room. 4-acre grounds. Derwent Water 3 miles. Unsuitable for &.
Location 6 miles S of Keswick on B5289 to Borrowdale. Just before village turn left over small hump-backed bridge. Bus: Keswick-Borrowdale.
Restrictions No smoking. No children under 11. No dogs in public rooms.
Credit cards Access, Visa.
Terms D,B&B £46. 3-night breaks Mar, Nov. 1-night bookings sometimes refused.

ROUGHAM Suffolk   Map 2

Ravenwood Hall   NEW   *Tel* (01359) 270345
Rougham   *Fax* (01359) 270788
nr Bury St Edmunds IP30 9JA

Historic building, Tudor in origin (carved oak and inglenook fireplace in restaurant; 16th-century wall paintings); "welcoming, if not smart, with country atmosphere". In 7-acre grounds, with swimming pool, tennis, croquet, off A14, 3 miles SE of Bury St Edmunds. Courteous, animal-loving owner, Craig Jarvis. "excellent, varied" breakfasts; cream teas; French classical/ modern dinners; informal meals in cosy bar. Functions in former cricket pavilion. Golf nearby; hunting, shooting available. 14 bedrooms, best in main house, smaller ones in Victorian stables; 5 on ground floor. No smoking: restaurant, bedrooms. No dogs in public rooms. All major credit cards accepted. B&B: single £65–£85, double £85–£115. Full alc £35. More reports, please.

RUSHLAKE GREEN East Sussex   Map 2

Stone House   *Tel* (01435) 830553
Rushlake Green   *Fax* (01435) 830726
Heathfield TN21 9QJ

This beautiful old house, built in 1495 and extended in Georgian days, is run on country house lines by Peter and Jane Dunn (he is a descendant of the original owners). It stands in a walled garden in a vast estate on the Kent/Sussex border; plenty of outdoor activities are on offer (see below). Mrs Dunn is a Master Chef, whose "delicious and varied" cooking, served in the panelled dining room, has earned a *Michelin* red "Meals". "High standards of old-fashioned service and civility," wrote a regular *Guide* correspondent. "Quite unhotel-like. You are cherished and cosseted from the moment you arrive. Cases vanish upstairs, tea (real tea, exquisite china and silver, home-made fruit cake, moist and crumbly) is served in the drawing room amid antiques, family heirlooms, portraits, photos in silver frames." The bedrooms all have antique furniture, good fabrics and ornaments, a telephone and TV; two have a four-poster and a large bathroom; the twin-bedded ones in the Tudor wing are on the small side. A good traditional breakfast is served downstairs; a simple continental one is brought to the bedroom. Picnic dinner hampers for nearby Glyndebourne can be ordered. Local sights include Kipling's house, Batemans, and Battle. More reports, please.

Open 2 Jan–23 Dec.
Rooms 1 suite, 5 double, 1 single.
Facilities Hall, drawing room, library, billiard room, dining room. 1,000-acre estate: 4½-acre garden, tennis, croquet, archery, off-road driving, shooting, ballooning, pheasant/clay pigeon-shooting, lake, fishing. Sea at Eastbourne 13 miles.
Location 4 miles E of Heathfield. Take B2096 towards Battle; 4th right to Rushlake Green. At green turn left; keep green on right; entrance on far left at crossroads.
Restrictions No children under 9. No dogs in public rooms.
Credit cards None accepted.
Terms B&B: single £55–£71.25, double £99.50–£169.50, suite £130–£169.50. Set lunch £18.95, dinner £24.95. Weekend house parties.

RYE East Sussex   **Map 2**

Jeake's House	BUDGET	*Tel* (01797) 222828
Mermaid Street		*Fax* (01797) 222623
Rye TN31 7ET		*E-mail* jeakeshouse@BtInternet.com

♛ *César award in 1992*

This delightful town was one of the Cinque Ports. Nowadays, it is two
and a half miles inland, perched above a plain between the rivers
Rother and Tillingham. In one of its most photogenic streets stands
Jenny and Francis Hadfield's civilised B&B. One visitor this year was
critical of the housekeeping, and would have appreciated a little more
pampering, but for a Japanese traveller, "it was the best, and the best
value, of our holiday". "Their approach is hands-on, but never offi-
cious," another guest has written. The hotel is composed of two venerable buildings, furnished with brass or mahogany bedsteads, antiques,
old pictures, samplers and lots of books. There's a Victorian parlour
with an upright piano complete with period sheet music, and a quiet
sitting room with a bar. Breakfast (vegetarian or traditional) is served
to soft classical music in a large adjoining galleried room – formerly a
Quaker meeting house – with high windows, good paintings and
china, books, plants, and a fire on cold days. Other visitors admired
their "charming bedroom, full of character, at the top, with sloping ceiling, beams, a dormer window, and a view over the garden to the sea".
One bedroom is small. Francis Hadfield also owns a laundry, and his
"excellent and prompt shirt laundering" is appreciated. *Jeake's House*
was the home of the writer Conrad Aiken for 23 years. Rye has many
other literary associations: it was immortalised as Tilling by EF Benson
in his much-loved Mapp and Lucia novels, and Henry James lived in
Lamb House, now owned by the National Trust. (*Kyoko Kosuge; also
John and Susan Colby, and others*)

Open All year.
Rooms 1 suite, 10 double, 1 single. 10 with *en suite* facilities.
Facilities Sitting room, bar/sitting room, breakfast room (piped classical music).
Beaches, bird sanctuary nearby. Unsuitable for &.
Location Central. Carpark nearby. Train/bus station 5 mins' walk.
Restrictions No smoking in breakfast room. No dogs in public rooms.
Credit cards Access, Visa.
Terms [1997] B&B: single £24.50, double £45–£61, suite £87. Reductions for 4 or
more days; 15% midweek reduction Nov–Feb, except Christmas, New Year.
Reductions for children sharing parents' bedroom. 1-night bookings generally
refused weekends.

The Old Vicarage	BUDGET	*Tel* (01797) 222119
66 Church Square		*Fax* (01797) 227466
Rye TN31 7HF		

A pink ex-vicarage with literary connections, now a civilised B&B.
Situated on a pretty square by the church, it was the birthplace of the
Elizabethan playwright John Fletcher, and Henry James wrote *The
Spoils of Poynton* here before moving to nearby Lamb House. The cheerful bedrooms, with flowery fabrics, drinks tray, TV and magazines,
have "a wonderful view of the 15th-century church whose golden
cherubs chime on the quarter-hour". In the small bay-windowed room

overlooking the walled garden, there's ample choice for breakfast, continental or English. Tea is properly brewed, marmalade home-made and the bread home-baked, the eggs are new-laid and the sausages award-winning. Paul and Julia Masters, "a pleasant couple", will help guests to book tables in local restaurants and to plan sightseeing. "They showed real concern for our well-being." Tea on arrival, a newspaper, and a glass of sherry are included in the price. (*Paul Evans and Samantha Stevenson, Robin Oaten*)

   Note: Not to be confused with *The Old Vicarage Hotel* in East Street.

Open All year, except Christmas.
Rooms 1 suite, 5 double. 5 with *en suite* facilities.
Facilities Lounge, reading room, breakfast room. Walled garden. Tennis, bowling, putting, beach (safe bathing) 2 miles. Unsuitable for &.
Location By St Mary's church. Follow signs to town centre. Through Landgate Arch to High St, 3rd left into West St. Private parking nearby.
Restrictions No smoking: breakfast room, bedrooms. No children under 8. Guide dogs only.
Credit cards None accepted.
Terms B&B: single £34–£55, double £40–£60. Winter breaks Nov–Mar; weekly discounts. Apr–Oct weekends 2 nights min. Reductions for children sharing parents' room. *V* (Nov–Feb, Sun–Thurs)

ST AUSTELL Cornwall   Map 1

Boscundle Manor   *Tel* (01726) 813557
Tregrehan, St Austell PL25 3RL   *Fax* (01726) 814997
🖤 *César award in 1997*

"A blissful four nights. Ideal for an upmarket country house stay where guests are treated with respect and attention, albeit in a laid-back atmosphere." "A divine place, comfortably lived in, with uncontrived style." Recent tributes to Andrew and Mary Flint, though some visitors this year have found the atmosphere "too intimate". The manor house, part medieval, mainly 18th-century, is near the sea at Carlyon Bay. It is reached up winding stone steps through charming gardens, with interesting plants, lovely views, secluded seats, ponds, a small lake and a sheltered heated swimming pool. Inside are thick walls, beams, low ceilings, and antique furniture and prints. The bedrooms have "comforts ancient and modern aplenty, including a little fridge with fresh milk". Some have a spa bath, some a patio. The garden cottage has the best views. An indoor swimming pool is new this year. The "competent dinner party-style" cooking on a short menu with choices, is based on fresh local ingredients. The wine list "is long and covers all continents"; if you can't finish your bottle you are charged only for what you consume. Breakfast is in a pretty conservatory. The manor is run on country house lines: no reception desk, no bedroom keys (though most rooms have a small safe). A bit casual for some, but its fans enjoy "the combination of easy cordiality and understated luxury". Plenty of outdoor activities are available (see below). St Austell, named for a 6th-century monk and saint, is a centre of the china-clay industry. Caerhays Castle, in a large woodland garden, is close by, so are the recently restored Lost Gardens of Heligan; many other Cornish gardens, as well as beaches, coastal walks and fishing villages, are easily reached. (*Charles Moncrieffe, Walter W Stork, and others*)

Open End Mar–end Oct. Dining room closed midday, to non-residents Sun.
Rooms 4 suites, 4 double, 2 single. 2 in garden, 2 in cottage (can be self-catering).
Facilities Sitting room, bar, games room, dining room, conservatory; private dining room; indoor swimming pool. 12-acre grounds: garden, swimming pool, exercise room, croquet, golf practice, badminton, small lake, ponds, woodlands. Beaches, riding, golf, coastal walks, fishing nearby. Unsuitable for &.
Location 2 miles E of St Austell. 200 yds off A390 on road to Tregrehan. Bus every half-hour.
Restrictions No smoking in dining room. No dogs in public rooms.
Credit cards Access, Amex, Visa.
Terms B&B: single £70–£75, double £120–£130, suite £140–£170; D,B&B: single £90–£100, double £160–£180, suite £180–£220. Set dinner £25. Reductions for longer stays.

ST BLAZEY Cornwall   Map 1

Nanscawen House   *Tel/Fax* (01726) 814488
Prideaux Road   *E-mail* 101756.2120@compuserve.com
St Blazey, nr Par PL24 2SR

"A wonderful two days; delightful bedroom; we were superbly looked after," wrote the nominator of this no-smoking B&B. It is a spacious old family home, wisteria-covered, in secluded grounds with a heated swimming pool and whirlpool spa. Only three bedrooms, all large, with flowery fabrics, garden view, TV and a bathroom with a spa bath; one has a four-poster. Breakfast, in a conservatory, includes freshly squeezed orange juice, a large choice of starters, and local smoked salmon. The drawing room has a small bar, with a selection of drinks and wines. The proprietors, Janet and Keith Martin, will advise guests about local restaurants. Tregrehan, a large wooded garden with magnificent Victorian greenhouses, is half a mile away; Llanhydrock (National Trust) is ten minutes' drive. The town of St Blazey is named for a 4th-century martyr, St Blaise. More reports, please. (*DG*)

Open All year, except Christmas.
Rooms 3 double.
Facilities Drawing room, conservatory/breakfast room. 5-acre garden: swimming pool (heated Apr–Sept), whirlpool spa. Golf, riding, beaches, fishing nearby. Unsuitable for &.
Location 4 miles NE of St Austell; 5 miles NW of Fowey. After level-crossing in St Blazey, from A390 turn right opposite Texaco garage into Prideaux Road. *Nanscawen* is ¾ mile on right (row of trees marks foot of drive).
Restrictions No smoking. No children under 12. No pets.
Credit cards (*3% surcharge*) Access, Visa.
Terms [1997] B&B: single £40–£58, double £68–£78.

ST HILARY Cornwall   Map 1

Ennys   NEW/BUDGET   *Tel/Fax* (01736) 740262
St Hilary
nr Marazion TR20 9BZ

Seventeenth-century Grade II-listed manor house in 2-acre gardens with grass tennis court, heated swimming pool (not available 12.30–4 pm) on working farm on river Hayle. 5 miles E of Penzance. Cordial hosts, Sue and John White; convivial atmosphere: drinks at 7 pm for dinner 7.30/8. Home-cooked food in generous portions: home-baked bread, home-grown vegetables, locally caught fish. 3 double rooms (1 minuscule) with antique beds, patchwork quilts, shower en suite; 2 family suites in courtyard; children welcomed. Peaceful setting, but beaches, fishing, sailing, windsurfing, riding, gardens, houses nearby. Closed Christmas. No smoking. No dogs. Amex, Visa accepted. B&B: single £35–£40, double £45–£60. Set dinner £18 [1997]. More reports, please.

ST IVES Cornwall   **Map 1**

The Garrack   *Tel* (01736) 796199
Burthallan Lane   *Fax* (01736) 798955
St Ives TR26 3AA   *E-mail* garrack@compuserve.com

St Ives, beloved by artists, is the home of the Tate Gallery of the West and the Barbara Hepworth museum and garden. In summer, surfers flock to its magnificent Porthmeor beach, which has a European blue flag for cleanness. This traditional hotel, a stone building with a modern extension, is on a hill with stunning views over the beach and the bay towards Trevose Head. The town and the Tate are within short but steep walking distance. The Kilby family, who have been here for 30 years, cater for all ages, and for the disabled. *Guide* readers praise its friendly style. "The staff are really keen to please," wrote one. "The bedrooms are well appointed. High standards all round." Some rooms are in the old house; the ones in the new part have less character, but better views. The restaurant, with a conservatory extension, is in the care of chef Benjamin Reeve. It attracts outside diners and has a short but varied daily set menu and a large *carte*, which includes "good vegetarian dishes served in generous helpings". There is a comprehensive wine cellar, reasonably priced. "On the first night," said one diner, "there was only one lobster in the tank, with someone else's name on it. Michael Kilby apologised profusely, and promised he would man the next boat with us in mind. It was worth the wait. The chef rightly warned us against starters and served our lobster with home-grown new potatoes. The wine waiter was concerned that we select the right bottle, without suggesting that we were viticulturally challenged. Service was informal but never slapdash. Michael Kilby was unstinting with his time, pointing out local walks, boat trips, etc." Breakfasts are generous. The small leisure centre has a swimming pool, sauna, solarium, exercise machines, and an all-day snack bar. No ban on smoking, but the Kilbys write: "Our guests seldom do." (*Deirdre Pushman, Louise Chase, also Susie and Bill Harding-Edgar*)

Open All year.
Rooms 17 double, 2 single. 2 in cottage. 1 designed for &.
Facilities Lounge, TV lounge, bar, restaurant (CDs "when appropriate"); conference facilities; leisure centre: small swimming pool, sauna, whirlpool, solarium, fitness room, coffee shop, bar. 2-acre grounds. Beaches 5–10 mins' walk.
Location 1 mile from centre. From Penzance on B3311 turn right on to B3306 towards St Ives. Hotel off this, to left.
Restriction Dogs in designated bedrooms; not in public rooms.
Credit cards All major cards accepted.
Terms B&B: single £64–£67, double £92–£134; D,B&B: £63.50–£84.50 per person. Snack lunches. Set dinner £19.50; full alc £27.50. Off-season breaks; Christmas programme. 1-night bookings sometimes refused. ***V***

ST JUST-IN-ROSELAND Cornwall   Map 1

Rose-da-Mar NEW/BUDGET   *Tel/Fax* (01326) 270450
St Just-in-Roseland
nr Truro, TR2 5JB

The lovely Roseland peninsula derives its name not from the flower, but from "ros", the Celtic word for heath. Here, this unpretentious small hotel has a peaceful setting overlooking the Carrick Roads on the river Fal. It is recommended by a fellow hotelier, as much for its dog-friendliness as for the kindness of the hostess, Rowena Lilley, who runs the place almost single-handed. "She accorded a warm welcome to our elderly labrador, and was willing to dog-sit and dog-walk (but two rooms are dog-free zones). The views from the bedrooms, dining room and garden are a constant delight, and quite Mediterranean. The evening meals (no choice except dessert, but they can be pre-negotiated) are splendid value. They included excellent soups, carefully sauced main dishes, vegetables with some crunch left in them, and warm crusty bread; desserts were a class act. Breakfast is carefully cooked, but the choice was rather limited." The public areas are bright and modern. The spotless bedrooms are spacious, with attractive soft fittings and robust furniture. Only snags: steep steps to the first floor, "and low water pressure made showering impossible". St Just's beautifully situated church, with a steep graveyard, is close by. A good base for visiting St Mawes, King Harry Ferry and Trelissick garden (National Trust). Children are welcomed. (*David Wallington*)
   Note: St Just-in-Roseland is not to be confused with St Just, four miles north of Land's End.

Open Easter–end Oct. Lunch not served.
Rooms 6 double, 1 single. Most with facilities *en suite*. 1 on ground floor. No telephone.
Facilities Lounge, dining room (piped music, depending on guests). Garden, 3-acre paddock.
Location ¼-mile N of St Mawes by B3289. Train: Truro, 15 miles.
Restrictions No smoking: restaurant, bedrooms.
Credit cards None accepted.
Terms B&B: £27–£33; D,B&B £45–£48. 3-day breaks in low season. Children accommodated free in parents' room. Off-season rates. 1-night bookings refused in high season. *V*

ST KEYNE Cornwall   Map 1

The Well House   *Tel* (01579) 342001
St Keyne, Liskeard PL14 4RN   *Fax* (01579) 343891

"We have never wholeheartedly recommended a hotel to anyone before, but we could find no fault here. Our reception was warm. Our bedroom was tastefully furnished, comfortable, quiet and warm, with lovely views, fresh flowers, and enormous fluffy towels in the bathroom. Everything worked. The owner is a delightful man who takes a personal interest in his guests, and has trained his young staff to a very high standard." A recent accolade for this Victorian stone house in an unspoilt spot in the Looe valley. It has an informal garden, with duckponds, a tennis court and a swimming pool, an "enjoyably idiosyncratic" host, Nick Wainford, and four Cavalier King Charles spaniels. "It is not a full-service hotel," another visitor wrote. "You feel that you are staying with someone who wants you to be happy. The lounge is what one would expect in a private house, with floral settees, commodious chairs, flowers, and an amazing array of current glossy magazines. The dining room is arranged so that every table is private. The wine list is a treat, and only modestly marked up. Real value for money." Food at the *Well House* has long been admired. David Woolfall, who ran the kitchens before, returned in April 1997, so we'd be grateful for reports on his modern British cooking. Breakfast

 includes fresh orange juice and good croissants. St Keyne is famous for its holy well; the first one of a married couple to drink from it will, according to legend, dominate the other. The picturesque fishing villages of Fowey, Polperro and Looe are nearby. (*Mrs Wheeldon, SH; also Mike and Judi Taylor-Evans*)

Open All year.
Rooms 9 double.
Facilities Lounge, bar (piped classical/"easy listening" music), restaurant. 4-acre grounds: tennis, swimming pool. Walking, fishing, riding, golf nearby; coast, beaches 4 miles. Unsuitable for &.
Location 3 miles S of Liskeard by B3254. At church fork left to St Keyne Well; hotel ½ mile on left.
Restriction No dogs in public rooms.
Credit cards All major cards accepted.
Terms [1997] B&B: single £70, double £95–£145. Set meals (2–4 courses) £22.50–£32.50. Winter breaks. 1-night bookings refused bank holidays.

ST MARTIN'S Isles of Scilly   Map 1

St Martin's On The Isle   NEW   *Tel* (01720) 422092
St Martin's, Isles of Scilly   *Fax* (01720) 422298
Cornwall TR25 0QW   *Freephone* 0800 834056 (reservations only)

A cluster of cottages built in 1980s under supervision of Prince of Wales (he is also Duke of Cornwall). Only hotel on third largest of Scillies. "Stunning views; spectacular sunsets. Utter peace." Sandy beach adjacent. Good for families – up to two children under 16 accommodated free in parents' room (but no under-12s in restaurant at night). Welcoming manager, Keith Bradford. Sophisticated French cooking by Patrick Pierre Tweedie (ex-Gavroche, London) in Tean restaurant (no smoking); lighter meals in bar/grill. 45-foot Bermudan cutter, with skipper, available free to guests. Indoor swimming pool; snooker; clay pigeon-shooting. Reached by short flight or boat ride from St Mary's (see next page); hotel will arrange all-in travel package. "No-quibble" guarantee of refund if anything under hotel's control (ie, not weather or travel) does not perform as advertised. Open Mar–Oct. 2 suites, 28 bedrooms. No dogs in public rooms. All major credit cards accepted. D,B&B £95–£223 [1997]. More reports, please.

ST MARY'S Isles of Scilly   Map 1

Star Castle   *Tel* (01720) 422317
St Mary's, Isles of Scilly   *Fax* (01720) 422343
Cornwall TR21 0JA

In a stunning location, overlooking the town and harbour of the largest
of the Scillies and the surrounding islands (fine sunsets), this 16th-
century castle, built in the shape of an eight-pointed star, is surrounded
by a dry moat and 18-foot ramparts. It was opened as a hotel in 1933 by
the Prince of Wales (later Edward VIII). Modest and welcoming, it is
now owned and run by John and Mary Nicholls, There is a small
lounge and an atmospheric bar in the former dungeon, and the dining
room is the former officers' mess. In its grounds there is a wealth of
subtropical plants, suntrap lawns enclosed by high hedges, a covered
swimming pool, and two modern blocks with large bedrooms, and
suites suitable for families. The most characterful rooms are in the main
house (two have a four-poster). Three singles are in guard rooms on the
battlements. Last year's nominator, on a family visit, was impressed:
"The hands-on owner remembers the names of the guests and makes a
point of talking to them at breakfast. He often takes them in the hotel's
launch to visit other islands (he is the pilot for large ships visiting the
island, and head of the lifeboat service). The staff are friendly. The food
is imaginative, with plenty of choice; there's a reasonable wine list." A
conservatory fish restaurant is new this year. A good base for island-
hopping. More reports, please.

Open Mid-Mar–mid-Oct.
Rooms 4 suites, 26 double, 4 single. 23 in 2 garden annexes.
Facilities Lounge, games room, bar, restaurant, conservatory/fish restaurant
(piped classical music). 4-acre grounds: covered swimming pool; private motor
launch. Beach 10 mins' walk. Golf, cycle hire, riding, sailing, diving, fishing
available. Unsuitable for &.
Location ¼ mile from town centre. Boat (2¾ hours), helicopter (20 mins) from
Penzance; Skybus (15 mins) from Land's End (except Sun); hotel will meet.
Restrictions No smoking in restaurants. No dogs in public rooms.
Credit cards Access, Visa.
Terms B&B £45–£80; D,B&B £65–£90. Light lunch £2–£5. Set dinner £24; full alc
£35. Children accommodated in parents' room: 5–50% of adult rate. Inclusive
breaks (including travel) Sept–May.

SALCOMBE Devon   Map 1

Tides Reach   *Tel* (01548) 843466
South Sands, Salcombe TQ8 8LJ   *Fax* (01548) 843954

Salcombe has one of the loveliest settings in south Devon, on a wide
estuary beloved by yachtsmen. This plain white building, with balconies overlooking a large duck pond, has been owned by the Edwards
family for 30 years. A tidal beach is across a small road. The town
centre, a mile away, can be reached by a passenger ferry, combined at
low tide with a sea tractor, as an alternative to the narrow road, which
can get crowded. The hotel has conservatory-style lounge, a bar with
an impressive sea-water aquarium, and bright bedrooms, most sea-
facing (a few are small, with a restricted view). Its leisure centre has a
large swimming pool with sliding panels, which open in summer to let

in fresh air. The food has been thought "good if not amazing" by some visitors this year, but others have been critical: "Elaborately described dishes failed to live up to their promise. But the extensive breakfast buffet was a delight. Tea on the lawn in the company of wildfowl very pleasant." Good snack lunches, too, and there is much else to enjoy: "A splendid hotel in an enviable location," wrote one guest. "The dining room is pleasantly laid out. Our bedroom was of a good size, well furnished and well lit, with a super view. Service by senior staff was excellent." "The staff set out to make your holiday enjoyable." "We cannot fault the relaxed atmosphere." There is entertainment by a magician on Saturday nights in season. Miles of wonderful walking on National Trust cliffs nearby, and also a delightful National Trust property, Overbecks, set in a lovely garden perched above the estuary. (*J Bickderdike, EA and G Smith, JP Berryman; also Ray and Angela Evans*)

Open Feb–Dec.
Rooms 3 family suites, 35 double.
Facilities 3 lounges, 2 bars, restaurant (piped "easy listening" music all day); leisure centre: swimming pool, sauna, solarium, spa bath, squash, beauty salon, bar/coffee shop. ½-acre garden. Sandy beach opposite. Sailing, fishing, windsurfing, golf, tennis nearby.
Location Through Salcombe: follow signs to South Sands. Carpark.
Restrictions No smoking: restaurant, 1 lounge. No children under 8. No dogs in public rooms.
Credit cards All major cards accepted.
Terms [1997] B&B £48–£93; D,B&B £58–£108. Set dinner £25.75; full alc £41.50. Bargain breaks; winter rates; early booking discount scheme; children's tariffs. 1-night bookings occasionally refused bank holiday weekends.

SALISBURY Wiltshire *See SHORTLIST*   **Map 2**

SANDGATE Kent   **Map 2**

Sandgate Hotel and   NEW/BUDGET   *Tel* (01303) 220444
  Restaurant La Terrasse   *Fax* (01303) 220496
The Esplanade
Sandgate, Folkestone CT20 3DY

This Victorian hotel is part of a terrace on the seafront of a village on the smart side of Folkestone; it overlooks a wide beach. It has a *Michelin*-starred restaurant, *La Terrasse*, serving French classical cuisine, and an intensely French atmosphere – chef Samuel Gicqueau, from the Loire valley, has worked at two other starred restaurants, *L'Auberge de Condé* at La-Ferté-sous-Jouarre, and *Le Manoir aux Quat'Saisons*, Great Milton (*qv*). His English partner, Zara Jackson, is front-of-house; the staff is mainly French. The smart public rooms have floor-to-ceiling windows overlooking the sea. In the lounge there are antique mirrors and in winter an open fire, while the restaurant, yellow and blue, with silver candelabras, opens on to a terrace, with sunshades in summer. "Dinner was absolutely excellent," writes the delighted nominator, "and the house wine was good value at £6 for a half bottle. Breakfast was continental in the true sense, with delicious croissants and pains chocolat; hearty English is also available. The bedrooms, though small, are elegantly decorated in pastel colours; the best have a balcony with a sea view. Our midweek break was excellent value."

Sandgate has many antique shops and a well-restored Tudor castle. The Channel Tunnel is five minutes' drive; Dover is eight miles away. (*Mrs JC Smye*)

Open All year, except mid-Jan–mid-Feb. Restaurant closed Sun evening/Mon (except bank holidays).
Rooms 13 double, 2 single.
Facilities Lounge with bar, restaurant (piped classical music); terrace. Unsuitable for &.
Location On seafront, 3 miles W of centre of Folkestone, on A259 coastal road to Hythe (some traffic noise). Train: Folkestone; then bus.
Restrictions No smoking in restaurant. No dogs.
Credit cards All major cards accepted.
Terms [1997] B&B: single £39, double £49–£67. Set lunch/dinner £18.50 weekdays, £24.50 weekends; full alc £36.50. Weekend/midweek breaks.

SCARBOROUGH North Yorkshire *See SHORTLIST*   **Map 4**

SCOTSDYKE Cumbria   **Map 4**

March Bank   NEW/BUDGET   *Tel* (01228) 791325
Scotsdyke, nr Longtown CA6 5XP

On main A7 Galashiels road, 3 miles N of Longtown, close to Scottish border, simple establishment (winner of Les Routiers Casserole Award) with friendly family owners, the Moores. Bar with sporting trophies; small dining room, serving consistently good simple food. 4 bedrooms, plain but comfortable. 3-acre grounds. Lovely views across Esk valley (fishing for salmon and sea trout); freezer and drying facilities. No smoking: restaurant, lounge. No dogs in public rooms. Access, Amex accepted. B&B: single £35, double £50. Full alc £20. More reports, please.

SEAVIEW Isle of Wight   **Map 2**

Seaview Hotel   BUDGET   *Tel* (01983) 612711
High Street   *Fax* (01983) 613729
Seaview PO34 5EX

♥ *César award in 1988*

Seaview is an old-fashioned sailing village on the north-east shore of the island. In the 19th century, Queen Victoria admired its quietness, and it is still a peaceful place, except in high season. This small hotel stands at the foot of the High Street, Union flag flying, and is something of a maritime museum – the proprietors, Nicholas and Nicola Hayward, are collectors of naval prints and things nautical. They welcome children (there's a wholesome high tea) and dogs, and number business folk and "slightly older couples" among their regular visitors. Pretty bedrooms, serviced at night, have good fabrics, antiques and a smart bathroom. They vary in size; rear ones are quietest (some overlook the carpark); front ones have a sea view. Traditional English/French cooking, specialising in seafood, is served in the restaurant and generally much enjoyed. At busy times there are two sittings; tables are close together, "which leads to amicable conversations", though one couple disliked being seated close to the kitchen door. There are two bars, the more formal of which serves imaginative brasserie-type meals. Much enthusiasm this year: "The service is outstanding. We thoroughly enjoyed the food. A perfect place to stay with children. They were made very welcome, but dinner was an adult affair, after they were tucked up in bed." "The owners and their staff could not have been more helpful. Everything done efficiently and without fuss. Large, quiet bedroom, recently redecorated." "First-rate house-keeping." "Good breakfast." (*Rosemary Tusa, RD Batcheller, and others*).

Open All year, except Christmas. Restaurant closed Sun evening, except bank holidays (bar meal available).
Rooms 3 suites, 13 double. 2 on ground floor. 3 with balcony.
Facilities Lounge, 2 bars, restaurant; function room; patio. Sea, sandy beach 50 yds: sailing, fishing, windsurfing.
Location Village centre. Follow signs for seafront. Small carpark. Bus, taxi from Ryde, 3 miles, Cowes, 10 miles.
Restrictions No smoking: 1 room in restaurant, lounge. No children under 5 in restaurant at night. No dogs in public rooms.
Credit cards All major cards accepted.
Terms [1997] B&B: single £45–£70, double £70–£100, suite £115; Set Sun lunch £12.95; full alc £23. Reductions for children under 12 sharing parents' room. Weekend, midweek, Christmas, New Year, painting breaks. *V*

SHEFFIELD South Yorkshire *See SHORTLIST*　　　　　**Map 4**

SHEPTON MALLET Somerset　　　　　**Map 1**

Bowlish House　**BUDGET**　　　　　*Tel/Fax* (01749) 342022
Wells Road
Shepton Mallet BA4 5JD

Linda and Bob Morley's restaurant-with-rooms in beautiful Palladian house in small garden. ¼ mile outside old market town on A371 to Wells, on edge of Mendip Hills. "Not grand, but elegant and comfortable; owners strike just the right note, not too fussy, not too casual." Good antiques, intimate sitting room and bar. Panelled restaurant, with portraits and conservatory extension. Sophisticated cooking on 3-course menu with plenty of choice, including vegetarian main dish (red "Meals" in Michelin). Wide-ranging wine list. 3 spacious bedrooms. Closed 1 week autumn, 1 week spring. Lunch by arrangement. Unsuitable for &. No dogs in public rooms. Access, Amex, Visa accepted. B&B double £48, including generous continental breakfast; cooked breakfast £3.50 extra. Set lunch (1st Sun of month) £12.50, dinner £22.50 [1997]. No recent reports; we'd like some, please.

Charlton House　**NEW**　　　　　*Tel* (01749) 342008
Charlton Road　　　　　*Fax* (01749) 346362
Shepton Mallet BA4 4PR

Elegant small hotel in Domesday-old manor, opened in 1997 by Roger and Monty Saul, who have for 25 years run Mulberry Design Company (furniture, fabrics, home fittings) close by. "Charming and unusual decor (many items for sale); delightful staff." Good modern British cooking in red dining room (pianist Sat night). Large conservatory for breakfast, tea, etc. Sauna, plunge pool. 8-acre grounds: pretty gardens, tennis, croquet, trout lake, river (fishing); but traffic noise from nearby road. 17 bedrooms (5 in lodge). Unsuitable for &. Dogs in 1 bedroom only. No smoking: restaurant, conservatory, bedrooms. B&B: single £85–£105, double £95–£135, suite £150–£250. Set lunch £18.50, dinner £32. More reports, please. ***V***

SHERBORNE Dorset   Map 2

The Eastbury   *Tel* (01935) 813131
Long Street   *Fax* (01935) 817296
Sherborne DT9 3BY

Thomas and Alison Pickford recently bought and restored this Georgian house in Dorset's loveliest town, famed for its abbey church, castles and public school. It is in a quiet street a short walk from the centre. Inside, the period decor has many original features, and there is a library of antiquarian books. The bedrooms are named for English flowers. Some (and some beds) are small, but one occupies most of the top floor. The dining room and its conservatory extension overlook the pretty walled garden. "The management and staff are consistently helpful and cheerful," wrote the nominator. "Every request we made was quickly met. Our bedroom was bright and clean, with flowers, sherry and mineral water. The cooking was best traditional English, with a light touch, on a varied *table d'hôte* menu." "Everyone was very welcoming," runs an endorsement this year. Food and service outstandingly good. Excellent breakfast." A good base for exploring Hardy country. The coast is 30 minutes' drive away. *(JSS, Colin and Stephanie McFie)*

Open All year.
Rooms 9 double, 6 single.
Facilities Lounge, library, 2 bars, restaurant (piped classical music/jazz at night); conference/banqueting room. 1-acre garden: croquet, *boules*. Unsuitable for &.
Location Near centre; hotel will send directions. Carpark.
Restrictions Smoking discouraged in restaurant, banned in library. No dogs.
Credit cards Access, Amex, Visa.
Terms [1997] B&B £39.50–£49.50; D,B&B (min. 2 nights): £53.50–£63.50. Set lunch £15.95, dinner £19.50; full alc £29. Romantic breaks: £68.50 a night per person (min. 2 nights). ***V***

SHIPTON GORGE Dorset   Map 1

Innsacre   **NEW/BUDGET**   *Tel/Fax* (01308) 456137
Shipton Gorge
Nr Bridport DT6 4LJ

Sydney Davies's informally run 17th-century farm guest house has a sheltered setting in a south-facing valley amid lovely countryside. It is reached up a cobbled drive through large grounds, with a flowery terrace, gardens, an orchard and rare breeds of farm animals. Inside are a lounge with a huge inglenook fireplace, and a beamed, stone-walled dining room, with yellow silk curtains and oak tables and chairs. Bedrooms, some of which are suitable for families, vary in size; they are simple but pretty, with cottage-style or antique French beds, and TV. There's warm approval this year: "We visited in a party of seven to dispel winter gloom and could not have made a better choice. The hosts, say our boys, are 'mega-friendly', but they are not intrusive." "We were welcomed into the family," writes an inspector. "Our bedroom was a converted hayloft with original stone walls and beams. Its bathroom was good-sized, but needed a face-lift. Delicious tea, with home-made carrot cake. No choice for supper, but each course was a treat (Jane Davies is an ex-restaurateur). You serve yourself from dishes on the table. Our only criticism was that all the food was quite robust; one lighter course might have been welcome. Breakfast was good too, with a choice of cereals and cooked dishes, home-made jam, and cafetière coffee in large French cups. We liked the goats, birds and sheep in the garden, and the family cats." The sea and the National Trust coastal path are three miles away. (*Dru Esam, and others*)

Open All year, except Christmas. Restaurant closed midday; also Sat evening, Easter–Oct.
Rooms 4 double. No telephone.
Facilities Lounge/bar, dining room. 10-acre grounds. Fishing nearby; shingle/sand beach 2½ m. Unsuitable for &.
Location 1½ miles SE of Bridport. Take A35 west from Dorchester. After *c.* 12 miles take *2nd* left to Shipton Gorge; go round hill; entrance on left after *c.* ⅓ mile.
Credit cards Access, Visa.
Terms [1997] B&B: single £45, double £58–£65; D,B&B: single £50–£65, double £90–£108. Evening meal £11.50. 10% reduction for 5 or more nights. 1-night bookings refused bank holidays. Children half-price in parents' room.

SHIPTON-UNDER-WYCHWOOD Oxfordshire   Map 3

The Lamb Inn   *Tel* (01993) 830465
Shipton-under-Wychwood OX7 6DQ   *Fax* (01993) 832025

This trim stone 18th-century building has a quiet setting in a large village in the Evenlode valley, once the centre of the ancient Forest of Wychwood (fine old houses and interesting church). There are new licensees this year, Michael and Jennie Eastick, but 1997 visitors confirm that everything is just as good as ever, and that last year's description is still valid: "It is intimate, and rather select, with a civilised clientele. There's a patio in front with tables for drinks and snacks. Inside are rough stone walls, wood panelling, polished floors, beamed ceilings, good wooden tables and chairs. Newspapers on sticks in the bar. Log fires in the tiny, cosy lounge. Everything beautifully kept; potted plants and flowers everywhere. The small dining room and the bar serve English dishes, copious and decently cooked. Pleasant young waiters. Excellent breakfasts include salmon kedgeree, smoked kippers and mixed grill. Bedrooms are named after local villages. Ours, Bruern, was white-walled, beam-ceilinged, and well equipped; the bathroom was medium-sized and adequate." Only reservation: "The pretty beamed ceiling doesn't allow for much insulation; rooms above the bar can be noisy until late. But this was reflected in the reasonable price; we had no regrets about staying." (*Carolyn Mathiasen; also Good Pub Guide*)

Open All year.
Rooms 5 double.
Facilities Lounge, bar, restaurant. ¼-acre garden. Unsuitable for &.
Location S edge of village, 4 miles NE of Burford. Carpark. Train: Charlbury, 5 miles.
Restrictions No smoking in restaurant. "Well-behaved children and dogs only."

Credit cards Access, Amex, Visa.
Terms B&B: single £47–£58, double £68–£95; D,B&B £55–£70. Bar meals. Set dinner £21.

SHREWSBURY Shropshire   Map 3

Albright Hussey   *Tel* (01939) 290571
Ellesmere Road   *Fax* (01939) 291143
Shrewsbury SY4 3AF

This "strangely wonderful" hybrid moated house, half black-and-white early Tudor, half 17th-century brick and timber, is full of history. It is listed in the Domesday Book under the name of Elbretone; to this was added the name of the Hussey family, its owners from the 13th to the 17th century; royalist troops were garrisoned here during the civil war. Since 1988, it has been owned by Franco and Vera Subbiani, whose son Paul is the manager. It has a "delightful situation, well away from traffic", a well-maintained garden complete with a moat with black swans, a pleasant atmosphere, and "extremely friendly owners and staff". The bedrooms with the most character are in the main house; one suite has a four-poster bed and a four-poster spa bath in the centre of the bedroom, another is "huge, with a lovely bathroom with a spa bath". Many have good views (some are in the attic, up steep stairs). But their chairs are said to be "of a non-relaxing variety". A recent extension added nine bedrooms, some quite small, a large function room and a lounge ("less comfortable than the older one"). The restaurant, "with a charming period decor", is popular with local diners for modern British/French cooking by a team of three chefs; there is a good wine list. The Subbianis also own a restaurant, *Henry's*, in nearby Shrewsbury, which has been an important town since Norman times, and has many historic buildings. Fans of Brother Cadfael, the sleuthing monk of Ellis Peters' novels, may visit the Shrewsbury Quest, where his medieval gardens have been recreated. (*John H Bell, Joy and Raymond Goldman, and others*)

Open All year.
Rooms 1 suite, 13 double. 1, on ground floor, suitable for &. 12 more planned.
Facilities 2 lounges, 2 bars, restaurant (piped classical music); large function room. 4-acre grounds.
Location On A528 to Ellesmere, 2 miles N of Shrewsbury,
Restrictions No smoking in restaurant. No children under 3. Dogs by arrangement, not in public rooms.
Credit cards All major cards accepted.
Terms [1997] B&B: single £65–£80, double £85–£120. Set lunch £12.50, dinner £19.50; full alc £25.

SHURDINGTON Gloucestershire   Map 3

The Greenway   *Tel* (01242) 862352
Shurdington,   *Fax* (01242) 862780
nr Cheltenham GL51 5UG

"David and Valerie White are splendid hosts. It is difficult to fault this well-controlled establishment. The staff are young, courteous and efficient, and radiate an air of quiet enthusiasm. Our room was large and well furnished. The housekeeping was first class. Breakfast is comprehensively good, with an extensive menu." "Warm welcome on a cold day, with a crackling log fire. Total peace and serenity; we were never bothered by the A46, 500 yards away." Recent tributes to this creeper-clad mansion, just outside Cheltenham. It is named for the pre-Roman path which runs beside it to the Cotswold Hills beyond (good walking). Set in a lovely garden amid parkland, it is Elizabethan in origin, with a flagstoned hall and a traditional decor. Bedrooms are spacious, with good fabrics, and well-equipped bathroom. The restaurant, which is quite formal (male guests are required to wear a tie), has a bright conservatory opening on to a pretty terrace. The English country house cooking is generally thought "agreeable" and the fish "particularly good"; the pastry chef comes in for special praise. More than one guest has found the lighting too dim in both public areas and bedrooms; and one couple had shower problems: "The thermostat at peak times caused us to perform mini-aerobics." Plenty to visit nearby: Cotswold villages and towns, castles, stately homes, gardens and churches. (*Sir Neil Shields, Michael and Maureen Heath; also Joy and Raymond Goldman*)

Open All year, except 5 days in 1st week Jan. Restaurant closed Sat midday, bank holidays.
Rooms 17 double, 2 single. 8 in coach house. 4 on ground floor.
Facilities Hall, drawing room, bar, restaurant (piped classical music); function facilities. 7-acre grounds: croquet. Golf, riding, tennis, swimming, clay pigeon-shooting available.
Location 2½ miles SW of Cheltenham, on A46. Train: Cheltenham; then taxi.
Restrictions No smoking in 8 bedrooms. No children under 7. No dogs.
Credit cards All major cards accepted.
Terms [1997] B&B: single £87.50, double £130–£190; D,B&B (min. 2 days): single £112, double £175–£215. Set lunch £17.50, dinner £30. Off-season rates; 2-day breaks.

SIMONSBATH Somerset   Map 1

Simonsbath House   *Tel* (01643) 831259
Simonsbath, nr Minehead TA24 7SH   *Fax* (01643) 831557

"Spectacular position, large comfortable bedrooms, delightful lounge and dining room; very high standards of cleanliness." "November is a perfect time to visit, when Exmoor lies undisturbed and the river sparkles in winter sunlight, or lies shrouded in mist and dripping beech trees. Sue and Mike Burns remember their guests from previous visits. The local staff are friendly and efficient." Recent reports on this 17th-century hunting lodge, long, low and white, off a small road in a tiny village in the heart of the Exmoor National Park. It faces south across the Barle valley; excellent walks start from the grounds. A massive oak door leads into the hall and the library, both with stout walls, panelling, log fires, subdued lamps, and "welcoming sofas". The dining room is a newer addition, with pale green walls, dark red tablecloths covered with white, and pictures of Exmoor. One couple this year were disappointed by the dinners, but others have enthused: "Such is the quality of the home-cooked food that locals eat here regularly. Portions are generous. Huge bowls of clotted cream accompany puddings. At breakfast, the smoked haddock overflows the plate." "Very good soups. Excellent home-made ice creams." There's plenty of choice on the wine list, including some unusual bottles. The bedrooms have a four-poster bed, magazines, books and TV; some bathrooms are small. Light meals and teas ("delicious warm scones and cream") are served, from 10 am to 5.30 pm, in a café/bistro at the foot of the drive, run by the Burnses' daughter. (*NP, Josephine Eglin, ER, and others*)

Open 1 Feb–30 Nov.
Rooms 7 double.
Facilities Lounge, library, dining room, café/bistro. 1-acre grounds. Riding, shooting, fishing nearby; coast 10 miles. Unsuitable for &.
Location On B3223, 7 miles SE of Lynton. Carpark. Train: Taunton, 34 miles; then taxi.
Restrictions No smoking in dining room. No children under 10. No dogs in house.
Credit cards All major cards accepted.
Terms [1997] B&B: single £54–£64, double £92; D,B&B: single £74–£84, double £132. Full alc £22.50. Bargain breaks.

SLAIDBURN Lancashire   Map 4

Parrock Head   BUDGET   *Tel* (01200) 446614
Woodhouse Lane   *Fax* (01200) 446313
Slaidburn, Clitheroe BB7 3AH

This low, whitewashed 17th-century farmhouse has a remote and beautiful setting amid the fells and pastureland of the Forest of Bowland. It makes an excellent base for touring, walking and bird-watching. The valley of the river Hodder is nearby. "What a relaxing place," wrote recent visitors. "Terry and Kath Hesketh, the owners since June 1996, run it competently, with cheerful friendliness, and offer remarkably good value. The staff is sizeable and efficient." Three spacious bedrooms, the best, are in the main building; those in the garden may have less character, "but they are pleasantly furnished in modern style, and well supplied with amenities". Guests may sit by the fire in the large beamed upstairs sitting room (once the hay loft) or browse over local information in the timbered library. The restaurant in the low-beamed former milking parlour, which is also open to non-residents, serves "good, plentiful country-style meals". Breakfast "sets you up for the day". (*John and Joan Wyatt, Eric Lee, and others*)

Open All year, except Jan.
Rooms 1 family, 8 double. 6 in garden cottages. 1 with & access.
Facilities Lounge, library, bar, restaurant (piped instrumental music); terrace. 1-acre grounds. Fishing, birdwatching nearby.
Location 9 miles N of Clitheroe. 1 mile NW of Slaidburn village.
Restrictions No smoking in dining room. Dogs with "kind nature and good manners" welcomed, but not in public rooms, unattended in bedrooms.
Credit cards Access, Visa.
Terms [1997] B&B: single £37.50–£47.50, double £55–£75; D,B&B (min. 2 nights) £45–£65 per person. Set Sun lunch £14.50, dinner £21.75. Bar/lounge lunches Mon–Sat from £4.25. Winter breaks. Christmas, New Year packages. 1-night bookings sometimes refused weekends.

****

Traveller's tale Service in this Welsh hotel, though obliging, was slightly marred by the "So what have you been doing today?" touch.

****

SLINFOLD West Sussex   Map 2

Random Hall   *Tel* (01403) 790558
Stane Street   *Fax* (01403) 791046
Slinfold, nr Horsham RH13 7QX

Nigel and Cathy Evans's converted farmhouse, part 16th-century,
stands on the outskirts of an old village near the market town of
Horsham. It has oak beams, flagstone floors, and a fine inglenook fireplace in its lounge, and upstairs, on the way to the bedrooms, there is
an impressive framed collection of cigarette cards. Visitors like its welcoming feel and unpretentious style – "friendly but not gushing".
Bedrooms are un-designerish, well lit, with TV, a large desk, plenty of
pillows, "no silly extras", and a good bathroom. Some have a four-
poster. Owing to the house's age, sound isolation is not always perfect;
and, because the hotel is set back from the busy A29, some rooms get
traffic noise. Meals (good traditional/modern British cooking by
Jonathan Gettings) are served in the candlelit Tudor-style restaurant,
which is hung with tapestries, or, on warm evenings, on the Vinery
Terrace. Light suppers and breakfast may be served in the bedrooms.
There is an attractive garden, and the reed-ringed pond on the edge
of the carpark may be of interest to birdwatchers. The hotel offers
chauffeur-driven tours of local attractions, for example, Brighton,
Portsmouth and Chichester; plenty of historic buildings and gardens
are nearby. Gatwick airport is 20 minutes' drive away. We'd like more
reports, please.

Open All year, except: hotel 27–30 Dec, restaurant 1–6 Jan.
Rooms 11 double, 4 single.
Facilities Lounge, bar, restaurant; conference/function facilities. 1-acre grounds:
terrace. Golf, ballooning, clay pigeon-shooting (tuition available) nearby.
Unsuitable for &.
Location Village 4 miles W of Horsham. Set back from A29 (some traffic noise).
Train: Horsham, Billingshurst.
Restrictions No smoking in restaurant. No children under 8. No dogs.
Credit cards Access, Amex, Visa.
Terms [Until July 1998] Rooms: single/double £62.50. Breakfast: continental
£6.50, English £8.50. Set lunch £15, dinner £22.50. Single room reduction at week-
ends. Golf, gardens, Christmas breaks.

SOAR MILL COVE Devon   Map 1

Soar Mill Cove Hotel   *Tel* (01548) 561566
Soar Mill Cove   *Fax* (01548) 561223
nr Salcombe TQ7 3DS

"Once again, a perfect visit. The sea mist prevented our seeing the view
for the first two days, but the hotel was as warm and welcoming as
ever." So writes a regular visitor to the Makepeace family's purpose-
built, single-storey hotel at the head of an isolated cove near Salcombe,
surrounded by National Trust land. Superb cliff walks start from the
grounds; a fine beach is a short walk down the hill. There is a small
heated pool outside and a very warm one indoors. The loyal clientele
love the mixture of sea, sand and comfort, and the welcome extended
to all generations: "A fine place to take children, while enjoying adult
comforts," one guest wrote: "Our four-year-old loved the indoor pool

and the play room, which is excellently equipped, with good seating thoughtfully provided for parents." Other praise: "The Makepeaces, who are always around, combine professionalism with individual care for their guests." "Impeccable housekeeping." The food draws mixed reviews, however. "Imaginative, but unfussy"; "better than ever," say the fans, but others have thought that the extensive menu was over-ambitious and failed to deliver on its promise. Service, on the other hand, is praised. One guest who lost her way, arrived "weary, fractious and famished" at midnight, to be soothed with a trolley laden with "a superb array of sandwiches and a good bottle of wine". The bedrooms, many of which have a private patio, are spacious and well equipped, though the reading lights are thought inadequate. Excellent laundry facilities, and a freshly cooked supper for children at 5.30 pm. A car is essential if you want to explore. Entertaining cookery classes are held during the low season. (*Mrs M Box, Rose Gayner, AS-M, Sue Kichenside, and others*)

Open 7 Feb–Nov, Christmas and New Year.
Rooms 3 suites, 16 double. All on ground floor.
Facilities 2 lounges (pianist twice weekly), bar, restaurant; indoor swimming pool; beauty salon. 5-acre grounds: swimming pool, tennis, putting. Sea 500 yds.
Location 3 miles W of Salcombe. From A381 turn right through Marlborough; follow signs for Soar, then Soar Mill Cove.
Restrictions No smoking in restaurant. No dogs in public rooms.
Credit cards Access, Visa.
Terms B&B: double £130–£170, suite £200–£250; D,B&B: double £180–£225, suite £270–£340. Set lunch £15, dinner £36. 3-day packages all year from £195.

SOUTHWOLD Suffolk   Map 2

The Crown   **BUDGET**   *Tel* (01502) 722275
High Street   *Fax* (01502) 727263
Southwold IP18 6DP

Adnams, the award-winning wine merchants, own most of the hostel-ries in this unspoilt seaside town. The *Crown* is a lively pub. Its beamed main bar, with pine tables, wooden settles and chairs and a fine carved wooden fireplace, is popular among locals, one of whom writes: "A queue builds up for the dinner menu, which appears at 7 pm (no book-ing). Eclectic dishes with a rustic approach are served as a starter or a main course. The same interesting menu is offered in the restaurant, where you may book, but you won't get to sit opposite a Suffolk Dr Johnson, hogging the fire." Other visitors have, however, enjoyed dining in the restaurant off crisp white table linen with silver cutlery: "The food was well presented, and of a high standard. The wine list was so extensive that decisions were difficult, but mark-ups were not excessive, and there is a wide range of wines by the glass." Breakfast includes fresh fruit, sliced and elegantly arranged "and excellent cooked dishes". The bedrooms upstairs are small "but adequate, with old pieces of furniture and a good modern bathroom". "Good value; a most enjoyable place to stay," some visitors have written, but others have thought the treatment of residents a bit offhand, and repeated the advice given in an earlier edition of the *Guide*: "Best eat here, but stay at the *Swan* [see below]." Southwold's beach has a European blue flag for cleanliness. (*AG, Good Pub Guide, and others*)

Open All year, except 2nd week Jan.
Rooms 1 family, 9 double, 2 single. All with private facilities, 3 not *en suite*.
Facilities Lounge/parlour, bar, public bar, restaurant; patio. Sea, pebble beach nearby. Unsuitable for &.
Location Central (front rooms might get traffic noise). Limited private parking.
Restrictions No smoking: restaurant, parlour. Dogs in public bar only.
Credit cards All major cards accepted.
Terms [1997] B&B: single £43, double £65, family £72. English breakfast £6.50. Bar meals; set meals (2/3 courses): lunch £13.50/£15.50, dinner £18.50/£21.50.

The Swan   *Tel* (01502) 722186
Market Place   *Fax* (01502) 724800
Southwold IP18 6EG

This stately building, with white-framed windows, iron balconies, and Union flag flying, stands by the town hall in the market place. Also owned by Adnams, it is smarter, pricier, and larger than *The Crown* (see previous entry). It has a flagstoned hall, a fine staircase with wrought-iron banisters, and a spacious lounge with an open fire. The large, stylish dining room serves food on three different menus, considered by most visitors to be "good, but not great"; they are, of course, accompanied by "superb" wines. There are reasonably priced bar snacks. The bedrooms in the main house are spacious, "with a pleasingly old-fashioned decor", and well equipped. The ones in the garden, round what was once a bowling green at the back, are good for dog-owners. They have been much disliked in the past, but they were recently refurbished and are now much more attractive. The hotel does a busy trade in afternoon teas and bar meals, which can lead to overnight visitors feeling neglected (there is no residents' lounge), and service can be pressed at times. But recent visitors have been satisfied on the whole: "Room spacious, with everything we needed for a relaxing evening." "Service excellent of its type, by local people doing a good and careful job." "Highly enjoyable Christmas package." One visitor this year, however, complained that the "freshly squeezed" orange juice was *not* freshly squeezed. A garden break, including tours of local gardens, is sometimes offered. (*Bernard Phillips, Denis Tate, and others*)

Open All year. Restaurant closed for lunch Mon–Fri Jan–Easter.
Rooms 2 suites, 38 double, 5 single. 18 in garden annexe, 5 with access for &.
Facilities Lift, ramps. 2 lounges, bar, restaurant; function facilities. Garden. Sea 200 yds.
Location Central. Rear parking. Train: Halesworth, 9 miles, Darsham, 11 miles; then taxi.
Restrictions No smoking in restaurant. No under-5s in restaurant after 7 pm. Dogs in garden rooms only.
Credit cards All major cards accepted.
Terms [Until Easter 1998] B&B: single £40–£58, double £86–£123, suite £145–£155; D,B&B (Oct–Mar) £52–£80 per person. Set lunch: weekdays £13.50–£15.50, Sun £15.50–£17.50; set dinner £21, £27.50, £33. Christmas package.

We quote either prices per room, or else the range of prices per person – the lowest is likely to be for one person sharing a double room out of season, the highest for a single room in the high season.

STADDLEBRIDGE North Yorkshire Map 4

McCoy's *Tel* (01609) 882671
The Cleveland Tontine *Fax* (01609) 882660
Staddlebridge
Northallerton DL6 3JB
❦ *César award in 1989*

This Victorian stone restaurant-with-rooms is at the Cleveland Tontine, where two busy roads converge, but effective double-glazing keeps the bedrooms surprisingly quiet, and there are good views. It is exuberantly run by the three McCoy brothers, Peter (front-of-house), Tom and Eugene (the chefs), with a friendly staff. "We accept our guests on the basis that they accept us as we are," says the jokey brochure. "A stance on ceremony cuts no ice." A recent visitor was delighted. "A must for connoisseurs of mild eccentricity coupled with enthusiasm. If only there were more places like it. I booked for one night, but it was so enjoyable that I stayed a second. Wonderful breakfast: fresh eggs and dry-cured bacon; real tea; home-made bread." The decor is "a curious mixture of homeliness, glitz, and riotous colour". Bedrooms have an eclectic mixture of furniture, comfortable beds and a good bathroom. The bar is furnished with pre-war sofas and lamps, and potted palms. The dimly lit restaurant, open three days a week, has bare floorboards, more palms, good napery and cutlery, and a similar menu to that of the busy bistro downstairs, with its close-packed tables and blackboard menus. Meals, accompanied by loud thirties music, are "straightforward but stylish, with strong sauces and flavours". (*AR, and others*)

Open All year, except 25/26 Dec, 1 Jan. Restaurant open Thurs, Fri, Sat.
Rooms 6 double.
Facilities 2 lounges, breakfast room, bar, bistro, restaurant (loud piped thirties music). Small garden. Unsuitable for &.
Location 6 miles NE of Northallerton, at junction of A19/A172 (rooms double-glazed); enter via southbound lane of A172. Staddlebridge not on map.
Restriction No dogs in restaurant, bistro.
Credit cards All major cards accepted.
Terms [1997] B&B: single £79, double £99. Full alc from £30.

STAMFORD Lincolnshire Map 2

The George *Tel* (01780) 755171
71 St Martin's *Fax* (01780) 757070
Stamford PE9 2LB *E-mail* georgehotelofstamford@btinternet.com
❦ *César award in 1986*

"A bustling, sprawling hotel with an incredibly competent staff, and food of the highest order." "Full of character and life. Interesting, reasonably priced wine list. Lovely walled garden." "A perfect example of what such an establishment should be." Recent admiration for this historic, creeper-covered coaching inn. It has a cobbled, flower-tubbed courtyard, mullioned windows, a flagstoned entrance hall, panelled rooms and creaking floorboards. In its London Room and York Bar, travellers once waited for their south- or north-bound coach. In the hall there is a portrait of its fattest customer, Daniel Lambert, who died in 1809 weighing over 52 stone. Bedrooms vary greatly in size and shape, and some are a considerable walk from reception; best ones are spacious, stylishly decorated and well lit; many have antiques. Meals in the panelled dining room are mainly traditional, with roasts on a silver carving wagon, and cheeses and puddings on trolleys. Recent visitors thought them excellent and efficiently served. On busy Saturdays, dinner is sometimes served in two shifts. Light meals and breakfast – "an array of wonderful things" – are served in the pretty garden lounge. Stamford is an unspoilt old market town with many fine Georgian buildings; it starred as Middlemarch in the TV adaptation of George Eliot's novel. Burghley House, a magnificent stately home set in a 300-acre deer park, is on its outskirts. (*Stephen and Ellise Holman, Kenneth Smith, and others; also Good Pub Guide*)

Open All year.
Rooms 1 suite, 34 double, 12 single.
Facilities Ramps. 2 lounges, 2 bars, 2 restaurants; 4 private dining rooms, business centre. 2-acre grounds: patio, monastery garden, croquet.
Location ½ mile from town centre (front rooms double-glazed; quietest overlook courtyard). Large carpark. Railway station 100 yds.
Restrictions No smoking in some bedrooms. No dogs in restaurant.
Credit cards All major cards accepted.
Terms [1997] B&B: single £72–£78, double £95–£160, suite £125–£160. Light meals in Garden Lounge. Set lunch £13.50–£16.50; full alc dinner £30–£35. Weekend, August breaks; Sunday reductions; Christmas, New Year packages.

STOKE GABRIEL Devon   **Map 1**

Gabriel Court   *Tel* (01803) 782206
Stoke Gabriel, nr Totnes TQ9 6SF   *Fax* (01803) 782333

"A nice-to-come-back-to hotel, undemanding and gentle. The Beacom family are always there, welcoming and helpful. One day, an octogenarian bused in 40 relatives for his birthday celebration; we were the only other guests, but we were not neglected." So writes a devotee of this pretty white-painted manor in a lovely old village on an inlet of the river Dart, not far from Totnes. It was owned by one family from 1487 until 1928, and it has a terraced Elizabethan garden, with clipped yew arches, magnolias and box hedges, and a swimming pool and grass tennis court. A major redecoration was recently carried out. "Wonderfully quiet," adds an inspector. "The corridors are a bit bleak, and housekeeping can be variable, but the bedrooms are comfortable and well lit and the bathrooms efficient. Breakfast included good scrambled eggs and coffee, and lots of toast. Dinner lives up to its plain English billing; the vegetables unfortunately were also of the English school." There is almost always a traditional roast; the hot puddings are thought to be the best way to end a meal. Children and dogs are welcomed. Afternoon tea is included in the half-board price. Trips on the Dart are available. Paignton and the coast – safe beaches – are three miles away; Dartmoor is 14 miles inland. (*Richard Creed, and others*)

Open All year. Dining room closed midday, except Sun.
Rooms 17 double, 2 single. 1 self-contained chalet.
Facilities Bar lounge, library, TV/meeting room, dining room. 2½-acre grounds: swimming pool, tennis. River Dart, fishing, 300 yds. Golf, riding nearby. Beach 3 miles. Unsuitable for &.
Location In village 3 miles SW of Paignton; turn S off A385 to Totnes. Train: Totnes; hotel will meet.

Restriction No smoking in dining room.
Credit cards All major cards accepted.
Terms B&B: single £51–£55, double £78; D,B&B: single £75–£80, double £126. Packed lunches available. Set Sun lunch £12.50, dinner £24. Christmas house party.

STOKE ST GREGORY Somerset   Map 1

Slough Court   NEW/BUDGET   *Tel/Fax* (01823) 490311
Stoke St Gregory
Nr Taunton TA3 6JQ

B&B in 14th-century moated farmhouse (oak beams, mullioned windows, open fires) on working farm in Somerset Levels (low, flat former marsh, with much wildlife). "Home-like feel; well heated throughout; charming, generous hostess, Sally Gothard, spares no effort on behalf of guests." 3 simple bedrooms, each with small bathroom. Lavish breakfasts. Restaurants, pubs, National Trust properties nearby. ¾-acre well-kept garden with tennis, croquet, small swimming pool. Open Mar–Nov. No smoking. No children under 12. No dogs. Credit cards not accepted. B&B double £52–£56.

STON EASTON Somerset   Map 2

Ston Easton Park   *Tel* (01761) 241631
Ston Easton, nr Bath BA3 4DF   *Fax* (01761) 241377
                                          E-mail stoneaston@cityscape.co.uk

❧ *César award in 1987*

Peter and Christine Smedley's magnificent Palladian mansion (Relais & Châteaux) stands in a large park between Bath and Wells. Its gardens were designed by Humphry Repton in the 18th century; the river Norr flows over his flight of shallow cascades. The sitting rooms and library are grand, with antiques, fine paintings, comfortable sofas, elegant flower arrangements. The dining room, which has a modern decor of white-painted panelling, bamboo chairs, flowers and candles, is supplied with fruit, vegetables and herbs from an impressive kitchen garden. Mark Harrington's "traditional English/classical French" cooking is described as "simply marvellous" by some; others have thought it over-flavoured at times. There is an "expertly described and served" cheeseboard, and the wine list is wide-ranging. Breakfasts "are beyond reproach, from fresh juice through platters of fruit, to brilliant cooked dishes, and some of the best croissants outside France". A lavish afternoon tea is served in the lounge. Immaculate bedrooms are luxuriously decorated and equipped. Those on the first floor have huge windows and fine proportions; smaller ones are on the floor above; there are two spacious, air-conditioned suites in a garden cottage. Accommodation tends to be upgraded

whenever possible. The new manager, David Jennings, "pleasant, skilful and efficient", leads a "particularly caring staff". "A final bonus: it is made quite clear that no service charge is levied, nor is any additional payment expected." Dogs are kennelled in a heated basement and are fed and exercised in the morning. (*David Crowe, David and Kate Wooff, and others*)

Open All year.
Rooms 2 suites (in cottage), 20 double.
Facilities Drawing room, saloon, library, restaurant; private dining room; terrace. 28-acre grounds: tennis, croquet, river, fishing. Only restaurant suitable for &.
Location On A37 Bristol–Shepton Mallet. Train: Bath, etc; then taxi.
Restrictions No smoking in restaurant. No children under 7. No dogs in house (kennelling in heated basement).
Credit cards All major cards accepted.
Terms [To March 1998] Room: single £145–£165, double £175–£380, suite £300–£320. Breakfast: continental £8.50, English £12.50. Set lunch £26, dinner £39.50; full alc £50. Christmas programme; winter tariff.

STONOR Oxfordshire   Map 2

The Stonor Arms   NEW   *Tel* (01491) 638345
Stonor   *Fax* (01491) 638863
nr Henley-on-Thames RG9 6HE

"Country atmosphere, log fire, delicious food. Breakfast in the conservatory, huge, tasty and leisurely. A great retreat from city living." So write recent visitors to this 18th-century inn on the edge of a tranquil hamlet in the Chiltern Hills. It was dropped from the *Guide* last year, following a change of management and chef. A change of style has followed too, along with much redecoration and renovation, and inspectors agreed with much of the above: "It is very attractive, in a lovely setting. The manager, Guy Hodgson, is charming, and the staff are friendly if a bit edgy, but service can be haphazard at times. The lounges have a warm pink decor and open fires; the dining room is beautiful, with lovely old furniture, pictures, good silver and glass, but we thought the food a little solid." The same *à la carte* menu (British/ French modern) is served both in the restaurant and in the bar, which has "a very Henley decor of rowing memorabilia". Guests may take as many or as few courses as they like, and there are bar snacks at lunchtime (the place is popular with locals). The wines are well chosen and reasonably priced. The bedrooms, in a converted barn at the back, are bright, quiet and spacious, and have old pine furniture, appealing soft furnishings and marble bathroom; but the lighting has been thought inadequate, and one visitor complained of noisy plumbing. Stonor House, adjacent, the seat of the Stonor family, has gardens and a deerpark; it is sometimes open to the public. Handy for the regatta at Henley-on-Thames, and a good base for visiting Oxford and Windsor. (*Richard and Katie Hardwick, TB; also JE Howard, and others*)

Open All year, except 1–19 Jan.
Rooms 10 double. Some on ground floor. 1 suitable for &.
Facilities Ramps. Sitting room, bar (live jazz Wed, pianist Fri), restaurant. Private dining/conference room. 1-acre garden. River Thames 4 miles. Carpark.
Location 5 miles NW of Henley off A4130 to Oxford. After 1 mile turn on to B480. Hotel 3 miles further, on right. Train: Henley; then taxi.

Restriction No dogs in restaurant.
Credit cards Access, Amex, Visa.
Terms B&B: single £90, double £105. Light meals; full alc £30. Champagne breaks all year. 1-night bookings refused Henley Week (1st week July). *V*

STRATFORD-UPON-AVON Warwickshire   Map 3

 Caterham House   BUDGET   *Tel* (01789) 267309
58/59 Rother Street   *Fax* (01789) 414836
Stratford-upon-Avon CV37 6LT

César award: Best B&B for Bard lovers

"A very special small hotel, where no labour of love is lost, and all ends well – exactly as you like it. There are numerous hotels and guest houses in Shakespeare's birthplace, but this easily stands out from the rest. Dominique Maury presides over the bar in the charming lounge which spills out on to a small flowery patio in warm weather. His wife, Olive, is responsible for the extraordinary decor of the rooms, each with its own character and English and French antique furniture. They are both great fans of the theatre. Perceptive discussions of the current season's offerings begin over a post-theatre drink and continue at breakfast." A recent tribute to this coral-pink Georgian house, popular with theatre-goers and actors, a short walk from the Royal Shakespeare Theatre. A literary editor adds: "Our fourth visit. We were more impressed than ever, by the quirky and comfortable bedrooms, the cheerful, helpful staff and the hearty breakfasts, with wonderful crois-sants and excellent home-made jams. M. Maury knows and enjoys his Shakespeare, and speaks his mind with gusto. Not for those in search of obsequious service." Others enjoyed the "bright continental atmos-phere, with unusual pictures, painted furniture, brass bedsteads (some are narrow), plants and flowers" and have written: "Superb hosts, not intrusive, but intelligently friendly." A generous pre-theatre supper for residents is available by arrangement. Rooms in the house are pre-ferred to those in the annexe. (*Patricia Zich, Tony Thomas, and others*)

Open All year, except Christmas.
Rooms 1 family, 13 double. 2 in annexe, 2 in cottage. No telephone (payphone available).
Facilities Lounge with TV, bar, breakfast room; small patio. Unsuitable for &.
Location Central, opposite police station (some traffic noise possible). Carpark.
Restriction Dogs by arrangement, not in public rooms or unattended in bed-rooms.
Credit cards Access, Visa.
Terms B&B: single £40–£60, double £44–£71. Pre-theatre snack by arrangement. Children under 10 accommodated in parents' room half price.

STRETTON Rutland   Map 2

Ram Jam Inn   BUDGET   *Tel* (01780) 410776
Great North Road   *Fax* (01780) 410361
Stretton LE15 7QX

♥ *César award in 1993*

A popular "motel with a difference" on the Great North Road (A1M), owned by Tim Hart of nearby *Hambleton Hall*, Hambleton (*qv*). Its curious name may come from a popular 18th-century drink. It offers comfort but not luxury, a warm welcome, kindly attention, food well above average and good value. In the snack bar, guests perch on stools to tuck into home-made soups, giant sandwiches, steaks, pasta, salads and calorific puddings, or breakfast from a *carte*. The restaurant menu is similar, with a short but adequate wine list. Bedrooms are cheerful, simple, spacious and modern, with large bathroom; all but one overlook the garden and apple orchard at the back. (*JM*)

Open All year, except 25/26/31 Dec.
Rooms 1 family, 6 double.
Facilities Lounge, snack bar, restaurant; conference room. 2-acre grounds. Only restaurant suitable for &.
Location W side of A1 9 miles N of Stamford. Travelling S leave A1 on B668 to Oakham; travelling N leave A1 through Texaco garage just past B668 turnoff. Large carpark.
Restrictions No smoking in restaurant. No dogs.
Credit cards All major cards accepted.
Terms Rooms: single £43, double £53, family £68. English breakfast £4.45. Full alc from £18.

STURMINSTER NEWTON Dorset   Map 2

Plumber Manor   *Tel* (01258) 472507
Sturminster Newton DT10 2AF   *Fax* (01258) 473370
 César award in 1987

This handsome Jacobean house, with trout stream and tennis court, is set amid pasture in the heart of Hardy country. The home of the Prideaux-Brune family since the early 17th century, it has a genuine family feel. It has for years been run, informally but highly professionally, as a restaurant with particularly comfortable bedrooms. Six are in the house, off a gallery hung with family portraits; ten larger ones are in the converted stable block. Lavish public rooms and comprehensive cosseting are not on offer, but visitors are warmly welcomed by the convivial proprietor, Richard Prideaux-Brune and Bertie the labrador. In the restaurant, which runs through three interconnecting rooms, Richard's brother Brian serves traditional cooking in generous portions. The dessert cart has been called "heaven on wheels". "Imaginative snacks with pre-dinner drinks and excellent wines," reports one visitor. "My dinner could not be faulted, although my wife was not too impressed with her vegetarian main course. Breakfast was first-class, with enormous cafetières of decaffeinated and caffeinated coffee; it passed my 'scrambled egg test' with flying colours. Delightful, impeccably fitted bedroom – a nice touch was the two bottles of mineral water (one still, one sparkling). Utterly peaceful grounds. Excellent value." Another visitor thought the three-course Sunday lunch "exceptional value". Sturminster Newton is centrally placed for many Dorset attractions, including Sherborne Castle, Old Wardour Castle, and Kingston Lacy. There is fine walking locally; hunting with the Portman can be arranged, and shooting parties accommodated. (*Dr KR Whittington, and others*)

Open All year, except Feb. Restaurant closed for lunch, except Sun.
Rooms 16 double. 10 in stable courtyard (2 with & access).
Facilities 2 lounges (1 with bar), gallery, restaurant. 7-acre grounds: garden,

tennis, croquet, trout stream; stabling for visiting horses. Golf, swimming, fishing, clay pigeon-shooting nearby.
Location 2 miles SW of Sturminster Newton; turn off A357 to Hazelbury Bryan.
Restrictions Smoking discouraged in dining room. No dogs (except owners') in public rooms.
Credit cards All major cards accepted.
Terms B&B: single £75–£90, double £90–£130. Set Sun lunch £17.50, dinner £17.50–£30. Off-season breaks on application.

Stourcastle Lodge   NEW/BUDGET   *Tel* (01258) 472320
Gough's Close   *Fax* (01258) 473381
Sturminster Newton DT10 1BU

Ken and Jill Hookham-Bassett's old house (slate roof, tall white chimneys), in traffic-free close off high street of small market town. Cottage-style accommodation in 5 double bedrooms, all with antique brass bedstead; some have whirlpool bath. Farmhouse breakfasts; Aga-cooked dinners using traditional recipes, home-grown herbs and vegetables. Garden with terrace, sculpture, hedgehogs and pigs. Ample parking. Bicycles for hire. River Stour (fishing) 300 yds; castles, stately homes and gardens, notably Stourhead, nearby. No smoking: dining room, bedrooms. No dogs. Access accepted. B&B £26.50–£42; D,B&B £42.50–£58. More reports, please. *V*

SWAFFHAM Norfolk   **Map 2**

Stratton House   *Tel* (01760) 723845
4 Ash Close   *Fax* (01760) 720458
Swaffham PE37 7NH

Leslie and Vanessa Scott's Grade II listed Palladian villa has an almost rural setting, though it is only a few yards from the market place of this delightful old town with its elegant 18th-century buildings. The decor is highly individual: antiques, paintings (some for sale), patchwork, family photographs, cat cushions, china cats, and a "regal resident Siamese". There are bantams, guinea fowl and ducks under old trees in the garden. Children are welcomed. Traditional English/French meals are served in the rustic dining room (one of the *Good Food Guide*'s restaurants of the year in 1997). Mrs Scott's daily-changing menu has a choice of five starters and three main courses. "We live in the heart of agricultural country," she writes. "Local produce – pheasants, venison, goat's cheese, plums and much else – is left on our doorstep, or bartered for dinner or for our home-made cakes, biscuits and ice creams. This way of life has operated here for centuries and keeps us in touch with the seasons." Many visitors this year have admired the food, the "decorative, informative and well-chosen" wine list, and the relaxed family atmosphere. "I loved the mild eccentricity. By the end of my stay, we were firm friends. The cooking is inspired. Leslie Scott will perform a vivid description of dishes. Visits to the kitchen are welcomed. My attic room, with teddies, rubber ducks and bath toys was very comforting." "Peaceful and well maintained. Hosts friendly, but never intrusive." "The best breakfast coffee we have had in any UK hotel accompanied winter fruit salad and kedgeree." Major changes are ahead. There will be fewer, but larger, rooms, all with a living or dining area. We'd like reports on these developments, please. Swaffham has a traditional market on Saturday. Houghton and many medieval churches are nearby; the North Norfolk Heritage Coast is 30 minutes' drive. (*Jackie Rochester, Deborah Loveluck-Newman, Sheena Canham; also Barbara Blake, and others*)

Open All year, except 24–26 Dec. Lunch by arrangement.
Rooms 6 double, 1 single.
Facilities 2 lounges (1 with TV), restaurant (piped jazz/folk/classical music at night); terrace. 1-acre garden: croquet. Unsuitable for &.
Location Enter Ash Close at N end of Market Place, between estate agent and Express Cleaners. Ample private parking. Train/bus: King's Lynn/Downham Market; then taxi.
Restrictions No smoking, except in 1 lounge. No dogs in restaurant.
Credit cards Access, Visa.
Terms B&B: single £60, double £80–£130, suite £140. Set dinner £25. 1-night booking sometimes refused bank holiday weekends.

TALLAND-BY-LOOE Cornwall   Map 1

Talland Bay Hotel   *Tel* (01503) 272667
Talland-by-Looe PL13 2JB   *Fax* (01503) 272940
♦ *César award in 1996*

Annie and Barry Rosier's hotel stands high above an unspoilt bay, in carefully tended sub-tropical gardens with a good-sized swimming pool. Architecturally, it is an interesting mix, 16th-century in origin, much altered in the 1930s and 1940s. Some rooms in the oldest part have walls three feet thick; some are quite small, but were described by an American visitor last year as "charming and functional". She also liked the professional style: "No pretence that you are staying in someone's home. The decor is country house style, but not overly feminine or knick-knacked. The food is neither 'gourmet' nor home-cooking; menus are suited for a long stay, different every night, with plenty of choice. Very good snack lunches, teas (included in the price) and breakfasts, too. Not for rumbustious teenagers or those who want fast-paced service or an active night life." Some guests this year have thought the reception lacked cordiality; one couple warned that "the back of the restaurant is depressingly dark", while another thought the beach unkempt. But most have echoed the earlier enthusiasm. "The idyllic situation would be hard to equal," writes a regular *Guide* correspondent. "The views are stunning. Our bedroom was attractively decorated and quite spacious. The staff were some of the nicest we have encountered in any hotel." "Delicious sandwich lunches." "Dinners varied and well cooked. We left the table feeling that the day had ended on a high note." Heligan, with its gardens, and several National Trust properties are nearby. (*SH, Joan A Powell, Ann Lawson Lucas, A Gradon; also Ian C Dewey, Virginia Pearce, Ken and Anne Sutton, and others*)

Open Mid-Feb–end Dec.
Rooms 1 suite, 12 double, 3 single. 3 in grounds, 1 across lane.
Facilities Sitting room, lounge, bar, restaurant; patio. 2½-acre grounds: garden, swimming pool, sauna, putting, croquet. Beach 5 mins' walk. Unsuitable for &.
Location 2½ miles SW of Looe. Left at hotel sign on Looe–Polperro road. Train: Liskeard, 8 miles; then branch line or taxi to Looe.
Restrictions No smoking: restaurant, 1 lounge. No under-5s in restaurant at night. Dogs by arrangement only, not in public rooms.
Credit cards All major cards accepted.

Terms [1997] B&B: single £39–£79, double £78–£158, suite £98–£138; D,B&B: single £54–£94, double £108–£188, suite £128–£168. Snack lunches. Set dinner £21; full alc £36.50. Off-season breaks, painting holidays; Christmas, New Year packages. *V*

TAPLOW Buckinghamshire   Map 2

Cliveden   *Tel* (01628) 668561
Taplow SL6 0JF   *Fax* (01628) 661837

♦ *César award in 1995*

This magnificent stately home – "a wonderful evocation of the Edwardian era," wrote one visitor – stands in huge National Trust grounds (open to the public in summer) on the Thames. It has a colourful past: three dukes lived here; it was the home of the Astor family for four generations; its many famous visitors included John Profumo who fatefully met Christine Keeler by the side of its swimming pool. Nowadays, it is a grand country house hotel, managed by Stuart Johnson, with air-conditioning and fax machines in the bedrooms and an international clientele. It is popular with honeymooners – Heathrow Airport is 20 minutes' drive away. The public rooms are spectacular, with tapestries, armour and fine paintings, but one visitor this year thought the new colour schemes inappropriate. Bedrooms in the main house are grand; those in the wings are attractive but less characterful. The large, quite formal *Terrace* restaurant serves "English modern and traditional" food; in the smaller, pricier *Waldo's* (*Michelin* star), modern British dishes are cooked by chef Ron Maxfield. Light meals are served in a conservatory. Three vintage boats are available for river trips. Many sporting facilities (see below) are included in the room price; so is afternoon tea. Children are welcome. *Cliveden* is host to functions of all kinds, and we get occasional reports of casual service, but there is also warm praise. "I stay regularly on my own," wrote one visitor. "Despite the sophistication, one feels at home. The staff are exceptional; without their warmth and care, it would not be the great hotel it is." The company also owns the *Royal Crescent Hotel*, Bath (*qv*) and the *Cliveden Town House* (formerly *The Draycott*) in London, on both of which we'd like more reports, please. (*Lady Napley*)

Open All year. *Waldo's* closed midday, Sun/Mon.
Rooms 15 suites, 23 double. 12 in wings. 9 on ground floor. 14 air-conditioned.
Facilities Lift, ramp. Great hall (pianist in evening), 2 lounges, library, billiard room, club room, breakfast room, 2 restaurants, conservatory; function facilities; crèche; pavilion: swimming pool, sauna, jacuzzi, gym, health and beauty treatments. 375-acre grounds: swimming pool, tennis, squash, riding, practice golf, fishing, jogging routes; 3 boats for river trips.
Location 10 miles NW of Windsor. M4 exit 7. On B476 opposite *Feathers* pub. Train: Burnham, 2 miles.
Restrictions No smoking in restaurants. No dogs in restaurants.
Credit cards All major cards accepted.
Terms [1997] (*Excluding donation to National Trust*) Rooms: single £230, double £230–£350, suite £410–£725. Breakfast: continental £12, English £17. *Terrace*: set lunch £28, dinner £40; full alc £65. *Waldo's*: set dinner £45–£75. Fitness, Christmas, New Year packages. Children under 14 accommodated free in parents' room. 1-night bookings refused weekends.

TAUNTON Somerset
Map 1

The Castle
Castle Green
Taunton TA1 1NF

Tel (01823) 272671
Fax (01823) 336066
E-mail reception@the-castle-hotel.com

♀ *César award in 1987*

The county town of Somerset has modern shopping malls and office blocks, but its historic centre, with some fine buildings, has survived. Here, the Chapman family's 300-year-old hostelry, wisteria-covered and castellated, stands on the site of a 12th-century castle. "Reeking history", it has a suitably traditional decor (oak furniture, tapestries and paintings), a fine wrought-iron staircase, and high standards of comfort. Fellow *Guide* hoteliers were well pleased: "After a stressful journey we stepped into peace and calm. The welcome was fantastic. We had champagne in our bedroom to unwind, and they delayed dinner for us. The food was sublime, the service attentive and friendly. Though there was a coach load of German gardeners, we were made to feel special." Philip Vickery ("an enthusiastic chef with a delightful personality") presides over the restaurant, which has always made a point of serving British cooking, both traditional and modern. Could this be why *Michelin* withdrew its star this year? The local suppliers are given credit on the menus. There is a long wine list, "generally good value". Bedrooms vary in size and style; the best and quietest overlook the moated garden at the back; they are "not too gadget-minded, and well maintained". The penthouse suite and roof garden have far-reaching views. Continental breakfast may be served in the bedrooms; there's a good cooked one in the dining room. (*David and Diane Skelton*)

Open All year.
Rooms 5 suites, 19 double, 12 single.
Facilities Lift, ramp. Lounge, lounge/bar (piped light classical music all day), restaurant; private dining/meeting rooms; roof garden. 1-acre grounds.
Location Central (follow signs for castle). Garages (£10), parking. Bus station 2 mins; railway station 5 mins.
Restrictions No smoking in restaurant. Small dogs by arrangement; not in public rooms.
Credit cards All major cards accepted.
Terms [1997] B&B: single £80, double £120, suite £195; D,B&B (2 nights min.) £80–£110 per person. Set lunch from £9, dinner from £23; full alc from £42. West Country breaks; musical weekends; Christmas, New Year packages. Special rates for honeymooners, old boys/parents from local schools. *V*

TEFFONT EVIAS Wiltshire
Map 2

Howard's House   NEW
Teffont Evias
nr Salisbury SP3 5RJ

Tel (01722) 716392
Fax (01722) 716820

Teffont Evias, like its partner, Teffont Magna, stands on the Teff, a little river "teeming with trout". It is a beautiful, quiet village which has been owned since the 17th century by one family, who have permitted little change. This unusual house, with a steeply pitched, broad-eved Swiss-style roof, is set in a romantic garden, and run in relaxed style: children and dogs are welcome; there is no dress code. It has a popular restaurant, with an agreeably restrained decor, where owner/chef Paul Firmin's modern British cooking is served by dignified local ladies. This year it regained *Michelin*'s red "Meals" for good food at a moderate price. *Howard's House* fell from the *Guide* last year when overnight visitors complained of a lack of welcome, and of poor maintenance of some bedrooms. This year, reports are mostly enthusiastic: "Wonderful in every way: lovely room, good service." "Exemplary dinner, and a comprehensive wine list which led to some super discoveries." "Smallish bedroom, decorated in good taste. Reasonable, if small, bathroom." "Good breakfast, apart from dreary coffee." But there are still criticisms: "We were disappointed to be presented with the same menu on both nights of our stay, and were told it was changed every six weeks." "Only one lounge, for diners as well as residents, which can cause congestion." And some have felt the place is expensive for what is on offer. So we'd like more reports, please. (*John Hall, D Lodge, NM Mackintosh*)

Open All year. Restaurant closed for lunch, except Sun.
Rooms 9 double.
Facilities Lounge, restaurant. 2-acre grounds. River fishing nearby. Unsuitable for &.
Location From A303 1½ miles S of Wylye, turn left, marked Teffont. After ½ mile turn left. Proceed 2 miles through Teffont. At *Black Horse* pub, turn right. Train: Tisbury, 3 miles; then taxi.
Restrictions No smoking in dining room. No dogs in dining room.
Credit cards All major cards accepted.
Terms [1997] B&B: single £65–£95, double £95–£115; D,B&B: single £90–£120, double £145–£165. Set lunch (Sun) £18.50, dinner £25. 2-night breaks; Christmas package. *V*

TEIGNMOUTH Devon   Map 1

Thomas Luny House   BUDGET   *Tel* (01626) 772976
Teign Street
Teignmouth TQ14 8EG

  César award in 1995

"This Wolsey Lodge epitomises the values which the *Good Hotel Guide* so ably champions," write recent visitors. "John and Alison Allan are a delightful couple, welcoming yet discreet, and very professional. We were welcomed with tea and chocolate cake. We enjoyed breakfasting with a chemistry professor and a microbiologist, and dining with a journalist from a national newspaper and a retired schoolmaster who had taught Paddy Ashdown. Only reservation: we would have liked brighter reading lights in the lounge and the bedroom." The Allans' beautifully proportioned Georgian house, named for the marine artist who built it, is approached from the street through an archway in a whitewashed wall. Though central, near the fish quay in the old quarter of town, it is quiet. The double drawing room and dining room, both with an open fire, lead through French windows on to a small walled garden. Three bedrooms are spacious, the fourth is small; all have fresh flowers, Malvern water, books and magazines. The place is run in house party style. Dinner is communally served (no choice of menu). There's a short, reasonably priced wine list. Teignmouth's days as an elegant bathing resort are long gone, but it is admirably placed for excursions to the Devon coast and moors, and to Exeter. There is excellent birdwatching on the Exe estuary. From 1998 the Allans will be offering B&B only. (*Anne and Robin Sharp, Marilyn Frampton, and others*)

Open 1 Feb–mid-Dec. Lunch not served.
Rooms 4 double.
Facilities 2 lounges, dining room. Small walled garden. Sea, sandy beach 5 mins' walk. Unsuitable for &.
Location Central. From dual carriageway, follow signs to quay. First left into Teign St. Courtyard parking.
Restrictions No smoking in dining room. No children under 12. No dogs.
Credit cards None accepted.
Terms [1997] B&B £25–£35; D,B&B £53.50.

TEMPLE SOWERBY Cumbria   **Map 4**

Temple Sowerby House   *Tel* (01768 3) 61578
Temple Sowerby   *Freephone* 0800 146157
nr Penrith CA10 1RZ   *Fax* (01768 3) 61958

In a pretty village on the A66 in the Eden Valley, with a large green surrounded by sandstone Georgian houses, this extended Cumbrian farmhouse was once the principal residence. It stands in a formal walled garden overlooking Cross Fell, the highest peak in the Pennines. The dramatic landscapes of the Pennines and Lake District are a few miles away on either horizon. "Cécile and Geoffrey Temple run the place with friendly professionalism," say recent visitors. "The traditional cooking by Andrew Walker was of a consistently high standard, and personal whims were cheerfully catered for. Geoffrey Temple is knowledgeable about his wines." "Staff friendly and attentive; good breakfast. A useful stop on the way north." The decor is traditional, with antiques and open fires in the lounges, and two candlelit areas, one white-panelled and beamed, for dining. Bedrooms (some in a coach house) vary in style; some are traditional, some modern. The tea shop serves light meals all day, and cream teas. Children are welcomed. Acorn Bank, a short walk away, is a National Trust garden with a stream and a mill, orchards and shrubs, and the largest collection of culinary and medicinal herbs in the north. (*Tony Thomas, also Beverly Brittan*)

Open All year.
Rooms 12 double. 4 in coach house (2 on ground floor). Some with access for &.
Facilities Ramps. 2 lounges, bar, restaurant (classical CDs in evening), conservatory; function facilities; tea shop; courtyard, terrace. 2-acre walled garden: croquet. River, fishing 400 yds.
Location On A66, 6 miles NW of Appleby. (Some traffic noise; front rooms double-glazed.)
Restriction No smoking in restaurant.
Credit cards Access, Amex, Visa.
Terms [1997] B&B: single £55–£60, double £80–£90; D,B&B: single £80–£85, double £130–£140. Full alc £30. 2-day breaks *V*

Please don't be shy of writing again about old favourites. Too many people feel that if they have written once, years ago, there is no need to report on a revisit.

TETBURY Gloucestershire   Map 3

Calcot Manor   *Tel* (01666) 890391
nr Tetbury GL8 8YJ   *Fax* (01666) 890394

"Cheerful atmosphere, helpful staff, appetising food. We loved the privacy of our spacious suite in beautifully renovated old stables; the six-foot bed was a total delight. The whole weekend was excellent value." So writes a recent visitor to this family-friendly hotel, run in relaxed style by Richard Ball. "The staff is not an army of uniformed bellmen and waiters," a visitor wrote last year, "but young professionals who do a bit of everything and grant every request with an indulgent 'of course'." The public rooms have a country house decor. Most bedrooms are spacious, and all are stocked with shortbread, fruit, toiletries, etc; a few have a whirlpool bath. Some are in the main house, a mellow Cotswold manor, others are in venerable barns and stables, complete with beams. There are five new ones this year, by the swimming pool. The family suites have a lounge with bunk or sofa beds. The *Gumstool Inn* provides casual meals; the restaurant, with a new conservatory extension, serves unfussy international cooking by chef Michael Croft. Breakfasts include fresh orange juice, local sausages, etc. Tetbury has lovely old houses, particularly in its market place, and it is home to the 600-acre Westonbirt Arboretum. On Woolsack Day in the spring, local inhabitants race up the steep Gumstool Hill, with heavy sacks of wool. (*AS-M*)

Open All year.
Rooms 4 family suites, 21 double. 15 in converted outbuildings. Some on ground floor.
Facilities Ramps. 2 lounges, restaurant, bar/restaurant (piped music); private dining room, conference facilities. 9-acre grounds: children's play area, swimming pool, tennis, croquet; bicycles. Golf, fishing, riding nearby.
Location 3 miles W of Tetbury, on intersection of A4135 and A46. Train: Kemble, 6 miles; then taxi.
Restriction No dogs.
Credit cards All major cards accepted.
Terms B&B: single £85, double £97–£145, suite £150. English breakfast £6. Pub meals. Full alc £26. 2-day breaks. 2 children under 14 accommodated free in family suites.

The Close   NEW   *Tel* (01666) 502272
8 Long Street   *Fax* (01666) 504401
Tetbury GL8 8AQ

Sixteenth-century wool merchant's rambling house on main street, with secluded walled garden, croquet lawn. Bills itself as Richard Branson's Cotswold retreat (it is part of the Virgin consortium). Nominator liked personal style: help with luggage, names remembered. Spacious public rooms, smart country house decor. 24-hour room service. Imaginative cooking ("portions just right"), in restaurant overlooking garden (pianist in evening Fri/Sat). 15 bedrooms (3 with 4-poster), some large, with sitting area. Unsuitable for &. No smoking: dining room, bedrooms. No children under 8 at dinner. No dogs. All major credit cards accepted. B&B: single £95, double £130–£170; D,B&B: single £123, double £165–£225. Set lunch £18.50, dinner £26.95; full alc £40. More reports, please. *V**

THEBERTON Suffolk   Map 2

Theberton Grange   NEW/BUDGET   *Tel/Fax* (01728) 830625
Theberton, nr Leiston IP16 4RR   *E-mail* Paul Rosher@compuserve.com

Red brick farmhouse, mainly Victorian with Tudor elements, in 4-acre grounds with woods and lily pond. In rural village with pretty church, 2 miles N of Leiston. Bright and warm, comfortable rather than luxurious, with friendly hosts, Paul and Dawn Rosher. Impressive pine staircase; large drawing room with log fire. Simple Aga-cooked dinner (3 courses, no choice, for residents only); adequate breakfast (home-made preserves). Light classical music during meals. Handy for Suffolk coast, Aldeburgh, Snape, Minsmere bird reserve; sailing, fishing, golf nearby. Closed 5 days over Christmas. Unsuitable for ♿. No smoking: dining room, bedrooms. No children under 7. No dogs. 7 bedrooms, all with private facilities (not all en suite). B&B: single £35–£40, double £60–£85; set dinner £19.50 [1997]. More reports, please.

THORNBURY South Gloucestershire   Map 3

Thornbury Castle   *Tel* (01454) 281182
Castle Street   *Fax* (01454) 416188
Thornbury, Bristol BS12 1HH

"Near perfect, and good value for what it offers. It stands isolated above the busy modern world of Thornbury which laps at its walls," notes a satisfied visitor to this imposing hotel. It is an early 16th-century castle, which Henry VIII seized from the Duke of Buckingham; he visited it with Anne Boleyn, and Mary Tudor later lived here. It is now owned by Maurice and Carol Taylor (aka the Baron and Baroness of Porthlethen). It has baronial public rooms, with huge fireplaces, mullioned windows, and antique furniture and tapestries. Some of the bedrooms are equally impressive, with views of the oldest Tudor garden in England, surrounded by the castle wall. The singles are small. Chef Steven Black's daily-changing menu, with a bias towards game and fish, is mainly English with a Mediterranean influence, and draws much praise: "Beautifully presented food – one hesitated to spoil the arrangements – and very fresh. The sea bass seemed to have jumped from net to table with just a brief interlude in the kitchen. Desserts include traditional British hot puddings, such as treacle tart adorned with a cage of spun sugar – utterly delicious – and butterscotch pudding. Service excellent, unobtrusive and effective; they read customers well." "The extensive wine list still contains some treasures from previous owner Kenneth Bell's day, as well as skilfully selected recent purchases." The castle is licensed for civil marriages. Thornbury is handy for touring South Wales and the Cotwolds. (*JS Rutter, Jo Winslow, and others*)

Open All year, except 3 days Jan.
Rooms 1 suite, 15 double, 2 single. 7 across small courtyard.
Facilities Lounge, library, 3 dining rooms (piped music all day). 15-acre grounds: garden, croquet, small farm, vineyard. Unsuitable for ♿.
Location 12 miles N of Bristol. From Thornbury on B4061 continue downhill to monumental water pump; bear left. Entrance to left of parish church 300 yds. Train: Bristol; then taxi.
Restrictions No smoking in dining rooms. "No children under 12 unless known to us." No dogs.

Credit cards All major cards accepted.
Terms B&B: single £75–£95, double £125–£145, suite £175–£225. Set lunch (2/3-course) £16.50/£18.50; dinner £34.50. *V*

THORNTON-LE-FYLDE Lancashire   **Map 4**

The River House   *Tel* (01253) 883497
Skippool Creek   *Fax* (01253) 892083
Thornton-le-Fylde
nr Blackpool FY5 5LF

This 1830s gentleman farmer's house, quietly set on a river estuary, has been owned by the Scott family for 40 years. Now a restaurant-with-rooms run by Bill Scott (he is chef) and his wife Linda, it offers a refuge from the rigours of Blackpool, 15 minutes' drive away. "Gentle, warm welcome from Bill Scott," wrote the nominator. "His dogs will accompany you on the walk along a well-kept path by the water; you see only boats and birds. The house is crammed with well-chosen antiques. Our bedroom had a mahogany bureau with secret drawers, an enormous built-in wardrobe, beds with a velvet headboard, tea tray with delicate china, and a shining new bathroom with upmarket soaps, etc." Mrs Scott tends the dark, pub-like bar, and serves the meals in the pretty restaurant, which has deep green walls, old mahogany tables, good cutlery and lace mats. The food on an eclectic menu, which includes ostrich, venison, and "ticky tacky pudding", is "fresh, light and original, and vegetables are out of this world". Breakfast includes freshly squeezed orange juice, home-made marmalade, cooked dishes to order, and make-your-own toast in an interesting eight-slice toaster. There is a Victorian conservatory, with basket chairs and glossy magazines. (*MA*)

Open All year. Restaurant closed Sun.
Rooms 5 double.
Facilities Lounge with TV, bar, restaurant (piped "easy-listening" music), conservatory. 1¼-acre garden on river. Clay pigeon/duck-shooting, golf nearby.
Location 5 miles NE of Blackpool. From N: M6 exit 33; A6 S past Garstang, then A586/A585 towards Fleetwood. At roundabout after 3 sets of traffic lights take 3rd exit. Follow signs to Skippool Creek. From S: M6; M55 to exit 3; A585 towards Fleetwood; then as above. Bus from Blackpool.
Restriction No dogs in restaurant.
Credit cards Access, Visa.
Terms [1997] B&B: single £65, double £80. Set lunch/dinner £20; full alc £40. Weekend breaks: D,B&B £85–£90. *V*

TINTAGEL Cornwall   **Map 1**

Trebrea Lodge   *Tel* (01840) 770410
Trenale, Tintagel PL34 0HR   *Fax* (01840) 770092

"A winner in every way." "The owners, though caring and welcoming, remained unobtrusive throughout. Delicious meals." "More a home than a hotel; old-fashioned, leisured and comfortable. High standards of decor and housekeeping." Recent tributes to a welcoming small establishment owned by John Charlick, Sean Devlin and Fergus Cochrane. It has a wonderful position on a wooded hillside, looking across open country to the Atlantic. It is a pretty Grade II* listed building, 14th-century in origin, only one room deep, with a symmetrical Georgian façade. There is a smart upstairs drawing room with antique furniture, and a cosier sitting/smoking room with an honesty bar and a log fire. Bedrooms, "full of charm", are of varying shapes and sizes; one has a wooden carved four-poster; a small one with beamed ceiling is reached up a steep stairway; one has a separate entrance. Dinner ("good private house cooking", no choice, but menus are discussed in advance) is served at 8 pm in the panelled dining room. There's a small but well-chosen wine list. Good breakfast too, with fresh orange juice and a buffet on a sideboard, followed by cooked dishes. Tintagel, with Arthurian connections, is a touristy village, but is worth visiting for the romantic ruined castle spectacularly set on a cliff. The old post office, in a 14th-century building, is owned by the National Trust. Excellent walking nearby. (*John and Susan Colby, John and Ann Smith, and others*)

Open All year, except Christmas, 4 Jan–13 Feb. Dining room closed midday.
Rooms 7 double. 1 with separate entrance.
Facilities Lounge, lounge/bar, dining room (piped classical music/jazz). 4½-acre grounds. Sea ½ mile. Unsuitable for &.
Location ½ mile SE of Tintagel. From Boscastle road, right by modern Roman Catholic church, right at top of lane. Hotel 300 yds on left. Train: Bodmin Parkway; then taxi.
Restrictions Smoking in lounge/bar only. No children under 12. "Well-behaved dogs", by prior arrangement.
Credit cards Access, Amex, Visa.
Terms B&B: single £55–£60, double £78–£88; D,B&B: single £76–£81, double £110–£130. Set dinner £21. Special breaks; winter rates. New Year packages.

TOWERSEY Oxfordshire   **Map 2**

Upper Green Farm   `BUDGET`   *Tel* (01844) 212496
Manor Road   *Fax* (01844) 260399
Towersey OX9 3QR

Euan and Marjorie Aitken's no-smoking B&B has a rural setting on the edge of a peaceful little village, and lovely views of the Chilterns. Accommodation is in a thatched 15th-century cottage, an 18th-century barn called Paradise, and a milking shed, all surrounded by flowers in tubs and a delightful garden, with a large pond complete with ducks and a skiff. Marjorie Aitken was formerly in the antiques business, and country antiques and knick-knacks, lace and patchwork abound. "We were made very welcome," say recent guests, "and were impressed by the beautifully laundered and ironed linen in the pretty bedroom. It had TV and tea-making kit, and a fridge containing fresh milk and with space for picnic materials was available for guests." The barn also houses a lounge, warmed in winter by a log fire, and the beamed breakfast room, where a generous spread includes home-grown fruit, home-made jams, local honey, free-range (often home-laid) eggs, and sausages and black pudding from an award-winning butcher in Thame. Nearby, are many eating places, ranging from *Le Manoir aux Quat'Saisons*, Great Milton (*qv*), to the village pub. Waddesdon Manor, home of the Rothschilds (now run by the National Trust), is 15 minutes' drive away; and there is easy motorway access to Oxford, Heathrow Airport and London. (*Ian and Anne Steel*)

Open All year, except Christmas/New Year.
Rooms 9 double, 1 single. 8 in converted barn and milking shed. 2 on ground floor, with access for &. No telephone.
Facilities 2 lounges, breakfast room. 7-acre grounds: pond with rowing boat, mini-golf, croquet.
Location Take Towersey road off Thame ring road. Hotel on left just after Towersey Manor.
Restrictions No smoking. No children under 14. No pets.
Credit cards None accepted.
Terms [1997] B&B: single £38, double £45–£60. 1-night bookings refused bank holidays, some weekends.

TREBARWITH STRAND Cornwall   Map 1

The Old Millfloor   BUDGET   *Tel* (01840) 770234
Trebarwith Strand
Tintagel PL34 0HA

"Downright wonderful; cosy and hospitable. Janice Waddon-Martyn made us and our children most welcome. She is an excellent cook." A warm endorsement in 1997 for this individual small guest house, which other visitors have described as "pleasantly old-fashioned". It is set in a fern-filled glen by a millstream, well away from trippery Tintagel. Inside are light and colour, gleaming wood, fresh flowers and cleverly used fabrics. Bedrooms have white walls, pure white linen, lots of lace, and big feather pillows. The home-cooked dinner, with limited choice, is served by candlelight in the small beamed dining room; menus feature home-made soups and ice-creams, organic and free-range meat, fresh vegetables and clotted cream. Rolls are freshly baked, as are the scones for tea (no charge). Good breakfasts too. No licence, bring your own wine. Not for the disabled or infirm, as there is a steep path down from the road (best to take the minimum of luggage), but perfect for families: lots of pets, large grounds; the sandy beach is a short walk away. No private facilities; there is one large shared bathroom. "The plumbing might not reach the standard expected by some pernickety people," one reporter has written, "but that is part of the charm of the place." "Amazing value" is the consensus. (*Jim and Melissa Fogle; also Elizabeth Goldby, and others*)

Open Easter–Nov.
Rooms 3 doubles with wash-basin.
Facilities Restaurant/lounge. 10-acre grounds: garden, orchard, paddocks, stream. Beach 10 mins' walk. Riding nearby. Unsuitable for &.
Location 2 miles S of Tintagel by B3263.
Restrictions No smoking. No dogs.
Credit cards None accepted.
Terms (*Not VAT-rated*) B&B £20 (£18 for 2 or more days). Dinner £15 (unlicensed: bring your own wine). 1 child accommodated free in parents' room; otherwise half price.

The "Budget" label by a hotel's name indicates an establishment where dinner, bed and breakfast is offered at around $80 per person, or B&B for about $48 and dinner for about $32. These are only rough guides and do not always apply to single accommodation; nor do they necessarily apply in high season.

TRESCO Isles of Scilly   Map 1

The Island Hotel   *Tel* (01720) 422883
Tresco, Isles of Scilly   *Fax* (01720) 423008
Cornwall TR24 0PU

Tresco is a private island, two miles by one, warmed by the Gulf
Stream, and renowned for its subtropical Abbey Gardens. No cars;
there are bicycles for hire, and a tractor and trailer convey guests and
their luggage from quay or heliport to this smart modern hotel, set in
beautiful gardens overlooking the rocky coastline. "It must be one of
the most beautifully situated hotels in the world," one visitor wrote this
year. Others praised its "recuperative charms", the personal style of the
manager, Ivan Curtis, and the "competent and friendly, but never
obsequious staff". Honeymooners "felt they had discovered paradise",
though they warned: "The atmosphere at dinner is quite staid; men
should bring a jacket and tie." The decor may lack character, but public areas are spacious and comfortable. A floor-to-ceiling glass wall in
the sitting room gives dramatic views of other islands. Suites have their
own balcony, and the best bedrooms (in the Flower wing) have picture-
windows opening on to a private patio, and views over the garden to
the sea. There is dissent about the food: one guest sent a paean of
praise. Another wrote: "If you stay long enough, you are gradually
promoted to a table by the window. But the food is entertainment
enough if you are denied a view. Dining room staff whirr like Swiss
clockwork through splendid, lavish meals." However, the dinners
have also been called "ambitious-sounding but rather bland" and the
breakfasts have come in for criticism too. The bar serves lunches, and
snacks, tea, coffee and drinks all day. Children are welcomed; there are
cots, chairs and high teas. (*Rosemary Wright, Richard and Katie Hardwick,
Lindsay Hunt, also Rosemary Inge, and others*)

Open Mid-Mar–end Oct.
Rooms 2 suites, 33 double, 5 single. 2 on ground floor.
Facilities Lounge/bar, library, restaurant. 8-acre grounds: tennis, croquet,
bowls, swimming pool, beach. Tresco not really suitable for &.
Location From Penzance: boat via St Mary's, or scheduled helicopter flight (not
Sun). Hotel will make travel arrangements; guests met on arrival.
Restriction No dogs allowed on Tresco.
Credit cards Access, Amex, Visa.
Terms D,B&B: single £75–£110, double £190–£290, suite £220–£370. Snack
lunches; packed lunches. 5-course set dinner £30. Gardeners', painters', writers'
holidays.

TROUTBECK Cumbria   Map 4

The Mortal Man   `BUDGET`   *Tel* (01539 4) 33193
Troutbeck, Windermere LA23 1PL   *Fax* (01539 4) 31261

"An excellent establishment, immaculately maintained." "Nothing
much changes here. Guests are cosseted by hands-on management.
The food, with plenty of choices and served in generous portions, is
especially good – varied and interesting vegetables and an exceptional
sweet trolley." "Warm, charming, laid back hostess; unfailingly courteous host. A combination of stalwart local staff and cheerful young

seasonal workers provides excellent service." Endorsements for
Annette and Christopher Poulsom's 300-year-old inn set in carefully
maintained gardens in an unspoilt village surrounded by the wonderful scenery of the Troutbeck valley. Outside hangs a sign depicting a
man with a tankard in conversation with a woman: "O, mortal man,
that lives by bread,/What is it makes thy nose so red?/Thou silly fool,
that look'st so pale,/'Tis drinking Sally Birkett's ale." Inside are oak
beams, thick walls and a simple decor. The residents' lounge, which
has an open fire, old hunting prints, easy chairs, and gleaming brass-
topped tables, is quite small "but arranged so you can converse within
your own party, chat to fellow guests, or ignore everyone and read a
book". The traditional bar serves good pub food. The restaurant, with
a separate kitchen and picture windows, is popular locally for dinner
and Sunday lunch. The bedrooms are small, as are the bathrooms, but
they have "solid, attractive furniture". Good drying facilities. Dogs are
welcome. Beatrix Potter lived at Troutbeck Farm in the village; her
flock of Herdwick sheep still survives. (*SC Law, Anne E Sharp; also JH
Astle-Fletcher, and others*)

Open Mid-Feb–mid-Nov.
Rooms 10 double, 2 single.
Facilities Residents' lounge, bar, restaurant. 2-acre grounds. Unsuitable for &.
Location 3 miles N of Windermere on A592.
Restrictions No smoking in restaurant. No children under 5.
Credit cards None accepted.
Terms D,B&B £50–£60. Set Sun lunch £12.50, dinner £22.50. Bar meals.
Reductions for longer stays; off-season rates. *V*

TWO BRIDGES Devon   **Map 2**

Prince Hall   NEW   *Tel* (01822) 890403
Two Bridges, Yelverton PL20 6SA   *Fax* (01822) 890676

Two Bridges is a hamlet at a road junction in the middle of Dartmoor,
named for its bridges (one built in 1780) across the West Dart river. Set
well back from the road in large grounds, with panoramic views across
the Dart valley, is this white-walled, grey-roofed house, which was
built in the 18th century as a private home for a famous High Court
judge, Sir Francis Buller. It featured in earlier editions of the *Guide*
under previous owners. Now Adam and Carrie Southwell, who have
been here since 1995, have earned warm praise: "A delightful place;
wonderfully restful." "Charming and efficient hosts and staff.
Wonderful views from dining room, bar and sitting room. Our attractive 'standard' bedroom had patchwork quilts, kettle, etc (but no fresh
milk). It overlooked a courtyard with a horse, two geese, a cockerel,
swifts and house martins. Next time, we would pay extra for a larger
room on the first floor, overlooking the moors. Breakfasts were good,
dinners very good, well cooked by Adam Southwell, and attractively
presented, with plenty of choice on a daily-changing menu; delicious
locally caught fish." The wine list is "interesting (particularly strong on
New World wines) and reasonably priced". Dogs are welcomed. You
can walk from the grounds straight on to the moor. The dramatic landscape is said to have inspired Sir Arthur Conan Doyle, a visitor in the
late 19th century, to write *The Hound of the Baskervilles*. (*Mr M Shennan,
Nadia Young*)

Open Mid-Feb–end Dec. Lunch not served (packed lunches available).
Rooms 8 double, 1 single.
Facilities Lounge, bar, restaurant (piped classical music/light jazz at night). 6-acre grounds. Fishing in river Dart, 3 mins' walk; riding, shooting, golf nearby. Unsuitable for &.
Location 1 mile SW of Two Bridges, on B3357 to Ashburton. Train: Plymouth, Exeter; taxi arranged.
Restrictions No smoking in restaurant. No children under 8. No dogs in restaurant.
Credit cards All major cards accepted.
Terms [1997] B&B: single £35, double £65–£75; D,B&B £52.50–£57.50 per person. Packed lunch £4.75. Set dinner £22. Children under 8 sharing parents' room half price.

TYNEMOUTH Tyne and Wear   Map 4

Hope House   BUDGET   *Tel/Fax* (0191) 257 1989
47 Percy Gardens
Tynemouth NE30 4HH

This civilised small guest house, once the home of a 19th-century merchant, overlooks the magnificent beach of a clifftop Victorian town at the mouth of the Tyne. Its original features have been carefully retained, and the nominator admired the decor, with its bright colours and antiques. "Our large, comfortable room had a marvellous sea view and a small but adequate shower room. The host is a charming Frenchman, Pascal Delin; his English wife, Anna, is the cook. Dinner is served communally, normally for residents only. It was delicious, beautifully served, and ended with unlimited coffee." The Delins write: "We never forget that you are our guest, not a room number; we can provide attention and service which many large hotels can no longer afford." Cooking is traditional English/French, with much use of local produce, particularly seafood. Tynemouth has a ruined Benedictine priory and castle, and it is the burial place of the ancient kings of Northumbria. Newcastle International Airport, and the North Shields terminal, with ferries to Scandinavia and northern Europe, are close by. More reports, please.

Open All year. Dining room closed midday, 2-week annual holiday.
Rooms 3 double (1 with bath, 2 with shower). No telephone.
Facilities Drawing room, dining room. Beach across road. Unsuitable for &.
Location A1058 to Tynemouth. To seafront, then right for ½ mile. Garages. Tyneside Metro, almost to door.
Restriction No dogs.
Credit cards All major cards accepted.
Terms B&B: single £40, double £65; D,B&B £50–£56 per person. Set dinner £17.50.

UCKFIELD East Sussex   Map 2

Hooke Hall   *Tel* (01825) 761578
250 High Street   *Fax* (01825) 768025
Uckfield TN22 1EN

This busy little town has modern suburbs but an attractive high street on a hill with some old buildings, including Juliet and Alister Percy's Queen Anne house, which 1997 visitors thought "beautifully decorated and furnished". Panelled public rooms have designer fabrics, antiques, ancestral paintings and open fires. The bedrooms (keys are not given) are named after famous mistresses and lovers, eg, Nell Gwynn and Madame de Pompadour, but their lighting is said to be poor. Attic rooms are small, with beams and a sloping ceiling, but well equipped. The pink-walled restaurant, *La Scaletta*, specialises in northern Italian regional cooking from the Veneto and Liguria. One couple enjoyed their dinner, but another thought it variable, and warned: "take care when ordering the wine." The breakfast, too, has been criticised. But there is praise for the "generous, interested hosts" and the "courteous, efficient staff". Light lunches are served. Parking can be "a nightmare". Plenty of castles, stately homes and gardens are nearby; Glyndebourne is 15 minutes' drive. (*CHN Mackey, and others*)

Open All year, except Christmas. Restaurant closed last 2 weeks Feb.
Rooms 1 suite, 8 double.
Facilities Lounge, study, restaurant (piped Italian music during dinner); function facilities; small garden. Golf nearby. Unsuitable for &.
Location Central (traffic noise in some rooms). Parking adjacent (can be difficult).
Restrictions No smoking in restaurant. No children under 12. No dogs.
Credit cards All major cards accepted.
Terms [1997] Rooms: single £40–£75, double £60–£75, suite £95–£115. Breakfast: continental £5.50, English £7.50. Set lunch £11.50–£14; full alc dinner £22. *V*

ULLINGSWICK Herefordshire   Map 3

The Steppes   *Tel* (01432) 820424
Ullingswick, nr Hereford HR1 3JG   *Fax* (01432) 820042

"A peaceful hotel, with easy access to an incomparable swathe of rural England. Henry and Tricia Howland's sensitivity to guests' needs is acute yet seemingly inadvertent." "Home-like comfort. Quality at a fair price." Recent accolades for this Grade II listed house, part 14th-, part 17th-century, carefully converted by the Howlands, who have been here since 1980. The public rooms are in the old farmhouse, which has exposed beams, uneven cobbled floors, huge inglenook fireplaces, rustic antiques, "and pleasing touches, such as swags of hops in the cellar bar". The generously proportioned bedrooms, with good *en suite* facilities, are in former stables and a timber-framed barn. Mrs Howland was a winner in the Logis of Great Britain regional competition in 1993. Her eclectic cooking is served "with unobtrusive solicitude" by her husband in the candle-lit dining room; there is a four-course set meal, or a *carte* by arrangement. Generous breakfasts include a wide choice of smoked fishes and fresh croissants. Ullingswick is a tiny hamlet in the Wye valley, not far from the Welsh border. Local attractions include the Mappa Mundi in Hereford cathedral, and Elgar's birthplace at Broadheath. (*Patricia Stone, BA Orman; also Mrs JG Kemp*)

Open All year, except 2 weeks before Christmas, 3 days after New Year, "other odd days for a rest".
Rooms 6 double, all in barn and stable.
Facilities Lounge, bar, dining room (piped classical music). 1½-acre garden with pond. Unsuitable for &.
Location 8 miles NE of Hereford, off A417 Gloucester–Leominster.
Restrictions No smoking, except in lounge. No children under 10. No dogs in public rooms.
Credit cards Access, Amex, Visa.

Terms B&B: single £45, double £80–£90; D,B&B: single £69, double £124–£138. Leisure breaks all year from £55 per person half board; Christmas, New Year house parties. 1-night booking sometimes refused Sat. *V*

ULLSWATER Cumbria   Map 4

Howtown Hotel   BUDGET   *Tel* (01768 4) 86514
Ullswater, nr Penrith CA10 2ND
Ɔ *César award in 1991*

An unsophisticated former farmhouse, set back from a road in a beautiful position on the eastern shore of the second-largest lake in the Lake District. Well placed for yachting, windsurfing and other water sports, it is a favourite of walkers and climbers, too, and so popular that it is often fully booked. It is run on old-fashioned lines by Jacquie Baldry and her son David, the fourth generation of the family to be involved. "The style of our food," writes Mrs Baldry, "hasn't changed over 37 years: home-made soups and puddings, traditional roasts and pies." Furnishings, if "a bit hugger mugger", are unpretentious and comfortable. Few bedrooms have private facilities, none has telephone or TV; keys are not given. But early morning tea is brought to the room, and beds are turned down during dinner, which is at 7 pm (tables are quite close together). "Just as a country hotel should be," wrote recent visitors. "No nonsense, attractive and satisfying. Substantial packed lunches. Walkers come rushing down from the hills for 4 pm tea: perfect scones and cake. Excellent value." The Baldrys' "enchanting" dog, Tad, something of a mongrel, has been joined by Zingara, a Rhodesian ridgeback. More reports, please.

Open End Mar–1 Nov.
Rooms 12 double, 3 single. 3 with bath, 1 with shower. 2 in annexe. 4 self-catering cottages.
Facilities 4 lounges, TV room, 2 bars, dining room. 2-acre grounds. 300 yds from lake: private foreshore. Walking, climbing, riding, golf nearby. Unsuitable for &.
Location E shore of lake, 4 miles S of Pooley Bridge.
Restrictions No children under 7. Dogs at management's discretion, not in public rooms.
Credit cards None accepted.
Terms [1997] D,B&B £38–£42. Cold weekday lunch from £7, set Sun lunch £9.25, dinner from £13.25; cold Sun supper from £9. 1-night bookings sometimes refused.

Sharrow Bay   *Tel* (01768 4) 86301 and 86483
Ullswater, nr Penrith CA10 2LZ   *Fax* (01768 4) 86349
Ɔ *César award in 1985*

In a lovely setting on the eastern shore of Ullswater stands the first English country house hotel, for many years a Relais & Châteaux member. Now entering its 50th season, it has had a *Guide* entry since our first edition. Its César award, all of 13 years ago, was "for distinguished long service". Supported by co-directors Nigel Lawrence and Nigel Lightburn, and a large staff, many long-serving, the founders, Francis Coulson and Brian Sack, still preside. Traditional British cooking on an extensive menu is served in the *Michelin*-starred restaurant. At times the public areas are crowded, and the whole experience is too much for

some tastes: "Meals are an obstacle course for gourmets." "The ceremony of 'looking at the puddings' at the start of the meal only served
to hold things up." But most visitors succumb to the hedonism, and the
majority verdict is strongly positive: "The genuinely warm welcome,
the constant cosseting, and the scrupulous attention to detail were
unsurpassed in our experience. Everything bespoke comfort and
expense." "The style is of opulent clutter: cupids peeping from extrav-
agant drapes; bows and gilt in abundance; porcelain, flowers, plants,
pictures and pot-pourri everywhere. All adds up to the atmosphere of
a well-loved home." "Superb scenery. Fantastically generous breakfasts. Packed lunch so large it lasted us two days." "There is an air of
camaraderie among the guests." Bedrooms are "splendid, with everything you could want, including a fridge with a sensible selection of
drinks, Scrabble, backgammon, glossy books on the Lake District".
Some of those in the main building are small; larger ones are in *Bank
House*, a mile away (transport provided). (*Michael Wareham, Kay
Thomson, CA Hutchinson; also Kim Maidment, Ann Farrow, and others*)

Open 20 Feb–7 Dec.
Rooms 4 suites, 20 double, 4 single. 17 in cottage, lodge, *Bank House*.
Facilities Main house: 3 lounges, 2 dining rooms; *Bank House*: lounge, breakfast
room. 12-acre grounds: gardens, woodland; ½-mile lake shore, safe (cold)
bathing, private jetty, boathouse. Unsuitable for &.
Location E shore of Ullswater, 2 miles S of Pooley Bridge. M6 exit 40. Turn on to
Howtown La by small church in Pooley Bridge.
Restrictions Smoking banned in dining room, discouraged in lounges, bed-
rooms. No children under 13. No dogs in house (kennels nearby).
Credit cards None accepted.
Terms [1997] D,B&B: single £93–£135, double £196–£340, suite £320–£340. Set
lunch £33.75, dinner £44.75. Midweek reductions off season. 1-night bookings
sometimes refused weekends.

UPPINGHAM Rutland   **Map 2**

The Lake Isle   *Tel/Fax* (01572) 822951
16 High Street East
Uppingham LE15 9PZ

"Hard to beat at the price. Excellent dinner – including a small loaf of
freshly baked bread on the table, with a good sharp knife. Delicious
and copious breakfast." "I thoroughly enjoyed all aspects of my stay.
Generous extras in the bedroom, including sherry, fresh fruit, good biscuits. Impressive wine list, with pages of halves. Difficult to reach by
car, owing to the one-way system, but worth the effort." Recent praise
for Claire and David Whitfield's small restaurant-with-rooms (he is
chef). It is on the main street of a delightful small market town, with
mellow stone houses and a famous public school. You approach
through a neat flower-filled yard. The old building has had many uses.
Its bar was once a barber's shop, known as "Sweeney Todd's", where
the schoolboys had their hair cut. The restaurant has pine panelled
walls and pine furniture, and serves three- to five-course meals on a
weekly-changing menu. Cooking is straightforward English/French,
with the emphasis on fresh ingredients. There's a pretty pink-walled
lounge, and a small garden. Bedrooms, at the back, are named after
French wines and wine regions; some are small, but Dom Pérignon is
large, with a whirlpool bath; Bordeaux has a power shower. The suites,

on two floors, with a spacious living area, are in adjacent cottages. Breakfast in the restaurant includes exotic fruits, grilled kidneys, and home-made preserves; a continental one may be delivered to the bedroom. When the restaurant is closed, simple meals are provided for residents. (*Mrs M Dwan, CK; also Joy and Raymond Goldman*)

Open All year. Restaurant closed to non-residents Sun evening/midday Mon.
Rooms 2 suites (in cottage), 9 double.
Facilities Lounge, bar, restaurant, meeting room. Small garden. Unsuitable for &.
Location Town centre. Entrance at rear of hotel. On foot approach via Reeves Yard, by car via Queen Street. Private parking. Train: Oakham, 7 miles, Kettering, 14 miles.
Restriction No dogs in public rooms.
Credit cards All major cards accepted.
Terms [1997] B&B: single £43–£54, double £60–£74, suite £75–£79. Set lunch £10.50, dinner £25.50. Champagne breaks. *V*

VELLOW Somerset   Map 1

Curdon Mill BUDGET   *Tel* (01984) 656522
Vellow, Williton TA4 4LS   *Fax* (01984) 656197

"Delightful setting; lots of character." "The conversion is a triumph of imagination and execution. Relaxing atmosphere, enhanced by the sound of the millstream." "Welcoming hosts, devoted to their enterprise. Good value." Recent endorsements for Richard and Daphne Criddle's old pink sandstone mill, complete with waterwheel, in a quiet hamlet at the foot of the Quantock Hills. It is on a large working farm, in a pretty garden with a swimming pool; a lake is under construction this year. Inside are exposed beams, log fires, and a chintzy sitting room ("its small size makes socialising inevitable"). The pretty bedrooms are small too, but well equipped. The large dining room, on the first floor, serves wholesome, traditional food using local game, meat, fish and vegetables. A vegetarian main course is always offered. The short wine list is reasonably priced. The mill is licensed for weddings. The Exmoor National Park and the North Devon coast are close by. (*KA Dann, and others*)

Open All year (for lunch only 25 Dec). Restaurant closed evening Sun, midday except Sun.
Rooms 6 double. No telephone.
Facilities Lounge, bar, restaurant. On 200-acre farm: garden, swimming pool, river, fishing; stabling for visiting horses. Sea, sandy beaches nearby. Unsuitable for &.
Location 2 miles SE of Williton. Follow signs for Vellow and Curdon Mill. Train: Williton/Bishop's Lydeard; then taxi.
Restrictions No smoking: restaurant, bedrooms. No children under 8. No dogs in house.
Credit cards Access, Amex, Visa.
Terms [1997] B&B: single £35–£50, double £50–£70; D,B&B £44.50–£69.50 per person. Set Sun lunch £12.50, dinner £19.50 (£22.50 to non-residents). Weekly rates: 7th night free. Winter breaks.

When you nominate a hotel, do please, if possible, send us its brochure.

VERYAN Cornwall   Map 1

The Nare   *Tel* (01872) 501279
Carne Beach   *Fax* (01872) 501856
Veryan, nr Truro TR2 5PF

Surrounded by National Trust land on the Roseland peninsula – "a breathtakingly beautiful setting" – this traditional hotel stands in sub-tropical gardens with a swimming pool, a tennis court, secluded corners for sunbathing, and direct access to a safe, sandy, clean beach. For inclement weather there's an indoor pool, heated all year. *The Nare* is run by Mrs Gray and her grandson Toby Ashworth, the fourth generation of a hotel-keeping family, though recent visitors have seen more of the manageress, Daphne Burt. "She runs an efficient ship," one wrote. It has a country house decor – antiques, oriental rugs, ornaments and flowers. The bedrooms vary in size; the best-designed ones, at the back, have a sea view; many have a balcony or patio. Old-fashioned services – shoe-cleaning, room-tidying in the evening, and hot water-bottles in beds – are on offer. Dinner in the restaurant is a quite formal five-course affair; light suppers and lunches are available in the Gwendra Room. There are inter-communicating bedrooms for families, and a nursery tea for under-sevens. Reactions are mixed this year: some redecoration is said to be needed, and there are reports of complaints unsympathetically dealt with. But there is also warm praise: "Excellent dinners, good light lunches, nearly all staff friendly and willing." "Beautifully furnished bedroom, with a more than adequate bathroom. We could walk straight out to the garden. We could not leave our poodle puppy alone, so dinner, with two superb lobsters, was brought to the room. Excellent breakfasts with lots of choice. Wonderful cream teas." Veryan's name is a corruption of St Symphorien, to whom the village church is dedicated. Its Regency round houses were so constructed to give the Devil no corners in which to hide. (*JH Bell, Peter and Pam Barrett*)

Open 1 Feb–3 Jan.
Rooms 2 suites, 30 double, 4 single. 5 on ground floor.
Facilities Lift. 4 lounges, 2 bars, billiard room, light lunch/supper room, restaurant, conservatory; drying room; indoor swimming pool, whirlpool spa, sauna, solarium, gym. 5-acre grounds: gardens, swimming pool (heated end May–mid-Sept), tennis, children's play area, safe sandy beach, sailboards, fishing. Concessionary golf at Truro Golf Club.
Location From A390 take B3287 towards Tregony; then A3078 towards St Mawes *c.* 1½ miles. 1st left to Veryan; through village, leaving *New Inn* on left; 1 mile straight towards sea.
Restriction Only guide dogs in public rooms.
Credit cards Access, Visa.
Terms B&B: single £56–£120, double £112–£208, suite £192–£420; D,B&B (min. 3 nights): single £86–£150, double £172–£268, suite £250–£480. Set lunch: weekdays £14, Sun £16, dinner £30; full alc £50. Winter, spring, bridge breaks. Christmas, New Year house parties.

British hotels nowadays have private facilities in most bedrooms, and many have TV, baby-listening and tea-making facilities. To save space we do not list all of these; if any is particularly important to you, please discuss with the hotel.

WALLINGTON Northumberland   **Map 4**

Shieldhall **NEW/BUDGET**   *Tel/Fax* (01830) 540387
Wallington by Kirkharle
Morpeth NE61 4AQ

This guest house, set in rolling Northumbrian countryside, overlooks the National Trust estate of Wallington, which has gardens designed early in his career by Capability Brown, who was born locally. It is an 18th-century stone farmhouse with guest suites in converted farm buildings grouped round a courtyard. "The owners are welcoming, and the service efficient and unobtrusive," wrote the nominator. "Good dinners and breakfasts. The whole place has considerable charm, and is very peaceful." The decor is based on types of wood: each bedroom is named for the one it features: oak, mahogany, etc. In his workshop in the courtyard, the proprietor, Stephen Gay, makes copies of antique furniture, many of which are to be seen the house. Guests have the use of a lounge and a library in the main house. They meet for drinks before dinner (ordered in advance), cooked by Celia Gay and served individually or communally. Plenty to see and do in the locality. Wallington Hall has fine plasterwork, an important dolls' house collection, and a 19th-century central hall decorated by Ruskin and others; nearby are other historic houses, as well as neolithic, settlements, Roman fortifications, moorland and coast. (*Olga Leapman*)

Open Mar–Nov.
Rooms 1 suite, 3 double, 1 single. Some on ground floor. No telephone.
Facilities Lounge, library, dining room (piped classical music on request). Garden: croquet. Fishing, pony-trekking nearby.
Location 1 mile S of Cambo. On B6342 east of junction with A496 at Kirkharle.
Restrictions No smoking. No children under 12. No dogs in house.
Credit cards Access, Visa.
Terms B&B: single £20–£35, double £38–£50. Set dinner £15. Reductions for 3 or more nights.

WAREHAM Dorset   **Map 2**

The Priory   *Tel* (01929) 551666
Church Green   *Fax* (01929) 554519
Wareham BH20 4ND

♦ *César award in 1996*

King Alfred defeated the Danes at Wareham in AD 876 and built a nunnery there. In the Middle Ages the site was occupied by a priory, which has now been converted into a luxurious hotel, with a decor in keeping with its historic past. Its gardens, sweeping down to the river Frome, have distant views of the Purbeck hills. "Lovely setting, magnificent grounds, outstanding service. A delightful experience, with memories to last a lifetime," writes one visitor. "Deserves all superlatives," echoes another. "The food was something to anticipate with pleasure at the beginning and end of each day." In the evening, chef Stephen Astley's modern English cooking is served in an atmospheric dining room in the vaulted cellars; another, used mainly for breakfast and lunch, overlooks the grounds. On fine days lunch may be taken alfresco. A full breakfast is served until 10.30 am. Two beamed lounges

WARMINSTER

229

overlook the grounds; in one a pianist plays on Saturdays and bank
holidays. The bedrooms have been described as romantic and charming "with lots of cushions and bits and pieces". Most are large and
grand; those in the converted boathouse are particularly luxurious,
with a riverside balcony or patio. "Staff are consistently polite and
friendly, without being obtrusive in any way. The whole set-up is most
attractive." The owners, the Turner family, also own the *Casterbridge
Hotel*, Dorchester (*qv*). Corfe Castle is close by; wonderful walking in
the Purbeck countryside and on the South West Coast Path. (*Dr T and
M McGhie, Gillian Comins, John Mainwaring, Robin Oaten, and others*)

Open All year.
Rooms 2 suites, 14 double, 3 single. 4 in boathouse. Some on ground floor.
Facilities 2 lounges (1 with TV, 1 with pianist Sat/holiday evenings), bar,
2 dining rooms; 4-acre gardens: croquet, river frontage, mooring, fishing, bicycle
hire. Sea 4 miles.
Location From A351 by-pass at station roundabout, take North Causeway/North
St. Left into East St, 1st right into Church St; hotel between church and river.
Restrictions No smoking in dining rooms. No children under 8; over 8 by prior
arrangement. Guide dogs only.
Credit cards All major cards accepted.
Terms [1997] B&B: single £75–£105, double £90–£215, suite £215. Light lunches.
Set lunch (2/3-course) £12.95/£14.95 (weekdays), £17.95 (Sun), dinner £24.50
(£26.50 Sat); full alc from £35. Off-season breaks; summer half-board rates.

WARMINSTER Wiltshire   **Map 2**

Bishopstrow House   *Tel* (01985) 212312
Boreham Road   *Fax* (01985) 216769
Warminster BA12 9HH   *E-mail* Bishopstrow House Hotel@msn.com

This late Georgian country house stands in large grounds, most of
which are reached through a tunnel under a road, with gardens,
ancient trees, temples, a lovely stretch of the river Wylye, and plenty to
amuse its guests (see below). Under the same ownership as *The
Feathers*, Woodstock (*qv*), it has an "amiable and enthusiastic manager,
David Dowden, and a welcoming staff, attentive at all times". It was
recently extensively refurbished, and given a "state of the art" spa, "but
the unhurried country house atmosphere still prevails". The public
rooms are dramatic, with vibrant colours, tartan carpets, mirrors of
gargantuan proportions, and heraldic motifs. The bedrooms vary
greatly. A 1997 visitor occupied the Weymouth Suite, "a two-storey
miniature house, with a cosy sitting room, and an enormous bathroom
with a huge jacuzzi and every potion and lotion possible". Other rooms
are likewise spacious and luxurious; smaller ones at the top (a steep
climb) are "comfortable, but lack character". There is a formal restaurant, where Chris Suter's cooking "with the accent on healthy eating"
is much enjoyed: "The menu is eclectic and tempting, and the food
cooked with enthusiasm, with lots of herbs and vegetables. The wine
list is good, but priced in the upward direction." Lighter meals and teas
are served in the conservatory. "Breakfast, served by jolly ladies, consists of a self-help buffet and a good choice of cooked dishes – perfect
eggs." Children and dogs are welcomed. Guests able to tear themselves
away from *Bishopstrow's* charms may visit Longleat, three miles away,
and Stourhead, Stonehenge, Bath and Salisbury, further afield. (*Louise
Medcalf, Jan Chalmers, and others*)

Open All year.
Rooms 6 suites, 24 double, 1 single. 6 on ground floor.
Facilities Hall, lounge, library, conservatory, restaurant (piped classical music); function facilities; health spa: swimming pool, sauna, sunbed, tennis, gym, hairdresser. 28-acre grounds: tennis, swimming pool, sauna, solarium, river, fishing. Golf nearby. Unsuitable for &.
Location On B3414, 1½ miles E of Warminster. Train: Westbury, 8 miles; then taxi.
Restriction No smoking in restaurant.
Credit cards All major cards accepted.
Terms [Until Mar 1998] B&B: single £80–£85, double £125–£180, suite £175–£240. English breakfast £5. Set lunch £14–£16, dinner £29; full alc £32. Summer/winter breaks. 1-night bookings refused Sat. B&B £25 for child sharing parents' room.

WASDALE HEAD Cumbria   Map 4

Wasdale Head Inn   `BUDGET`   *Tel* (01946 7) 26229
Wasdale Head   *Fax* (01946 7) 26334
nr Gosforth CA20 1EX

Mr and Mrs Hammond's unsophisticated old gabled pub has been popular for many years among walkers and climbers. It is in a magnificent isolated setting at the head of Wasdale, surrounded by steep fells. The decor is traditional, with solid old furniture, much panelling, and plenty of climbing mementos. The main bar, with an open fire, is named after the inn's first landlord, Will Ritson, reputed to be the world's biggest liar – lying competitions are held once a year in his memory. Beer festivals are held, and there is a "Bah Humbug" Christmas package – "no crackers, no silly hats". The robust humour of the place may not be to everyone's taste, but a regular visitor thought that things had improved under the self-styled "site director", Howard Christie, "an excellent, committed Scotsman": "The staff are friendly and efficient. The food and wine are better now. Perhaps the most starkly beautiful setting in England." Good, simple bar meals and cream teas are served. Traditional dinners on a set menu in *Abraham's*, the large panelled restaurant, end with home-made puddings. A substantial breakfast is served from 7.30 am. There is a comfortably old-fashioned residents' lounge. The bedrooms are small, but clean and well lit, with private facilities, plenty of hot water and lovely views. The atmosphere is relaxed – no dress rules. There is a large drying room, and a full laundry service. The self-catering apartments have been turned into suites. Wast Water, England's deepest lake, is a mile away. (*Ben Whitaker, and others*)

Open All year.
Rooms 1 triple, 5 double, 3 single. 4 suites with TV in annexe 20 yds.
Facilities Residents' lounge, residents' bar, public bar, restaurant; drying room; beer garden. 3-acre grounds. Lake 1 mile, sea 12 miles. Unsuitable for &.
Location 10 miles from Gosforth and Holmrook. Follow signs from A595.
Restrictions No smoking: restaurant, lounge. No dogs in public rooms.
Credit cards Access, Amex, Visa.
Terms [1997] B&B £34–£39. Bar meals; packed lunches. Set dinner £18. Reductions for 2 or more days.

All our inspections are carried out anonymously.

WATER YEAT Cumbria   Map 4

Water Yeat Guest House   BUDGET   *Tel/Fax* (01229) 885306
Water Yeat
nr Ulverston LA12 8DJ

Pierre and Jill Labat's little 17th-century farmhouse is at the southern tip of Coniston Water. Its simple bedrooms have a floral, chintzy decor, and lovely views of the Crake valley and the fells. It has a devoted regular clientele, including the nominator, who love the peace, the country air and the "wonderful food", for which locals come from far and wide. "Pierre appears at 7.15 pm to describe the evening's choice: just two options for the first two courses, plus a vegetarian dish. Even so, decision is agonising. And the real hush comes after the adventurous cheeseboard, when anxiously swivelling eyes scan the pudding trolley, with plenty of sensational offerings, and second helpings offered. The superb ingredients are from local suppliers; Jill is a brilliant cook. Pierre is a perfect host, sensing whether you are feeling sociable or hermit-like, and behaving accordingly. The place is beautifully kept, pretty and spotlessly clean. Arriving here is to shed the troubles of the world. Bliss." The cooking is "a mixture of hearty French home cooking and modern English". Breakfast includes yogurt, muesli, croissants, and a hearty Cumbrian affair, with oatcakes. The house is at the foot of Beacon Tarn with a walk up to lovely views over Coniston Water and the Cumbrian summits. Guests may go sailing – Arthur Ransome's Wild Cat Island is half-way down the lake. Plenty to visit nearby, including Holker Hall, Levens Hall and John Ruskin's home, Brantwood House. (*Christina Hardyment; endorsed this year by Judith Barraclough*)

Open Mid-Feb–mid-Dec. Closed 1 week July, Sun except bank holidays.
Rooms 5 double. No telephone/TV.
Facilities Lounge, dining room (piped music). 3-acre garden. Mountain bikes, canoe available. Lake ½ mile. Unsuitable for ♿.
Location S tip of Coniston Water. On A5084, 2½ miles N of Lowick, 3 miles S of Torver. Bus twice daily.
Restrictions No smoking: dining room, bedrooms. No children under 4. No dogs in house.
Credit cards None accepted.
Terms B&B: single £30–£36, double £49.55–£52.58. Set dinner £17.50 (£19 to non-residents). Off-season breaks; creative textile courses. *V*

WATERHOUSES Staffordshire   Map 3

The Old Beams   *Tel* (01538) 308254
Leek Road   *Fax* (01538) 308157
Waterhouses ST10 3HW

"A gem. Our bedroom was beautiful and the food was gorgeous. Expensive, but worth it." So write American visitors to this restaurant-with-rooms in a hamlet on the edge of the Peak District. An earlier guest admired "the feeling of France, with delightful touches everywhere – quality abounds in the fixtures, the fittings, and above all in the service". Nigel Wallis, the owner/chef, runs it with his wife Ann ("exuberantly front-of-house") and son Simon. *Michelin* awards a star for the modern English/French cooking, which is served in a beamed dining room with frescoes of an italianate landscape, and a conservatory extension overlooking the sloping garden. The menu includes copious coffee and petits fours; on weekdays a two-course option for £29 is available as an alternative to the full six-course dinner. The bedrooms are across a major road, in a stone cottage – double-glazing mitigates traffic noise, and umbrellas are provided for inclement weather. Each is named for a local pottery, and tea is served in the room on the relevant china. They have a sophisticated decor, with quality fabrics, marble bathroom and hand-embroidered sheets, and home-made biscuits and fudge, books and glossy magazines are provided. Some are small. The quietest ones, Royal Doulton and Royal Stafford, overlook a millstream. A simple continental breakfast, with home-made croissants, brioches and jam, is included in the room rates. (*Marjorie and Charles Berg, and others*)

Open All year, except early Jan, Sun evening/Mon; restaurant also closed midday Tues/Sat.
Rooms 5 double. All in annexe across road. 1 with & access.
Facilities Lounge, bar, restaurant. ½-acre garden.
Location On A523 Ashbourne–Leek (all rooms double-glazed).
Restrictions No smoking: restaurant, bedrooms. No dogs.
Credit cards All major cards accepted.
Terms [1997] B&B: single £55–£72, double £70–£89.95. English breakfast £6.50. Set lunch £21, dinner £39.50 (weekday 2-course option £29).

WATERMILLOCK Cumbria   Map 4

Old Church Hotel   *Tel* (01768 4) 86204
Old Church Bay   *Fax* (01768 4) 86368
Watermillock, Penrith CA11 0JN   *E-mail* oldchurch@ullswater.co.uk

Reached by a long drive through large grounds, this 18th-century house, built on the site of a 12th-century church, has a peaceful position on the shore of Ullswater and lovely views of the fells. There's good walking all around. It is informally run by the owners, Kevin and Maureen Whitemore, and their family – "don't expect beds to be turned down, or crumbs swept from the table between courses," one guest has said. There is praise for the decor, which includes warm colours, flowers, pot plants, books and magazines, and plenty of evidence of Mrs Whitemore's enthusiasm for soft furnishings (she runs upholstery courses during much of the year). The English home cooking, with particularly good fish and vegetables and ample choice, is admired too. Breakfasts are "generous and varied enough to satisfy the most demanding of appetites". Bedrooms vary in size and style and this is reflected in their prices; some have lake views. One couple this year felt that "a little more warmth from the staff" was required. But most visitors have thought the service "cheerful and efficient, yet unpretentious", and visitors last year wrote: "Everyone was very kind to our small children, and adaptable about their needs." We'd like more reports, please.

Open Apr–Oct. Restaurant closed midday, Sun evening.
Rooms 10 double.
Facilities 2 lounges, bar, dining room. 2-acre grounds on lake: mooring, fishing, rowing boat. Unsuitable for &.

Location Off A592, 3 miles S of Pooley Bridge; 5 miles from M6 exit 40. Train: Penrith; then bus.
Restrictions No smoking in dining room. No children in dining room, bar after 7 pm. No dogs.
Credit cards Access, Amex, Visa.
Terms [1997] B&B £59–£99; D,B&B £85–£125; full alc £25. 1-night bookings sometimes refused. Soft-furnishing courses Mar–Oct.

Rampsbeck *Tel* (01768 4) 86442
Watermillock, Penrith CA11 0LP *Fax* (01768 4) 86688

This 18th-century house, white-walled and bay-windowed, is set in manicured gardens, with formal flower beds and precisely trimmed hedges. Its large grounds lead down to the shore of Ullswater. It is owned by Thomas and Marion Gibb and Mrs Gibb's mother, Marguerite MacDowall. "They are a charming family," wrote the nominator, "and the style is slightly old-fashioned, and pleasingly unlike the contrived slickness of so many country house hotels. The huge hall is friendly, with a crackling log fire, and someone always at reception. We took tea in a high-ceilinged lounge with lovely plaster work, a large marble fireplace, Victorian furniture, current newspapers, plants and flowers. In the spacious dining room the menu was imaginative, Andrew McGeorge's cooking was precise and attractively presented, and the service was well paced. The wine list is comprehensive and moderately priced." "Beautiful setting; hospitable atmosphere; very good home-baking," add visitors this year. The best bedrooms are spacious, with antique furniture and a lake view; some have a balcony. (*PH*) More reports, please.

Open Mid-Feb–early Jan, except few days Dec.
Rooms 1 suite, 18 double, 2 single.
Facilities Hall, 2 lounges, bar, restaurant. 19-acre grounds: croquet, lake frontage: fishing, sailing, windsurfing, etc. Golf, clay pigeon-shooting, archery nearby. Unsuitable for &.
Location From M6 exit 40, follow signs for A592 to Ullswater. At T-junction on lake shore turn right. Hotel 1¼ miles. Train: Penrith; then bus or taxi.
Restrictions No smoking: restaurant, 1 lounge, 2 bedrooms. No children under 5 in dining room at night. Dogs by prior arrangement only; not in public rooms.
Credit cards Access, Visa.
Terms [1997] B&B £45–£90; D,B&B £65–£116. Set lunch £22, dinner £26, £38.50. Midweek breaks. 1-night bookings sometimes refused.

WENLOCK EDGE Shropshire **Map 3**

Wenlock Edge Inn **BUDGET** *Tel* (01746) 785678
Hilltop, Wenlock Edge TF13 6DJ *Fax* (01746) 785285

"A fine example of an honest, old-fashioned inn, with owners as chatty and friendly as you could wish." "The whole family (two generations of Warings, Harry and Joan, Diane, Stephen and Jonathan) help with the running and, what's more, seem thoroughly to enjoy it. They cheerfully draw guests into the stream of things, which ensures an interesting flow of conversation." Two recent tributes to this traditional inn on the dramatic wooded ridge made famous by AE Housman and Mary Webb. Nowadays, it is a designated area of outstanding natural beauty, largely owned by the National Trust. The pub stands right by the Ippikins Rock viewpoint, with stunning views to west and south, and it makes an excellent base for walking along the Edge. The simple, pretty bedrooms, with beams, sloping ceiling and smallish windows with a padded window seat, are "fair-sized and slightly cluttered", with TV, lots of goodies and a spotless shower room with water from the pub's own well (the plumbing can be noisy). Most overlook a minor road, but traffic noise has not worried our reporters. One bar has wooden pews, a fine oak counter and an open fire; the other has an inglenook fireplace with a wood-burning stove. The busy little dining room serves good home-cooked dinners, chosen from a blackboard menu; there is a short but adequate selection of wines. The robust traditional breakfast includes thick brown toast. The pub is at its most convivial on the second Monday of the month, when it is host to a story-telling club. (*HR, Good Pub Guide*)

Open All year, except 24–26 Dec. Dining room closed midday Mon, to non-residents evening Mon (except bank holidays).
Rooms 4 double. 1 on ground floor, with ♿ access, in adjacent cottage. No telephone.
Facilities Ramp. Lounge bar, public bar, dining room. Patio; wildlife pool. Walking, riding, fishing, mountain biking nearby; gliding, hang-gliding 9 miles.
Location On B4371, 4 miles W of Much Wenlock.
Restrictions No smoking in dining room. Children under 8 not accommodated. No dogs in dining room, lounge, main house bedrooms.
Credit cards Access, Amex, Visa.
Terms [1997] B&B: single £45–£50, double £70–£75. Full alc £17. 10% discount for 3 or more nights. ***V***

WEOBLEY Herefordshire   Map 3

Ye Olde Salutation Inn   **BUDGET**   *Tel* (01544) 318443
Market Pitch   *Fax* (01544) 318216
Weobley HR4 8SJ

"A lovely place in a gorgeous part of the country. Genial host. First-rate breakfast with home-made jams." "Charming bedroom, spotlessly clean, with lots of character. Very good food." "Particularly good service; enjoyable atmosphere." Recent praise for Chris and Frances Anthony's sophisticated pub. It is one of many black-and-white buildings in a medieval village with a tall-spired 900-year-old church. The beamed restaurant, with a conservatory extension, serves traditional cooking based on local produce, accompanied by a serious wine list. Meals in the bar, which has stone walls, a collection of tankards and much shining copper, are "delicious, quickly served and reasonably priced". There is a residents' lounge with a log fire in a large stone fireplace "and a relaxed feel". The bedrooms upstairs have antique beds and flowery fabrics. The best one is spacious, with a four-poster and a smart bathroom. The one above the bar is to be avoided because of the noisy juke box below. The timbered cottage across the road, with a simpler decor and a well-equipped kitchen, is good for a family. Guests arriving between 3 pm and 7 pm, when the bars are closed, have a special point of entry. Wonderful walking in the Wye Valley, to the south. (*NM Mackintosh, Good Pub Guide*)

Open All year. Restaurant closed Sun evening/Mon (bar meals available).
Rooms 4 double. Also 2-bedroom self-catering cottage across road.
Facilities Residents' lounge with TV, lounge bar, public bar, restaurant, conservatory; fitness room; small patio. River Wye 6 miles: fishing. Unsuitable for &.
Location Top of main street of village 12 miles NW of Hereford. Carpark. Local buses.
Restrictions No smoking: restaurant, conservatory, bedrooms. No children under 14. Dogs by arrangement (in public bar only).
Credit cards All major cards accepted.
Terms [1997] B&B: single £37, double £60–£65. Bar meals. Set Sun lunch £9.75. Full alc £27.

WEST CLIFFE Kent   **Map 2**

Wallett's Court   *Tel* (01304) 852424
West Cliffe   *Fax* (01304) 853430
St Margaret's at Cliffe
Dover CT15 6EW

"The strong sense of history combines with modern comforts and an English ambience to create a welcoming impression. Excellent dinner, ending with inventive desserts." "The owners have everything under control with the minimum of fuss. Relaxed atmosphere. Good value." "High standards of service, good housekeeping, friendly part-Siamese cat." Praise from recent visitors to this Grade II* listed manor house, high above the sea in a designated area of outstanding natural beauty. Mentioned in the Domesday Book, developed in the 17th century, it was rescued from dereliction 21 years ago by Chris and Lea Oakley. It has exposed brickwork, moulded plaster fireplaces, black wood-burning stoves, antiques, a large, comfortable lounge and an ancient staircase – "to be treated with respect". The setting is rural, but the Dover ferries and the Channel Tunnel are nearby. The bedrooms with most character are in the main house (one has an oak-panelled four-poster); the more modern ones in converted barns were recently upgraded. Early leavers may ask for breakfast from 6.30 am, or a continental tray in their room. Those in less of a hurry enjoy a "splendid cooked breakfast in a charming conservatory". The restaurant, managed by the Oakleys' sons, Gavin and Craig, is popular locally for Chris Oakley's sophisticated modern British cooking. On weekdays and Sunday, a three-course dinner is served; on Saturday it is a more expensive five-course affair. A charming little seaside resort, St Margaret's Bay, is at the bottom of the cliff; Canterbury is 15 miles away. (*John Hall, Dr Arthur and Mrs Irene Naylor, and others*)

Open All year, except Christmas. Restaurant closed midday.
Rooms 1 suite, 10 double, 1 single. 9 in converted barns, 10–40 yds.
Facilities Lounge/bar, 2 dining rooms (piped classical music on quiet evenings), conservatory. 8-acre grounds: tennis, croquet, swings, tree house. Golf nearby. Not really suitable for &.
Location 3 miles N of Dover. From A2 take A258 to Deal. 1st right to West Cliffe; hotel ½ mile on right, opposite church. Train: Dover Priory; bus: Deal.
Restrictions No smoking in restaurant. No children under 8 in restaurant after 8 pm. No dogs.

Credit cards All major cards accepted.
Terms [1997] B&B: single £40–£75, double £65–£90. Set Sun lunch £15, dinner £23 (Sat £28).

WEST DEAN East Sussex   Map 2

The Old Parsonage   BUDGET   *Tel* (01323) 870432
West Dean, nr Seaford BN25 4AL

Medieval house, remarkably well preserved, with Victorian extension. By 12th-century church in quiet conservation village 5 miles W of Eastbourne, in heart of Friston Forest. Thick stone walls, small mullioned windows, beams, stone spiral staircases. Only 3 bedrooms: 1, with 4-poster, in old Hall; 1 in Solar; 1 in Middle Room, between Solar and Crypt. Private facilities (not en suite); no telephone/TV. Friendly owners, Raymond and Angela Woodhams. Excellent breakfasts. 2-acre grounds. Sea, safe bathing 1 mile. Closed Christmas, New Year. No children under 12. No smoking. No dogs. Credit cards not accepted. B&B double £55–£70. No restaurant; Hungry Monk, Jevington, *warmly recommended. More reports, please.*

WEST PORLOCK Somerset   Map 1

Bales Mead   BUDGET   *Tel* ((01643) 862565
West Porlock TA24 8NX

Stephen Blue and Peter Clover's no-smoking B&B is set amid National Trust land beneath the wooded hills of the Exmoor National Park, in a hamlet between Porlock and Porlock Weir. There are wonderful views over the surrounding countryside to the sea. "It is a stunning Edwardian country house, with an aura of peaceful elegance, and attention to detail in every respect," said one of many enthusiastic visitors this year. "The decor has a distinct retro feel, reminiscent of the 1920s and 1930s, with sufficient quirks to make it feel home-like and lived-in." Others wrote: "The owners like their creature comforts and want their guests to enjoy their own high standards." "More taste than any five-star hotel can match, for amazingly little money. They go out of their way to make your stay special." Each bedroom has a different colour scheme, hand-stencilled wall borders, canopies and drapes in fine fabrics, unusual touches such as pot-pourri in a chamber pot, sherry and amaretti, Spanish bathroom tiles, crystal decanters with different bath oils and salts – "we bathed in luxury, like Victorian aristocrats." Breakfast – "worth getting up for" – includes fresh fruit salad, home-made granola and yogurt, hot pastries, and the full cooked works for those who can manage that as well. In fine weather it is served in the immaculate small garden. Porlock Weir, close by, is a picturesque, tiny harbour; Local attractions include Dunster Castle, Arlington Court, National Trust villages, gardens and much else. (*Moira Thompson, Uli Lloyd Pack, Peter Hanssen, Kristine Sandrick, and others*)

Open All year, except Christmas/New Year.
Rooms 3 double, 2 with private facilities. No telephone.
Facilities Lounge, breakfast room (piped classical music). ½-acre garden. Shingle beach, harbour ½-mile; bathing, fishing, boating.
Location Off A39, between Porlock village and harbour at Porlock Weir.
Restrictions No smoking. No children under 14. No dogs.

Credit cards None accepted.
Terms [1997] B&B: single £32–£42, double £52.

WHEELOCK Cheshire   Map 3

The Grove House   NEW/BUDGET   *Tel* (01270) 762582
Mill Lane, Wheelock   *Fax* (01270) 759465
nr Sandbach CW11 4RD

Restaurant-with-rooms in Georgian house owned by Brenda Curtis with daughter and son-in-law Katherine and Richard Shaw (he is chef). In village on Trent and Mersey Canal, on A534 2 miles S of Sandbach; near M6 exit 17 and Crewe railway station. Welcoming feel: flowers, potted plants, knick-knacks, family photos; soothing colour scheme. Background music in public rooms. Ambitious modern cooking on daily-changing menu in locally popular restaurant. Good service. Golf, fishing, riding nearby; also Jodrell Bank, Little Moreton Hall. 9 airy bedrooms upstairs (no lift). Closed Christmas/New Year. Unsuitable for &. Access, Amex, Visa accepted. B&B: single £25–£45, double £45–£70. Set lunch £12.50, dinner £17, £23. More reports, please.

WHIMPLE Devon   Map 1

Woodhayes   *Tel* (01404) 822237
Whimple, nr Exeter EX5 2TD   *Fax* (01404) 822337

This large white Georgian house stands in a well-tended garden in a peaceful cider-apple village. Run in a generous spirit by Katherine and Frank Rendle and their son Michael, "charm personified", it has many admirers among *Guide* readers. "It combines elegant living with perfect relaxation," one has written. "You are pampered from the moment you arrive." The decor is "smart and home-like, with peach-coloured lounges, chintzes, and flowers everywhere – in fresh arrangements, and in delicately painted watercolours, oils and prints". The tariff includes early morning tea delivered to the bedroom, afternoon cream tea, newspapers, full English breakfast, tea and coffee during the day, and light laundry. One bedroom is small, with a small bathroom, but the others are spacious, with Edwardian furniture, ample wardrobe accommodation, sofa and comfortable chairs, and a roomy bathroom with big bottles of toiletries. At night, Mr Rendle performs in the bar and serves dinner. Everyone eats at the same time. Dinner (six courses, no choice until dessert) is "imaginatively cooked and beautifully presented", with home-grown fruit and vegetables, home-baked rolls, and a good wine selection. It is mostly greatly enjoyed, but those with a small appetite find it a lengthy affair. Breakfast includes a buffet of fresh fruit salad, etc, and an interesting choice of cooked dishes. Dartmoor, Exmoor, Exeter and the coast are all within striking distance. (*FM Leake, Mr and Mrs DG Elliott, Heather Sharland, and others*)

Open All year, except Christmas. Lunch not served.
Rooms 6 double.
Facilities 2 lounges, bar, dining room (piped light classical music). 4-acre grounds: garden, croquet, paddock. Unsuitable for &.
Location 8 miles E of Exeter. ¾ mile off A30, on right just before village. Train: Exeter/Whimple.
Restrictions No smoking in dining room. No children under 12. No dogs.

Credit cards All major cards accepted.
Terms [1997] B&B: single £65, double £90; D,B&B: single £90, double £140. Set dinner £27.50. Reduced rates for children sharing parents' room.

WHITEWELL Lancashire   Map 4

The Inn at Whitewell
Forest of Bowland
nr Clitheroe BB7 3AT

Tel (01200) 448222
Fax (01200) 448298

This inn, which shares its premises with a wine merchant, an art gallery and a shirtmaker, is a long, low stone building, part 14th-century, owned by the Duchy of Lancaster. It stands by the green of a tiny village in the beautiful valley of the river Hodder, deep in the Forest of Bowland. It is on a road with little traffic, quiet at night. The sheltered garden overlooks the river on which it owns six miles of trout-, sea trout- and salmon-fishing. Children and dogs are welcome. The place is so popular that bedrooms must be booked well in advance, and the bar and dining room are often crowded. Richard Bowman, the innkeeper, describes it in the jokey brochure, as "chaotically welcoming", but our inspectors thought it altogether too disorganised: "No host figure visible, long waits in the dining room, food a strange mixture of good and bad." But they liked the "unpretentiously tasteful" decor, and their bedroom. "It had a river view, a peat fire, a sophisticated tape/radio system, a comfortable sofa, a rather squeaky wood and brass bed, antique bedside tables, smart lamps, and interesting *objets*, including a telescope and an antique calendar. The bathroom had a large window, a large bath, and remarkable old scales." Luckier visitors have thought the service "charming and helpful" and admired the "authentically English, old-fashioned feel, more like a hospitable country house than a pub, with gleaming brass, log fires, fresh flowers and sporting paraphernalia". Bar meals are served in generous portions, and there is an extensive *à la carte* dinner menu. A new chef, Rosemary Shragel, arrived in August 1997. There are Neolithic cave dwellings across the river; Browsholme Hall and Clitheroe Castle are nearby. The hotel is handy for Manchester airport. More reports, please.

Open All year.
Rooms 1 suite, 10 double. Some with peat fire (£5). 4 more (2 in annexe 800 yds) planned for 1997.
Facilities Lounge, bar, dining room; 2 private dining rooms, function facilities. 3-acre grounds: garden, river frontage, fishing.
Location 6 miles NW of Clitheroe. Large carpark. Bus from Clitheroe (3 daily).
Restriction "Dogs if amiable allowed almost everywhere except the dining room, but no alsatians, rottweilers or moody dogs in public rooms."
Credit cards All major cards accepted.
Terms [1997] B&B: single £49.50–£79, double £69–£78, suite £98. Bar meals. Full alc dinner £29. Weekly rates negotiable.

WHITNEY-ON-WYE Herefordshire   Map 3

Rhydspence Inn   BUDGET
Whitney-on-Wye HR3 6EU

Tel (01497) 831262
Fax (01497) 831751

"Good food, reasonable rooms, delightful gardens and a friendly atmosphere. Peter Glover is a charming and attentive host. If only all hoteliers were like him." A recent tribute to this 14th-century black-and-white timbered inn on the road on the west side of a village in the valley of the lovely river Wye. It is just in England – the stream in the garden marks the border with Wales. The bar is "all an English pub should be, with old wooden furniture, gleaming copper, and fresh flowers". Traditional food is served in generous portions in the blue-carpeted, pink-tableclothed, candlelit restaurant. The bedrooms, up a narrow staircase, are pretty, with flowery fabrics and a simple bathroom. Good breakfast. Only snag: no residents' lounge. Hereford, Hay-on-Wye, and Bruce Chatwin's Black Hill are among many local attractions. (*AL*)

Open All year, except Christmas.
Rooms 6 double, 1 single. No telephone.
Facilities 2 bars, restaurant, small dining room, family room. ½-acre garden: terrace, patio, stream. Unsuitable for &.
Location Just off A438 Hereford–Brecon, 4 miles N of Hay-on-Wye.
Restrictions Smoking discouraged in dining room. No dogs.
Credit cards Access, Amex, Visa.
Terms [1997] B&B £27.50–£37.50. Bar meals; full alc £27. Off-season breaks. 1-night bookings occasionally refused.

WICKHAM Hampshire   Map 2

The Old House   *Tel* (01329) 833049
The Square   *Fax* (01329) 833672
Wickham, nr Fareham PO17 5JG

Wickham, some say, is one of the finest villages in southern England. Its huge square, protected in its entirety by a preservation order, contains buildings in a striking variety of architectural styles, including this red brick, creeper-covered Grade II listed early-Georgian town house. Here, Richard Skipwith and his French wife, Annie, have presided for 27 years. Inside, the house is panelled and beamed, with antique and period furniture. The bar is French provincial in style. The restaurant, in timber-framed former stables overlooking the attractive small garden, serves French regional cooking, which our readers have found imaginative and well executed. The pretty bedrooms are "full of old-world charm": most are large, and those on the second floor – the old servants' quarters – have beams, sloping ceiling and flowery wallpaper. "Though professionally run," wrote a visitor last year, "it retains the atmosphere of a family house." The walk from Wickham down the disused railway line to Alton is recommended after the hearty breakfasts. The New Forest, Beaulieu Abbey and many other attractions are close by. (*Endorsed this year by Pat Atkin*)

Open All year, except 2 weeks Christmas, 1 week Easter, 2 weeks August, Sun night. Restaurant closed Sat midday, Sun, midday Mon.
Rooms 9 double, 3 single. 3 in cottage 50 yds.
Facilities 2 lounges, bar, restaurant; private dining room, function room. ¼-acre grounds. Unsuitable for &.
Location Centre of village at junction of A32 and B2177, 3 miles N of Fareham (front rooms double-glazed). Carpark. Train: Fareham; then bus.
Restriction No dogs.
Credit cards All major cards accepted.
Terms [1997] Rooms: single £70–£80, double £85–£95. Breakfast: continental £6, English £10. Set lunch £12–£30, dinner £23–£30. 2-day breaks. *V*

WILLESLEY Gloucestershire   **Map 3**

Tavern House   BUDGET   *Tel* (01666) 880444
Willesley, nr Tetbury GL8 8QU   *Fax* (01666) 880254

This pretty 17th-century B&B, once a coaching inn, is in a hamlet on the
Tetbury to Bath road. "It is furnished in good taste," wrote the nominator, "with antiques and country furniture. The bedrooms are immaculate. There is a pleasant lounge, a charming breakfast room and a
flowery walled garden. The delightful owners, Janet and Tim
Tremellen, are helpful with local know-how. We dined well at the
Rattlebone Inn in the nearby village of Sherston, which for sheer beauty
warrants a visit. A peaceful base for exploring the Cotswolds." There is
lovely walking all around; the Westonbirt Arboretum, the largest in
Europe, is a mile away; Badminton is three miles away; Berkeley Castle
and the Wildfowl and Wetlands Trust at Slimbridge are not far. (*ULP*)

Open All year.
Rooms 4 double.
Facilities Lounge, breakfast room. ¾-acre garden. Golf, hunting, horse- and
motor-racing nearby. Unsuitable for &.
Location 4 miles SW of Tetbury on A433 (quiet at night; rooms double-glazed).
Limited local bus service.
Restrictions No smoking, except in lounge. No children under 10. No dogs.
Credit cards Access, Visa.
Terms [1997] B&B: single £45–£55, double £61–£66. 2/3-day mini-breaks. 1-night
bookings refused Christmas, bank holidays, Badminton horse trials (early May).

WILLITON Somerset   **Map 1**

The White House   *Tel* (01984) 632306 and 632777
Williton TA4 4QW

♀ *César award in 1988*

"A taste of the Côte d'Azur, with the courtyard garden, shingle and
palms, and trailing geraniums," was the first impression for one visitor
to this restaurant-with-rooms which owner/chefs, Dick and Kay
Smith, have run for 30 years (it has appeared in almost every edition of
the *Guide*). Another writes: "My 89-year-old mother and I much
enjoyed our stay. The very nice Smiths create a relaxed atmosphere.
Wonderful food, with some exotic sauces. The excellent system of pre-
ordering dinner meant that we were able to enjoy delicious soufflés as
our first course. Splendid poached eggs and grilled tomatoes, and good
coffee for breakfast (none of these simple things can be taken for
granted)." The cooking is French and modern British, on a daily-
changing menu with four choices for each course. Dick Smith prepares
the starters and main courses; his wife does the vegetables and the
puddings. An extensive wine list includes some good ones sold by the
glass. The house is filled with paintings, prints and ceramics, old and
modern, chosen with taste. Bedrooms in the main house are a good
size, and thoughtfully equipped; not all have private facilities ("but the
bathroom on the hall is gorgeous, with a huge tub, thick carpets and
large mirrors"). Those in the converted stables and coach house are
smaller, but avoid noise from the busy road in front. Williton, a large
village with a 19th-century core, lies between Exmoor and the

Quantocks. It has a late medieval manor, Orchard Wyndham, open to the public by arrangement. Cleeve Abbey, an impressive monastic site, is an easy drive away. (*DGH Jones, Gillian Comins, and others*)

Open Mid-May–early Nov. Restaurant closed midday.
Rooms 12 double, 9 with private facilities. 4 in ground-floor annexe around courtyard, 1 suitable for ♿.
Facilities Lounge, bar, restaurant. Sea, beaches nearby.
Location On A39 in centre of village (rear rooms quietest). Forecourt parking. Train: Taunton, 15 miles; then bus or taxi.
Restrictions No smoking: lounge, restaurant. No dogs in public rooms.
Credit cards None accepted.
Terms B&B: single £33–£54, double £58–£90; D,B&B: single £62.50–£83.50, double £117–£149. Set dinner £29.50. Bargain breaks all year. *V*

WILMINGTON East Sussex   Map 2

Crossways Hotel   BUDGET   *Tel* (01323) 482455
Lewes Road   *Fax* (01323) 487811
Wilmington BN26 5SG   *E-mail* crossways@fastnet.co.uk

David Stott and Clive James's white-painted, green-shuttered restaurant-with-rooms is set in a garden with a duckpond, rabbits and a herb garden. It has an attractive decor and a large collection of cheese dishes. Bedrooms range from a good-sized double, with a sofa and a balcony, to well-equipped singles. "The owners are a cheerful, welcoming couple," wrote a 1997 visitor. "Meals are generous and rich." The popular small restaurant, "just the right mix of smartness and informality", serves four-course dinners with plenty of choice (the second course is soup), using locally produced or home-grown ingredients; portions are generous. Wilmington is an affluent village in the South Downs, handy for Glyndebourne. Its chalk-cut Long Man, date unknown, is said to be the largest representation of the human figure in Europe, and it has a ruined 13th-century Benedictine priory, and a string of cottages along its main street. Good for walkers – the Southdown Way and the Weald Way are close by; and the Newhaven ferry is only 20 minutes' drive away. The hotel is on a busy road, but rooms are double-glazed. There is no residents' lounge, and one visitor, on a sunny weekend, regretted the absence of loungers in the pretty garden. (*HR*)

Open 23 Jan–23 Dec. Restaurant closed midday, Sun, Mon.
Rooms 5 double, 2 single.
Facilities Breakfast room, restaurant (occasional piped classical music). 2-acre grounds. Sea 3 miles. Unsuitable for ♿.
Location 6 miles N of Eastbourne on A27 (rooms double-glazed). Large carpark. Train: Polegate, 2 miles; then taxi.
Restrictions No smoking in restaurant. No children under 12. No dogs.
Credit cards Access, Amex, Visa.
Terms B&B: single £46, double £70–£75; D,B&B (min. 2 nights) £59.50–£62 per person. Set dinner £26.95. Gourmet, Glyndebourne breaks.

Please never tell a hotel you intend to send a report to the *Guide*. Anonymity is essential for objectivity.

WIMBORNE MINSTER Dorset   Map 2

Beechleas   *Tel* (01202) 841684
17 Poole Road   *Fax* (01202) 849344
Wimborne Minster BH21 1QA

Josephine McQuillan's red brick Grade II listed Georgian house stands
on the road to Poole in a handsome market town on the river Stour. It
has a pretty sitting room with an open fire and a chintzy decor. "The
dining room with a conservatory extension, is charming," say recent
readers. "It overlooks the garden, and has well-spaced tables, candles,
gleaming cutlery and glass. The Aga-cooked dinners are delicious and
well presented: organically produced meat; vegetables *al dente* but not
excessively so; good vegetarian dishes; delectable desserts." Service
can be leisurely, and one reader thought the wine list "unbalanced – it
lacked middle-of-the-range bottles". The smartest bedrooms, with high
ceilings and a Georgian-style decor, are on the first floor. Those in the
attic are cottagey in style, "with weathered pine furniture, dried flower
arrangements, and a spacious, immaculate bathroom". There are also
pretty beamed ones in a converted coach house and a lodge. "Morning
tea was brought to the room for no charge. Breakfast included freshly
squeezed orange juice. We were cosseted throughout our stay," one
couple wrote. A National Trust house, Kingston Lacy, with an outstanding collection of paintings is one-and-a-half miles to the west of
town. (*CHN Mackey, A and S Webster, and others*)

Open 13 Jan–24 Dec. Restaurant closed midday, to non-residents Sun/Mon.
Rooms 9 double. 2 in coach house, 2 in lodge. 2 on ground floor.
Facilities Lounge, restaurant (piped music at night). Small walled garden. Coast
8 miles. Unsuitable for &.
Location 5 mins from centre (possible traffic noise). Small carpark.
Restrictions No smoking: restaurant, bedrooms. No dogs.
Credit cards Access, Amex, Visa.
Terms [1997] B&B: single £65–£98, double £78–£98. Set dinner (2/3-course)
£16.75/£19.75. Weekend breaks. 1 child accommodated free in parents' room;
2nd child £10; food for under-10s half-price. ***V***

WINCHCOMBE Gloucestershire   Map 3

Wesley House   *Tel* (01242) 602366
High Street   *Fax* (01242) 602405
Winchcombe GL54 5LJ

Winchcombe is an ancient town in the Isbourne valley, in the Cotswold
Area of Outstanding Natural Beauty. It is Saxon in origin, and came to
prosperity with the wool trade in the Middle Ages. It has a grand
church, and a main street with half-timbered buildings, including this
restaurant-with-rooms, named for the Methodist preacher, who is
believed to have visited in 1779. Last year's nominator has returned
and found it as good as ever: "Unpretentious charm, genuine friendliness, and excellent food in the modern manner. Co-owner Matthew
Brown, front-of-house, could not do enough for us. The ambience is
charming. You enter straight into a parlour, with a huge fireplace (blazing fire). Before dinner, fresh olives on every table in the sitting room,
and generous measures of champagne. Then a superb dinner, cooked

by Jonathan Lewis, attentively but unintrusively served. The tasting plate of all the desserts is a must." Another guest ordered a glass of wine and was pleased to be given a bottle, and charged only for what he consumed. Breakfasts "have the same attention to detail: freshly squeezed orange juice, warm rolls and croissants, butter and jams in little bowls and excellent cooked dishes". Morning coffee, bar lunches and afternoon teas are served. The bedrooms are up a steep beamed staircase. All but one are small, but they are stylish, with blackened beams, rich fabrics, antiques, *objets d'art*, and a tiny bathroom. The best one has panoramic views across fields towards Sudeley Castle (once the home of Henry VIII's last wife, Katherine Parr), where the gardens were recently restored to their original glory. (*Jon Hughes, F Opitz*)

Open All year, except 30 Jan–12 Feb.
Rooms 5 double, 1 single.
Facilities Lounge/bar (piped classical music at night), restaurant; function facilities. Horse-racing, riding, golf nearby. Unsuitable for &.
Location High street of town 6 miles NE of Cheltenham (4 rear rooms quietest). Street parking. Bus from Cheltenham.
Restrictions No smoking: restaurant, bedrooms. No dogs.
Credit cards Access, Amex, Visa.
Terms [1997] B&B £48; D,B&B £55–£70. Set lunch £16.50, dinner £26. Dinnerdances, cookery demonstrations. 1-night bookings sometimes refused bank holidays.

WINCHESTER Hampshire   Map 2

 Hotel du Vin & Bistro   *Tel* (01962) 841414
14 Southgate Street   *Fax* (01962) 842458
Winchester SO23 9EF

César award: a town house for wine connoisseurs

Gerald Basset was recently named Best Sommelier in Europe in the Trophée Ruinart competition in Reims. Before that, he was the much admired *sommelier* at *Chewton Glen*, New Milton (*qv*). He co-owns, with Robin Hutson (also ex-*Chewton Glen*), this Georgian red-brick town house in the heart of the cathedral city. Its name declares its purpose: it is dedicated to the encouragement of good drinking, by offering a wide range of bottles with a modest mark-up, accompanied by affordable food. The decor is dedicated to wine. Walls are densely hung with vinous pictures, labels, menus and old photographs. Each bedroom is sponsored by a wine house. They are sophisticated, with subtle colours, good fabrics and pristine white linen, but, reflecting the owners' policy of providing style without frills, they lack extras. Some are in the main house; others are in a purpose-built building in the walled garden. Garden-facing rooms are quietest (the house is on a busy road). The centre of the operation is the lively bistro, pale yellow, softly lit and picture-bedecked, with wooden floors and small polished mahogany tables. Here chef James Martin serves modern Mediterranean cooking in generous portions. The high-ceilinged sitting room has a beautiful *trompe l'oeil* painting, and huge sofas and squashy armchairs; there is a café-style bar opening off the street, where locals drop in for a snack. "A really nice place with a pleasant staff; reasonably priced for the quality," wrote one recent guest. Another admired "the generous spirit, the lack of palaver, the absence of a dress code, and the fact that children are welcomed". Messrs Hutson and Basset recently bought the 30-bedroom *Calverly Hotel* in Tunbridge Wells, Kent. This is to undergo a major refurbishment and reopen, also with the name *Hotel du Vin*, in late 1997. (*Sir William Goodhart, HR, and others*)

Open All year.
Rooms 1 suite, 22 double. 4 in garden. 1 on ground floor with &. access.
Facilities Drawing room, bar, bistro. Small walled garden.
Location Central (back rooms quietest). Hotel will send directions. Carpark.
Restriction Guide dogs only.
Credit cards All major cards accepted.
Terms Rooms: single from £75, double £75–£115, suite £150. Breakfast: continental £6, English £9.50. Full alc £35.

The Wykeham Arms
75 Kingsgate Street
Winchester SO23 9PE
❂ *César award in 1996*

Tel (01962) 853834
Fax (01962) 854411

"A gem of hospitality in a jewel of a place. Caters for those who prize individuality and a care for comfort above lavish furnishings and lists of amenities. The menu is enticing, the food is well prepared and presented, the friendly young staff are interesting to talk with." "We loved the buzz of the place, and the bonhomie dispensed by Graeme and Anne Jameson." Some of this year's praise for this ever-popular hostelry, a historic building close by the cathedral and handy for sightseeing, yet quiet – it's on a cul-de-sac. Military memorabilia, hats, tankards, pictures of royalty and framed collections of cigarette cards fill the public rooms. The main bar has old school desks from the college. In a series of small eating areas, traditional cooking is served in generous portions. The list of wines is long and reasonably priced; many are available by the glass. The attractive small bedrooms upstairs have a mini-bar with fresh milk for tea-making, hot water-bottles, two single duvets on the double bed to prevent marital strife, and an efficient bathroom. This year the Jamesons opened an annexe, *The Saint George*, in a 16th-century building opposite, which formerly contained shops and a post office. It has a sitting room, five bedrooms, a suite on two floors, and a courtyard garden. Breakfast includes "delicious wholemeal toast; nothing packaged or wrapped". Difficult to find, but confirmations of reservation are accompanied by good instructions, and Mr Jameson has been known to park cars for arriving guests. Frequent concerts in the College and Evensong in the cathedral provide entertainment on the doorstep. (*Margaret and Alan Clark, HR, Lt. Col. Robin Laird; also Good Pub Guide*)

Open All year, except 25 Dec.
Rooms Pub: 7 double; *St George*: 1 suite, 4 double, 1 single.
Facilities Pub: 2 bars, 5 eating areas, breakfast room; sauna; small garden. *St George*: sitting room, kitchen; garden. Unsuitable for &.
Location Central, between college and cathedral; hotel will send directions. Carpark.
Restrictions No smoking: 3 eating areas, breakfast room. No children under 14.
Credit cards All major cards accepted.
Terms [1997] B&B: single £69.50, double £79.50. Full alc: £20–£25.

WINDERMERE Cumbria	Map 4

The Archway BUDGET	*Tel* (01539 4) 45613

13 College Road
Windermere LA23 1BU

"I could happily spend a month here. Anthony and Aurea Greenhalgh are wonderfully friendly and helpful. The food is fabulous. The breakfasts keep you going until afternoon, and the dinners, ending with luscious puddings, are a treat after a day of hitchhiking and sightseeing." "A comfortable and memorable stay. We felt like house guests. The Greenhalghs are a mine of local information." Recent tributes to this no-smoking Victorian terrace guest house, filled with antiques, paintings, flowers, and books, and with an open view of green field and trees. It is in a quiet road, near the rail and bus stations of this busy town. Steep steps lead to bedrooms with flowery fabrics, Victorian quilts and duvets, pine furniture, home-made biscuits, hot water-bottles and TV. One is large, with a dressing area; one has a bath; the others have a shower room. Some have a view of the lake, half a mile away (one overlooks a carpark). Lavish breakfasts include dried fruit, home-made yogurt, bread and marmalade, and a huge choice of cooked dishes. The evening meal is at 6.45 pm with no choice – three courses in winter, two in summer: imaginative traditional English cooking, with an emphasis on fresh organic produce. Bread and yogurt are home-made. Vegetarians are catered for. The wine list is "brief but good". (*Susan Bari, Howard M Jones; also the Ven. Arthur Hawes, Archdeacon of Lincoln*)

Open All year. Dinner not served Wed, Sun.
Rooms 4 double.
Facilities Sitting room, dining room. Small front garden. Lake 15 mins. Unsuitable for &.
Location 2 mins' walk from centre; W of Main Road. Parking for 2 cars.
Restrictions No smoking. No children under 10. No dogs.
Credit cards Access, Visa.
Terms B&B £20–£28. Set dinner £12.50. Bargain breaks; Christmas, New Year breaks. 1-night bookings sometimes refused summer.

Gilpin Lodge	*Tel* (01539 4) 88818
Crook Road	*Fax* (01539 4) 88058

Windermere LA23 3NE

This old white Lakeland house is set well back from the road in large grounds with gardens and woodland. It has large public rooms, with bright colours, stylish Chinese pottery, open fires and flowers. Many of the bedrooms are spacious and have a sitting area, fine textiles, antiques and original pictures and lovely views. Many bathrooms have Victorian fittings. There is one report this year of a poor welcome, but other guests have been enthusiastic: "The owners, John and Christine Cunliffe, and their staff work hard to make everything as comfortable as possible. The food is quite fancy, with interesting combinations, and attractively presented, with an excellent cheeseboard. Our bedroom had many windows and was bright and spacious. It had antiques, and pictures with an eastern theme." Others have written of the dedication and professionalism of the hosts – "their kindness to their guests inspires the staff." "They are perfectionists. Hotel warmth in low season is a real test – they passed with flying colours. The ambience was relaxing and friendly, but not exaggeratedly so; the decor interesting, but not distracting." Breakfast includes a generous Cumbrian spread. The restaurant, with a conservatory extension, is popular locally for its attractive ambience and the modern English/French cooking of Christopher Davies. There is plenty of choice on the fixed-price dinner menu. Lunches are flexible, ranging from a full meal in the dining room to a light one served in the lounge. Local attractions include places associated with Beatrix Potter, William Wordsworth and John Ruskin, and two stately homes: Livens Hall and Sizergh Castle. (*Margaret Reid, JD, and others*)

Open All year.
Rooms 14 double, some with access for &.
Facilities 2 lounges, 3 dining rooms (piped music). 20-acre grounds: gardens, croquet. Lake Windermere 2 miles: fishing, boating, etc. Free access to Parklands country club nearby: swimming pool, sauna, squash, badminton, snooker.
Location On B5284 Kendal–Bowness. M6 exit 36.
Restrictions No smoking in restaurant. No children under 7. No dogs.
Credit cards All major cards accepted.
Terms B&B: single £75–£100, double £90–£140; D,B&B: single £95–£120, double £130–£180. Light lunches; full alc lunch £20; set Sun lunch £15.50, dinner £28.50. Off-season reductions; reductions for longer stays. Christmas, New Year packages.

Holbeck Ghyll   *Tel* (01539 4) 32375
Holbeck Lane   *Fax* (01539 4) 34743
Windermere LA23 1LU

"Outstanding bedrooms, exceptional service, delicious meals." "Cheerful welcome from friendly young staff, who are keen to please, but do not fuss. Great attention to creature comforts. Stunning view from bedroom with large balcony. Beautiful grounds with walk down to lakeside. We enjoyed sitting by the log fire in the company of Roker, the labrador. Fair value too. Altogether a fine hotel." Recent praise for David and Patricia Nicholson's large late-Victorian former hunting lodge. It stands up a steep drive off the road to Ambleside, and has stunning views of Lake Windermere and Langdale Fells. Streams run through the landscaped garden. Public areas have Art Nouveau features such as stained glass in the style of Charles Rennie Macintosh, high ceilings, wood panelling, large pieces of antique furniture, mirrors, and good quality curtains and carpets. Bedrooms are similar in style; many are spacious. There are two dining rooms: the older, panelled one is "distinctly more opulent" than the new Terrace Restaurant ("could do with better chairs," one visitor thought), the French doors of which lead on to a patio where alfresco meals may be served. Cooking by Jake Watson is English with a French influence. There's an extensive cheeseboard, and a good choice of wines, with plenty of half bottles – although one couple thought the mark-ups were high. Good breakfasts too. A small health spa was recently added. The homes of Wordsworth and Beatrix Potter are nearby. (*JI, Mark Tattersall and Scott Darby*)

Open All year.
Rooms 3 suites, 10 double, 1 single.
Facilities 2 lounges, bar area, billiard room, 2 dining rooms; function facilities; small health spa: sauna, exercise equipment, etc. 7-acre grounds: streams, woods to lakeshore, jogging track. Golf, watersports nearby. Unsuitable for &.

Location 3 miles N of Windermere off road to Ambleside. Pass Brockhole Visitor Centre on left, right turn (Holbeck La) to Troutbeck. Drive ½ mile on left. Station 3 miles.
Restrictions No smoking in restaurant. No children under 8 at dinner. No dogs in public rooms.
Credit cards All major cards accepted.
Terms B&B £65–£105 per person; D,B&B: single £79–£125, double £138–£240, suite £178–£260. Set Sun lunch £14.95 (weekdays alc), dinner (3/4 courses) £25/£30. 10% reduction for 5 or more nights. Off-season, Christmas, New Year breaks. 1-night bookings sometimes refused Sat in winter. ***V***

Miller Howe   *Tel* (01539 4) 42536
Rayrigg Road   *Fax* (01539 4) 45664
Windermere LA23 1EY   *E-mail* miller.howe.hotel@dialin.net

♀ *César award in 1986*

John Tovey has presided for 27 years over this "truly individualistic", famously pampering hotel. Perched above Windermere, it overlooks statue-dotted lawns that slope down to the water, and has magnificent views to the great peaks beyond. It is an Edwardian house, whose decor, one guest has written, is "a throwback to the seventies, with gold-painted cherubs in the bathroom and a crown above the draped double bed". The "warm, friendly atmosphere" is praised, as is Chris Blaydes' modern cooking "with strong flavours and textures". Dinner (7.30 pm for 8; four courses, no choice until dessert) is theatrically served in a two-tier dining room with a *trompe l'oeil* Tuscan landscape; lights are dimmed as the meal begins; five small portions of vegetables accompany the main dish. Bedrooms are "a delight, and unusually well equipped: a music centre, excellent bedside lights, books, binoculars, backgammon, Scrabble *and* a dictionary". Some have a terrace. The lounges are luxurious, with leather sofas and chairs. "Lovely breakfast, with a huge choice, including home-made bread", is preceded by Buck's Fizz in the hall. Light lunches and traditional afternoon teas are available. (*JR, and others*)

Open Mar–Dec.
Rooms 12 double.
Facilities 3 lounges, restaurant (piped classical music at night), conservatory; terrace. 4-acre grounds: landscaped garden. Walking, climbing, tennis, sailing, fishing, water sports nearby. Unsuitable for &.
Location On A592 N of Bowness. Lake-facing rooms quietest. Train: Windermere; then taxi.
Restrictions No smoking in restaurant. No children under 8. No dogs in public rooms.
Credit cards All major cards accepted.
Terms [1997] (*Excluding 12½% service charge*) D,B&B £75–£125. Set lunch £16, dinner £32. Off-season breaks; spring stand-by bargain breaks: D,B&B £60–£80; cookery courses Mar/Nov.

WINSTONE Gloucestershire   **Map 3**

Winstone Glebe   NEW/BUDGET   *Tel/Fax* (01285) 821451
Winstone, nr Cirencester GL7 7JN

In a Domesday-old village in a designated area of outstanding natural beauty, this Georgian rectory, quietly set in gardens and paddocks, overlooks a Saxon church and has lovely views. It is the family home of Susanna (an ex-restaurateur) and Shaun Parsons. "She is a superb cook; he genially dispenses pre-prandial drinks and appropriate table wines by the glass," wrote the nominators, "They are delightful, relaxed hosts. The house is charming. We appreciated the fire in the drawing room on a chilly May evening. Our bedroom was very comfortable and well appointed. Winstone is unexciting, but the Duntisbournes, just down the valley, are some of the loveliest, most unspoilt villages in the Cotswolds." Nearby are polo at Cirencester; medieval castles, old churches, stately homes and gardens. (*Roger and Jytte Hardisty*)

Open All year, except Christmas.
Rooms 1 suite, 2 double. 1 in coach house 30 yds.
Facilities Drawing room, dining room. 5-acre grounds: garden, tennis, paddocks; bicycles available. Unsuitable for &.
Location Off A417 between Cirencester and Gloucester. House is 300 yds short of church, by public footpath sign.
Restriction No smoking.
Credit cards Access, Visa.
Terms B&B: single £27.50–£35, double £55–£60. Set dinner £18.

WINTERINGHAM North Lincolnshire   Map 4

Winteringham Fields	*Tel* (01724) 733096
Winteringham DN15 9PF	*Fax* (01724) 733898
	E-mail EuroAnnie@aol.com

🎗 *César award in 1996*

Michelin bestows a star and four red crossed spoon-and-forks on Germain and Annie Schwab's restaurant-with-rooms. It has an unlikely setting, at a crossroads in a nondescript village "surrounded by mangel wurzel fields", on the southern bank of the Humber estuary. A 16th-century farmhouse facing on to a flowery courtyard, it has exposed beams, low doorways and ceilings, oak panelling and period fireplaces, narrow corridors, and Victorian furniture and *objets d'art*. Bedrooms, "while not especially luxurious, lack nothing in terms of thoughtful extras". Those in the main house are "wonderfully atmospheric, with uneven floors and chintzy fabrics". One has a four-poster and a bathroom down a tiny flight of stairs in what was the apple store – "quite magic". There are spacious ones in converted stables across a courtyard. The smart, if rather dark, restaurant has large, elegantly dressed tables, ornamental pillars, and an open fire in an antique range. One visitor thought the dining room over-formal, but otherwise the rave reviews continue: "What distinguishes it from the norm is the sheer niceness of the Schwabs – he a shy genius in the kitchen, she, front-of-house, a powerhouse of enthusiasm." "The Schwabs' love for their work sheds a glow; they encourage staff enthusiasm by taking them to sample other establishments." "Outstanding food, with particularly enticing fish dishes, using the local catch; impressive *maître d'*; the biggest cheese trolley I have ever seen." "Germain's highly sophisticated modern cooking never loses sight of the down-to-earth principles of his native Jura. Breakfast is impeccable." (*Pat and Jeremy Temple, Gillie Bolton; also David and Kate Wooff, GED Clarkson, Martin Chatt*)

Open All year, except Sun, bank holidays, 1st week Aug, 2 weeks Christmas. Lunch served Tues–Fri, dinner Mon–Sat.

Rooms 1 suite, 6 double. 3 in courtyard. 3 on ground floor (one with ♿ access).
Facilities Lounge, bar, restaurant, conservatory; private dining room. 1-acre grounds. Unsuitable for ♿.
Location Centre of village 4 miles SW of Humber Bridge. Train: Scunthorpe; bus: Winteringham.
Restrictions No smoking: restaurant, bedrooms. No children under 8, except babies. No dogs (kennels nearby).
Credit cards Access, Amex, Visa.
Terms B&B: single £65–£75, double £85–£115, suite £135. English breakfast £8.50. Set lunch £18.50, dinner £29; full alc £58.

WOODSTOCK Oxfordshire   Map 2

The Feathers   *Tel* (01993) 812291
Market Street,   *Fax* (01993) 813158
Woodstock OX20 1SX

This lively former coaching inn, "not too grand, but comfortably smart", is in the centre of this showplace town, a few minutes' stroll from Blenheim Palace. It has expanded over the years into neighbouring buildings, acquiring a rambling nature, "with interesting nooks and crannies". The small lounges have low beamed ceilings, log fires, interesting furniture, books and flowers. The old-fashioned bar, with stuffed fish and birds and a live parrot, opens on to a small courtyard where lunches, drinks and teas are served in fine weather. Bedrooms vary in size; the best have a high ceiling and a modern bathroom. The partly panelled restaurant, with starched white linen tablecloths, crystal and candles, serves "progressive modern cooking" by chef David Lewis on a daily-changing menu. The food is generally admired, but there are grumbles about high prices, particularly since a "suggested gratuity" of 15% is added to the restaurant bill. "No one need pay it," says the hotel, but it leaves an unhappy impression. And one couple complained about breakfast: "If you want, for example, kippers as an alternative to the not very satisfying continental breakfast (stale croissants, tough toast), or the usual cooked dishes, you pay extra." But the "courteous and cheerful" young staff are regularly praised, and one couple could find no wrong: "Standards were high in every respect. We had one of the cheaper rooms; though slightly dark, it was comfortable and elegant, with a good bathroom with, for once, a shelf to put things on. Dinner in the wonderfully elegant dining room was a triumph, with polished service." Children are welcomed. *Bishopstrow House*, Warminster (*qv*), is under the same management. (*Richard and Caroline Faircliff, and others; also Good Pub Guide*)

Open All year. Bar meals not served weekend evenings.
Rooms 4 suites, 12 double.
Facilities 2 lounges, bar (piped jazz), restaurant (piped classical music); function facilities; courtyard. ¼-acre garden. Golf, fishing, riding, gliding nearby. Unsuitable for ♿.
Location Central (generally quiet at night). Street parking; public carpark nearby.
Restriction No smoking in restaurant. No dogs in bar, restaurant.
Credit cards All major cards accepted.
Terms [1997] B&B: single occupancy from £88, double £105–£155, suite £195–£250. Bar meals. Set lunch £16.95; full alc £36–£40. 2-day breaks. ***V***

WOOLTON HILL Berkshire   Map 2

Hollington House   *Tel* (01635) 255100
Woolton Hill   *Fax* (01635) 255075
nr Newbury RG20 9XA

This Edwardian house, in rolling Berkshire countryside, is informally
run by Australian owners, John and Penny Guy, with an Antipodean
staff. It is set in large wooded grounds with gardens designed by
Gertrude Jekyll. "From the lovely terrace which runs the length of the
house you can see neither buildings, pylons nor poles, nor can you hear
traffic," one visitor wrote. Inside are high-ceilinged, tall-windowed
lounges with fires in cold weather, a large panelled hall and dining
room, an imposing wooden staircase, an interesting mixture of paintings and artefacts, including a collection of model ships in glass cases,
and a full-sized snooker table. "Mr Guy is charming and interested,"
wrote a visitor from California. "The staff were delightful; keen to
make us comfortable, but not overly stuffy. They were very kind to our
young daughter who was not feeling well. We were impressed by the
New World wine list." A new chef, Simon Rogan, arrived in October
1996, and recent diners thought the food had improved. Sunday lunch
is a family affair, with a joint carved by Mr Guy. The "huge, well-
equipped bedrooms" have flowers, fruit, mineral water, books, fine
views, and turned-back beds at night; some have a spa bath. "The
flower arrangements, cleanliness and attention to detail make for much
contentment". An indoor swimming pool is new this year. (*Mrs WK
Norman, Michael and Maureen Heath, and others*)

Open All year.
Rooms 1 suite, 19 double.
Facilities Lift, ramp. Lounge, snooker room, 2 dining rooms; 3 meeting rooms;
indoor swimming pool; terrace. 25-acre grounds: swimming pool, croquet, ten-
nis, helipad; chauffeur available. River Kennet nearby: fishing.
Location 3 miles SW of Newbury, off A343 to Andover. Turn right to Woolton
Hill; hotel next to Hollington Herb Garden. Train: Newbury.
Restrictions No smoking in 2 bedrooms. No dogs except guide dogs (kennels
nearby).
Credit cards All major cards accepted.
Terms [1997] B&B: single £95, double £120–£175, suite £250. Set lunch (2/3-
course) £14.50/£19; full alc £50. Children under 7 accommodated free in parents'
room. 2-day unwinder break: D,B&B from £90. Christmas, New Year packages.

WORFIELD Shropshire   Map 3

The Old Vicarage   *Tel* (01746) 716497
Worfield, Bridgnorth WV15 5JZ   *Fax* (01746) 716552

"Peter and Christine Iles are unpretentious hosts, who give guests'
comfort their priority. We had a most happy visit." "One of the most
pleasant away-from-home settings you could find." "Breakfasts unsurpassed." Recent tributes to this red brick Edwardian parsonage by the
impressive medieval church of a peaceful old village in the valley of the
river Worfe. Its spacious public rooms are handsomely furnished with
a mixture of antique and repro furniture, and have remarkable collections of watercolours and clocks. Drinks and coffee are served in a conservatory. Bedrooms have fruit, sweets, mini-bar and books. The best,

in a coach house, have a whirlpool bath, and "the feel of a country cottage". Two of these have access for a wheelchair. *Michelin* awards a red
"Meals" for the four-course dinners served in the small, smart dining
room. As we went to press a new chef arrived – Richard Arnold, whose
modern British cooking at *The Lake*, Llangammarch Wells, Wales (*qv*),
was admired. So we'd like reports on the food, please. The Ileses offer
special breaks including a visit to the Ironbridge Gorge, close by. The
wines are sometimes thought expensive, but the long list of half bottles
is appreciated; extras can make the bill mount up. (*Prof. and Mrs
Bantock, and others*)

Open All year, except Christmas, New Year. Weekday lunch by arrangement.
Rooms 1 suite, 13 double. 4 (with jacuzzi) in coach house, 2 with ♿ access.
Facilities Lounge/bar, restaurant (piped classical music), conservatory. 2-acre
grounds.
Location 4 miles NE of Bridgnorth. 1 mile from A454, by cricket ground. Regular
buses from Bridgnorth.
Restrictions No smoking: restaurant, bedrooms. No dogs in public rooms.
Credit cards All major cards accepted (except for special breaks).
Terms [1997] B&B: single £70–£95, double £107.50–£142.50, suite £152.50; D,B&B
£78.75–£95. Set lunch (Sun) £16.50, dinner £25–£32.50. Special breaks, including
entrance to Ironbridge Gorge Museum.

YORK North Yorkshire Map 4

4 South Parade NEW/BUDGET *Tel/Fax* (01904) 628229
4 South Parade
York YO2 2BA

*Anne and Robin McClure's small B&B in Georgian terrace in quiet cobbled
street close to Micklegate Bar, 10–15 mins' walk from centre. Private house
atmosphere; elegant decor. Personal service: guests met at station; early morning tea brought to bedroom; itineraries organised for guests. Good breakfast in
pretty beamed basement room. Cream tea by arrangement in second-floor
drawing room. Small garden. 3 bedrooms, with original fireplace, flowers,
fruit, shower en suite facilities. Bathroom with whirlpool bath available.
Closed Christmas/New Year. No smoking. Unsuitable for ♿. No children
under 14. No dogs. Credit cards not accepted. B&B: single £63–£73, double
£73–£93 [1997]. More reports, please.*

The Grange *Tel* (01904) 644744
1 Clifton *Fax* (01904) 612453
York YO3 6AA

Jeremy Cassel's Regency town house is within walking distance of the
minster. It has a striking period decor, "more private house than hotel",
with panelling, smart wallpapers, family portraits, and open fires in the
large drawing room and morning room, and a grand staircase. The
bedrooms have fine fabrics, antiques, good lighting and a smart
bathroom, but some are small and on the dark side. Number 20, with a
four-poster, was admired by recent guests: "Quiet, comfortable, large
and luxurious, with all the amenities one could want." One visitor this
year was critical of the service but others were enthusiastic. "A lovely,
well-kept hotel," runs an endorsement this year. "Attractive public
rooms and bedrooms. Breakfasts to suit trenchermen as well as dieters.

Our group of eight adults and three children, staying for a 70th birthday celebration, was well looked after. All the staff were cheerfully and effectively helpful." The restaurant, hung with pictures of racehorses, serves modern British cooking by the new chef, Michael Whiteley, who arrived in early 1997; there is also a brasserie in a vaulted cellar, open for lunch and until late in the evening, and a seafood bar. We'd be grateful for reports on the food. The hotel is on a busy road, but front rooms are double-glazed. (*Dr and Mrs Viola, Roger Hole*)

Open All year. Restaurant closed Sun evening; brasserie closed Sun midday; seafood bar closed Sat/Sun.
Rooms 1 suite, 26 double, 3 single. Some on ground floor, 1 suitable for &.
Facilities Ramps. Drawing room, morning room, library, restaurant, brasserie, seafood bar (piped jazz/easy listening music); conference facilities.
Location 500 yds from city wall, on A19 N to Thirsk (front rooms double-glazed). Carpark.
Restriction Small dogs only, not in public rooms.
Credit cards All major cards accepted.
Terms B&B: single £99, double £108–£160, suite £190. Set meals: seafood bar £12, restaurant: lunch £11.50, dinner £24; full alc: restaurant £28, brasserie £16. 2-day breaks; Christmas, New Year breaks.

Hobbits   BUDGET   *Tel* (01904) 624538 and 642926
9 St Peter's Grove   *Fax* (01904) 651765
Clifton, York YO3 6AQ

Rosemary Miller's civilised B&B is an Edwardian house in a quiet, leafy street a short walk from the city centre (easy parking). It is her family home, complete with a "podgy, friendly dog called Jess" and a collection of jugs, and, says a returning visitor, it is "warm, comfortable and welcoming". The spacious bedrooms (some, reached by a winding staircase, are in an attic) have a well-stocked fridge, TV, a writing table, books, etc. The "absolutely delicious" breakfast (full English or vegetarian) is generally served communally, but there is a small table for those wanting privacy. It includes muesli, yogurt, home-produced stewed gooseberries, home-made jams and good coffee. "Nothing is packaged – a real test. Standards are consistently high. They treat you as a house guest. Excellent value." There are plenty of eating places close by. (*CC, Antony Hill*)

Open All year, except Christmas.
Rooms 4 double, 2 single.
Facilities 2 lounges, breakfast room. Small garden. River Ouse nearby: fishing, boating. Unsuitable for &.
Location Entering York from N on A19, turn left just before footbridge in Clifton. Private and street parking.
Restrictions No smoking: 1 lounge, dining room, bedrooms.
Credit cards Access, Diners, Visa.
Terms B&B £25–£30. *V*

Middlethorpe Hall   *Tel* (01904) 641241
Bishopthorpe Road   *Fax* (01904) 620176
York YO2 1QB

This noble Grade II listed William III house, near York racecourse, was the home of the diarist Lady Mary Wortley Montagu. It has been immaculately restored and converted into a luxurious hotel by Historic

House Hotels Ltd, who have done the same for *Hartwell House*, Aylesbury, *The Cadogan*, London, and *Bodysgallen Hall*, Llandudno, Wales (*qqv*). It has an imposing façade, a black-and-white marble-floored hall, an intricately carved staircase and stately public rooms with chandeliers, fine furniture, paintings and *objets d'art*. It stands in magnificent large grounds with parkland, a walled garden and a small lake, just off a busy road (there is some traffic noise). The best bed-rooms, in the main house, are enormous, "with every creature comfort"; some have a large sitting room and a walk-in wardrobe; at least one has two bathrooms. Smaller rooms in converted stables are also carefully decorated, and well provided with pampering extras. Some walls are thin. Accomplished traditional English cooking by chef Andrew Wood is served in the panelled dining room overlooking the garden; there is also a simpler grill room. "The whole ambience is highly civilised," wrote visitors last year. "The staff were professional, and seemed to enjoy their work." Others marvelled: "It was as if our names had been stamped on our foreheads when we registered – we

were greeted by name throughout our stay, which made us feel very welcome." "Expert porterage and room service; good housekeeping." Peter Phillips, formerly deputy manager, has been promoted to manager this year. A spa is due to open by the end of 1998. (*AD, and others*)

Open All year. Restaurant closed Christmas Day to non-residents.
Rooms 7 suites, 19 double, 4 single. 19 in courtyard.
Facilities Drawing room, library, bar, restaurant, grill room (pianist Fri/Sat evening May–Sept); private dining rooms, function facilities. 26-acre grounds: croquet, walled garden, lake. Racecourse, golf nearby. Unsuitable for &.
Location 1½ miles S of centre, by racecourse. From A64(T) follow signs to York West, then Bishopthorpe.
Restrictions No smoking in restaurant. No children under 8. No dogs.
Credit cards Access, Amex, Visa.
Terms (until 31.3.98) Rooms: single £95–£110, double £131–£145, suite £165–£215. Breakfast: continental £7.95, English £11.50. Set lunch £14.50, dinner £28.95; full alc £43.45. Champagne breaks Nov–Apr; 2-day summer breaks; Christmas, New Year packages.

Mount Royale	*Tel* (01904) 628856
The Mount	*Fax* (01904) 611171
York YO2 2DA	*E-mail* oxtoby@uk.com

"Our third visit. A different bedroom each time, each one comfortable and varied in style. Once we were upgraded to a garden suite – a pleasant surprise. We love the place, and feel completely at home. The friendly staff are always willing to assist (for example, with last-minute ironing)." "An excellent place for breaking the journey to Scotland. We could not fault the bedroom, apart from the bedside lights. A friendly cat joined us for a while." "Excellent dinner; delicious vegetarian dishes; plenty of bargains on the wine list." "Breakfast a treat, with fresh fruit, a host of cereals, and a magnificent kedgeree." "Lovely swimming pool in the garden – a great plus for a city hotel." Much praise this year for this traditional hotel, mainly William IV with modern extensions, where the decor is "an interesting mixture of fifties, sixties and seventies". It is near the racecourse and Micklegate Bar and three-quarters of a mile from the minster. Run by two generations of the Oxtoby family with a long-serving staff, it has had a *Guide* entry for many years. Best bedrooms, with a sitting area and a private verandah, are in the garden annexe, connected to the main building by a covered walkway filled with orange trees, figs, and sub-tropical plants. Bathrooms are "stocked with useful goodies". Some rooms in the main house are quite small and old-fashioned; front ones have triple-glazing to cut out the noise from the busy road outside; back ones overlook the pretty garden. There is a full-sized snooker table. (*Fr Gordon Murray, David G Felce, NM Mackintosh, H Medcalf, Mike Hutton*)

Open All year.
Rooms 6 suites (4 in garden annexe), 17 double. Some on ground floor.
Facilities Lounge, TV room, bar, conservatory, restaurant (pianist 6 nights a week, piped music); meeting room; beauty centre. ½-acre grounds: swimming pool (heated May–Sept). Unsuitable for &.
Location Past racecourse on A1036 from Tadcaster (front rooms triple-glazed), at junction with Albemarle Rd. Parking. Bus from centre.
Restrictions No smoking in restaurant. No dogs unattended in bedrooms.
Credit cards All major cards accepted.
Terms B&B: single £70–£95, double £80–£95, suite £120. Full alc £34.50. 2-day breaks: D,B&B double £230.

See also SHORTLIST

****

Traveller's tale London: This is one of those places that prides itself on being "not a hotel". The only indication outside that we had arrived at the right place was the street number. I rang the bell, and asked if it was the hotel I sought, only to become enmeshed in a childish, pompous and annoying word game. "Do I have the right place? This is a hotel?" "No, this is not a hotel. It is a private home." "Oh, I'm sorry. I was looking for an inn in this street." "This is a private house, but we take paying guests." "Oh, then this is a guest house?" "No, it is a private home, but do come in, and I will show you round."

****

Traveller's tale Oxfordshire: We settled down for an afternoon nap and were woken by a horrendous noise, like the sound of 100 bombers warming up for take-off. The manager seemed surprised at our concern and told us soothingly that the kitchen extractor fan was the culprit, but it was only ever on briefly, and never after 10 pm. At 11.15 that night, my husband went down in his dressing gown to ask that it be turned off. It was, but started up again early next morning, wafting the smell of breakfast through our window. When we left, we asked if others had complained about the noise. We were told that some had, and perhaps the extractor needed some attention.

****

Wales

Carlton House, Llanwrtyd Wells

ABERSOCH Gwynedd

Map 3

Porth Tocyn Hotel
Abersoch LL53 7BU

Tel (01758) 713303
Fax (01758) 713538

"Good accommodation, very good food, relaxed and warm atmosphere – altogether a delightful experience. Excellent value out of season." A recent tribute to this long-established family-friendly hotel – 1998 will be the Fletcher-Brewer family's fiftieth season. It has a peaceful setting above a popular yachting village, with glorious views of Cardigan Bay and Snowdonia. The owner, Nick Fletcher-Brewer, writes: "Over the last two winters we have upgraded well over half our bedrooms to create much better family accommodation, for which there is a huge demand." The interconnected lounges are traditionally decorated with country antiques and fresh flowers, and there's a small children's sitting room with games, TV, video etc. Under-sevens high tea, to avoid a "summer camp" atmosphere at dinner. The has had a *Good Food Guide* entry for forty years, and Louise Fletcher-Brewer's cooking continues to be praised. "We enjoyed our fifteenth dinner just as much as the first." There's a two-course option for those unable to cope with the five-course daily-changing menu. The disabled are well catered for too. Guests are encouraged to discuss any special requirements in advance. The October "blackberry-pickers" package gives a 25 per cent discount to an entire party when previous guests introduce new ones to the hotel. (*Mr and Mrs PJ Hussey*)

Open Week before Easter–mid-Nov.
Rooms 14 double, 3 single. 3 on ground floor.
Facilities 6 sitting rooms, 1 children's room, bar, restaurant. 25-acre grounds: outdoor swimming pool (heated May–Sept), tennis. Beach, safe bathing, sailing, fishing, golf, riding, clay-pigeon shooting nearby.
Location 2½ miles S of Abersoch, through hamlets of Sarn-bach and Bwlch-Tocyn. Follow blue bed symbol and signs: Gwesty/Hotel.
Restrictions No smoking in restaurant. No children under 7 in restaurant at night (high teas until 6.15 pm). No dogs in public rooms.
Credit cards Access, Visa.
Terms [1997] B&B: single £45–£58.50, double £60–£108. Set lunch (Sun) £16.25, dinner (2/5 courses) £21/£28. Reductions for longer stays. 1-night bookings occasionally refused. Children accommodated free in parents' room.

BEAUMARIS Anglesey   Map 3

Ye Olde Bulls Head   NEW   *Tel* (01248) 810329
Castle St   *Fax* (01248) 811294
Beaumaris
Isle of Anglesey LL58 8AP

Beaumaris is a resort and sailing centre, medieval in origin, on the Menai Strait, just south of the eastern tip of the Isle of Anglesey. It has many historic buildings, including this hostelry, which dates from 1472 and was commandeered by Cromwell's General Mytton when he besieged the castle in 1645. Previous guests include Samuel Johnson and Charles Dickens. The bedrooms, which are named for characters in the latter's books, are beamed and cottagey; some have brass beds or a four-poster. One without private facilities, called the Artful Dodger, is suitable for young children. The nominator, a regular visitor, writes: "We love the blend of modern comfort and 'olde worlde' charm. The food is superb. They wisely serve restaurant meals only in the evening, but the bar lunches are superior to what you get in many a restaurant. Breakfasts are excellent, too – no package butter or jam here." The rambling bar, popular with locals, is full of reminders of the inn's interesting past, including a rare 17th-century brass water clock, a collection of antique weapons and the town's oak ducking seat, as well as much shining copper. There's a large lounge with a log fire. The sophisticated cooking of chefs Soames Whittingham and Keith Rothwell (co-owner with David Robertson, the manager) makes imaginative use of local ingredients – freshly caught fish, Conwy samphire, Llanrwst goat's cheese, etc. Beaumaris Castle, built by Edward I, is a designated World Heritage site, owing to its unique concentric fortifications. Two National Trust properties, Plas Newydd and Penrhyn Castle, and Bodnant gardens are nearby. (*JW Makinson, Good Pub Guide*)

Open All year, except Christmas.
Rooms 14 double, 1 single. 1 in annexe. Some on ground floor.

Facilities Lounge, bar, restaurant, courtyard. 100 yds from Menai Strait; small sand/pebble beach. Sailing, fishing, shooting, golf available.
Location Central, in main street. Train: Bangor, 7 miles.
Restrictions No smoking: restaurant, 4 bedrooms. No children under 7 in restaurant. No dogs.
Credit cards Access, Amex, Visa.
Terms B&B £39.50–£49. Bar lunches Mon–Sat. Set Sun lunch £14.95, dinner £20.95; full alc £30. Off-season breaks.

BUILTH WELLS Powys   Map 3

Dol-llyn-wydd   BUDGET   *Tel* (01982) 553660
Builth Wells LD2 3RZ

Seventeenth-century farmhouse B&B, off B4520, in lovely countryside 1 mile S of old-fashioned spa town; you can walk on to the hills from the door. "Wonderfully welcoming hostess, Biddy Williams; charming decor; plentiful, excellent home-cooked evening meal by arrangement." 4 bedrooms, 1 with bath en suite; showers available. 20-acre grounds. Fishing, golf, tennis, riding nearby. Open Mar–Dec. No smoking. No children under 14. No dogs in house. Credit cards not accepted. B&B £15–£20; D,B&B £25–£30 [1997]. More reports, please.

CAERSWS Powys   Map 3

Maesmawr Hall   NEW   *Tel* (01686) 688255
Caersws SY17 5SF   *Fax* (01686) 688410

This impressive Grade I listed half-timbered 16th-century hunting lodge is set back from the main road up a long tree-lined drive in attractive gardens. It has been well modernised by the two couples who own and run it, Isabel and Alan Hunt, and Marilyn and John Pemberton (he is the chef). "We have visited three times, and the standards have remained consistent," writes the nominator. "The traditional food is first-class, if almost too plentiful – masses of fresh vegetables. There's an extensive and reasonably priced wine list." The lounge has wood panelling, oak beams and a garden view "but is not very inviting". The best bedrooms are in the main house; they are good-sized and comfortable; some have a sloping ceiling and a four-poster. Newer ones are in the coach house across the lawn. The hotel has fishing rights on the Severn and can arrange rough shooting nearby. Caersws village, in the Severn valley, is close to good walking country in the Montgomeryshire hills and the Shropshire Mynd. (*J Rudd*)

Open All year, except Christmas.
Rooms 16 double, 1 single. 6 in coach house, some on ground floor.
Facilities Lounge, bar, restaurant (piped "easy listening" music); function room. 4-acre gardens. River Severn 250 yds, fishing; pony-trekking, shooting, golf nearby. Unsuitable for &.
Location 5 miles W of Newtown, off A489 1 mile before Caersws (300-yd drive on right). Train: Caersws.
Restrictions No smoking in restaurant. Well-behaved small dogs only.
Credit cards Access, Amex, Visa.
Terms B&B: single £53.50, double £69.50; D,B&B: single £75, double £112.50. Set lunch £11.50, dinner £22.50; full alc £28.50. 2-night break £55 per night.

CAPEL GARMON Gwynedd   **Map 3**

Tan-y-Foel   NEW   *Tel* (01690) 710507
Capel Garmon   *Fax* (01690) 710681
nr Betws-y-Coed LL26 0RE   *E-mail* sjones@imaginet.co.uk

Janet and Peter Pitman's stone manor house – the name means "under
the hillside" – is peacefully set up a bumpy drive in wooded grounds at
the heart of Snowdonia. It has magnificent views over the Conwy valley. Dinners, cooked by Mrs Pitman and served only to residents (at
7.45 pm; they make their choice at breakfast), rate an entry in the *Good
Food Guide*. Our readers, too, are enthusiastic about the food: "definitely
nouvelle, beautifully cooked and presented"; "outstanding sauces, carefully and knowledgeably chosen wine list"; "the menu is small, but
over several days it offered a wide choice to suit most tastes." A number of visitors last year complained of a regimented atmosphere, but
most reports are favourable this year: "The welcome is warm and
friendly; they willingly help with luggage. The decor may not be to
everyone's taste, but it is compellingly warm and cheerful, even on the
dullest days." "Lovely, peaceful setting. Large bedrooms." Some rooms
have a king-size, four-poster or canopy bed; they are supplied with
chocolates and flowers, and have a good-size bathroom. Breakfast is
"good and, if you want it, vast". The swimming pool is no longer in
operation. (*Dr and Mrs RR Evans, Tina Upchurch, RAL Ogston, and others*)

Open Jan–mid-Dec.
Rooms 7 double. 2, with own entrance, adjoining main house.
Facilities 2 lounges, restaurant. 8 acre grounds. Unsuitable for &.
Location 1½ miles SE of Betws-y-Coed. Right to Capel Garmon and Nebo off
A470 to Llanrwst. 1¼ miles up hill; sign on left.
Restrictions No smoking. No children under 7. No dogs.
Credit cards All major cards accepted.
Terms B&B: single £65–£85, double £80–£150; D,B&B: single £90–£110, double
£130–£200. Set dinner (3/4 courses) £24/£28. Special breaks (min. 2 nights) from
£128. 1-night bookings often refused.

CARDIFF *See SHORTLIST*   **Map 3**

CRICKHOWELL Powys   **Map 3**

Gliffaes   *Tel* (01874) 730371
Crickhowell NP8 1RH   *Fax* (01874) 730463
                                      Freephone (0800) 146719
                      E-mail gliffaehotel@compuserve.com

The Brabner family have owned this imposing italianate mansion,
complete with campanile, since 1948. It has a lovely setting above the
Usk valley, and is popular with fishing people – it has rights on two
stretches of the river. *Gliffaes* has a loyal following: "Our 25th visit and
probably our most enjoyable," runs one recent report. "We had begun
to take the gardens for granted, but this week they were outstanding."
Some visitors have thought the atmosphere a little impersonal, but
others have written of the "nice, unobtrusive owners". The decor is
comfortable and traditional – "no hint of interior design". Bedrooms

are simple, and housekeeping may not always be perfect. Plenty of places for sitting: a large lounge, a pretty conservatory and a terrace overlooking the valley. The hotel is informally run: no room servicing at night, pour-yourself tea at breakfast and in the afternoon, etc, but service is friendly and generally efficient, and staff are available when needed. Mealtimes are elastic. Mark Coulton's cooking is admired: "Light first courses, good fish dishes, pretty, delicately flavoured desserts. Breakfast good too, with large self-service buffet and freshly cooked eggs, kippers, etc." Bar lunches range from light snacks, served wherever you want, to a substantial meal; tea is laid out in the lounge each afternoon. Bedrooms are priced according to view; some are small. There is wonderful walking in the Brecon Beacons National Park and in the Black Mountains, both nearby. Three more bedrooms and three meeting rooms in an annexe are planned for the end of 1997. (*Col. AJW and Mrs HM Harvey, and others*)

Open All year.
Rooms 22 double. 3 in lodge 450 yds. 3 more planned for 1998.
Facilities 2 sitting rooms, TV room, billiard room, conservatory bar, dining room (pianist Sat evening); meeting rooms. 34-acre grounds: gardens, tennis, croquet, putting, fishing. Unsuitable for &.
Location 2½ miles W of Crickhowell, 1 mile off A40; follow *Gliffaes* sign.
Restrictions No smoking in dining room. Dogs in lodge only.
Credit cards All major cards accepted.
Terms B&B: single £37.50, double £75–£111; D,B&B: single £59, double £118–£155; full board (2–6 nights): single £68.50, double £137–£173. Bar lunches. Set Sun lunch £17, dinner £21.75; full alc £26.50. 2–6-night breaks off season; fishing, history, cookery, flower arranging, courses. ***V***

EGLWYSFACH Ceredigion   Map 3

Ynyshir Hall   *Tel* (01654) 781209
Eglwysfach   *Fax* (01654) 781366
nr Machynlleth SY20 8TA

Q *César award in 1997*

"The scenic setting, the brilliant decor, the exciting paintings, and the charm of the proprietors combine to make this a bright star in the 'rural charm and character' league." "Caring owners and staff." "A gorgeous house with much to delight the eye and cosset the senses: beautiful furniture, oriental rugs, *objets d'art*, spectacular flower arrangements. Our bedroom had everything we could wish for; its bathroom was yellow and blue, with white clouds floating across the ceiling. The food was of the same high standard, served by candlelight, with gleaming silver and crystal and snow-white china. In four days we never heard noises of housework. A haven of peace and beauty." Recent praise for Rob and Joan Reen's white Georgian longhouse, set in large landscaped gardens surrounded by the 365 acres of the RSPB's Ynyshir bird reserve, on the southern shore of the Dyfi estuary. The young chef, Chris Colmer, who recently won the title of National Chef of Wales, has spent some time at the *Michelin* triple-starred *Troisgros* in Roanne. His modern British cooking has a strong emphasis on Welsh produce. Breakfast is a lavish affair with home-made marmalade and jams; after-noon tea comes with home-made scones and jams. Apart from the bird reserve, places of interest nearby include the Centre for Alternative Technology just north of Machynlleth, and Harlech castle and Portmeirion village are not too far away; there are also plenty of sport-ing activities (see below), and opportunities for walking and climbing in the Snowdonia National Park. Rooms vary in size and outlook, and one couple this year were disappointed in a small double "with over-sized furniture and a restricted view of the mountains". (*Richard and Sheila Owen, MW Atkinson, Ruth West, and others*)

Open All year.
Rooms 4 suites, 4 double. 1 on ground floor.
Facilities Drawing room, bar lounge, breakfast room, restaurant (piped harp/classical music at night). 14-acre landscaped gardens in 365-acre bird reserve: croquet, putting. Near Dyfi estuary: beaches 8 miles; sailing, river and sea fishing, riding, pony trekking, golf nearby.
Location Just W of A487, 6 miles SW of Machynlleth, 11 miles NE of Aberystwyth. Train: Machynlleth; then taxi.
Restrictions No smoking: drawing room, restaurant, 4 bedrooms. No children under 9. Dogs by arrangement, not in public areas.
Credit cards All major cards accepted.
Terms B&B: single £75–£95, double £100–£150, suite £150–£170. Set lunch from £20, dinner from £30. Gourmet, bird-watching weekends; Christmas, New Year packages. 1-night bookings sometimes refused high season weekends.

FISHGUARD Pembrokeshire   Map 3

Gilfach Goch Farmhouse   **BUDGET**   *Tel/Fax* (01348) 873871
Fishguard SA65 9SR   *E-mail* devgg@netwales.co.uk

Simple guest house in Pembrokeshire Coast National Park 2 miles E of Fishguard, S of A487. 18th-century stone farmhouse with original features (beams, inglenook), but modern comforts. In 10-acre grounds with sheep, don-keys, lovely views. Children warmly welcomed. Run by husband-and-wife team, June and Vernon Devonald; she cooks, he waits at table. "High stan-dards all round." 6 immaculate bedrooms with TV and good bathroom. Wholesome evening meals, except Wed. Open Easter–end Oct. No smoking. No dogs. Credit cards not accepted. B&B £23–£25; D,B&B £35–£37 [1997]. Children half-price in parents' room. 1-night bookings refused July, Aug. More reports, please.

GLYNARTHEN Ceredigion   Map 3

Penbontbren Farm   **BUDGET**   *Tel* (01239) 810248
Glynarthen, nr Cardigan SA44 6PE   *Fax* (01239) 811129

"A pleasant, peaceful setting." "Hosts friendly but not overbearing." "Good value." "A good base for exploring the beautiful countryside and beaches nearby." So say recent visitors to this unpretentious Welsh farmhouse hotel, an attractive conversion of old farm buildings, set

amid fields with grazing sheep. It is full of Welsh atmosphere: Barrie
and Nan Humphreys and their staff speak Welsh; the menus and information are bilingual. The locally popular restaurant has friendly waitresses and well-spaced tables. It serves reasonably priced dinners in
generous portions, on a large *carte* with regional specialities and high-
cholesterol puddings. Some guests have thought the food ordinary and
complained that "the menu never changes", but others praise the
"imaginative choice and standard of food". Breakfast includes
Glamorgan sausages; bar lunches are available. Meals are sometimes
accompanied by a harpist, but one visitor was irritated by the repetitive
piped music in the restaurant. Bedrooms, with pine furniture, are in
outbuildings around the farmyard. The conversion is in no way luxurious, but all the important elements are there: good lighting, TV,
rough but decent-sized towels in spotless bathrooms. Some rooms are
small and dark. The farm has a little countryside museum and a nature
trail. The sea and the coastal path are two-and-a-half miles away. (*Ruth
Davis, Brenda J Weatherill, Mrs C Wright*)

Open All year.
Rooms 10 double. 2 on ground floor, suitable for &.
Facilities Ramp. 2 lounges, games room, bar, restaurant (harpist, piped
Welsh/classical music). 90-acre farm: nature trail. Coast 10 mins' drive.
Location Travelling S from Aberystwyth on A487, 1st left at hotel sign, just S of
Sarnau; N from Cardigan, 2nd right, 1 mile N of Tan-y-groes.
Restrictions No smoking in restaurant. No dogs in public rooms, unattended in
bedrooms.
Credit cards All major cards accepted.
Terms [1997] B&B £34–£43; D,B&B £46–£55. Bar lunches £6–£8; full alc £22. 2-
night breaks; weekly rates.

GOVILON Monmouthshire   **Map 3**

Llanwenarth House   *Tel* (01873) 830289
Govilon, nr Abergavenny NP7 9SF   *Fax* (01873) 832199

"The house is magnificent, as was our meal, rather like a first-class dinner party. The bedrooms are elegant, spacious and comfortable, with
high quality antiques. Marvellous views." "A quiet country home in
delightful grounds by a canal, with two huge copper beeches, horses,
chickens and lurcher dogs. We enjoyed the communal dinners – you
get to visit with everyone." "After dinner we relaxed with coffee by the
log fire in the Georgian drawing room, chatting to our fellow guests.
Many were walkers, who love this area. Breakfast is superb, with haddock, kippers, etc, and home-made jams." Praise from London and
Texas for Bruce and Amanda Weatherill's family home, a fine tall-
windowed, thick-walled, 16th-century manor house, built of warm
grey limestone, in the Brecon Beacons National Park. Its grounds overlook the Usk valley, and border the Brecon and Monmouthshire canal,
where boats may be hired by the day – an agreeable way to explore the
area. Many of the vegetables are home-grown, so is much of the fruit;
honey comes from hives in the orchard. Abergavenny, three miles
away, is an old market town. A good base for visiting the castles and
archaeological sites of the Welsh marches, Offa's Dyke and the Black
Mountains. Plenty of sporting activities are available (see next page).
(*Robert Hill, Diane Camp, Mrs E Hiam; also P Rudd, and others*)

Open All year, except mid-Jan–late Feb; Christmas/New Year by arrangement. No lunches.
Rooms 5 double, 1 on ground floor. No telephone.
Facilities Drawing room, dining room. 10-acre grounds: croquet, canal (boat hire); stabling for visiting horses. Trout/salmon-fishing, golf, pony-trekking, shooting nearby.
Location From junction of A40/A465/A4042, take A465 towards Merthyr Tydfil for 3½ miles. At roundabout take 1st exit to Govilon; the hotel's half-mile drive is 150 yards on right.
Restrictions No smoking: dining room, bedrooms. No children under 10. No dogs in public rooms.
Credit cards None accepted.
Terms [1997] B&B: single £50–£56, double £72–£78. Set dinner £23.

KNIGHTON Powys   **Map 3**

Milebrook House   BUDGET   *Tel* (01547) 528632
Milebrook, Knighton LD7 1LT   *Fax* (01547) 520509
                              E-mail hotel@milebrook.kc3ltd.co.uk

"As agreeable as ever. Wonderful situation, idyllic views." "This small hotel has a real country house feeling: warm lighting and log fires kept us comfortable even with outside temperatures below freezing. Our bedroom was large and thoughtfully equipped with hot water-bottles, plenty of storage space. "Delightful, if isolated; staff and owners very helpful." Praise this year for Rodney and Beryl Marsden's 18th-century grey stone house in the Teme valley, just over the border from England and close to some of the best stretches of the Offa's Dyke path. There are four luxurious bedrooms in the smart new wing, opened in September 1996 by the explorer Wilfred Thesiger, who once lived there. They have thick carpets and curtains, excellent lighting, and the bathrooms are blue-tiled, with marble floors. Beryl Marsden's cooking is admired: "unpretentious and good"; "strong and satisfying daubes"; "beautifully cooked vegetables". But some readers have reported inadequate heating in bedrooms, and an "erratic hot water supply"; and one found the service slow at breakfast. The hotel has a mile-long stretch of the Teme for trout-fishing and Rodney Marsden is happy to advise on birdwatching and walking expeditions. The bar menu provides reasonably priced light lunches. (*Janet and Dennis Allom, Sonia Cohen, and others*)

Open All year. Restaurant closed Mon midday.
Rooms 10 double. 2 on ground floor.
Facilities Ramps. Lounge, bar, dining room. 3-acre grounds: croquet, fishing.
Location 2 miles E of Knighton on A4113 (rooms double-glazed). Train: Knighton.
Restrictions No smoking: dining room, bedrooms. No children under 4. No dogs.
Credit cards Access, Amex, Visa.
Terms B&B: single £46.50–£50, double £68–£75. Set lunch £10.95, dinner £17.50 or £21.50. Special breaks. Christmas, New Year packages.

We ask hotels to estimate their 1998 tariffs, but many prefer not to think so far ahead and give their 1997 tariffs. Prices should always be checked on booking.

LLANDDEINIOLEN Gwynedd   Map 3

Ty'n Rhos   *Tel* (01248) 670489
Seion, Llanddeiniolen   *Fax* (01248) 670079
nr Caernarfon LL55 3AE

"Highly recommended. Very large room with view and all amenities.
Pleasant and helpful hosts. Extremely good value." "A beautiful hotel
in a beautiful setting. Perfect food." Recent praise from regular correspondents for Nigel and Lynda Kettle's former farmhouse. It has a
rural setting in the plain between Snowdonia and the coast, with pleasant views towards the beaches of Anglesey and the Menai Strait.
Inside, the house is cosy and light. There's a large lounge, with
antiques, books and games. The pretty, unfussy bedrooms have pine
furniture, fresh flowers, and a hospitality tray. Two, on the ground
floor, have a sliding picture window and a patio overlooking the garden and the fields beyond; three new ones are in converted farm buildings. In the restaurant (a *Good Food Guide* restaurant of the year in 1997),
local produce and home-grown vegetables are used for the tradi-
tional/modern cooking. There's a set dinner, or a more expensive *carte*,
priced according to the main course. Kippers and kedgeree are offered
for breakfast as well as the usual eggs-and-bacon-plus, and excellent
home-made preserves; nothing packaged. The farm, with its carp lake,
is separately operated, but open to *Ty'n Rhos*'s guests. (*RAL Ogston,
Sonia Cohen, and others*)

Open 1 Jan–23 Dec, except 1 week Jan. Restaurant closed midday, to non-
residents Sun.
Rooms 11 double, 3 single. 3 in outbuildings. Some on ground floor.
Facilities 2 lounges, restaurant/bar. 72-acre farm: 1-acre garden, carp lake. Sea
9 miles.
Location 6 miles NE of Caernarfon, in hamlet of Seion, between B4366 and
B4547.
Restrictions No smoking: restaurant, bedrooms. No children under 6. No dogs
in house.
Credit cards Access, Amex, Visa.
Terms [1997] B&B: £45–£49, double £60–£85. Set dinner £19; full alc £29. ***V***

LLANDEILO Carmarthenshire   Map 3

The Cawdor Arms NEW   *Tel* (01558) 823500
Rhosmaen Street   *Fax* (01558) 822399
Llandeilo SA19 6EN

"Sumptuous luxury without sky-high prices" was enjoyed by the nominators of this Georgian former coaching inn, owned by Peter Grey-
Hughes and Delyth Wilson (the manager is Marc Williams). The
exterior, on the pleasant main street of this small town, belies the space
and elegance within. Flagstoned hall, polished oak floors, leather chairs
and fresh flowers downstairs. Upstairs, the bedrooms, recently refurbished, are individually styled, using William Morris designs. Some
are named after famous past visitors: Sarah Siddons, Charles Wesley
and Howard Hughes (who stayed in 1927). Chef Rod Peterson's cooking is sophisticated, with a Mediterranean flavour; we'd be grateful for
reports on it. Llandeilo lies on the Tywi river, which is famous for

salmon and trout, and is well placed for exploration of the Brecon
Beacons National Park and, a little further off, the Carmarthenshire and
Pembrokeshire coasts. (*Nannw Williams*)

Open All year.
Rooms 2 suites, 12 double, 2 single.
Facilities Lounge, bar, restaurant (piped music during day).
Location Centre of town (front rooms double-glazed).
Restrictions No smoking: restaurant, bedrooms. No dogs: public rooms, some
bedrooms.
Credit cards Access, Visa.
Terms [1997] B&B: single £55, double £65–£75, suite £85; D,B&B: single £75,
double £115, suite £135. Set lunch £14; full alc £30. 2-night breaks.

LLANDRILLO Denbighshire   Map 3

Tyddyn Llan   *Tel* (01490) 440264
Llandrillo, nr Corwen LL21 0ST   *Fax* (01490) 440414

♦ *César award in 1989*

"The Kindreds get everything right: a sincerely friendly greeting;
generous-sized public rooms; beautifully furnished and spotlessly
clean bedrooms; delightful bathrooms, mostly with proper shower as
well as bath. Delicious food, well presented, with great attention to
detail: home-made rolls in many flavours, extra strong cafetière coffee
when requested at breakfast. Good value too." "Not many hotels
would willingly accept a family party of 12 adults and five children
under ten celebrating a milestone birthday and a ruby wedding. The
staff were delightful – a sausage and chip supper provided for the children was much appreciated. Altogether a happy family occasion."
"One of the best country hotels I have visited." Many compliments
again this year for Peter and Bridget Kindred and their grey stone
Georgian country house, tranquilly set in the Vale of Edeyrnion. The
decor is in quiet good taste, with antique and period furniture, and
clever use of colour. The pretty, high-ceilinged restaurant is popular
with outside diners: chef Jason Hornbuckle, who was trained by the
well-known chef Bruno Loubet in London, "really knows his craft".
There is a good, reasonably priced wine list. The light lunches are
"imaginative and fairly priced", and the Welsh breakfasts, served until
10 am, are much admired. In November and March, Peter Kindred,

 whose work can be seen
throughout the hotel, runs
painting weekends. There's
lovely walking in the surrounding Berwyn moun-
tains. The hotel has a
four-mile stretch of the river
Dee, with fishing mostly for
grayling. (*Rosemary Viner,
Mrs JC Smye, Braham
Murray, Joy and Raymond
Goldman*)

Open All year.
Rooms 10 double.
Facilities Lounge, bar, restaurant (piped classical music). 3½-acre grounds:

water garden, croquet. River fishing (ghillie available), riding, golf, sailing, walking nearby. Only restaurant suitable for &.
Location From A5 W of Corwen take B4401 to Llandrillo.
Restrictions No smoking in restaurant. Early supper for children under 8. No dogs in public rooms.
Credit cards All major cards accepted.
Terms [Until Mar 1998] B&B: single £49–£70, double £98–£110; D,B&B: single £76.50–£97.50, double £130–£165. Set lunch £15.50, dinner £27. Special interest weekends, painting courses, in low season. Christmas, New Year house parties. *V*

LLANDUDNO Conwy   Map 3

Bodysgallen Hall   *Tel* (01492) 584466
Llanrhos, Llandudno LL30 1RS   *Fax* (01492) 582519
Q *César award in 1988*

"My third visit this year. It is one of the nicest hotels I know." So writes a regular visitor to this impressive Grade I listed house, mainly 17th-century, with skilful later additions. Restored to its original splendour by Historic House Hotels Ltd (see also *The Cadogan*, London, *Hartwell House*, Aylesbury, and *Middlethorpe Hall*, York), it stands in 200 acres of parkland on a hillside outside the agreeable Victorian seaside resort. Its 17th-century knot garden and 18th-century walled rose garden are much admired, as is its fine interior with panelled rooms, ancestral portraits, splendid fireplaces and stone mullioned windows. Most bedrooms are spacious and elegant. Some are in cottages grouped around a secluded courtyard. A friendly staff is led by manager, Matthew Johnson. In the restaurant, which has fine views of the grounds, chef Michael Penny's menus include both traditional and modern dishes, and there's a five-course gourmet menu. The original stone-built farm in the grounds has been converted into a spa, with a 54-foot swimming pool, a club room, a gymnasium and three beauty salons. The cottage suites, close to the spa, are good for families (as long as the children are over eight). The splendid gardens at Bodnant are among many local attractions, as is Conwy castle, and Caernarfon and Beaumaris castles are only a short drive. (*Sir Timothy Harford*)

Open All year.
Rooms 16 cottage suites, 13 double, 2 single.
Facilities Hall, drawing room, library, bar, restaurant (pianist Fri, Sat); conference centre. 200-acre parkland: gardens, tennis, croquet; spa: swimming pool, gym, sauna, beauty treatment, club room (light meals and drinks). Riding, shooting, fishing, sandy beaches nearby.
Location Off A470, 1 mile N of junction with A55.
Restrictions No smoking: restaurant, 3 bedrooms. No children under 8. Dogs in cottages/parkland only (not in gardens).
Credit cards Access, Amex, Visa.
Terms [1997] Rooms: single £85–£95, double £125–£135, suite £145–£155. Breakfast £10.50. D,B&B £86–£100 per person. Set lunch £14.50–£15.50, dinner £27.50–£36; full alc £35. Special breaks; Christmas package. *V*

If you are recommending a bed-and-breakfast hotel and know of a good restaurant nearby, please mention it in your report.

St Tudno Hotel   *Tel* (01492) 874411
The Promenade   *Fax* (01492) 860407
Llandudno LL30 2LP
♢ *César award in 1987*

Martin and Janette Bland's Grade II listed house is on the seafront of
this attractive Victorian seaside resort. It has a Victorian-style decor:
lounges with much drapery, potted plants, and patterned wallpaper;
bedrooms with lots of frills and pastel colours – also fresh milk for tea,
iced water, and sweets on pillows at night. The best rooms are in the
front, overlooking the promenade. There is a new suite this year,
named for Alice Liddell, of Lewis Carroll fame, who holidayed here in
1861. Some rooms are small – "the hotel's limited size," one visitor
wrote, "is part of its charm." There is praise for the modern British
cooking with a Welsh emphasis and classic French influences, served
in the pretty, garden-style restaurant: "beautifully cooked and presented"; "wonderful seafood"; "thoroughly enjoyable, due both to the
pleasant, attentive and enthusiastic staff, and to the flexibility of choice
– you can mix and match between a daily and a 'gourmet' menu. A nice
touch was the proprietor's selection of wines from the excellent list,
rather than the more customary house wines." There is good family
accommodation, and a small indoor swimming pool. Parking can be
difficult, but the staff will help. Bodnant garden, Conwy, Caernarfon
and Penrhyn castles, and Plas Newydd, the home of the Marquess of
Anglesey, are nearby. (*Ann and Norman Leece, AJ, and others*)

Open All year.
Rooms 1 suite, 17 double, 2 single. 1 on ground floor.
Facilities Lift. Sitting room, coffee lounge, lounge bar (harpist Sat evening),
restaurant; small indoor swimming pool; 2 patios. Sandy beach 60 yds.
Unsuitable for severely &.
Location Central, opposite pier. Secure carpark, garaging.
Restrictions No smoking: dining room, sitting room. No very young children in
restaurant at night. "Well-behaved dogs only", not in public rooms, unattended
in bedrooms.
Credit cards All major cards accepted.
Terms B&B: single £70–£90; double £90–£160, suite £230; D,B&B £74.50–£144.50
per person. Set lunch £16.50, dinner £23–£29.50. Bar lunches. Mid-week, weekend, off-season, Christmas, New Year breaks. 1-night bookings occasionally
refused bank holidays.

LLANFIHANGEL CRUCORNEY Monmouthshire   **Map 3**

Penyclawdd Court   *Tel* (01873) 890719
Llanfihangel Crucorney   *Fax* (01873) 890848
nr Abergavenny NP7 7LB

A Wolsey Lodge, owned by Julia Evans and Ken Peacock, reached up
a bumpy track at the foot of Bryn Arw mountain, in the Brecon Beacons
National Park. It is a Grade II* listed Tudor manor house, "oozing
antiquity, with beams, original panelling, crooked walls and sloping
floors". The grounds contain a listed Norman motte and bailey, a traditional herb garden and a knot garden. The quality of the restoration
has been recognised by awards from the Prince of Wales and others.
Heating is beneath the flagstone floor, so no need for radiators. There's

no electricity in the dining room – dinner and breakfast are served by candlelight. Tudor feasts are sometimes held. Lots of oxblood-red paint in the public areas, which our inspectors found gloomy. "But our bedroom, the Granary, up a steep, winding stone staircase, was a pleasant surprise: cream paint, low beams, beds cleverly contrived from church pews (with the prayerbook rests full of books and magazines), TV, and modern bathroom (but no shower). The Oak Room has an open fireplace and a free-standing bath. Dinner, at 8 pm – good home cooking – was communally served; we sat on excruciatingly hard benches; lighting was by candles in a black wrought iron coronet overhead, dripping wax. It was very dark, but we enjoyed talking to our fellow guests. Breakfast, served between 8.30 and 9 am, included good cooked items and home-made marmalade. Friendly owner; all very informal. The setting is deeply peaceful. Wonderful walking all around." More reports, please.

Open All year.
Rooms 3 double. No telephone.
Facilities Lounge, dining room. 6-acre grounds: Norman motte and bailey, herb and knot gardens, maze. Walking, biking, pony-trekking nearby. Unsuitable for &.
Location 4 miles NE of Abergavenny. Turn off A465 on to Old Hereford Road, signed Pantgelli; cross railway line. Drive 2nd right, between Victorian house and modern bungalow (follow B&B sign). Train: Abergavenny; then taxi.
Restrictions No smoking: bedrooms. No children under 12. No dogs.
Credit cards Access, Visa.
Terms [1997] B&B: single £45, double £70; D,B&B: single £65, double £117. Set dinner £22. Christmas, New Year breaks; 2-night midweek breaks Nov–Mar. 1-night bookings refused bank holidays.

LLANGAMMARCH WELLS Powys   Map 3

The Lake   *Tel* (01591) 620202
Llangammarch Wells LD4 4BS   *Fax* (01591) 620457
♦ *César award in 1992*

"Epitomises how country hotels should be run." "Excellent and welcoming. Young and enthusiastic staff. Lovely light rooms, with a beautiful view and nuthatches scurrying up and down the tree outside." "Atmosphere and courteous service hard to beat. Food extremely good. I was impressed to find a credit note when I got home as they had forgotten to offset the GHG voucher – characteristic, and much-appreciated, honesty." Recent praise (there is just one demur) for Jean-Pierre and Jan Mifsud's half-timbered turn-of-the-century purpose-built hotel, set in large grounds with plenty of wildlife, above lawns that slope down to a river. You can walk along the banks by fields with sheep or to the well-stocked trout lake. Bedrooms and suites, though not large, are well insulated and uncluttered, with chintzy canopied or four-poster beds, sherry and fruit. Rooms are serviced during dinner; morning tea is brought up. A "sumptuous" afternoon tea is served in a huge lounge with deep sofas and armchairs, a log fire, a gently ticking clock, and photographs and magazines (one guest found its light too dim for reading). The large dining room, with candlelit tables at night, serves modern English/French cooking by Richard Arnold, with plenty of choice; some ingredients are organically produced locally. "The cheeseboard is worth a detour; the wine list is of exceptional variety, quality and value." Generous Welsh breakfasts include "wonderful toast made from thick slices of home-made bread". Red kites are sometimes seen in the area. (*Michael and Maureen Heath, Ben Bradshaw, Bruce Douglas-Mann; also Jane Pullee, and others*)

Open All year.
Rooms 10 suites, 9 double. 1 on ground floor.
Facilities Ramp. 2 lounges, bar, billiard room, restaurant. 50-acre grounds: tennis, 9-hole par 3 golf course. Riding, pony-trekking, golf, rivers, fishing (tuition available) nearby.
Location 8 miles SW of Builth Wells. From A483 Builth–Llandovery follow signs to Llangammarch Wells, then to hotel. Train: Swansea/Shrewsbury, then scenic Heart of Wales line to Llangammarch Wells; guests will be met.
Restrictions No smoking: restaurant, some bedrooms. No children under 7 in dining room after 7.30 pm (high tea provided). No dogs in public rooms.
Credit cards All major cards accepted.
Terms B&B: single £80–£130, double £125–£136, suite £157–£190; D,B&B (min. 2 days) £91–£123 per person. Set lunch £16.50, dinner £28.50. Winter breaks; Christmas, New Year breaks. *V*

LLANSANFFRAID GLAN CONWY Conwy   Map 3

The Old Rectory   *Tel* (01492) 580611
Llanrwst Road   *Fax* (01492) 584555
Llansanffraid Glan Conwy
nr Conwy LL28 5LF

Q *César award in 1994*

This sophisticated Georgian house stands in carefully tended grounds up a steep drive, with glorious views over the Conwy estuary towards Snowdonia. It has garnered much admiration from *Guide* readers over the years: "A lovely old building with superb antique and repro furniture, pictures, family photos, lots of bric-à-brac and beautiful flowers." "Michael and Wendy Vaughan, the kindly, thoughtful hosts, work hard to achieve a perfect balance. The atmosphere is quiet and calm." This is one of only two establishments in Wales with a red "Meals" in *Michelin*, for the quality of Mrs Vaughan's cooking, and her "brilliant use of local produce", and in 1997 she was the first woman in Wales to be nominated a World Master Chef. The no-choice menu, served at 8 pm, may be taken communally at a long mahogany table, but there are separate tables for those who wish to dine alone. The good wine list includes a wide selection of half bottles. After dinner, guests may socialise in the pine-panelled drawing room, or play cards or chess.

The place has a strong Welsh atmosphere, and the Vaughans are knowledgeable about Welsh history and culture. The bedrooms (some are a little small) are luxuriously kitted out, and fresh fruit and bottled water are renewed each day; some have a four-poster or a half-tester bed. Breakfasts include freshly squeezed orange juice and Welsh rarebit made with Welsh ale. Bodnant gardens are just down the road, and there is a clutch of castles – Conwy, Caernarfon, Beaumaris, Rhuddlan and Denbigh – within 25 miles. The Conwy Estuary Bird Sanctuary and three championship golf courses are close by. More reports, please.

Open 1 Feb–30 Nov. Dining room closed for lunch, occasionally for dinner (guests warned when booking).
Rooms 6 double. 2 on ground floor in coach house.
Facilities Lounge, restaurant. 2½-acre grounds. Sea, safe bathing 3 miles; fishing, golf, riding, sailing, dry ski-slope nearby.
Location On A470, ½ mile S of junction with A55. Train: Conwy, 2 miles.
Restrictions No children under 5, except babies under 9 months. Smoking/dogs in coach house only.
Credit cards All major cards accepted.
Terms [1997] D,B&B: single £109–£129, double £179–£189. Set dinner (2/3-course) £25/£29.50. 2-day breaks. 1-night bookings refused high season weekends, bank holidays. *V* (Oct, Nov, Feb, Mar, Apr)

LLANWDDYN Powys   Map 3

Lake Vyrnwy Hotel   NEW   *Tel* (01691) 870692
Llanwddyn SY10 0LY   *Fax* (01691) 870259
                                      E-mail res@lakevyrnwy.com

This substantial late-Victorian half-timbered "Tudor" mansion stands 150 feet above a man-made lake, which was created in 1881 to supply Liverpool with water (it took two years to fill). The views it commands down the four-and-a-half-mile length of the lake are magnificent. The surrounding 24,000 acres of meadow and forest, which include a large RSPB reserve, miles of forest tracks, and an eleven-mile scenic route around the lake for bikers, can be crowded at the weekend. The hotel was dropped from the *Guide* last year following criticisms, but regular correspondents have written enthusiastically: "It was good in 1996, but it is now more professional, with an obliging staff." "A most enjoyable stay. Our large room had a balcony and magnificent view. Dinner was traditional British cooking of a high standard." Some have enjoyed the breakfast, but others thought it "ample, but disappointing, with leathery scrambled eggs". Sporting activities, especially fishing, are a major draw. The large lounges and the restaurant enjoy the stunning view. Off-season Brolly Breaks – "make the most of the winter rain" – include an extra night's free accommodation if you have stayed two. A tavern in the grounds, where light meals are served, is said by some visitors to lack charm. (*Frank Davies, MW Atkinson*)

Open All year.
Rooms 1 suite, 34 double.
Facilities Lift. Drawing room, lounge, cocktail bar, restaurant with conservatory; function facilities; tavern adjacent. 33-acre grounds: sporting rights on 24,000 acres meadow, moorland and forest; 1,100-acre lake for fishing, sailing. Unsuitable for &.
Location At SE corner of Lake Vyrnwy, well signed from Shrewsbury, Oswestry, Welshpool.
Restrictions No smoking in restaurant. No dogs in public rooms.
Credit cards All major cards accepted.
Terms B&B: single £68–£112, double £88–£150; D,B&B (min. 2 nights) single £84–£134, double £115–£186. Set lunch £15.95, dinner £25.50. Off-season, fishing, Christmas, New Year breaks. 1 night bookings refused weekends. *V*

LLANWRTYD WELLS Powys   Map 3

 Carlton House   `BUDGET`   *Tel* (01591) 610248
Dolycoed Road   *Fax* (01591) 610242
Llanwrtyd Wells LD5 4RA

César award: for gastronomic wizardry in the heart of Wales

This old spa town, which claims to be the smallest town in Britain, nestles at the foot of the Cambrian mountains and is a popular base for pony-trekking and mountain-biking. In its centre stands Alan and Mary Ann Gilchrist's restaurant-with-rooms, a solid bow-windowed Edwardian villa. The exterior is somewhat stark but inside the atmosphere is warm and the decor original and stylish, with strong colours and oriental artefacts. Mrs Gilchrist's modern British cooking is served in a small dining room with just six tables. This is one of only three restaurants in Wales to have a *Michelin* red "Meals". "We cannot speak too highly of the food," writes a regular visitor. "Fantastic dishes, crying out to be photographed. Succulent meat; sauces which are out of this world in terms of flavour and artistry. The wine list is well chosen, with good-value New World bottles. Outstanding value." Breakfast includes home-made breads and marmalade, and local honey. Bedrooms are "home-like and quaint" and well-equipped. One at the top is large and light, with a small, elegantly tiled *en suite* bathroom; the suite has a view of the Cambrian mountains. Another guest wrote: "The Gilchrists seem thoroughly to enjoy what they do, and they love mid-Wales. Their enthusiasm is infectious." Devotees of George, the basset hound, will be sorry to hear that he has finally retired, but, says Dr Gilchrist, "an understudy named Cecily is waiting in the wings". Llanwrtyd Wells is at the centre of Wales's red kite country; they can be seen feeding at Gigrin, to the north, or at the RSPB's Dinas Reserve. (*Stephen and Judy Parish, and others; endorsed by Tony Thomas*)

Open All year. Restaurant closed midday.
Rooms 1 suite, 5 double, 1 single. No telephone.
Facilities Lounge, restaurant. Tiny garden. Golf, pony-trekking, riding, mountain biking, birdwatching nearby. Unsuitable for &.
Location Town centre. No private parking. Train: Llanwrtyd Wells is on the scenic Heart of Wales line (Shrewsbury to Swansea).
Restrictions No smoking in restaurant. No dogs in public rooms.
Credit cards Access, Visa.
Terms B&B: single £30, double £56, suite £70. Set dinner £20; full alc £28.50. 2-night breaks: D,B&B from £36; seasonal breaks. *V*

LLYSWEN Powys   Map 3

Llangoed Hall   *Tel* (01874) 754525
Llyswen   *Fax* (01874) 754545
Brecon LD3 0YP   *E-mail* llangoed-hall-co-wales-uk@compuserve.com

♀ *César award in 1990*

This fine 17th-century mansion, redesigned in the 20th century by Sir Clough Williams-Ellis of Portmeirion fame, is set back from a main road, in formal gardens. Behind are lovely views across the river Wye to the Black Mountains. Many country pursuits are available in the area (see next page). The public rooms are impressive: great hall with deep sofas and stone fireplace, morning room with piano, library with snooker table. Owner Sir Bernard Ashley's magnificent collection of pictures is lavishly distributed throughout; antiques and oriental rugs abound. Bedrooms have high ceilings, period furniture (some four-posters), garden views, sherry, mineral water, fruit, splendid bath-rooms. Chef Ben Davies' cooking is "modern British with imaginative use of local ingredients". Breakfasts include local sausages, black pud-ding and laver bread. Some criticisms again this year, of a lack of wel-come and too much emphasis on corporate entertainment. But other reports are enthusiastic: "Faultless. Airy, spacious rooms, with good furniture and outstanding bathrooms. The restaurant fully deserves its *Michelin* star. The whole atmosphere is relaxed, but professional. Not cheap, but you get full value for money." "The best, and best value, of any 'grand' country house hotels we know. Weekend break outstand-ing value." "A dream hotel, with excellent food and service." Tintern Abbey, Chepstow Castle and Raglan Castle are within easy reach, as is Hay-on-Wye, and there's fine walking in the Black Mountains and the Brecon Beacons nearby. (*SP Edwards, P Fisher, and others*)

Open All year.
Rooms 3 suites, 18 double, 2 single.
Facilities Ramps. 2 lounges, garden room, orangery, dining room, billiard room. 17-acre grounds: tennis, croquet. River Wye 200 yds: fishing (ghillie). Riding, golf, gliding, clay pigeon-shooting, canoeing nearby. Not suitable for &.
Location On A470, 1 mile N of Llyswen.
Restrictions No smoking in dining room. No children under 8. No dogs in house (heated kennels in grounds).
Credit cards All major cards accepted.
Terms B&B: single £100, double £155–£195, suite £195–£285; D,B&B: £60–£165 per person. Set lunch £17, dinner £29.50; full alc £42. 2-day breaks; Christmas, New Year house parties. 1-night bookings refused weekends 1 May–31 Oct. *V*

MUMBLES Swansea   Map 3

Hillcrest House   BUDGET   *Tel* (01792) 363700
1 Higher Lane   *Fax* (01792) 363768
Mumbles, Swansea SA3 4NS

*On edge of Swansea, convenient for visiting Gower peninsula, quirky estab-lishment with Scottish hostess, Yvonne Scott, and international flavour. Themed bedrooms, eg Wales (with mining memorabilia), Scotland (tartan decor). Adequate, if not gourmet food; reasonably priced wines; obtrusive back-ground music during dinner and breakfast. 6 bedrooms; some overlook busy road (effective double-glazing). Terrace, small garden. Beaches, golf, tennis nearby. Closed Christmas week. Unsuitable for &. No smoking in restaurant. No dogs. Access, Amex, Visa accepted. B&B: single £45–£50, double £63–£80. Set dinner £14.95–£17. No recent reports; we'd like some, please. *V*

****

Traveller's gripe Why do so few hotels provide space for two suitcases in a double room? Neither a second luggage stand, nor a flat surface.

****

NANTGWYNANT Gwynedd   Map 3

Pen-y-Gwryd Hotel   BUDGET   *Tel* (01286) 870211
Nantgwynant
Llanberis LL55 4NT

꙳ *César award in 1995*

Brian and Jane Pullee's hotel, in an isolated position near the foot of the
Llanberis Pass in the heart of the Snowdonia National Park, is famous
among mountaineers. In 1953, Hunt and Hillary and most of the
Everest team stayed here before flying to Nepal. Nine pairs of well-
worn boots, relics of famous climbs, hang from the ceiling of the public snug; the slate-floored climbers' bar doubles as a rescue post. It is
well equipped for walkers and fishermen, too. No frills, but bedrooms
are adequate and comfortable; five were recently given *en suite* facilities, and there are five public bathrooms, some with a massive old bath.
There is a panelled lounge for residents, spartanly furnished, perhaps,
but with a blazing log fire. The large games room with pool, bar billiards, etc, is good for younger guests. Outside, among the trees, there
is a natural spring-fed pool, and a sauna, The chef, Lena Jensen, from
Jutland, produces five-course dinners – "wholesome, tasty, plentiful
and hot" – announced by a gong at 7.30 pm. "Unique hospitality," one
visitor has written. "The Pullees draw you into their family; no TV, but
convivial evenings in the bar." The "charming young staff", the breakfasts – "no portion control" – and the cream teas on the lawn are all
admired. Prices are "incredibly low". More reports, please.

Open Mar–early Nov, New Year, weekends Jan/Feb.
Rooms 15 double, 1 single. 4 with bath, 1 with shower. 1 ground-floor room in
annexe (with four-poster).
Facilities Lounge, bar, smoke room, games room, dining room. 2-acre grounds:
natural swimming pool, sauna. River/lake fishing nearby.
Location On A498 Beddgelert–Capel Curig, at junction with A4086. Local buses,
frequent in summer.
Restriction No smoking in dining room, discouraged in bedrooms.
Credit cards None accepted.
Terms B&B £20–£25. Bar, packed lunch from £4. Set dinner £15. 1-night bookings
occasionally refused weekends.

NEWPORT Pembrokeshire   Map 3

Cnapan   BUDGET   *Tel* (01239) 820575
East Street   *Fax* (01239) 820878
Newport, nr Fishguard SA42 0SY

A pink listed restaurant-with-rooms in an attractive small town (not to
be confused with Newport in Gwent) in the Pembrokeshire Coast
National Park, and close to the coast. Here, John and Eluned Lloyd and
their daughter and son-in-law, Judith and Michael Cooper, dispense
innovative evening meals, accompanied by a good wine list (mother
and daughter are the chefs). For a set price, residents choose items from
the extensive *carte*, which includes plenty of vegetarian dishes. The
place has a homely style: a traditional Welsh dresser, crowded with
family treasures, stands in the hall; a woodburning stove burns in the
guests' sitting room; books and local information are everywhere. Each

of the "comfortably cluttered" bedrooms has a shower, but guests wanting a good soak may avail themselves of the massive bath along the corridor. Huge breakfasts, with home-made bread, set you up for the day. In summer, drinks and tea are served in the sheltered garden. "Wonderful value for money," our correspondents have written. "The proprietors get the balance between friendliness and reserve right." The road in front of the house is busy by day. There's good coastal path walking nearby. More reports, please.

Open Mar–Dec. Restaurant closed Tues.
Rooms 5 double. No telephone.
Facilities Lounge, bar, restaurant. Small garden. 10 mins' walk to sea; fishing, birdwatching, pony-trekking, golf, boating nearby. Unsuitable for &.
Location Centre of small town (quiet at night). Private parking. Train: Haverfordwest/Fishguard.
Restrictions No smoking: restaurant, bedrooms. No dogs.
Credit cards Access, Visa.
Terms B&B £26; D,B&B £42. Full alc £21.50. 1-night bookings occasionally refused.

PENMACHNO Conwy   Map 3

Penmachno Hall   NEW/BUDGET   *Tel* (01690) 760207

Victorian ex-rectory, quiet and beautifully situated (wooded hillside, water-falls), on edge of village in Snowdonia National Park, 4 miles SE of Betws-y-Coed. Friendly, idiosyncratic owners, Ian and Modwena Cutler, offer communal hospitality on their own terms. 4 large bedrooms, with wide choice of books, some risqué. No telephone/TV. Excellent no-choice dinners around refectory table – "just like a meal with way-out friends," wrote inspectors. Good-value wine list. Free tea/coffee always available. Piped music at times – can be obtrusive. 2½-acre grounds. Closed Christmas, New Year. No smoking: dining room, bedrooms. Access, Visa accepted. B&B £25–£30. Set lunch £10, dinner £15. Weekend breaks: D,B&B (2 nights) £87.

PENMAENPOOL Gwynedd   Map 3

George III   NEW   *Tel* (01341) 422525
Penmaenpool   *Fax* (01341) 423565
Dolgellau LL40 1YD

John and Julia Cartwright's hotel, 1 mile W of Dolgellau, between old railway and Mawddach estuary. "Magnificent views. Historic atmosphere of toll-roads, sea, river and railways." 12 bedrooms, 6 in lodge, part of old Victorian station; most face estuary. Good bar food in Cellar Bar, popular with tourists, walkers, fishermen, locals. Straightforward cooking in upstairs dining room; local produce, old-fashioned puddings. Extensive wine list. Birdwatching (RSPB centre adjacent), pony trekking, fishing. Bicycle hire. Closed 25 Dec. No smoking: Cellar Bar before 9.30 pm, dining room. No dogs: dining room, residents' lounge. Access, Visa accepted. B&B: £44–£50; D,B&B: £58–£62. Set lunch (Sun) £11.95; full alc £27. Child sharing parents' room: B&B £12.50. More reports, please.

Give the *Guide* positive support. Don't leave feedback to others.

PORTHKERRY Vale of Glamorgan   **Map 3**

Egerton Grey   *Tel* (01446) 711666
Porthkerry, nr Cardiff CF62 3BZ   *Fax* (01446) 711690
                               E-mail info@egertongrey.co.uk

A 19th-century rectory, full of country charm, with ornate mouldings,
acres of beautiful panelling, antiques, porcelain, paintings, and a collection of old clocks. It stands in a wooded valley 20 minutes' drive
from Cardiff, looking towards the Somerset coast over Porthkerry Park
and the Bristol Channel, and though near the airport, is generally
peaceful. It is stylishly run by the owners, Anthony and Magda Pitkin,
with a courteous staff, and the welcome has been universally praised
this year. "Superb balance between professionalism and friendliness;
help was always at hand if needed, but in a quiet efficient way."
"Hospitality simply excellent, not over-fussy, but always appropriate."
The spacious bedrooms have bold colour schemes, antiques, thick carpets, and carefully restored Edwardian bathrooms, some with enormous tubs. A nice touch is the placing of guests' names on their door.
Menus offer a choice of elaborate dishes, and Craig Brookes's cooking
is admired by most visitors. Excellent cheeseboard. Good wine list.
Lots of interesting choices for breakfast. The hotel is licensed for wed-
dings. It is only a short drive to the Gower Peninsula or Caerphilly
Castle. (*Squadron Ldr DA Wood, BB Woodham, and others*)

Open All year.
Rooms 2 suites, 7 double, 1 single.
Facilities Drawing room, library, loggia, restaurant (piped classical music); pri-
vate dining room, function facilities. 3½-acre garden: croquet, tennis. Beach
200 yds; golf nearby. Only restaurant suitable for &.
Location 10 miles SW of Cardiff. From M4 exit 33 follow signs to airport, by-
passing Barry. Left at small roundabout by airport, signposted Porthkerry; after
500 yds left again, down lane between thatched cottages. Train: Barry, 3 miles.
Restrictions No smoking in dining room. No dogs in public rooms.
Credit cards All major cards accepted.
Terms [1997] B&B: single £60–£75, double £90, suite £120; D,B&B: single £82–£97,
double £96–£120, suite £120–£145. Set lunch/dinner £18–£25.50. 3-day Christmas
break. *V*

PORTMEIRION Gwynedd   **Map 3**

Hotel Portmeirion   *Tel* (01766) 770228
Portmeirion LL48 6ET   *Fax* (01766) 771331
                            E-mail hotel@portmeirion.wales.com

𝒬 *César award in 1990*

"The village is an italianate gem in a verdant Welsh setting. The hotel
is a centre of charm and comfort, its decor nostalgically reminiscent of
the Raj." "A magical place." So write recent visitors to Sir Clough
Williams-Ellis's fantasy village, set on the steep hillside of a sheltered
wooded peninsula, above a wide estuary. It is busy with tourists by
day, but the hotel's guests are well protected in Mediterranean-style
gardens with peacocks and a swimming pool, and they have the place
to themselves in the evening. Behind its unpretentious early Victorian
exterior, the hotel is exuberantly decorated with bright fabrics, carved

panels, and furniture and ornaments imported from Rajasthan. It's very Welsh, with bilingual staff, bilingual menus, and live Welsh music (a harpist and a resident bard). The accommodation ranges from lavish suites in the main house to quite simple but well-maintained rooms with old-fashioned bathrooms in houses in the village. The food, in the handsome, curvilinear dining room, is modern Welsh. Service is friendly, but can be slow at busy times (package tours are sometimes catered for). Breakfast includes fresh fruit and a good choice of cooked

dishes. There are miles of paths along the headland, leading through the woods to coves and sandy beaches. The great mountains of Snowdonia are within easy reach, as are the castles of Caernarfon, Harlech, Criccieth and Dolwyddelan. (*Mrs Sian Williams, Denis W Tate, and others*)

Open All year, except 11 Jan–6 Feb. Restaurant closed Mon midday, except bank holidays.
Rooms 9 suites, 28 double. 23 in village. Some on ground floor. Also self-catering cottages. Not really suitable for &.
Facilities Hall, 2 lounges, 2 bars, restaurant, children's supper room; function room. 120-acre grounds: garden, swimming pool (heated May–Sept), tennis, lakes, sandy beach. Free golf at Porthmadog Golf Club.
Location SW of Penrhyndeudraeth, SE of Porthmadog, off A487 at Minffordd. Street parking.
Restrictions No smoking: restaurant, 1 lounge. No dogs in village.
Credit cards All major cards accepted.
Terms [1997] B&B double £98–£153, suite £113–£193. Set lunch £13.50, dinner £26.50. Christmas, New Year, 2-day breaks.

PWLLHELI Gwynedd   Map 3

Plas Bodegroes   NEW   *Tel* (01758) 612363
Nefyn Road, Pwllheli LL53 5TH   *Fax* (01758) 701247

In 1994, Chris and Gunna Chown put their *Michelin*-starred restaurant-with-rooms (its name is pronounced "Bod-egg-royce") on the market. They did not sell, however, so decided to stay. Though they also own the famous *Hole in the Wall* in Bath, they are mainly based in Wales. They have carried out a major refurbishment: some of the smaller bedrooms have been enlarged, there are new ones in a cottage at the rear, overlooking a new courtyard garden, and the old Georgian building has been given a Scandinavian interior (Mrs Chown is Faroese). "One of the nicest places I have stayed in for some years," wrote an inspector. "The effect is understated in an attractive way. The setting is in wooded grounds is beautiful and blissfully quiet. We were greeted by the elegant Mrs Chown, who served us tea and buttered bara brith in the pretty sitting room. Our attic room was small and less attractive than the ones on lower floors, but it was comfortable enough. Service was outstanding throughout." The lounge is quite small too, and can get crowded with non-resident diners. The restaurant is decorated in shades of green, with crisp white linen, but one guest thought the lighting a little harsh, and meals can be a let-down when Chris Chown himself is not cooking. Breakfast is "excellent, with plenty of choice, delicious Greek yogurt and apricots, properly cooked hot dishes, and a selection of newspapers. Pwllheli is the main town of the southern shore of the Lleyn Peninsula, which, with its rocky shores, cliffs and beaches, and small villages and farms inland, separates Caernarfon Bay from Ceredigion (Cardigan) Bay. More reports, please.

Open 1 Mar–1 Dec. Closed Mon, except bank holidays.
Rooms 10 double (2 in annexe), 1 single.
Facilities Lounge, bar, breakfast room, restaurant (occasional piped jazz/classical music). 6-acre grounds. Safe, sandy beach 1 mile. Golf nearby. Unsuitable for &.
Location 1 mile W of Pwllheli, on A497 to Nefyn. Train: Pwllheli; then taxi.
Restrictions No smoking: restaurant, bedrooms. Dogs by arrangement.
Credit cards Access, Amex, Visa.
Terms [1997] B&B £45–£75; D,B&B £70–£100. Single supplement £20. Full alc £39.50. 1-night bookings sometimes refused bank holidays. *V*

REYNOLDSTON Swansea   **Map 3**

Fairyhill   *Tel* (01792) 390139
Reynoldston, nr Swansea SA3 1BS   *Fax* (01792) 391358

This 18th-century house is peacefully set in large grounds, with woodland, a trout stream and a lake with wild ducks, amid lovely scenery and with easy access to the Gower Heritage Coast. For one 1997 visitor it represents "a benchmark" for other hotels: "A super place to unwind. There is always a very personal welcome. They have done wonders with the decor." One couple this year complained of a sub-standard bedroom, but others have been enthusiastic: "It combines the efficient atmosphere of a well-staffed establishment with the informality of a family-run hotel. Andrew Hetherington (co-owner with Jane and Peter Camm, and Paul Davies, the chef) is an excellent front-of-house *patron*, friendly, helpful and efficient. Our good-size bedroom had a lovely view and a CD player; there is a huge library of discs downstairs." The carefully cooked modern British food served in the green-and-yellow restaurant is generally much admired, though one visitor considered it expensive, and outside diners can detract from the ambience. The award-winning wine list includes many reasonably priced bottles. There's a leafy patio for alfresco drinks and tea, and a cosy bar. (*Mrs C Wright, Stephen and Judy Parish; also Anne-Marie Sutcliffe, and others*)

Open All year, except 25/26 Dec.
Rooms 8 double.
Facilities Lounge, bar, 2 dining rooms (piped classical music). 24-acre grounds: croquet, woodland, stream, lake. Beaches, water sports nearby. Unsuitable for &.
Location 11 miles W of Swansea. M4 exit 47 to Gowerton; then B4295 for 9 miles.
Restrictions No smoking in restaurant. No children under 8, except at lunch. No dogs in public rooms.
Credit cards Access, Amex, Visa.
Terms [1997] B&B £42.50–£75. Set lunch £14.50, dinner £29.50. 2-day breaks. 1-night bookings refused Sat in Aug.

Report forms (Freepost in UK) are at the end of the *Guide*.

RHYDGALED Ceredigion Map 3

Conrah Country House *Tel* (01970) 617941
Rhydgaled, Chancery *Fax* (01970) 624546
nr Aberystwyth SY23 4DF

Fine country house with 20th-century extensions, up long drive in 22-acre rolling grounds with woods, fine views, just outside main town of mid Wales. Beautiful gardens; vegetables home-grown for "superb" dinners – traditional/modern cooking, fine cheeseboard. Bar snacks Mon–Sat. Excellent breakfast, with Welsh delicacies. Impeccable service. 3 attractive lounges. 20 bedrooms of varying size: 11, traditional, in main house; more modern ones, much less attractive, on ground level, round courtyard. Indoor swimming pool, sauna; croquet, table tennis. 3½ miles S of Aberystwyth on A487 coast road. River ½ mile, sea 3½ miles. Closed Christmas week. Unsuitable for &. No smoking in restaurant. No children under 5. No dogs. All major credit cards accepted. B&B: single £61–£71, double £88–£110; D,B&B (min. 2 nights): single £78–£88, double £120–£140. Set lunch and dinner £23.50–£29.50 [1997]. More reports, please.

TALSARNAU Gwynedd Map 3

Maes-y-Neuadd *Tel* (01766) 780200
Talsarnau LL47 6YA *Fax* (01766) 780211
E-mail myn@marketsite.co.uk

"Like arriving in Shangri-La. Friendly hosts, excellent service, lovely bedroom. Tea on the patio was a treat." "Beautiful building, beautiful views, professional and friendly owners, immaculate housekeeping, extensive though pricey wine-list, outstanding breakfast and wonderful people-free walking nearby." With one demur from a returning visitor who felt "a loss of spontaneity among the staff", there is praise again this year for this grey granite-and-slate mansion, 14th-century in origin, with 16th- and 17th-century extensions. Owned and run by two couples, the Horsfalls and the Slatters, it stands amid lawns, orchards and paddocks, on a wooded hillside with glorious views across to the Snowdonia National Park. The approach is by a narrow lane up a one-in-five hill. Inside are oak beams, decorated plasterwork, good antique and modern furniture, and a bar with an inglenook fireplace. Bedrooms vary greatly in style and size; some have pine furniture, others antiques; three have a spa bath. Some are in the main house; others in a converted coach house. In the panelled dining room, with service by young men and women, mostly French, guests may choose three or five courses, and ask for a simpler treatment of some dishes if they prefer it. Opinion differs on the cooking of chef Peter Jackson. "A memorable treat, especially Diweddglo Mawreddog (the grand finale – a four-part dessert)," one couple wrote. But another felt there was "an element of overkill", and that "the menus promise more than they deliver". June Slatter also runs "Steam and Cuisine", a weekly dining service on the narrow gauge Rheilffordd Ffestiniog steam railway. The Royal St David's golf course, Harlech Castle, and Portmeirion are nearby. (*MJA Lewis, and others*)

Open All year.
Rooms 2 suites, 13 double, 1 single. 4 in coach house 10 yds. 3 on ground floor.

Facilities Exterior lift, ramps. Lounge, bar, conservatory, 2 dining rooms; terrace. 7½-acre grounds: croquet, orchard, paddock. Sea, golf, riding, sailing, fishing, climbing nearby.
Location 3 miles NE of Harlech, signposted off B4573. ½ mile up narrow, steep lane. Train: Harlech/Blaenau Ffestiniog; hotel will meet.
Restrictions No smoking in restaurant. No children under 8 in dining room at night. Dogs by prior arrangement only; not in public rooms.
Credit cards All major cards accepted.
Terms [1997] D,B&B: single £65–£76, double £135–£209, suite £161–£201. Set lunch £13.75, dinner (3/5-course) £24/£31. 2-night breaks all year; 3-day breaks Nov–Mar. Christmas, New Year packages. 1-night bookings refused bank holidays. *V*

TALYLLYN Gwynedd   Map 3

Minfford Hotel   BUDGET   *Tel* (01654) 761665
Talyllyn, Tywyn LL36 9AJ   *Fax* (01654) 761517

"A wonderful place. It bridges the gap between top B&B and country house. Rooms, though not large, are delightful and beautifully kept; Mary McQuillan and Mark Warner are even more delightful hosts, willing, helpful, friendly and warm in a way that escapes professional hotel-keepers; Aga-cooked food plainish but delicious; wine good and very cheap. When we got soaked on Cader Idris, Mary bore off all the wet clothes at night and returned them, dried and laundered. Satisfaction guaranteed to anyone you send." "Bedrooms were spotless, towels and sheets changed every second day, water always hot, excellent early morning tea facilities." Recent encomiums for this rambling 300-year-old drovers' inn which has retained its old-world atmosphere alongside 20th-century comfort. It has a glorious setting at the head of the Dysynni valley; flocks of sheep graze in the surrounding fields. The footpath to the top of Cader Idris starts by its front gate. It is not for the misanthrope: the smallness of the public rooms makes socialising inevitable, although there are "private little corners for the dinner tables". Excellent breakfasts, too. (*David Lipsey, Mrs MM Church; also J Rudd and others*)

Open Mar–end Nov, weekends only, Nov. Restaurant closed for lunch.
Rooms 6 double. 3 on ground floor. No TV.
Facilities Sun lounge, parlour, bar, dining room; drying facilities. 4-acre grounds: garden, paddock, river, fishing. Golf, shooting, lake with fishing, sailing, nearby. Unsuitable for &.
Location 8 miles S of Dolgellau; at junction of A487 and B4405. Train: Machynlleth, 6 miles; then taxi, or owner will fetch if not too busy.
Restrictions Smoking in lounge bar only. No children under 5. Guide dogs only.
Credit cards Access, Visa.
Terms [1997] D,B&B £47.50–£65 (B&B terms by arrangement). Set dinner £18.95. Packed lunches available. Off-season breaks. *V*

THREE COCKS Powys   Map 3

Three Cocks Hotel   *Tel/Fax* (01497) 847215
Three Cocks, nr Brecon LD3 0SL

This 15th-century inn, built around a tree that is still visible in one of its lounges, is a restaurant-with-rooms in a village on the A438, close to the river Wye. It has a cobbled forecourt, ivy-clad walls, worn steps, great oak beams and a small flowery garden. The owners, Michael Winstone (the chef) and his Belgian wife, Marie-Jeanne (front-of-house), previously ran a restaurant in Belgium. There's a continental accent to the decor of the spacious dining room, with lace table cloths, a massive French *armoire*, and tapestries on the stone walls. Here, "one of the best restaurant meals we have had in ages" was eaten by recent visitors. "Classic cooking at its non-fussy best. Delicious bass in a herb sauce. Those who chose the succulent duck and lamb were offered a second helping. Puddings were light and lovely. Service was quiet and efficient." Others wrote: "Tables are well spaced, the menu varied each day. Vegetables were inventive and superb. Breakfasts were delicious, cooked to order. Our room and bathroom were small (we were warned in advance) but comfortable, with an attractive Welsh wardrobe, and without TV, which we liked. The half-board package was very good value." Bread is freshly baked. There is an "excellent French wine list, fairly priced", and a good choice of Belgian beers. The Brecon Beacons National Park, with wonderful walking, is close by; so is the great second-hand book centre of Hay-on-Wye. (*CR, Kate Davey and Gareth Hughes, Prof. G Jones, and others*)

Open Mid-Feb–end Nov. Restaurant closed Tues, midday Sun.
Rooms 7 double. No telephone/TV.
Facilities 2 lounges, TV lounge, breakfast room, restaurant (piped classical music on quiet evenings). ½-acre grounds. Golf, canoeing, riding, fishing nearby. Unsuitable for &.
Location 5 miles SW of Hay-on-Wye on A438 Hereford–Brecon. Rear rooms quietest. Large carpark. Local buses.
Restriction No dogs.
Credit cards Access, Visa.
Terms [1997] B&B: single £40–£65, double £65; D,B&B double (min. 2 nights) £99–£117. Set lunch/dinner £27; full alc £35.

TINTERN Monmouthshire   Map 3

Parva Farmhouse   *Tel* (01291) 689411
Tintern, nr Chepstow NP6 6SQ   *Fax* (01291) 689557

"Friendly and helpful; lovely meals; good service." "Very good value." Recent praise for this unpretentious old creepered stone building, bedecked with flowers in hanging baskets and tubs. It is set in compact grounds beside a small church above an oxbow of the river Wye, a mile from the famous ruined abbey. The comfortable beamed lounge has a wood-burning stove, an honesty bar, and lots of board games; some think it is too dimly lit. There's a huge inglenook fireplace in the restaurant, which has been refurbished this year; the four-course dinner, prepared by chef/proprietor Dereck Stubbs, includes traditional Welsh dishes, and the wine list features Parva wine, made from local grapes. There is a good traditional breakfast. Vickie Stubbs is "very much in evidence, helpful and friendly, but never pushy". The "simple but charming" bedrooms vary in size; some are good for a family. They have tea-making facilities, muted TV, and river or garden views. There is a busy road nearby, but most rooms face away from it. Castles, ruins and ancient monuments and Offa's Dyke are nearby, and there are miles of footpaths; Forestry Commission wardens conduct guided walks most weekends. (*Leslie M Case, Perdita Burlingame, and others*)

Open All year.
Rooms 3 family, 6 double.
Facilities Lounge with honesty bar, restaurant (piped classical music). Small lawn alongside river. Fishing, golf, riding, shooting nearby. Unsuitable for &.
Location At N end of village, just off A466 Chepstow–Monmouth. Train: Chepstow, 5 miles; local buses.
Restrictions No smoking in dining room.
Credit cards Access, Amex, Visa.
Terms [1997] B&B £45–£64; D,B&B (min. 2 nights) £55–£99. Set dinner £17.50. Special breaks; 2 nights for price of 1 Oct–end Mar; weekly rates. 1-night bookings occasionally refused. Children under 12 accommodated free in parents' room. ***V***

WHITEBROOK Monmouthshire   **Map 3**

The Crown at Whitebrook   *Tel* (01600) 860254
Whitebrook, Monmouth NP5 4TX   *Fax* (01600) 860607

"Our fourth visit in five years. As good as ever in all respects. The atmosphere is cheerful, the decor unprotentious and in keeping with the general feel of the place. Our dinners were faultless and cooked to perfection, from the canapés to the petits fours." A 1997 accolade for this restaurant-with-rooms, an extended and modernised 17th-century inn, with "exceptionally friendly hosts", Sandra and Roger Bates. It is peacefully set in a steeply wooded valley near the river Wye, a designated area of outstanding natural beauty. Bedrooms are on the small side, but they are well equipped, with comfortable beds and good bedside lights; the best one has a four-poster and a whirlpool bath. In contrast with the decor, Sandra Bates' cooking, served in the beamed restaurant, is sophisticated, with a strong French accent. Dishes, using "the best of Welsh ingredients", are accompanied by wines from "an excellent list, with good descriptions and helpful guidance from Roger Bates". "Breakfast has everything one could wish for, properly cooked; plenty of choice, lots of coffee and, above all, fresh hot toast." "No matter how busy he is, Roger Bates always finds time to chat and to check on detail. Very good value for money." There's excellent walking all around – the Wye Valley and Offa's Dyke footpaths are within a mile. A good base for visiting Tintern Abbey, Chepstow, and Raglan and Goodrich castles. (*RL and HJ Marks, and others*)

Open All year, except Christmas, 2 weeks Jan, 2 weeks Aug.
Rooms 12 double. 1 on ground floor.
Facilities Lounge, bar, restaurant; function room; terrace. 3-acre garden. Fishing in Wye 1 mile; golf nearby. Unsuitable for &.
Location 5 miles S of Monmouth on unclassified road from A466 and B4293 W of Bigsweir Bridge.
Restrictions No smoking in restaurant. No dogs in public rooms.
Credit cards All major cards accepted.
Terms [1997] B&B £40–£50; D,B&B £60–£75. Set lunch £15.95, dinner £26.95. Midweek, off-season, New Year breaks. ***V***

Don't keep your favourite hotel to yourself. The *Guide* supports; it doesn't spoil.

Scotland

Minmore House, Glenlivet

ABERDEEN *See SHORTLIST*   **Map 5**

ABERFELDY Perthshire and Kinross   **Map 5**

Farleyer House   *Tel* (01887) 820332
Aberfeldy PH15 2JE   *Fax* (01887) 829430
                      E-mail AndyCole@compuserve.com

Aberfeldy has a beautiful stone bridge, built across the Tay, one of Scotland's finest salmon rivers, by the Hanoverian General Wade in 1733. Close by is the impressive Castle Menzies, where Charles Stuart took refuge during the 1745 rebellion. Its white-walled 16th-century dower house is now this smart hotel, which stands in huge grounds with mature trees on a hillside overlooking the valley. "The atmosphere is that of the perfect Scottish country house," wrote winter visitors. "The public rooms are comfortably furnished, and were beautifully warm, despite thick snow outside. The intimate feel made the cost worthwhile." The "young and enthusiastic staff" are admired too: "They are unobtrusively pleasant and helpful." Chef Richard Lyth supervises two restaurants, the smart set-menu, dinner-only *Menzies* – "wonderfully appointed; each of the four courses was perfect" – and the cheaper *Scottish Bistro*, which serves "good regional fare" at reasonable prices. The bedrooms vary considerably; some have antiques and a canopied bed. There are four luxurious new ones in the Keeper's Cottage in the garden, and four simpler ones in the Ghillie's Cottage. There's a "challenging" six-hole golf course in the grounds; *Farleyer*'s residents may use a nearby country club with indoor swimming pool and other sporting and leisure facilities. Devotees of Aberfeldy Malt Whisky enjoy visiting the distillery close by. *(Scott Darby and Mark Tattersall, John C Gillett)*

Open All year. House party only at Christmas.
Rooms 19 double. 4 in Keeper's Cottage, 4 in Ghillie's Cottage (1 adapted for &).
Facilities Drawing room, TV lounge, library, bar, 2 restaurants. 45-acre grounds: garden, croquet, golf, children's playground, woods; opposite river Tay, fishing arranged. Shooting, riding, country club with leisure facilities nearby.
Location From Aberfeldy, take B846 for 2 miles, towards Kinloch Rannoch. Local bus.
Restrictions No smoking in 12 bedrooms. No dogs.
Credit cards All major cards accepted.
Terms B&B £75–£90 per person, D,B&B £95–£110. Full alc: (*Menzies*) £32, (*Scottish Bistro*) £22.50. 2-night breaks. Children under 14 accommodated free in parents' room.

ACHILTIBUIE Highland   Map 5

Summer Isles Hotel   *Tel* (01854) 622282
Achiltibuie   *Fax* (01854) 622251
by Ullapool IV26 2YG
♦ *César award in 1993*

"A hotel apart, in a world apart," writes a regular visitor to Mark and Geraldine Irvine's "seriously addictive haven", on a remote stretch of coast, reached by 15 miles of narrow winding road between mountains and lochs. "We know nowhere else where we relax so completely and feel so much at home. Public rooms are attractive, with a welcome log fire, and splendid views. Guests chat together before, during and after dinner. Chef Chris Firth-Bernard's cooking (red "Meals" in *Michelin*) is a major attraction. The langoustines silence the dining room as guests dismantle them. In winter there is often a hot pudding; in summer, passion fruit sorbet and lemon ice cream. There can be few Scottish hotels with a better cheese trolley, 28 kinds, knowledgeably presented. Breakfasts are equally good: juices, yogurt, artistically arranged fruit, local kippers, home-made bread." Bar meals are also available. The bedrooms vary: some are "comfortable but not luxurious"; those in the log cabins are said to lack charm; some overlook the carpark and have poor sound insulation. Some visitors therefore feel the place is better described as a restaurant-with-rooms. But everyone praises the warmth of welcome and the service. The Gulf Stream means weather can change from Arctic to Aegean inside a week; guests are advised to bring wellingtons, binoculars, paint-boxes and midge cream. The *Hectoria*, a local boat, takes visitors to see seals and rare birds, and the underwater scenery can be explored with the local diving school. (*Margaret Box; also Prof. Robert Cahn*)

Open Easter–mid-Oct.
Rooms Suite (sleeps 2–4), 11 double. 8 in annexe. Some on ground floor. No TV.
Facilities Sitting room, sun lounge, study with TV, 2 bars, dining room. Small garden. Sea 100 yds; beaches, lakes, fly-fishing nearby. Unsuitable for &.
Location NW of Ullapool; after 10 miles turn off A835 on to single-track road skirting lochs Lurgain, Badagyle and Oscaig. Hotel just past village post office, 15 miles. Bus from Ullapool twice daily.
Restrictions No smoking in dining room, discouraged in bedrooms. No children under 6. No dogs in public rooms.
Credit card Access.
Terms B&B: single £50–£72, double £75–£106, suite £156. Bar meals. Set dinner £35. 10% discount for 6 or more nights. High tea for children 6 pm, or half-price at dinner.

ARDUAINE Argyll and Bute   **Map 5**

Loch Melfort Hotel   *Tel* (01852) 200233
Arduaine, by Oban PA34 4XG   *Fax* (01852) 200214
♢ *César award in 1996*

Philip and Rosalind Lewis's white-walled Edwardian hotel on the coast road between Oban and Crinan has a nonpareil position looking towards Jura and Scarba. Most visitors have enjoyed it again this year: "Tranquil, beautiful location. Our room was vast, comfortably furnished with wall-to-wall windows giving on to the view. The Sunday evening seafood buffet is a visual and gastronomic delight, and the dessert trolley is irresistible." "A comfortable and satisfying place to stay." "The Lewises run the hotel with exactly the right mixture of friendliness and professionalism." "Cheerful, courteous staff." The best bedrooms are in the main house (although one of these was this year thought to need redecoration, and some are small, with thin walls). The majority are in the custom-built Cedar Wing, which is good for families. They are comfortable and have their own terrace or balcony, but the sound insulation is poor, particularly on the ground floor. Yapping dogs and "clodhopping" neighbours are frequently mentioned. Philip Lewis's cooking has been much praised, especially his excellent use of local shellfish and seafood. Lunches and suppers "to suit all ages" are served in the bar. Breakfasts are substantial. The hotel's lawn runs down to the water's edge, and passing yachtsmen use its moorings, drying facilities and hot showers. Adjoining is Arduaine Garden (National Trust of Scotland), and 20 other gardens are within easy reach. (*Kay Hickman, John Campbell, Anne Laurence, and others; also Stephen and Ellise Holman, JR Holland, Good Pub Guide*)

Open 23 Feb–5 Jan.
Rooms 26 double. 20 in Cedar Wing. Some on ground floor.
Facilities Ramps. Lounge, bar (piped music), dining room. 20-acre grounds: small sandy beach, fishing, windsurfing.
Location 19 miles S of Oban, on A816. Large carpark. Train: Oban, 19 miles; then taxi.
Restrictions No smoking in dining room. No dogs in main house.
Credit cards Access, Amex, Visa
Terms B&B £35–£64.50; D,B&B £59.50–£82.50. Bar meals. Set dinner from £28.50. Off-season, Christmas, New Year breaks. ***V***

ARDVOURLIE Western Isles   **Map 5**

Ardvourlie Castle   *Tel* (01859) 502307
Aird a Mhulaidh   *Fax* (01859) 502348
Isle of Harris HS3 3AB

More praise this year, from regular *Guide* readers, for this "wonderful
Victorian pile". Built as a shooting lodge rather than as a castle, it
stands on the shores of Loch Seaforth, in the far reaches of the Western
Isles. "An absolute triumph. The quiet, unassuming care and attention
to detail shines out in every respect." "What a delightful experience.
The wonderful brother and sister, Pam and Derek Martin, who run this
place are 'worth a journey'; they are so warm and helpful. Only problem: their gentle over-feeding! Our room was extremely comfortable
and roomy, though we had to walk down the hall to our private bathroom, nearly as large as the bedroom, with the tub in majestic isolation
in the middle." "Our third visit. *Ardvourlie* lived up to all expectations.
It is a blend of traditional Victorian furnishings with modern standards
of comfort. Gas lights in the dining room, open fires in the lounge and
library, lots of hot water. An ideal place to relax after a hard day tramp-
ing the hills. Superb food." No choice on the menu; the traditional
dishes cooked by Derek Martin might include halibut casserole or
steak, and end with brown betty with plums and custard, and unusual
Scottish cheeses. A good base, particularly for wild flower and bird
spotters, and for exploring the mountains and lochs of North Harris on
foot. (*JP Marland, Stephen and Ellise Holman, Mr and Mrs D Scull*)

Open Apr–Oct. Dining room closed to non-residents.
Rooms 4 double. 1 on ground floor. Telephone/tea-making facilities available.
Facilities Lounge with TV, library with piano, dining room. 13-acre grounds.
Sandy beaches, loch and river fishing nearby. Unsuitable for &.
Location Off A859 11 miles NE of Tarbert, 24 miles S of Stornoway. Occasional
buses from both.
Restriction No smoking in restaurant, by arrangement with other guests in
lounges, discouraged in bedrooms. Children must be old enough to dine with
parents. Dogs by arrangement only.
Credit cards None accepted.
Terms D,B&B £75–£85. Children under 12 sharing parents' room half price.

ARISAIG Highland   **Map 5**

Arisaig House   *Tel* (01687) 450622
Beasdale, by Arisaig PH39 4NR   *Fax* (01687) 450626
                              E-mail arisaighse@aol.com

"Our favourite hotel in Scotland," writes a returning *aficionado* of the
Smither family's hotel (Relais & Châteaux), a grand 19th-century
laird's mansion in a wonderful position at the end of one of the most
spectacular roads to the isles. "The food under award-winning Gary
Robinson, ex *Inverlochy Castle* (*qv*) among others, has become outstandingly good, particularly fish. Variety on the dinner menu was well
maintained during a week's stay; appetisers with pre-dinner drinks
were different every night. Breakfasts too are excellent, with a wide
choice, and bar lunches surprisingly reasonably priced." On this most
visitors agree, though others found it "pretentious", and inattentive
restaurant service and dim lighting have also been mentioned. But to a

regular American visitor the hotel is: "As lovely as ever: beautiful old trees, rhododendrons in full bloom, immaculate lawns, public rooms filled with flowers; our pretty blue-and-white room had a wonderful view out to Loch nan Uamh. A superb main course of Barbary duck and guinea fowl in red wine and bacon sauce. Expensive, but worth it for a special occasion – this was our wedding anniversary." The house has an entrance hall with high windows, oriental rugs and a carved oak

staircase, a drawing room with vaulted ceiling and log fire, and a billiard room decorated with college oars. In summer, light lunches and teas are served on a terrace. Bedrooms, priced according to size and view (most are spacious), are traditional; best ones overlook the sea. (*J and D Rednall, Martha Prince, and others*)

Open Easter–end Oct.
Rooms 2 suites, 12 double.
Facilities 3 lounges, lounge bar, billiard room, dining room; meeting room. 20-acre grounds: croquet, helipad. Sea loch 15 mins' walk. Unsuitable for &.
Location On A830 Fort William–Mallaig. 1 mile past Beasdale railway station; 3 miles before Arisaig village.
Restrictions No smoking in restaurant. No children under 10. Guide dogs only.
Credit cards Access, Amex, Visa.
Terms B&B £84–£126. Set dinner £36.75. Reductions for 5 or more nights May, July, Sept; off-season breaks.

AUCHENCAIRN Dumfries and Galloway   Map 5

Balcary Bay Hotel   *Tel* (01556) 640217
Auchencairn   *Fax* (01556) 640272
nr Castle Douglas DG7 1QZ

Lamb family's large white country house, peacefully set in 3-acre grounds on bay (sand/rock beach), 2 miles S of Auchencairn. Attractive exterior, lovely gardens, traditional decor. Straightforward Scottish/French cooking. Close by are well-signposted walks along Solway Firth; good for golfers, birdwatchers. Highly popular with some: "A hotel for all seasons, all types and all tastes; charming young staff." But also reports this year of lack of welcome. Open 6 Mar–mid-Nov. Unsuitable for &. Access, Amex, Visa accepted. 17 rooms. B&B £47–£53; D,B&B (min. 3 nights) £58–£64. Set lunch (Sun) £9.75, dinner £22.50 [1997]. ***V***

BALLANTRAE South Ayrshire   Map 5

Cosses Country House   **NEW/BUDGET**   *Tel* (01465) 831363
Ballantrae KA26 0LR   *Fax* (01465) 831598
                              E-mail 100636.1047@compuserve.com

Robin and Susan Crosthwaite's Wolsey Lodge in secluded valley in unspoilt area of SW Scotland, 2 miles E of fishing village that was made famous by

RL Stevenson. Charming decor: antiques etc from Middle and Far East. 12-acre gardens and woodland; owners' dogs will take guests for walks. Scottish/French dinners, communally served, using home-grown vegetables, fruit and herbs. Breakfast in kitchen – "tasty and generous". 2 suites across courtyard, 1 small double in house. Golf, walking, cycling, famous gardens, sea, safe bathing nearby. Open 17 Jan–17 Dec. Unsuitable for &. No smoking: dining room, bedrooms. No dogs in public rooms. Access, Visa accepted. B&B £30–£40; D,B&B £50–£60. More reports, please.

BALLATER Aberdeenshire   **Map 5**

Balgonie Country House   *Tel/Fax* (01339 7) 55482
Braemar Place
Ballater AB35 5NQ

John and Priscilla Finnie's Edwardian country house is on the outskirts of Ballater, in the heart of Royal Deeside and the "Malt Whisky Trail". It is set in lovely grounds with mature trees and lawns, and overlooks the golf course, with the hills of Glen Muick beyond. "A real gem," writes one satisfied customer this year. "John Finnie's ebullient charm was evident from the initial telephone enquiry to our reluctant departure. Our peaceful bedroom, with a wonderful view, was well lit, warmly decorated in peach and beige, and furnished with oak in harmony with the hotel's origins. Good pictures too, and crisp sheets on the high brass bed, which was turned down during dinner. It had a well-equipped bathroom. The comfortable lounge had games and plenty to read; binoculars stood on the bar windowsill, but sadly the red squirrels declined to make an appearance." Local game, beef and fish star on the menus of the two new chefs, Stuart Morrison and Steven Leitch, who arrived in early 1997; we'd be grateful for reports on their modern British cooking, served in the smart blue-and-white dining room. The "gargantuan" breakfast has been criticised by some visitors, but others have enjoyed it. Balmoral and Corgarff castles are a few miles away, *en route* to the ski slopes at Glenshee and the Lecht. If you go to church at Crathes you might see the Queen. Salmon fishing can be arranged, with notice. (*David and Jennifer Williams, M Heath, Val Ferguson*)

Open All year, except early Jan–mid-Feb.
Rooms 9 double.
Facilities Sitting room, bar, restaurant. 3½-acre grounds: croquet. Fishing on river Dee, golf, hill-walking, skiing nearby. Unsuitable for &.
Location On outskirts of Ballater, off A93 Aberdeen–Perth. Bus from Aberdeen, 40 miles.
Restrictions No smoking in restaurant. No children under 5. No dogs in public rooms, unattended in bedrooms.
Credit cards Access, Amex, Visa.
Terms [1997] B&B £40–£60. Set lunch £17.50, dinner £29.50–£30.50. ***V***

Darroch Learg   *Tel* (01339 7) 55443
Braemar Road   *Fax* (01339 7) 55252
Ballater AB35 5UX   *E-mail* darroch.learg@exodus.uk.com

"A splendid setting with lovely walks. A warm welcome from Nigel and Fiona Franks. A delightful, spacious bedroom. Superb dinners, a blend of *nouvelle cuisine* and the finest traditional cooking with a Scottish flavour. Excellent value for money. Altogether a happy visit." So runs a recent report on this hotel whose Gaelic name means an oak wood on a sunny hillside. Perched in wooded grounds on the side of a mountain, ten minutes' walk up from Ballater, overlooking the Dee Valley and the Grampians, it is composed of two pink-and-grey granite listed country houses, one a former hunting lodge, the other baronial and turreted. The bedrooms vary: those on the upper floors can be slightly cramped, but most have lovely views. The "exceptionally pleasant staff" are also praised; so is the welcome accorded to children, though there are no specific facilities for them. The dinners cooked by chef David Mutter have two choices for each course, and include local venison, lamb and beef; there are two menus, one changing daily, the other monthly. The wine list "includes some excellent bottles, and there is a fixed mark-up per bottle, rather than a percentage, which means that the higher quality wines, which have been selected with discrimination, are exceptionally good value". Breakfasts are generous. A good base for a golfing or fishing holiday. (*Ian Hughes Smith, and others*)

Open Feb–Dec.
Rooms 17 double, 1 single, 6 in separate building. 1 on ground floor.
Facilities Ramp. 2 lounges, smoking room, restaurant, conservatory; drying room. 4-acre grounds. River Dee ¼ mile, fishing. Birdwatching, shooting, golf, hang-gliding, riding nearby.
Location On A93, ½ mile W of Ballater. Bus from Aberdeen.
Restrictions No smoking: restaurant, 1 lounge, 4 bedrooms. No dogs in public rooms.
Credit cards All major cards accepted.
Terms B&B: single £42.50–£47.50, double £75–£115; D,B&B: single £56–£82, double £92–£164. Set lunch £15.75, dinner £27.50. Winter breaks, 7-day rates; New Year package. Children under 12 accommodated free in parents' room. ***V*** (Oct–Mar)

BALQUHIDDER Stirling   **Map 5**

Monachyle Mhor   BUDGET   *Tel* (01877) 384622
Lochearnhead FK19 8PQ   *Fax* (01877) 384305

On the narrow road, mentioned in Stevenson's *Kidnapped*, that winds along Loch Voil, through the Braes o' Balquhidder, stands this pink-washed converted farmhouse, with stunning views on all sides. It is surrounded by a large estate with a working farm, and there are plenty of activities for the sportingly inclined (see below). The "genial and caring" hosts, Rob, Jean and Tom Lewis, offer excellent value to those prepared to make the detour from the Stirling to Crianlarich road. The compact dining room in a covered verandah running along the front of the house serves French-influenced cooking on two fixed-price menus. One visitor this year was accommodated in the self-catering cottage at the back, which he thought "a little dingy", but otherwise there is endorsement for last year's enthusiastic review: "Our bedroom was spacious and well furnished, and exuded a feeling of warm friendship. The food was delicious – every item prepared and presented with care. Excellent local fish and game. We did not expect scrambled eggs and smoked salmon for breakfast at such a moderately priced hotel." "The real culinary strength is the baking of bread and scones," added a visitor this year, who praised "the welcoming Australian staff". Good bar meals too. Rob Roy McGregor is buried in the church in Balquhidder village, four miles away. (*Margaret and Alan Clarke, Denis Durno*)

Open All year, except last two weeks of Jan.
Rooms 3 suites, 7 double. 5 in courtyard. Self-catering cottages.
Facilities Lounge, lounge bar, sitting room with TV, restaurant (piped classical music). 2,000-acre estate: walking, salmon/trout-fishing, deer stalking, grouse moor.
Location 11 miles NW of Callander. Turn off A84 at Kingshouse; hotel 6 miles along glen.
Restrictions No smoking: restaurant, bedrooms. No children under 12. No dogs.
Credit cards Access, Visa.
Terms [1997] B&B £29–£37.50. Set dinner £19.50–£23.50. Sunday lunch £17.50.

BANAVIE Highland   Map 5

Torbeag House   BUDGET   *Tel/Fax* (01397) 772412
Muirshearlich, Banavie
by Fort William PH33 7PB

"A real home from home, with a relaxed atmosphere." So wrote visitors after a ten day visit to Ken and Gladys Whyte's modern house, in a superb location overlooking Ben Nevis and the Great Glen. "It was furnished with good taste throughout. Our bedroom was spacious, with fresh fruit and flowers, home-made biscuits and a view to rival any in Britain. The bathroom was the perfect match. The food, cooked by Ken Whyte, who is self-taught, was imaginative and well presented." Dinner is at 7.30 pm: four courses, no choice; preferences discussed in advance. It is served at separate tables in a dining room with dark Georgian-type furniture, good silver and china, and old oil paintings of prize cattle. The menu might feature Mallaig seafood chowder, roast beef and hot Seville orange pudding. Unlicensed; bring your own drink (no corkage charge). Breakfast is a "real Scottish" affair. No smoking. A good base to explore the West Highlands or to stop *en route* to the Isles. The moving Commando memorial is at Spean Bridge (they trained near here). (*John and Mona Taylor, and others*)

Open All year except Christmas. Guests should not arrive before 4 pm except by prior arrangement. Dinner for residents only (not Sunday).
Rooms 3 double.
Facilities Drawing room, dining room. 2½ acre garden: tennis. Walking, climbing, fishing, sailing, skiing nearby. Unsuitable for &.
Location 5 miles N of Fort William. A830 towards Mallaig 1 mile, then B8004 Banavie–Gairlochy 2½ miles. Entrance on left.
Restrictions No smoking. No children under 12. No pets in house.
Credit cards Access, Visa.
Terms [1997] B&B £27–£35; D,B&B £46–£54. Single supplement £10. Set dinner £19.50. Reductions for 3–7-night stays.

BANCHORY Aberdeenshire   Map 5

Banchory Lodge   *Tel* (01330) 822625
Banchory AB31 3HS   *Fax* (01330) 825019

Salmon leap upstream at Brig O'Feugh, close to this 17th/18th-century black and white former coaching inn on the banks of the river Dee, in the heart of salmon country. The hotel is filled with Victorian and

Edwardian furniture collected over 30 years by resident owner, Mrs Margaret Jaffray, and has many loyal regulars, many of them fishers and golfers (there are three courses close by). A reader called in for lunch, and reports: "The real thing: real antique furniture, real log fire, colourful country house decor, lots of flowers. The waitress was pleased to see us, although it was after two. We sat in velvet chairs and were served excellent ham and smoked salmon open sandwiches and cafetière coffee. Sun poured through the windows and sparkled on the Dee. The succulent dinner menu featured crab, beef, pheasant and small halibut. It felt like somebody's home – friendly and not too smart." Traditional afternoon teas are also served. The bedrooms continue the country home feeling, with bright chintzy fabrics, old furniture and flowers. Mrs Jaffray offers several specialist breaks, including one devoted to the artist Joseph Farquharson RA, who lived nearby and whose work she and her late husband collected. Crathes, Craigievar and Drum castles are not far away. We'd like more reports, please. (CJC)

Open All year, except Christmas (but open for Christmas lunch), New Year, 1st week Jan.
Rooms 1 suite, 21 double.
Facilities 2 lounges, cocktail bar, pool room with TV, 2 dining rooms; conference facilities. 10-acre grounds: children's playground, river with salmon/trout-fishing (book well in advance). Golf, tennis, bowls, clay pigeon-shooting nearby. Unsuitable for &.
Location 5 mins' walk from centre. Private carpark. Train: Aberdeen, 18 miles; then bus/taxi.
Restriction No dogs in public rooms.
Credit cards All major cards accepted.
Terms [1997] B&B £55–£78; D,B&B £71–£99. Set dinner £25.50. Bar lunches. Packed lunches available. 3-night specialist breaks: gardens, fishing, golf. Special meals, reduced rates for children.

BRIDGE OF MARNOCH Aberdeenshire   **Map 5**

The Old Manse of Marnoch   *Tel/Fax* (01466) 780873
Bridge of Marnoch   *E-mail* manse.marnoch@nest.org.uk
by Huntly AB54 7RS

"A treasure, with a lovely walk down to the river," says a recent visitor to Patrick and Keren Carter's immaculate early 19th-century house in a tranquil setting half-way between Banff and Huntly. Standing in large grounds on the banks of the river Deveron, it is surrounded by mature gardens with old-fashioned roses and a herb parterre, and is popular with the fishing fraternity. Its decor reflects the many years the Carters spent in the Middle East: bold colours predominate, as in the dark red dining room. Dinner, "modern Scottish", with choices, includes such dishes as roast pepper soup, and Barbary duck breast with rowan sauce. Fruit and vegetables come from the walled kitchen garden. The large breakfast menu is eclectic, ranging from Turkish figs and Afghan apricots to venison sausages and kedgeree, via "rough meal porridge, served in a wooden bowl with horn spoon". Tea, with two sorts of cake and biscuits, is served without charge, outdoors in fine weather. Ideal base for exploring Castle, Whisky and Coastal Heritage Trails. Duff House Art Gallery, an outpost of the National Galleries of Scotland, is a few miles away, as are the fishing villages and stunning beaches of the Banffshire coast. Not everyone appreciates the owners' enthusiastic dogs. More reports, please. (*Michael and Maureen Heath*)

Open All year, except 2 weeks Oct/Nov, Christmas, New Year.
Rooms 5 double. No telephone.
Facilities Lounge, dining room. 4-acre grounds: garden, herb parterre; river: fishing. Stalking, shooting arranged. Unsuitable for &.
Location On B9117 less than 1 mile W of A97 Huntly–Banff.
Restrictions No smoking in dining room. No children under 12. No dogs in public rooms.
Credit cards Access, Visa.
Terms B&B: single £54–£60, double £81–£90; D,B&B: single £79–£85, double £131–£140. Set dinner £25. 10% reduction for 3 nights or more. Reduced rates for children sharing parents' room.

BUNCHREW Highland   Map 5

Bunchrew House   `NEW`   *Tel* (01463) 234917
Bunchrew, Inverness IV3 6TA   *Fax* (01463) 710620

Fairytale silver-spired, castellated 17th-century mansion in fabulous position overlooking Black Isle, on shores of Beauly Firth, 2½ miles from Inverness. Converted by Stewart and Lesley Dykes into comfortable, friendly 15-bedroom hotel in 20-acre grounds with landscaped gardens. Fishing on property; golf, skiing, sailing nearby. French-influenced food "adequate and reasonably priced". Unsuitable for &. No smoking in restaurant. No dogs in public rooms. Access, Visa, Amex accepted. B&B: single £50–£85, double £60–£140; D,B&B: single £75–£110, double £100–£200. Full alc £30. We'd like some more reports, please.

BUNESSAN Argyll and Bute   Map 5

Assapol House   `NEW/BUDGET`   *Tel* (01681) 700258
Bunessan, Isle of Mull, PA67 6DW   *Fax* (01681) 700445

The Robertson family's 200-year-old white former manse, with some walls two feet thick, has a lovely setting on the fishing loch of the same name, in south-west Mull. "Our visit was a delight," write the nominators. "This is one of the most hospitable and comfortable guest houses we have ever stayed in. Mrs Onny Robertson is a charming and entertaining hostess. She is the chef; her husband Thomas serves drinks in the lounge; son Alex waits at table. The food is of high quality: always a soup or salad starter; no choice of main course, but different vegetables each day; the amazing cheeseboard might make you regret that you had eaten both of the delicious puddings. The full Scottish breakfast includes "truly free-range eggs". Tables in the small dining room are spaced to ensure privacy or allow conversations with fellow guests, according to preference. The family treat their guests with easy courtesy, never intruding but always happy to advise about local attractions, expeditions, etc." The menus are limited (guests choose their starter and wine by 6.30 pm), drinks are reasonably priced. The bedrooms are well equipped: fresh flowers, sewing kit in a small wicker basket, supply of current magazines, bath or shower *en suite*. Plenty of reading matter in the public rooms, and a collection of CDs which guests may play. Secluded beaches are close by; the ferry to Iona leaves from Fionnphort, six miles away, so do boats to Staffa, famous for puffins, and to Fingal's Cave. (*John and Margaret Myring*)

Open Apr–Oct.
Rooms 4 double, 1 single.
Facilities 2 lounges (CDs for guests to play), dining room. 3½-acre grounds, on fresh-water loch: boating, fishing. Unsuitable for ᙙ.
Location 1½ miles S of village. From Craignure take A849 to Fionnphort; approaching village, pass school on right; take road on left signposted *Assapol*. Bus stops ½ mile away on request.
Restrictions Smoking in 1 lounge only. No children under 10. Dogs in car only.
Credit cards Access, Visa.
Terms D,B&B: £49–£56. Set dinner £17. £2 reductions for 3 or more nights.

BUSTA Shetland   Map 5

Busta House	*Tel* (01806) 522506
Busta, Brae ZE2 9QN	*Fax* (01806) 522588
	E-mail busta@mes.co.uk

This white-painted house, built in the 16th century by the Gifford family, who were lairds of the island, is said to be the oldest continuously inhabited building in Shetland. It lies in a remote and sometimes windswept position overlooking the sea, and has its own small harbour, and fine views over Busta Voe. The owners, Peter and Judith Jones, cater both for tourists and for business visitors to the Sullem Voe oil terminal nearby, and their bar and restaurant are kept busy. "An island on the island," *Guide* readers have written. "Friendly, informal, competent and warm-hearted, with a charming staff." The upstairs library, with a good collection of books about Shetland, and the large sitting room, with flowery fabrics, a polished wooden floor, oriental rugs and fresh flowers, are "inviting places to spend a wet or lazy day". The bedrooms have a Laura Ashley-style decor; some are very small. Recent visitors thought the restaurant meals over-ambitious at times, "but the bar meals are generous, good and hot". Breakfast includes scrambled eggs with smoked salmon. Trips are organised, with expert guides, to see Shetland wildlife – seals, otters and whales, puffins, falcons, merlins, snowy owls, etc. There is fishing for brown trout in many freshwater lochs nearby. More reports, please.

Open 3 Jan–22 Dec.
Rooms 1 suite, 17 double, 2 single.
Facilities Lounge, library, bar, restaurant. 4-acre grounds on loch: small harbour, loch/sea fishing. Sailing, diving, pony-trekking, indoor swimming pool nearby. Unsuitable for ᙙ.
Location Clearly signposted from A970 Voe–Hillswick, 1 mile N of Brae. Hotel will help with travel arrangements from mainland. Bus: Lerwick to Brae; then taxi.
Restrictions No smoking: restaurant, library. No dogs in public rooms.
Credit cards All major cards accepted.
Terms B&B: single £65, double £89, suite £113. Set dinner £19.50–£23. Short day packages; off-season breaks: painting, archaeology, etc.

> If you are nominating a hotel, please err on the side of saying too much. Many suggestions have to be rejected only because they are too brief. We find brochures very helpful.

CALLANDER Stirling   **Map 5**

Arran Lodge   `NEW`   *Tel* (01877) 330976
Leny Road
Callander FK17 8AJ

*Robert and Pasqua Moore's no-smoking guest house, a 150-year-old house
with verandah in ½-acre garden on banks of river Leny (with fishing). On A84
just W of Callander. Charming decor, luxurious fittings; four-posters. House
party atmosphere. "Delicious, eclectic dinner," writes nominator, whose
birthday was celebrated with large cake serenaded by bagpipes. 4 bedrooms.
Open mid-Mar–end Oct. No children under 12. No dogs. Credit cards not
accepted at present. B&B £30.50–£63; D,B&B £57.50–£90. Unlicensed: bring
your own drink (no corkage). More reports, please.*

Brook Linn   `BUDGET`   *Tel/Fax* (01877) 330103
Leny Feus, Callander FK17 8AU

Fiona and Derek House's elegant but unpretentious no-smoking guest
house was once the home of a prosperous Victorian wool merchant. It is
set on a hill, ten minutes' walk from the town centre, in a large garden
with stream and waterfall (*linn* in Gaelic) and fine views over the
Trossachs. "First class in every respect," wrote a visitor who admired
the beautiful, quiet setting, "the happy atmosphere provided by Mr and
Mrs House, and the excellent service". The hotel is "spacious, warm and
comfortable" and the atmosphere is informal; children are welcome.
Food – slightly adventurous traditional – includes the intriguing Steak
Marlène and Fat Boy Pudding; vegetarians are catered for, and there is
excellent home baking. Mealtimes are fixed: breakfast at 8.15–8.45 am;
dinner at 7 pm. On a clear day you can see the Forth Bridge 40 miles to
the south and Ben Lawers 20 miles to the north. For sightseers there are
castles, stately homes, gardens and distilleries. (*JD, and others*)

Open Mid-March–mid-Nov.
Rooms 6 double, 1 single. No telephone.
Facilities Residents' lounge, dining room. 2-acre garden. Fishing, walking, bik-
ing, water sports, golf nearby. Unsuitable for ♿.
Location Through town on A84 from Stirling; right at *Pinewood* nursing home
into Leny Feus; right, up hill, at hotel's sign. Private parking. Bus from Stirling.
Restrictions No smoking. No dogs in public rooms.
Credit cards None accepted.
Terms B&B £18–£26; D,B&B £30–£38. Packed lunches £3.50. Weekly rates.
Children in parents' room: under 2 £5; under 13 half-price.

The Priory   `NEW/BUDGET`   *Tel/Fax* (01877) 330001
Bracklinn Road
Callander FK17 8EH

*Victorian manse, now a no-smoking guest house with young owners, Karin
Warren and Ian Wylie (he will give guests a game of golf). On A84
Stirling–Crianlarich, ¼ mile from centre. 7 bedrooms, mostly spacious, overlooking 1-acre walled garden. Beautiful view of Ben Ledi. Golf course adjacent,
fishing, sailing, beach nearby. "Scrumptious breakfasts: home-made breads
and jams, cheeses, omelettes." Well-prepared dinners at 7 pm (except on
Tues, Wed), with healthy emphasis. Children welcomed; cot, high chair,*

*baby-listening available. Open Easter–end Oct. No dogs. Credit cards not
accepted. B&B £25–£27. Set dinner £14.50.* ***V***

The Roman Camp   *Tel* (01877) 330003
off Main Street   *Fax* (01877) 331533
Callander FK17 8BG

A Roman fort is said to have stood on the site of this house, which was
built in 1625 as a hunting lodge for the dukes of Perth, and still retains
many original features. Though it is just off Callander's main street, it
is set in large, romantic grounds on the banks of the river Teith. There's
private fishing, and access to the local golf course nearby. "The old-
world character combines with a welcoming atmosphere; the personal
touch of the owners, Eric and Marion Brown, is evident everywhere,"
wrote one enthusiastic visitor. Another said: "I was taken by the
country house atmosphere; piles of antique leather suitcases, log
baskets, walking sticks. Best of all was the drawing room, which has
log fires, interesting furniture, and is perfect for sitting around in, or
having tea, light lunches or drinks." There is an oak-beamed bar, and a
panelled library. The accommodation varies: a family suite at the top of
the house is said to be dark and cramped; some bedrooms are high-
ceilinged, with an ornate fireplace; others are "small and cosy, with
coombed walls, and furniture dating back 200 years". Spacious modern
ones in a new wing have "a rather pink and bland decor", but some
have "a door leading on to the grounds; you could walk straight out to
the river – brilliant in the early morning". A new chef, Ian McNaught,
arrived at the end of 1996; his contemporary Scottish cooking is
admired by some, but thought pretentious by others. A new dining
room is planned for late 1997. Copious breakfasts include clootie
dumpling, haggis and black pudding as well as more conventional
items. (*Sue Gerrard, Joanna Carey*)

Open All year.
Rooms 3 suites, 11 double. 7 on ground floor (1 adapted for &).
Facilities Drawing room, library, bar, conservatory, restaurant; conference/
function facilities. 20-acre grounds: river, ¾-mile fishing. Golf nearby.
Location E end of Main St (small driveway between 2 pink cottages). Bus from
Stirling.
Restrictions No smoking in restaurant. No children under 5 in restaurant after
7 pm. No dogs in public rooms.
Credit cards All major cards accepted.
Terms B&B: single £70–£105, double £90–£140, suite £115–£155; D,B&B: single
£104–£139, double £158–£208, suite £183–£223. Set lunch £18.50, dinner £34; full
alc £55. 2-day breaks off season. ***V***

CANONBIE Dumfries and Galloway   **Map 5**

Riverside Inn   *Tel* (01387 3) 71512 and 71295
Canonbie DG14 0UX

Robert and Susan Phillips's black and white Borders inn close to the
river Esk has long been a favourite staging post for travellers on their
way north or south (the northern end of the M6 is only 12 miles away).
For those who can afford to linger, it is a good base for exploring
Hadrian's Wall and the Solway coast. It is popular with fisher folk, too.

The bedrooms, which vary in size, have been described as "homely, rather than sophisticated". They have a chintzy decor, electric blankets, flowers and baskets of fruit. Some get traffic noise. Two are in a secluded cottage, overlooking the river. The place has long been admired for the food served in the beamed, cottagey dining room with wooden tables and candles in brass candlesticks. "The cooking is of exceptionally high standard," wrote a visitor this year. "The wonderful five-course dinner will stay in our memory for many years. The initial welcome was restrained, but we all ended up the best of friends. We had a most comfortable room. Everything was lovely." Others have written of the "delightful, helpful hosts", the "unobtrusive and quietly friendly service", and the high-quality meals served in the bar, which offers "plenty of good cheer, real ale, a huge variety of malts, pictures on the wall, and some stuffed wildlife". On Sundays a traditional lunch is served in the restaurant. Breakfasts include home-made bread, marmalade and jams. Canonbie is at the eastern end of the Scots Dyke, a ditch three-and-a-half miles wide, marking the border between England and Scotland. (*John C Gillett, Good Pub Guide*)

Open All year, except 2 weeks Nov, Christmas, 2 weeks Feb
Rooms 7 double, 2 in cottage in garden. 1 on ground floor. No telephone.
Facilities 2 lounges, lounge bar, dining room. Small garden. River Esk 50 yds, fishing.
Location M6 exit 44. 10 miles N on A7; turn into Canonbie. Bottom of hill by Esk bridge. Private carpark. Bus from Carlisle, Edinburgh, Galashiels.
Restrictions No smoking: dining room, lounges. No dogs in public rooms.
Credit cards Access, Visa.
Terms B&B: single £55, double £75. Bar meals £5–£15. Set Sun lunch £11.95, dinner £18.50–£22.50. 2-day winter breaks.

CHIRNSIDE Scottish Borders — Map 5

Chirnside Hall NEW — *Tel* (01890) 818219
Chirnside, Duns TD11 3LD — *Fax* (01890) 818231

Handsome sandstone building, in Borders baronial style, on hillside in village 6 miles NW of Berwick-upon-Tweed. Recently restored by young owners (since 1995), Alan and Karla White. 10 bedrooms. 5-acre lawns and woodlands. Recently won Best Eating Place in the Borders award: exotic dishes by chef Tom Rowe (traditional Scottish with strong French influence), served to easy listening music. Full-size snooker table in basement; fishing, golf, riding, off-road driving nearby; also castles, stately homes, eg, Manderston at Duns. Open Feb–Dec. Unsuitable for ♿. No smoking: restaurant, bedrooms. No dogs in public rooms. Access, Amex, Visa accepted. B&B £40–£55; D,B&B £59.50–£74.50. Lunch £15.50 [1997]. More reports, please. *V*

COLONSAY Argyll and Bute — Map 5

Isle of Colonsay Hotel — *Tel* (01951) 200316
Isle of Colonsay PA61 7YP — *Fax* (01951) 200353
E-mail: hotel@premier.co.uk

César award in 1988

This "lovely hotel, run with flair and versatility" overlooks Scalasaig harbour on Argyll's remotest island (population 112). Two years ago, because it was on the market, it lost its *Guide* entry, but Kevin and Christa Byrne have decided to stay for the moment – they are taking bookings for 2000 – and regular visitors say that it is as good as ever. "The Byrnes are thoroughly nice people who make their guests welcome, but remain unobtrusive unless approached." "Cheerful and helpful staff. Excellent breakfasts: marvellous eggs and bacon, homemade bread and marmalade; wide-ranging bar meals; well-prepared dinner at 7.30 pm – no choice, but alternatives when Colonsay oysters are served. Extensive low-to-medium-priced wine list, with a sensible system for ordering in advance. Bedrooms are spotless and tidy by 10 am. Large, fluffy towels changed every day." The bedrooms vary in size; the doubles have a high-quality shower; the two public bathrooms are "exceptionally pleasant". Children are welcomed; there is good family accommodation. The hotel minibus does a circuit of the island twice a day and will drop and pick up walkers. Colonsay has golden beaches, dramatic rocky cliffs, heathland, lochs, plenty of wildlife, good cycling and challenging golf. The ferry generally goes to the mainland three times a week, but when guests are marooned by storms, the Byrnes cope with good humour. Special events are arranged, eg, sheep shearing, wildlife walks and talks; archaeological remains abound, and Oransay's ruined priory can be reached on foot at low tide. (*Peter Mahaffey, Nancy and John Lawson, Roger Hole; also Christina Johnston*)

Open 1 Mar–5 Nov, New Year.
Rooms 7 double (including 1 family) with shower, 3 single. 2 on ground floor. Garden bungalow for families. No telephone.
Facilities Lounge, sun room, public bar, cocktail bar, dining room; café, bookshop. ¾-acre garden. Near sandy beach (safe bathing); sea and loch fishing, golf nearby.
Location Ferry from Oban Mon, Wed, Fri (2¼ hrs), and from Kintyre via Islay in summer; details from Caledonian MacBrayne, *tel* (0990) 650000. Hotel is 400 yds W of harbour; mini-bus will meet ferry.
Restrictions No smoking in dining room. No dogs in public rooms.
Credit cards All major cards accepted.
Terms [1997] D,B&B (min. 2 nights because of ferry) £60–£80. Set dinner £23. Low season house parties. Special breaks. 15% discount Apr–Sept for last-minute reservations (ie, within 1 week of arrival). Children accommodated free in parents' room. *V*

CRINAN Argyll and Bute   Map 5

Crinan Hotel   *Tel* (01546) 830261
Crinan PA31 8SR   *Fax* (01546) 830292

"An elegant refuge for anyone seeking a culinary paradise." Thus a longtime friend of the *Guide* describes this incomparably positioned hotel at the seaward end of the eight-mile Crinan Canal, which connects Loch Fyne to the Atlantic. The large white building has stunning views over the tiny village, the lighthouse and the fishing boats and yachts, across to the mountains of Mull and the Isle of Jura. Its garden is listed in the *Good Gardens Guide*. The owners, Nick and Frances Ryan (the artist, Frances Macdonald), who have been here for nearly 30 years, are much in evidence; daughter Julia is now working in the kitchens, and son Ross helps his mother with the artistic side of things (interior design, paintings, menus, etc). The staff have been described as "outstanding". Simple but comfortable bedrooms (some are small) have Designers Guild fabrics, crisp white Egyptian cotton sheets and pine furniture; nine have a private balcony. One, suitable for a family, has bunk beds. Mrs Ryan says the poor sound insulation complained of last year has been attended to. There are two restaurants. Nick Ryan is chef in the top-floor gourmet seafood *Lock 16* (the last lock on the canal is number 15), where diners may watch a magnificent sunset through picture windows, while eating jumbo prawns landed only two hours earlier. The cheaper ground-floor restaurant, the *Westward*, serves seafood too, as well as Angus beef, local venison and hill lamb. The local weather forecast is printed on both menus. There is a rooftop bar with a colonial-style decor; light lunches are served in the public bar; the coffee shop serves home-made cakes including clootie dumpling. "Well-behaved" dogs are welcomed. (*Derek Cooper; also Good Pub Guide*)

Open All year, except 1 week Christmas. Restaurants closed midday; *Lock 16* also closed Oct–May, Sun/Mon.
Rooms 1 suite, 19 double, 2 single.
Facilities Lift, ramp. 2 lounges, 3 bars, 2 restaurants, coffee shop. ½-acre garden. Safe, sandy beaches nearby; fishing. Boat trips.
Location At centre of Lochgilphead follow A83 over small roundabout; right at next roundabout on to A816 to Oban; left after 2 miles on to B841 to Crinan. Train: Glasgow; then bus.
Restrictions No smoking in restaurants. No dogs in restaurants.
Credit cards Access, Amex, Visa.
Terms [1997] B&B £90; D,B&B £100–£120 (dinner in *Westward*). Bar lunches. Set dinner: *Westward* £30; *Lock 16* £40. Winter rates. Reduced rates for children.

DAIRSIE Fife   **Map 5**

Todhall House   NEW/BUDGET   *Tel/fax* (01334) 656344
Dairsie, by Cupar KY15 4RQ

A warm nomination from distinguished fellow hoteliers for John and Gill Donald's handsome, stone no-smoking guest house near Cupar, in the kingdom of Fife: "We were warmly welcomed by Mrs Donald, who showed us to a spacious, immaculately clean bedroom with fresh flowers, fruit, electric blanket, and a lovely view across the valley. Immaculate bathroom equipped with all refinements, and excellent breakfast." An evening meal is available by arrangement. Traditional cooking uses many Scottish ingredients, such as venison, salmon, beef and haggis. Breakfast includes locally smoked kippers. Golfers are spoilt for choice, with St Andrews and many other famous courses on the doorstep, and golf widows/widowers can choose between several National Trust of Scotland properties, eg, Hill of Tarvit and Kellie Castle, or maybe explore the East Neuk fishing villages. The owners write of "how much beauty there is to offer the discerning visitor willing to strike east from the M90". Unlicensed: bring your own (no corkage). (*Gunn Eriksen and Fred Brown*)

Open Apr–Oct. New Year for private parties.
Rooms 3 double. No telephone.
Facilities Lounge, dining room. 2-acre garden: unheated swimming pool, golf practice net. Beach 7 miles: safe bathing. Unsuitable for &.
Location Off A91, 2 miles E of Cupar. Sign by tall beech tree on left, house ½ mile from main road. Train: Cupar/Leuchars; hotel will meet.

Restrictions No smoking. No children under 12. No dogs.
Credit cards Access, Visa.
Terms [1997] B&B £24–£37; D,B&B £42–£55. Set dinner (by arrangement) from £18. Discounts for 5 or more nights.

DERVAIG Argyll and Bute   **Map 5**

Druimard Country House   *Tel/Fax* (01688) 400291
Dervaig, Tobermory
Isle of Mull PA75 6QW

"A winner! We loved every aspect of this place. Great food, pleasant people, comfortable room." Thus a recent endorsement from faithful American correspondents for Haydn and Wendy Hubbard's Victorian house on a hillside just outside a pretty village at the head of Loch Cuin, on the north-west side of the island. It has stunning views across the glen and the river Bellart. A converted cow byre in its grounds houses the world's smallest professional theatre, the popular 43-seat Mull Little Theatre, which plays from April to October. There's a pretty conservatory and a cosy lounge. Bedrooms are of reasonable size, and simply furnished, with flowery fabrics, fresh flowers and small but well-equipped shower or bathroom. Mrs Hubbard's excellent cooking puts the emphasis on local produce – Mull salmon and scallops, Croia oysters, lobster, venison, local cheeses. Calgary beach, a wide expanse of white sand, is close by, and boat trips can be arranged to see puffins on Lunga, Minke whales, and the legendary Fingal's Cave on Staffa. (*Stephen and Ellise Holman*)

Open End Mar–Nov. Restaurant closed midday, to non-residents Sun evening.
Rooms 1 suite, 5 double.
Facilities Lounge, conservatory, bar, restaurant (piped classical/Scottish music). 1 acre grounds: theatre. Golf, beaches, fishing (ghillie available) nearby. Only restaurant has &. access.
Location From Craignure ferry, A849 W through Salen. Left to Dervaig after 1½ miles. Hotel on right before village.
Restrictions No smoking in restaurant. No dogs in public rooms.
Credit card Access.
Terms [1997] B&B (3 nights min.) £37.50–£52.00, suite (2–4 persons) £110–£165; D,B&B £57.50–£72, suite £150–£245. Set dinner £26. Special meals and reduced rates for children. ***V***

DULNAIN BRIDGE Highland   **Map 5**

Auchendean Lodge   **BUDGET**   *Tel* (01479) 851347
Dulnain Bridge
Grantown-on-Spey PH26 3LU

Ian Kirk and Eric Hart's Edwardian hunting lodge, gloriously set in Cairngorms, just off road to Aviemore; wonderful views of Spey valley. Salmon fishing; capercaillie and other wildlife; good walking in Cairngorms. Art Nouveau/traditional decor, dotted with knick-knacks – a bit kitsch for some tastes. French/Scottish menus, with emphasis on game; wild mushrooms a speciality. Extensive wine list. Closed 4 weeks in winter (Nov or Jan). Lunch not served. No smoking: restaurant, drawing room. Only restaurant suitable for &. Dogs in bedrooms, 1 lounge only. All major credit cards accepted (2½% commission added). B&B £17–£49; D,B&B £40.50–£71. Set dinner £24.50;

full alc £28.50. Christmas, New Year packages [1997]. More reports badly needed.

DUNDEE *See SHORTLIST*   **Map 5**

DUNKELD Perthshire and Kinross   **Map 5**

Kinnaird   *Tel* (01796) 482440
Kinnaird Estate   *Fax* (01796) 482289
by Dunkeld PH8 0LB

"Wonderful reception from manager Douglas Jack. Restful cedar-panelled lounge, impressive snooker room, and the best raspberry soufflé ever." So write recent visitors to Constance Ward's luxurious yet unstuffy 18th-century Grade B listed house (Relais & Châteaux). It is set in a vast estate in the heart of Perthshire, with magnificent views over the valley of the river Tay, one of Scotland's finest fishing rivers. *Kinnaird* offers salmon-fishing on the Tay, and trout-fishing in its own lochs; many other activities are available on the estate (see below). Indoors there is billiards, backgammon and bridge. The public rooms are much as they would have been 80 years ago, when the then dower house to Blair Atholl Castle was filled with house parties: family por-traits, fishing trophies, antiques and flowers. Bedrooms, each with a gas log fire, are sumptuously decorated. In the impressive chande-liered and frescoed restaurant, chef John Webber (Mosimann-trained), serves such dishes as shellfish minestrone, and millefeuille of pigeon and potato. The wine list is comprehensive, with many half bottles. (*Michael and Maureen Heath*)

Open All year. Thurs–Sun only 1 Jan–1 Mar.
Rooms 1 suite, 8 double, 1 on ground floor suitable for &. 7 holiday cottages.
Facilities Lift. Drawing room, morning room, study, billiard room, 2 dining rooms; function facilities. 9,000-acre estate: gardens, bowling lawn, tennis, cro-quet, shooting, walking, birdwatching, 3 trout lochs. Riding, golf, clay pigeon-shooting nearby. Salmon/trout-fishing on river Tay ½ mile.
Location NE of Dunkeld. From A9 Perth–Pitlochry left on to B898 to Dalguise/Balnaguard. *Kinnaird* 4½ miles on right.
Restrictions No smoking in dining rooms. No children under 12. No dogs in house (kennels available).
Credit cards Access, Amex, Visa.
Terms B&B: single £220, double £275, suite £295. Set lunch (2/3-course) £19.50/£24, dinner (4-course) £39.50. Off-season rate (not Christmas, New Year): D,B&B double £225.

DUNOON Argyll and Bute   **Map 5**

Enmore Hotel   *Tel* (01369) 702230
Marine Parade   *Fax* (01369) 702148
Kirn, Dunoon PA23 8HH   *E-mail* enmorehotel@btinternet.com.

"A real gem," runs a recent report on this Victorian villa, on the water-front, overlooking the Firth of Clyde. Originally the retreat of a rich Glasgow businessman, it is reached by an enjoyable short ferry ride from Gourock, or overland via Loch Lomond. Some bedrooms have a four-poster or a waterbed; some bathrooms have a jacuzzi, and there are plenty of extras: tins of sweets, a good selection of books, towelling dressing-gowns, and – an innovation – a *digital* trouser press. The slightly over-the-top decor, and the parchment scroll menu, chummily naming the hotel's guests, were too much for one reader this year. But other visitors have enjoyed Angela Wilson's hospitality, and David Wilson's "English/Scottish modern eclectic" cooking, which uses lots of seafood, home-grown vegetables and local cheeses. Evening walks along the boardwalk are an added attraction. Breakfast includes fresh orange juice and local kippers. The hotel has two international standard squash courts with video playback facilities, and there are dozens of gardens to visit on the Cowal peninsula. Children and dogs are welcomed. (*RM Flaherty*)

Open All year, except Christmas week.
Rooms 1 suite, 7 double, 2 single. 2 on ground floor.
Facilities 2 lounges (piped music in 1 at night), bar, dining room; conference room; shop; 2 squash courts. 1-acre grounds. Private shingle beach across road: safe but cold bathing, boating. Golf, swimming pool, tennis, pony-trekking nearby. Unsuitable for &.
Location On Marine Parade between 2 ferries, 1 mile W of town centre. Private parking. Train: Gourock; then ferry.
Restrictions No smoking in dining room. No dogs in dining room.
Credit cards Access, Amex, Visa.
Terms [1997] B&B: single £35, double £80, suite £130; D,B&B £55–£95 per person. Set lunch £10, dinner £25; full alc £30. Romantic, New Year, winter, spring, garden, etc, breaks. Special meals for children. Children under 12 sharing parents' room free. *V*

DUNVEGAN Highland   Map 5

Harlosh House   *Tel/Fax* (01470) 521367
by Dunvegan
Isle of Skye IV55 8ZG

"A delightful visit. Warm and cosy bedrooms with sofa, books, fruit and a Scandinavian feel; good bathrooms with lots of hot water, fluffy towels and extras. The friendly staff can't do enough for you. The food is truly outstanding: tasty soups, beautifully cooked fish, puddings of the gods. Huge breakfasts served when you want – a welcome change." "Peter and Lindsey Elford are charming hosts. He is a magnificent cook, mostly self-taught. A peaceful, wonderful place." More praise this year for this small white croft-style house in a remote setting on a peninsula jutting into Loch Bracadale, in the north-west of Skye, with a view of the Cuillins. Peter Elford's cooking has earned a red "Meals" in *Michelin*. Bread, pasta, ice-cream and sorbets are homemade; there is a special cheese menu and a wide range of malt whiskies. Through a telescope in the lounge, otters, seals and eagles may be spotted. Excellent walking nearby; also Dunvegan Castle, the Skye Heritage Centre and the Clan Donald Centre. (*Val Ferguson, Mary Milne-Day; also Stephen and Ellise Holman, David and Mary Lodge*)

Open Easter–Oct.
Rooms 6 double. No telephone; TV on request.
Facilities Lounge with bar, sun lounge, dining room (piped classical/Gaelic music in evening). Sea, rocky shore 50 yds: fishing, sailing; walking, pony-trekking, shooting nearby. Unsuitable for &.

Location 4 miles S of Dunvegan by A863. Between Roag and Caroy take minor road, signposted to Harlosh, for 2 miles.
Restrictions No smoking, except in sun lounge. No dogs.
Credit cards Access, Visa.
Terms B&B £35–£95; D,B&B: single £60–£120, double £135–£145. Set dinner £25.

EDINBURGH   Map 5

Channings   NEW   *Tel* (0131) 315 2226
South Learmonth Gardens, EH4 1EZ   *Fax* (0131) 332 9631
                          E-mail reserve@channings.co.uk

Half a mile from the west end of Princes Street, five Edwardian houses, on a quiet cobbled street, have been transformed into a comfortable hotel. The decor is traditional and club-like: oak panelling, moulded ceilings, tile-surrounded fireplaces, antiques and old prints in the public rooms. The bedrooms, of varying size, have period furniture, and some look over the Firth of Forth to the hills of Fife beyond. "It must be one of the few places in Edinburgh where you can sleep with the windows open," wrote a seasoned traveller. "The youthful staff manage the trick of combining friendliness with efficiency." The bar has a good selection of malt whiskies, and a chess board. The brasserie in the basement, a popular meeting place, serves Scottish and continental dishes. The chef, Richard Glennie, took charge in May 1997, so we'd like comments on the food please. Food and drink are served in the terraced garden in fine weather. *Channings'* owner, Peter Taylor, also owns the *Howard* (see below). (*Desmond Balmer*)

Open All year, except 24–28 Dec.
Rooms 1 suite, 32 double, 15 single.
Facilities Lift. 3 lounges, brasserie; patio. Gardens.
Location W of centre, off Queensferry Rd.
Restrictions No smoking: brasserie, 1st-floor bedrooms.
Credit cards All major cards accepted.
Terms B&B: single £95–£120, double £125–£175, suite £195–£220. Set lunch £9.95, dinner £21. Short breaks all year. *V*

Drummond House   *Tel/Fax* (0131) 557 9189
17 Drummond Place, EH3 6PL

Many of our Edinburgh entries are discreet B&Bs (no hotel sign) in elegant houses in the city's Georgian New Town, with Princes Street and major sights only a short walk away. This one is in Drummond Square, which, curved on one side, is a cobbled street surrounding a garden (closed to the public). Here, Alan and Josephine Dougall's fine Georgian house, with spacious rooms, high ceilings, tall windows, a pillared hallway, and a spiral staircase beneath a cupola, remains popular with *Guide* readers. "A special place," wrote a visitor from Hawaii. "Everything well thought out. As much attention to detail in the service as in the decor. The soft colours, and the fabrics, rugs and prints of quality, blend perfectly with the architecture to create an understated elegance. My spacious bedroom looked on to a back garden. The bathroom was so large I would have been quite happy to live in it. I enjoyed my conversations with fellow guests at breakfast, which contained some light touches – yogurt and fruit, as well as a cooked Scottish affair and home-made preserves. Helpful but never intrusive hosts." (*Cheryl Tipton*)

Open All year, except Christmas.
Rooms 3 double, 1 single. No TV.
Facilities Sitting room with TV, breakfast room. Unsuitable for &.
Location Just N of St Andrew Sq and Waverley Stn, at E end of Gt King St. No.10 bus from centre.
Restrictions No smoking. No children under 12. No dogs.
Credit cards Access, Visa.
Terms B&B: single £60, double £90.

The Howard   NEW   *Tel* (0131) 557 3500
34 Great King Street, EH3 6QH   *Fax* (0131) 557 6515

Unlike our other New Town entries, the *Howard* is a "proper", pricey, small hotel. It is composed of three adjoining Georgian houses on a cobbled street, with some traffic by day, but quiet at night. Behind its discreet brass sign are a formal reception, a smart sitting room with an open fire, where drinks and tea are served, a pretty breakfast room, and a fashionable basement restaurant, where a cheerful young staff serve Scottish/international cooking by chef Malcolm Warham. The clientele is a mix of business visitors and tourists, and the single rooms, often a hotel's weak point, are unusually attractive, apart from one with a claustrophobic four-poster. The hotel dropped from last year's *Guide* following a change of ownership. It is now in the hands of Peter Taylor, who also owns *Channings* (above). An inspector was mostly in favour. "The decor is traditional – chandeliers, marble fireplaces, brocade curtains and antiques in the public rooms, old-fashioned telephones in the bedrooms, and wooden loo seats in the well-stocked bathrooms. Service is willing and accommodating: offers of help with luggage, free tea served on arrival. Only caveats: the 'freshly squeezed' juices at breakfast were not; bedroom lighting is on the dim side." We'd like more reports, please.

Open All year, except 24–28 Dec.
Rooms 2 suites, 10 double, 3 single.
Facilities Lift. Drawing room, breakfast room, restaurant, meeting room.
Location New Town, 5 mins' walk from Princes Street. Carpark.
Credit cards All major cards accepted.
Terms B&B: single £110–£150, double £195, suite £275. Set lunch £12, dinner £25; full alc £34. 5-night discounts. Winter weekend rates.

Malmaison   *Tel* (0131) 555 6868
1 Tower Place   *Fax* (0131) 555 6999
Leith EH6 7DB

The Edinburgh and Glasgow *Malmaisons* opened with a flourish two years ago. The brainchild of Ken McCulloch, owner of the much grander *One Devonshire Gardens* in Glasgow (*qv*), they are stylish conversions of interesting old buildings. Crisply designed bedrooms have good fabrics, TV and CD player and a smart bathroom. Bistro-style food is served in an informal café and in a brasserie. The lack of frills and bedroom extras produces reasonable prices. Recent visitors have admired this imposing building (the old Sailors' Rest), its "marvellous atmosphere", and the "impressive decor – curtains as thick as door-mats and lovely colours everywhere, stylish both inside and out". The food and drink in the café and the brasserie have also been enjoyed. But there are criticisms too: service, though generally friendly, can be dis-organised; room maintenance is not always perfect; a stronger man-agerial hand is said to be needed. This *Malmaison* is due to more than double, with the opening of 35 new bedrooms in 1997; the Glasgow one, too, will expand, and further *Malmaisons* will open in Manchester and Newcastle. We'd be grateful for reports on the effect of this expan-sion. (*Joanna Carey*)

Open All year.
Rooms 6 suites, 19 double. 35 more planned for late 1997.
Facilities Lift. Café/bar, brasserie (piped music all day); private dining room, meeting room.
Location Leith dockside, 10 mins' drive from city centre and Waverley station. Bus from centre.
Restrictions No smoking in bedrooms. No dogs in public rooms.
Credit cards All major cards accepted.
Terms [1997] Rooms (single/double) £85, suite £120, Breakfast: continental £6, Scottish £10. Set lunch/dinner £9.95–£12.95. Full alc £22. Numerous special breaks

---

7 Danube Street NEW   *Tel* (0131) 332 2755
7 Danube Street, EH4 1NN   *Fax* (0131) 343 3648

Fiona Mitchell-Rose opened her home, in the Stockbridge area of New Town, to guests in mid-1996 when her daughters flew the nest. It is a fine, unspoiled Georgian house, with a beautiful cupola-ed staircase. There is evidence everywhere that it is a family house – skis and dogs' cushions in the hallway, and inherited pictures and furniture, all in excellent taste. The guest bedrooms are on the lower floor (guests are given a key to the basement door). The best one, with a four-poster, overlooks the lovingly tended garden. All are kitted out with a plethora of extras; beds have an electric blanket. Spick and span bathrooms have a power shower and innumerable toiletries – even dental floss. "Civilised, friendly hostess (an opera and theatre buff and skiing en-thusiast), with two dogs in attendance," write inspectors. "She serves breakfast at a large table in the dining room: freshly squeezed juice, fresh fruit salad, home-baked scones and the cooked works if required, set us up for the day. Danube Street is a charming curved cobbled street, quiet by night and not very busy by day." More reports, please.

Open All year, except Christmas.
Rooms 2 double, 1 single.
Facilities Drawing room, breakfast room. Garden. Unsuitable for &.
Location Just N of St Andrew Sq and Waverley Stn, at E end of Gt King St. Meter parking 5 mins' walk.
Restrictions No smoking: restaurant, bedrooms.
Credit cards Access, Visa.
Terms B&B: single £40–£50, double £75–£85. Reductions for long stays. *V*

---

17 Abercromby Place   *Tel* (0131) 557 8036
17 Abercromby Place, EH3 6LB   *Fax* (0131) 558 3453

This handsome New Town house was built by Edinburgh's famous architect, William Henry Playfair; now it is the home of Mrs Eirlys

Lloyd, advocate and barrister, who takes paying guests. She welcomes them with "unforced, easy friendliness," say recent guests. "We felt we were staying with friends." The house, which looks across the road to a leafy square, has private parking, and it is five minutes' walk (uphill) from Princes Street. The bedrooms are large, with flowery curtains and a good bathroom. Two are in the mews at the back, suitable for a family. Breakfast, communally served in the handsome green-walled dining room, has a large buffet, and is generally enjoyed: "Proper food, not a packet in sight." An evening meal is available by arrangement between 7.30 and 11 pm. No licence: guests should bring their own wine. (*Stephen Wrigley-Hare; also Judith Barraclough, and others*)

Open All year.
Rooms 7 double, 2 single.
Facilities Sitting room, breakfast room. Access to communal gardens across street. Unsuitable for &.
Location 5 mins' walk from city centre. Private parking.
Restrictions No smoking. No dogs.
Credit cards Access, Visa.
Terms B&B £40–£45. Set dinner £25.

See also SHORTLIST

ERISKA Argyll and Bute   Map 5

Isle of Eriska   *Tel* (01631) 720371
Ledaig, by Oban PA37 1SD   *Fax* (01631) 720531

"Heaven: tranquillity, labradors and a golf course (of sorts)." "More country home than hotel." Recent endorsements for the baronial granite and sandstone mansion, turreted and crenellated, which has been the Buchanan-Smith family's fiefdom for 20 years. Built in 1884 by the wondrously named Hippolyte Blanc, it is on the tiny private island of *Love Lilt* fame, off the west coast (linked by a wrought-iron bridge to the mainland). "Robin Buchanan-Smith, Church of Scotland minister, raconteur and character, has created an ambience of warmth and bonhomie," wrote visitors last year, former super-hoteliers themselves. "He and his wife, Sheena, continue to be hospitable hosts and to provide essential backup. But day-to-day management is now in the hands of their energetic son Beppo, who has breathed fresh life into the Scottish baronial pile. The large, light bedrooms are decorated with flair and attention to detail. Bathrooms are smart and tiled. The house-keeping fairy still tucks hot water-bottles into beds each night. Tame badgers come to the library door for their supper of bread and milk; wildlife abounds on the island – otters, seals, herons and deer." The decor is old-fashioned, rather than smart, with panelling, leather chairs and chintzes. Plenty of sporting facilities are available (see

below). Oban, Mull, Iona and Inverary can be visited from here. A new
chef arrived in May 1997; reports on the traditional Scottish food would
be welcome. (*Michael and Maureen Heath, Eve and Ron Jones*)

Open All year, except Jan.
Rooms 15 double, 2 single. 2 on ground floor.
Facilities 3 drawing rooms (1 with piano), bar/library, dining room; indoor
swimming pool, gymnasium, games room, spa, sauna. 300-acre island: tennis,
golf, water sports, riding, croquet, clay pigeon-shooting.
Location 12 miles N of Oban. 4 miles W of A828.
Restrictions No smoking in dining room. No children under 5 in dining room at
night, or in swimming pool; no under-15s in gymnasium. No dogs in public
rooms.
Credit cards Access, Amex, Visa.
Terms [1997] B&B: single £160, double £195–£225; D,B&B (low season only):
single £110, double £220. Set dinner £35. Bar lunch for residents only. Advance
reservations for 2 nights min. Weekly rates. Off-season breaks.

EVIE Orkney   **Map 5**

Woodwick House   BUDGET   *Tel* (01856) 751330
Evie KW17 2PQ   *Fax* (01856) 751383

This small guest house, run by Ann Herdman, is set in some of
Orkney's only woods. It has an overgrown garden with bluebells, a
noisy rookery and a small stream running down to the lapping waters
of Woodwick Bay, where seals are sometimes seen. The lounges have
open peat fires; one has TV, videos and books, another has a baby
grand piano. The bedrooms are a bit basic for some visitors – not all
have private facilities, and the plumbing can be noisy. Mrs Herdman
does much of the work on her own, so service can be spasmodic at
times. But visitors find her "friendly, interesting and adaptable" and
praise the breakfasts, which include home-made marmalade, and the
"healthy, varied and imaginative" dinners. Food can be simply or more
elaborately prepared according to guests' requirements, and will include local specialities: salmon, crab, lobster, oysters and Orkney lamb,
as well as fresh herbs and organic produce when possible. Special diets
are catered for, too. Notices and leaflets proclaim the house's affiliation
with the Dandelion Trust (see also *Hazelwood House*, Loddiswell,
England). Concerts, poetry readings and musical recitals in aid of the
charity are held once a month, and there is sometimes a spontaneous
ceilidh in the evening. Stromness and Kirkwall, the two main towns of
Orkney, are 20 minutes' drive away. The Tingwall ferry just down the
river makes regular trips to other islands. The RSPB at Birsay, and Loch
Harray (famous for fishing) are nearby. More reports, please.

Open All year.
Rooms 7 double, 1 single. 4 with *en suite* facilities. 2 on ground floor. No tele-
phone/radio/TV.
Facilities Lounge, TV lounge, dining room; room with piano for entertainments.
12-acre grounds on bay: fishing, birdwatching; guided tours.
Location From A965 turn off to Evie. After *c*.15 mins, right at *Woodwick House*
sign, then left; house in trees at end of road.
Restriction No smoking in bedrooms, discouraged in restaurant.
Credit cards None accepted.
Terms [1997] B&B £22–£37; D,B&B £35.50–£57.50; full board £40.50–£68.50.
Lunch from £3.50, dinner from £14.50. Terms negotiable. Christmas, New Year
packages. *V*

FORSS Highland   Map 5

Forss House   NEW   *Tel* (01847) 861201
Forss, nr Thurso KW14 7XY   *Fax* (01847) 861301

*James and Jacqueline MacGregor's Grade II listed house, built in 1810, out-
wardly austere, inside full of home-like comfort. 4 miles W of Thurso on A836.
In 24-acre wooded grounds by river; 100 yards from falls on river Forss.
Leaping salmon, riverside walk to sea; seals, sea birds, rookery, heronry.
"Traditional Scottish/unusual" cooking. 10 spacious, stylish bedrooms,
5 (good for fisherfolk) in lodges in grounds; 1 suitable for &. Closed 23 Dec–
6 Jan. No smoking: restaurant, conservatory. Dogs by arrangement. Access,
Amex, Visa accepted. B&B £42.50–£52.50; D,B&B £62–£72. Set lunch £9,
dinner £19.50–£20.50. More reports, please.*

FORT WILLIAM Highland   Map 5

Crolinnhe   *Tel* (01397) 702709
Grange Road
Fort William PH33 6JF

Flora Mackenzie's unassuming no-smoking B&B is set in a large garden in a quiet residential area a short walk from the town centre. Its
Gaelic name ("Above the Linnhe") describes its position on a hillside,
with a fine view over the loch to the North Western Highlands. It is a
carefully renovated Victorian villa, with a pretty, home-like decor. The
spacious bedrooms all have TV; most have *en suite* facilities and a loch
view. "Breakfast was the best of our trip, and included award-winning
haggis," wrote one American couple. "If you're trying haggis for the
first time, this is the place." "Deserves the highest praise," said another
reporter, who knows it well. Rates are "amazingly reasonable". Fort
William, at the foot of Ben Nevis, is a major tourist centre for the
Highlands; there are many outdoors activities in the wonderful
countryside around. (*ML, and others*)

Open Mar–Nov.
Rooms 5 double. No telephone.
Facilities Lounge, dining room. 1-acre grounds. Loch 200 yds. Unsuitable for &.
Location 10 mins' walk from centre. From High St take Lundavra Rd; fork right
into Grange Rd. Private parking. Station ½ mile.
Restrictions No smoking. No children under 12. No dogs.
Credit cards None accepted.
Terms B&B £33–£36.

The Grange   NEW   *Tel* (01397) 705516
Grange Road
Fort William PH33 6JF

"Joan Campbell is a charming hostess, with a welcoming smile and an
acute awareness of what genuine Highland hospitality should be." So
writes the nominator of this small no-smoking B&B, a white-painted
Victorian villa on the shores of Loch Linnhe, a short walk from the
town centre. "It is spotlessly clean, with a cheerful coal fire in the
lounge. Amazing attention to detail: real linen scalloped napkins tied
up with tartan ribbon, fresh flowers and sherry in the bedroom. Many

so-called superior hotels would not go to half the trouble." Breakfast, ordered the night before from an extensive menu, includes fruit compôte, Mallaig kippers, haggis and "Turkish eggs" (poached with yogurt). The actress Jessica Lange took the place over for several weeks during the filming of *Rob Roy*. Her room, with a colonial-style bed and

a view of the garden and the loch, has been rechristened the Rob Roy Room in her honour. In 1996 *The Grange* won the Scottish Tourist Board's Best Bed and Breakfast award. No dinners, but *Crannog*, "an excellent seafood restaurant", is recommended, and *Inverlochy Castle* (*qv*) is only five miles away. (*Michael Leonard; also Colin MacLeod*)

Open March–Nov.
Rooms 3 double. No telephone.
Facilities Lounge, breakfast room. 1-acre garden. Loch 200 yds. Unsuitable for &.
Location 10 mins' walk from centre. From High St take Lundavra Rd: fork right into Grange Rd. Private parking. Station ½ mile.
Restrictions No smoking. No children under 12. No dogs.
Credit cards Access, Visa.
Terms [1997] B&B double £66–£72. Reduced rates for 3 nights or more.

Inverlochy Castle   *Tel* (01397) 702177
Torlundy, Fort William PH33 6SN   *Fax* (01397) 702953

This 19th-century Scottish baronial house (Relais & Châteaux) is set in huge grounds amid magnificent Highland scenery – "I never saw a lovelier or more romantic spot," wrote Queen Victoria, visiting when it was in private hands. Today it is one of Britain's most luxurious country house hotels. Its chief architectural glory is the Great Hall with crystal chandeliers and a frescoed ceiling with cherubs among clouds. There's a splendid billiard room with a high ceiling and a marbled fireplace. The drawing room has open fires and comfortable sofas and armchairs. Bedrooms are equally sumptuous. In the formal dining room, chef Simon Haigh, who trained with Raymond Blanc, serves classic cookery in generous portions, with a strong emphasis on local fish and game; he will also turn out a good haggis. There is an outstanding wine list. In November 1996, a group of overseas investors bought the hotel from the long-time owner, Grete Hobbs. They have completed a massive refurbishment, adding fax and ISDN lines to bedrooms, a helipad "and a new corporate identity". Five more bedrooms are also planned. Michael Leonard, the exemplary longtime managing director, is staying on. "Simple bedroom, with understated but luxurious decor," wrote 1997 visitors. "Dinner was an elegant, if expensive, affair; creative cuisine, superbly served." The *Factor's House*, nearby, which was run in simpler style by Mrs Hobbs's son, Peter, has now closed. (*Michael and Maureen Heath; also David and Mary Lodge*)

Open 1 Mar–6 Jan.
Rooms 1 suite, 16 double.
Facilities Great Hall, drawing room, 3 dining rooms (pianist Fri/Sat/Sun),

billiard room; function facilities. 50-acre grounds in 500-acre estate: gardens, tennis, loch, fishing. Golf, skiing nearby. Chauffeur-driven limousines for hire. Unsuitable for &.
Location On A82 3 miles NE of Fort William, just past golf club. Follow signs to hotel; ignore signs to Inverlochy village/Inverlochy Castle (ruins).
Restrictions No smoking, no mobile phones in dining rooms.
Credit cards Access, Amex, Visa.
Terms [1997] B&B: single £175–£210, double £280–£330, suite £375–£425. Set lunch £20–£30, dinner £45–£52.50.

GLASGOW   Map 5

Babbity Bowster   Tel (0141) 552 5055
16–18 Blackfriars Street, G1 1PE   Fax (0141) 552 7774

Q César award in 1995

This lively, stylish café/bar/restaurant/hotel, named for an obscure 18th-century wedding dance, is owned by bearded Fraser Laurie, an energetic and convivial host. Much frequented by journalists, the ground floor is the café and bar. The restaurant is above, and bedrooms are on the second floor. No reception (you apply to the bar), but the welcome is warm and informal; staff carry bags up and down. Rooms are small and very simple, but clean, with good wardrobe space; no "goodies", no TV. The listed Robert Adam building is in a pedestrian street in Merchant City, not far from the centre. You might expect it to be quiet but the noise of the pub, the sounds of cheerful street voices, and city activity bounce off the stone walls of the surrounding buildings – earplugs are recommended. Breakfast in the café can be haphazard. The popular restaurant, *Schottische*, with an Auld Alliance menu of Scottish venison, lamb, salmon, and fish stew, has cartoons of the owner/chef and staff on white walls, caricature sculptures, potted greenery and café-style furniture. The café serves haggis, seafood and croques all day, and there's a floodlit *boules* court. (*Good Pub Guide, and others*) More reports please.

Open All year, except Christmas Day, New Year's Day. Restaurant closed Sun.
Rooms 4 double, 2 single. All with shower. No TV/telephone. Family flat opposite.
Facilities Café/bar, restaurant; live music at weekends; patio, *boules*. Unsuitable for &.
Location Pedestrian precinct in centre, between Glasgow Cross and cathedral. Small carpark. Station 10 mins' walk.
Restriction No dogs.
Credit cards Access, Amex, Visa.
Terms B&B: single £45, double £65. Café: set lunch (with wine) £10; full alc £25; restaurant: set lunch £14, dinner £24.50.

Malmaison   Tel (0141) 221 6400
278 West George Street   Fax (0141) 221 6411
G2 4LL   E-mail glasgow@malmaison.com

Smart, stylish, no frills, reasonable cost – the *Malmaison* concept is the brainchild of Ken McCulloch, owner of the far grander and more expensive *One Devonshire Gardens* (*qv*). This *Malmaison* – the name is that of Joséphine Bonaparte's Paris home – already has an Edinburgh sibling (*qv*), and the leisure developer Arcadian International has now joined the company, which will expand to Manchester, Leeds, Newcastle, Birmingham and London in the next few years. Situated in the Georgian area of the city, close to the centre, the original hotel occupies a former Greek Orthodox church that was built at the turn of the century. Inside, is a magnificent Art Nouveau central staircase with ironwork of blue and gold – the decor, like the name, is inspired by the Paris Malmaison. The bedrooms vary in size; some are "spacious, with a good-size bathroom", others are "small but well-arranged". Each has a CD player and TV, but extras, room service and porterage are not offered, and some are not particularly well thought-out – one switch for both bedside lights, for example. The ventilation may not always be perfect. The young staff are mostly praised as "outstandingly friendly and relaxed", though at times they are thought "over-relaxed". The basement brasserie, with its vaulted ceiling, stone pillars and mahogany bar has "buzz, vitality and a relaxed atmosphere", helped along by taped jazz. There's white linen on the tables, and a classic French brasserie menu, which recent visitors thought "excellent and reasonably priced, with an unusually imaginative choice of dishes, and a high standard of cooking". An extension with 51 new bedrooms was due to open in July 1997. (*John C Gillett, Stephen and Ellise Holman, and others*)

Open All year.
Rooms 8 suites, 65 double. Some on ground floor. 4 adapted for &.
Facilities Lift. Café bar, brasserie (taped jazz all day); fitness room.
Location Corner of West George and Pitt Sts, opposite police station. NCP parking nearby. Bus, train to city centre.
Restrictions No smoking in some bedrooms. No dogs in bar, brasserie.
Credit cards All major cards accepted.
Terms [1997] Rooms: single/double £90, suite £120–£165. Breakfast £7.50–£10.50. Full alc £25. Weekend rates.

One Devonshire Gardens   *Tel* (0141) 339 2001
1–3 Devonshire Gardens, G12 0UX   *Fax* (0141) 337 1663

"Opulent" and "decadent" are two adjectives which have been used to describe Ken McCulloch's theatrical establishment in the fashionable West End, a short distance from the city centre. It stands at a busy intersection of two roads, but windows are double-glazed. The three town houses of which it is composed are not interconnected; reception is in Number 3, the restaurant in Number 1. The hotel aims at a Victorian private house atmosphere; guests must ring the bell to enter; maids wear white pinnies. Bedrooms, many huge, with a four-poster, are richly endowed with heavy fabrics and drapes in deep colours, lights with dimmer switches, fruit, magazines, a CD player, and a marble bathroom with luxurious bath robes. One visitor this year wrote: "It remains my favourite hotel in the UK, even though the atmosphere is quite impersonal, and the room service breakfast is a disaster." Another guest admired the food, the service, and the decor, "but having to pay extra for the Sunday paper at such prices is ridiculous". One couple had no complaint: "We felt at home, despite the opulence." Andrew Fairlie, named Scottish Hotel Chef of the Year in 1996, has a *Michelin* star for his modern French-influenced cooking, using mainly Scottish ingredients. (*David Felce, WL Coggans, Michael and Maureen Heath, and others*)

Open All year. Restaurant closed Sat lunch.
Rooms 2 suites, 25 double. 1 on ground floor.
Facilities 2 drawing rooms, bar/club room, study, restaurant (piped classical music); board room, private dining room; patio. Unsuitable for &.
Location 2 miles from centre at intersection of Great Western and Hyndland roads. Back rooms quietest. Off-street parking in front.
Restrictions No smoking in restaurant. No dogs in public rooms.
Credit cards All major cards accepted.
Terms [1997]: Rooms: single £120–£135, double £120–£170, suite £150–£200. Breakfast: continental £8.50, Scottish £13.50. Set lunch £27, dinner £43. Weekend breaks.

The Town House   *Tel* (0141) 357 0862
4 Hughenden Terrace, G12 9XR   *Fax* (0141) 339 9605
                                E-mail thow@cityscape.co.uk

Bill and Charlotte Thow's B&B ("an oasis", one visitor has called it) is in a quiet street in a conservation area in Glasgow's West End. It overlooks Hughenden rugby ground (the Thows' guests may use its bar). "Behind its imposing double-fronted late-Victorian sandstone exterior," writes a recent guest, "the modest furnishings are rather at odds with deep cornices, high ceilings and elaborately carved architraves. But our room was spacious, light and quiet, overlooking playing fields." Others have praised the "young well-trained staff" and admired the extensive book collection in the lounge. Rooms at the top are tiny, with a minuscule shower. Guests are given a front door key, and though the "very helpful and pleasant" owners are not much around, they can be summoned by internal telephone. A simple *à la carte* evening meal is available ("a bit overpriced", one couple thought), and some dishes may be brought to the bedroom. Breakfast, ordered the night before, is "generous, if unimaginative". The restaurants and shops in Byres Road are 15 minutes' walk away. (*JMR Irving, Claire Wrathall, JC Gillett, and others*)
    Note: Not to be confused with the grander, pricier *Town House Hotel* in Nelson Mandela Place; make sure the taxi driver knows which one you are heading for.

Open All year, except Christmas/New Year.
Rooms 10 double.
Facilities Lounge, dining room. Small garden. Unsuitable for &.
Location 1½ miles W of centre. Leave A82 at Hyndland Rd, 1st right into Hughenden Rd, then right at mini-roundabout. Street parking. Bus no.59 from centre.
Restrictions No smoking in dining room. No dogs.
Credit cards Access, Visa accepted.
Terms B&B: single £58, double £68. Full alc £26. Special meals, reduced rates for children.

See also SHORTLIST

The 1999 volume of the *Guide* covering Great Britain and Ireland will be published in the United States in December 1998. Reports are particularly useful in the spring, and they need to reach us by 1 June 1998 if they are to help the 1999 edition. Nominations of new hotels are needed by 25 May 1998.

GLEN CLOY North Ayrshire   Map 5

Kilmichael Country House   NEW   *Tel* (01770) 302219
Glen Cloy, by Brodick   *Fax* (01770) 302068
Isle of Arran KA27 8BY

Fulsome praise from the nominator of Geoffrey Botterill and Antony Butterworth's country house, possibly the oldest on Arran – late 17th-century. It stands in large grounds, on land granted to the forebears of its builder by Robert the Bruce in 1307: "A remarkable place, with a warm welcome, unobtrusive service, great attention to detail. Entirely lives up to its stated aim in the brochure – an escape to the welcoming peace and tranquillity of a friend's home in the country. White-gloved waiters introduce themselves: 'I'm Angus,' with engaging lack of formality. Exotic and exciting food, for example, chocolate ravioli stuffed with minced hare, or a turban of sea bass with tiger prawns and spinach. Breakfast brought the offer of a fresh duck egg, the donor of which waddles round the garden. Even the shoe-cleaning kit is packed artistically into a lovely wooden box. Puccini the dalmatian takes his owners for walks, and everything is in exquisite taste and harmony." Chinese porcelain, oriental rugs and antique furniture decorate the drawing room. The individually designed bedrooms range from Grizel's Room, named after the 1681 love plaque set into the wall, to the Forest Room, which has a four-poster and a corner bath big enough for two; all the "lavishly appointed" bathrooms are stocked with expensive toiletries. (*James Kavanagh*)

Open Jan–Dec.
Rooms 2 suites, 7 double. 8 on ground floor. 4 in stable block (1, with ramp, suitable for &).
Facilities 2 drawing rooms (1 with bar), dining room (piped classical music during meals). 30-acre grounds. Beach 1 mile, sailing; golf, walking nearby.
Location From Brodick ferry terminal go N on A841; turn inland at golf course; follow signs to long drive leading to house. Taxi from ferry.
Restrictions No smoking, except in 1 drawing room. No children under 12. No dogs in public rooms.
Credit cards Access, Visa.
Terms B&B £40–£62; D,B&B £68.50–£90. Set dinner £28.50, full alc £29. Discounts for 3 or more nights.

GLENELG Highland   Map 5

Glenelg Inn   BUDGET   *Tel* (01599) 522273
Glenelg Bay   *Fax* (01599) 522373
by Kyle of Lochalsh IV40 8JR

"An out-of-the-ordinary establishment – the one we most enjoy visiting," write fans of this venerable inn on Glenelg Bay. "It manages to achieve a blend of tranquillity, comfort, well-observed but easy-going interiors, and good food. All this in an unspoilt setting – shimmering sea and islands, tree-laden shore with the mountains of Skye as a backdrop. The informal style of the host, Christopher Main, is just right for an inn which succeeds in linking the demands of the discerning visitor with the needs of the local community in such a splendid place." Another couple wrote: "Our room had not seen a duster for a long time, but with the view from the window across the Sound of Sleat to Skye, what's a speck of dust? *Glenelg* would not do for anyone allergic to a pub atmosphere and the odd spot of carousing into the small hours, or to perching on an upturned fish box to order dinner, but the dining room is a haven, and dinners are of a very high standard." The emphasis is on seafood and local produce: "excellent herring cooked in oatmeal"; "the most delicious salmon with hollandaise sauce we have ever tasted." But the breakfasts have been criticised. The large, rather dark panelled bar with a roaring fire is the village pub; occasional *ceilidhs* are held. The residents' dining room is separate, and quiet, with candlelight and roses. Christopher Main is one of only a few young Scottish/local innkeepers on the West Coast. There's plenty of wildlife and lots to do out of doors. (*Janey and Adrian Stevens, and others*)

Footnote A far cry from the visit paid by James Boswell and Dr Johnson in 1774. "Our room," Boswell reported, "was damp and dirty, with bare walls and a variety of bad smells. Dr Johnson was calm. I said he was so from vanity. *Johnson*: 'No sir, it is from philosophy.'"

Open Easter–end Nov, New Year. Bar open all year.
Rooms 6 double. 1 on ground floor. No telephone.
Facilities Morning room for residents, bar (piped traditional music all day), dining room. 2-acre grounds: garden down to sea, sailing, fishing; trips in hotel powerboat sometimes possible. Birdwatching, hill walking, golf nearby.
Location Seafront of village on Sound of Sleat.
Restrictions No smoking in dining room. No dogs in bedrooms.
Credit cards None accepted.
Terms D,B&B £49–£89. Bar lunch from £3. Set dinner £19. Off season 4-day rates: D,B&B £50. ***V***

GLENLIVET Moray   **Map 5**

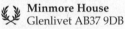
Minmore House   *Tel* (01807) 590378
Glenlivet AB37 9DB   *Fax* (01807) 590472

César award: Scottish hotel of the year

There is much praise again this year for this Victorian house in the beautiful Glenlivet valley, run with enthusiasm by Belinda Luxmoore. "Our eighth visit. Still unrivalled value. She has welded together a new staff and the atmosphere remains friendly but totally professional." "Our room had a well-worn feel, but was clean, comfortable and warm, with new carpets. Friendly Australian staff. No TV but a lovely mix of guests; we stayed in the bar till midnight. Scrumptious teas (included in daily rates) – three types of leaf tea, fruit cakes, hot muffins and scones. The scenery is wonderful and there are many good walks on the Glenlivet Estate." "We liked the relaxed informality of the staff. Wonderful breakfasts; my husband loved his scrambled eggs and smoked salmon, and I discovered a taste for haggis from the local butcher. Dinner was the highlight of the day – five courses of absolute bliss, and we always managed to find room for the home-made fudge served with coffee in the wonderful oak-panelled bar." The no-choice menu features local salmon, beef, venison and organically grown vegetables; breakfast includes freshly squeezed orange juice, and eggs from the hens in the paddock. Dogs are allowed into the house via the fire escape. Generous packed lunches can be provided. There is a secluded garden with a swimming pool above the river Livet, on which *Minmore* has fishing rights, and nearby are many castles and gardens, almost a score of golf courses, and skiing at the Lecht. Mrs Luxmoore tells us the top-floor single rooms mentioned in a cavil last year have been redecorated, and that no single supplement is charged. (*John and Phyllis Bowes, Janice Carrera, Theresa Dougall; also Clive Mackey*)

Open May–mid-Oct. Dining room closed for lunch.
Rooms 8 double, 2 single. No TV.
Facilities Hall, drawing room, lounge bar (occasional *ceilidhs*), dining room (piped classical music during dinner). 4-acre grounds: terraced garden, croquet, tennis, swimming pool (unheated). Fishing, golf nearby. Unsuitable for ბ.
Location Take A95 Grantown-on-Spey–Ballindalloch. Right on to B9008 at *Delnashaugh Inn*. Follow signs to Glenlivet Distillery.
Restrictions No smoking: dining room, drawing room, some bedrooms. No dogs in public rooms.
Credit card Access.
Terms [1997] B&B £45; D,B&B £65. Set dinner £25. 3/7-day rates. 1-night bookings occasionally refused. *V*

GUILDTOWN Perthshire and Kinross   Map 5

Campsie Hill   NEW   *Tel* (01821) 640325
Guildtown, by Perth PH2 6DP   *Fax* (01821) 640785

This turn-of-the-century mansion was built by Arthur Bell of whisky fame, and later was the family home of Garry Barnett, who now runs it with his wife, Jenny, as a private house taking paying guests. It has a wonderful setting: there are views across the valley of the Tay (one of Scotland's great fishing rivers) for 30 miles to the west, and excellent walking straight from the door. Dunsinane and Birnam Wood, known to Macbeth, are close by. A family party were well pleased: "A lovely house, set in a beautiful garden. Our sons were made welcome. We had two huge bedrooms. The excellent four-course dinners, served in the grand manner at about 8 pm, included roast beef one night, gallina fowl the next, and finished with delicious home-made puddings. Generous Scottish breakfast." Unlicensed; bring your own wine. The Barnetts like guests to arrive in time for tea and gingerbread at about 4.30 pm. We dine with our guests unless they ask us not to," they write. "No one has yet." Picnic lunches are available by arrangement. There is tennis and "non-serious" croquet in the grounds, and plenty of wildlife, including red squirrels, roe deer and birds of prey, in the surrounding woods and farmland. Blair and Glamis castles, Scone Palace and Perth race course are nearby; so are several golf courses. (*Sara and Andrey Kidel*)

Open All year, except Christmas, New Year.
Rooms 1 suite with 4-poster, 2 double. No telephone/TV. Also 1 self-contained flat.
Facilities Hall, drawing room, dining room. 2-acre grounds surrounded by farmland. Tennis, croquet. River Tay ¼ mile, fishing; shooting, golf nearby. Unsuitable for ბ.
Location 7 miles N of Perth on A93 to Braemar. Go through Guildtown village, pass sign to Stormontfield on left; hotel 150 yds on right, after bend (letter box at bottom of drive).
Restrictions No smoking: dining room, bedrooms. No children under 12. Dogs by arrangement; not in public rooms.
Credit cards None accepted.
Terms [1997] B&B £33–£35. Set dinner £20.

INNERLEITHEN Scottish Borders   Map 5

The Ley   *Tel/Fax* (01896) 830240
Innerleithen EH44 6NL

"Willie and Doreen McVicar are charming and helpful hosts. It is
clearly a pleasure to them to entertain their guests," wrote the nominator of this fine country house, set in large wooded grounds in Border
country. "They have three large, beautifully furnished guest rooms,
each with an excellent bathroom and fine views over extensive and
beautifully kept gardens. Dinner (four courses, no choice, cooked by
Mrs McVicar) was a splendid affair, served by Mr McVicar and accompanied by a carefully chosen bottle from the adequate wine list. After
dinner, we sampled malts in the lounge, advised by our host." There's
a nine-hole golf course at the bottom of the drive. Walter Scott's
Abbotsford, and many Border abbeys and castles are close by.
Edinburgh is 40 minutes' drive. (*CK*) More reports, please.

Open April–Sept.
Rooms 3 double. No telephone; TV on request.
Facilities Small lift. Drawing room, sitting room with TV, dining room. 30-acre
grounds, woodland walks. Golf nearby. Unsuitable for &.
Location 2 miles N of Innerleithen on B709 towards Heriot. Pass through golf
course, then left over white bridge.
Restrictions No smoking: dining room, bedrooms. No children under 12. No
dogs.
Credit cards None accepted.
Terms B&B £36–£39; D,B&B £58–£61; single occupancy supplement £12. Set
dinner £22.

INVERNESS Highland   Map 5

Culduthel Lodge   NEW/BUDGET   *Tel/Fax* (01463) 240089
14 Culduthel Road
Inverness IV2 4AG

*Georgian Grade II listed guest house, 10 mins' walk from centre. Friendly
owners, David and Marion Bonsor and labrador, Shelley. Quite ambitious
evening meal, which nominators thought "excellent"; but breakfast "patchy".
12 bedrooms, some on ground floor; some with 4-poster or half-tester, all with
CD/cassette player, sherry, fruit, flowers. Garden terrace overlooking river
Ness. Eden Court Theatre on opposite bank; Culloden battlefield nearby.
Closed Christmas/New Year. No smoking: dining room, bedrooms. No children under 10 at dinner. No dogs in public rooms. Access, Visa accepted. B&B
£37.50–£45; D,B&B £55–£63.50. Set dinner £18.50.*

Dunain Park   *Tel* (01463) 230512
Inverness IV3 6JN   *Fax* (01463) 224532

"We were extremely impressed: our suite was beautifully furnished
with every possible amenity; the hotel is impeccably maintained."
"We were made to feel welcome from the moment we arrived." "The
service is understated and discreet, quite lacking obsequiousness, in
keeping with the nature of this small hotel. Food of a consistently
high standard." Recent praise for Edward and Ann Nicoll's italianate

19th-century mansion, set in large gardens and woodland, overlooking the river Ness and the Caledonian Canal. It has a traditional decor, with leather settees, comfortable armchairs, family photographs, fires in cold weather, and "a relaxed atmosphere, conducive to sitting around and chatting". Huge windows overlook the grounds. The bedrooms, especially the six suites in the new wing (each with a sitting room and a marble bathroom), are attractive and spacious. Ann Nicoll's cooking, "traditional Scottish with French influence", might include field mushrooms and chanterelles in pastry, or venison in oatmeal, accompanied by vegetables from the hotel's garden. There's a separate steak menu. Edward Nicoll offers a choice of over 200 malt whiskies. Plenty to see in the area, including Loch Ness, Cawdor Castle and Culloden battlefield. (*Kathie and Eliot Bernstein, Angela Newman, HJ Hamilton*)

Open All year.
Rooms 6 suites (2 in cottages, 1 with access for ♿), 6 double, 1 single.
Facilities Drawing room, lounges, restaurant; indoor swimming pool, sauna. 6-acre grounds: badminton, croquet. Fishing, shooting, golf, tennis, winter sports nearby.
Location 1 mile S of Inverness. Turn left off A82 after Craig Dunain hospital (on right). Station 2½ miles; taxi.
Restrictions No smoking in restaurant. "Well-behaved children welcomed." Dogs by arrangement; not in public rooms.
Credit cards All major cards accepted.
Terms [1997] B&B £55–£79; D,B&B £75–£104. Set lunch £17.50; full alc £34. Low season rates; Christmas/New Year breaks.

ISLE ORNSAY Highland   Map 5

Eilean Iarmain Hotel   *Tel* (01471) 833332
Isle Ornsay, Sleat   *Fax* (01471) 833275
Isle of Skye IV43 8QR

This bilingual Gaelic/English inn (also known as the *Isle Ornsay Hotel*), in a pretty, wooded area, overlooks the Sound of Sleat and the Knoydart hills. Last year's American nominator writes: "Again we were pleased with this small inn, on a wee road lined with bluebells, ferns and yellow broom, only minutes from the Armadale–Mallaig ferry. Our spotless white room in the garden house was attractive and comfortable, set right on the sea, with views across the water to a picture-perfect lighthouse. Excellent croissants at an otherwise typically Scottish breakfast. We enjoyed the gardens at the Clan Donald Centre and there is a lovely drive to the north shore at Ord, where we like to picnic." "Civilised and attractive inn; Gaelic is the first language of the charming staff." Sound insulation is not always perfect in the bedrooms. Half of the bedrooms are in a garden house across the drive. In the restaurant, the bay windows of which overlook sea and mountains, the new chef, Roger Brown, serves local fish, shellfish and game on a short menu; we'd be grateful to hear from recent diners. The inn's owner, Skye Bridge chairman Sir Iain Noble, "whose special interest is all things Gaelic", also owns a small shop and a small distillery. (*Martha Prince, Good Pub Guide*)

Open All year.
Rooms 2 family suites, 10 double. 6 in garden house. Some with TV.
Facilities Lounge, bar (live Scottish music once a month), restaurant (piped

music); Loch fishing, safe bathing, pony trekking, climbing, shooting, stalking nearby. Unsuitable for &.
Location Above Isle Ornsay Bay; 15 mins' drive from Skye bridge and from Mallaig-Armadale ferry. Take A852, then A851. Coach/ferry to Broadford; then taxi.
Restrictions No smoking: restaurant, some bedrooms. No dogs in public rooms.
Credit cards Access, Amex, Visa.
Terms B&B £47.50–£69.50. Set lunch £16.50, dinner £29. Winter breaks. Special meals, reduced rates for children.

KILCHRENAN Argyll and Bute Map 5

Taychreggan *Tel* (01866) 833211
Kilchrenan, by Taynuilt PA35 1HQ *Fax* (01866) 833244
E-mail taychreggan@btinternet.com

This old stone drovers' inn, in a perfect position on the banks of Loch Awe, has been extended and much smartened. The buildings are arranged around a cobbled flowery courtyard, where lunch can be eaten in fine weather. One wing houses a billiard room and some new bedrooms; these have less character than the older rooms, and poor sound insulation, but all the rooms are lavishly draped, attractively furnished and well equipped. There are mixed reports this year. Several visitors have described a chilly welcome and over-formal service. But things seem to improve when the owner, Annie Paul, is around. One visitor wrote of her "friendliness and professionalism", and the "atmosphere of quality". Another said: "The setting is unbeatable. We enjoyed the relaxed and crisp feeling of the bar, and the atmosphere in the dining room, which has antique tables with candles, and a watchful French *maîtresse d'*. Breakfast had excellent porridge, kippers and bacon." Martin Wallace recently took over the kitchens; reports on his modern European cooking would be welcome. There is lots to do in the area: fishing and boating on the loch; walking in the magnificent forests; historic houses and castles to visit; Inverawe Smokehouse for gourmets; 13 Munros (mountains over 3,000 feet) within an hour's drive; the Nervous Wreck diving school in Oban. (*IHK Flinter, Nick and Myriam Whalley, Dr D Wilkie, and others*)

Open All year.
Rooms 20 double. No TV.
Facilities 2 lounges, TV lounge, bar, dining room (piped music during meals); function rooms; snooker room. 25-acre grounds on loch: boats, water sports, fishing (ghillie available). Riding, deer-stalking, walking, climbing, golf nearby. Unsuitable for &.
Location 19 miles SE of Oban. Off B845, at end of 7-mile single track. Train/bus: Taynuilt; hotel will meet.
Restrictions No smoking in dining room. No children under 14. Dogs by arrangement, not in public rooms. One-night bookings sometimes refused.
Credit cards Access, Amex, Visa.
Terms B&B £52–£82; D,B&B £80–£110. Set lunch £18, dinner £32. Autumn, winter, spring, themed breaks. *V*

Before making a long detour to a small hotel, do check that it is open. Some are known to close on impulse.

KILDRUMMY Aberdeenshire   Map 5

Kildrummy Castle Hotel   Tel (01975 5) 71288
Kildrummy, by Alford AB33 8RA   Fax (01975 5) 71345

Thomas Hanna, with a long-serving and loyal staff, has been running
his turn-of-the-century Scottish baronial house in the heart of Donside
for 18 years. It adjoins the grounds of a ruined 13th-century castle (the
gardens with their alpines, shrubs and specimen trees are open to
guests), and has a private stretch of the river Don, two miles away, for
trout- and salmon-fishing. The public rooms are large and comfortable,
with masses of books and magazines. A fine carved wooden staircase
leads up from the panelled hall to the bedrooms, which vary greatly in
shape, size and outlook. Some have thought the atmosphere impersonal, but there is lots to admire. Chef Kenneth Whyte's four-course
dinner menu offers plenty of choice – "good plain cooking, efficiently
served; much local produce and plentiful helpings; sweet trolley

irresistible". And a recent
visitor has written of "a
wonderful setting, pleasant
bedroom and pretty public
rooms". Gardens, castles and
distilleries abound locally
and the Grampian Transport
Museum is a popular excur-
sion. Skiing at the Lecht.
(*M Heath*)

Open 6 Feb–3 Jan.
Rooms 15 double, 1 single.
Facilities Drawing room, lounge bar, library, billiard room, restaurant. Adjacent
to 15-acre castle gardens. 3½ miles private fishing on river Don. Unsuitable
for &.
Location NE of Ballater off A97 Ballater–Huntly.
Restrictions No smoking in restaurant. No dogs in public rooms.
Credit cards Access, Amex, Visa.
Terms B&B £60–£80; D,B&B (min. 2 nights) £63–£108. Set lunch £14.95, dinner
£29; full alc £34. Short breaks; Christmas, New Year packages. Reduced rates for
children sharing parents' room.

KILFINAN Argyll and Bute   Map 5

Kilfinan Hotel   NEW   Tel (01700) 821201
Kilfinan   Fax (01700) 821205
nr Tighnabruaich PA21 2EP

*Former coaching inn on 4,000-acre private estate on Cowal peninsula (eastern
shore of Loch Fyne), amid wonderful Highland scenery. Reached overland or
by road/ferry from Dunoon. Excellent cooking on daily-changing "modern
classical" menu by Rolf Mueller, a Master Chef of Great Britain, who runs
hotel with wife, Lynne. Game, salmon from estate, seafood from Loch
Fyne/Kyles of Bute. Numerous gardens nearby; free golf for residents on local
course; free fishing in Kilfinan Burn. Good walks. Open all year, except Feb.
No smoking in restaurant. No children under 12. No dogs (kennels available).
Access, Amex, Visa accepted. 11 bedrooms, simple but pretty, with bath,*

power shower. B&B £36–£48. Full alc lunch £20. Set dinner £26 [1997]. More reports, please.

KILLIECRANKIE Perthshire and Kinross · · · · · · · · Map 5

Killiecrankie Hotel · · · · · · · · · · · · · · · · · · *Tel* (01796) 473220
Pass of Killiecrankie · · · · · · · · · · · · · · · · · · · *Fax* (01796) 472451
by Pitlochry PH16 5LG

"As good as ever. Colin and Carole Anderson, most helpful, continue to improve and refurbish. There is now a pleasant sitting room with a door into the garden. The well-furnished bedrooms, with comfortable chairs, have views across the gorge, or over the garden to the hills beyond. A flourishing bar meal trade does not interfere with the residents; indeed some prefer to eat there. The young, mainly Australian, staff are friendly and well-trained. Opposite the hotel is one of the loveliest riverside walks we know." "Well run and comfortable; lovely grounds, dramatic views." More praise this year for this small hotel in a beautiful wooded setting at the entrance to the Pass of Killiecrankie, overlooking the river Garry. Chef John Ramsay's menus are "Scottish with continental and Asian influence"; main courses include bouilla-baisse, guinea fowl, perfectly cooked venison, and pudding might be marinaded fruit with home-made ice cream. One visitor this year thought the food pretentious, but others thought it excellent. The wine list is well chosen, with a good selection of half bottles. Pre-theatre suppers are served to guests visiting the nearby Pitlochry Festival Theatre. Plenty of wild life – roe deer, red squirrels, etc – in the grounds; there's an RSPB bird reserve across the river, and the drive through the beeches to the Queen's View of Loch Tummel is recommended, especially in October. Glamis, Scone and Blair castles are nearby. (*Margaret Box, Good Pub Guide, and others*)

Open 7 Mar–2 Jan. Closed 10 days mid-Dec.
Rooms 1 suite, 7 double, 2 single.
Facilities Lounge, bar, restaurant. 4-acre grounds: garden, putting, croquet. Fishing on river Garry ¼ mile; bird reserve nearby. Unsuitable for &.
Location 3 miles N of Pitlochry, just off A9. Train/bus: Pitlochry; then taxi/occasional bus, or hotel will collect.
Restrictions No smoking: 2 bedrooms, restaurant. No children under 5 in restaurant at night.
Credit cards Access, Visa.
Terms [1997] B&B £55; D,B&B £70–£83. Set dinner £29.50. 2-night off-season breaks, wine-tasting weekends, Christmas, New Year programmes. 1-night bookings occasionally refused. Special meals, reduced rates for children.

KINCLAVEN Perthshire and Kinross · · · · · · · · · · Map 5

Ballathie House · *Tel* (01250) 883268
Kinclaven, Stanley PH1 4QN · · · · · · · · · · · · · · · *Fax* (01250) 883396

This sturdy, creeper-clad Victorian mansion, "with Rapunzel-style towers", is set in a vast estate on the banks of the Tay, one of Scotland's finest salmon rivers. It has been admired this year: "Wonderful, remote location. Welcoming and charming staff." "A well-run hotel; lovely walks in extensive grounds with red squirrels and oystercatchers.

Comfortable and relaxing public rooms. Charming restaurant overlooking the river, serving good, varied and well-presented food. Breakfast first-rate, with plenty of choice, including kippers." Chef Kevin MacGillivray's modern Scottish cooking makes inventive use of local produce, eg, warm venison salad with smoked bacon and lentils, Skye scallops with couscous and creamed leeks. But one visitor thought the vegetables undercooked. A grand staircase leads up to the bedrooms. They vary greatly in size and style; some are regally draped; singles are "snug". There is also a luxurious garden suite, and simple accommodation for sportsmen in a lodge in the grounds. Local attractions include golf at Blairgowrie, skiing at Glenshee, the Perth leisure complex, Glamis Castle and Scone Palace. (*June Godding, Val Ferguson, Sir Neil Shields*)

Open All year.
Rooms 1 suite, 20 double, 7 single. 2 on ground floor. Also Sportsman's Lodge in grounds
Facilities Drawing room, morning room, lounge bar, restaurant; small function/conference room. 1,500-acre estate: garden, tennis, croquet, putting, salmon-fishing (ghillie available). Golf, skiing nearby.
Location 8 miles N of Perth. A9 for 2 miles; B9099 through Stanley; right at sign for Kinclaven/Ballathie. From A93: follow Kinclaven/Ballathie signs from Beech Hedges. Train: Perth; then taxi.
Restrictions No smoking in restaurant. No dogs in public rooms.
Credit cards All major cards accepted.
Terms B&B £60–£100; D,B&B £80–£120. Set lunch £12.95–£15.95, dinner £27–£30. Special breaks Oct–Easter £69 per person per night half board. Special meals for children by arrangement. Some reduced rates for children. ***V***

KINGUSSIE Highland   **Map 5**

The Cross   *Tel* (01540) 661166
Tweed Mill Brae   *Fax* (01540) 661080
Kingussie PH21 1TC

"An oasis in a culinary desert," writes a regular visitor to Tony and Ruth Hadley's restaurant-with-rooms. It is a well-converted 19th-century stone-built tweed mill on the edge of the village . The Gynack burn runs alongside the building, and through the wooded grounds, which are filled with native trees and wild flowers, and plenty of wildlife, including red squirrels. A magnet for local gourmets, Ruth Hadley's stylish "Scottish eclectic" cooking makes inventive use of local ingredients: scallop mousse, ceviche of hake, guinea fowl with lemon grass; puddings such as white chocolate and Drambuie cheesecake. Vegans are catered for. There is an outstanding wine list; Tony Hadley writes: "We aim to please people who enjoy wine, rather than wine buffs, and to encourage them to try new things." "He advises, without urging you to break the bank," wrote one gourmet. Another reporter agreed about the meals, but found the bedrooms, many of which overlook the burn, "a bit basic". Local sports of the great outdoors include skiing at Aviemore, water sports at Loch Insh, pony trekking and gliding. (*PN Paterson Brown, and others*)

Open 1 Mar–1 Dec, 27 Dec–10 Jan. Restaurant closed Tues evening.
Rooms 9 double. TV on request.
Facilities Ramp. 2 lounges (1 with TV), restaurant. 4-acre grounds, river: fishing. Golf, walking, climbing nearby. Only restaurant suitable for &.

Location 350 yds up Ardbroilach Rd from traffic lights at town centre. Left at sign down private road. Train/coach; then taxi.
Restrictions No smoking: restaurant, bedrooms. No children under 12. No dogs.
Credit cards Access, Visa.
Terms D,B&B £85–£190. Set dinner £35. Guests staying 1 night only are expected to dine in. Wine weekends; New Year breaks.

KIRKCUDBRIGHT Dumfries and Galloway   Map 5

Gladstone House   NEW/BUDGET   *Tel/Fax* (01557) 331734
48 High Street
Kirkcudbright DG6 4JX

Susan and James Westbrook's handsome Georgian house stands on the main street (a conservation area) of what was once a thriving port and is now much favoured by artists – the name is pronounced "Kurcoobrie". In the 17th century it was the home of a prosperous merchant; today the Westbrooks run it as a no-smoking B&B. It fell from the *Guide* for lack of reports, but is brought back by a mainly positive inspection report. "The welcome was warm. Our bedroom was comfortable, if a little chilly, but might not do for a honeymoon, as the bed was squeaky and the walls were thin. The bathroom had a power shower and an electric towel rail, but minuscule towels. The cosy residents' lounge had tartan cushions, and dim lighting. Breakfast was excellent, with cafetière coffee and plenty of choice, including scrambled eggs and smoked salmon – good ingredients unfussily served." Tea is served in the garden in summer. No restaurant, but *La Dolce Vita* is recommended. The street is quiet, apart from a clock which chimes nearby. Broughton House, a National Trust for Scotland property, is just down the road. An excellent base for touring this fascinating area, with good walking, golf, gardens and the Burns trail.

Open All year.
Rooms 3 double. No telephone.
Facilities Lounge, breakfast room. 2 gardens. Harbour 5 mins' walk. Unsuitable for &.
Location Centre of town, behind Maclellan's Castle, two doors away from Tollbooth. Street parking. Train: Dumfries; then bus.
Restrictions No smoking. No children under 12. No dogs.
Credit cards Access, Visa.
Terms [1997] B&B: single £34–£40, double £54–£60.

KNIPOCH Argyll and Bute   Map 5

Knipoch Hotel   NEW   *Tel* (01852) 316251
Knipoch, by Oban PA34 4QT   *Fax* (01852) 316249
                              E-mail 100745.1315@compuserve.com

The Craig family's yellow-walled hotel is on the A816 in beautiful surroundings overlooking Loch Feochan, an arm of the sea stretching four miles inland, just south of Oban. Inside it is spruce and polished, with log fires, Persian rugs on stripped-pine floors, deep leather armchairs, fabrics and antiques of quality, fine paintings and attractive flower arrangements. It was dropped from the *Guide* last year for lack of reports, but praise from a recent visitor brings it back: "Our room was good-sized. The young staff, who are almost entirely from the

Antipodes, are well-trained, agreeable and adept. The food is outstanding. Every dish we ate was cooked to perfection. Sauces were
excellent complements, not obtrusive. We had no problem with a menu
without choice. The wine list ranges widely, in type and cost – two
bottles were the most expensive (justly so) that we have seen in any
hotel in the UK, but you can drink something entirely acceptable at a
fraction of these prices. The area is beautiful, especially in June, when
the rhododendrons and azaleas are in bloom. The National Trust garden at Arduaine demands a visit, and there are other gardens within an
easy journey." A short list of alternatives to the no-choice menu is available; smoked salmon is home-produced; water comes from the house's
own spring. (*Sir Alan Cook*)

Open Mid-Feb–mid-Nov.
Rooms 1 suite, 15 double.
Facilities Lounge, bar (piped classical music), 3 dining rooms. 2-acre grounds.
Rock beach on sea loch close by.
Location 6 miles S of Oban on A816. Bus from Oban.
Restrictions No smoking in dining rooms. No dogs.
Credit cards All major cards accepted.
Terms [1997] B&B: single £35–£80; double £70–£160, suite £100–£200; D,B&B:
single £65–£110, double £100–£190, suite £130–£260. Lunch by arrangement. Set
dinner (2/3-course) £29.50/£39.50. Children under 10 accommodated free in
parents' room.

KYLESKU Highland   Map 5

Kylesku Hotel   BUDGET   *Tel* (01971) 502231
by Lairg IV27 4HW   *Fax* (01971) 502313

Marcel and Janice Klein's small white hotel at the ferry dock, now by-
passed by the new Kylesku bridge, makes an ideal base for a tour of the
wild and dramatic scenery of the far north-west of Scotland. "A long
drive, but worth it," wrote the nominator. "Superb location – the views
from the dining room conservatory are breathtaking. Marcel Klein is a
congenial host, and the staff are friendly and helpful. Fabulous food.
Local fishermen land fresh fish daily, which Marcel cooks in the
evening. He is something of a wine buff, and has assembled an impressive cellar. Very good bar food in the pub, where friendly locals con-
gregate. The hotel has been recently refurbished and is very warm,
with plenty of hot water; our room had a sofa and a large comfortable
bed with good linen; our dogs were made welcome, too." The hotel has
fishing rights on several lochs. The new Kylesku bridge gives easy
access to the dramatic scenery of the north-west. Handa Island, ten
minutes' drive, is "a paradise for birdwatchers", and Eas Coul Aulin,
Britain's highest waterfall, four times the height of Niagara, can be
visited in Captain Willy Watson's boat, along with the seal islands. (*JC*)

Open 1 Mar–23 Oct.
Rooms 1 suite, 7 double. 6 on ground floor. No telephone.
Facilities Lounge with TV, lounge bar (piped music in evening), restaurant; drying
room. Fishing (tuition arranged), boating, walking, climbing, birdwatching nearby.
Location 35 miles N of Ullapool, on A894. Bus from Ullapool.
Restrictions No smoking in restaurant. No dogs in public rooms.
Credit cards Access, Visa.
Terms B&B £25–£35. Full alc dinner £23. Special meals, reduced rates for
children. *V*

LAIDE Highland   Map 5

Obinan Croft   `NEW/BUDGET`   *Tel* (01445) 731548
Opinan, Laide IV22 2NU   *Fax* (01445) 731635
                                          E-mail obinan@dircon.uk

"A magical place: total peace and outstanding beauty," writes one of
several enchanted nominators of Roger and Mairi Beeson's far-flung
croft, a few yards from the sea at Gruinard Bay, on a peninsula in the
top left-hand corner of Scotland. Rooms can be small, and not all will
have private facilities until 1998, but the compensation is "sinking into
piles of crisp linen pillows on a comfortable bed". "In the morning you
wake to the smell of baking bread – Mairi also bakes girdle scones and
oatcakes daily, and makes her own jams." Her "magnificent" cooking
uses local fish, meat and poultry: "We saw the scallops delivered by
sea, and they tasted excellent in a dill sauce." "Mairi's bread and butter
pudding is out of this world. Everyone dined together and afterwards
conversation flowed over coffee in a comfortable sitting room with a
log fire. We enjoyed smoked salmon and coddled eggs for breakfast."
Another satisfied customer adds: "Such attention to detail: the napkins
and linen changed between breakfast and dinner, and all the feathered
bedclothes, to which I am allergic, were replaced." Dinner is at 8 pm.
The Beesons write: "Our menus are unashamedly British, with a strong
Scottish bias, without fussiness or pretension. We believe nothing beats
fresh food simply prepared, generously served, and enjoyed in an
informal atmosphere." Inverewe Gardens are a few miles south, and
the beach at Mellon Udrigle has spectacular views of the Summer Isles.
(*J Wood, M Edwards, Prof. J Davidoff*)

Open 1 Mar–31 Oct.
Rooms 4 double. 3 on ground floor, with access for ♿. 1 in Old Croft House
15 yds. No telephone/TV.
Facilities Sitting room, dining room. ½-acre garden, surrounded by common
land. Sea 50 yds: safe bathing, fishing. Walking.
Location From A835 12 miles SE of Ullapool take A832 towards Gairloch; right
at Laide, 4 miles to Opinan; hotel is last house. Train: Inverness; then bus.
Restrictions No smoking: dining room, bedrooms. Dogs by arrangement, not in
house. No children under 12 at dinner (high tea 5.30 pm).
Credit cards Access, Visa.
Terms B&B £30. Set dinner £20. Packed lunches £5. .pa

LOCHINVER Highland   Map 5

Inver Lodge   `NEW`   *Tel* (01571) 844496
Lochinver IV27 4LU   *Fax* (01571) 844395
                              E-mail 101322.3315@compuserve.com

This modern clifftop hotel, overlooking the bay, popular with seals, of
a north-west fishing port, was dropped from the *Guide* last year for lack
of feedback. But, apart from one mention of chilly rooms during a particularly cold snap, recent reports are almost all favourable. "The exterior is unprepossessing, but inside it's a nice, well-run, comfortable
place to stay, with spectacular views across to Lewis, particularly at
sunset." "Attentive service and friendly atmosphere. The impressive
Sunday night buffet included salmon, beef, oysters, langoustines, ham,

and home-made puddings. Two stags were grazing 20 yards from the
dining room window. The hotel is frequented by fisher folk, some of
whom come year after year." The decor may be unexciting, but the
spacious bedrooms include video films nightly, fruit renewed daily,
flowers and freebies. They are named after local lochs and peaks, such
as Canisp, Suilven and Assynt – don't try asking for the key after a few
drams – and all have views, and extra-large beds. Bathrooms are well
fitted. Public rooms are large. The manager, Nicholas Gorton, is "ever-
present and cordial", and the owners, Anne and Edmund Vestey, who
have a small house above the hotel, "keep a close eye on everything".
Inverpolly Nature Reserve is nearby, as is ruined Ardvreck Castle,
where Montrose was imprisoned before his execution. (*Ruth West, Jean
Dundas, Sir John B Hall, and others*)

Open 10 Apr–1 Nov.
Rooms 20 double.
Facilities 2 lounges, bar, restaurant (piped music), sauna, solarium, snooker
room, gift shop. 1-acre garden. Sea ½ mile. Loch/river trout-fishing (free for
guests), birdwatching, walking, stalking nearby. Unsuitable for &.
Location A837 from Ullapool. Hotel ½ mile from village, above Lochinver Bay.
Train: Lairg; then bus.
Restrictions No smoking in dining room. No children under 7 in restaurant at
night. No dogs in public rooms.
Credit cards All major cards accepted.
Terms B&B £60–£80; D,B&B £80–£100. Set dinner £27; full alc £32. Discount for
7 nights or more B&B. Special meals, reduced rates for children. *V*

LOCHRANZA North Ayrshire   **Map 5**

Apple Lodge   BUDGET   *Tel/Fax* (01770) 830229
Lochranza
Isle of Arran KA27 8HJ

"Our fourth visit: we enjoy it more each year. John and Jeannie Boyd
are perfect hosts, the decor is in excellent taste, with paintings, embroi-
deries, antiques and local crafts, and the food is superb. Hills on three
sides provide the ideal location for deer- and eagle-spotting from the
bedroom windows." So runs a recent report on this small hotel, originally the village manse, which stands in a small well-kept garden in the
north of the island, a mile from the Kintyre ferry. The bedrooms are
well supplied with books and local information. Dinners, at 7 pm for
7.15, are served by candlelight, with crystal and fresh flowers. Jeannie
Boyd's no-choice menu might include roulade of wild mushrooms,
brie and spinach, and "boozy bread-and-butter pudding with mango";
she will take guests' preferences into account, and promises "no dish
repeated during your stay". No licence; bring your own wine, and
make your own bedtime and early-morning drinks in the kitchen, too.
There is excellent hill-walking on the doorstep, and a golf-course too.
Brodick castle and gardens are worth a visit, and if you're lucky the
deer may come down from the hills and cross the road as you return to
see the romantic ruins of Lochranza at sunset. (*John and Mona Taylor*)

Open All year, except Christmas.
Rooms 1 self-contained suite, 3 double. No telephone.
Facilities Lounge, dining room (piped classical music at night). ¼-acre garden.
200 yds from loch: rocky beach. Walking, golf, fishing, sailing nearby.
Unsuitable for &.

Location N side of island, on A841, ½ mile past village sign, opposite golf-course. Bus from ferry.
Restrictions No smoking: dining room, bedrooms. No children under 12. No dogs.
Credit cards None accepted.
Terms B&B £27–£45; D,B&B £42–£60. Packed lunch from £4.50. Set dinner £15. Weekend, midweek off-season breaks. 1-night bookings refused in advance for high season. Child half-price in parents' room.

MARKINCH Fife   Map 5

Balbirnie House   *Tel* (01592) 610066
Balbirnie Park   *Fax* (01592) 610529
Markinch   *E-mail* hotline.balbirnie@btinternet.com
by Glenrothes KY7 6NE

This Grade A Georgian mansion stands in a Capability Brown-style landscaped park, with mature trees and an important collection of rhododendrons. It has been carefully restored by the Russell family, and has original plaster ceilings, a long gallery with *trompe-l'oeil* paintings, a library bar well stocked with malt whiskies, and a comfortable drawing room; antiques are everywhere and the style is luxurious. "Well-furnished, extremely comfortable bedrooms, high-quality food; excellent breakfast," reads a report this year, endorsing last year's praise: "Well worth the price for such pampering. Most bedrooms are spacious, with sofa, armchairs, lots of extras. Staff are without exception pleasant and friendly." David Kinnes, a runner-up in the Northern Chef of the Year competition, is now head chef. His cooking – "classical with a Scottish approach" – won the AA's top award (four red stars) in 1996, when *Balbirnie* was also the Macallan/Taste of Scotland Hotel of the Year. All manner of country pursuits are available (see below); there's an 18-hole golf course "just a chip shot away", and 100 others within an hour's drive. Falkland Palace, and St Andrew's Abbey and Castle are a short drive away. A new "events venue" is due to open in early 1998; we'd like to know if the corporate overtakes the personal style. (*SC Law, and others*)

Open All year.
Rooms 2 suites, 26 double, 2 single. 1 on ground floor.
Facilities Ramp. Gallery, drawing room, 2 bars, library, snooker room, 2 dining rooms, bistro (piped music throughout); function/conference facilities. 420-acre estate: 2-acre garden, croquet, golf, fishing, riding, shooting, falconry, jogging.
Location NW of Markinch, off B9130. Half-way between Edinburgh and St Andrews. Train: Markinch; then taxi.
Restriction No smoking in restaurant.
Credit cards All major cards accepted.
Terms B&B £80–£112.50; D,B&B £128–£141. Set Sun lunch £15.75, dinner £28.50; full alc £34.50. Weekend, golfing, Christmas, New Year, Celebration breaks.

MARYCULTER Aberdeenshire   Map 5

Maryculter House   *Tel* (01224) 732124
South Deeside Road   *Fax* (01224) 733510
Maryculter, Aberdeen AB12 5GB

Former Templar priory in 5-acre wooded grounds on river Dee, 8 miles S of Aberdeen. Ample public rooms. Efficient management. Somewhat functional decor; business/function-oriented clientele (riverside setting popular for wed-dings). 23 comfortable bedrooms (some overlooking river) with pine furniture, flowery fabrics; 12 no-smoking; some on ground floor, with ramps. Good bar meals; very good traditional French dinners in restaurant (closed Sun). Obliging staff. Golf, fishing, shooting nearby. Open all year. All major credit cards accepted. No-smoking: bar, restaurant. No dogs in public rooms. Rooms: single £65–£105, double £65–£115, suite £90–£120; D,B&B single £75–£82, double £100–£118. Set dinner £29.50. *V*

MOFFAT Dumfries and Galloway   Map 5

Beechwood House   NEW   *Tel* (01683) 220210
Harthope Place   *Fax* (01683) 220889
Moffat DG10 9RS

Country house in 1½-acre grounds with beech trees, overlooking river Annan on edge of small market town just off A74 – a useful staging post to and from the north. Owners, Lynda and Jeff Rogers, have completely renovated in last 2 years. "Blissfully quiet," writes nominator. "Bedrooms equipped with every extra imaginable; lounges well furnished, and with log fire; quite ambitious cooking; friendly proprietors." Golf, fishing, riding, pony-trekking nearby. Glasgow and Edinburgh, west and east coasts just over an hour's drive. Closed Jan. Only restaurant suitable for ☐. No-smoking restaurant, main lounge. 7 bedrooms. B&B £36.50–£51; D,B&B £55–£66. Set lunch £14.50, dinner £23. More reports, please. *V*

MUIR OF ORD Highland   Map 5

The Dower House   *Tel/Fax* (01463) 870090
Highfield, Muir of Ord IV6 7XN

"Lovely, lovely, lovely," writes a recent ecstatic visitor to Robyn and Mena Aitchison's welcoming and colourful *cottage orné* in mature grounds, close to some of Scotland's most spectacular scenery. "Our four days here were the highlight of our holiday: I felt like Alice in Wonderland. On our arrival, Robyn came dashing out; he picked up the cases and led us to our bedroom: great floppy ribbons floated across a pink and white wallpaper, flowers streamed across the sofa, pictures and family photos were on the walls, there was a view of the garden, and the enormous Victorian bath nearly filled the little bathroom – tow-els were changed twice daily – all so *gemütlich*. The standard of excel-lence the hotel has set for itself runs through every aspect. Robyn produced high quality food night after night: gorgeous home-made soups, chicken and mushroom risotto, poached wild salmon, interest-ing sauces and vegetables. He makes his own after-dinner chocolates. Lovely coffee, poached eggs and heather honey for breakfast, brought by Mena in a long blue dress. Robyn tells stories about Culloden, just down the road, which will make your hair stand on end. Apparently, the ghosts of the Jacobites still roam the moor, even in daylight." Some bedrooms are small, but they are cosily decorated. (*Ruth West*)

Open All year, except Christmas, 1 week Oct, 2 weeks Mar.
Rooms 1 suite, 4 double. All on ground floor. 3 in lodge (also let as a self-catering unit).

Facilities Lounge, dining room. 4-acre grounds: small formal garden, swings, tree house. Walking, fishing, beach, golf, beaches nearby.
Location 15 miles NW of Inverness. 1 mile N of Muir of Ord, on A862 to Dingwall: left at double bend sign; through maroon gates.
Restrictions No smoking: dining room, bedrooms. No dogs in public rooms.
Credit cards Access, Visa.
Terms [1997] B&B: single £45–£70, double £90–£120; suite £100–£120. Set lunch £17.50, dinner £30. Winter, group rates. Discounts for 3 or more nights D,B&B.

NAIRN Highland   Map 5

Clifton House   *Tel* (01667) 453119
Viewfield Street   *Fax* (01667) 452836
Nairn IV12 4HW

◊ *César award in 1987*

"We have been visiting J Gordon Macintyre's delightful and somewhat eccentric inn, with pleasure, for ten years. We always feel most welcome. The public rooms are bright and richly attractive, with flowers on every surface. There are books everywhere, and *objets d'art* on walls, stair landings and table tops. The white cat, Zauberflöte, now joined by fluffy Oberon, supervises everything. The food is always delicious. Mr Macintyre is a knowledgeable collector of cheeses and wines. Breakfast is served when you want it." Praise from a regular American visitor to this Victorian seaside villa, which others have called "one of the most distinctive hotels in Scotland". It looks across the Moray Firth towards Ross-shire and the Sutherland hills, and has an owner as theatrical and exuberant as its Victorian interiors. His welcome, style and personal concern for his guests have been much praised over the years, and so has the "most helpful staff". The restaurant serves local fish, meat and game. There is plenty of choice on the daily-changing menu; cooking is French, with well-executed traditional dishes, followed by British puddings and Scottish cheeses. Breakfast includes home-made bread, oatcakes, muesli and preserves. Snack lunches and picnics are available. Stylish bedrooms (some quite small) have antique furniture; duvets on beds can be changed to conventional bedding on request. The hotel has a theatre licence; in winter, plays, concerts and recitals are staged. A good centre for sight-seeing: Brodie and Cawdor castles, Culloden, Loch Ness, etc. (*Martha Prince; also Anne and Ian Steel*)

Open Mar–Nov.
Rooms 9 double, 3 single. No telephone/TV.
Facilities Sitting room, drawing room, TV room/library, 2 dining rooms (piped classical music in evening); plays, concerts, recitals Oct–Mar. Beach, golf, tennis, public swimming pool, fishing, shooting, riding nearby. Unsuitable for &.
Location Turn E at roundabout on A96 in town centre. Private parking. Train/bus stations nearby.
Restrictions No smoking in 1 dining room. No dogs in dining rooms.
Credit cards All major cards accepted.
Terms B&B: single £54, double £91–£96. Full alc £30–£35.

We need feedback on all entries. Often people fail to report on the better-known hotels, assuming that "someone else is sure to".

NEWPORT-ON-TAY Fife   Map 5

Forgan House   NEW/BUDGET   *Tel/Fax* (01382) 542760
Newport-on-Tay DD6 8RB

This small B&B is a listed Georgian manse set in farmland (with ponies) three miles south of the Tay bridge. "It is like a small Irish country house, if less stylish, but with great charm," writes the Belfast nominator. "There is a large walled garden with a fine tree house in a magnificent chestnut tree. Inside, all is spick and span, with pine doors and comfortable furniture. Our bedroom was roomy and pleasant. A large bath was set in the middle of its bathroom. There is a cosy library/sitting room with a log fire. Communal dinners, simple home-cooking, extremely palatable to anyone with a decent appetite, are served in the small but characterful dining room. Wine is chosen from a rack in the kitchen. Breakfast is substantial, and rapidly served. The owners, Doug and Patricia Scott, radiate good humour." There are two self-catering cottages in the early 18th-century steadings. St Andrews, with its famous golf courses and *Chariots of Fire* beaches, and the Fife fishing villages are nearby. (*Esler Crawford*)

Open All year, except Christmas.
Rooms 1 suite, 3 double, 1 single. No telephone. 2 self-catering cottages.
Facilities Library/lounge with TV, conservatory, dining room. 3-acre grounds: walled garden. Golf, sea nearby. Unsuitable for &.
Location From Forgan roundabout take A92 towards St Andrews; 1st left after ¾ mile, signed Tayport. Hotel ¼ mile on left.
Restrictions Smoking in library only. No dogs.
Credit cards Access, Visa.
Terms B&B £29.50–£39.50; D,B&B £51–£61. Set dinner £21.50. Reduced rates for children; special meals on request.

NEWTON STEWART Dumfries and Galloway   Map 5

Creebridge House   *Tel* (01671) 402121
Minnigaff   *Fax* (01671) 403258
Newton Stewart DG8 6NP   *E-mail* creebridge.hotel@daelnet.co.uk

This peaceful grey stone former shooting lodge stands amid flowery gardens on the edge of a fairly unremarkable town close to the Galloway hills, convenient for the Stranraer ferry and Ayr racecourse. A visitor this year found "a very friendly and unpretentious hotel, with delicious food, especially breakfast: wonderfully tender haggis and black pudding". The public rooms are large and comfortable, with fresh flowers and pot-pourri everywhere. Bedrooms vary in size and standard; the best have views over the garden. The owners, Chris and Sue Walker, are originally from Yorkshire. He does the "Scottish/French" cooking: the four-course dinners offer a limited choice, but always include fish or game and often an unusual combination, such as herring fillet with prawns and scallops, or lemon and green apple sorbet. Bar meals, too, are popular: "Meats are local and well-hung, presentation is careful with good attention to detail." The hotel makes a good base for a fishing holiday, and offers many country pursuits and sports, including free golf for guests at the local course. Children and dogs are welcome. (*Mary and Rodney Milne-Day, Good Pub Guide*)

Open All year.
Rooms 2 suites, 15 double, 2 single. 1 on ground floor.
Facilities 2 lounges, bar (with bar billiards), brasserie, restaurant (piped classical music in evening). 3-acre grounds: croquet, putting. Fishing, golf (free at local course), walking, shooting, pony-trekking, birdwatching, sailing, beach nearby. Unsuitable for &.
Location Left over bridge in town, towards Minnigaff. Hotel 200 yds on left, after petrol station. Train: Dumfries, 47 miles; then bus.
Restriction No smoking in restaurant.
Credit cards Access, Amex, Visa.
Terms B&B: single £42–£49.50, double £62–£84; D,B&B: single £57–£70, double £94–£120. Set dinner £22. Bar meals. 3-day rates. Off-season breaks. Fishing, shooting, golf packages. Children under 12 accommodated free in parents' room; special meals. *V*

OBAN Argyll and Bute   Map 5

Dungallan House   *Tel* (01631) 563799
Gallanach Road   *Fax* (01631) 566711
Oban PA34 4PD

"Bliss," wrote our sorely tried inspector last year. "At last somewhere I can unreservedly recommend. Welcoming, accommodating owners, delightful smiley young staff. Delicious dinners. Excellent value. An oasis in an otherwise unexciting town." Now an American stalwart endorses George and Janice Stewart's new clifftop venture on the outskirts of Oban: "A great discovery. The handsome stone inn is set high on a hill, with panoramic views through lovely old trees down to the town and harbour, and across to Mull. Our bedroom was bright and spacious, and friends had a tower room upstairs, complete with resident ghost. Janice Stewart is the chef: lobster vol au vent and venison paté were fine starters, braised steak with burgundy sauce a good choice, and strawberry meringue roulade made a delicious ending." Bedrooms are floral, with a good simple *en suite* bathroom (plenty of hot water). The best are at the front – you can lie in bed watching the ferries go by in the distance. The large, handsome striped dining room, warmed by a fire, overlooks the bay (fine sunsets). A good place to stop before catching a ferry to Mull and the islands – or on the return journey; and there are half a dozen castles and public gardens to visit in the area. (*Martha Prince*)

Open All year, except Nov, Feb.
Rooms 11 double, 2 single. 1 on ground floor. No telephone.
Facilities Lounge, bar, dining room. 5-acre grounds. Sea 50 yds. Sandy beaches, sea/loch fishing, golf nearby. Unsuitable for &.
Location ½ mile from town centre. Follow signs to Gallanach, left 500 yds past ferry terminal.
Restrictions No smoking in dining room. Dogs by arrangement; not unattended in bedrooms.
Credit cards Access, Visa.
Terms B&B £37.50–£45; D,B&B £63.50–£71. Full alc lunch £15, dinner £30.50; set dinner £20–£26. Discounts for 5 or more nights. Special meals, reduced rates for children. *V*

Please make a habit of sending in a report as soon as possible after a visit when details are still fresh in your mind.

PEEBLES Scottish Borders   Map 5

Cringletie House   Tel (01721) 730233
Peebles EH45 8PL   Fax (01721) 730244
                                  E-mail res@cringletie.prestel.co.uk

*Pink stone baronial mansion, turreted, gabled, dormer-windowed, built in
1861 by renowned Scottish architect David Bryce for Wolfe Murrays of
Quebec fame; owned by Maguire family for 25 years. On large estate 2 miles
N of Peebles on A703. Extensive views over surrounding hills and Tweed valley. Tennis, putting, croquet, children's play area; golf, fishing nearby;
Edinburgh 30 mins' drive. Old-fashioned decor. Panelled lounge with painted
ceiling, marble fireplace, antique furniture; conservatory with lovely views.
"Hearty, excellent home-cooking; good, unobtrusive service; extensive, reasonably priced wine list. Fruit and vegetables home-grown in large walled
kitchen garden. 13 bedrooms, varying in size and quality; some up 3 flights of
steps, a few thought dingy. Open 10 Mar–2 Jan. Unsuitable for &. No smoking: dining rooms, 1 lounge. No dogs in public rooms, unattended in bedrooms. Access, Amex, Visa accepted. B&B £57.50–£62.50. Set Sun lunch £16,
dinner £25.50 [1997]. More reports, please.*

PENNYGHAEL Argyll and Bute   Map 5

Pennyghael Hotel   **BUDGET**   Tel (01681) 704288
Isle of Mull PA70 6HB   Fax (01681) 704205

"A more beautiful location could not be imagined," wrote the nominators last year of the Bowman family's informally run small guest house.
It is a low white 17th-century farmhouse on the rocky shore of Loch
Scridain, a deep inlet on the west coast of the island, with wonderful
views across to Iona. Visitors this year have written enthusiastically of
the "varied evening meals, beautifully cooked by Mrs Jess Bowman,
with excellent seafood, and fresh flavours". Local wild salmon, scallops, venison and cheese feature on the limited menus. "The enormous
breakfast fry-up is a great start to the day; it's the only place we know
that can properly scramble eggs." "Mrs Bowman seems to do most of
the work – with the greatest good nature and warmth of spirit." The
bedrooms and bathrooms are "scrupulously clean, if a bit basic". Not
for those in search of luxury: "You couldn't describe the place as cosy,"
one couple wrote: "No open fire, and the only sitting area is around the
bar and not very inviting." But Mrs Bowman is a "welcoming, considerate" hostess, and her staff are "genuinely friendly". Plenty of
wildlife, including herons and sea otters. (*John C Gillett, Dr H Garmany,
Carolyn Mathiasen, and others*)

Open All year, except New Year.
Rooms 6 double. 2 on ground floor. Also self-catering cottages.
Facilities Lounge, dining room.
Location On A849, beside Loch Scridain. Ferry from Oban.
Restrictions No smoking in dining room. No dogs in public rooms.
Credit card Access.
Terms B&B £35–£45; D,B&B £40–£70. Reductions for 3 or more nights; 3 nights
for price of 2 Nov–Mar. Christmas package.

PIEROWALL Orkney   Map 5

Cleaton House   NEW/BUDGET   *Tel* (01857) 677508
Pierowall, Westray KW17 2DB   *Fax* (01857) 677442
                                          E-mail cleaton@orkney.com

*On Westray, one of northern-most Orkneys, "a find": small hotel, also acting
as local pub, with hands-on proprietor, Malcolm Stout. 2 miles SE of Pierowall
village, reached by ferry from Kirkwall. Simple decor; wonderful views; large,
well-equipped bedrooms; beach a short walk across fields. Good dinners: local
ingredients, freshly caught fish; good bar meals too. Ethnic Orcadian music in
public rooms. Island offers daylight until midnight in summer; wonderful
walking and birdlife; cliffs, sandy beaches; free golf at local course, trout-
fishing; day trips to Papa Westray ("one of the most beautiful of the islands").
No dogs in public rooms. B&B £20–£32; D,B&B £35; full alc £25.* *V*

PLOCKTON Highland   Map 5

The Haven   BUDGET   *Tel* (01599) 544223
Plockton IV52 8TW   *Fax* (01599) 544467

This unassuming hotel is a converted merchant's house owned by
Annan and Jill Dryburgh. It is situated on the palm- and flowering
shrub-lined shore of an inlet of Loch Carron, in a delightful West
Highland village ("a crescent of white cottages opposite steep blue
hills") owned by the Scottish National Trust. Simple bedrooms vary in
size and position; the best are spacious and light. There are two new
suites, one with a four-poster. The large dining room, with a gold-
toned pipe organ, is popular with non-residents (you need to book well
in advance). Cooking is traditional Scottish, with plenty of choice on
the menu, including local salmon, prawns and venison. "Very good
value. Willing and friendly staff. We stayed four nights and were never
disappointed with the meals," said one couple. Another thought the
lighting in the dining room gloomy, but wrote: "The hotel eases the
cost of crossing the Skye bridge, close by, by purchasing books of tickets – a considerable saving." A long-established yachters' haven,
Plockton is also the setting for TV's *Hamish MacBeth*. (*John and Phyllis
Bowes, and others; also Good Pub Guide*)

Open 1 Feb–20 Dec.
Rooms 2 suites, 12 double. 1 single.
Facilities 2 lounges, conservatory, bar, restaurant (piped Scottish music). Sea
30 yds: beach, boating, fishing, seal trips.
Location Centre of village 7 miles N of Kyle of Lochalsh. Small carpark.
Restrictions No smoking: restaurant, 1 lounge, conservatory. No children
under 7. No dogs in public rooms.
Credit cards Access, Visa.
Terms [1997] B&B £35–£37; D,B&B £51–£68. Set dinner £23.50 (non-residents).
3-day breaks.

We asked hotels to quote 1998 prices. Not all were able to pre-
dict them in the late spring of 1997. Some of our terms will be
inaccurate. Do check latest tariffs at the time of booking.

POLLOCHAR Western Isles   Map 5

Polochar Inn NEW/BUDGET   *Tel* (01878) 700215
Pollochar, Lochboisdale   *Fax* (01878) 700768
South Uist HS8 5TT

*Ewen and Tiag MacInnes' simple white-painted inn (named in Gaelic for
nearby standing stone). "Heavenly location" on beach at SW tip of island.
Views of Sound of Barra, seals, dolphins, sunsets. Reached by ferry from Oban.
Lively style: discos, karaoke, quizzes, live and piped music; also quiet lounge.
Scottish country cooking. Bathing, hill-walking, sea/trout-fishing, birdwatching (many corncrakes). Eriskay/Barra ferries 2 miles. Closed New Year's Day,
Good Friday. Only public rooms suitable for &. No smoking: dining room,
bedrooms. Access, Visa accepted. 10 rooms ("OK to good"). B&B: single
£30–£35, double £50–£55, family £60–£70. Bar meals. Set lunch £10, dinner
£15; full alc £30.*

PORT APPIN Argyll and Bute   Map 5

The Airds Hotel   *Tel* (01631) 730236
Port Appin PA38 4DF   *Fax* (01631) 730535
Q *César award in 1994*

"We spent New Year there: natural foliage Christmas decorations,
bowls of clove-studded oranges, ribboned garlands, pyramids of tan-
gerines combined with log fires and unstinted central heating to make
Airds a warm bower in a wintry landscape. Kenneth, the unflappable
manager, had his staff well drilled in the ritual of brushing away the
errant crumb from the spotless white damask. Graeme Allen's
Michelin-starred menus surpassed themselves: mousse of scallops, crab
sausages, a memorably intense red pepper and fennel soup, prune and
armagnac ice cream. There are gorgeous home-made chocolates with
coffee. People chat, in a friendly atmosphere. Undoubtedly expensive,
but worth it." One report of many which sum up the Allen family's
small but sybaritic hotel (Relais & Châteaux), overlooking Loch
Linnhe. A few caveats this year, however: repetition of dishes, an
expensive and patchily stocked wine list, infrequent sightings of the
Allens. Bedrooms and bathrooms are designer mix-and-match chic and
pretty, as are the two cosy drawing rooms, with open fires, and masses
of flowers. For those who can haul themselves out of the squashy sofas
with chintz and tartan cushions, a short walk leads to Port Appin and
a boat trip to Lismore. (*George and Jean Dundas, J and D Rednall; also S
and E Holman, and others*)

Open All year. Restaurant closed 9–31 Jan.
Rooms 1 suite, 10 double, 1 single. 2 on ground floor. Also 4 double in Linnhe
House 60 yds.
Facilities 2 lounges, bar, restaurant, conservatory. 1-acre garden. Near loch:
shingle beach, bathing, fishing, boating; pony-trekking, forest walks, stalking
with camera.
Location 2 miles off A828, 25 miles from Fort William (N) and Oban (S). Parking.
Restrictions No smoking: restaurant, Linnhe House bedrooms; discouraged in
main hotel bedrooms. No dogs.
Credit cards Access, Visa.
Terms [1997] D,B&B £98–£138 (Linnhe House £80). Set dinner £35. Off-season

reductions. Extra bed for child in parents' room £30. Special meals for children.
One-night bookings occasionally refused.

Pierhouse   **NEW**   *Tel* (01631) 730302
Port Appin PA38 4DE   *Fax* (01631) 730400

"An unpretentious, endearing restaurant-with-rooms, right at the
water's edge, with outstanding food and a warm welcome." Thus an
American visitor nominates this former ferry house on Loch Linnhe, in
the heart of RL Stevenson's *Kidnapped* country. It is very much a family
affair: Sheila MacLeod is the cook and "well deserves her *Good Food
Guide* entry"; her husband, Alan, is self-styled "dogsbody"; daughter
Julie runs the bar; son Callum is front-of-house and does a lot of the
waiting. "He is one of those special people who make guests feel
they've made his day by showing up. The bedrooms are simple, with
pine furniture, cheerful curtains and bedspreads, and a lovely view
across the loch to the islands and the Morvern Hills beyond". "All our
seafood is caught within sight of the restaurant," write the MacLeods,
and our inspector rhapsodised: "The 'water's edge simplistic' cookery,
served in the buttermilk and blue restaurant is matchless: a towering
pile of prawns plucked straight from creels at the pier, scallops and langoustines, perfectly cooked, abundant vegetables, and a definitive
sticky toffee pudding. Delicious kippers or scrambled eggs and
smoked salmon for breakfast. Though the hotel side of things is a little
basic, the food makes up for a lot." The *Pierhouse* is also the local pub
and is popular with yachting people. The passenger ferry to Lismore
leaves every two hours, and a boat can be hired to visit Castle Stalker
and the Seal Islands. (*Carolyn Mathiason, and others*).

Open All year.
Rooms 1 suite, 10 double. 5 on ground floor, some with access for &.
Facilities Ramp. 2 lounges, bar (with pool table), restaurant (piped classical
music). On loch: bathing for strong swimmers, boat trips, sailing (moorings
available); fishing; riding; cycling.
Location From A828 Oban–Fort William, follow sign for Appin, then Lismore
Ferry: hotel is at pier. Bus: Appin, 3 miles; then taxi.
Restriction No dogs. No children in bar after 8 pm.
Credit cards Access, Visa.
Terms B&B £35–£45. Full alc lunch £17, dinner £25. Packed lunches. Discounts
for 2 or more nights.

PORT OF MENTEITH Stirling   **Map 5**

The Lake Hotel   *Tel* (01877) 385258
Port of Menteith FK8 3RA   *Fax* (01877) 385671

This tiny village is the main holiday centre on the only lake in Scotland.
The hotel, a much-added-to manse beside a church, has a beautiful,
peaceful setting on the shore, looking across the island of Inchmahome
(where Mary, Queen of Scots, once took refuge in an Augustinian
monastery, now in ruins) to the Trossachs. Some rooms are very small.
It is worth paying extra for one with a lake view; those on the ground
floor open on to a terrace, almost on the water's edge. The lawn is like
a wildlife sanctuary," wrote an inspector, "with oystercatchers,
plovers, ducks, swans and garden birds galore, almost within arm's

length. The conservatory restaurant, which has a very pleasant atmosphere, is dominated by the view. Dinner was mostly very good. Breakfast included a wide selection of porridge, cereals, and cooked dishes; toast was replenished as fast as we ate it. We thought the lounge a bit unappealing. The place lacks the personal touch of a resident owner, and housekeeping can be a little casual, but the manager, Douglas Little, and his staff are very pleasant. We would certainly return if we could have a bedroom on the lake." Other visitors enjoyed "lingering over coffee and home-made petits fours, watching the fishermen making their nightly sortie", and added: "Absolutely quiet. Absolutely relaxing." (*Lois Lyman, and others*)

Open All year. Closed Sun pm–Tues pm Nov–Mar, except Christmas, New Year.
Rooms 16 double.
Facilities Lounge, lounge bar, restaurant (piped light classical music during dinner). 1-acre grounds on lake: fishing. Golf, hill walking, mountain biking nearby. Unsuitable for &.
Location Take A85 to Port of Menteith, B8034 to Arnprior. Hotel on right after 250 yds. Bus from Stirling/Glasgow.
Restrictions No smoking in restaurant. No children under 12. No dogs in public rooms.
Credit cards Access, Amex, Visa.
Terms [1997] B&B £44–£80; D,B&B £54–£97. Set lunch £14.50, dinner £23.90. Off-season breaks.

PORTPATRICK Dumfries and Galloway   **Map 5**

The Crown   NEW   *Tel* (01776) 810261
9 North Crescent
Portpatrick DG9 8SX

On harbour of charming village facing Irish Channel, friendly small inn. Bustling bar, attractive conservatory/dining room, serving fish and lobster – sometimes caught by owner, Bernard Wilson, or chef, Robert Campbell; "service sometimes slow, but food worth waiting for". Good-value bar snacks. Piped music in public rooms. 12 small bedrooms, "full of character", particularly those at top, with harbour view. Southern Upland Way starts close by; golf, sea angling, pony-trekking available. Access, Amex, Visa accepted. B&B £36–£48. Winter breaks. Set lunch £15–£20; full alc £20–£25.

Knockinaam Lodge   *Tel* (01776) 810471
Portpatrick DG9 9AD   *Fax* (01776) 810435

"We could not fault the atmosphere, the food or the service," runs a hearty endorsement this year for this "small but perfect" hotel in the far south-west corner of Scotland. It stands in subtropical gardens at the end of a three-mile track, in a spectacular setting, with cliffs on three sides and the sea on the fourth. The setting is so secluded that Churchill and Eisenhower were able to meet here secretly during World War II. On a clear day you can see the coast of Ireland. It has refreshingly informal Canadian owners, Michael Bricker and Pauline Ashworth, "and beautiful furnishings", and the bedrooms have every sort of country house comfort. The food prepared by head chef Tony Pierce retains the *Michelin* star earned by his predecessor. "The no-choice dinner menu of four courses, *canapés* and an *amuse-gueule*, was quite excellent in flavours, cooking and presentation. Packed lunch in a wicker basket was provided one day, and on another sandwiches at very short notice." Cuisine is "modern English with international touches" – and lots of seafood. Breakfast is traditional Scottish, and Michael Bricker's

collection of 104 malt whiskies may be sampled in the bar. Children are welcomed. Logan, Castle Kennedy and Ardwell House gardens are nearby, and a trip to watch the dangerous tidal race at the Mull of Galloway is recommended. (*Dr and Mrs P Tattersall, Julie and Mike Taylor-Evans*)

Open All year.
Rooms 9 double, 1 single.
Facilities 2 lounges, bar, dining room (piped classical music at night). 30-acre grounds: garden, croquet; private beach 50 yds. Sea fishing, golf nearby.
Location 7½ miles SW of Stranraer. Turn left off A77 at *Knockinaam* sign 2 miles W of Lochans; follow signs for 3 miles to hotel.
Restrictions No smoking in restaurant. No children under 12 in dining room at night (high tea 6 pm). No dogs in public rooms.
Credit cards All major cards accepted.
Terms D,B&B £75–£120. Set lunch £25, dinner £35. Off-season 3-day breaks. Reduced rates for children sharing parents' room. *V*

PORTREE Highland   **Map 5**

Viewfield House   BUDGET   *Tel* (01478) 612217
Portree, Isle of Skye IV51 9EU   *Fax* (01478) 613517

🗘 *César award in 1993*

"We grew to like it greatly, though on arrival we thought we had made a mistake: the hall was full of dusty stuffed birds, animals and stags and nobody was there to greet us. But our enormous bedroom was superb, and the bath water was boiling hot." "As good as ever: the mild eccentricity of the owner, Hugh Macdonald, with his pre-dinner interrogation of guests; the fire lit, just for effect, on a warm day, in the gorgeous sitting room; the 'common table' where guests sat together, and which was soon buzzing with conversation; and the food as delicious as before." So write recent visitors to this baronial house, in large wooded grounds just outside Skye's main town. It has been the Macdonald family home since the 18th century and, apart from the plumbing, has hardly changed since before the first world war. It is a repository of imperial mementos – Persian carpets, Burmese gongs, Benares brass, and bric-à-brac of the Raj. Guests "dine in Victorian splendour" (there are separate tables for those who prefer to sit alone), with gleaming family silver and crystal. Hugh's Californian wife, Linda, produces five-course traditional Scottish dinners which might include some unusual items, eg, gravadlax mousse, or apple, ginger and mustard soup. Vegetarian dishes, and a fish option for the main course are always available. (*David and Anna Berkeley, Dr Bryan Sykes*)

Open Mid-Apr–mid-Oct.
Rooms 9 double, 2 single. No telephone/TV.
Facilities Drawing room, TV room, dining room. 20-acre grounds: croquet, swings, woodland walks. Sea 200 yds; fishing. Unsuitable for ♿ (a ground floor room is planned).
Location S side of Portree, 10 mins' walk from centre. Take A850 towards Broadford; turn right just after BP station on left. Bus from Portree passes door.
Restrictions No smoking in dining room. No dogs in public rooms.
Credit cards Access, Visa
Terms B&B £30–£45; D,B&B £45–£60. Set dinner £15. 3/5-day rates. 1-night group bookings sometimes refused.

ROTHES Moray   Map 5

Rothes Glen   NEW   *Tel* (01340) 831254
Rothes   *Fax* (01340) 831566
by Elgin AB38 7AQ   *E-mail* 101516.1660@compuserve.com

Grand Victorian baronial-style Speyside hotel, with many original features: plaster ceilings, panelling, marble fireplaces. 7 miles S of Elgin on A941. Bought May 1996 and extensively refurbished by Frederic Symonds and Michael MacKenzie. "Food much improved," says nominator. Menus include game, fish, old-fashioned puddings, home-made truffles. 10-acre grounds with rhododendrons, putting, croquet, highland cattle, trout pond, visiting deer. Fishing, golf, shooting, stalking, birdwatching, Cawdor, Culloden, Moray Firth, many famous whisky distilleries nearby. Unsuitable for ♿. No smoking in dining room. No children under 7 at dinner. Dogs by arrangement. Access, Amex, Visa accepted. 16 bedrooms. B&B £50–£85, D,B&B £75–£105. Set lunch £11.95–£14.50, dinner £30. *V*

ST ANDREWS Fife   Map 5

Rufflets   NEW   *Tel* (01334) 472594
Strathkinness Low Road   *Fax* (01334) 478703
St Andrews KY16 9TX   *E-mail* rufflets@standrews.co.uk

Ann Russell's long-established Edwardian hotel, turreted and creepered, on B939, 1½ miles W of golfers' mecca. Chintz, checks and tartan decor, and collection of works by local artist, Sir William Russell Flint. "Staff helpful, room relaxing, food average, wine excellent," write recent visitors. 25 bedrooms: best ones in turrets and garden cottage; some have ♿ access. Modern Scottish cooking on 3-course menus; home-grown vegetables. Impressive topiary in 10-acre grounds. No smoking: dining room, library, bedrooms. No dogs. All major credit cards accepted. B&B £60–£90. Bar lunches. Set lunch £18, dinner £29. 1-night bookings occasionally refused. Special breaks. More reports, please.

ST BOSWELLS Scottish Borders   Map 5

Dryburgh Abbey Hotel   *Tel* (01835) 822261
St Boswells, Melrose TD6 0RQ   *Fax* (01835) 823945

The Grose family's luxuriously restored baronial mansion (Best Western) is adjacent to the romantic ruins of Dryburgh Abbey, in a village, near Melrose, with the largest green in Scotland. It has mostly received plaudits this year: "Combines the charm of the small hotel with the slicker comforts of a chain. Lovely approach and grounds, light and airy room with a view, Roman-style pool, free fishing in the Tweed 50 yards away. Very good for business or pleasure." A 90th birthday party was well catered for, and a wheelchair user found facilities and staff "excellent". In the beautiful dining room overlooking the Tweed, Patrick Ruse's dinners, "served with decorum", always include a vegetarian dish and several "Taste of Scotland" options (with supplements). The meals have been enjoyed by some, but thought a touch pretentious by others. There is a cheaper supper menu in the new bistro-style courtyard bar. Children are welcomed. Fourteen golf courses are within half an hour's drive, and the hotel will organise fishing and shooting parties. Traquair, Scotland's oldest inhabited house, and Floors Castle are also nearby. (*Stephen Wrigley-Hare, Eric Cameron Lee, S Gillian Comins; also John Campbell, and others*)

Open All year.
Rooms 2 suites, 20 double, 6 single. Some in lodge 100 yds. Some on ground floor, suitable for &.
Facilities Lift, ramp. 3 lounges, 3 bars, dining room (piped music throughout all day), indoor swimming pool. 9-acre grounds: putting. Fishing, shooting, clay pigeon-shooting, golf nearby.
Location From St Boswells take B6404 towards Dryburgh Abbey for 2 miles, then B6356 for just over 1½ miles. Bus: St Boswells; then taxi.
Restrictions No smoking: 1 lounge, dining room. No dogs in public rooms.
Credit cards Access, Amex, Visa.
Terms B&B £42–£77.50; D,B&B £52.50–£102.50. Bar meals. Set dinner £22.50. 2/5-night, Christmas, New Year, off-season, breaks. Golfing, shooting, fishing, off road driving packages. Special meals, reduced rates for children. ***V***

SHAPINSAY Orkney   Map 5

Balfour Castle   *Tel* (01856) 711282
Shapinsay KW17 2DY   *Fax* (01856) 711283

An evocative report from a faithful American correspondent: "The sight of *Balfour Castle* looming ever larger on the horizon during the ferry crossing to Shapinsay is but a taste of the 'world apart' atmosphere awaiting the visitor to this lush green island. The hotel itself is a historic gem, with which Catherine Zawadzki will enthusiastically acquaint her guests. We had planned to tour many of the other Orkney Isles, but found ourselves so completely content with Shapinsay's quiet attractions that we ended up spending several days walking the beautiful coastline, visiting the island's very own Stone Age broch, and thrilling to our first sighting of puffins, grey seals and nesting arctic terns. The RSPB bird hide is perhaps the best we have ever seen. Arrangements for touring Shapinsay are gladly arranged by the family or staff. With the comforts of *Balfour* just a short walk away, even being caught out in the notoriously changing Orkney weather poses no problem, for a welcome cup of tea, heated towel rails, and electric blankets await. Meals were ample, with a set three-course dinner (substitutions for my diabetic husband were cheerfully offered), beginning on one occasion with the freshest of scallops poached in a herb broth, followed by a roast leg of lamb served with crisp vegetables, and finishing with hot gooseberry tart, using home-grown fruit, with sinfully thick cream. Wines are served with each meal, and guests are charged according to their con-

sumption. Our huge, twin-bedded room, complete with turret, had splendid views down to the sea, and we enjoyed watching the ferry and fishing boats ply back and forth, and eider ducks with their tiny broods drifting on the seaweedy waves. A unique bit of timeless escapism." *(Mrs Romney Bathurst)*

Open All year.
Rooms 4 suites, 3 double, 1 single. No telephone/TV.
Facilities Drawing room, library with bar, TV room, billiard room, 2 dining rooms. 2-acre garden on 70-acre estate. Sea, beaches, boat trips, birdwatching, fishing close by. Unsuitable for &.
Location 25-minute ferry from Kirkwall. Travel information sent to guests.
Restriction Dogs by arrangement.
Credit card Access.
Terms [1997] D,B&B £80. Light lunch £4.50. 30% reduction for children. Weekly rates; house parties.

SHIELDAIG Highland   Map 5

Tigh an Eilean   *Tel* (01520) 755251
Shieldaig   *Fax* (01520) 755321
by Strathcarron IV54 8XN

Callum and Elizabeth Stewart's small inn is in a row of old buildings peacefully set by a sea loch in a fishing village amid the glorious Torridon hills of Wester Ross. It opens directly on to the village street, where hens and ducks wander. No garden but, as one visitor wrote, "in fine weather most people want to be out in this magnificent area, and you can easily find sheltered places on the Shieldaig peninsula nearby to sit and admire the views". One correspondent this year thought the meals expensive, and another disliked the "ubiquitous artificial flowers", but most reports are enthusiastic: "A real gem." "Elizabeth Stewart is a delightful hostess who seems to be everywhere at once." "Informally run and not luxurious, it is wonderful for walking and relaxing. The staff are friendly. The food is tasty and filling, with lots of fresh fish and hot puddings, just what you need after being in the open all day. Plenty of hot water and fluffy towels to wrap yourself in." Local crab, lobster, game and wild Atlantic salmon feature on the dinner menu. Breakfasts are "splendidly sustaining, with excellent porridge". The residents' lounge and the bar are small, but the dining room has a modern decor and a "light, open feeling". The bedrooms are plainly but adequately furnished; some, at the top ("quite a climb"), are very small and lack a view. Simple bar meals are available. *(Clive Mackay, and others; also Good Pub Guide)*

Open Apr–mid-Oct.
Rooms 8 double, 3 single. No telephone/TV.
Facilities Lounge, TV lounge, bar, dining room; drying room. Unsuitable for &.
Location Centre of village off A896 (but quiet). Parking opposite. Train: Strathcarran; bus connects with lunchtime train.

Restrictions No smoking: dining room, TV lounge. No dogs in public rooms.
Credit cards Access, Visa.
Terms B&B: single £46, double £100.50. Bar meals. Set dinner £22.50. Reductions for 5 or more nights. Children under 8 accommodated free in parents' room.

SKIRLING Scottish Borders   Map 5

Skirling House BUDGET   *Tel* (01899) 860274
Skirling, Biggar ML12 6HD   *Fax* (01899) 860255
                                        E-mail skirlinghouse@dial.pipex.com

"Perfect. We arrived in May, with snow falling, and immediately a log fire was roaring. Our room was large, with every possible comfort. Service could not be faulted." "A lovely stay. Food imaginative and beautifully presented." Two endorsements this year for Bob and Isobel Hunter's home, an Arts and Crafts period piece, with sloping roofs and bay windows, now an upmarket no-smoking private home taking paying guests. It is in the midst of splendid Border countryside teeming with castles, abbeys and stately homes. The drawing room has a 16th-century carved wood Florentine ceiling, and pieces of ironwork specially commissioned for the house, which was built in 1908. The cooking is "modern Scottish, with influences from the southern and south-western US". Four-course no-choice dinners, served at 8 pm, might include courgette soufflé, game pie and damson frangipane tart. "For breakfast there is fresh orange juice and home-made cherry, plum and walnut muffins; home-made bread and marmalade too." (*Elizabeth Brice, M Kershaw*)

Open Mar–Dec. New Year.
Rooms 3 double. 1 on ground floor. Also 2-bedroom self-catering wing.
Facilities Drawing room, dining room, conservatory. 5½-acre garden: tennis, croquet. Fishing on river Tweed. Not really suitable for &.
Location Centre of village 2 miles E of Biggar, facing green. Local buses.
Restrictions No smoking. Dogs by arrangement.
Credit cards None accepted.
Terms B&B £27.50–£39. Set dinner £17.50. Weekly rates. Reduced rates for children. *V*

SPEAN BRIDGE Highland   Map 5

Corriegour Lodge BUDGET   *Tel* (01397) 712685
by Spean Bridge PH34 4EB   *Fax* (01397) 712696

*Victorian hunting lodge on Loch Lochy, between Spean Bridge and Invergarry. Owned since Oct 1996 by Christian and Steven Kerr (he is chef). Traditional Scottish cooking. Friendly service, comfortable accommodation; simple decor; stunning views. 6-acre grounds with beach, jetty, waterfall. Skiing, climbing, fishing, sailing nearby. Open Feb–Dec (except Christmas). No smoking in dining room. No children under 8. No dogs. Unsuitable for &. Access, Amex accepted. 9 bedrooms. B&B £28, D,B&B £47–£59. Set dinner £20.50 [1997]. More reports, please. *V*

Don't let old favourites down. Entries are dropped when there is no endorsement.

STRATHTUMMEL Perthshire and Kinross   Map 5

Queens View   NEW   Tel (01796) 473291
Strathtummel   Fax (01796) 473515
by Pitlochry PH16 5NR

*Tayside baronial hotel 15 mins' drive W of Pitlochry, with magnificent views
of Loch Tummel. Extensively refurbished (Edwardian/Sanderson/Laura
Ashley decor) by new owners, (since 1995) Richard and Norma Tomlinson.
She cooks "varied and interesting" meals; he is front-of-house. 4½-acre
grounds with mature trees sloping down to loch. Queen Victoria's picnic site,
complete with view, 5 mins' drive; golf, sailing, fishing, distilleries, Blair
Atholl castle nearby. Open Mar–mid-Jan, except Christmas. Only dining
room suitable for &. No smoking in dining room. No dogs in public rooms,
unattended in bedrooms. Access, Visa accepted. 9 rooms. B&B £37–£50;
D,B&B £57–£70. Bar lunches. Set dinner £23.50.* *V*

STRONTIAN Highland   Map 5

Kilcamb Lodge   Tel (01967) 402257
Strontian PH36 4HY   Fax (01967) 402041
♧ *César award in 1997*

The Blakeway family's stone house, Georgian with Victorian additions,
stands on the edge of a tiny village on Loch Sunart, on the way to the
Ardnamurchan peninsula. It is reached via a scenic road through Glen
Tarbert, after a short ride on the Corran ferry. In spring its large
grounds are ablaze with rhododendrons, azaleas and rare wild flowers.
There's plenty of wildlife too: red deer, squirrels, otters and seals,
hawks and golden eagles. The lounges have fires, fresh flowers, decorative plates, and a "home-like feel". Bedrooms are priced according to
size; the best ones are spacious, with armchairs and a coffee table. The
senior Blakeways have now retired and son Peter, and his wife, Annie,
are in charge. Apart from one report of a 1997 visit when a number of
things went wrong, *Guide* readers continue to be enthusiastic. "Peter
Blakeway looks after young and old with the same charm and kindness
as his parents. Annie runs the place with easy professionalism."
"Tranquillity combined with efficiency and genuine friendliness.
Totally unpretentious." "We booked for three days and stayed a
week." Neil Mellis, formerly of *Taychreggan*, Kilchrenan (*qv*), is in
charge of the kitchens, and the food "is perfect for a long stay. Superbly
and straightforwardly cooked ingredients: always a huge dish of
simply cooked help-yourself vegetables; always fresh fruit as an option
to delicious puddings; and they are adaptable – for example, you can
opt to have two first courses." Stakker, an ebullient labrador, welcomes
one and all. The Gordon Girls – free-range chickens – provide fresh
eggs every day. A day trip to Mull is possible, via the ferry from
Lochaline, a few miles to the south. (*Padi Howard, Lady Davenport-
Handley, JC Gillett, David Lipsey; also Mary Milne-Day, JMR Irving,
and others*)

Open Mar–Nov, New Year.
Rooms 10 double, 1 single. No telephone. 2 self-catering cottages in grounds.
Facilities Drawing room, lounge/bar, dining room. 28-acre grounds on loch:

private beach, fishing, boating; mountain bikes available. Pony-trekking nearby.
Unsuitable for &.
Location From A82 S of Fort William take Corran ferry, then A861 to Strontian.
Restrictions No smoking: drawing room, dining room, bedrooms. No dogs in
public rooms.
Credit cards Access, Visa.
Terms [1997] D,B&B £62–£85. Set dinner £25. Discounts for 3/6 nights.

SWINTON Scottish Borders   Map 5

The Wheatsheaf   BUDGET   *Tel/Fax* (01890) 860257
Main Street
Swinton, nr Duns TD11 3JJ

Alan and Julie Reid's popular inn is in a village in the rolling agricultural land of the Merse, four miles from the river Tweed. The bedrooms
are simple but comfortable; four have *en suite* facilities. Those on the
road side can be noisy. "Room 5 is yellow and rather small, and the residents' lounge is unappealing," wrote a recent visitor, "but this is a
must for the food. We waited in the dining room with others equally
keen. Everything, oh, so fresh: great starters, fish just caught, served in
good quantities. For breakfast Alan Reid asked what we would like
and did it with style, generosity and verve. Home-made oatcakes,
smoked salmon, and a mixture of fresh and poached fruit." "A most
enjoyable place to stay, with a warm welcome. Carefully decorated bar,
with attractive long oak settle, green-cushioned window seats, sporting prints. Superb pub meals: local seafood every day, delicious puddings." A good base for touring the Border countryside and the
Berwickshire coast. (*Philip Chklar, Good Pub Guide*)

Open All year, except last 2 weeks Feb, last week Oct. Closed Mon.
Rooms 5 double, 4 with *en suite* facilities. No telephone/TV.
Facilities Residents' lounge, lounge bar, 2 dining rooms. ½-acre garden: chil-
dren's play area. River Tweed 4 miles; fishing by arrangement.
Location Centre of village 12 miles W of Berwick-upon-Tweed, on road to Kelso.
Parking. Train: Berwick; then taxi.
Restrictions No smoking: dining rooms, bedrooms. No dogs in bedrooms.
Credit cards Access, Visa.
Terms B&B £26–£44. Full alc £25. 3-night rates. *V*

TANGUSDALE Western Isles   Map 5

Isle of Barra Hotel   NEW/BUDGET   *Tel* (01871) 810383
Tangusdale Beach   *Fax* (01871) 810385
Isle of Barra HS80 5XW   *E-mail* barrahotel@aol.com

*In "glorious, pristine setting", modern hotel, overlooking bay, on W of tiny
furthest Western* Whisky Galore *Isle. Reached by 5-hour ferry trip (4 a week)
from Oban or Mallaig, shorter one from South Uist, or flight from Glasgow,
landing on Cockle Shell beach. Personal welcome from owners, the
Worthingtons, and dog, Thomas. 30 bedrooms, most spacious and pretty,
some suitable for* &. *Public rooms with stunning views. Good food: lots of
choice on four-course menu. Weekly band in public bar. 5-acre garden. Golf,
pony trekking, trips to Vatersay/Mingulay, walking, birdwatching. Open 21
Mar–17 Oct. No dogs in public rooms. Access, Visa accepted. B&B £30–£44;
D,B&B £48–£56. Set dinner £18.95. Occasional groups.* *V*

TARBERT Western Isles
Map 5

Leachin House
Tarbert, Isle of Harris HS3 3AH

Tel (01859) 502157

"Linda and Diarmuid Evelyn Wood's wee inn is completely charming, with a welcoming fire always lit in the drawing room," writes a returning visitor to this Wolsey Lodge, whose name (pronounced lee-ak-in) means house among the rocks. "The Woods are most helpful hosts. Everything is spick and span, in a nautical way, with ships' models, paintings and other treasures. Our bedroom was large and comfortable, with a lovely view and thoughtful amenities in the ample bathroom. The pretty dining room has the original 100-year-old hand-painted French wallpaper, and the communal table is set with good china, attractive linens, silver and flowers. Linda is an excellent cook: a fragrant, creamy smoked haddock chowder was followed by some of the best lamb we have ever tasted, in a redcurrant and port sauce. The sweet was a heavenly chocolate rum truffle with cream. There is a garden with a burn running down to the loch, and beautiful sunsets are a treat on good days." Guided trips to look for seals, otters and eagles can be arranged, also fishing. Rugged, treeless Harris, home of the eponymous tweed, is a paradise for walkers and naturalists: orchids in April and May, and in June and July the hills are alive with wild flowers. (*Martha Prince*)

Open All year, except Christmas/New Year.
Rooms 3 double, 1 with facilities *en suite*. No telephone.
Facilities Drawing room, dining room. ½-acre garden. Sea 60 yds: safe bathing; fishing, walking nearby. Unsuitable for &.
Location 1 mile W of Tarbert on A859. Signposted on loch side. Bus from Tarbert/Stornoway.
Restrictions No smoking: dining room, bedrooms. No children under 10. Dogs by arrangement.
Credit card Access.
Terms B&B £37; D,B&B £60. Set dinner (with carafe of house wine) £23. 5-day breaks. ***V*** (Nov–Feb, as alternative to house discounts)

TIMSGARRY Western Isles
Map 5

Baile-na-Cille   BUDGET
Timsgarry, Uig
Isle of Lewis HS2 9JD

Tel (01851) 672242
Fax (01851) 672241

♕ *César award in 1990*

The *César* citation for this "unique place" (a description last year) read: "Shangri La of the Outer Hebrides". One of the remotest hotels in the *Guide*, it lies by a huge white sand beach on the wild west coast of Lewis. Informally run by Richard and Joanna Gollin, the proprietors for 18 years, it consists of an old manse and converted stables, with simple but well-appointed bedrooms. Some can be combined to make a family unit. Three others, in the converted cowshed are fairly basic, and priced accordingly. Recently there has been a thorough redecoration. The quirky charm of the place has brought it many devotees. "We welcome children, dogs and grannies," writes Richard Gollin. "And we have been a refuge, in the last ten years, for a number of Labour politicians during their exile. We offer hills to climb, historic sites to visit, lochs to fish and 200 square miles of wilderness for peace and quiet. Twenty-three other beaches are within eight miles. Our two dogs will take guests for walks." Uproarious games of cricket sometimes take place on the beach during the long summer evenings. Dinners are communal (no choice, preferences discussed in advance; vegetarians are well catered for), and Joanna Gollin's "imaginative, but not fancy cooking" is much admired: "interesting soups and main courses, delicious puddings, home-made bread, always a good cheese board and fruit bowl". No wine list: bottles at two prices: £8.50 and £12.50. Breakfasts include generous amounts of porridge, black pudding, eggs, bacon, etc. Tea and coffee are willingly produced at any time of day. Richard Gollin drives frequently to Stornoway (about an hour away) and will drop guests off for walking and climbing. Mrs Gollin, a keen amateur flyer, will take visitors aloft "if we have a machine staying". A few visitors this year have reported problems due to over-booking. (*MR; also SP Edwards, and others*)

Open 2 weeks Easter; 1 May–1 Oct.
Rooms 2 family suites, 8 double, 2 single. 8 with bath. 3 in cottage annexe. Some on ground floor. No telephone/TV.
Facilities 3 lounges (1 with TV, 1 with music), dining room, conservatory; games room, drying room. 3-acre grounds: walled garden, tennis, children's play area, beach (dinghy, windsurfer, fishing rods available). Beaches: safe bathing, fishing, sailing. Not really suitable for &, "but an increasing number come and everyone helps".
Location 34 miles W of Stornoway. By air: Glasgow/Inverness to Stornoway; ferry from Ullapool. A858 to Garynahine, B8011 towards Uig; at Timsgarry shop (brown sign) turn right to shore. Post bus from Stornoway twice daily.
Restriction No smoking: dining room, 2 lounges, bedrooms.
Credit cards Access, Visa.
Terms B&B £22–£39; D,B&B £44–£63. Snack lunch £2–£10. Set dinner £24. Child in bunk room: B&B £14. Weekly rates.

ULLAPOOL Highland   Map 5

Altnaharrie   *Tel* (01854) 633230
Ullapool IV26 2SS
✪ *César award in 1987*

This old drover's house is idyllically set on the southern shores of Loch Broom. When it first entered the *Guide* in 1984, visitors were ferried over from the mainland in Fred Brown's "wee motor boat" (cars are left on the mainland). Nowadays, pilgrims to the only Scottish establishment with two *Michelin* stars make the ten-minute crossing in a comfortable launch. "Every serious hotel-lover should visit at least once," writes a connoisseur of such matters. "It *is* expensive, but that reflects the remoteness of the location, and the quality of the food. Fred Brown's interest in wine is obvious from the extensive and sensibly priced list." An Scottish visitor adds: "Porridge at breakfast was the best I have ever eaten (I was reared on it). We have never eaten better; the presentation of the food was beautiful, as was the dining room. We loved the freshness of the decor. Uncompromising all-round excellence." An earlier report: "Fred Brown's quiet way of making each guest's stay perfect has rubbed off on his young staff. The welcome and the friendliness throughout make for a special experience. I know no hotel with fewer notices." Many of the ingredients for Norwegian-born Gunn Eriksen's five-course menus (no choice until dessert; preferences discussed at the time of booking) are grown or caught locally. Some bedrooms in the main house are small; larger ones are in a cottage annexe; one is by a stream. They have a simple Scandinavian style decor with a king-size bed, and the bathrooms are both lavish and functional. No radio or TV; lots of books. No mains electricity supply: the generator is turned off after bedtime; a torch by the bed helps out in the dark. There is limited walking from the house, up a steep track; further afield there are heather-clad hills. Plenty of wildlife, including golden eagles, seals and otters. Stout footwear is recommended. (*Sir Timothy Harford, Prof. NC Craig Sharp, and others*)

Open Easter–Nov.
Rooms 8 double. 2 in cottage near house, 1 in grounds 100 yds. No telephone/TV.
Facilities 2 lounges, dining room. 2-acre garden on loch: stream, pond, pebble beach, safe (cold) bathing; trout/salmon-fishing by arrangement. Unsuitable for &.
Location On S shore of Loch Broom, reached by regular ferry (telephone from Ullapool). Free private parking in Ullapool. Bus from Inverness to Ullapool.
Restrictions No smoking. No children under 8. No dogs in main house bedrooms, public rooms.
Credit cards Access, Visa.
Terms [1997] D,B&B: single £155–£230, double £310–£380. Set dinner £70. 1-night bookings occasionally refused Sat.

The Ceilidh Place   BUDGET   *Tel* (01854) 612103
14 West Argyle Street   *Fax* (01854) 612886
Ullapool IV26 2TY   *E-mail* jean@ceilidh.demon.co.uk
♥ *César award in 1986*

This exuberant, idiosyncratic establishment started out as a coffee shop, but then grew to include bar, hotel, bunkhouse, wholefood shop, bakery, and much else besides. It is run by Jean Urquhart, widow of co-founder Robert Urquhart. She writes this year: "We are endlessly 'tweaking' the *Ceilidh Place* to make it more comfortable. We differ from other hotels in that we run a serious bookshop, an arts venue and exhibition spaces. We are busiest in summer; in winter prices are lower, and there is less choice on the menus, but standards remain the same." Plays, poetry readings and *ceilidhs* are held regularly. *Aficionados* found the place "better than ever" this year: "Beautifully warm despite bitterly cold weather, with an open wood-burning stove. We arrived at 11 pm and were warmly greeted even though a *ceilidh* was in full

swing. The food was perfect for the season and location. They were extremely kind to our boisterous two-year-old." Another guest has written: "The welcome is warm and genuine, the rooms homely and comfortable, and the individually crafted furniture in the lounges quite exquisite. If only there were more such

places in the world." Accommodation in the Bunkhouse across the
street is basic (bunk beds, some shared rooms) and cheap. Cooking is
"Scottish eclectic", with an emphasis on local seafood and vegetarian
dishes. Breakfasts are robust. Some might find the place too laid-back,
but many appreciate the relaxed atmosphere, the myriad entertainments and the genuine friendliness. Ullapool, which was laid out in a
grid pattern in the 18th century, is a pleasant little fishing port near the
mouth of Loch Broom, amid lovely Highland scenery. (*RT Macey, and
others; also Stephen and Ellise Holman, Good Pub Guide*)

Open All year.
Rooms 10 double, 3 single. 11 more in Bunkhouse across street.
Facilities Lounge, 2 bars, restaurant, coffee shop (piped music); conference/
function facilities; games room, book shop. ¼-acre garden. Rocky beach, sea
angling, waterskiing; loch fishing; pony-trekking. Unsuitable for &.
Location 1st right after pier at W end of Main St, then 2nd right. Large carpark.
Bus from Inverness, 64 miles.
Restrictions No smoking: restaurant, some bedrooms. No dogs in public rooms.
Credit cards All major cards accepted.
Terms Hotel: B&B £35–£55; Bunkhouse: bed £10–£14, breakfast in hotel
£6–£8.50 or alc in coffee shop. Full alc dinner £28. Half board rates for 3 nights
or more.

WALLS Shetland Islands   **Map 5**

Burrastow House   NEW   *Tel* (01595) 809307
Walls ZE2 9PD   *Fax* (01595) 809213

"The journey is long, but it is worth making. Bo Simmons and Henry
Anderton have achieved what no one else in Shetland seems to have
dreamed of – true country house accommodation, with charm and
ease." That report by an American visitor brings back to the *Guide* this
small Georgian house in a magnificent setting on the west side of the
island. It fell from the *Guide* last year for lack of reports – hardly sur-
prising, in view of its remoteness. It looks across a deep blue bay to the
island of Vaila; sightings of black-headed gulls, red-throated divers,
seals and otters are not unusual. The two large bedrooms in the main
house have a draped and canopied four-poster; one has a twin-bedded
room adjoining, complete with children's books and games. Other bedrooms in a newer extension lack the view, but it is seen from the large,
much-windowed lounge above. Pre-dinner drinks are taken in a small,
eclectically furnished drawing room, which has a peat fire. Dinner is
served in a conservatory, amid scented pelargoniums, clematis and
nasturtiums. "Bo Simmons offers the finest food for miles around,
cooked with expertise and enthusiasm," says our reporter. "Our only
problem was making a choice. Everything – crab, lobster, salmon – is
sublimely fresh, never abused by over-cooking or saucing. Bread is
warm and freshly baked, flavourful new potatoes and vegetables come
from the garden. Puddings range from home-made ice creams to traditional trifle, well sherried. We retired each evening feeling well fed but
not over-stuffed." Breakfast includes kedgeree. (*Romney Bathurst*)

Open 1 Mar–Oct, other times by arrangement. Restaurant closed to non-resi-
dents for dinner Sun/Mon.
Rooms 1 family, 4 double. 1, on ground floor, suitable for &. 1 with telephone.
TV on request.
Facilities Sitting room, lounge, library, dining room (occasional local musicians),

conservatory; small conference room. 1-acre grounds in large estate; on sea, safe (cold) bathing, hotel boat; indoor swimming pool in village 2 miles.
Location 27 miles NW of Lerwick. Take A970 N, then A971 W. Through Walls; left on brow of hill; 2 miles to dead end. Bus: Lerwick to Walls (daily, except Sun); hotel will meet.
Restrictions No smoking: dining room, bedrooms. Dogs by arrangement; not in dining room.
Credit cards Access, Visa.
Terms B&B £50–£55, D,B&B £59.50–£80. Full alc £32. Off-season rates by arrangement. Music, painting, massage, decorating courses.

Traveller's tale Wiltshire: Dinner looked promising at £19.50 for four courses. There was nothing wrong with the seafood starter, though it was a bit small and not what I would call seafood – taramasalata and a sardine. The pan-fried steak which I had ordered rare was grey, and the pepper sauce was a Bisto-coloured brown. We sent this back, and the replacement did have a touch of pink, but had probably come straight out of the freezer. I made my views known to the head waiter who agreed that it was unfortunate that the chef couldn't cook a rare steak. Still, the conversation ended on a cheery note when he said: "Anyway, glad you're enjoying your meal, Sir."

Traveller's tale Norfolk: Breakfasts were dreadful. They charge £9 for a continental breakfast, not the whole shebang. This is a lot to pay for juice, cornflakes, cold toast made from undistinguished bread, and a dreadful doughy croissant. One day we didn't get coffee until almost the end of the meal; the next day we got a pot of coffee but had a dreadful time getting cups. Meanwhile members of the substantial staff entertained themselves setting up tables for lunch.

Perpetual plaint Why is one obliged to sit interminably in some sitting room or bar before being allowed into the dining room? In one Kent hotel, it took 15 minutes for the menu to arrive, 15 minutes for the order to be taken, and another 15 before we were shown to the table. Then, to add insult to injury, it was another 15 minutes before the first course arrived. If I book a table for 8 pm, I like to eat at that time, not an hour later.

Personal Preference Suffolk: We thoroughly applaud two aspects of the management of this hotel: 1) The proprietors are always about. 2) They don't try to pretend you are "staying in their home". In too many "country house" hotels the proprietors give the impression that they are trying to fund the life to which they aspire by graciously taking in guests and making them pay through the nose, while never acknowledging the commercial relationship. I much prefer hoteliers who are completely straightforward about the fact that money is changing hands.

Channel Islands

La Sablonnerie, Sark

ROZEL BAY Jersey   **Map 1**

Château La Chaire   *Tel* (01534) 863354
Rozel Bay, St Martin JE3 6AJ   *Fax* (01534) 865137

This elegant small hotel has an "idyllic" setting, on the slopes overlooking the Rozel valley at the north-eastern tip of Jersey. It is set in
terraced gardens above a picturesque fishing harbour, with good cliff
walks, safe beaches and splendid views nearby. "It is truly lovely,"
wrote one enthusiastic visitor. "All the staff were charming; service
was at all times efficient, polite and welcoming. The food was excellent
in both quality and choice." It has a spacious rococo lounge with chandeliers and fine mouldings with cherubs and intricate scrollwork, and
an oak-panelled restaurant with a conservatory extension, where chef
Simon Walker serves modern British cooking, specialising in seafood.
Some bedrooms are large and luxurious "with everything you could
think of: fresh fruit, towelling robes, even a Scrabble board". Some

have a jacuzzi; some have a balcony; the galleried suite has two bath-rooms. Smaller rooms under the roof have sloping ceilings. Sean Copp has taken over the day-to-day running of the hotel from Alan Winch, who has been promoted to managing director. (*VG, and others*)

Open All year. Restaurant closed Christmas evening.
Rooms 1 suite (on ground floor), 13 double.
Facilities Lounge, bar, restaurant with conservatory (piped classical music). 6-acre garden. Sandy beach, safe bathing, golf, riding, fishing nearby. Unsuitable for &.
Location 5 miles NE of St Helier. Follow signs for St Martin's church, then Rozel. 1st left in village; hotel carpark 200 yds on left.
Restrictions No children under 7. No dogs.
Credit cards All major cards accepted.
Terms [1997] B&B: single £65–£105, double £85–£135, suite £160–£180; D,B&B: single £81.50–£121.50, double £118–£168, suite £193–£213. Set lunch £15.50, dinner £21.50; full alc £32.50. Winter breaks. Child 7–12 sharing parents' room: B&B £25. 1-night bookings sometimes refused in season.

ST ANNE Alderney   **Map 1**

Inchalla NEW/BUDGET	*Tel* (01481) 823220
Le Val	*Fax* (01481) 824045

Valerie Willis has presided for 17 years over this unpretentious modern house in the middle of the tiny island. It is set in a large garden on the edge of St Anne, a charming little town with cobbled streets and colour-washed houses. From its elevated position, there are views across the English Channel towards the bird sanctuary island of Burhou. Regular *Guide* correspondents thought it a winner. "We very much enjoyed our stay. It is simple, but with a charming conservatory lounge, attractive bedrooms, and a wonderful dining room serving English/French cooking by the talented young Irish chef, Anne Marie Burbidge, who is self-taught." On weekdays there is a four-course *table d'hôte* menu and a *carte*; on Sunday there is a traditional lunch and an evening supper tray. There is good family accommodation; baby-sitters are available, and children are charged according to age. Plenty of good beaches, and a scenic nine-hole golf course are close by. (*Stephen and Ellise Holman*)

Open All year.
Rooms 9 double. 3 on ground floor.
Facilities Lounge, conservatory, restaurant/bar ("mellow" piped music during dinner); banqueting/conference facilities; sauna, spa bath. Large garden. Golf, tennis, sandy beach nearby.
Location 4 mins' walk from centre of town.
Restrictions No smoking in restaurant. No dogs.
Credit cards Access, Amex, Visa.
Terms [1997] B&B £25–£40.50. Set lunch £12, dinner £15; full alc £22.50. Packages including air fare from Jersey/Guernsey.

There is no VAT in the Channel Islands.

ST BRELADE Jersey   **Map 1**

Atlantic Hotel   *Tel* (01534) 44101
St Brelade JE3 8HE   *Fax* (01534) 44102
                                                  E-mail atlantic@itl.net

"Exceptional staff." "The high point of our visit to Jersey: the location,
the beautiful rooms, the view, above all the food." "The decor is quite
exceptional; the designer's talents combine cleverly with the beauty of
the situation." "We could find no fault." More plaudits this year for a
luxurious modern hotel, adjoining the La Moye championship golf
course and overlooking the wonderful five-mile beach of St Ouen's
Bay. It was opened 26 years ago by the father of Patrick Burke, the
present owner. Its manager, Simon Dufty, is a member of the hotel-
keeping family of *Longueville Manor*, St Saviour (*qv*). Behind its plain
exterior are a wrought iron staircase, rich carpeting, urns, fountains,
antiques and specially designed modern furniture. All the bedrooms
have a balcony overlooking the sea or the golf course. The suites
are spacious, but some rooms are on the small side. Tom Sleigh's
modern British cooking is generally thought exceptional: "original
and lively, never too heavy, with every day a vegetarian main
dish". "Mouth-watering hot soufflés for dessert." But one visitor
thought breakfast was not quite as good as the rest. Light lunches are
served, by the pool in fine weather. The airport is ten minutes'
drive away. (*Lynda Gillinson, Stephen and Ellise Holman, EB Schaffer,
and others*)

Open Mar–Dec.
Rooms 2 suites, 48 double.
Facilities Lounges, cocktail bar, restaurant (piped music throughout); fitness
centre: swimming pool, sauna. 3-acre grounds: tennis, swimming pool. Golf
club, beach nearby. Unsuitable for &.
Location 5 miles W of St Helier. Bus, taxi.
Restriction No dogs.
Credit cards All major cards accepted.
Terms [1997] B&B: double £120–£210, suite £190–£350. Set lunch £15, dinner
£22.50; full alc £40. Special breaks.

St Brelade's Bay Hotel   *Tel* (01534) 46141
St Brelade's Bay JE3 8EF   *Fax* (01534) 47278

This large hotel has been owned by the Colley family for five generations. It is set in large landscaped gardens, in a fine position overlooking the vast expanse of the bay, though separated from the beach
by a road. Behind the modern exterior is an old-fashioned, elegant
decor, with moulded ceilings, chandeliers and lots of fresh flowers.
Traditional food is served in the panelled restaurant. There are plenty
of outdoor facilities (see below) and evening entertainment. Sea-facing
bedrooms have a balcony; others overlook the garden. Children are
welcomed: there's good family accommodation, a playroom for
toddlers, and a TV room for the sole use of children. Recent visitors
wrote: "We had a lovely suite, with comfortable chairs for reading, and
current magazines. The food was enjoyable. The staff seemed
genuinely to want to please the guests, and the quality of service per-
meated the hotel." (*CW, and others*)

Open End Apr–mid-Oct.
Rooms 5 suites, 73 double, 4 single.
Facilities Lift. Lounge, TV room, bar (CD music at night), restaurant; entertainments, disco twice weekly; games room, snooker room; sun verandah. 7-acre grounds: swimming pool with bar, barbecue, sauna, solarium, exercise room; children's swimming pool, lifeguard; tennis, croquet, putting, table-tennis, *boules*, children's play area. Beach across road. Golf nearby.
Location 5 miles W of St Helier. Bus.
Restrictions No smoking in restàurant. No dogs.
Credit cards Access, Visa.
Terms B&B: single £52–£90, double £76–£220; D,B&B: single £60–£102, double £100–£236. Set lunch £12, dinner £20; full alc £25. Child in cot free of charge.

ST MARTIN Guernsey   Map 1

Bella Luce   NEW/BUDGET   *Tel* (01481) 38764
La Fosse   *Fax* (01481) 39561
St Martin GY4 6EB

This old house, built as a manor in the 12th century, is at the top of Moulin Huet valley, not far from St Peter Port, and within easy reach of three lovely bays. "It is a comfortable hotel in country lanes," writes the nominator. "Small but well-equipped bedrooms; good evening meals with several choices on the residents' menu, ample English breakfasts. The staff is friendly and efficient: our three-year-old son was made welcome. Pleasant gardens with small swimming pool. The little beach of Moulin Huet is 10 minutes' walk down a steep lane, and the hotel is a good base for those who like coastal walks: Guernsey's south coast path – 20 miles of splendid and little-developed cliffs and occasional beaches – passes near the hotel. You might imagine that the hotel's name was Italian, and pronounced accordingly, but it derives from a previous owner named Luce, and is pronounced, unexotically, 'Bella Loose'." For those who prefer to do without a car, there's a regular bus service from outside the hotel. Bicycles can be hired through the hotel, and a tennis club and a riding school are within ten minutes' walk. (*Graham Avery*)

Open All year.
Rooms 16 suites, 11 double, 3 single. 3 on ground floor.
Facilities Lounge, bar (piped classical music at night), restaurant. 1-acre garden: swimming pool (heated during season). Safe beach, golf, tennis, riding nearby.
Location 2 miles S of St Peter Port. Bus from centre.
Restriction Dogs at management's discretion; not in public rooms.
Credit cards Access, Amex.
Terms B&B £26–£50; D,B&B £39–£63. Bar lunches from £4. Set dinner £13; full alc £17. Winter breaks; Christmas package.

ST PETER PORT Guernsey   Map 1

La Frégate   *Tel* (01481) 724624
Les Côtils   *Fax* (01481) 720443
St Peter Port GY1 1UT

"The hotel is in a little time-warp, but then so is Guernsey. Austrian proprietor, Spanish *maître d'*, Scottish receptionist – and an extensive view over the bonny off-shore banks towards Herm and Sark." "Our room was spacious, with a lovely view of the port, and exceptionally comfortable. Staff particularly cosseting." Two recent reports on an old manor, much converted, set in terraced gardens on a hill above the harbour, which most bedrooms overlook. Some of the rooms have a balcony; those in the old house don't, "but a magnificent camellia more than made up". Bathrooms are large, too, with "man-sized" towels. "We enjoyed sitting at our window eating the room-service breakfast (this is encouraged); the view was so good that my wife got out her water colours. Apart from the gentle noises from the town, all was quiet." The restaurant is popular with locals for its mainly French cooking, and is considered by some to be the best in the island. One *Guide* reporter thought the food "old-fashioned", but others were enthusiastic, and considered both the *table d'hôte* menu and the wine list "good value". (*Christine and Stephen Wright, Stephen and Ellise Holman, Julian Currie*)

Open All year.
Rooms 9 double, 4 single.
Facilities Lounge, bar, restaurant. Terraced garden.
Location 3 mins' walk from centre. Hard to find; hotel will send directions. Carpark.
Restrictions No children under 14 in hotel, under 8 in restaurant. No dogs.
Credit cards All major cards accepted.
Terms [1997] B&B: single £55, double £70–£95. Set lunch £12.50, dinner £18; full alc £25–£35. 1-night bookings sometimes refused May–Sept. *V*

ST SAVIOUR Jersey Map 1

Longueville Manor *Tel* (01534) 25501
Longueville Road *Fax* (01534) 31613
St Saviour JE2 7WF *E-mail* longman@itl.net
♦ *César award in 1986*

This luxurious hotel (Relais & Châteaux) is set in large grounds at the foot of a wooded valley, just inland from Jersey's capital, St Helier. It has been owned for three generations by the Lewis family and is currently run by Malcolm Lewis and Sue Dufty, his sister. "They are charming," wrote a recent visitor, "and the staff (many are Portuguese) are exceptionally hard-working and keen to please." The decor is "smart without being brash or contrived" – swagged chintz curtains, colourful oriental rugs, original paintings, antiques, good repro furniture. Bedrooms and suites are spacious, with sofas and fresh flowers. "Excellent" lunches are served by the swimming pool. In the *Michelin*-starred restaurant (one of only two in the Channel Islands), Andrew Baird's "modern English cooking with strong French classical influence" is interesting and varied. The emphasis is on fresh meat, freshly caught fish, home-grown vegetables and such luxuries as hand-collected scallops – three full-time divers provide 100 dozen a week. "Wonderful vegetarian dishes too." Children and dogs are welcomed. The Royal Jersey Golf Club is close by. The winter package, which includes car hire, is considered good value. More reports, please.

Open All year.
Rooms 2 suites, 30 double. 8 on ground floor.
Facilities Lift. 2 lounges, bar lounge, restaurant; conference facilities. 16-acre

grounds: gardens, woodland, croquet, tennis, swimming pool. Golf, bowls, squash nearby. Sandy beaches ¾ mile.
Location On left 1 mile E of St Helier by A3.
Restriction No dogs in public rooms.
Credit cards All major cards accepted.
Terms B&B: single £137.50–£167.50, double £155–£235, suite £280–£330; D,B&B £30 per person added. Set lunch £21, dinner £36; full alc £41.75. Winter weekend breaks; Christmas/New Year package.

SARK   Map 1

Hotel Petit Champ   BUDGET   *Tel* (01481) 832046
Sark, via Guernsey GY9 0SF   *Fax* (01481) 832469

*Caroline and Chris Robins's 19th-century granite hotel in secluded area on headland of west coast, well away from day trippers – magnificent views, spectacular sunsets. Rooms comfortable, but not luxurious (no telephone, TV, etc). Sun lounges, TV lounge, library, bar. 1-acre grounds: putting, solar-heated pool; steep walk down to sandy beach. Good food: fresh lobster, fresh fish, etc, "served with style and panache". Open Easter–early Oct. 16 bedrooms, some arranged for families. Sark unsuitable for &. No smoking: dining rooms, library. "Children must be old enough to sit with parents at dinner." All major credit cards accepted. B&B £32–£39.50; D,B&B £43–£51. Set Sunday lunch £9.50, dinner £17.25; full alc £21. More reports, please. *V**

La Sablonnerie   BUDGET   *Tel* (01481) 832061
Little Sark   *Fax* (01481) 832408
Sark, via Guernsey GY9 0SD

Sark, only three-and-a-half miles long, but with nearly 40 miles of coastline, is the smallest of the four main Channel Islands. No cars, but all parts of the coast are easily reached on foot, by barouche, or on a bicycle. This "charming and idiosyncratic" 16th-century farmhouse is the only hotel in Little Sark, the southernmost part of the island. It has been owned by the Perrée family for over 40 years, and is currently run by Elizabeth Perrée. "A hotel with genuine character; not for those looking for nightlife," writes a Sark enthusiast. "Peace, beautiful scenery, attractive walks; no traffic other than the occasional tractor. Many guests return year after year." "My annual visit was as enjoyable as ever," says another devotee. "The place is spotlessly clean; staff are attentive without being overbearing, friendly but never familiar. A nice touch this year was a regularly replenished bowl of fruit in our room. Consistently high standards of cuisine, with a well-varied choice, beautifully cooked and presented; in 17 days I did not experience an unsatisfactory meal." Beef, fruit and vegetables come from the hotel's own farm. Desserts are "exceptional" and there's a groaning cheeseboard. Breakfasts include "whatever you want". Light lunches are served in the tea garden. No TV or telephone in bedrooms, but, writes Mrs Perrée, "all rooms now have heating, and are far more luxurious since the recent refurbishment." (*ET Boddye, David Brimble; also Sylvia Anton, and others*)

Open Easter–Oct.
Rooms 1 suite, 15 double, 6 single. Accommodation also in nearby cottages.
Facilities 3 lounges, 2 bars (piped classical music), restaurant. 1-acre garden: tea

garden, croquet. Bays, beaches, rock pools nearby. Sark unsuitable for &.
Location Southern part of island. Hotel will meet boat from Guernsey.
Restrictions No smoking in some bedrooms. Dogs by arrangement.
Credit cards Access, Amex, Visa.
Terms (*Excluding 10% service charge*) B&B £38–£72; D,B&B: £49.50–£86. Set lunch
£19.50, dinner £22.50; full alc £32.50.

Stocks Island Hotel   BUDGET   *Tel* (01481) 832001
Sark, via Guernsey GY9 0SD   *Fax* (01481) 832130
                                                    E-mail stocks@sark.net

*Armorgie family's old-established hotel (recently renamed), an 18th-century
granite farmhouse, centrally situated in south-facing wooded valley,
20 minutes' walk from harbour. Welcoming lounge; 24 simple bedrooms (7 in
Dower House); good family accommodation. Informal courtyard bistro serves
moderately priced lunches, cream teas.* Cider Press *restaurant specialises in
local fish, shellfish, meat, on quite ambitious menu. Food and location recently
admired, "but atmosphere a bit regimented". 1-acre garden: heated swimming
pool. Bicycle hire. Sandy beach nearby. Sark unsuitable for &. Smoking discouraged throughout. Open 9 Apr–3 Oct. Dogs by arrangement; not in public rooms. All major credit cards accepted. B&B £30–£40; D,B&B £42–£52.
Set lunch £13, dinner £18; full alc £25. Good packages, inclusive of travel.*

****

Traveller's tale Devon: Our meal was served by our hostess,
keeping up a non-stop flow of trivia, popping in from the kitchen
whenever a new snippet entered her head. The sound of her husband's incessant coughing was heard from the kitchen throughout dinner. She confided to me that she was worried about his
smoking and thought a doctor's advice should be sought. I
thought privately that the local public health inspector might
have an opinion on the subject.

****

Traveller's tale I arrive weary, worn, wet and windblown, having sought this remote pub up and down dark, muddy Devon
lanes. I am hung about with bags, macs, cameras, brolly; I am
specless. What is the first thing the host insists? Not "Come in",
or "You must be exhausted", or "What a dreadful night." No, it
was "Sign in, please." Why do they do this? They have my name,
address, telephone number and credit card number from the
original booking routine. As for my car registration number, I
never remember that, even when asked by a policeman. The host
was so cross with me for being uncooperative that he walked
past my suitcase and left me to haul it upstairs unaided. I could
have cried.

****

Diner's plaint Hampshire: The presentation of a large menu all
in French can be a stressful experience. It is one thing to identify
the boeuf and the agneau, even a pintade or a magret. But what
is a poulard en vessie? Chicken in a little vest? And how about a
petoncle with your huître, or a veggie gargouillou accompanied
by a pain in the écrevisses? A glossary of terms is clearly needed.

****

Northern Ireland

Tempo Manor, Tempo

ANNALONG Co. Down   **Map 6**

Glassdrumman Lodge   NEW   *Tel* (01396 7) 68451
85 Mill Road   *Fax* (01396 7) 67041
Annalong BT34 4RH

"The Mountains o' Mourne sweep down not quite to the sea, in fact, for between them and the coast is a broad pastoral stretch, where this stylishly converted old farmhouse, long, low and white, stands amid fields." It fell from last year's *Guide* for lack of reports, but was warmly liked by inspectors in 1997. "We weren't wild about the setting (those brooding heights can seem aptly named), but inside all is a delight, sophisticated yet intimate. It is very well run by its friendly owner, Joan Hall, and her family, helped by an excellent young English chef, Stephen Webb, and his wife Bronagh, a true Irish charmer, who plays front-of-house. The lounge is graceful yet cosy – old beamed ceiling, imposing open fireplace (real log fire), velvety sofas, nice lamps, lots of books. The candlelit dining room has good silver. And the piped music, for once, was enchanting: flautist James Galway playing old Irish airs created just the mood for enjoying Webb's 'country house cooking' – good leek-and-potato and seafood soups, steak, home-made apple pie (but poor salmon). Breakfast was good, too, with lovely home-made breads. And our large bedroom was superb, with panoramic windows, big sofa, luxury bathroom, gas fire to welcome us in chilly April (other rooms vary in size). There's a well-kept garden with loungers. And guests can watch, even take part in, the life of the small home farm (pigs, poultry, horses, golden retrievers being bred). It also has an equestrian centre. Many guests are American golfers with Irish roots, who are said to burst into tears when the young Hall daughter sings them *Danny Boy*, etc. Dining is communal or at separate tables, as you wish. 'Americans and Southern Irish like it communal,' says Joan, 'but with Northerners it can obviously be a problem.' Ian Paisley is sometimes a visitor. Once, at breakfast, he shared a long table with a group of Dubliners, who at first retreated nervously. 'Och, I'm nae going to aaaate yer!' – and soon they were all chatting aimably. What ever could they find to agree on? Perhaps, that this *is* the best hotel in the North."

Open All year.
Rooms 2 suites, 8 double. 2 in annexe. Unsuitable for &.
Facilities Drawing room, library, bar, 2 dining rooms (piped classical music during dinner). 7-acre grounds: equestrian centre. Golf nearby. Unsuitable for &.
Location 8 miles S of Newcastle, 1 mile inland from Annalong (turn off at *Halfway House* pub). Bus from Newcastle.
Restrictions No smoking: restaurant, bedrooms. No dogs.
Credit cards Access, Visa.
Terms [1997] B&B £55–£85. Set dinner £30; full alc £35. *V*

BELFAST   Map 6

Ash-Rowan   *Tel* (01232) 661758
12 Windsor Avenue   *Fax* (01232) 663227
Belfast BT9 6EE

Not far from Queen's University, this solid Victorian house in residential south Belfast is run as a very *soigné* B&B guest house by Evelyn and Sam Hazlett – "charming hosts". It was recently refurbished, and has been liked again: "Cosy rooms with lovely linen, perhaps a touch frilly; genuinely kind and warm welcome; lovely bread." The house is full of old furniture, lace and curios. Breakfast includes two types of home-baked bread, "gorgeous" home-made jams, fresh fruit salad, and a large choice of cooked dishes, notably the Ulster Fry, "not for the faint-hearted". Bedrooms are well fitted out, and all have a shower. There's a lounge for residents, with daily papers. We'd like more reports, please. (*AF*)

Open All year, except Christmas/New Year.
Rooms 4 double, 1 single.
Facilities Lounge, breakfast room. ½-acre garden. Unsuitable for &.
Location Just off Lisburn Rd, 2 miles SW of centre. Carpark. Bus from centre.
Restrictions No smoking: breakfast room, 2 bedrooms. No children under 12. No dogs.
Credit cards Access, Visa.
Terms B&B: single £46, double £66–£79.

See also SHORTLIST

DERRY Co. Londonderry   Map 6

Beech Hill House   *Tel* (01504) 349279
32 Ardmore Road   *Fax* (01504) 345366
Derry BT47 3QP

Two miles outside Derry, in its own broad parkland, stands this hand-some white country house. Once the home of a judge, now a hotel owned by local people, the Donnellys, it is one of the most highly reputed in the North. "The garden is lovely, beds and bedrooms are comfortable; the food is excellent – they have a wonderful chef, James Nicholas," wrote one visitor. Another said: "My room was bright and spacious, with a lovely view. Staff were friendly and flexible and the food superb – best fresh salmon and soup, best cooked breakfast I can remember." The owners describe the cooking as "classical French with an Irish influence". Bedrooms are mostly quite large, and well equipped. Local people use the big lounge as a kind of pub: "Everyone who is anyone in Northern Ireland seems to turn up there." The piped classical music in the public rooms did not please one visitor, who added: "But the kindness and willingness of the proprietors overcame everything." The marvellous scenery of Donegal is nearby. More reports, please.

Open All year, except 24/25 Dec.
Rooms 2 suites, 15 double.
Facilities Ramps. Lounge, morning room, bar, restaurant (piped classical music all day); conference facilities. 32-acre grounds: tennis, ponds, waterfall.
Location 2 miles SE of Derry, off Belfast road (signposted to right). Carpark.
Restrictions No smoking in restaurant. No dogs.
Credit cards Access, Amex, Visa.
Terms B&B: single £57.50–£62.50, double £75, suite £100. Set lunch £15.95, dinner £22.95; full alc from £34. Weekend, midweek breaks.

ENNISKILLEN Co. Fermanagh   Map 6

Killyhevlin Hotel   *Tel* (01365) 323481
                                    Fax (01365) 324726

One mile S of town, on Belfast road, large 2-storey building in "splendid position" amid 5-acre grounds on shores of Lough Erne (boating, coarse fishing). Rebuilt after serious 1996 bomb damage, it is modern and functional, but bright, cheerful and spacious. 43 pleasant bedrooms, some with balcony (lovely views of lake and hills); large bathrooms. Bar meals in boathouse-style bar, and lounge (pianist Tues–Sat). Extensive restaurant menu, with English cooking; large helpings. Excellent value on long wine list. Good breakfasts. Closed 25 Dec. 14 self-catering chalets on lake shore; conference complex. 1-acre grounds. No smoking in restaurant. No dogs in restaurant. All major credit cards accepted. B&B: single £50–£60, double £70–£90, suite £100–£125. Set lunch £14, dinner £19.50; full alc £22.50. *V*

We are particularly keen to have reports on italicised entries.

PORTAFERRY Co. Down

Map 6

Portaferry Hotel   NEW
10 The Strand
Portaferry DT22 1PE

Tel (01247 7) 28231
Fax (01247 7) 28999
E-mail portferry@iol.ie

"One of the most sympathetic hotels in the North." It's a traditional old quayside pub, set by the ferry landing in a pleasant village at the mouth of Strangford Lough, a long inland sea studded with tiny islands. Two enthusiastic reports restore it to the *Guide* this year. "Full of antiques, it has a warm atmosphere aided by friendly, smartly dressed and courteous staff. The food was excellent, with the accent on seafood. Our room was well furnished, but the canopied double bed was small. A delightful residents' lounge overlooks the harbour." "Quite plain outside, the hotel has been decently modernised inside but remains unpretentious, and is *gemütlich* more than elegant. Much is due to the owner, John Herlihy, a charming, urbane and breezy man, omnipresent, chatting up his guests. The dining room is a bit under-decorated; the sleek bar is more attractive, with a lively informal ambience, good food and superb youthful service. Both these rooms face the broad estuary-like sound, as do the pleasant front bedrooms. We loved the peaceful waterside setting. This enterprising hotel does a busy tourist trade in season. It offers painting, sailing and riding courses, and there are fine walks and cycle trails all round. It could make a good base for a quiet holiday, in an unspoilt area." Strangford Lough may be visited by ferry from the quay – a five-minute trip. (*SC Law, JA and KA*)

Open All year, except 24/25 Dec.
Rooms 12 double, 2 single.
Facilities 3 lounges, bar, dining room (piped instrumental music). Golf, riding, sailing, cycling nearby. Unsuitable for &.
Location In village, on seafront. Parking. Bus from Belfast.
Restriction No dogs.
Credit cards All major cards accepted.
Terms [1997] B&B £40–£55. Set lunch £15, dinner £22.50. Reduced rates and special meals for children. 1-night bookings refused bank holidays. *V*

TEMPO Co. Fermanagh

Map 6

Tempo Manor   NEW
Tempo BT94 3PA

Tel (01365 5) 41450
Fax (01365 5) 41202
E-mail tempo.manor@btinternet.com

Young John Langham receives guests in his ancestral home, a grey stone Victorian manor (1863), just outside Tempo village. "The best feature," write inspectors in 1997, "is the lovely romantic estate and garden, notably the big lakes among tall trees, where spaniels and alsatians came for walks with us. The house has been carefully preserved in authentic 1860s style – lots of stuffed birds, good Victorian furniture, family portraits and other memorabilia. Visitors might find it all enchanting or a bit melancholy. In our bathroom, the huge bath and period bath-taps were truly Victorian. Our bedroom had a four-poster, with lots of stuffed toy animals, and a privately printed volume of our host's grandmother's very personal poems. He was affable, giving us port after dinner by the fire in the grand drawing room. The cooking,

by a local lady, was wholesome traditional, eg, roast pork with crackling, then trifle. Good breakfast, with muesli, home-made jams, etc. All
in all, a peaceful, personal, Anglo-Irish experience." Children and dogs
are welcomed, though the latter may not come into the house. Guests
may fish for trout, pike, perch and bream in the manor's stream and
lakes. There is coarse and game fishing on Lough Erne and many rivers
nearby, and sea fishing can be arranged. Plenty of golf courses in the
area, and Castle Coole, a magnificent neo-classical house, designed by
James Wyatt.

Open 1 Mar–31 Oct.
Rooms 1 suite, 4 double. No telephone/TV.
Facilities Drawing room, dining room. 300-acre estate: 11-acre gardens, lake,
stream, fishing. Golf, lake/river fishing nearby. Unsuitable for &.
Location 8 miles NE of Enniskillen. In village, take Brookeborough road; drive
1st on left, marked "private road". Taxi from Enniskillen.
Restriction No dogs in house (kennels in grounds).
Credit cards Access, Visa.
Terms B&B £50–£60. Set dinner £25.

UPPERLANDS Co. Londonderry   Map 6

Ardtara Country House   NEW   *Tel* (01648) 44490
8 Gorteade Road   *Fax* (01648) 45080
Upperlands BT46 5SA

*Outside village famed for linen production, 4 miles NE of Maghera, in Seamus
Heaney country. Sturdy Victorian manor recently converted into pleasant
country hotel, full of antiques. Comfortable modern bedrooms, some with view.
Interesting food in no-smoking restaurant. Large garden with tennis court.
Fishing nearby. Royal Portrush golf course and Belfast airport both 30 mins'
drive. Closed 25/26 Dec. Access, Amex, Visa accepted. 8 rooms. B&B single
£60–£80, double £110–£130. Set lunch £13.50; full alc £32.*

****

Traveller's tale Cornwall: Our bedroom was over a function
room where a stag party was taking place. The noise was intol-
erable. At about 2.30 am we phoned down to ask the management if the noise could be reduced. They rather cheekily
suggested that we move to another room. We felt we should
have been given that option before going to bed. The party dis-
charged into the garden below our window at 3.30. We thought
they might have offered compensation when we paid the bill,
but they did not.

****

Traveller's tale Cheshire: Getting up in the middle of the night
was a nightmare. The light switch was cunningly hidden behind
the bed's dainty drapes, so I felt my way to the bathroom, bump-
ing into the lethal iron bed frame on the way. I was misguided
enough to flush the loo. The reverberations throughout the hotel,
which has the noisiest plumbing I've ever come across, sounded
like the blitz. This of course set off other guests, and the thunder-
ing of water cisterns that ensued had to be heard to be believed.

****

Republic of Ireland

Castle Leslie, Glaslough

Dublin is today more popular than ever, and its tourist boom has led to the building of several ambitious new hotels. Only a few belong to the big international chains, which are little represented either in Dublin or in the rest of Ireland. There are one or two small Irish chains, notably Fitzpatrick's and Jurys, but they do not feature in this section. Almost all Irish hotels are privately owned and run, and indeed this country is a paradise of the kind of smallish hotel of character that the *Guide* seeks out.

Many of them are stately homes still lived in by their ancestral owners, often the Anglo-Irish gentry, who have turned them into private hotels or guest houses to defray the cost of keeping up a big estate. Or newer owners have acquired them and now run them in the same very personal way. The aim is to give guests the feeling that they are personal friends on a visit. They may be surrounded by old family portraits and heirlooms, fine old family antiques and furniture. Often the wife of the house does the cooking, in "country house" style, using local ingredients, and guests dine communally round one big table.

The hosts will sometimes preside. Conversation is general, as at a private dinner party. This can work well, or less well, depending on the mix of guests and the hosts' personality: often they are great fun, full of local anecdotes and information. Most of the best of these stately homes are in this guide.

In town and country alike, there are also guest houses of all kinds, private homes offering B&B, and – an Irish speciality – farmhouses providing simple bedrooms, big breakfasts, sometimes an evening meal too. You can stay in converted farm buildings or outhouses, get to know the country people, even share briefly in the life of the farm. The Irish Tourist Board, Bord Fáilte, grades all kinds of accommodation: the places it approves generally display at the gate its green shamrock sign.

All Irish accommodation provides a cooked breakfast, with bacon, sausages, eggs, etc – ample, but somewhat monotonous, and coffee is sometimes poor. Food in Irish hotels has been improving considerably, as witness some of the entries in this chapter. French or Italian influences have been creeping in, and many young chefs have received training abroad. But standards remain variable, and attempts at sophistication do not always succeed. Just a few places win a *Michelin* star or red "Meals" for quality, and we identify these. As in Britain, VAT is included in bills, but service is not, and you are expected to add about 10 per cent for this. Service, usually by local people, may sometimes lack polish: but it makes up for this by an almost universal Irish cheerfulness and obligingness.

ADARE Co. Limerick   **Map 6**

Dunraven Arms   *Tel* (061) 396633
Main Street   *Fax* (061) 396541

Adare, near Limerick, is a pretty village on the banks of the river Maigue, with black and white timbered houses and an ancient church. This handsome old traditional inn (1792), long, low and yellow, with a pretty garden, today specialises in sports and is popular with local horse-riders: its manager, Louis Murphy, a keen huntsman, will arrange for guests to hunt with famous local packs. The hotel has recently added new bedrooms and is now quite large for rural Ireland. But a recent visitor found it had kept the personal touch: "I was given an excellent, quiet large room, facing the garden. The food was good – not gourmet, but well cooked and presented. The service was a bit amateur, but full of charm. The half board rate was good value. It might be a bit noisy in the fox-hunting season." The decor is traditional. Chef Mark Phelan has won awards for his cooking, enticingly described on the menu, for example, "whole roasted native wild partridge on an artichoke and potato boxty". The leisure centre includes a large swimming pool, a computerised gym studio and a steam room. Other attractions for the sportingly inclined include an 18-hole championship golf course and fishing for trout and salmon in the river Maigue. More reports, please.

Open All year.
Rooms 14 suites, 57 double, 4 single. Some on ground floor.
Facilities Lift. Lounge, writing room, TV room, residents' bar (pianist at weekends), public bar, restaurant, conservatory; conference/function facilities;

leisure centre: swimming pool, steam room, gym. 3-acre garden. River, fishing,
golf, riding, fox-hunting nearby.
Location In village 10 miles SW of Limerick. Private parking. Bus from Limerick.
Restriction No smoking in writing room. No dogs.
Credit cards All major cards accepted.
Terms [1997] *(Excluding 12½% service charge)* Rooms: single IR£70–£87, double
IR£95–£115, suite IR£170. Breakfast IR£9.95. Set lunch IR£13.95, dinner IR£23.95.

AGLISH Co. Tipperary   Map 6

Ballycormac House   *Tel* (067) 21129
Aglish, nr Borrisokane   *Fax* (067) 21200

"Herb and Christine were gracious hosts. Their rooms were excellent
and their food outstanding, especially the rack of lamb" – more praise
in 1997 for this ancient farmhouse east of Lough Derg, run with
American-style comfort by its American owners, Herbert and Christine
Quigley. The location is not spectacular, but the house and small gardens are charming. Other recent praise: "We had such a successful
hunting weekend that we returned with all the family for two-and-a-
half weeks – it was the best holiday of our life." "Our suite had a four-
poster, and was delightfully decorated. The food was very good,
plentiful and reasonably priced." The Quigleys call their cuisine "modern eclectic, with diverse ethnic menus using the best produce Ireland
has to offer"; vegetarians are catered for. Families and people on their
own are welcomed, and programmes of outdoor activities (riding, fox-
hunting, golf, shooting, etc) can be arranged. So can packed or light
lunches; and "old-fashioned teas" are served by the fire. (*Morgan
Howells, and others*)

Open All year.
Rooms 1 suite, 3 double, 1 single. No TV/telephone.
Facilities Sitting room, dining room; drying room. 2-acre gardens. Lough Derg
5 miles; fishing, sailing, riding, golf nearby. Fox-hunting, shooting arranged.
Location From Nenagh, N on N52 to Borrisokane, then N65. Right at signs to
hotel. Bus from Nenagh.
Restrictions No smoking: dining room, bedrooms. No young children. Dogs by
arrangement; not in house.
Credit cards Access, Visa.
Terms B&B: single IR£35, double IR£70, suite IR£80; D,B&B IR£55–£64 per person. Set lunch IR£6–£10, dinner IR£20–£24. Off-season breaks; activity programmes; Christmas, New Year, golf packages. 1-night bookings refused bank
holidays. *V*

BALLINA Co. Mayo   Map 6

Mount Falcon Castle   NEW   *Tel* (096) 21172 and 70811
                                                     Fax (096) 71517
                                         E-mail mfsalmon@iol.ie

Ballina, home town of the Irish president, Mary Robinson, lies close to
the lovely wild countryside of Co. Mayo. Just to the south is this grey
stone creeper-covered mansion, dating from 1876, set in a large estate
on the banks of the river Moy, on which it has eight miles of fishing
rights. It was bought in 1932 by the Aldridge family, as somewhere to
entertain their fishing friends, and they have run it ever since as a

country house hotel, grand yet informal. After some years with no reports, it makes a welcome return to the *Guide*: "Constance Aldridge, now in her eighties, has 'retired', but she still dominates, even if the day-to-day running is now in the hands of her grandson, Steven Hannick. Dinner was a real experience, with above-average food, and Mrs Aldridge presiding at the head of the table. Our bedroom was spacious, though the plumbing was a little unpredictable. The public rooms and the grounds are all part of the experience." There are log fires and fresh flowers in the reception rooms. In country house style, dinner is at a fixed time, and all guests dine round one long table. Much use is made of local salmon, meat and game, and vegetables grown on the home farm. Co. Mayo has the highest concentration of megalithic tombs in Ireland; and some of the country's best golf courses are in the area. (*R Rennison*)

Open All year, except Christmas, Feb, Mar.
Rooms 1 suite, 7 double, 2 single.
Facilities Hall (piped classical music at night; entertainments in summer), drawing room, TV room, dining room. 100-acre grounds: tennis, woodland, pasture, river frontage with fishing. Golf, riding nearby. Unsuitable for &.
Location 4 miles S of Ballina on N26 to Foxford. Bus from Ballina.
Restrictions No smoking in dining room. No dogs in public rooms.
Credit cards All major cards accepted.
Terms B&B IR£44–£49. Set lunch IR£18, dinner IR£25. Weekly rates. Reduced rates for children.

BALLINA Co. Tipperary   Map 6

Waterman's Lodge   NEW   *Tel* (061) 376333
Ballina, Killaloe

Peacefully set on hill overlooking broad Shannon river, 16 miles NE of Limerick, outside Ballina village, small and friendly country hotel, with delightful owner, Brid Ryan. Charming decor: antiques throughout, open fire in lounge, flowers, plants, books. Spacious no-smoking bedrooms; impressive beds. Interesting cooking (using organic produce) by Thomas O'Leary in Courtyard *restaurant (closed Mon). Fishing (ghillie available) in village; golf nearby. Open early Mar–31 Dec (except Christmas). Access, Visa accepted. 10 rooms, all on ground floor. B&B IR£30–£45. D,B&B IR£55–£70. Set dinner IR£26.50 [1997].*

BALLINDERRY Co. Tipperary   Map 6

Kylenoe   BUDGET   *Tel/Fax* (067) 22015
Ballinderry, Nenagh

Virginia Moeran's 18th-century house stands on a hilltop near Lough Derg. It is set in large grounds with meadows, woods, apple orchards, plenty of wildlife – foxes, deer, red squirrels – and a small horse-breeding farm. Again in 1996–97, readers were happy here. "It's a charming stone house with enchanting views. Our hostess gave us a gracious welcome and is a superb cook – smoked eel, and casseroled wild duck. In February, we revelled in the warmth of the house: log fires, antique furniture, very comfortable beds." "Altogether delightful, with personal, thoughtful service." "Like staying with friends." "Our children were made particularly welcome. Uncomplicated, friendly atmosphere." (*PM Knatchbull-Hugessen, Sylvia Thomas-Ferrand, Dieter Beck, and others*)

Open All year, except Christmas. Advance booking required.
Rooms 3 double, 1 single. No telephone.
Facilities Drawing room, dining room. 150-acre grounds. Lake 1 mile: fishing; water sports, golf, riding nearby. Unsuitable for &.
Location Between Ballinderry and Terryglass (signposted). 7 miles NW of Borrisokane.
Restriction Dogs by arrangement only.
Credit card Visa.
Terms B&B IR£25. Set lunch IR£8.50, dinner IR£19.

BALLINGARRY Co. Limerick   Map 6

The Mustard Seed at Echo Lodge   NEW   *Tel* (069) 68508
                                                           Fax (069) 68511

On outskirts of village, 18 miles SW of Limerick, a yellow mansion, built 1884, set in large grounds. Once a convent, but recently converted into ambitious restaurant-with-rooms by owner Daniel Mullane, "a convivial and friendly host" (former owner of Mustard Seed *restaurant in nearby Adare). Excellent cooking, large wine list, good breakfasts; friendly staff. Lounges with log fires, somewhat over-decorated. 12 bedrooms, some no-smoking, some with views, individually furnished in period style, but awkwardly designed. 1 suitable for &. Closed mid-Jan–end Feb, Christmas. Riding, shooting, angling nearby. No dogs. Access, Amex, Visa accepted. B&B: single IR£65–£90, double IR£120–£150; D,B&B IR£93–£103 per person.* ***V***

BALLYLICKEY Co. Cork   Map 6

Sea View House   *Tel* (027) 50073 and 50462
Ballylickey, Bantry Bay   *Fax* (027) 51555

Set in large well-kept gardens, this solid white Victorian house over-looks Bantry Bay and the far mountains. It is owned and run in cheery personal style by Kathleen O'Sullivan. The decor and ambience might not appeal to the sophisticated, but it has many devotees among our readers: "Such a warm welcome, excellent food." "A friendly atmos-phere, attentive service by well-trained young waitresses." "Our spa-cious room overlooked the garden, a mass of colour. The staff were delightful and amusing." There are large public rooms, and good bed-rooms with plenty of cupboard space and personal touches: but not all have views of Bantry Bay. There is plenty of good local fish and seafood on offer, also Irish potato pancakes for breakfast. Portions are gener-ous. (*J Tudor-Craig, RMJ Kenber, EB Schaffer, L Evans and others*)

Open Mid-Mar–mid-Nov.
Rooms 2 suites, 14 double. 1 on ground floor, suitable for &.
Facilities Lounge, bar, TV room, 2 dining rooms. 5-acre grounds. Fishing, boat-ing, beaches, riding, golf nearby.
Location 3 miles N of Bantry towards Glengarriff; 70 yds off main road. Bus from Cork.
Restrictions: No smoking in dining room on request. No dogs in public rooms.
Credit cards All major cards accepted.
Terms [1997] B&B: IR£45–£55; D,B&B (min. 3 days) IR£65–£80. Set dinner IR£25. Special breaks all year. ***V***

BALLYMOTE Co. Sligo   Map 6

Temple House   *Tel* (071) 83329
                                                      Fax (071) 83808

This Georgian mansion is in huge grounds with farmland and woods, beside a lake and the ruins of a castle built by the knights templar in 1200. Sandy Perceval's family has lived here for three centuries, and he and his wife Deb now run it as a private hotel ("outstanding value", is a recent comment). They are friendly, and the style is informal, despite the grandeur of the main hall and stairway. Some of the five bedrooms are huge too – one is nicknamed "the half-acre" – and all are comfortably kitted out; beds have an electric blanket. At dinner, guests sit round one table, and Deb Perceval's cooking ("Irish with French connections") is much admired. Mr Perceval, something of a Green, is proud to show visitors around his estate, which is a European lichen conservation area. It has a farm stocked with sheep and Kerry cattle, and abounds with wildlife and flora. Fishing is available on the lake and shooting parties are held in winter. Children are welcomed. All around is the beauty of County Sligo: mountains, lakes and beaches, archaeological sites, and places associated with Yeats. Because of Mr Perceval's allergies, guests are asked not to wear scented products. More reports welcome.

Open 1 Apr–30 Nov.
Rooms 4 double, 1 single. No TV/telephone.
Facilities Sitting room, snooker room, dining room. Terraced garden: croquet. 1,000-acre farm and woodlands; lake: coarse fishing, boating. Golf, riding nearby. Unsuitable for &.
Location 14 miles S of Sligo on N17. Signposted beyond Esso garage in Ballymote. Train: Ballymote; then taxi.
Restrictions No smoking in dining room. Dogs in car only.
Credit cards Access, Amex, Visa.
Terms B&B IR£40. Set dinner IR£18. Weekend breaks. Reductions for long stays. 1-night bookings refused public holidays.

BEAUFORT Co. Kerry   Map 6

Beaufort House   *Tel/Fax* (064) 44764

A handsome Georgian family home, complete with two children and a dog, in a small village near Killarney. The river Laune (with fishing for salmon and trout) runs through its large grounds. It is "unreservedly recommended" by a seasoned Irish traveller: "The setting by the river is idyllic; from the upper rooms there is a good view of the mountains – MacGillicuddy's Reeks. The owners, Rachel and Donald Cameron, are a charming, attentive couple, with an eye for interior design. They have spent lavishly on beautifully coordinated curtains and carpets; walls are painted to match. Our large front bedroom was superb, with a view of the river and mountains, a double bed wide enough for four, and a very adequate bathroom with good quality towels. Dinner is communal and the Camerons join their guests over dessert and coffee; the no-choice set menu was excellent, with a carefully chosen wine list. Breakfast is generous Irish." (*EC*)

Open 1 Apr–30 Sept. Groups at other times by arrangement.

Rooms 4 double. No telephone/TV.
Facilities Drawing room, library, dining room. 40-acre grounds: river, trout/salmon-fishing. Golf nearby.
Location 6 miles W of Killarney on R562. Left over bridge opposite petrol station. House immediately on left.
Restrictions No smoking, except in library. No dogs in house.
Credit cards Access, Visa.
Terms B&B IR£50–£60. Set dinner IR£25.

BIRR Co. Offaly   Map 6

Tullanisk   *Tel* (0509) 20572
                                                       Fax (0509) 21783

George and Susan Gossip's 18th-century dower house stands amid fields where sheep graze, in the wooded deer park of the Earl of Rosse's vast Birr Castle estate. Its elegant rooms are filled with the owners' own antique furniture, china and pictures, giving it a personal atmosphere – "pleasantly relaxed and informal, run with taste and care", according to 1997 visitors. George Gossip is "a colourful character and a great sportsman". "He continues to preside with tremendous style," writes a regular visitor, "and goes to great lengths to talk to everyone." Dinner is taken communally and served by candlelight. No menu or choice, but preferences are discussed. Food is "quite adventurous" and cooked "with enthusiasm"; game is a speciality. Breakfasts are also admired. Birr castle gardens may be visited, and all manner of sporting activities (see below) are available. (*EC, and others*) *V*

Open 1 Apr–15 Oct. Other times (except Feb) by arrangement. Lunch not served.
Rooms 6 double. 5 with facilities *en suite*. 1 on ground floor.
Facilities Drawing room, sitting room, playroom, dining room. 2-acre grounds in 2,000-acre estate. Shooting, fishing, riding, golf nearby. Unsuitable for &.
Location 1½ miles NW of Birr.
Restrictions No smoking in dining room, discouraged in bedrooms. Dogs in 1 bedroom only.
Credit cards Access, Amex, Visa.
Terms [1997] B&B: single IR£39–£52, double IR£70–£90. Set dinner IR£22.50. Negotiable rates for longer stays. *V*

BUNCLODY Co. Wexford   Map 6

Clohamon House   *Tel* (054) 77253
                                                       Fax (054) 77956

"Friendly, relaxed and informal, with first-class cooking, beautiful bedrooms, lovely scenery." "Charming and amusing hosts." So runs this year's praise for Sir Richard and Lady Levinge's 18th-century manor, which stands, surrounded by beechwoods, in gardens with rare trees and shrubs. Its huge grounds slope down to the river Slaney (salmon-and trout-fishing in season), and contain a stud of Connemara ponies. Family antiques and portraits spanning 250 years fill the house. There are just four bedrooms, each with a pretty decor and a bath or shower *en suite*. Guests eat together at the candlelit table. The "excellent, straightforward" meals prepared by Maria Levinge include home-grown vegetables and Irish cheeses. Vegetarian choices are good, while dishes such as chicken breasts with orange, honey and ginger might also feature on the set menu. The house has fine furniture and paintings. Its interior has been called "grand, if worn", but carpets and showers are new this year. Gardening tuition and painting sessions can be arranged, if booked in advance. The nearby village of Ferns, former capital of Leinster, has a newly restored castle, a ruined 12th-century abbey, and even a cathedral. *(Barbara Clauson, and others)*

Open End Mar–Nov.
Rooms 4 double. No telephone/TV.
Facilities Drawing room, dining room. 180-acre grounds: 3-acre garden, fishing, riding. Golf, tennis nearby. Unsuitable for &.
Location Off Carlow–Enniscorthy road, 2 miles SE of Bunclody: in village, cross river, turn right towards Clohamon. Bus from Bunclody.
Restrictions No smoking in bedrooms. No children. Dogs by arrangement.
Credit cards Access, Visa.
Terms B&B IR£36–£48. Set supper (June/July/Aug) IR£16, set dinner IR£23. Gardening, painting breaks. 1-night bookings sometimes refused.

CARAGH LAKE Co. Kerry   Map 6

Caragh Lodge   *Tel* (066) 69115
                                                       Fax (066) 69316

"A genuine country house feel. Superb decor, warm ambience and wonderful food." "A perfect place to unwind; quiet and secluded. Mrs Gaunt was welcoming and enthusiastic; the staff were courteous. We enjoyed high teas on the verandah by the garden, and cycled round the lake on locally rented bicycles." Recent praise for Mary Gaunt's Victorian fishing lodge, a low white building "with a colonial feel". It stands in magnificent large gardens with rare trees and shrubs, on the shore of Caragh Lake, with views of Ireland's highest mountains, MacGillycuddy's Reeks. The Ring of Kerry is a mile away. The spacious bedrooms in the main building have splendid views. Rooms in the annexe are smaller and simpler, and can be noisy. The cooking is modern in style: very good fish, chicken and Irish cheeses; bread is home-baked, wines are fairly priced. Service can be rushed at weekends, when the restaurant is open to the public. Good breakfasts: freshly squeezed orange juice, scrambled eggs with smoked salmon. There is unpolluted swimming in the lake. Sandy beaches are a short drive away; there are eight golf courses nearby. *(RM, and others)*

Open 25 Apr–28 Oct.
Rooms 1 suite, 12 double, 2 single. 6 in garden annexe. Some on ground floor.
Facilities 2 lounges, dining room. 7-acre grounds: garden, tennis, sauna; lake: swimming, fishing, boating. Sea 4 miles. Unsuitable for &.
Location 22 miles W of Killarney. N70 from Killorglin along Ring of Kerry, 2nd road signposted Caragh Lake; left at lake.
Restriction No smoking in restaurant. No children under 7. No dogs.
Credit cards Access, Amex, Visa.
Terms [1997] *(Excluding 10% service charge)* B&B: single IR£65, double IR£45–£90. Set dinner IR£26.

Inevitably some hotels change hands or close after we have gone to press. It may be prudent to check the ownership when booking, particularly in the case of small establishments.

CARRICK-ON-SUIR Co. Tipperary   Map 6

Cedarfield House   NEW/BUDGET   *Tel* (051) 640164
Waterfield Road   *Fax* (051) 641580

On N24 Rosslare–Limerick, 1 mile E of Carrick, 16 miles NW of Waterford, Penelope Eades' pink 18th-century house in 3½-acre garden, set in open country. Friendly welcome, pleasant bedrooms, lounges with log fires. Good cooking, with French/Spanish overtones; good wine list. Fishing, golf, riding, etc nearby. Unsuitable for ﹩. No dogs in house. Closed 23 Dec–last week Jan. Access, Diners, Visa accepted. 6 rooms. B&B single IR£27.50–£35, double IR£45–£60. Set dinner IR£19. *V*

CARRIGBYRNE Co. Wexford   Map 6

Cedar Lodge   *Tel* (051) 428386 and 428436
Carrigbyrne, Newbawn   *Fax* (051) 428222

This well-furnished modern hotel, west of Wexford and handy for the Rosslare ferry, is set beneath the slopes of the Carrigbyrne Forest. It was again liked this year for its comfort and good food, though some thought prices too high. "Friendly owner, fantastic rooms, good walks in local forest." "No beauty outside, inside it has a smart decor and a warm and friendly atmosphere. The spacious bedrooms are prettily decorated, with impressive marble bathrooms. The omnipresent owner, Tom Martin, keeps things running smoothly." "Excellent dinner with good service in attractive restaurant with a big log fire in the middle of the room. Delicious home-made bread." The menus include local mussels, oysters and scallops. There's a garden, but front rooms by the main road might be noisy. Many attractions nearby, including the John F Kennedy Arboretum, with trees and shrubs from all over the world. (*Dr CH Cannon, Ruth West, J Tudor-Craig*)

Open 1 Feb–1 Dec.
Rooms 28 double. Some on ground floor.
Facilities Lounge (live Irish music 3 times a week), lounge bar, breakfast room, restaurant (piped music all day). 1½-acre garden. Golf nearby, sandy beaches 12 miles.
Location On N25, 14 miles W of Wexford.
Restrictions No smoking in restaurant. Dogs by arrangement, not in public rooms.
Credit cards Access, Visa.
Terms [1997] B&B IR£45–£75. Set lunch IR£15, dinner IR£25. 3-day rates.

CASHEL BAY Co. Galway   Map 6

Cashel House   *Tel* (095) 31001
                                                    Fax (095) 31077

Kay and Dermot McEvilly's civilised manor house (Relais & Chateaux) stands at the head of Cashel Bay, amid the wilds of Connemara. De Gaulle stayed here for a fortnight (guarded by 63 Irish police) when he retired in 1969, and today there are still many French guests. But the Gallic influence goes little further: "It's all chintz and Victoriana," was one comment this year. Another: "Breakfast was good and copious and dinner excellent, as was service. Our bedroom and bathroom were a bit small but very comfortable, with luxurious bath towels." Others wrote earlier: "The proprietors are visibly present, and the staff are superbly trained to provide the facilities of a first-rate hotel." Public rooms include a comfortable lounge with antiques and fresh flowers, a library and a spacious modern bar. Breakfasts, in the large conservatory dining room, and snack lunches in the bar, are much praised. The food at dinner, found "wonderful" in 1997, could include terrine of quail, casserole of guinea fowl, poached brill with champagne sauce. Some bedrooms have a sea view; the suites in the modern section are "superb and good value". (*Mrs JC Smye, and others*) The hotel has its own tennis court, riding stable and tiny beach, and golf and fishing are close by.

Open All year, except 10 Jan–10 Feb.
Rooms 13 garden suites, 17 double, 2 single. Some on ground floor.
Facilities Drawing room, lounge, lounge bar, library, dining room/conservatory. 50-acre grounds: 15-acre gardens, tennis, riding, private beach, fishing.
Location 42 miles NW of Galway. 1 mile S of N59 at Recess.
Restrictions No children under 5. No dogs in public rooms.
Credit cards All major cards accepted.
Terms (*Excluding 12½% service charge*) B&B: IR£50–£91. Set dinner IR£30; full alc IR£24–£38. Spring, autumn breaks.

Zetland House   *Tel* (095) 31111
                                                               Fax (095) 31117

John and Mona Prendergast's handsome white 1850s hunting lodge stands in large grounds on the edge of Cashel Bay, amid the wild Connemara landscape. More eager praise has come this year: "We had a wonderful stay in beautiful surroundings, among delightful people. The owners and staff are charming, and service is excellent. The young Irish chef, Paul Neehan, has enormous talent, with the accent on seafood, exquisitely presented." Others have written: "The views are breathtaking." "Genuine Irish hospitality." "Spacious, comfortable bedroom." The lounges are large, with peat fires, antiques, soft colour schemes, fresh flowers, books, porcelain and a wide-ranging collection of paintings. *Zetland House* has its own sea trout fishery, the Gowla, which has 20 lakes and three-and-a-half miles of river. Recently there have been problems, and the fish have become scarce. John Prendergast is part of the "Save Our Seatrout" organisation and there are hopes for a better season in 1997–98. Meanwhile there are plenty of other sporting activities (see below); wonderful beaches are nearby, with safe swimming, and this as a good base for touring Connemara. (*Mrs PM Falconer Smith, Mr and Mrs TI Frith, and others*)

Open Apr–Oct.
Rooms 17 double, 3 single. 1 on ground floor.
Facilities Drawing room, lounge, snooker room, bar, restaurant. 6-acre grounds: tennis, croquet, fishing; rocky shore 200 yds. Golf, water sports, sea angling, cycling, shooting, pony-trekking available.
Location 40 miles W of Galway, on N59. Bus from Galway.
Credit cards All major cards accepted.
Terms [1997] B&B IR£48–£75. Set lunch IR£17, dinner IR£28; full alc IR£38. Off-season rates. ***V***

The international dialling code for Ireland is 353.

CASTLEBALDWIN Co. Sligo   **Map 6**

Cromleach Lodge   *Tel* (071) 65155
Ballindoon   *Fax* (071) 65455
Castlebaldwin, via Boyle

Christy and Moira Tighe, a local couple, have enlarged their own home
into a sophisticated guest house. It's a striking modern building, grey-
gabled and glass-fronted, in a panoramic setting alone on a hillside in
large wooded grounds above Lough Arrow, which all the bedrooms
overlook. The decor in the public areas has been thought "a bit over-
the-top" by some guests, but visiting hoteliers thought otherwise:
"Absolutely lovely, both in layout and design. Our bedrooms were
superb, with plenty of space, magnificent views, fresh fruit, varieties of
tea, complimentary whiskey and a well-appointed bathroom." The
"skilful modern cooking" is well above average, and has a *Michelin* red
"Meals" for good value. Some visitors have thought the breakfast
"over-formal", and have been irritated by the piped music at mealtimes
and in the corridors. Others wrote: "All is still very friendly, though
with less of a homely feel than before. But it is a wonderful place for a
few nights' pampering." There is a private dining room which families
with young children may use. (*Diane Skelton, Sara Price, and others*)

Open 6 Feb–2 Nov. Lunch not served.
Rooms 10 double.
Facilities 2 lounges, 3 dining rooms, conservatory. 30-acre grounds. Private
access to Lough Arrow: fishing, boating, surfing; walking, hill climbing.
Unsuitable for &.
Location 9 miles NW of Boyle, off N4 Dublin–Sligo. Turn E at Castlebaldwin.
Restrictions No smoking: dining rooms, 1 lounge, 5 bedrooms. No children
under 7 in dining room. No dogs in house (kennels provided).
Credit cards All major cards accepted.
Terms [1997] B&B IR£59–£99; D,B&B IR£84–£124. Set dinner IR£25–£38; full alc
IR£31. Midweek, weekend rates. Cookery courses out of season.

CLIFDEN Co. Galway   **Map 6**

The Ardagh   *Tel* (095) 21384
Ballyconneely Road   *Fax* (095) 21314

The distinguished name "Ardagh" means "high point" in Irish – and
the high point here is the "excellent cooking" of Monique Bauvet. She
and her husband Stephane, a young Belgian couple, own and run a
very spruce modern hotel in a splendid isolated setting, looking out
over Ardbear Bay. "They are friendly, charming and helpful," wrote
the nominator. "Our large sea-facing room was well equipped and had
a good-sized bathroom. This makes a fine base to explore the western
end of the Connemara peninsula. At the end of the day you return to
be greeted by the smiling staff and the really delicious food." The
emphasis is on fish – for example, "*Ardagh*'s famous seafood chowder"
or brill on spinach with a saffron sauce. (*RMS*)

Open End Mar–end Oct.
Rooms 3 suites, 14 double, 4 single.
Facilities 2 lounges, bar, restaurant. Small garden. Beach, lake fishing, golf, rid-
ing nearby.
Location 2 miles S of Clifden, on R341 towards Ballyconneely.

Restriction No dogs.
Credit cards All major cards accepted.
Terms [1997] B&B IR£42–£70. Set dinner IR£30.35.

The Quay House   *Tel* (095) 21369
                                                Fax (095) 21608
                                      E-mail bluebook@iol.ie

Clifden's oldest building, a trim white Georgian house, has a "quiet and charming" position by the water, in a garden with tropical plants. It has in this century been harbourmaster's house, convent and Franciscan friary; now it is a restaurant-with-rooms, owned and run by the "delightful" Paddy and Julia Foyle. This year, their "friendly informality, with assortments of children, cats, candles and teapots" was again enjoyed. The decor is amusingly eccentric and colourful ("a blend of antiques and Art Deco, creating an avant-garde style," say the Foyles). "The hall was full of deer with huge antlers, a tiger or two and an ocelot," wrote one visitor. Another described her huge room: "Blue-painted and wood-panelled, it had a vast bed with a wide rococo mirror behind it. All was beautifully clean, but with slightly decaying gentility. The pictures were fascinating but hardly jolly – Joan of Arc at prayer, the death of General Wolfe, various dogs." Many rooms have garden or bay views, and most are comfortable and spacious, though one at the top was found cramped and basic. The dining room is in two parts; one blue-walled, with large round tables; the other white and bright. The cooking has long been admired; a new chef, Valerie Marcus, came in 1997, and we'd like to know whether she is keeping up the high standards. Breakfasts are "of high quality, with generous servings of fresh orange juice, good plain yogurt, and scrambled eggs and smoked salmon". (*Sara A Price, Noel and Sheila Marriott, and others*)

Open All year, except Christmas/New Year.
Rooms 14 double. Some on ground floor.
Facilities Ramps. 2 sitting rooms, dining room, conservatory. 1-acre garden. Fishing, sailing, golf, riding nearby.
Location Harbour; 3 mins' walk from centre. Courtyard parking.
Restrictions No smoking in some bedrooms. No dogs in house.
Credit cards Access, Visa.
Terms B&B IR£30–£50. Set lunch IR£7, dinner IR£22. Children under 12 accommodated free in parents' bedroom. Weekend rates negotiable. ***V***

Rock Glen   NEW   *Tel* (095) 21035
                                                Fax (095) 21737

"Just to see again the moon rise over Clifden," crooned Bing Crosby. And that is what you can do from this low white building, a converted 1815 hunting lodge, set by a fjord beside the wild Connemara hills. Owned by John and Evangeline Roche, whose daughter Siobhán is manageress, it is warmly nominated this year. "Delightful, with a young and friendly staff. Dinner and breakfasts, in the handsome dining room, both had at least five courses, with excellent cooking. One drawing room has a bar and a piano. Real country house feel. Bedroom elegantly decorated. Some guests really smart, but children welcome." "Brilliant family-run hotel in large grounds. Front bedrooms light and attractive, some rear ones less so, but OK. Small bathrooms. Nothing was too much trouble for the staff – they cooked for breakfast the mackerel we caught, and dried our rain-sodden clothes. It was like staying with friends. Huge drawing-room complete with chess, Scrabble, etc. Food delicious – scrambled eggs with smoked salmon for breakfast." Sandy beaches are nearby. (*Simon Jones, Dr CH Cannon*)

Open Mid-Mar–30 Oct.
Rooms 1 suite, 23 double, 5 single. 15 on ground floor.
Facilities Sitting room, bar (pianist 3 nights a week), billiard room, restaurant. 50-acre grounds: tennis, croquet, putting. Horse-riding, pony-trekking, fishing available.
Location 1½ miles S of Clifden on Ballyconneely road. Buses from Galway.
Restriction No dogs in bedrooms, public rooms.
Credit cards All major cards accepted.
Terms [1997] B&B: single IR£67–£73, double IR£99–£110. Set dinner (*excluding 12½% service charge*) IR£25. ⅓ reduction for children sharing parents' room.

CLONES Co. Monaghan   Map 6

Hilton Park   *Tel* (047) 56007
Scothouse, Clones   *Fax* (047) 56033
Q *César award in 1994*

"'Great windows open to the south', Yeats wrote of another Irish country house, but it could have been this one. All the rooms have floor-to-ceiling windows commanding views of the landscaped park." So writes a recent visitor to this stately italianate mansion, which has been the family home of the Maddens for some 250 years. It is set amid rolling parkland, with pleasure gardens laid out by John Madden in the 1870s, three lakes, and a golf course. "The style is relaxed and informal, but everything runs like clockwork." "The food continues to be a delight," adds another enthusiast. Lucy Madden makes use of "the best raw materials locally available, and organically grown vegetables often only picked at 5 pm". Evening meals, in the baronial dining room, are served communally or at separate tables, according to preference. Breakfast, by contrast, is in a "cosy, cheerful annexe to the kitchen". The "warmly hospitable" Maddens run the place on house party lines; they are always around to advise or to chat, but do not impose themselves on their guests. Bedrooms are huge, and public rooms elegantly furnished, with memorabilia from past times. More reports, please.

Open 1 Apr–30 Sept. Dining room closed midday, and to non-residents.
Rooms 6 double. No telephone/TV.
Facilities Drawing room, sitting room, games room, smoking room, dining room, breakfast room. 500-acre grounds: gardens, park, golf, 3 lakes: swimming, boating, fishing. Unsuitable for &.
Location 4 miles S of Clones, on L46 to Ballyhaise. Bus: Clones; then taxi.
Restrictions No smoking: dining room, bedrooms. Children under 7 by arrangement. Dogs on lead only, not in house.
Credit cards Access, Visa.
Terms [1997] B&B IR£49–£67.50 (single supplement £10). Set dinner IR£25. 2-night reductions.

The length of an entry need not reflect the merit of a hotel. The more interesting the report or the more unusual or controversial the hotel, the longer the entry.

CORK   Map 6

Lotamore House BUDGET   *Tel* (021) 822344
Tivoli   *Fax* (021) 822219

This fine Georgian manor, recently refurbished and now a Grade A
guest house, stands on a hill just east of Cork. Rooms are nicely furnished, with some period pieces. Front ones have views of hills and the
river Lee, with some industry in the foreground; rear ones are quietest.
A family with children in 1997 found the welcome poor and the breakfast service very slow, but there is otherwise praise for the comfort, and
the "very good and generous" breakfasts. The "charming" Mr and Mrs
Harty are efficient hosts, and service has been called "friendly and personal". (*Bob Morrissey, Ray and Angela Evans*)

Open All year, except Christmas.
Rooms 20 double. Some on ground floor.
Facilities Lounge, breakfast room. 4-acre garden.
Location 3 miles E of city centre, off N25.
Restriction No smoking in bedrooms.
Credit cards Access, Amex, Visa.
Terms B&B IR£20–£27.50. Winter weekend break. *V*

CROSSMOLINA Co. Mayo   Map 6

Enniscoe House   *Tel* (096) 31112
Castlehill   *Fax* (096) 31773

Set in its own large and pleasant grounds beside Lough Conn, this
graceful Georgian country house has been the home of Susan Kellett's
family for generations, and today she owns and runs it as a private
hotel. Its plain façade belies the 18th-century plasterwork and sweeping
staircase inside, where two big sitting rooms have their original furniture, paintings and bookcases; family memorabilia are everywhere, and
polished wood floors with rugs. A recent report: "We were greeted
warmly by Mrs Kellett and given a *massive* room overlooking the lough.
Plenty of hot water and a most comfortable four-poster bed. Good
dinner and Irish breakfast." Others, too, have thoroughly enjoyed this
experience of country house living. "Mrs Kellett was tireless in her
efforts to keep things running smoothly." "She is neither fussy nor over-
powering, but always there when needed. Bedrooms, some of which
have been renovated this year, are large and comfortable, with modern
bathrooms. Dinner, with limited choice, is Irish country house style
with French touches – "good beef, turbot, salmon; delicious desserts" –
served on a charming eclectic mixture of china. There's a working farm
on the estate. Mrs Kellett also runs a heritage centre, helping returning
emigrants to trace their Irish roots. The hotel makes a good base for
exploring the many attractions of north Mayo. (*R Rennison*)

Open 1 Apr–14 Oct, 31 Dec–1 Feb. Lunch not served.
Rooms 2 suites, 4 double. Self-catering units in yard behind house.
Facilities 2 sitting rooms, dining room. 150-acre estate: garden, farm, heritage
centre, lake frontage, fishing (tuition, ghillie). Golf, riding, cycling, shooting
nearby. Unsuitable for &.
Location 2 miles S of Crossmolina on R315 to Castlebar. Train/bus: Ballina,
10 miles; then taxi.
Restrictions No smoking: restaurant, 2 bedrooms. Dogs by arrangement.

Credit cards Access, Amex, Visa.
Terms B&B: single IR£54–£60, double IR£88–£112; D,B&B IR£66–£82 per person.
Set dinner (book by 4 pm) IR£22 (IR£25 for non-residents). 10% reduction for 3 or
more nights. Children under 2 accommodated free in parents' room. *V*
(except July/Aug).

DINGLE Co. Kerry   Map 6

Doyle's Townhouse and Seafood Bar   *Tel* (066) 51174
John Street   *Fax* (066) 51816

This old fishing port, on the scenic Dingle peninsula, is the most westerly town in Europe. Here the Doyles run the much-admired *Seafood
Bar* restaurant (red "Meals" in *Michelin*) plus a small hotel next door,
the *Townhouse*, the sitting room of which is furnished nostalgically in
the style of a traditional Irish small-town hotel. In the bedrooms are
brass bedsteads, pine furniture and good fabrics, as well as "white
starched sheets and gigantic towels", and some have a marble bathroom. Four suites are in annexes down the street. The operation
remains popular. This year, one visitor praised "the quality of Stella's
cooking, John's cheerful welcome, the reasonable prices, the character
and comfort of the *Townhouse*", while another wrote of "fish and
seafood of excellent quality, beautifully presented, home-made bread
to die for, a spacious bedroom with a view". The local fish on the menu
will include oysters, hot poached lobster, salmon in puff pastry with
sorrel sauce, and grilled mussels with garlic stuffing. The substantial
breakfasts are "the best we have tasted, with scrummy scrambled eggs
and smoked salmon, and a waitress with a lovely smile". Service is
"very fast, because there are lots of American guests". (*John and Helen
Wright, Marc and Margaret Wall, and others*) One complaint about
unhelpful service late in the evening. The Doyles are contemplating
selling, though not in the immediate future. You should check the
status when booking.

Open Mid-Mar–mid-Nov. Restaurant closed Sun.
Rooms 4 suites (in nearby annexe), 4 double. 2 on ground floor.
Facilities Residents' lounge, cocktail bar, 2 dining rooms. Beaches, sea angling,
golf, riding, windsurfing nearby.
Location Central (quietest rooms at rear). Bus from Tralee, 31 miles.
Restrictions No smoking in 1 dining room. Not really suitable for young chil-
dren. No dogs.
Credit cards Access, Diners, Visa.
Terms (*10% service charge added to meals*) B&B: single IR£40–£44, double IR£68.
Set dinner IR£14.75; full alc IR£28.

Milltown House   *Tel* (066) 51372
                                                        Fax (066) 51095

*John and Angela Gill's unpretentious B&B in beautiful situation, 1 mile out-
side Dingle, overlooking bay. Bright, large bedrooms, with pleasant decor,
excellent bathroom fittings. Welcoming owners and staff. Good breakfasts
(emphasis on home-baking). Several restaurants within walking distance. 1-
acre grounds; riding stable on premises (pony-trekking holidays). 10 bedrooms, some with private patio, 1 suitable for &. Open 15 Mar–15 Nov. No
smoking in conservatory lounge. No dogs in public rooms. Access, Visa
accepted. B&B IR£30–£40 [1997].*

DUBLIN   Map 6

Anglesea Town House   NEW   *Tel* (01) 668 3877
63 Anglesea Road   *Fax* (01) 668 3461
Ballsbridge, Dublin 4

Sean and Helen Kirrane's handsome Edwardian house in the select
Ballsbridge area is now a stylish B&B, winner of a National Breakfast
Award in 1989. Its nominators this year were lyrical: "This place is
special, and, boy, are we enjoying it. Why haven't we found this haven
before? A welcoming smile, a soft warm bed, a room like a spring
morning. Dining room with family portraits; oak table set with fine
china, silver; Celtic music gently awakening. Poached salmon, calves'
kidneys, home made breads and chutney. Succeeds in pampering." "A
delightful balance of family home with first-class hotel service. Here
Johnson would eat well on only one breakfast a day: fresh fruit salad,
marinated dried fruits, salmon omelette – and what is the secret recipe
for the baked cereal?" (*AJ Strickland, Robert Matthew*)

Open All year.
Rooms 6 double, 1 single.
Facilities Drawing room, breakfast room (piped music). Small garden.
Unsuitable for &.
Location 2 miles SE of centre (rooms double-glazed). Buses from centre.
Restrictions No smoking: dining room, bedrooms. No dogs.
Credit cards Access, Amex, Visa.
Terms B&B: single IR£40–£45, double IR£67.50–£90.

Ariel House   *Tel* (01) 6685512
52 Lansdowne Road   *Fax* (01) 6685845
Ballsbridge, Dublin 4

*B&B 1850s house in residential Ballsbridge area. 3 mins walk from rapid
transport to centre. Hospitable owner Michael O'Brien. Generous Irish breakfasts in Victorian room with conservatory overlooking garden. Wine bar, but
food not served. Ramps. 2 suites, 26 bedrooms in modern extension; some on
ground floor. Open 12 Jan–24 Dec. No smoking in breakfast room, bedrooms.
No children under 12. No dogs. Access, Visa accepted. Double room
IR£70–£90, suite IR£90–£150. Breakfast IR£7.50. More reports, please.*

Belcamp Hutchinson   *Tel* (01) 8460843
Carrs Lane, Malahide Road   *Fax* (01) 8485703
Balgriffin, Dublin 17

On the north-east fringe of Dublin, off the Malahide road, stands this
handsome creeper-covered Georgian manor, smartly furnished, and
very well run by Doreen Gleeson, who co-owns it with Count
Waldburg. Its name comes from its first owner, Francis Hely-
Hutchinson, third earl of Donoughmore. More plaudits came this year.
"A perfect spot with splendid hostess. Great place for a house party."
"Very peaceful, with a nice garden, large and comfortable bedrooms."
"Wonderful: marvellous welcome, a superb Irish breakfast, and they
kindly drove me to the conference centre when my taxi failed to turn
up." Dinner, taken communally, is by arrangement. It is 15 minutes'
drive to Dublin airport, and ten to bathing beaches; Malahide, one of

Ireland's oldest and prettiest villages, is close by. (*David Taylor, D Kaars Sypesteyn, William Keegan*)

Open All year, except 23 Dec–31 Jan.
Rooms 8 double.
Facilities Drawing room with TV. 4-acre garden.
Location 20 mins' drive NE from Dublin: take Malahide road, turn left at Balgriffin. Buses from Dublin.
Restriction No children under 10.
Credit cards Access, Visa.
Terms B&B IR£38. Set dinner IR£24.

The Grey Door   *Tel* (01) 676 3286
22–23 Upper Pembroke Street   *Fax* (01) 676 3287
Dublin 2

Two-restaurants-with-seven-bedrooms, centrally located near St Stephen's Square. Food found "wonderful" again this year, alike in modern Grey Door *(contemporary Irish cooking) and traditional* Pier 32 *(Irish seafood dishes; Irish folk music most nights). Antiques in public areas; friendly, humorous, if sometimes casual, staff. 9 pretty bedrooms with "excellent" bathroom (but front ones get traffic noise, 4 are up many steps); some criticisms of house-keeping this year. Closed 24–30 Dec.* Grey Door *closed bank holidays. Guide dogs only. All major credit cards accepted. Rooms: single IR£75, double IR£95. Breakfast IR£5–£6.95. Set meals IR£10–£14.50. More reports, please.*

The Hibernian   *Tel* (01) 668 7666
Eastmoreland Place   *Fax* (01) 660 2655
Ballsbridge, Dublin 4   *E-mail* info@hibernianhotel.ie

Twenty minutes' walk from central Dublin, down a quiet street in select residential Ballsbridge, this stylish and luxurious hotel occupies a sturdy red brick late-Victorian building that was once a nurses' home. It is furnished with rich fabrics, deep upholstery and bright colours; public rooms are designed in country house style. Bedrooms are small-ish but comfortable, with pocket-sprung mattresses and superior toiletries; some in the new wing are said to be poorly insulated. "Under the supervision of manager David Butt," wrote one visitor, "the young staff give the impression that they genuinely want you to enjoy your stay." But another thought them disorganised at times. The sophisticated cooking of chef David Foley, "modern Irish with French influences", is generally admired. More reports, please.

Open All year, except 24–28 Dec.
Rooms 10 suites, 30 double. 2 adapted for &.
Facilities Drawing room, library, restaurant (classical guitarist Fri/Sat evening), sun-lounge (piped classical/Irish music 24 hrs throughout). Garden.
Location Off Baggot St Upper, ⅔ mile SE of St Stephen's Green. Private parking. Buses from centre.
Restrictions No smoking in drawing room, 13 bedrooms. No dogs.
Credit cards All major cards accepted.
Terms [1997] (*Excluding 12½% service charge on meals*) B&B: single IR£110–£180, double IR£145–£180. Set lunch IR£13.95, dinner IR£24.50. 50% discount for child in parents' room.

We need detailed fresh reports to keep our entries up to date.

Kingswood Country House   *Tel/Fax* (01) 459 2428
Naas Road
Clondalkin, Dublin 22

Once the home of the Irish tenor Joseph Locke (whose story is told in the film *Hear My Song*), this handsome Georgian country house lies seven miles west of central Dublin, within a walled garden. It is now an elegant restaurant with seven bedrooms, well run by a young couple, Tom and Sheila O'Byrne. Recent accolades: "My room was charming and cleverly decorated to suit the mood of the building – lace curtains and shutters, bare polished boards in the bathroom (but all washing facilities new). Home-made marmalade for breakfast." "We arrived late. Mrs O'Byrne produced an excellent light meal which we ate in the pleasant conservatory. Friendly and helpful staff." "Breakfast at 6 am was 'no trouble at all'." Dinner has been warmly praised, also breakfast, with "stupendous" porridge and a fire blazing in winter. The setting is no longer rural; there is some industry near by, and a motorway, but out of earshot. (*Mrs J Gilbert, and others*)

Open All year, except 3 days Christmas, Good Friday.
Rooms 7 double.
Facilities Lounge/bar, restaurant (piped music); function facilities. 1-acre garden. Riding, shooting, golf nearby. Only restaurant suitable for &.
Location 7 miles W of Dublin centre, on left side of N7 towards Naas, 1½ miles after Newlands Cross.
Restriction Guide dogs only.
Credit cards All major cards accepted.
Terms [1997] (*Excluding 12.5% service charge*) B&B: single IR£55, double IR£80. Set lunch IR£13.95, dinner IR£22.95. Weekend breaks.

Number 31   NEW   *Tel* (01) 6765011
31 Leeson Close   *Fax* (01) 6762929
Dublin 2   *E-Mail*: number31@iol.ie

In the heart of Georgian Dublin, Brian and Mary Bennett have this year expanded their B&B hotel from five to 18 bedrooms, by acquiring a new building. First they had just a converted coach-house, formerly the home of the controversial architect Sam Stephenson, an unabashed modernist, who gutted its centre to create a huge drawing room in a sunken area beside a bar. Now they have taken over the fine Georgian mansion across the garden, which it once served. The teething troubles of the transition led to criticisms last year, and *Number 31* fell from the 1997 *Guide*. But this year three reports (one from a *Guide* hotelier) recommend its return: "The owners were charming. We had a huge room, warm, comfortable and well lit, with a good bathroom. Excellent breakfast." "We enjoyed our stay in the new house, in a large, well-decorated room facing the garden. Breakfast, served in a rooftop conservatory round one long table, is an informal affair with the Bennetts officiating. I found myself chatting to people from all over the globe." The menu includes smoked salmon, kippers, eggs and home-made jams, etc. The informal style (first names tend to be used) won't suit everyone. There is no lift in the new building, and some rooms are up several flights of stairs. Rooms on the street are sound-proofed. (*Carol Heaton, Bridget Kindred; also Katharine Lounsbery*)

Open All year, except Christmas week.
Rooms 4 suites, 14 double. Some on ground floor.
Facilities Lounge, bar, rooftop conservatory/breakfast room; patio garden.
Location Central (all rooms sound-proofed), off St Stephen's Green. Garage.
Restrictions No smoking in breakfast room. No children under 10. No dogs.
Credit cards Access, Amex, Visa.
Terms B&B: single IR£35–£50, double IR£58–£84, suite IR£68–£90. *V*

See also SHORTLIST

DUNLAVIN Co. Wicklow   **Map 6**

Grangebeg House   *Tel/Fax* (045) 401367

West of the Wicklow mountains, a beautiful Georgian house set in
huge grounds, amid lush farmland. "Mrs Aine McGrane is a warm,
loquacious and kindly host, and serves an excellent breakfast," says
one visitor this year. "A haven of peace with a lovely atmosphere,"
adds another. All agree about the "delicious" breakfasts, served round
an antique table, with no time limit. The drawing room is spacious,
heated by a big open fire on chilly days. Bedrooms, too, are large, furnished in a mixture of antique and traditional, but with also "a touch of
schmaltz". Dinners are available on request, with huge helpings but
uncertain quality, says a 1997 report. Decent house wines. This part of
Ireland is famous for its racehorses, and Mrs McGrane's daughter runs
a stables behind the house; there is a cross-country course for enthusiasts. The lake in the grounds has just been cleaned out. (*Esler Crawford,
Michael O'Flaherty, J Maxwell-Brown, and others*)

Open All year, except 20–28 Dec.
Rooms 5 double, 1 single. 2 with TV, no telephone.
Facilities Drawing room (piped classical music), TV room, dining room. 86-acre
grounds: parkland, gardens, tennis, lake, stables. Walking, shooting, fishing,
water sports, golf, racing nearby. Unsuitable for &.
Location 1¼ miles N of Dunlavin, off R412.
Restriction No dogs in house.
Credit cards Access, Visa.
Terms B&B: single IR£30–£54, double IR£64–£84. Set dinner (by arrangement)
IR£19.95.

ENNISCORTHY Co. Wexford   **Map 6**

Salville House   **NEW/BUDGET**   *Tel* (054) 35252

*Two miles S of town, off N11 to Wexford, a mid-19th-century hilltop house,
light and bright, in 5-acre grounds with tennis. Now a trim guest house with
friendly owners, Gordon and Jane Parker. His cooking, on no-choice set menu,
is admired, as are breakfasts. Closed Christmas, New Year except for group
bookings. Bird sanctuaries, golf, nearby. No smoking in bedrooms. No dogs in
house. Credit cards not accepted. B&B IR£20–£22.50. Dinner IR£17.50. No
wine licence, no corkage charge. More reports, please.*

At the time of going to press, the Irish punt is worth 97p in
pounds sterling.

GALWAY   Map 6

Norman Villa   BUDGET   *Tel/Fax* (091) 521131
86 Lower Salthill

Galway City is today the boom town of the West. A Mecca for youth and a hub of artistic exuberance, it is full of fringe theatres, musical pubs and folksy bistros, and is home to Ireland's biggest summer arts festival. Less trendy in style is this restored Victorian coach house on the edge of town, now a B&B well run by Mark and Dee Keogh. A comment this year: "Excellent: comfortable, efficient and friendly – tea and cake offered on arrival." It has a pretty decor, with old pine furniture, plenty of paintings and sculpture, and good linen on antique brass beds. "Best breakfast ever." (*June Hexton, JF*)

Open All year.
Rooms 5 double. No telephone/TV.
Facilities Drawing room, breakfast room (piped classical music/jazz). Sandy beach, river, fishing nearby.
Location 1 mile W of centre, at Salthill. Courtyard parking.
Restrictions No smoking: breakfast room, bedrooms. Unsuitable for children under 3. No dogs.
Credit cards Access, Visa.
Terms B&B IR£26–£34. 25% reduction for children under 12. Christmas breaks.

GLASLOUGH Co. Monaghan   Map 6

 Castle Leslie   NEW   *Tel* (047) 88109
                                                      Fax (047) 88256
                                    E-Mail: ultan@castle-leslie.ie

César award: for utterly enjoyable mild eccentricity

"Outrageous, but fun, and charmingly eccentric," write inspectors of this hefty Victorian castle in a 1,000-acre estate near the Border. "The titled Leslie family, migrants from Scotland, have lived on this site since 1661; they built this castle in 1878. Crammed to the rafters with Victoriana, it has changed little, save for the addition of modern comforts. It is run in high Victorian style, partly tongue-in-cheek. The urbane Sir John, fourth bart, aged 80, presides. But the driving spirit is his ebullient young niece Samantha (Sammy), owner and co-manager, who also does much of the cooking – very well, in dinner party style. In the imposing candlelit banqueting hall, the waitresses wear Victorian dress. Our bedroom (big four-poster, red velvet drapes, antique silver hair-brushes) was authentically Victorian, and its bathroom even more so – a Victorian wooden 'thunder box' loo, a vast bath (with faulty plug), and basin-taps marked *froid* for hot and *chaud* for cold. Other bedrooms are in wacky Victorian style, some intentionally comic (odd-shaped bath-tubs), some truly beautiful. In the family nursery, now a bedroom, a vast dolls' house façade conceals the bathroom. The huge public rooms have fine old tapestries, family portraits, suits of armour, and other heirlooms of this much-travelled family – a lovely painted Della Robbia fireplace from a chapel in Florence, a harp given by Wordsworth, an emerald bracelet from the empress of China. The Leslies host many business seminars and tourist banquets, at the end of which Sammy, in hooded Victorian cloak, regales diners with ghost stories of this haunted house (a child was murdered in one bed). The Leslies have long been thought a curious lot. Winston Churchill, a cousin, when asked in 1940 why he had not put Sir Shane Leslie into his cabinet, replied: 'I am running a government, not a comedy show.' This hotel may be a comedy show, but it's worth a visit for its sense of fun, as the Leslies cheerfully send themselves up."

Open All year, except 2 weeks Jan.
Rooms 1 suite, 13 double. No telephone/TV.
Facilities Drawing room, dining room, gallery. 1,000-acre grounds: tennis, wildlife, lake, boating, fishing. Unsuitable for &.
Location 5 miles NE of Monaghan. N2 towards Armagh/Derry; right after *Four Seasons* hotel. After 3 km, 1st left to Glaslough village. Go through village to castle gates at end of drive. Bus: Monaghan; then taxi.
Restrictions No smoking in bedrooms. No children. No dogs in house (kennels available).
Credit cards Access, Visa.
Terms [1997] B&B IR£48–£86. Full alc £ IR£23–£28. Weekend, midweek rates. 1-night bookings refused weekends in high season.

GOREY Co. Wexford   Map 6

Marlfield House   *Tel* (055) 21124
Courtown Road   *Fax* (055) 21572
                                                  E-mail: marlf@iol.ie

&) *César award in 1996*

"A wonderful place to stay" – more tributes came in 1996–97 for Mary and Ray Bowe's sophisticated country house hotel (Relais et Châteaux), once the dower house of the Courtown estate. Three miles from the coast, it is a Regency building set in award winning grounds with a lake and wildlife reserve. It was completely redecorated in 1997, and the entrance hall is now "dazzling", with smart antique furniture, spectacular flower displays, and goldfish ponds by the front door. The large domed conservatory, refurnished at the same time, "makes a glorious place to eat", and the cooking of the new chef, Jason Matthia, has been found "excellent" this year: he has worked at *Le Gavroche* in London, and his food is called "modern classical with Mediterranean influence", eg, lasagne of shellfish, roast quail in crepinette. "Mary Bowe, who circulates at dinner, is closely involved", and her daughter is the efficient general manager. Staff are friendly and the atmosphere is "totally unstuffy", though one couple thought the place "over-the-top", and service can be slow. Others wrote earlier: "The lounges and bedrooms are a joy. It is a real talent that can present luxury without a hint of vulgarity. The gardens, from bird sanctuary, through 'rain forest' to manicured lawns and burgeoning herb garden are pleasant and interesting. Mrs Bowe, entertaining and welcoming to the manner born, clearly enjoys meeting her guests in the dining room." Bedrooms have dramatic wallpapers and curtains, hand-embroidered sheets, real lace pillows, and "a splendid bathroom". They vary in size, and not all have a good view. (*Mrs M Lancaster, Sir Timothy Harford, and others*)

Open All year, except mid-Dec–late Jan.
Rooms 6 suites, 11 double, 2 single. Some on ground floor.
Facilities Reception hall, drawing room, library/bar, conservatory/restaurant. 36-acre grounds: tennis, croquet, wildfowl reserve, lake. Sea 1 mile: sandy beaches, safe bathing.

Location 1 mile from Gorey on Courtown road. Train: Gorey, from Dublin/Waterford.
Restrictions No smoking: dining room, bedrooms. Dogs by arrangement, not in public rooms.
Credit cards All major cards accepted.
Terms B&B: single IR£77–£99, double IR£155–£165, suite IR£250. Set dinner IR£34–£37. Off-season reductions. *V*

INISTIOGE Co. Kilkenny   Map 6

Cullintra House   NEW/BUDGET   *Tel/Fax* (051) 423614
                                                   E-mail Cullhse@indigo.ie

This 18th-century farmhouse lies down a long drive in a lovely peaceful setting at the foot of Mount Brandon, amid 230 acres of farmland. It has been the home of the Cantlon family for 100 years. Breakfasts till midday, and leisurely late candlelit dinners, are specialities. "It's for those who enjoy the idiosyncratic," says our beguiled nominator. "All hangs on the personality of Patricia Cantlon, the hostess, whose paintings fill the house. Dinner (good French-influenced home cooking), is scheduled for 9 pm, but we didn't eat till 10. All the guests sat round one table, and had a good time. At the end, Patricia said she would not think about serving breakfast till 9.30 am; we should tap on her door. We did, and got breakfast at 10." Children are fed early "and then to bed". Inspectors enjoyed the "delightfully pretty and individual bedrooms, in plush-rustic style, with period furnishings, but the *en suite* showers are simple and the only bathroom is communal. There is a conservatory studio with a piano, where guests can have fun. The ambience is unaffectedly bohemian, and many regulars are from the Dublin intellectual/artistic world. The hostess has been known to treat some guests more warmly than others. She has six adored cats, omnipresent, and will accept guests' dogs only if she is certain that they will behave." Bring your own wine. Nearby Kilkenny is a picturesque old town, with a splendid historic castle, one of Ireland's finest. (*Josie Mayers, and others*)

Open All year.
Rooms 1 suite, 5 double. 4 with shower.
Facilities Drawing room, dining room, studio conservatory. 230-acre grounds: 1-acre garden, woodland, private path to Brandon Hill with 4,000-year-old cairn. River bathing 4 miles; fishing nearby.
Location 6 miles NW of New Ross, off New Ross–Kilkenny road. Take turning E (signposted): hotel 1 mile. Bus to main road once a day.
Restrictions No smoking: dining room, 1 bedroom. Unsuitable for &. Dogs in car/on leash at all times.
Credit cards None accepted.
Terms [1997] B&B IR£20–£23. Set dinner IR£16.

KANTURK Co. Cork   Map 6

Assolas Country House   *Tel* (029) 50015
                                                   Fax (029) 50795

💫 *César award in 1995*

Always one of our most admired Irish hotels, this elegant 17th-century manor stands in beautiful grounds: in its little river are swans, a weir and a mini-island. It has been the Bourke family's home for over

70 years, and for the past 25 they have run it as a hotel with warmth and efficiency. This year, praise flowed again. "Our clear favourite. Joe Bourke has a quite unfair amount of the nicest Irish charm, plus engaging enthusiasm. We had a large bedroom slightly erratically furnished, with a tiny but well-equipped bathroom." "Our room was comfortable in an old-fashioned rather than antique-y way. Dishes at dinner were imaginative, and breakfasts were possibly the best I have enjoyed in Europe." "Splendid bathroom with jacuzzi. Friendly atmosphere among guests, though perhaps a touch formal." Earlier views: "As near to perfection as possible. Great personal attention." "As soon as you enter, a log fire is lit for you. You are offered umbrellas and wellingtons as well as recipes." Afternoon tea, with lemon or chocolate cake, is served in the garden or by the fire. There is sparkling glass in the dining room, and damask napkins. Mrs Bourke's Irish country house cooking puts its accent on fish and shellfish; many of the herbs and vegetables come from the hotel's walled kitchen garden; the soups, sauces and pastry are much admired, as are the brown scones and soda bread at breakfast;
and the wine list is well chosen. There is good hill and forest walking nearby. Also nearby are Millstreet country park and Annesgrove garden at Castletownroche; and Cork and Killarney are not far away. (*Sir Timothy Harford, Mike Hutton, RMJ Kenber, and others*)

Open 1 Apr–1 Nov.
Rooms 9 double. 3 in courtyard annexe.
Facilities Hall, drawing room, dining room; private dining room. 15-acre grounds: gardens, tennis, croquet, river, boating, trout-fishing. Salmon-fishing, golf nearby. Unsuitable for &.
Location 3½ miles NE of Kanturk; turn off N72 Mallow–Killarney towards Buttevant.
Restriction No dogs in house (accommodation in stables).
Credit cards All major cards accepted.
Terms B&B: single IR£53.50–£77, double IR£88–£164. Set dinner IR£30. 1-night bookings sometimes refused. *V* (in low season)

KENMARE Co. Kerry   Map 6

Hawthorne House   NEW/BUDGET   *Tel* (064) 41035
Shelbourne Street   *Fax* (064) 41932

Kenmare is a popular little resort by the lovely Ring of Kerry. Alongside its two very grand hotels, the *Park Hotel Kenmare* and *Sheen Falls Lodge* (*qqv*), the village has others more modest. One such is this pleasant B&B on its edge, which now returns to the *Guide* under new owners, Stephen and Mary O'Brien. "Mrs O'Brien, an infectiously bubbly lady, served us tea and cake in the drawing room, and escorted us to a pretty and comfortable room, tastefully furnished in pine. Rooms are of different shapes and sizes but all welcoming. Most have a shower rather than a bath. Breakfast is pleasant, with fresh porridge and Irish fries (but synthetic orange juice). All good value. There's a plethora of good restaurants close by." A convenient base for exploring the Ring of Kerry. (*Esler Crawford*)

Open All year, except Christmas.
Rooms 7 double, 1 single.
Facilities TV lounge, breakfast room. Sea ¼ mile; cycling, golf, water sports, fishing nearby.
Location On S edge of village, close to centre. Private parking.
Restrictions No smoking: restaurant, bedrooms. No dogs.
Credit cards Access, Visa.
Terms [1997] B&B IR£17–£23.

Park Hotel Kenmare *Tel* (064) 41200
Fax (064) 41402
E-mail phkenmare@iol.ie

Country house grandeur (five red *Michelin* gables) combines with sybaritic comfort and high gastronomy (*Michelin* star) in this superior Relais & Châteaux hotel. With one exception it has pleased our readers again this year. It has plenty going for it: an idyllic parkland setting, with beautiful views of the Kenmare estuary and the west Cork mountains; elegant public rooms with open fires, sculptures and flowers; "gorgeous" bedrooms with smart antiques, fine china and large modern bathroom; friendly and very helpful staff; excellent "progressive Irish" cooking by Bruno Schmidt. Outwardly, the hotel's long grey hulk is no beauty, but, as a devotee wrote this year: "Don't be put off by its rather dour looks. The rooms are superb, accompanied by dazzling paintings. Smashing place, terrific staff, marvellous food, superb breakfasts. Our first night, we were kept waiting forty minutes for dinner, but our polite complaint led to our getting a bottle of wine on the house. On our last night, we scored a major triumph in getting the rich international guests to join in an Irish sing-song, accompanied by the charming in-house pianist." Local attractions include the Ring of Kerry and Garinish Island. (*Mike Hutton; also Esler Crawford, HCM*)

Open 9 Apr–1 Nov; 23 Dec–2 Jan. Restaurant closed midday.
Rooms 9 suites, 36 double, 4 single. 1 equipped for &.
Facilities Lift, ramps. Lounge, TV room, bar lounge (live piano at night), restaurant; games room. 11-acre grounds: tennis, golf, croquet. Rock beach, safe bathing, fishing 5 mins' walk.
Location 60 miles W of Cork, adjacent to village. Signposted.
Restriction No dogs.
Credit cards All major cards accepted.
Terms [1997] B&B: single IR£118–£142, double IR£210–£302, suite IR£356–£420. Set dinner IR£40; full alc IR£75. Christmas, New Year programmes.

Sheen Falls Lodge *Tel* (064) 41600
Fax (064) 41386
E-mail sheenfalls@iol.ie

This Cromwellian manor house, much extended, is now a luxurious resort hotel (Relais & Châteaux), set in huge wooded grounds, beside the Sheen Falls. It has a stunning location amid green hills, woods and moors, with lovely views of Kenmare Bay. The ambience is cosmopolitan as well as Irish. A visitor this year commends "the wonderful library, with up-to-date magazines such as the *New Yorker*, and books in many languages". Others have written: "The warmth and friendliness of the staff is high even by Irish standards, the food and service are superb, and the bedrooms are huge, with crisp linen sheets and duvets, and large marble bathroom." "Kindness and food outstanding," adds another admirer. The *Michelin*-starred *La Cascade* restaurant serves stylish modern Irish cooking by chef Fergus Moore. All kinds of leisure activity are available, including falconry and water-skiing (see below). There is a discreet conference centre. Guests may be taken sightseeing in the hotel's 1936 Buick convertible. Twenty-one bedrooms and a swimming pool have been added this year. More reports, please. (*Catherine Fraher, and others*)

Open All year, except 3 Jan–6 Feb, 30 Nov–22 Dec.
Rooms 9 suites, 52 double. Self-catering cottage in grounds.
Facilities Lift, ramps. 2 lounges, bar, restaurant (pianist nightly); health and fitness centre: swimming pool, jacuzzi, sauna, gym, beauty treatments. 360-acre grounds: fishing, riding, croquet, tennis, clay pigeon-shooting. Falconry, golf, lake fishing, windsurfing, boating nearby. Sea 6 miles.
Location 1½ miles SE of Kenmare, just off N71 to Glengariff. Bus from Kenmare.
Restrictions No smoking in some bedrooms. Dogs in grounds only.
Credit cards All major cards accepted.
Terms Rooms: single IR£135–£185, double IR£160–£240, suite IR£255–£360. Breakfast IR£13. Set dinner IR£37.50–£40. Half board rates in low season.

KILLARNEY Co. Kerry   **Map 6**

Aghadoe Heights Hotel   NEW   *Tel* (064) 31766
Aghadoe   *Fax* (064) 31345

"A magnificent view of lakes and mountains – probably the best from any hotel in the area." So writes a recent visitor to this fairly luxurious and ambitious hotel, just outside Ireland's leading inland resort. "The long low building's rather plain exterior leaves one unprepared for the dramatic interior, where a designer has run riot with marble, glass and chromium, but which is saved from vulgarity by the excellence of the workmanship. These spectacular renovations are the work of the German owner, Frederick Lösel, who bought the hotel five years ago. His daughter, Patricia, is the manager, and they run it with brisk efficiency. Our bedroom, comfortably sized and very well equipped, had a magnificent view, but not all rooms share this. There are wonderful views from window seats in the top-floor restaurant, *Frederick's*, where we found the food excellent and lavish, and the wine list comprehensive but with high mark-ups. At breakfast, the 'fresh orange juice' was from a carton, I suspect. Staff are friendly and well informed." "A lovely breakfast buffet, and super view from the superbly designed swimming pool, overlooked by the dramatic bar." The hotel has an English sister, *Frederick's* at Maidenhead. (*Esler Crawford, Mrs C Wright*)

Open All year.
Rooms 3 suites, 56 double, 1 single. Some on ground floor.
Facilities Lounge, 2 bars, restaurant (pianist daily; jazz at Sunday brunch); function facilities; leisure centre: swimming pool, fitness room, sauna. 8½-acre grounds: river, fishing. Golf, sea/lake fishing, riding nearby. Unsuitable for &.
Location Off N22, 3 miles NW of Killarney.
Restriction No dogs.
Credit cards All major cards accepted.

Terms [1997] B&B: single IR£85–£125, double IR£120–£175, suite IR£175–£225. Set lunch IR£23.50, dinner IR£33.50; full alc IR£55. Christmas/New Year packages.

KILLEAGH Co. Cork   Map 6

Ballymakeigh House   BUDGET   *Tel* (024) 95184
Killeagh, nr Youghal   *Fax* (024) 95370

"A wonderfully relaxing place to stay, with outstanding food" – more enthusiasm this year for this modernised old farmhouse, now a well-decorated guest house, in a "beautiful, peaceful setting" amid the green countryside of prosperous east Cork. "Margaret Browne has a gift for making her guests feel at home." "Excellent value." Rooms are "attractive and spotless" and most are large, though some are a little cramped. The hot cheese and walnut soufflés, the turbot in wine-and-cream sauce and the elderberry fritters are all admired, though one guest did not care for the food's being "decorated with flower petals". The spacious flowery conservatory on the south side is a delightful place to sit and survey the Brownes' large dairy herd: "It was great to feel part of a working farm." Guests can watch the milking and other routines, or ride or play tennis. The breakfast has won a national award. Nearby are sandy beaches and the attractive old port of Youghal. (*Niki Gorick and Peter Hardy, and others*)

Open 1 Feb–1 Nov. Dining room open to non-residents by arrangement only.
Rooms 6 double.
Facilities Lounge, TV room, conservatory, dining room (piped classical music). 200-acre farm: 1-acre garden, tennis, children's play area. Unsuitable for &.
Location 6 miles W of Youghal, just NE of Killeagh. Buses from Youghal.
Restrictions No smoking in dining room. No dogs in house.
Credit cards Access, Visa.
Terms [1997] B&B IR£25–£38. Set dinner IR£22.50; full alc IR£28. 50% reduction for children.

KILMALLOCK Co. Limerick   Map 6

Flemingstown House   BUDGET   *Tel* (063) 98093
                                                       Fax (063) 98546

The interesting medieval town of Kilmallock, south of Limerick, has a fine Dominican friary. Nearby, set amid open country, is this large 18th-century farmhouse, now a guest house run with warmth and informality by a local farmer, Imelda Sheedy-King, whose cooking has quality. Praise came again this year: "A delight. Imelda couldn't have been more helpful, even writing out recipes for some of her delicious dishes. Especially good were the creamy soups, and the tiramisù with whipped cream fresh from her dairy herd. All bedrooms have been newly decorated, have *en suite* showers and are clean and bright. Our small daughter was made very welcome." Others too have enjoyed the rooms and the food, notably the salmon, the fresh vegetables and the luscious desserts, "unusual in rural Ireland". "A comfortable and friendly place to stay in away-from-tourists countryside." Visitors can be shown round the working dairy farm. (*Niki Gorick and Peter Hardy, and others*)

Open 1 Mar–1 Nov.
Rooms 5 double.
Facilities Lounge, dining room (with TV, piped music). 2-acre garden. Golf, rid-
ing, fishing, cycling nearby. Unsuitable for &.
Location 2 miles SE of Kilmallock on R512 to Fermoy. Bus from Kilmallock.
Restrictions No smoking. Dogs by arrangement.
Credit card Visa.
Terms B&B IR£20–£22.50 (single supplement IR£5–£8). Set dinner IR£17.

KINSALE Co. Cork   **Map 6**

The Old Presbytery   BUDGET   *Tel/Fax* (021) 772027
Cork Street

This old fishing-port is today rather fashionable, with an annual
gourmet festival: in 1996 it even won the European Union's top Prize
for Tourism and the Environment. Philip and Noreen McEvoy, the
owners of this tall, narrow house, are "a chatty and friendly couple,"
writes an admirer. "Our bedroom had a magnificent brass bed and pine
furniture. The march of time has definitely stopped in the sitting room
which is Victorian in every detail, right down to the music on the
upright piano." Breakfast is served in the old kitchen; dishes on offer
include fruit-filled crêpes, chicken livers, bacon and sausages, and "full
Irish breakfast with black and white pudding"; orange juice is freshly
squeezed. Dinner is not served, but there are plenty of good restaurants
nearby – *Man Friday*, overlooking the harbour, is recommended. (*EC,
Cilla Langdon-Down*)

Open All year, except Christmas.
Rooms 6 double.
Facilities Lounge with TV, conservatory, breakfast room. Sea, river, fishing close
by. Unsuitable for &.
Location 2 mins' walk from centre, near parish church. Private carpark. Buses
from Cork.
Restrictions Unsuitable for children. No dogs.
Credit cards None accepted.
Terms B&B IR£20–£40.

LEENANE Co. Galway   **Map 6**

Delphi Lodge   *Tel* (095) 42211
Leenane, Connemara   *Fax* (095) 42296
                                              E-mail delfish@iol.ie

Set alone by a lake amid unspoilt mountain country, in a large estate on
the northern edge of Connemara, is this former sporting lodge of the
Marquis of Sligo. It is now owned and run as a private hotel by Peter
and Jane Mantle; he is a keen fly-fisherman and golfer, "and very good
company". The Delphi fishery is famous for its salmon- and sea trout-
fishing on three lakes and the pretty Delphi river; fishing courses are
held, and a team of ghillies is available. Non-fishing enthusiasts enjoy
the peaceful atmosphere and walks amid wild scenery. "In a class of its
own," wrote a 1997 visitor. "It is just as hospitable to those who wish to
relax. The quality that pervades the place is demonstrated in food, service and accommodation. Peter Mantle has the knack of getting on with
most people and the evenings are always enjoyable." Other praise: "A

delightful setting." "It manages that tricky blend of friendliness and professionalism. Afternoon tea and chocolate cake served on arrival. Big well-furnished bedroom; huge fluffy towels and piping hot water. Excellent home-cooked dinner, taken at a huge oak table." Some rooms have a four-poster. There is a large but cosy library, and a billiard room. Several empty sandy beaches lie within easy reach, and the wildlife is exceptional: otters, badgers, peregrines, etc. (*R Rennison*)

Open All year, except Christmas, New Year.
Rooms 12 double. 2 on ground floor. 4 self-catering cottages.
Facilities Drawing room, library, billiard room, dining room; function facilities. 600-acre estate: 15-acre gardens, lake, fishing, bathing. Golf, riding, beaches nearby.
Location 9 miles N of Leenane on Louisburgh road. 20 miles SW of Westport.
Restrictions No children under 12. No dogs.
Credit cards Access, Visa.
Terms [1997] B&B: single IR£50–£70, double IR£90–£110. Set lunch IR£3–£7, dinner IR£28. Fly-fishing courses Thurs–Sun 2-3 times a year IR£350.

LETTERKENNY Co. Donegal   Map 6

Castle Grove   BUDGET   *Tel* (074) 51118
Ballymaleel   *Fax* (074) 51384

This handsome late-17th-century manor stands alone in broad gardens that slope down to Lough Swilly, a long sea inlet. Not far away is the glorious rugged Donegal coast, and Glenveagh National Park. Inspectors in 1997 enjoyed the peaceful setting, and the hotel itself: "The house belonged to the Duke of Abercorn, but the hotel today is not grand at all, nor very smart. Cosy and comfortable, with an easygoing family feel, it is owned and run by Raymond and Mary Sweeney, a local farmer and his wife. Their front-of-house, Eileen from Limerick, was an exuberant charmer, warm and witty, and all staff were friendly. The hotel is popular locally, and wedding parties were going on in the three lounges; but service remained attentive, and we liked dining with views of the lake. The young chef, Jason Byrne, has an inventive talent (eg, poached chicken roulade on couscous, panfried lamb with black pudding), though quality varied a little. A large wine list, and excellent breakfasts. Our decent-sized bedroom had some antiques, a view of the lake, an adequate if not very modern bathroom. Not all rooms have good views." Seven more bedrooms were added this year. Much produce comes from the huge home farm.

Open All year, except 22–27 Dec. Restaurant closed Sun/Mon Jan–Apr.
Rooms 2 suites, 13 double. 1 on ground floor.
Facilities 2 drawing rooms, library with TV, dining room (piped classical music throughout). 2-acre grounds in 350-acre estate. Beaches, fishing, golfing, riding nearby.
Location Off Ramelton road, 3 miles NE of Letterkenny by N13, R245.
Restrictions No smoking: restaurant, library, bedrooms. No children under 10. No dogs.
Credit cards All major cards accepted.
Terms B&B IR£35–£80. Set lunch IR£18, dinner IR£25. Weekend, midweek breaks. *V*

For details of the Voucher scheme see page xxviii.

LISMORE Co. Waterford   Map 6

Ballyrafter House   ▌NEW/BUDGET▐   *Tel* (058) 54002
                                                Fax (058) 53050

One mile W of attractive little town off N72 on river Blackwater, small, unpre-
tentious hotel in 19th-century building. Opposite impressive castle owned by
Duke of Devonshire. Well run by friendly owners, Joe and Noreen
Willoughby. "Nothing flash or fancy; what they do, they do well," writes nom-
inator. Good, simple cooking, using local produce, eg, fresh salmon. Pretty 4-
acre garden. Open Feb–end Oct. Unsuitable for &. No children under 10.
10 rooms. All major credit cards accepted. B&B IR£30–£45; D,B&B
IR£48–£64. Set lunch IR£12, dinner IR£22.

LOUGH ESKE Co. Donegal   Map 6

Ardnamona House   *Tel* (073) 22650
                                                 Fax (073) 22819
                              E-mail hiddenireland@indigo.ie

This early-Victorian shooting lodge has a splendid position beside
Lough Eske, amid wild Donegal scenery, off the road from Derry to
Donegal town. It is set in huge grounds with an ancient oak forest, and
a National Heritage garden with a famous array of rhododendrons.
Run with enthusiasm and charm by Kieran and Amabel Clarke, it has
a house party atmosphere, and was liked again this year: "Very comfortable and welcoming, the house rambles round a courtyard, with a
sun room and sitting room. It has lots of books, especially on music. Mr
Clarke is a musician and restores pianos – there were two or three
about, in various stages. We had a lovely bedroom with good bathroom. The dining room is elegant, with one large table for everyone.
There were fires here and in the lounge. The food was as good as one
could hope for. In May, the rhododendron forest was very beautiful,
with many varieties in flower." "A romantic setting, and vases of
heavenly scented lilies in public rooms." Bedrooms, south-facing, are
brightly decorated. Dinners are not always available (best enquire in
advance), but two miles away is *Harvey's Point*, "a rather expensive but
good Swiss-run restaurant". (*Donald H Brown, and others*)

Open All year, except Christmas/New Year.
Rooms 5 double. No telephone/TV.
Facilities Sitting room, sun room, dining room. 95-acre grounds: garden, lake:
fishing, swimming, boating. Unsuitable for &.
Location 8 miles NE of Donegal town. Turn left off N15 3 miles N of Donegal,
towards Harvey's Point.
Restrictions No smoking in bedrooms. No dogs in house.
Credit cards Access, Diners, Visa.
Terms B&B IR£35–£55. Set dinner IR£18. ▌*V*▐

MALLOW Co. Cork   Map 6

Longueville House   *Tel* (022) 47156
                                                          Fax (022) 47459

A splendid Georgian mansion (Relais & Châteaux) owned by the
O'Callaghan family; Aisling O'Callaghan is the manager, and her husband, William, is the chef. It stands in a large estate, with the river
Blackwater running through, and overlooks the ruins of Dromineen
Castle, owned by O'Callaghan ancestors and destroyed by Cromwell.
Recently much renovated, it has won warm praise: "It is tastefully furnished without being ornate, and a sense of history pervades. There are
portraits of all the Irish presidents in the dining room. Our room, more
like a suite, was immense, with a large well-equipped bathroom. The
hostess was charming, the waiting staff were cheerful and humorous,
and the dinners were memorable. The parkland setting offers gentle,
pleasant walks, but the garden is in need of attention. Not cheap, but
good value; nice atmosphere." The cooking is French-style, "with the

best of Irish ingredients". In
warm weather, guests may
dine in the Victorian conservatory. "An excellent base for
visiting the south-west corner
of Ireland, as a day out could
cover most places of interest
without a long drive over the
somewhat indifferent roads."
Blarney is not far away. (*PJ
and BA D'Arcy*)

Open Mid-Feb–22 Dec.
Rooms 7 suites, 11 double, 2 single.
Facilities Drawing room, bar, library, games room, restaurant, conservatory; pri-
vate dining room, function facilities. 500-acre estate: gardens, vineyard, walks,
river, salmon/trout-fishing, walking. Riding, golf nearby.
Location 3 miles W of Mallow on N72 to Killarney.
Restrictions No smoking: restaurant, 5 bedrooms. No dogs.
Credit cards All major cards accepted.
Terms [1997] B&B IR£55–£82. Set lunch IR£18–£20, dinner IR£30. Special breaks
by arrangement.

MIDLETON Co. Cork   Map 6

Glenview House   NEW/BUDGET   *Tel/Fax* (021) 631680
Ballinaclasha

"In most respects, the very model of a quality rural guest house," write
inspectors this year. "This trim white Georgian manor, secluded in
deep wooded country near Midleton village, the home of Irish
whiskey, has for twenty years been the home of Ken Sherrard, a local
gentleman farmer, and his Scottish wife, Beth. They have restored it in
perfect taste, with fine antique pieces, and they now take paying
guests, on a very personal basis. Each of the four bedrooms is large,
lovely and well equipped, with a superior bathroom. Downstairs is an
elegant residents' lounge, with a log fire on chilly days. Good silver

gleams in the dining room, where meals are served round one big table. Beth's cooking was excellent – lavish portions of seafood chowder, poached brill with asparagus, lemon syllabub; no choice, but preferences are discussed. Unlicensed; bring your own wine. Breakfast very good too, elegantly laid out, with home-made soda bread and jams. Rooms have views over the carefully landscaped flower garden and the fields beyond, where horses graze. Three Alsatian dogs, and Burmese and Siamese cats, add to the strong family ambience; but the high degree of personal attention might be a bit much for some." The gregarious owners write: "We take a warm approach to our guests. No TV or radio; we sit with them round the fire and talk, or we take them to a local pub; in summer we play tennis with them. We can arrange all types of fishing. There are 16 golf courses between two and 40 minutes' drive." The place is often taken over by house parties.

Open All year.
Rooms 4 double. 1 on ground floor, equipped for ♿. No telephone/TV.
Facilities Lounge, dining room. 20-acre grounds: tennis, croquet, woodland walks. River/lake fishing, golf nearby; sea, safe sandy beaches ½-hour's drive.
Location 15 miles E of Cork, 3 miles N of Midleton: from Midleton, take L35 towards Fermoy, turn left after 2½ miles (signposted).
Restrictions No smoking in dining room. Guide dogs only.
Credit cards Access, Visa.
Terms B&B IR£30–£35, D,B&B: single IR£55, double IR£80–£90. Set lunch IR£5, dinner IR£20. Children sharing parents' room: under 2 10% of adult rate; 2–12 years 25% reduction.

MONKSTOWN Co. Dublin — Map 6

Chestnut Lodge BUDGET — Tel (01) 280 7860
2 Vesey Place — Fax (01) 280 1466

In a tranquil area east of Dublin, quite near the ferry at Dun Laoghaire, stands this Regency terrace house, down a cul-de-sac facing a wooded park. "Nancy Malone runs it with exceptional efficiency," says a visitor this year. "Good housekeeping, with fresh flowers in hall, breakfast room and our bedroom, which was spacious and overlooked a small rambling garden. Breakfast, served communally at an antique table, or at separate tables, included fresh orange juice, hand-made brown bread, delicious scrambled eggs. Good value for money." Others have written: "It is furnished with good taste. Breakfast is a delight, as was tea with freshly baked scones and home-made jam. Everything is beautifully presented: starched table napery, proper tea." Among the many nearby restaurants, *Monkstown Brasserie* is recommended for fish. (*Andrew and Rosemary Reeves, and others*)

Open All year.
Rooms 4 double.
Facilities Lounge, breakfast room. Golf, riding, sailing nearby.
Location 6 miles SE of central Dublin, 1 mile W of Dun Laoghaire, off Monkstown Rd. DART rapid rail, bus no.7/8 from centre.
Restrictions No smoking: breakfast room, bedrooms. No dogs.
Credit cards Access, Visa.
Terms B&B IR£27.50–£45.

Always check latest tariffs with a hotel when booking.

MOUNTRATH Co. Laois   Map 6

Roundwood House   *Tel* (0502) 32120
                                             Fax (0502) 32711
                                   E-mail roundwood@tinet.ie

ॐ *César award in 1992*

Frank and Rosemarie Kennan's 18th-century Palladian mansion, "a gem", is set in large grounds, with donkeys, geese, ducks and chickens, at the foot of the Slieve Bloom mountains, in the almost empty Irish "Midlands". "Staying there is *fun*," writes one enthusiast. Another says: "A perfect place to stay – relaxed informality combined with good food." There is no television in the house, but plenty of late-night conversation, "lively and intelligent", led by Mr Kennan himself over dinner, and "resumed in the morning over a very enjoyable breakfast". Dining is communal, though you can have a separate table if you prefer. The Kennans' friendliness and welcome, in their beautiful old house full of books and pictures, make it easy to ignore a few creaking floorboards and cracked walls. *Roundwood* has been partly refurbished, but *aficionados* of its slightly shabby Irish charm need not worry. The Kennans say: "Our intention is to keep *Roundwood* as near as possible to what it should be – an aged beauty, dressed in her own slightly frayed clothes, not tarted up in modern fashion." Bathrooms are quaint, but the water is hot and some now have a shower. Dinners are substantial and well cooked, and the wine list is unusually good. Children are welcomed and encouraged to feed the animals. (*R Rennison*)

Open All year, except Christmas Day.
Rooms 10 double.
Facilities Drawing room, study, dining room. 20-acre grounds: croquet, swings, stables. Golf, river fishing nearby. Unsuitable for &.
Location N7 Dublin–Limerick. Right at T-junction in Mountrath, then left to Kinnitty. Hotel 3 miles exactly.
Restrictions No smoking in bedrooms. No dogs.
Credit cards All major cards accepted.
Terms [1997] B&B IR£38–£46. Set Sun lunch IR£13, dinner IR£22. ***V***

MUCKROSS Co. Kerry   Map 6

Muckross Park   *Tel* (064) 31938
                                             Fax (064) 31965

In the heart of Killarney's National Park, and conveniently placed for the lakes, is Raymond Kelliher's modernised version of Killarney's oldest hotel, in business since 1795. It offers an excellent base for riding and exploring lakeside and forest walks. "We didn't see the famed red deer, but we spotted a dappled Japanese deer within a couple of hundred yards of the hotel," wrote a recent visitor. "The staff could not have been more cheerful and helpful, and the food in *Molly's* (the thatched 'traditional Irish pub and restaurant' next to, and owned by, the hotel) was ample, wholesome and tasty. The bedrooms are prettily furnished – Laura Ashley with an Irish brogue – and the public rooms have a hearty charm." In the gourmet *Blue Pool* restaurant, Matthias Elbel's extensive menu uses plenty of fresh local produce: crab fritters with dill mayonnaise, seafood chowder, Cromane oysters and so on. Kerry is a golfer's paradise; there are several championship courses within easy reach. There is a new manageress this year, Patricia Shanahan. (*TT*) More reports, please.

Open Mar–Nov.
Rooms 2 suites, 25 double.
Facilities Drawing room, bar, restaurant (piped classical music throughout all day); function facilities; pub/restaurant next door. 8-acre grounds. Lakes, fishing, walking, riding, pony-trekking, golf nearby. Unsuitable for &.
Location 2½ miles S of Killarney, on N71 towards Kenmare. Bus from Killarney.
Restrictions No smoking: restaurant, 2 bedrooms. No dogs.
Credit cards All major cards accepted.
Terms B&B: single IR£60–£80, double IR£80–£120, suite IR£150–£300. Pub meals. Set dinner IR£23; full alc IR£33. Off-season breaks.

MULRANY Co. Mayo   Map 6

Rosturk Woods   **BUDGET**   *Tel/Fax* (098) 36264

This is real *Playboy of the Western World* country – the remote west coast of Mayo, between the high cliffs of Achill Island and the neat, historic town of Westport. Here, beside woodlands on the sandy seashore of a village by beautiful Clew Bay, stands this "delectable upper-crust guest house", much admired by our readers, with "exemplary hosts", Louisa and Alan Stoney. Though recently built, the house has an old feel, some antique furnishings and a cottage atmosphere; interesting books and pictures abound. Bedrooms have stripped pine doors, soft shades of blue, cotton prints, good lighting, and views across the bay. Alan Stoney grew up in the castle next door; Louisa, "friendly, intelligent and down to earth", runs the house and cooks simple dinners – good soups, freshly grilled salmon, etc. Breakfast includes smoked salmon and scrambled egg. There are also self-catering cottages, whose guests may dine in the main house. Very popular, the house is often booked out in advance. More reports, please.

Open Feb–Dec.
Rooms 1 suite, 3 double. 1 suitable for &. Also self-catering accommodation (available all year).
Facilities Sitting room with TV, games room, dining room. 5-acre wooded grounds: garden, tennis; seashore: bathing, sea angling. Riding, golf, lake/river fishing, sailing nearby.
Location 7½ miles W of Newport, between main road and sea.
Restrictions No smoking: dining room, bedrooms. No dogs in bedrooms.
Credit cards None accepted.
Terms B&B IR£20–£30. Set dinner IR£20.25.

NEWPORT Co. Mayo   Map 6

Newport House   *Tel* (098) 41222
                                               Fax (098) 41613

Close to the sea in a village on beautiful Clew Bay, between Achill Island and Connemara, stands this handsome creeper-covered Georgian mansion, former home of a branch of the O'Donels. Today, according to a regular visitor, it is "one of the finest hotels in Ireland". A Relais & Châteaux member, it has impressive public rooms, fine plasterwork and a splendid staircase with lantern and dome. "Great hospitality and a warm greeting from Thelma and Kieran Thompson and their staff; wonderful food." Endorsed this year: "Our room was gloriously old-fashioned: huge bed, linen sheets, towels changed daily in our green-and-white bathroom. You could doze by the sitting-room fire, amid antiques, or visit the vegetable garden." Chef John Gavin's cooking includes sophisticated dishes such as quail stuffed with mousseline of venison and wild mushroom sauce; you can have eggs Benedict for breakfast. The hotel is famous as an angling centre; it has its own fishery on the Newport river. (*CVB, Judith Davies*)

Open 19 Mar–5 Oct.
Rooms 16 double, 2 single. 5 in courtyard. 2 on ground floor.
Facilities Drawing room, sitting room, bar, billiard room, dining room. 20-acre grounds: walled vegetable garden. Private fishing; golf, riding, walking, shooting, hang-gliding nearby.
Location In village, 7 miles N Westport. Bus no.25 from Westport 3 times daily.
Restrictions No smoking in dining room. Dogs only in courtyard bedrooms.
Credit cards All major cards accepted.
Terms B&B IR£56–£83. Set dinner (6-course) IR£32.

OUGHTERARD Co. Galway   Map 6

Currarevagh House
Tel (091) 552312
Fax (091) 552731

ۉ *César award in 1992*

This mid-Victorian country house, set in huge grounds by the shore of Lough Corrib (some of the best fishing in Ireland), has been owned by the Hodgson family for five generations – Harry and June Hodgson have been resident hosts since 1970 – and it has featured in every edition of the *Guide*. This year, guests returning after 35 years found that little had changed. "The tiger-skin is still on the wall on the staircase! To stay is unique and pleasurable, the four-course set dinner was very good, with seconds offered." Others wrote: "It is warm, comfortable and welcoming, with a hotchpotch of carpets and furniture." Not at all smart, the house is openly old-fashioned and slightly run-down, and some bedrooms are small; but that is its appeal to many readers, who enjoy the huge beds ("nightly hot water-bottles") and Edwardian furniture: "Because it lacks formal elegance, it is comfortable and relaxing; the overall effect is home-like and friendly, like visiting an old relative." The no-choice, country house-style dinner menu might include

haunch of venison or roast Irish beef; service is by local women, and guests are expected to be punctual. Breakfast, an Edwardian-style buffet, includes a range of hot dishes on the sideboard. A good base for touring Connemara and the Aran Islands. (*Mrs JC Smye, CMH, and others*)

Open 9 Apr–24 Oct. Parties of 8 or more at other times (except Christmas, New Year). Lunch by arrangement (residents only).

Rooms 13 double, 2 single. 3, on ground floor, in mews.
Facilities Drawing room, sitting room, library, bar, dining room. 150-acre grounds: lake, fishing (ghillies available), boating, swimming, tennis, croquet. Golf, riding, hill-walking nearby. Not ideal for &.
Location 4 miles NW of Oughterard on Glann lakeshore road.
Restrictions No smoking in dining room. Children under 12 by arrangement. Dogs by arrangement; only on lead in public rooms.
Credit cards None accepted.
Terms (*Excluding 10% service charge*) B&B: single IR£47–£62, double IR£94–£98. 3–6 day D,B&B rate IR£62.50 per person. Set dinner IR£21. Weekly rates. 1-night bookings sometimes refused if too far in advance.

RATHMULLAN Co. Donegal   Map 6

Rathmullan House   *Tel* (074) 58188
Rathmullan, Letterkenny   *Fax* (074) 58200

Admired again this year for its "magnificent location" and its imaginative food – "it gets better every year" – this white 1800s mansion stands in its own wide gardens, beside Lough Swilly, which is not a lake but an inlet from the sea, with a broad sandy beach. The owners, Bob and Robin Wheeler, have been here since 1963. Their son Mark is manager, and Kevin Murphy is chef. More plaudits this year and last: "Superb lounges, with turf fires (scruffy bar best avoided). An excellent spacious bedroom. Friendly and attentive waiters." "Though professionally run, it still has the feel of a private house. Everyone very helpful; my heavy suitcase was rushed up the staircase." Public rooms have chandeliers, antiques, marble fireplaces and oil paintings. In the striking conservatory-style dining room, a lavish buffet lunch is served on Sundays. Breakfasts are hugely enjoyed. There are pleasant walks along the beach, up the lovely Fanad peninsula, and into Rathmullan, "a village full of unspoilt Donegal melancholy". A pretty indoor salt water swimming pool, and a sauna and steam room add to the pleasures. (*SC Law, Esler Crawford, DKS, and others*)

Open Early Mar–Nov.
Rooms 8 mini-suites, 11 double, 1 single.
Facilities Drawing room, Rajah room, library, smoking room, cellar bar, dining room; indoor salt water swimming pool, sauna, steam room. 10-acre grounds: tennis, croquet; direct access to sandy beach, safe bathing. Golf nearby. Unsuitable for &.
Location ½ mile N of village, 14 miles NE of Letterkenny. Bus: Letterkenny; hotel will meet.
Restrictions No smoking in dining room. No dogs.
Credit cards All major cards accepted.
Terms [1997] (*Excluding 10% service charge*) B&B IR£40–£62.50; D,B&B IR£65–£87.50. Set lunch IR£15, dinner IR£25. 1-night bookings refused bank holidays.

RATHNEW Co. Wicklow   Map 6

Hunter's Hotel   *Tel* (0404) 40106
Newrath Bridge   *Fax* (0404) 40338
                                   E-mail hunters@indigo.ie

This ancient coaching inn by a river, near the coast at Wicklow, has been owned and run by the Gelletlie family since 1825. Recent

modernisation has not spoilt its charm, as two devotees report: "My
memory was of old-fashioned comfort, perhaps a little time-worn.
Recently, however, I found the whole place gleaming with fresh paint,
new carpets and polished wood. My single bedroom was generous in
size; with a bed big enough for two, and no fewer than three mirrors.
The extensive dinner menu provided hearty fare, if not *haute cuisine*,
and breakfast was 'full house Irish' with freshly squeezed juice, linen
napkins and not a sign of pre-packed butter or preserves." "I have
loved this place for 30 years. Mrs Gelletlie is my ideal Irish hotelkeeper, and the hotel itself, with all its quirks, strikes me as the best
possible indoctrination into Irishness." Whiskey and tea are served
throughout the day, often simultaneously. Nobody bothers with keys.
There are 15 18-hole golf courses within an hour's drive. (*EC, JM*)

Open All year, except 3 days over Christmas.
Rooms 13 double, 3 single. 1 on ground floor.
Facilities Residents' lounge, TV room, bar lounge, dining room; conference
room. 2-acre garden: river, fishing. Golf, tennis, riding, sea, sandy beach, fishing
nearby.
Location 28 miles S of Dublin. From Dublin take N11; left at bridge in Ashford;
hotel 1½ miles. From S turn right off N11 on leaving Rathnew; hotel ½ mile.
Carpark. Bus from Wicklow.
Restrictions No smoking: dining room, some bedrooms. No dogs.
Credit cards All major cards accepted.
Terms B&B IR£47.50–£60; D,B&B IR£71.50–£84. Set lunch IR£15, dinner IR£24. 1-
night bookings refused holiday weekends.

Tinakilly House   *Tel* (0404) 69274
                                                       Fax (0404) 67806
                                          E-mail wpower@tinakilly.ie

This grey stone mansion was built in the 1870s as a retirement home
by the great navigator Captain Robert Halpin, one-time commander of
Brunel's *Great Eastern*. It stands in large wooded grounds, overlooking
the Irish Sea and Broadlough coastal lagoon (a bird sanctuary), and is
efficiently run as a superior country hotel by its owners, William and
Bee Power. One guest this year, who found the residents' lounge taken
over by a conference, thought the style was "commercial more than
personal", but another had nothing but praise: "This is the sort of
place that makes you glad that you bought the *Guide*. It would take a
pedant to find a fault. The welcome is warm and friendly, without
being overbearing. The bedrooms are the star of the show – as
spacious as they are characterful, with a huge bed, antiques, and a
wealth of attention to detail: fresh fruit *and* a finger bowl, bathroom
with excellent shower and towels ergonomically within reach. Superb
food, too." The furnishings include golden chandeliers and sconces,
polished dark wood, Rococo fireplaces, softly upholstered formal
sofas and chairs, red carpets, potted plants, assorted glittering bric-à-
brac, and good reproduction pictures. Glendalough monastery and
the Wicklow mountains are nearby. (*Stephen Wrigley-Hare; also Mrs M
Lancaster, and others*)

Open All year.
Rooms 27 suites, 14 double. 5 on ground floor, 1 equipped for &.
Facilities Large hall (pianist Fri/Sat), residents' lounge, bar, 3 dining rooms;
function/conference facilities. 7-acre grounds: tennis, putting green. Golf, sailing, hill-walking, bird sanctuary nearby.

Location Off N11 Dublin–Wicklow. Take R750 through Rathnew. Entrance on left after ¼ mile.
Restriction No dogs.
Credit cards All major cards accepted.
Terms [1997] B&B IR£60–£125. Bar lunches. Set lunch IR£18, dinner IR£30; full alc IR£38. Short breaks, Dickensian Christmas, New Year programme.

RECESS Co. Galway   **Map 6**

Ballynahinch Castle   *Tel* (095) 31006
                                                           Fax (095) 31085
                                                    E-Mail 6hinch@iol.ie

This splendid crenellated house stands on the banks of a river (excellent salmon fishing) in a large wooded private estate in the wild heart of Connemara. It was enjoyed in 1997 by a fellow *Guide* hotelier: "A charming, rambling house in a peaceful setting with glorious views (spectacular sunsets over the river). The rooms are spacious and well furnished, the food and service were good, and the welcome and attention to detail was full of homely warmth." This backed last year's view: "We love its stunning location, relaxed style, and atmosphere of a private home. Fires burn in the hall in winter, and guests are encouraged to sit around drying off walking gear and having tea or drinks. The restaurant and the bedrooms in the new annexe have wonderful views of the river, from huge windows. Food is very good, with plenty of local fish and game. We enjoyed the sense of history." This is the ancestral home of the Martin family: "Humanity Dick" Martin was the founder of the RSPCA. The English county cricketer and sportsman, Maharajah Ranjitsingh, also once lived here. Local activities including mountain climbing on the Twelve Bens, day trips to the Aran Islands, and excellent golfing. (*Richard Quinlan, LF*)

Open All year, except Christmas, Feb.
Rooms 23 double, 5 single.
Facilities Lounges, pub, dining room. 350-acre grounds: river, fishing, tennis, walking, shooting. Golf, pony-trekking, sea fishing nearby. Unsuitable for &.
Location 36 miles NW of Galway. Turn towards Roundstone off N59: entrance 2 miles. Bus from Galway.
Restriction No dogs.
Credit cards All major cards accepted.
Terms [1997] (*Excluding 10% service charge*) B&B: single IR£63–£80, double IR£92–£140. Set dinner IR£23. 50% reduction for child sharing parents' room.

RIVERSTOWN Co. Sligo   Map 6

Coopershill   *Tel* (071) 65108
                                                         Fax (071) 65466

♔ *César award in 1987*

Set in a large estate south of Sligo town, near the knobbly hills that Yeats
loved, this grey stone mansion has been the home of the O'Hara family
since they built it in 1774. Brian and Lindy O'Hara are today thought
"excellent hosts", and again this year their "really special" hotel has
won eager praise, especially for its house party style. "A real country
house with plenty of old-world charm. It is amazingly beautiful inside,
and our rooms and bathroom were huge. The good honest Irish cooking
was enjoyable" (eg, beef Wellington, roast monkfish). "It gives a wonderful feeling of entering a viable family estate. Our hosts were so welcoming and caring." "The staff were exceptionally nice and helpful. The
good plain cooking was lavishly served; breakfasts were probably the
best of our trip." Others have written: "We liked the walks through the
woods, the dogs, the peacocks, and the gathering of guests in the drawing room before and after dinner. The house is filled with antiques;
everything is impeccably cared for. Wonderful fudge and chocolate
with coffee, afternoon tea with cakes, fresh orange juice at breakfast."
"The interior is something of a time warp, with spears, hunting trophies, and ancestors decorating the walls." Most bedrooms have a four-
poster or a canopied bed. Dinner, by candlelight, starts at 8.30 pm and
can be very leisurely, since all guests are served each course together.
(*Diane Skelton, Richard Creed, Sir Timothy Harford, and others*)

Open 1 Apr–31 Oct. Out-of-season house parties by arrangement.
Rooms 8 double.
Facilities 2 halls, drawing room, TV room, dining room; table-tennis. 500-acre
grounds: garden, tennis, woods, farmland, river with coarse fishing. Trout-
fishing, sandy beach, championship golf course 18 miles. Unsuitable for &.
Location 11 miles SE of Sligo: turn off N4 towards Riverstown at Drumfin, then
follow *Coopershill* signs. Train: Ballymote; plane: Sligo, Knock.
Restrictions No smoking: dining room, bedrooms. No dogs in house.
Credit cards All major cards accepted.
Terms B&B: IR£45–£62.50; D,B&B IR£70–£87.50. Light or picnic lunch IR£6; set
dinner IR£25. Discounts for 3 or more nights.

SHANAGARRY Co. Cork   Map 6

Ballymaloe House   *Tel* (021) 652531
                                                         Fax (021) 652021
                                                  E-mail bmaloe@iol.ie

♔ *César award in 1984*

"We loved it." "A unique, peaceful atmosphere. Fantastic food; dinner
is a five-course celebration of fresh Irish cuisine." "A very friendly
atmosphere in the restaurant, everyone talking and laughing. A beautiful house, clean, bright and airy. No pretension anywhere." Ivan and
Myrtle Allen's renowned hotel/restaurant has remained popular this
year, apart from a few grumbles ("a victim of its own success").
Gracious and rambling, more or less Georgian, with a Norman keep, it
is surrounded by a large home farm, which provides much of what you

eat. The Allens have developed a special brand of graceful hospitality, helped by their extended family. Daughter Hazel is manageress; head chef is Rory O'Connell, brother of daughter-in-law Darina Allen, who runs the Ballymaloe Cookery School. The cooking remains careful and traditional, "unspoilt by *nouvelle* pretensions", and includes "wonderful home-made puddings"; the wine list is splendid, if pricey. The restaurant, drawing a civilised clientele from many countries, has five rooms and a conservatory. Lounges are comfortable, with log fires in winter; walls are hung with Ivan Allen's collection of modern Irish paintings. "By day we swam, played tennis and strolled in the wooded gardens, accompanied by peacocks," ran a report this year. "After dinner, by the wood fire, we unwound to Rory's Irish singing, and guests were encouraged to join in." Bedrooms vary in size; those in the main house tend to be larger than annexe ones. Children are welcomed. (*Mrs M Lancaster, James Skelton, Diane Skelton, and others*)

Open All year, except 24–26 Dec.
Rooms 30 double, 3 single. 10 in courtyard. 3 on ground floor.
Facilities Drawing room, sitting room, TV room, conservatory, 5 dining rooms. 350-acre farm: gardens, tennis, swimming pool, 6-hole golf course, croquet, children's play area; craft shop. Cookery school nearby. Sea 2 miles: sand and rock beaches; fishing, riding by arrangement.
Location 20 miles E of Cork; 2 miles E of Cloyne on L35 Ballycotton road. Train: Cork; then taxi.
Restrictions No smoking in some dining rooms. No dogs in house.
Credit cards All major cards accepted.
Terms [1997] B&B IR£50–£90; D,B&B IR£81.50–£121.50. Set lunch IR£16.50, dinner IR£31.50. Child sharing parents' room half-price. Winter, conference rates.

THURLES Co. Tipperary   Map 6

Inch House   NEW/BUDGET   *Tel* (0504) 51348 and 51261
Inch, Thurles   *Fax* (0504) 51348

Four miles W of Thurles on Nenagh road, 300-year-old manor set in 250-acre grounds. Family feel – friendly hosts, John and Nora Egan, have 8 children. Pleasant service. Large bedrooms with antiques, good bathrooms. Lavish breakfasts. Cordon Bleu cooking in elegant dining room with log fire. Drawing room in William Morris style. Golf, riding, fishing nearby. Children welcomed, but not at dinner. 5 rooms. Closed Christmas week. Access, Visa accepted. B&B IR£25–£30; D,B&B IR£47.50–£52.50.

YOUGHAL Co. Cork   Map 6

Aherne's   *Tel* (024) 92424
163 North Main Street   *Fax* (024) 93633
                                                   E-mail ahe@iol.ie

꘎ *César award 1997*

This historic fortified port and market town sits at the mouth of the Blackwater river, east of Cork. Its name means "yew wood", and ancient yew trees are still found in the town. The Fitzgibbon family's small restaurant-with-rooms is outwardly modest-looking but inwardly very stylish. Again this year, it has been one of the most admired of our Irish entries, above all for its "flair with freshly caught seafood" and its "wonderful, extremely Irish hospitality". "We have visited for many years, and the warm welcome improves every time. We had one of the new rooms in the modern wing: these are spacious, bright and airy, with high-quality fabrics enhanced by antique furniture." That 1997 report from a *Guide* hotelier backs earlier plaudits: "A delight in every way." "A perfect stay. The most helpful of staff; friendliness and hospitality of the highest order." "Our room had a lavishly fitted bathroom, plus a sitting room with a peat fire and breakfast area; the overall effect was that of the best sort of French hotel." "The food was marvellous: perfectly cooked seafood at dinner, and a mammoth breakfast with freshly squeezed orange juice, scrambled egg and smoked salmon and fresh fish, if required." Meals are also to be had in the bar, where the solicitous service was praised in 1997. (*Richard Quinlan, Rachel Burridge, N Williams; also Bill and April Hancock, and many others*)

Open All year, except Christmas.
Rooms 12 double. 3 on ground floor, 1 with facilities for &.
Facilities Drawing room; 2 bars, restaurant (piped "easy listening" music). Beach, bathing, sea/river fishing, riding, golf nearby.
Location At N end of main street, on N25. Courtyard parking. Bus from Cork.
Restriction No dogs.
Credit cards All major cards accepted.
Terms [1997] B&B IR£50–£80. Bar meals. Set lunch IR£15.50, dinner IR£27; full alc IR£20.

****

Suggestion Box One of the characteristics of a country house hotel of a certain type is that one is made to feel like a house guest of the family, therefore criticism of any kind is bad manners. Maybe the *Guide* could introduce a new symbol: TLOOF, meaning "treated like one of the family", or even RBA: "run by amateurs", meaning amateur in the true, not pejorative, sense.

****

Traveller's tale No staff were in evidence in the dining room of this Yorkshire hostelry, so we found a table and waited. Eventually a waitress appeared with menus. Some time later, our first courses arrived, but they were not what we had ordered. The waitress, who had the interpersonal skills of an ox, uttered a mild expletive and took them away without so much as "sorry". After an hour, we asked when we might receive some food. The waitress said she would check, "but starters often took rather a long time". One of our starters was a plate of smoked salmon, which could not have involved much preparation.

****

In the dark Hotel proprietors seem to think that a bedside lamp need be no more than sufficient to enable the intended user to make his or her way across the room without colliding with the furniture. They seem not to realise how cheap electricity has become in recent years. And though some diners like dim lighting for romantic reasons, many would prefer to be able to read the menu (and the prices).

****

Shortlist

The following hotels, guest houses and B&Bs are in, or within commuting distance of, major cities and towns that do not at present have a *Guide* entry, or that are inadequately represented. Apart, that is, from London, where we are well covered, but where there is a huge unsatisfied demand for budget accommodation and hotels that do not cost an arm and a leg, which most of these recommendations do not.

Most of these Shortlist hotels are not typical *Guide* entries, but some could be. The information is taken from various sources, including reports from readers and inspectors. A few of the hotels are large, but we have, as usual, tried to seek out small, owner-managed establishments. Some lack the character of a true *Guide* entry. Some may be altogether too flamboyant. Many cater for business visitors during the week, so offer good weekend reductions. As this is the Shortlist's first year, it is of necessity somewhat haphazard, and the standards may be inconsistent. We'd like reports and nominations, please.

Those places which do not also have a full entry in the *Guide* are indicated in the maps with a triangle. The rates quoted are for 1997.

ENGLAND

ALDEBURGH Suffolk   Map 2
The Wentworth, Wentworth Road, IP15 5BD. *Tel* (01728) 452312, *fax* (01728) 454343. Traditional hotel, across quiet road from seafront, owned and run since 1920 by Pritt family. "Bright and welcoming. Pleasant local staff. Good value." 38 bedrooms with good quality fittings and *Orlando, the Marmalade Cat* books by Kathleen Hale (Aldeburgh features as Owlbarrow). Attractive lounge: antiques and Russell Flint prints. "Enjoyable, if not outstanding" meals in pleasant dining room, with wines from Adnams. D,B&B £56.50–£69.50.

BRIGHTON East Sussex   Map 2
Adelaide, 51 Regency Square, BN1 2FF. *Tel* (01273) 205286, *fax* (01273) 220904. Ruth and Clive Buxton's Grade II listed Regency house, recently renovated, on seafront square. Handy for centre. NCP carpark opposite. 12 bedrooms. B&B: single £39, double £57–£68. Evening meal by arrangement.
Prince Regent, 29 Regency Square, BN1 2FH. *Tel* (01273) 329962, *fax* (01273) 748162. Alan Ashworth and Stuart Corson's B&B in Regency mansion close to *Adelaide* (above). 20 bedrooms, some with 19th-century 4-poster (one has a mirrored canopy). B&B: single from £35, double from £55.

BRISTOL   Map 2
Berkeley Square Hotel, 15 Berkeley Square, Clifton, BS8 1HB. *Tel* (0117) 925 4000, *fax* (0117) 925 2970. Flagship of group of 4 hotels in

Clifton area, close to university, museum and art gallery; ½ mile from centre. Garage. Conversion of 2 houses in sedate Georgian square. Helpful staff. Pleasant if anodyne decor. Modern English cooking in restaurant, *Nightingales*. No residents' lounge; trendy bar in basement. 41 rooms (25 are singles). Access to square garden. B&B: single £49–£81, double £80–£102.

CAMBRIDGE Cambridgeshire   Map 2
Arundel House, 53 Chesterton Road, CB4 3AN. *Tel* (01223) 367701, *fax* (01223) 367721. Across road from Cam and Jesus Green, a short walk from centre, well-run privately owned hotel composed of Victorian town houses. "Lacks the individual character prized by the *Guide* but gives good value at a reasonable price. Food good, if not distinctive; delightful staff." 105 unfussy bedrooms, most with facilities *en suite*; 50% no-smoking. Small garden. Private parking. Some conference trade, but families warmly welcomed. B&B: single £28–£65, double £39.50–£89. Cooked breakfast £3.25 extra. Set lunch £9.75/£10.95, dinner £15.95.
Quy Mill, Newmarket Road, Stow-cum-Quy, Cambridgeshire CB5 9AG. *Tel* (01223) 293383, *fax* (01223) 293770. On E side of Cambridge (car or taxi to centre), 19th-century water mill (with original wheel), in 11-acre grounds, with wildlife, fishing in river Quy (pronounced "Kwai"). 23 bedrooms. B&B: single from £52, double from £68. Bar meals from £8.
Further afield:
Purlins, 12 High Street, Little Shelford, Cambridgeshire CB2 5ES. *Tel/fax* (01223) 842643. In quiet, picturesque village, 4 miles S of Cambridge, Olga and David Hindley's charming family house, relatively new, but in medieval manor style. 2 acres woodland and lawns. Conservatory lounge for guests; breakfasts – English, continental, vegetarian – in galleried hall. Buses to city every 2 hours till 5 pm (weekdays), or trains from Great Shelford (25 mins' walk). 3 bedrooms. B&B: single from £28, double £40–£48.
Melbourn Bury, Melbourn, Cambridgeshire SG8 6DE. *Tel* (01763) 261151, *fax* (01763) 262375. Country house, Tudor in origin, with attractive decor. 3 no-smoking bedrooms. Bus or train from nearby Royston to Cambridge (10 miles to N). B&B: single £50, double £80. Evening meal by arrangement (communal, residents only) £16.

See also entries for **DUXFORD** (9½ miles S of Cambridge) and **LITTLEBURY GREEN** (16 miles S of Cambridge).

CHESTER Cheshire   Map 3
Chester Grosvenor, Eastgate, CH1 1LT. *Tel* (01244) 324024, *fax* (01244) 313246. Luxurious hotel, owned by Duke of Westminster's Grosvenor Estates, in centre of historic city. Smart lounge and library; health suite. *Michelin*-starred *Arkle* restaurant (named for famous racehorse owned by Anne, Duchess of Westminster); light meals in informal brasserie. 86 bedrooms: single £141–£158.62, double £211.50–£235, suite £352.50–£470. Breakfast: continental £8.75, English £12.50. Set lunch £22.50, dinner (2/3-course) £38/£45.
Further afield
Craxton Wood, Parkgate Road, Puddington, Cheshire L66 9PB. *Tel* (0151) 339 4717, *fax* (0151) 339 1740. 7¼ miles NW of Chester, in wooded grounds, with lawns and rose gardens. 14-bedroom hotel,

owned by Petranca family for 30 years, with country home feel, good food, long-serving staff. Handy also for Liverpool (5 mins' walk to station, then 20-min train journey) and Manchester airport. B&B: single £63.85–£87.50, double £101.85–£118.50. Set dinner £19.85.

COVENTRY West Midlands   Map 2
Coombe Abbey, Brinklow Road, Binley, CV3 2AB. *Tel* (01203) 450450, *fax* (01203) 635101. 3½ miles E of city centre. Former Cistercian Abbey (11th-century, with moat and portcullis). Quiet setting in 500-acre park with 80-acre lake, and formal gardens by Capability Brown. "Owner Gordon Bear's love of the old and atmospheric apparent throughout." Medieval evenings with "monks", chanted music, flickering lighting, banquets in baronial hall. 63 bedrooms; "feature" ones with huge 4-poster and elaborate throne toilet. Single £115, double from £125. Breakfast: continental £8.50, "Full Abbey" £10.50.
Nailcote Hall, Nailcote Lane, Berkswell, West Midlands CV7 7DE. *Tel* (01203) 466174, *fax* (01203) 470720. 6½ miles W of centre on B4101 to Knowle; 10 mins from Birmingham airport. Rick Cressman's Tudor-style manor house, with subterranean extensions – "a stunning mixture of old and modern". 15-acre grounds. Extensive leisure facilities (swimming pool, golf, tennis, beauty treatments, etc). French cooking in *Oak Room* restaurant; "pasta and pizzazz in shamelessly noisy *Rick's Bar*, 20 feet under ground". Live music nights. 38 rooms. B&B: single £120, double £130. Set meals £25.50–£27.50.

DOVER Kent   Map 2
Loddington House, 14 East Cliff, CT16 1LX. *Tel/fax* (01304) 201947. Kathy and Mike Cupper's Grade II listed guest house in seafront Regency terrace, close to terminals and Hoverport. 6 bedrooms (4 with facilities *en suite*). B&B double £48–£56. Evening meal £15.50.
Further afield
Coldred Court Farm, Church Road, Coldred, Kent CT15 5AQ. *Tel/fax* (01304) 830816. 6 miles NW of Dover by A256 off A2. Truda and Peter Kelly's 17th-century brick and peg-tile farmhouse in 7-acre grounds, on hill (panoramic views over North Downs to Pegwell Bay). Home-baked bread, home-made preserves. 3 bedrooms. B&B £20–£22.50. Evening meal, by arrangement, £12.50.
    See also entry for **WEST CLIFFE** (4 miles NE of Dover).

HUDDERSFIELD West Yorkshire   Map 4
Elm Crest, 2 Queens Road, Edgerton, HD2 2AG. *Tel* (01484) 530990, *fax* (01484) 516227. Derek and Hilary Gee's no-smoking Victorian guest house, in residential area 1 mile N of centre. 8 bedrooms, most with facilities *en suite*. Home-cooked breakfast and evening meal (£15). Conservatory; lounge with log fire. Carpark. B&B double £45–£59.
The Lodge, 48 Birkby Lodge Road, Birkby, HD2 2BG. *Tel* (01484) 431001, *fax* (01484) 421590. Garry and Kevin Birley's substantial stone-built house in pretty garden in prosperous suburb, 1½ miles from city centre. Peaceful and clean; lovely sitting room with Art Nouveau panelled walls and plaster ceiling. Good modern food in popular restaurant. Children welcomed. 11 no-smoking bedrooms, 3 on ground floor. B&B: single £65, double £75. Set lunch £14.95, dinner £24.95.

LIVERPOOL Merseyside   **Map 4**
Woolton Redbourne, Acrefield Road, Woolton, L25 5JN. *Tel*
(0151) 428 2152, *fax* (0151) 421 1501. 6 miles SE of centre by A562. In
leafy suburb, Grade II-listed Victorian house in landscaped gardens
and lawns, built by industrialist Sir Henry Tate, now owned by Paul
Collins. Country house decor: antiques, fine fabrics; 4-poster bed *and*
4-poster jacuzzi in large suites. Opulent restaurant. 22 bedrooms.
B&B: single from £63, double from £92, suite from £120. Dinner
(residents only) £22.95.
Further afield
The Bowler Hat, 2 Talbot Road, Oxton, Birkenhead, Merseyside
L43 2HH. *Tel* (0151) 652 4931, *fax* (0151) 653 8127. 3 miles SW of centre.
Late Victorian house, with home-like decor, garden, in residential area.
32 bedrooms, some spacious; smaller ones in modern extension. B&B:
single £45–£65, double £72.50–£80. Set meals £10.95–£16.50.
The Old Hall, Main Street, Frodsham, Cheshire WA6 7AR. *Tel*
(01928) 732052, *fax* (01928) 739046. In village 3 miles S of Runcorn, 30
mins by car to Liverpool. Evocative of a country post house hotel, Mr
and Mrs Winfield's Tudor building on main street, with inglenooks,
roaring log fires, and "traditional British fare". 20 bedrooms. B&B:
single £57.50, double £73. Set lunch £8.95–£10.95, dinner £15.95.
Thornton Hall, Neston Road, Thornton Hough, Wirral, Merseyside
L63 1JF. *Tel* (0151) 336 3938, *fax* (0151) 336 7864. In village in central
Wirral, impressive house, built for 18th-century shipping magnate,
much extended. Some original features: oak carvings, restaurant with
leather and mother-of-pearl ceiling, serving food "of a traditional
British character". Conference centre. Large gardens. 63 bedrooms,
most in modern extension. B&B: single £73, double £83. Meals
£19.50–£20.50.

LONDON   **Map 2**
Abbey House, 11 Vicarage Gate, W8 4AG. *Tel* (0171) 727 2594.
Family-run B&B in Victorian house with attractive entrance hall and
staircase, in quiet road off Kensington Church St. Small lounge; basement breakfast room. 19 simple rooms, none with facilities *en suite*.
B&B double £58. (Underground: Kensington High St.)
Aster House, 3 Sumner Place, SW7 3EE. *Tel* (0171) 581 5888, *fax*
(0171) 584 4925. Rachel and Peter Carapiet's town house B&B at end
of pleasant tree-lined Victorian terrace in South Kensington. Public
carpark nearby. Pretty decor, "with home-like feel"; award-winning
garden. No lounge, but charming conservatory, with sitting area,
where health-conscious buffet breakfasts are served. No smoking.
12 rooms. B&B (*excluding VAT*): single £65, double £98–£110.
(Underground: South Kensington.)
Blair House, 34 Draycott Place, SW3 2SA. *Tel* (0171) 581 2323, *fax*
(0171) 823 7752. Modest, no-frills accommodation in Victorian house
in attractive, quiet street close to Sloane Sq. "Sweet-natured, helpful
staff, but imperfect housekeeping and basic breakfast." B&B: single
£85, double £105. (Underground: Sloane Sq.)
The Colonnade, 2 Warrington Crescent, W9 1ER. *Tel* (0171) 286 1052,
fax (0171) 286 1057. Victorian Grade II listed house in fashionable
residential area, Little Venice. Owned by Richards family since 1948;
home-like atmosphere. 48 rooms. B&B only: single £72.50, double
£110–£150. (Underground: Warwick Ave.)

Cranley Gardens Hotel, 8 Cranley Gardens, SW7 3DB. *Tel* (0171) 373 3232, *fax* (0171) 373 7944. Conversion of four Georgian terraced houses in South Kensington, looking across quite busy road to garden square. 85 bedrooms, some small. Clean and comfortable; simple decor, friendly staff. Basement breakfast room; bar snacks available. An outstanding restaurant, *Shaw's*, is just round the corner. B&B: single £69–£79, double £99–£110. (Underground: Gloucester Rd, South Kensington.)

Dorset Square Hotel, 39–40 Dorset Square, NW1 6QN. *Tel* (0171) 723 7874, *fax* (0171) 724 3328, *e-mail* firmdale@dircon. co.uk.kc. Lavishly decorated conversion of Regency town houses, on garden square near Marylebone Rd and Regent's Pk. Public carpark nearby. 37 rooms £95–£175 (*excluding VAT*). Breakfast: continental £9, English £12.50. Set lunch £14.95, dinner £13.95–£16.95. (Underground: Baker St.)

Five Sumner Place, 5 Sumner Place, SW7 3EE. *Tel* (0171) 584 7586, *fax* (0171) 823 9962. John Palgan's immaculate B&B, recently refurbished, in Victorian terrace, near *Aster House* (above). Buffet breakfast in pretty conservatory. Small garden. 13 rooms, most with facilities *en suite*. B&B (*excluding VAT*): single £69, double £99–£100. (Underground: South Kensington.)

La Gaffe, 107–111 Heath Street, NW3 6SS. *Tel* (0171) 435 8965, *fax* (0171) 794 7592, *e-mail* La-Gaffe@msn.com. Italian restaurant-with-rooms in Hampstead village, near heath and underground. Friendly proprietors (for 35 years) Bernard and Androulla Stella. Roof-garden for tea; breakfast in coffee bar. 16 small, no-smoking bedrooms, most with shower (3 4-poster rooms have bath); rear ones, overlooking garden square, are quietest. B&B: single from £50, double £60–£110. (Underground: Hampstead.)

The Gore, 189 Queen's Gate, SW7 5EX. *Tel* (0171) 584 6601, *fax* (0171) 589 8127. Peter McKay's hotel "of idiosyncratic charm and laid-back style" – 2 grand Victorian houses in tree-lined terrace, near Albert Hall, museums and Kensington Gdns. Attractive decor: antiques, oriental rugs, open fires, potted palms, over 5,000 paintings and prints. 54 bedrooms, varying greatly; best have a sitting room; some overlook adjacent Bulgarian embassy; some no-smoking. 2 popular restaurants. Public carpark nearby. Rooms: single £118, double £165, suite £240. Breakfast: continental £6.50, English £9.50. Bistro: set lunch £18, dinner £25; restaurant: alc dinner £45. (Underground: Gloucester Rd.)

A number of organisations in London offer B&B in private homes. They include:

At Home in London, 70 Black Lion Lane, London W6 9BE. *Tel* (0181) 748 1943, *fax* (0181) 748 2701. B&B in 70 private homes in central and west London, priced according to location. All close to public transport. B&B (2 nights min.): single £22–£34, double £42–£54.

Uptown Reservations: 50 Christchurch Street, London SW3 4AR. *Tel* (0171) 351 3445, *fax* (0171) 351 9383, *e-mail* uptown@dial.pipex.com. Upmarket accommodation in private homes in central London. B&B: single £55, double £75.

Hazlitt's, 6 Frith Street, W1V 5TZ. *Tel* (0171) 434 1771, *fax* (0171) 439 1524. Like *The Gore*, owned by Peter McKay: conversion of three 18th-century terraced houses (named for the essayist, who died here in 1830). In Soho, close to theatres, restaurants, museums. Victorian-style decor; informally run. 23 bedrooms, most light and airy; back ones quietest: (*excluding VAT*) single £115, double £148, suite £205; continental breakfast £6.75. (Underground: Tottenham Court Rd, Leicester Sq.)

Knightsbridge Hotel, 12 Beaufort Gardens SW3 1PT. *Tel* (0171) 589 9271, *fax* (0171) 823 9692. Conversion of Victorian terraced houses in quiet street off Brompton Road, close to Harrods and Hyde Pk. Bar, lounge, mini-health centre. Recently refurbished – unfussy modern decor. Helpful, unobtrusive staff. Good breakfast. 40 rooms, 10 apartments. B&B: single £90, double £135–£150, family £180. (Underground: Knightsbridge.)

The Pelham, 15 Cromwell Place, SW7 2LA. *Tel* (0171) 589 8288, *fax* (0171) 584 8444, *e-mail* firmdale@dircon.co.uk. Luxurious 44-bedroom hotel, with lavish decor – chandeliers, sumptuous drapes, etc. Modern, good-value cooking in blue-and-yellow basement restaurant. Rooms (*excluding VAT*): single from £130, double from £180. Breakfast £10.25–£13.25. Set lunch £10.95–£12.95; full alc £25. (Underground: South Kensington.)

La Reserve, 422–428 Fulham Road, SW6 1DU. *Tel* (0171) 385 8561, *fax* (0171) 385 7662. On Chelsea/Fulham border, by Chelsea Football Club. Public rooms with modern decor; restaurant open all day. 41 smallish bedrooms. B&B: single £79, double £95–£110. Set meals £12–£17.20. (Underground: Fulham Broadway.)

Searcy's Roof Garden Bedrooms, 30 Pavilion Road, SW1X 0HJ. *Tel* (0171) 584 4921, *fax* (0171) 823 8694. In small side street, close to Knightsbridge and Sloane Sq. No public rooms, no extras. 13 good-sized, well-equipped bedrooms; luxurious bathrooms; access to fully equipped kitchen. Single £83.50, double £119–£145.50. (Underground: Knightsbridge, Sloane Sq.)

The Stafford, 16–18 St James's Place, SW1A 1NJ. *Tel* (0171) 493 0111, *fax* (0171) 493 7121, *e-mail* info@thestaffordhotel.co.uk. In quiet backwater off St James's St, near Green Pk. Sedate, pricey hotel with 80 conventional, comfortable bedrooms and suites, 12 in converted carriage house. Traditional restaurant; American bar. Rooms (*excluding VAT*): single £180, double £195–£255, suite from £295. Breakfast £11.50–£15.50. Set meals £20.95–£26.25. (Underground: Green Pk.)

MANCHESTER   Map 4

In December 1997, the **Malmaison** group, which blazed a trail in Scotland, offering affordable accommodation (no room service or porterage) and bistro food in stylish conversions of interesting buildings, is opening a Manchester hotel on similar lines, thanks to a cash injection by the pop group Simply Red. In the former Joshua Hoyle building, opposite Piccadilly Station, it will have 116 bedrooms, a gym, a brasserie and a café.

Crescent Gate, Park Crescent, Victoria Park, Rusholme, M14 5RE. *Tel* (0161) 224 0672, *fax* (0161) 257 2822. Friendly guest house, run for many years by Terry Hughes, in quiet crescent 2 miles S of city centre, just off busy Wilmslow Rd, handy for university and airport. Carpark. 26 bedrooms, most with facilities *en suite*. B&B double £48. Evening meal £10.

The **Ox Noble**, 71 Liverpool Road, Castlefield, M3 4NQ. *Tel* (0161) 839 7740, *fax* (0161) 839 7760. Cheerful pub, recently renovated, in heritage area of city, across road from Museum of Science and Industry. 7 bedrooms, all with facilities *en suite* (most with shower only). Lancashire, vegetarian or continental breakfast. B&B double £39.95. Pub meals.

The **Victoria and Albert**, Water Street, M3 4JQ. *Tel* (0161) 832 1188, *fax* (0161) 834 2484. Considered by many to be the city's premier hotel. Conversion of two riverside warehouses, full of Mancunian character – decor themed to productions by Granada TV studios next door. Restaurant, café, pub. Wing for lone female guests (with CCTV, windows that are impossible to open from outside, ironing board, special toiletries, etc). 156 rooms. Midweek rate: single/double £140 (excluding breakfast, £11.95); B&B (weekends): single £85, double £95. Alc: restaurant from £25, café/brasserie £9.50–£17.50.

Further afield:

Alderley Edge Hotel, Macclesfield Road, Alderley Edge, Cheshire SK9 7BJ. *Tel* (01625) 583033, *fax* (01625) 586343. 14 miles S of Manchester; 7 miles from airport; city centre 20 mins by car/taxi. Red sandstone house, former home of wealthy cotton merchant. Classic French cooking in popular restaurant. 32 bedrooms (deluxe ones with whirlpool bath). Close to "The Edge", a famous beauty spot (stunning views of Cheshire Plain); 7 National Trust properties nearby, including Lyme Park ("Pemberley" exteriors in TV's *Pride and Prejudice*). Rooms: single £89.50–£102, double £99.50–£125; breakfast from £7.50. Set meals £22.95; alc £9.50–£21.95.

Hazeldean, 467 Bury New Road, Kersal, Salford, Greater Manchester M7 3NE. *Tel* (0161) 792 6667, *fax* (0161) 792 6668. Graham Chadwick's guest house in Victorian house in residential area of industrial city (painted by LS Lowry), 2½ miles from central Manchester. Pretty garden; carpark. 21 rooms. B&B: single from £30, double from £45. Evening meal £5–£10; bar snacks at weekend.

Normandie, Elbut Lane, Birtle, nr Bury, Greater Manchester, BL9 6UT. *Tel* (0161) 764 1170, *fax* (0161) 764 4866. In rural setting in Pennine foothills, 12 miles N of central Manchester (20 mins by car; awkward otherwise). Max and Susan Moussa's restaurant-with-rooms. French cooking in bright yellow dining room (with piped music). 23 bedrooms, large and comfortable but lacking character. B&B: single £59–£69, double £69–£79. Set lunch £12.50, dinner £15; alc (excluding wine) £30.

Etrop Grange, Thorley Lane, Manchester Airport, Greater Manchester M90 4EG. *Tel* (0161) 499 0500, *fax* (0161) 499 0970. Georgian Grade II listed country house, much extended, 12 miles from city centre (airport and road noise). Edwardian decor; antique and repro furniture; some original architectural features. Extensive function facilities. Friendly staff. Light meals and snacks all day; restaurant specialises in fish dishes. 40 bedrooms. B&B: single £105, double from £115.

Springfield Hotel, 99 Station Road, Marple, Greater Manchester SK6 6PA. *Tel* (0161) 449 0721, *fax* (0161) 449 0766. In attractive dormitory town, 11 miles SE of Manchester. Mr and Mrs Giannecchini's small Victorian hotel, 5 mins' walk from station with regular services to city, 25 mins' drive from airport; 10 mins to Stockport. 7 bedrooms. B&B: single £30–£40, double £45–£50. Home-cooked evening meal (weekdays only) £14.50.

Stanneylands Hotel, Stanneylands Road, Wilmslow, Cheshire SK9 4EY. *Tel* (01625) 525225, *fax* (01625) 537282. Luxurious Victorian country house in beautiful gardens. 12 miles from Manchester city centre, 3 miles from airport. 32 rooms: single £85, double £99. Breakfast £10.45. Set meals £13.75–£27.50.

PLYMOUTH Devon Map 1
Invicta, 11/12 Osborne Place, Lockyer Street, The Hoe, PL1 2PU. *Tel* (01752) 664997, *fax* (01752) 664994. Victorian house opposite Sir Francis Drake's bowling green and the Hoe (famous park); 5 mins' walk from centre and historic Barbican. Secure carpark. Plain decor. 23 bedrooms, most with facilities *en suite* (3 family). B&B: single £26–£39, double £50–£58; D,B&B £35–£45 per person.

PORTSMOUTH Hampshire Map 2
Beaufort, 71 Festing Road, Southsea PO4 0NQ. *Tel* (01705) 823707, *fax* (01705) 870270. Logis of Great Britain, in residential area, 1 min's walk from sea. Owned by Penny and Tony Freemantle for 10 years. Lounge, bar; restaurant, serving "good home-cooked fare". Garden, carpark. 20 bedrooms (8 no-smoking). B&B double £30. Set dinner £14.50.
Seacrest 12 South Parade, Southsea PO5 2JB. *Tel* (01705) 733192, *fax* (01705) 832523. Seafront hotel (good views) opposite D-Day museum. Resident proprietress, Antoinette Stretton. Simple decor. Comfortable lounge with leather seats. 27 bedrooms, varying in size. B&B double £48–£58. Evening meal £11.95.

REIGATE Surrey Map 2
The Cranleigh, 41 West Street, Reigate RH2 9BL. *Tel* (01737) 223417, *fax* (01737) 223734. Carol and Pino Bussandri's guest house at end of high street, in garden with swimming pool, tennis. Garden Room restaurant (dinners only) serves Italian cooking. 10 neat bedrooms: single £40–£55, double £75–£85. Dinner alc from £15 (excluding wine).

SALISBURY Wiltshire Map 2
Red Lion, Milford Street, SP1 2AN. *Tel* (01722) 323334, *fax* (01722) 325756. Michael Maidment's historic coaching inn (Best Western), in city centre, with creepered courtyard. Interesting old-world ambience, popular restaurant, clock collection. 54 bedrooms along rambling corridors. Parking awkward. Rooms: single £69.50–£85, double £84.50–£110. Breakfast: continental £5, English £9. Set lunch from £10.50, dinner from £17.50.
Milford Hall 206 Castle Street, SP1 3TE. *Tel* (01722) 417411, *fax* (01722) 419444. At uninteresting north end of town, close to A30, 10 mins' walk from centre. Georgian house in landscaped gardens. 35 bedrooms, most (plain but comfortable) in modern extension; food above average; parking easy. B&B: single £55–£67.50, double £69–£77.50; D,B&B: single £65–£78, double £99.50–£108.50.
Old Mill at Harnham, Town Path, Harnham SP2 8EU. *Tel* (01722) 327517, *fax* (01722) 333367. Historic building, once a paper mill, in lovely waterside setting, with millrace cascading through beamed restaurant. 1½ miles from city by A3094; 15-mins' walk across water meadow. 10 simple bedrooms. B&B: single £40, double £65.
Rose and Crown, Harnham Road, Harnham SP2 8JQ. *Tel* (01722) 399955, *fax* (01722) 339816. 13th-century half-timbered inn in

lovely setting on river Avon. 28 bedrooms, some in Tudor wing with old beams, modern ones in garden wing with cathedral views. Single £105, double £130–£145; breakfast £9.50. Bar snacks; alc in riverside restaurant *c.* £17.

Further afield
Little Langford Farmhouse, Little Langford SP3 4NP. *Tel* (01722) 790205, *fax* (01722) 790086. Patricia Helyer's B&B in spacious Victorian farmhouse, 8 miles N of Salisbury. Commanding position in Wylye valley, on Earl of Salisbury's estate; 1-acre grounds. Relaxed atmosphere, children welcomed. 3 simple bedrooms. B&B double £42.

SCARBOROUGH North Yorkshire Map 4
Interludes, 32 Princess Street, YO11 1QR. *Tel* (01723) 360513, *fax* (01723) 368597. Near castle and harbour: small guest house run by theatre *aficionados*, Ian Grundy and Bob Harris. Decorated with much theatrical memorabilia. 5 bedrooms. Continental, light or full English breakfast. 4-course evening meal at 6 pm (£13; limited choice, communally served at 2 mahogany tables). B&B £23–£36.
Tall Storeys, 131 Longwestgate, Old Town, YO11 1RQ. *Tel* (01723) 373696. Colin Milne's Grade II listed house, with simple decor, overlooking castle and harbour. 7 no-smoking bedrooms. B&B: single £30, double £48.

SHEFFIELD South Yorkshire Map 4
Staindrop Lodge, Lane End, Chapeltown, S30 4UH. *Tel* (0114) 284 6727, *fax* (0114) 284 6783. 6 miles N of centre. Bailey family's 19th-century house, ivy-covered, in mature gardens. Modern English cooking in large no-smoking restaurant. 13 bedrooms. B&B: single £59, double £74. Set lunch £9.25–£11.25; dinner £19.50 (including ½ bottle of wine weekdays)
Whitley Hall, Elliott Lane, Grenoside S30 3NR. *Tel* (0114) 245 4444, *fax* (0114) 245 5414. 4½ miles N of centre. Fearn family's part Elizabethan house: mullioned windows, flagged floors, balustraded gallery, oak panelling, country house decor. In 30-acre landscaped grounds: gardens, 2 lakes, croquet, putting, peacocks. 18 bedrooms. B&B: single £62, double £83–£99. English cooking in large restaurant: lunch (3-course) £12.95; dinner (5-course) £19.75.

YORK North Yorkshire Map 4
Dean Court, Duncombe Place, YO1 2EF. *Tel* (01904) 625082, *fax* (01904) 620305. Best Western hotel, recently refurbished, opposite Minster. Friendly staff, good facilities for children. Traditional restaurant serving adequate meals; conservatory tea room. Free valet parking. 40 bedrooms (12 no-smoking). B&B: single £70–£85, double £100–£115, suite £125–£145. Set lunch £13.50, dinner £21.

WALES

CARDIFF Map 3
Walton House, 37 Victoria Road, Penarth, CF64 3HY. *Tel* (01222) 707782, *fax* (01222) 711012. Vanessa and Gino Damiani's spacious Edwardian guest house in residential area. 10 mins' walk from Penarth seafront; 4 miles from centre. Plain decor; home-cooked meals £13.50. 12 rooms. B&B: single £25–£30, double £40–£47.

The Town House, 70 Cathedral Road, CF1 9LL. *Tel* (01222) 239399, *fax* (01222) 223214. B&B in Victorian gothic town house in conservation area by castle, with American owners, Iris and Bart Zuzik. 7 simple bedrooms. B&B: single £39.50, double £49.50.

SCOTLAND

ABERDEEN   Map 5
Craiglynn, 36 Fonthill Road, AB11 6UJ. *Tel* (01224) 584050, *fax* (01224) 212225, *e-mail* craiglynn hotel aberdeen@compuserve.com. Chris and Hazel Mann's Victorian granite guest house in residential area, between Duthie Park and Union Street. Smoking in lounge only. 9 simple bedrooms. B&B: single £29–£46, double £39–£65. Home-cooked evening meal in panelled, parquet-floored, former billiard room: £14.95.
The Marcliffe at Pitfodels, North Deeside Road, Pitfodels, AB15 9YA. *Tel* (01224) 861000, *fax* (01224) 868860, *e-mail* stewart@marcliff.win-uk.net. In 8-acre landscaped grounds in West End of city, off A93 Deeside road. Stewart and Sheila Spence's luxurious new, large, white hotel, traditional in style. Good food in smart restaurant and less formal conservatory. Large function facilities. 42 bedrooms (1 adapted for ఉ); 19 suites planned for 1998. B&B: single £105–£155, double £115–£175, suite £190–£290. Full alc £32.50.
Palm Court, 81 Seafield Road, AB15 7YU. *Tel* (01224) 310351, *fax* (01224) 312707, *e-mail* palm.court@exodus.uk.com. In quiet residential area in West End, Ricky Simpson's hotel with alc meals in conservatory restaurant, light meals in bar. 3 golf courses close by. 24 bedrooms. B&B: single £70–£80, double £80–£90. Bar meals *c.* £12.
Further afield
Cromlet Hill Guest House, Cromlet Hill, South Road, Oldmeldrum, Aberdeenshire AB51 0AB. *Tel* (01651) 872315, *fax* (01651) 872164. In historic old town, 16 miles (*c* 30 mins' drive) NW of Aberdeen, 15 mins from airport. John Page's listed neo-classical Georgian mansion (*c.* 1805) in conservation area. Quiet garden; fine views. 3 bedrooms. B&B £25–£30. Communal evening meal £15.
Meldrum House, Oldmeldrum, Aberdeenshire AB51 0AE. *Tel* (01651) 872294, *fax* (01651) 872464. In 15-acre park and garden, 1½ miles from town centre on A947. Douglas and Eileen Pearson's part 13th-century baronial house, with antiques, *objets d'art* and ancestral portraits. Traditional Scottish cooking. 9 bedrooms. B&B: single £80, double £105–£115. Set dinner £25.70–£27.70.
   See also entry for **MARYCULTER**, 8 miles S of Aberdeen.

DUNDEE   Map 5
Invercarse, 371 Perth Road, DD2 1PG. *Tel* (01382) 669231, *fax* (01382) 644112. On W side of city, near university. Extended Victorian silk mercer's mansion in large grounds on hill, overlooking river Tay (Best Western). Large function facilities. 35 bedrooms (17 no-smoking). B&B: single £32–£62, double £64–£80, suite £90. Set lunch £10, dinner £12–£14.95.
Shaftesbury Hotel, 1 Hyndford Street, off Perth Road, DD1 1HQ. *Tel* (01382) 669216, *fax* (01382) 641598. "An honest enterprise, with helpful staff" – former 19th-century jute baron's mansion in West End, 5 mins by car from centre. 3-course dinners in restaurant; garden room for light meals. 12 bedrooms. B&B: single £39.50–£44.50, double £58–£68.

Strathdon, 277 Perth Road, DD2 1JS. *Tel/fax* (01382) 665648. Ian and Carole Hornsby's Edwardian terrace house, close to university, city centre. 10 rooms, some with river view. B&B: single £25–£30, double £44. Modern British cooking alc in no-smoking restaurant.

Further afield

The Old Mansion House, Auchterhouse, by Dundee DD3 0QN. *Tel* (01382) 320366, *fax* (01382) 320400. 6 miles NW of Dundee. 16th-century mansion on knoll, with fine gardens, small stream, swimming pool, croquet, tennis. Fine plaster work in public rooms; restaurant with Jacobean fireplace serving Scottish/European cooking. Bar meals available. 6 bedrooms, some large. New owners in 1997 Mr and Mrs Bertschy. B&B £55–£75. Set lunch from £6.50, dinner £27.

EDINBURGH   Map 5

24 Northumberland Street, 24 Northumberland Street, EH3 6LS. *Tel* (0131) 556 8140, *fax* (0131) 556 4423. B&B in Grade I Georgian New Town house, owned by antique dealers David and Theresa Ingram. Classy decor: fine antiques, porcelain, pictures, rugs etc. 3 twin-bedded rooms. B&B: single £45, double £70.

GLASGOW   Map 5

Kirkton House, Darleith Road, Cardross G82 5EZ. *Tel* (01389) 841951, *fax* (01389) 841868, *e-mail* kirktonhouse@compuserve.com. Stewart and Gillian Macdonald's 160-year-old converted farmhouse built round courtyard, with superb views of the Clyde, offering "country guest accommodation". Unpretentious and informal; 6 simple double bedrooms, some suitable for families. Good plain country meals, excellent Scottish breakfasts. 2-acre grounds and paddock. 18 miles NW of Glasgow; 25 mins by car to airport. B&B: £31–£38.50. Set dinner £18.75.

NORTHERN IRELAND

BELFAST   Map 6

Duke's, 65–67 University Street, BT7 1HL. *Tel* (01232) 236666, *fax* (01232) 237177. 1 mile S of city centre, just behind Queen's University. Victorian residence in tree-lined street, well modernised, comfortable, with restaurant, bar; popular meeting point for business and university people. Well-equipped gymnasium. 21 bedrooms. B&B: single £55–£87.50, double £65–£105. Meals £10.50–£15.

Further afield

The Dunadry, 2 Islandreagh Drive, Dunadry, Co. Antrim BT41 2HA. *Tel* (01849) 432474, *fax* (01849) 433389. 15 miles NW of Belfast, 4 miles SE of Antrim, just off M2 motorway, and 5 miles NE of Belfast airport. Set amid quiet countryside, unusual modern white building, now fairly swish roadhouse-type hotel, much used for functions. Impressive public rooms; bedrooms with Scandinavian feel; good restaurant; vast breakfast. 10-acre grounds with country club, free to residents (huge indoor pool, jacuzzi, solarium, beauty salon); croquet, cycling, trout fishing. 67 bedrooms. B&B: single £50–£115, double £75–£140. Set meals £15–£20.

The Old Inn, 15 Main Street, Crawfordsburn, Co. Down BT19 1JH. *Tel* (01247) 853255, *fax* (01247) 852775. In village 10 miles E of Belfast, 3 miles W of Bangor, 1 mile from sea. Historic inn (1614), renovated in fancy style with much wood panelling, chintz, pastels; canopied four-posters; quaint honeymoon cottage. Conservatory-style restaurant serving seafood; simpler bistro. 32 bedrooms. B&B: single £45, double £65–£85. Meals £15–£20.

IRELAND

DUBLIN   Map 6
Albany House, 84 Harcourt Street, Dublin 2. *Tel* (01) 475 1092, *fax* (01) 475 1093. Central, off St Stephen's Green, converted Georgian house with new owner (since early 1997) Richard Byrne, genial host. Large rooms, elegant furnishings, good breakfasts. Carpark. 29 bedrooms. B&B: single IR£60–£80, double IR£90–£110.
The Clarence, 6–8 Wellington Quay, Dublin 2. *Tel* (01) 670 9000, *fax* (01) 670 7800. Central, on river Liffey, at Temple Bar. Dublin's top fashionable hotel, opened 1996; owned by Bono and the Edge of U2, who are often present and have just refurbished for £50 million. Crowded with rock stars, fashion designers, film directors, etc. Assertive contemporary decor in academic/ecclesiastical style, with bold colours. 49 super-equipped bedrooms rivalling Hollywood, bathrooms with glittery mosaics, excellent food in *Tea Room* restaurant. Roof terrace facing river. Rooms: single/double IR£165–£190. Breakfast IR£13. Set lunch IR£17.50; alc IR£19.85–£34.45.
Georgian House, 18 Lower Baggott Street, Dublin 2. *Tel* (01) 661 8832, *fax* (01) 661 8834. Central, near St Stephen's Green. Two fine Georgian houses comprise Annette O'Sullivan's elegant hotel, comfortable, quiet, with good service. Basement restaurant serves excellent breakfasts, goodish seafood dishes. Jolly bar. Lock-up garage. 33 bedrooms: single IR£55–£75, double IR£74–£98. Breakfast £2–£5.
Longfield's, Fitzwilliam Street Lower, Dublin 2. *Tel* (01) 676 1367, *fax* (01) 676 1542. Central, in heart of Georgian Dublin, small, select hotel formed from 2 Georgian houses. Elegant furnishings, attractive lounge; good food in basement restaurant. 26 bedrooms. B&B: single IR£70–£85, double IR£90–£105. Set meals IR£14.50–£27.50.
Raglan Lodge, 10 Raglan Road, Dublin 4. *Tel* (01) 660 6697, *fax* (01) 660 6781. In residential Ballsbridge, 1 mile SE of centre. Helen Moran's friendly, above-average guest house in restored Victorian mansion. Attractive rooms, some antiques. Excellent award-winning breakfasts. Small garden. Secure car park. 7 bedrooms. B&B: single IR£50, double IR£90.
Further afield
Moytura House, Saval Park Road, Dalkey, Co. Dublin. *Tel* (01) 285 2371, *fax* (01) 235 0633. In fashionable village by sea 8 miles SE of Dublin (18 mins by DART train), 2 miles from car ferry at Dun Laoghaire. Corinne Giacometti's small, much-admired B&B guest house with family atmosphere, in 1881 building; garden. 3 bedrooms. B&B IR£35–£45.

Even if all room prices are the same, hotels may give you a less good room in the hope of selling their better rooms to late customers. It always pays to discuss accommodation in detail when making a reservation and to ask for a free upgrade on arrival if the hotel isn't full.

Alphabetical list of hotels

(S) indicates a Shortlist entry

Maps

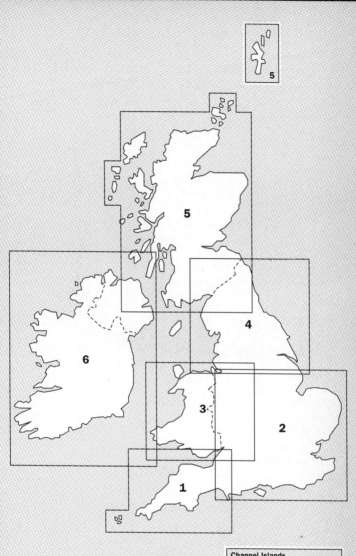

Channel Islands

1

Not to scale

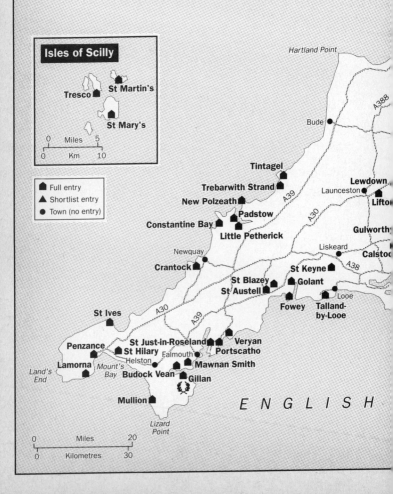

BRISTOL

Pembroke • Tenby

Hartland Point

Isles of Scilly

Tresco St Martin's

St Mary's

0 Miles 5

0 Km 10

■ Full entry
▲ Shortlist entry
● Town (no entry)

Bude

Tintagel

Trebarwith Strand

New Polzeath

Constantine Bay **Padstow**

Little Petherick

Newquay

Crantock

St Ives

Penzance

Lamorna

St Just-in-Roseland

St Hilary

Helston

Budock Vean

Mullion

Land's End

Mount's Bay

Lizard Point

Launceston

Lewdown

Lifto

Gulworth

Liskeard

Calsto

St Keyne

St Blazey **Golant**

St Austell

Fowey Talland-

by-Looe

Looe

A388

A39

A30

A38

Veryan

Portscatho

Falmouth

Mawnan Smith

Gillan

ENGLISH

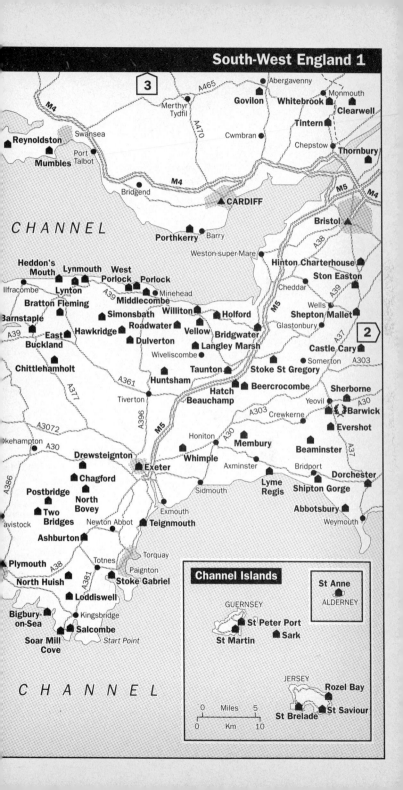

3

Abergavenny
Govilon Whitebrook Monmouth
Merthyr Clearwell
Tydfil Tintern
Cwmbran Thornbury
Reynoldston Swansea
Port Chepstow
Mumbles Talbot
M4 Bridgend M5 M4
M4
Bridgend CARDIFF Bristol
CHANNEL Porthkerry Barry A38
Weston-super-Mare
Hinton Charterhouse
Heddon's Ston Easton
Mouth Lynmouth West Porlock Cheddar
Porlock Minehead Wells A39 Shepton Mallet
Ilfracombe Lynton Middlecombe A39
Bratton Fleming Williton Holford Glastonbury A37
Barnstaple Simonsbath Roadwater Vellow Bridgwater Castle Cary
East Hawkridge Dulverton Langley Marsh
Buckland Wiveliscombe Somerton A303 2
Chittlehamholt Taunton Stoke St Gregory Sherborne
A377 Huntsham Hatch Beercrombe Yeovil A30
A361 Beauchamp Barwick
Tiverton A303 Crewkerne Evershot
A3072 A396 Honiton A30 Membury Beaminster A37
Okehampton A30 Drewsteignton Whimple Bridport Dorchester
A386 Chagford Exeter Axminster Lyme Shipton Gorge
Postbridge North Sidmouth Regis Abbotsbury
Two Bovey Exmouth Weymouth
Tavistock Bridges Newton Abbot Teignmouth
Ashburton Torquay
Plymouth Totnes Paignton
North Huish A381 Stoke Gabriel
Loddiswell
Bigbury- Kingsbridge
on-Sea Salcombe
Soar Mill Start Point
Cove

Channel Islands

St Anne
ALDERNEY
GUERNSEY
St Peter Port
St Martin Sark

JERSEY
Rozel Bay
St Saviour
St Brelade

0 Miles 5
0 Km 10

CHANNEL

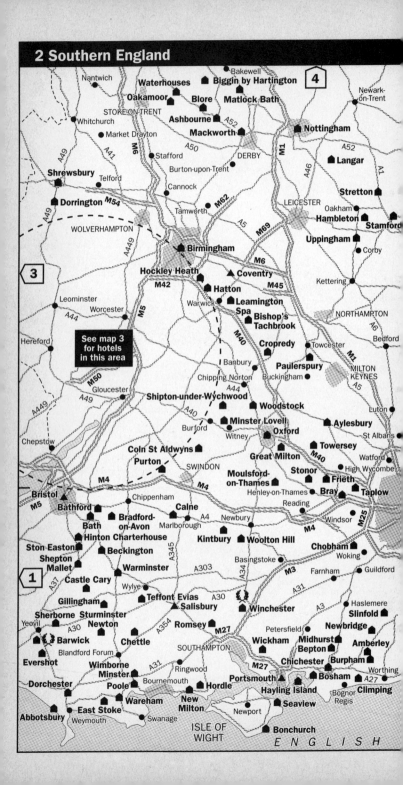

4

Nantwich
Waterhouses
Bakewell
Biggin by Hartington
Newark-on-Trent
Oakamoor
Blore
Matlock Bath
Whitchurch
Market Drayton
STOKE-ON-TRENT
Ashbourne
A52
Mackworth
Nottingham
Stafford
A50
Burton-upon-Trent
DERBY
M1
A52
Langar
Shrewsbury
Telford
Cannock
A46
A1
Dorrington
M54
Tamworth
A5
LEICESTER
Stretton
Oakham
Stamford
A49
WOLVERHAMPTON
M62
M69
Hambleton
Uppingham
A6
Leominster
Worcester
Birmingham
M6
Corby
Kettering
NORTHAMPTON
Bedford
Hockley Heath
Coventry
M42
Hatton
M45
Hereford
Warwick
Leamington Spa
Bishop's Tachbrook
Cropredy
Towcester
Paulerspury
MILTON KEYNES
A5
M50
Gloucester
A40
Banbury
Chipping Norton
Buckingham
A44
Luton
Chepstow
Shipton-under-Wychwood
Woodstock
Burford
Minster Lovell
Witney
Aylesbury
St Albans
Oxford
Towersey
Watford
Coln St Aldwyns
SWINDON
Great Milton
M40
Stonor
High Wycombe
Purton
Moulsford-on-Thames
Frieth
M4
M4
Henley-on-Thames
Bray
Taplow
Bristol
Chippenham
Reading
M25
M5
Bathford
Calne
Newbury
Windsor
M4
Bath
Bradford-on-Avon
Marlborough
A4
Kintbury
Woolton Hill
Chobham
Hinton Charterhouse
M3
Ston Easton
Beckington
Basingstoke
Woking
Shepton Mallet
Warminster
A303
Farnham
Guildford
Castle Cary
Wylye
A31
Gillingham
Teffont Evias
Salisbury
Winchester
A3
Haslemere
Sherborne
Sturminster Newton
A354
Romsey
M27
Petersfield
Slinfold
Yeovil
Chettle
Newbridge
Barwick
Blandford Forum
SOUTHAMPTON
Wickham
Midhurst
Bepton
Amberley
Evershot
Wimborne Minster
A31
Ringwood
Chichester
Burpham
Dorchester
Poole
Bournemouth
Portsmouth
Bosham
Worthing
A27
Wareham
New Milton
Hordle
Hayling Island
Climping
Bognor Regis
Abbotsbury
East Stoke
Weymouth
Swanage
Newport
Seaview
ISLE OF WIGHT
Bonchurch
ENGLISH

See map 3 for hotels in this area

A49
A41
A6
M6
A52
M1
A45
A44
A345
A37
A30
A354
M4
M5
A43

Skegness

Boston

A16

THE
WASH

A17

Spalding

King's Lynn

Bourne

Wisbech

A47

Peterborough

Downham
Market

A19

Huntingdon

Ely

Wells-
next-
the-
Sea

Burnham
Market

Blakeney

Morston

Cromer

Great Snoring

Erpingham

A149

Fakenham

Aylsham

Grimston

East Dereham

A47

Swaffham

Norwich

Wymondham

Great
Yarmouth

A11

A143

Thetford

Diss

A12

Cambridge

Bury St
Edmunds

Southwold

Newmarket

A45

Rougham

Theberton

Otley

Leiston

Aldeburgh

M11

Duxford

Bradfield
Combust

Lavenham

Campsea Ashe

Royston

Saffron
Walden

Woodbridge

A131

Hintlesham

Ipswich

Letchworth

Littlebury Green

A1(M)

Great
Dunmow

Dedham

Felixstowe

A10

M11

Bishop's
Stortford

Braintree

A12

Harwich

Hertford

Colchester

Chelmsford

Clacton-on-Sea

Basildon

LONDON

Southend-on-Sea

Tilbury

Canvey

Orpington

Rochester

Croydon

M25

Sittingbourne

Margate

M20

M2

Ramsgate

Maidstone

Canterbury

Reigate

Sevenoaks

Boughton Monchelsea

A2

West Cliffe

M23

East Grinstead

Ashford

M20

Dover

Horley

Hartfield

Tunbridge Wells

Frant

Bethersden

Folkestone

Lower Beeding

Cranbrook

Sandgate

Cuckfield

A259

Uckfield

Rushlake
Green

Rye

New Romney

Lewes

A21

Battle

Wilmington

Brighton

A27

Hastings

West Dean

Eastbourne

■ Full entry
▲ Shortlist entry
● Town (no entry)

0 ———— Miles ———— 40
0 ———— Kilometres ———— 60

C H A N N E L

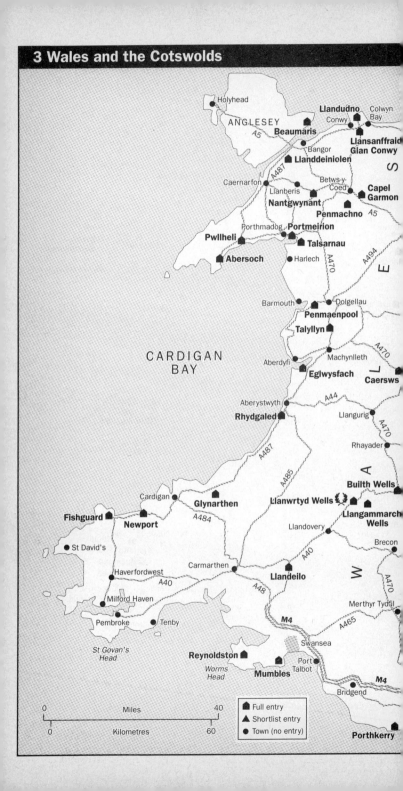

3 Wales and the Cotswolds

Holyhead

ANGLESEY

Llandudno
Colwyn Bay
Conwy

A5

Beaumaris

Llansanffraid Glan Conwy

Bangor

Llanddeiniolen

Caernarfon

Betws-y-Coed

Capel Garmon

Llanberis

Nantgwynant

Penmachno

A5

Porthmadog

Portmeirion

Pwllheli

Talsarnau

Abersoch

Harlech

A470

A494

Barmouth

Dolgellau

Penmaenpool

Talyllyn

CARDIGAN BAY

Aberdyfi

Machynlleth

A470

Eglwysfach

Caersws

Aberystwyth

A44

Llangurig

A470

Rhydgaled

Rhayader

A487

A485

Builth Wells

Cardigan

Glynarthen

Llanwrtyd Wells

Llangammarch Wells

Fishguard

A484

Newport

Llandovery

St David's

Brecon

Haverfordwest

Carmarthen

A40

Llandeilo

A40

Milford Haven

A48

Merthyr Tydfil

Pembroke

Tenby

St Govan's Head

M4

A465

A470

Swansea

Worms Head

Reynoldston

Port Talbot

Mumbles

M4

Bridgend

Porthkerry

| 0 | Miles | 40 |

| 0 | Kilometres | 60 |

■ Full entry
▲ Shortlist entry
● Town (no entry)

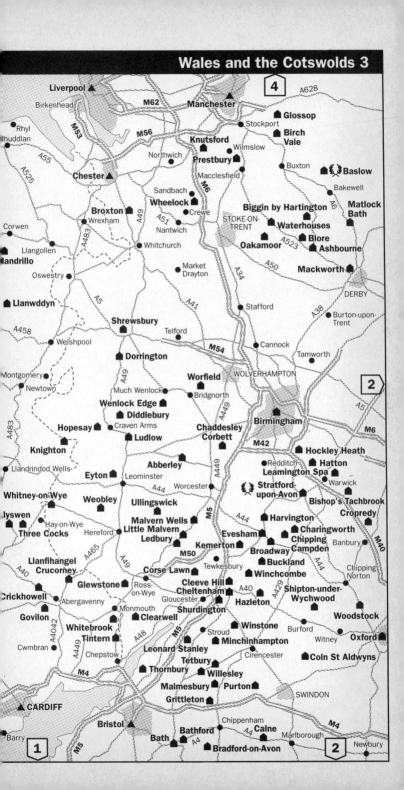

4

A628

Liverpool

Birkenhead

M62

Manchester

Glossop

Stockport

Birch Vale

Rhyl

Rhuddlan

A525

M53

M56

Knutsford

Wilmslow

Buxton

Baslow

Bakewell

Northwich

Prestbury

A55

Chester

Macclesfield

Matlock Bath

Sandbach

Wheelock

Broxton

Wrexham

Crewe

M6

Biggin by Hartington

Waterhouses

A6

Corwen

A49

A51

Nantwich

STOKE-ON-TRENT

Blore

Oakamoor

Ashbourne

A523

Llangollen

Llandrillo

Whitchurch

Mackworth

Oswestry

Market Drayton

A50

DERBY

Llanwddyn

A5

A41

Stafford

A38

Burton-upon-Trent

A458

Shrewsbury

Telford

Welshpool

Dorrington

M54

Cannock

Tamworth

2

Montgomery

Newtown

Worfield

WOLVERHAMPTON

A5

Much Wenlock

Bridgnorth

A49

M6

Wenlock Edge

Diddlebury

A483

Hopesay

Craven Arms

Chaddesley Corbett

Birmingham

M42

Hockley Heath

Knighton

Ludlow

Redditch

Hatton

Abberley

A449

Leamington Spa

Warwick

Llandrindod Wells

Eyton

Leominster

A44

Worcester

Stratford-upon-Avon

Bishop's Tachbrook

Cropredy

Whitney-on-Wye

Weobley

Ullingswick

Harvington

Charingworth

Llyswen

Hay-on-Wye

Hereford

Malvern Wells

Little Malvern

M5

A44

Evesham

Chipping Campden

Banbury

M40

Three Cocks

Ledbury

Kemerton

Broadway

A465

A49

M50

Buckland

Chipping Norton

Llanfihangel Crucorney

Corse Lawn

Tewkesbury

Winchcombe

Crickhowell

Glewstone

Ross-on-Wye

Cleeve Hill

A40

A429

Shipton-under-Wychwood

Abergavenny

Cheltenham

Hazleton

Woodstock

Govilon

Monmouth

Gloucester

Shurdington

A40

A4042

Whitebrook

Clearwell

Winstone

Burford

Oxford

Cwmbran

Tintern

A48

M5

Stroud

Minchinhampton

Witney

Coln St Aldwyns

Chepstow

Leonard Stanley

Tetbury

Cirencester

M4

Thornbury

Willesley

SWINDON

CARDIFF

Malmesbury

Purton

Grittleton

Barry

Bristol

Chippenham

Calne

Marlborough

M4

1

M5

Bathford

A4

2

Bath

Bradford-on-Avon

Newbury

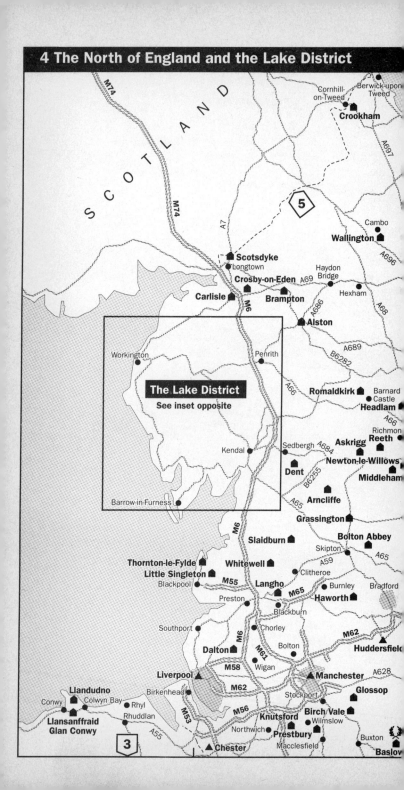

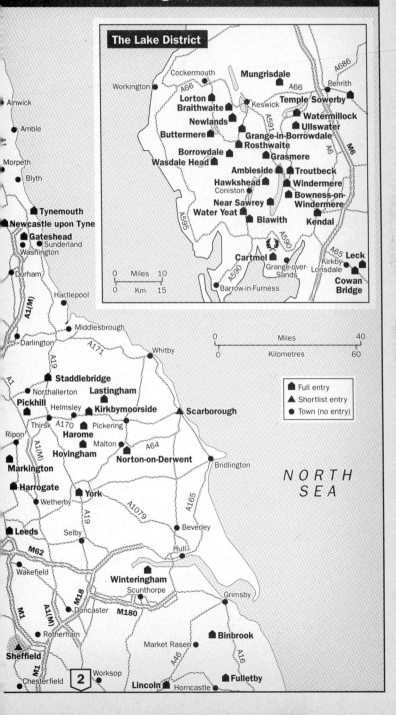

The Lake District

Cockermouth
Workington
A66
Mungrisdale
A66
Penrith
Lorton
Braithwaite
Keswick
Temple Sowerby
Newlands
A591
Watermillock
Buttermere
Grange-in-Borrowdale
Ullswater
Borrowdale
Rosthwaite
A6
Wasdale Head
Grasmere
Ambleside
Troutbeck
Hawkshead
Windermere
Coniston
Bowness-on-
Near Sawrey
Windermere
Water Yeat
Blawith
Kendal
A595
A590
A65
Leck
Cartmel
Kirkby
Grange-over-
Lonsdale
Sands
Cowan
Bridge
Barrow-in-Furness
A686
M6

0   Miles   10
0   Km   15

Alnwick
Amble
Morpeth
Blyth
Tynemouth
Newcastle upon Tyne
Gateshead
Sunderland
Washington
Durham
Hartlepool
A1(M)
Middlesbrough
Darlington
A171
Whitby
A19
A1
Staddlebridge
Northallerton
Lastingham
Pickhill
Helmsley
Kirkbymoorside
Scarborough
Thirsk
A170
Pickering
Ripon
Harome
Malton
A64
Hovingham
Markington
Norton-on-Derwent
Bridlington
A1(M)
Harrogate
York
Wetherby
A1079
A165
Beverley
Leeds
Selby
M62
Hull
Wakefield
A19
M18
Winteringham
Scunthorpe
M1
A1(M)
Doncaster
M180
Grimsby
Rotherham
Binbrook
Market Rasen
Sheffield
M1
A46
A16
Chesterfield
Worksop
Fulletby
Lincoln
Horncastle

NORTH
SEA

Legend:
■ Full entry
▲ Shortlist entry
● Town (no entry)

0   Miles   40
0   Kilometres   60

2

5 Scotland

The Uists & Barra

Lochmaddy
NORTH UIST
SOUTH UIST
Lochboisdale
Outer Hebrides
Pollochar
Tangusdale
BARRA
Castlebay

YELL
UNST
MAINLAND
Busta
Lerwick
Walls

Shetland Islands

0   Miles   40
0 Kilometres 60

Orkney Islands
WESTRAY **Pierowall**
SANDAY
Evie
Shapinsay
Kirkwall
MAINLAND
HOY

Outer Hebrides
LEWIS
Timsgarry
Stornoway
Scourie
Thurso
Forss
A836
Wick
A9
Kylesku
A836
Lochinver
A837
Lairg
Ardvourlie
Achiltibuie
Tarbert
Laide
Ullapool
HARRIS
Gairloch
A835
Dornoch
MORAY FIRTH
Dingwall
Dunvegan
Shieldaig
Nairn
Elgin
Portree
Plockton
Bunchrew
Rothes
A98
SKYE
A890
Muir of Ord
Inverness
A96
A92
Bridge of Marnoch
Kyle of Lochalsh
A9
Glenlivet
Glenelg
Grantown-on-Spey
Isle Ornsay
A82
Fort Augustus
Dulnain Bridge
Kildrummy
RUM
Mallaig
Ballater
Aberdeen
A830
Banavie
A86
Kingussie
Maryculter
Arisaig
Spean Bridge
Banchory
Braemar
A93
Strontian
Fort William
A9
A94
Tobermory
Killiecrankie
MULL
Dervaig
Strathtummel
Port Appin
Pitlochry
Pennyghael
Eriska
Aberfeldy
A82
Bunessan
Oban
Dunkeld
Kinclaven
Tyndrum
Guildtown
Knipoch
Kilchrenan
Arduaine
Balquhidder
Perth
Dundee
Crinan
Port of Menteith
Callander
Newport-on-Tay
Colonsay
Lochgilphead
Dairsie
St Andrews
Kilfinan
Stirling
Markinch
JURA
Dunoon
Glenrothes
FIRTH OF FORTH
Kirkcaldy
ISLAY
BUTE
Greenock
Falkirk
Dunbar
Glasgow
M8
A1
EDINBURGH
Lochranza
Brodick
Kilmarnock
Berwick-upon-Tweed
Peebles
Chirnside
Glen Cloy
ARRAN
A83
Innerleithen
Swinton
Campbeltown
Ayr
Biggar
Skirling
Selkirk
St Boswells
FIRTH OF CLYDE
A77
A76
M74
Moffat
Hawick
Jedburgh
A7
M6(9)
4
Ballantrae
Newton Stewart
Canonbie
ENGLAND
A75
Stranraer
Gatehouse of Fleet
Dumfries
Portpatrick
Kirkcudbright
Auchencairn
Carlisle
M6

■ Full entry
▲ Shortlist entry
● Town (no entry)

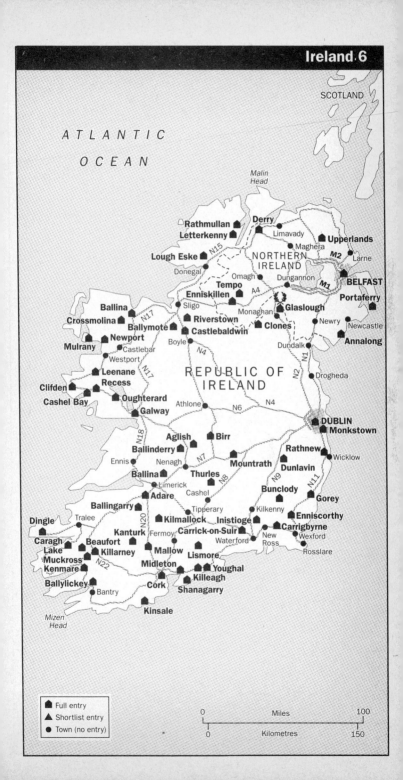

Ireland 6

SCOTLAND

A T L A N T I C

O C E A N

Malin Head

Rathmullan
Letterkenny
Derry
Limavady
Maghera
Upperlands
M2
Larne

Lough Eske
Donegal
NORTHERN IRELAND
Omagh
Dungannon
M1
BELFAST

Tempo
Enniskillen
Sligo
Monaghan
Glaslough
Portaferry

Ballina
Crossmolina
Riverstown
Clones
Newry
Newcastle

Ballymote
Castlebaldwin
Boyle

Newport
Castlebar
Annalong

Mulrany
Westport
Dundalk

Leenane
Recess
N4
REPUBLIC OF IRELAND
N2
Drogheda

Clifden
Oughterard
N17

Cashel Bay
Galway
Athlone
N6
N4
DUBLIN
Monkstown

Aglish
Birr

Ballinderry
Rathnew
Wicklow

Ballina
Ennis
Nenagh
N7
Mountrath
Dunlavin
N9

Adare
Thurles
N8
Bunclody
Gorey

Cashel
Kilkenny
Enniscorthy

Ballingarry
N20
Tipperary
Inistioge
Carrigbyrne

Dingle
Tralee
Kilmallock
Carrick-on-Suir
New Ross
Wexford

Caragh Lake
Kanturk
Fermoy
Waterford
Rosslare

Beaufort
Killarney
Mallow
Lismore

Muckross
N22
Midleton
Youghal

Kenmare
Cork
Kileagh

Ballylickey
Bantry
Shanagarry

Mizen Head
Kinsale

N15
N17
N18
N1

Legend:
- Full entry
- Shortlist entry
- Town (no entry)

0   Miles   100
0   Kilometres   150

Exchange rates

These rates for buying currency are correct at time of printing but in some cases may be wildly awry at the time of publication. It is essential that you check with banks or newspapers for up-to-date pound and dollar equivalents.

£1 (Pound sterling) = \$1.63 (US Dollars)

£1 (Pound sterling) = C\$2.27 (Canadian Dollars)

IR£1 (Punt) = \$1.58 (US Dollars)

IR£1 (Punt) = C\$2.20 (Canadian Dollars)

Champagne winners: Report of the Year competition

As usual we have awarded a dozen bottles of champagne for the best reports of the year. A bottle apiece will go to the following generous and eloquent readers for their contributions to this volume. A further dozen bottles will be awarded to readers who write to us about hotels on the Continent, when that volume is published early in 1998.

Mrs Romney Bathurst of Cashiers, North Carolina
Janice Carrera of London
Sebastian Chamberlain of Ringwood, Hampshire
Patricia Darby of Alcester, Warwickshire
Sir Timothy Harford of Evesham, Worcestershire
Ann Laurence of Oxford
Trevor Lockwood of Helston, Cornwall
Father Gordon Murray of London
Richard and Sheila Owen of Welwyn, Herts
Brian and Eve Webb of Taunton, Somerset
Ruth West of London
AP Wiltshire of Broadchalke, Wiltshire

Another case will be on offer for 1999. No special entry form is required; everything we receive in the course of the year will qualify. A winner may be someone who nominates a new hotel or comments on an existing one. We award champagne to those whose reports are consistently useful, as well as to individually brilliant examples of the art of hotel criticism.

Hotel reports

The report forms on the following pages may be used to endorse or criticise an existing entry or to nominate a hotel that you feel deserves inclusion in the *Guide*. But it is not essential that you use our forms or restrict yourself to the space available.

All reports (*each on a separate piece of paper, please*) should include your name and address, the name and location of the hotel, and the date and length of your stay. Please nominate only hotels you have visited in the past 12 months unless you are sure from friends that standards have been maintained. And please be as specific as possible, and critical where appropriate, about the character of the building, the public rooms and the bedrooms, the meals, the service, the nightlife, the grounds.

We should also be grateful for some impression of the location as well as of the hotel, particularly in less familiar regions. Comments about worthwhile places to visit in the neighbourhood and, in the case of B&B hotels, recommendable restaurants would also be much appreciated.

Do not feel embarrassed about writing at length. We want the *Guide* to convey the special flavour of its hotels, so the more time and trouble you take in providing small details that will help to make a description come alive, the more valuable to others will be the published result. Many nominations just don't tell us enough. We mind having to pass up a potentially attractive hotel because the report is inadequate. You need not bother with prices or routine information about the number of rooms and facilities; we obtain such details direct from the hotels. We want readers to supply information that is not accessible elsewhere. And we should be extremely grateful, in the case of foreign hotels and new nominations, if you would include brochures whenever possible. Nominations for the 1999 edition, which will be published in the US in December 1998, should reach us not later than 25 May 1998. The latest date for comments on existing entries is 1 June 1998. For the Europe volume we need nominations by 18 October 1998, and reports no later than 6 November 1998.

Please never tell a hotel that you intend to file a report. Anonymity is essential to objectivity.

Please let us know if you would like us to send you more report forms. Our address is: The Good Hotel Guide, Freepost PAM 2931, London W11 4BR, for UK correspondents (no stamp needed).

Reports can also be faxed to us on (0171) 602 4182, or sent by e-mail to Goodhotel@aol.com.

Reports posted outside the UK should be addressed to: The Good Hotel Guide, 50 Addison Avenue, London W11 4BR, England (stamped normally).

[1998]

To: *The Good Hotel Guide*, Freepost PAM 2931, London W11 4BR

NOTE: No stamps needed in UK, but letters posted outside the UK should be addressed to 50 Addison Avenue, London W11 4BR, England, and stamped normally. Unless asked not to, we shall assume that we may publish your name if you are recommending a new hotel or supporting an existing entry. If you would like more report forms please tick ☐

Name of Hotel _____

Address _____

_____

Date of most recent visit   Duration of visit
☐ New recommendation   ☐ Comment on existing entry
Report:

I am not connected directly or indirectly with the management or proprietors

Signed _____

Name (CAPITALS PLEASE)_____

Address _____

_____

To: *The Good Hotel Guide*, Freepost PAM 2931, London W11 4BR

NOTE: No stamps needed in UK, but letters posted outside the UK should be addressed to 50 Addison Avenue, London W11 4BR, England, and stamped normally. Unless asked not to, we shall assume that we may publish your name if you are recommending a new hotel or supporting an existing entry. If you would like more report forms please tick ☐

Name of Hotel _____

Address _____

_____

Date of most recent visit   Duration of visit
☐ New recommendation   ☐ Comment on existing entry
Report:

Please continue overleaf

I am not connected directly or indirectly with the management or proprietors

Signed _____

Name (CAPITALS PLEASE)_____

Address _____

_____

To: *The Good Hotel Guide*, Freepost PAM 2931, London W11 4BR

NOTE: No stamps needed in UK, but letters posted outside the UK should be addressed to 50 Addison Avenue, London W11 4BR, England, and stamped normally. Unless asked not to, we shall assume that we may publish your name if you are recommending a new hotel or supporting an existing entry. If you would like more report forms please tick ☐

Name of Hotel _____

Address _____

_____

Date of most recent visit   Duration of visit
☐ New recommendation   ☐ Comment on existing entry
Report:

I am not connected directly or indirectly with the management or proprietors

Signed _____

Name (CAPITALS PLEASE)_____

Address _____

_____

[1998]

To: *The Good Hotel Guide*, Freepost PAM 2931, London W11 4BR

NOTE: No stamps needed in UK, but letters posted outside the UK should be addressed to 50 Addison Avenue, London W11 4BR, England, and stamped normally. Unless asked not to, we shall assume that we may publish your name if you are recommending a new hotel or supporting an existing entry. If you would like more report forms please tick ☐

Name of Hotel _____

Address _____

_____

Date of most recent visit   Duration of visit
☐ New recommendation   ☐ Comment on existing entry
Report:

Please continue overleaf

I am not connected directly or indirectly with the management or proprietors

Signed _____

Name (CAPITALS PLEASE)_____

Address _____

_____

[1998]

To: *The Good Hotel Guide*, Freepost PAM 2931, London W11 4BR

NOTE: No stamps needed in UK, but letters posted outside the UK should be addressed to 50 Addison Avenue, London W11 4BR, England, and stamped normally. Unless asked not to, we shall assume that we may publish your name if you are recommending a new hotel or supporting an existing entry. If you would like more report forms please tick ☐

Name of Hotel _____

Address _____

_____

Date of most recent visit   Duration of visit
☐ New recommendation   ☐ Comment on existing entry
Report:

Please continue overleaf

I am not connected directly or indirectly with the management or proprietors

Signed _____

Name (CAPITALS PLEASE)_____

Address _____

_____

To: *The Good Hotel Guide*, Freepost PAM 2931, London W11 4BR

NOTE: No stamps needed in UK, but letters posted outside the UK should be addressed to 50 Addison Avenue, London W11 4BR, England, and stamped normally. Unless asked not to, we shall assume that we may publish your name if you are recommending a new hotel or supporting an existing entry. If you would like more report forms please tick ☐

Name of Hotel _____

Address _____

_____

Date of most recent visit   Duration of visit
☐ New recommendation   ☐ Comment on existing entry
Report:

Please continue overleaf

I am not connected directly or indirectly with the management or proprietors

Signed _____

Name (CAPITALS PLEASE)_____

Address _____

_____

To: *The Good Hotel Guide*, Freepost PAM 2931, London W11 4BR

NOTE: No stamps needed in UK, but letters posted outside the UK should be addressed to 50 Addison Avenue, London W11 4BR, England, and stamped normally. Unless asked not to, we shall assume that we may publish your name if you are recommending a new hotel or supporting an existing entry. If you would like more report forms please tick ☐

Name of Hotel _____

Address _____

_____

Date of most recent visit   Duration of visit
☐ New recommendation   ☐ Comment on existing entry
Report:

I am not connected directly or indirectly with the management or proprietors

Signed _____

Name (CAPITALS PLEASE)_____

Address _____

_____